BASEBALLHQ.COM'S 2024

MINOR LEAGUE BASEBALL ANALYST

PRESENTED BY BASEBALLHQ.COM | 19TH EDITION

BRENT HERSHEY, EDITOR | CHRIS BLESSING & JEREMY DELONEY, ASSOCIATE EDITORS

TRIUMPH
BOOKS

This book is available in quantity at special discounts for your group or organization. For further information, contact:

Triumph Books LLC
814 North Franklin Street
Chicago, Illinois 60610
(312) 337-0747
www.triumphbooks.com

Printed in U.S.A.
ISBN: 978-1-63727-322-7

Data provided by TheBaseballCube.com and Baseball Info Solutions

Cover design by Brent Hershey
Front cover photograph by Julio Aguilar/Getty Images

TABLE OF CONTENTS

MINOR LEAGUE BASEBALL ANALYST

Editor
Brent Hershey

Associate Editors
Chris Blessing
Jeremy Deloney
• • • • • •

Tech/Data/Charts
Matt Cederholm
Neil FitzGerald
Ray Murphy

Graphic Design
Brent Hershey

**Player Commentaries
by MLB Organization**
Chris Blessing:
Atlanta, Chicago (AL), Cincinnati,
Los Angeles (AL), Miami, New York (AL),
New York (NL), Tampa Bay
Jeremy Deloney:
Boston, Cleveland, Milwaukee, Minnesota,
Oakland, Pittsburgh, San Diego,
San Francisco, Seattle, Toronto
Rob Gordon:
Chicago (NL), Colorado, Detroit,
Los Angeles (NL), St. Louis
Brent Hershey:
Philadelphia, Washington
Trevor Hooth:
Baltimore, Kansas City
Doug Otto:
Arizona, Houston
Matthew St-Germain:
Texas

Articles
Chris Blessing, Jeremy Deloney
Rob Gordon, Brent Hershey,
Chris Lee, Doug Otto,
Shelly Verougstraete

HQ100
Chris Blessing, Jeremy Deloney
Rob Gordon, Brent Hershey,
Doug Otto, Nick Richards,
Matthew St-Germain,
Shelly Verougstraete

Editing Support
Ryan Bloomfield
Brandon Kruse

The MLBA and Redraft Leagues: A Case Study

by Brent Hershey

This publication is often thought of—by both readers and, frankly, authors—as primarily a keeper league or dynasty format tool. That notion certainly comes from the depth of our coverage here; the bulk of what follows in this volume is 900+ player scouting reports that dive deep in search of the next valuable fantasy prospect for your team(s). Having the *Minor League Baseball Analyst* (MLBA) nearby on draft day in those formats will give you a skills-based leg up in finding those reserve-list and farm-system gems.

But the book is also a great resource for in-season roster management. It can be useful specifically in redraft leagues, where the "now" performance of a recently-recalled minor leaguer can be a game- (or season-) changer. We hope that the commentary, lists and skills grades help guide your in-season pick-ups and free agent bids. Once the MiLB season gets going and prospects get promoted to the big leagues, the book takes the "same season" recency bias away, as it's written over the winter with our reporting and observations. The one-season, redraft format is what we'll explore a bit more in the following study, as we think about ways in which to incorporate the MLBA to that context.

As it turns out, we have a fascinating case study in which to delve into this relationship. The 2023 season has been rightfully recognized around MLB and our own fantasy baseball circles as an outlier in terms of the number and quality of in-season rookie player debuts. One only needs to scan back over April and May 2023 free agent budget (FAB) logs to see the impact that these high-profile players had on fantasy squads. Like many years, the early bids for perceived possible difference-makers were high, but the sheer number of these opportunities week after week contributed to a unique situation. And like every year, some rookies flourished from the start, and others, well, … did not.

With the above in mind, our main questions are these:

- How did the 2023 MLBA evaluate these players a year ago?
- In hindsight, what aspects of the book's grades, list placement and commentary were most (and least) useful in determining how hard to pursue an individual player?
- From this one-year sample, are there any practical takeaways we can apply for the coming 2024 in-season rookie callup class?

A few ground rules and assumptions before we proceed:

First, in redraft leagues, the value of any player plucked from the free agent pool is skewed towards the beginning of the season. This is straightforward: A player with the same rate stats who joins your team in early May is more valuable than if he joins your team in mid-August, because he has a longer time frame to influence your team's counting and rate stats. So for this exercise, we will focus almost entirely on players who debuted in the first two months of the 2023 season.

Second, this two-month period of course also corresponds with fantasy managers having the most remaining FAB to spend. As such, the bidding on free agents in April and May is the most competitive.

Third, we self-selected this group of 14 players due to their relative hype and competitive bidding in redraft leagues. (For this exercise, we assume that the list is more or less equally useful for 15-team mixed leagues or AL- or NL-only leagues.) We didn't include all rookie call-ups over this time of course but tried to select a sample of those with the biggest "buzz" around them.

Fourth, our lens to look at this group is fairly simple: To sort/group by 1) Debut date; 2) Upside grade (if not familiar, see our Player Grade Primer essay on page 5) as well as 2023 HQ100 rank (if applicable) and 3) End of season dollar earnings (as calculated by BaseballHQ.com). We also examined player-box commentaries to see if that revealed any relevant nuggets.

Again, we are mainly seeking correlations between our 2023 MLBA material and their seasonal performance/earnings to construct any lessons to take into the 2024 season and beyond. The list of fourteen 2023 rookies, in alphabetical order:

- Andrew Abbott (LHP, CIN)
- Logan Allen (LHP, CLE)
- Tanner Bibee (RHP, CLE)
- Taj Bradley (RHP, TAM)
- Elly De La Cruz (SS, CIN)
- Matt McLain (2B/SS, CIN)
- Matt Mervis (1B, CHC)
- Bobby Miller (RHP, LA)
- Bryce Miller (RHP, SEA)
- Mason Miller (RHP, OAK)
- Eury Pérez (RHP, MIA)
- Brandon Pfaadt (RHP, ARI)
- Gavin Stone (RHP, LA)
- Bryan Woo (RHP, SEA)

Let's jump in.

By Debut Date

Date	Name	Grade	HQ100	R$
12-Apr	Taj Bradley	8B	40	-6
19-Apr	Mason Miller	8D	-	-4
23-Apr	Logan Allen	8C	-	2
26-Apr	Tanner Bibee	9D	78	16
2-May	Bryce Miller	8D	-	6
3-May	Gavin Stone	8D	50	-16
3-May	Brandon Pfaadt	8C	51	-9
5-May	Matt Mervis	8D	77	-4
12-May	Eury Pérez	9C	9	8
15-May	Matt McLain	8D	-	17
23-May	Bobby Miller	9C	37	12
3-Jun	Bryan Woo	8D	-	1
5-Jun	Andrew Abbott	8D	-	4
6-Jun	Elly De La Cruz	9C	8	15

Observations: Looking mainly at debut date to R$, there is very little (any?) correlation. Bradley and Mason Miller were early busts, and of the double-digit earners, only Bibee debuted before May 15. Perhaps the fact that two of those four were hitters (McLain and De La Cruz) is notable? With four of five scoring stats being cumulative, it would make sense that the earlier a hitter debuts, the better chance he has to return positive value. Bobby Miller, on the other hand, is an example of how very good ratios (3.76 ERA, 1.10 WHIP) can affect pitcher value even over a smaller sample size.

By Rating Grade and HQ100 Ranking

Date	Name	Grade	HQ100	R$
6-Jun	Elly De La Cruz	9C	8	15
12-May	Eury Pérez	9C	9	8
23-May	Bobby Miller	9C	37	12
26-Apr	Tanner Bibee	9D	78	16
12-Apr	Taj Bradley	8B	40	-6
3-May	Brandon Pfaadt	8C	51	-9
23-Apr	Logan Allen	8C		2
3-May	Gavin Stone	8D	50	-16
5-May	Matt Mervis	8D	77	-4
2-May	Bryce Miller	8D		6
15-May	Matt McLain	8D		17
3-Jun	Bryan Woo	8D		1
5-Jun	Andrew Abbott	8D		4
19-Apr	Mason Miller	8D		-4

Observations: We combined these two (player potential grade and HQ100 ranking) because they are closely but not exclusively related. As we mention in the section that follows, the individual player grades are doled out by one BHQ analyst—the evaluator of that MLB team. The HQ100, on the other hand, is a collective exercise. For this treatment we group the list together by grade, but then within that group, rank by HQ100 rating.

A few things do come into focus in this iteration. Players with the higher individual grades fared better than their counterparts on a whole, in terms of rookie-year earnings. The four players with "9" upside averaged $12.8 in seasonal value, whereas only 5 of the remaining 10 players posted a positive dollar value. Stone, Pfaadt and Bradley—all with "8" upsides—were the three most damaging players to your roster via R$ on this list.

By End-of-Season Dollar Value

Date	Name	Grade	HQ100	R$
15-May	Matt McLain	8D		17
26-Apr	Tanner Bibee	9D	78	16
6-Jun	Elly De La Cruz	9C	8	15
23-May	Bobby Miller	9C	37	12
12-May	Eury Pérez	9C	9	8
2-May	Bryce Miller	8D		6
5-Jun	Andrew Abbott	8D		4
23-Apr	Logan Allen	8C		2
3-Jun	Bryan Woo	8D		1
19-Apr	Mason Miller	8D		-4
5-May	Matt Mervis	8D	77	-4
12-Apr	Taj Bradley	8B	40	-6
3-May	Brandon Pfaadt	8C	51	-9
3-May	Gavin Stone	8D	50	-16

Observations: We alluded to this above, but ranking these 14 by 2023 earnings only results in two of the three hitters in the overall top three. McLain's rise to the top of this list was unexpected, to say the least. In most leagues, he was eligible to be bid

on in the same week as fireballer Pérez. It seemed as if he was an afterthought given the string of pitchers who preceded Pérez in their debuts and the natural Fear of Missing Out that each subsequent one evoked. Even if you were in on the McLain bidding, you likely had one eye on (and a few auction units stashed for) Elly De La Cruz's eventual promotion. McLain's chart-topping $17 return under those circumstances proved especially fruitful.

By Commentary Nuggets

Observations: Scanning the player-box commentaries for these 14 provided few definitive markers. This could be a function of the individual choices of that box's author: there's often so much to write about once the author has completed player research that what gets included and what gets left out in those 70-80 words can be a bit arbitrary.

One separator on the pitching side could be number of pitches, and even ones that are graded highly. Bibee, Pérez and Bobby Miller's commentaries all noted their arsenals included four pitches (at least three of each graded out as plus), whereas Mason Miller and Taj Bradley's writeups indicated they had quality fastballs without much mention of their secondary offerings. Middle-of-the-road outcomes by Abbott and Allen noted their wide arsenals paired with pitchability/control qualities. But on the other hand, Pfaadt got mention of his 4-pitch arsenal and strike-throwing ability; Stone was noted for his 3-pitch mix and above-average command. [Insert shrug emoji here.]

For batters, there were some similar inconsistencies. Sure, De La Cruz was lauded for his exceptional power potential and double-plus run tool, but Mervis' advanced understanding of the strike zone and McLain's contact concerns proved to be off the mark.

In the end, the commentaries alone worked better as part of a bigger picture (overall grade, individual skills ratings) than as a standalone point of perspective.

Conclusions

So … how does one proceed with your 2024 MLBA in hand? With the enormous caveat of this study providing but a one-year sample, there are a couple things to keep in mind for 2024 redraft leagues when rookies come available.

1. Pay attention to player grades, especially the number portion (which represents peak upside). Our MLBA team attempts to be stingy giving out 9s, and it's in situations like an MLB debut where immense talent can withstand—and perhaps even thrive in—the challenges of playing in the majors. That "9" is an indicator of elite upside talent and a worthy separator.

2. Hitters are far more likely to have rookie-year success than pitchers. That's obviously not meant to be a blanket statement—those who rostered Bibee, Bobby Miller and Pérez got great returns in 2023. But it does back up other observations we've made in terms of in-season rookie pickups—that hitters are far more likely to succeed in that Year 1 than pitchers. It's part of the reason that in our recent Top Fantasy Impact (IE, this year) rookie rankings (found on page 129), we have included fewer pitchers than we have in seasons past.

3. While the "math" may tell you that a rookie rostered in mid-April has a greater chance of affecting your season than one added in June, don't take that as a hard-and-fast rule. Our inclination is that, as stated above, upside talent in many instances has more impact.

4. A wholistic approach of all the MLBA has to offer—where one considers rating, ranking, commentary and even MLB team context—is still most likely to give you the best chance of snatching up that rookie who can make a difference.

Oh, and then the players actually have to perform. May the 2024 rookie call-ups treat you well.

•

Long-time readers of the *Minor League Baseball Analyst* will no doubt recognize most of the elements of the pages that follow in this 19th Edition. For both the new readers and vets, let's quickly run through the featues and structure.

Last year we added a masthead on the Table of Contents page that makes it a bit easier to see just who is responsible for what in this publication. Perhaps most important is the list that attributes all player-based information in the boxes—including the skills grades, commentaries and player ratings—to one analyst per MLB team. Assignments are divided up by organization, and those are listed in the masthead.

That means, if you are reading a box commentary about a player in the Toronto system, that author is Jeremy Deloney. If it's a Marlin, those are Chris Blessing's words. Given our emphasis on seeing players in person—and the daunting task when the book covers 900+ players—we did share information and insights with each other, tapping the strength of our team. In addition, each writer filled in the gaps with various scouting and front-office contacts.

Though the player-box section is the meat of the book, there are many other great features and structure to help you prepare for your next minor-league game (or fantasy-league draft).

The Insights section provides some narrative details and tools you can use as you prepare for getting the most out of your farm system and the rookies that will emerge during the 2024 baseball season. All the essays are designed to help you assemble your teams, as well as give you some food for thought on the prospect landscape.

As usual, several of the essays address our unique player grading system and some perspectives on how we've used it in the past. Again this year, the first Insights essay is a "Primer" on the subject, where we explain in more detail the grading process, and give some real-life examples of what we mean when we give a player an "8C" grade, for instance.

Additional topics in this edition include an examination of how the experimental rule changes in the minors affect player development and evaluation; MLB outcomes for high school vs. college draftees; an appeal to reconsider shallow fantasy leagues; the reviews of the 2023 Arizona Fall League and the MLB First Year Player Draft; and previews of prospects to know about from 2024 college baseball and the 2024 prep ranks. If the past is any indication, no doubt many of these players mentioned in the essays will soon be fantasy cornerstones. For keeper leagues, the time to get on board is now.

Up next is the HQ100—our signature list of the top 100 fantasy baseball prospects for 2024. The HQ100 is a compilation of eight individual lists (MLBA authors Chris Blessing, Jeremy Deloney, Rob Gordon Brent Hershey, Doug Otto and Matthew St-Germain, as well as BaseballHQ.com prospect-savvy writers Nick Richards and Shelly Verougstraete). This list is ranked by overall fantasy value, in an attempt to balance raw skill level, level of polish/refinement, risk in terms of age/level, and overall potential impact value. And then Deloney suggests 10 more "Sleepers" just outside the HQ100, players who just missed in 2024 or who could make the jump to the list in 2025.

Though the player profiles make up the bulk of the book, don't miss the tools that follow: the Major League Equivalencies; the Organization Grades; the Top Prospects by organization, by position, and by specific skills; the Top 75 prospects for 2024 only; an archive of our Top 100 lists; the glossary and a list of minor league affiliates. Whew … there's a lot of information in these pages.

But for now—if you have a suggestion to share, email us at support@baseballhq.com. Otherwise, grab a shovel and dig in. A better fantasy farm system awaits.

Player Grade Primer

by Brent Hershey

What follows is a quick primer on our background and grading system that we hope gives you the proper context to consume the player grades you find in each player box, and referenced in some of the essays. Feel free to refer to this repeatedly as you work your way through this book. Our hope is that the context provides a clear sense of making the most out of our evaluations.

Background

Yes, these are prospect reports, and in one sense they are like the many other quality prospect lists and discussions you'll find in pre-season books and websites that aim to prepare you for the 2024 season. There is one specific characteristic, however, about the *Minor League Baseball Analyst* evaluations that we feel makes them stand out: They are compiled, evaluated and ranked *specifically with fantasy baseball in mind*. We know that you're not just looking for the best prospects; you want the best *fantasy* prospects. Our writers write and editors edit with the goal of how much a player will contribute to a fantasy baseball roster. Among a few of their considerations that may help you:

Position(s) matters. For instance, almost all fantasy leagues require a catcher. Given the lower bar offensively for that position, we attempt to adjust when we evaluate backstops. Finding a catcher who consistently contributes on offense can be a challenging endeavor. Given how much emphasis is put on a rookie catcher's defense, and learning to manage a big-league staff upon his promotion, it often takes time for the bat to "catch up." We attempt to account for that, because finding a reliable catcher who can contribute to your fantasy squad is a huge built-in advantage. And knowing who to stay away from can be just as valuable.

Speed matters. How about this one, after the 2023 SB explosion? Now more than ever, we're seeking out the prospects who have the characteristics and track record that indicate MLB SB are in their future. Of course, SB totals in the minors are not always the best proxy for MLB SB success—pitchers and catchers are better equipped at the majors, for one thing, there's always the question of whether the player can either hit or get on base enough. And of course having a manager (and/or front office) who recognizes that weapon is also invaluable. And with all the rule changes in 2023 and the results, many of those calculations have to be re-done. But our crew is taking as much of that info into consideration as we can to project how prospects translate their minor-league SB into MLB production.

Defense matters. This point has long been touted on the opposite side: Defense doesn't matter when evaluating MLB prospects for fantasy utility; we only worry about the bat. But given the growing importance in the real-life game on position flexibility and players able to play multiple positions, it's past time to consider defensive flexibility as an important part of prospect evaluation. Prospects who are able to play MLB-quality defense at several positions are many times more likely to get opportunities

to play (which equals more AB) than, say, a player who is merely adequate defensively at just one position. The MLB game's shift to carrying more pitchers on the active roster almost means that bench players especially *have* to be capable at several positions. And it's even better if some of a team's starting eight position players can "double up" on positions. So while no, it doesn't matter how many errors in the field a certain top-hitting shortstop makes for fantasy baseball purposes, it may matter just how many positions a player can adequately man; that could be the difference between a big-league roster spot and one at Triple-A.

A pitcher's "stuff" matters. With strikeouts, velocity and pitch design all the rage, standards have changed in what MLB orgs are looking for in successful pitchers. A pitcher needs to have some baseline of control, command, and secondary pitches, but the rising average velocity and the up-in-the-zone/down-in-the-zone cat-and-mouse game continues. Add to that the fact that non-closing relief pitchers can hold value in some formats, and the equation gets more complex. But in general, we'll rate a high-K, wild pitcher higher than a Low-A change-up artist with a 2.00 ERA. Yes, a pitcher's stuff can improve, but showing the raw skills of pitch movement and getting swings-and-misses seems to project better to fantasy success than pitchers cruising on pinpoint control but only average velocity and overall arsenal.

There are more elements to this complex process, of course, but those are just some examples of elements that this volume's writers take into account that may differ from other "baseball-only value" lists.

Then of course, in many cases our reports attempt to continue to account for a player development curve that was disrupted by the canceled 2020 season. It feels like, four years later, we're just about over that hump—though any smart MLB draft analyst will tell you that the stellar crop from this past summer was due to the pandemic. So maybe we're not over that hump yet; but the influx of talent has kept MLB farm systems strong. Again, our analysts are taking that into account as best they can as we attempt to project player performance forward with that once-in-a-lifetime event still visible (but fading) in the rear-view mirror.

Lastly, with the above, it may seem curious that we still break up our writing assignments by MLB team—after all, beyond -only leagues, which MLB team a player is on has very little bearing as to a player's future value. The answer, for now … is that it's just the easiest way to produce this material. In our case—like other outlets—we have one analyst solely responsible for each individual organization (see specific assignments in the introductory essay). It helps with our workload of attempting to see with live looks as many of these players as we can throughout the season. And it helps because each of the evaluators fills in the gaps with information from contacts who have seen the players in person.

The Grade

Minor League Baseball Analyst and BaseballHQ.com's unique grading system was developed by Deric McKamey, a former prospect writer and current scout for the St. Louis Cardinals. The system debuted in the 2007 edition of this book, and we've been using it in subsequent MLBAs and on our site ever since. While the scale is listed on the introductory Batters and Pitchers pages, sometimes there's some confusion for both new and old readers on the specifics of the system. So we'll take some time here to explain how we best intend to use it along with some examples of current MLB players.

The system is a two-part scale: A number grade comes first, which represents a player's upside—at full MLB maturity, not at the present day. And then a letter grade follows, which attaches some probability that the player reaches that upside. Let's break these elements down even further.

Upside

Upside, of course, is what we're all chasing in this prospecting endeavor. We want to get the highest-performing players onto our fantasy rosters, even if we have to wait a bit for the production to materialize. And that's exactly why we use this measure—we want to help identify which players have the highest upside, regardless of other factors.

As prospect analysts, our goal is to be as realistic as possible with this number grade. This is why not everyone is a 10—even though, in the purest technical sense, there is still the infinitesimal chance that you or I would be a Hall of Fame-caliber player. Each analyst brings their own perspective and experience to providing these number grades. It comes from years of scouting players, seeing comps, realizing who worked out, who improved, who didn't—and understanding to their best of their ability the "why"s behind those examples. Also, while we can be realistic, there are still players like Jacob deGrom (graded as a 7D in his final OrgReport year of 2014) and Jose Altuve (7C in 2011), as well as the flip side of Jay Bruce (10C in 2008) and Matt Wieters (10C in 2009). Remember: we will get these wrong. Full-time MLB scouts will get some wrong. It's the nature of the business.

Let's run through the top five levels of number grades here with the "key"—but also with several corresponding established MLB players at their current level to help level-set our expectations. And of course, some of these players can still move up or down a tier as their careers develop. This is just a snapshot of who they are now:

Gr	Description	Current Example Player
10	Potential Hall of Famer	Mookie Betts, Bryce Harper Gerrit Cole, Justin Verlander
9	Potential Elite Player	José Ramírez, Julio Rodríguez, Juan Soto Zack Wheeler, Luis Castillo, Devin Williams
8	Potential Solid Regular	Bryan Reynolds, Will Smith, Gleyber Torres Mitch Keller, Joe Ryan, Paul Sewald
7	Potential Average Regular	Keibert Ruiz, Nate Lowe, Jonathan India Jameson Taillon, Jose Quintana, Kyle Gibson
6	Potential Platoon Player	Joc Pederson, Luke Raley, LaMonte Wade Jr. J.T. France, Brandon Williamson, Jake Irvin

So as you consume these number grades, you may find the examples above helpful given some of their real-life production levels.

Probability/risk

The second part of the Grade is a letter, given in the A-E academic scale. The letter portion is best thought of as a proxy for risk: Essentially, it is the probability that the evaluator thinks the player will reach his upside grade. We break it down into percentages, like this:

A: 90% probability of reaching potential

B: 70% probability of reaching potential

C: 50% probability of reaching potential

D: 30% probability of reaching potential

E: 10% probability of reaching potential

It's best to remember that this is *not* how close a player is to the majors—though that is one small aspect of the letter grade—as in, proven production at higher levels of the minors usually increases a player's probability grade. For instance, a player who has performed well against AA competition has some aspect of a smaller risk than a Low-A teenager.

Other things that can affect a players' letter grade:

Quality makeup. Here are two examples of makeup that could affect a player's letter grade positively: A drivenness to put in the work to improve, and/or the ability to block out other distractions and keenly focus on his craft.

A sense of conquering foundational skills that can "set the table" for further overall improvement. Think of a Low-A pitcher with impeccable ability to throw strikes, or a Double-A hitter who can just put the bat on the ball. Even if there are other aspects of these players' skill sets that are deficient—say, the pitcher can't command his fastball and the hitter has not yet developed in-game power—sometimes the foundational skills are building blocks for skills that come later. Recognizing these different tools and knowing how to express them in the letter grade is one of the things we ask our evaluators to consider.

Note that a lower letter grade that indicates more risk may include:

Concerns about a player staying healthy. If he has trouble in the minors, how likely is that to continue as he climbs the ladder?

Lack of fundamental baseball skills. This is the flip side of the above. We see this in toolsy but undisciplined players, sometimes pure athletes who have come to baseball later in their youth and have to refine their hitting mechanics or strike zone judgment. A pitcher might throw hard and have a nasty offspeed swing-and-miss pitch, but can't find the plate.

Makeup that might hold a player back from improving. Of course, judging and grading makeup is one of the toughest calls. But that still goes into our thought process.

One essential takeaway: not all players with the same grade are created equal. That's why it's so important to not just look at the grade; the real work our crew does is in the written comments, where we break down a player's tools/skills and attempt to give a snapshot of the player's future. Related, don't obsess over the differences in the grade. Yes, for sure, an 8B and a 9C are very close and there is some merit to saying that every 8B could easily also be graded a 9C. But we ask our evaluators to make a call, and provide them space in the comments to give their understanding of this player's potential future. In the end, *you* make the call for *your* team. Some fantasy owners don't mind the risk, and just want to shoot for upside. It is likely those owners will have more 9Ds on their roster. Others may want more sure things, and are going to lean towards the 8As and 8Bs, or even 7As, who are meant to have lower risk in their profiles. It's just how this works.

Conclusion

We do all of this knowing that there will instances when we will be wrong; and those when we'll be right—such as our 2022 reports on the certainty of Julio Rodríguez (9B) and the ceiling for Spencer Strider (9D). Fantasy or not, both hits and misses are the nature of this business. But we hope you will find value in our work to help guide your decisions for your teams.

How Experimental Rules in the Minors are Affecting Development and Evaluation

by Chris Blessing

The Major League Baseball competition committee has approved several rule changes over the last few seasons to speed up the game and improve gameplay. This offseason, the committee announced MLB would be subtracting two seconds off the pitch timer with men on base (from 20 seconds to 18 seconds) and widening the base path between home plate and first base for the 2024 season. Neither of those changes are expected to have a major effect on MLB games.

These rule changes don't come out of thin air. Nearly all of these rule changes have been created and tested in the minor leagues or independent leagues with MLB partnerships. Some of these tested rule modifications have been successful, like increasing the base size, which has shortened the distance between bases; others have not worked out or are still being tinkered with, like the automated ball-strike system (ABS). These experimental rule changes have altered the way we evaluate certain leagues. Let's check out three ongoing experiments that are potentially affecting development and evaluation.

The Automated Ball-Strike System (ABS)

The ABS has been tested in the Florida State League (FSL) since the start of the 2021 season. Prior to 2023, looking at the data, there were certain prospects who outclassed the system. HQ100 prospect Emmanuel Rodriguez (OF, MIN) had a bunch of helium last offseason, sporting a .272/.493/.552 slash line with 57 walks to 52 strikeouts in 47 games. Throw in plus power potential, and Rodriguez looked like a budding superstar on the Twins FSL affiliate, Fort Myers (Low-A). Speaking to scouting sources throughout last offseason, I became convinced this elite zone discipline was fabricated by the ABS. One source, midway through the spring, questioned whether Rodriguez didn't swing because he knew he'd struggle to get to contact regularly.

In this instance, I was wrong about ABS helping Rodriguez's patience and right about the whiffs and hit tool concerns. In 2023 in the Midwest League, Rodriguez slashed .240/.400/.463 with 92 walks and 134 strikeouts in 99 games. With Cedar Rapids

(High-A), he showed an elite level of patience, like he did with the ABS in the FSL. His zone miss rate, which was over 25% in 2022, remained nearly in the same place last season, and his chase rate only increased by 4%, from around 10% to near 15%. In other words, ABS or no ABS, Rodriguez had an elite patience profile in 2022, which was verified in 2023.

However, looking at a select group of prospects who were active in the FSL in 2022, the vast majority had much higher swing rates in other leagues/levels in 2023. Other than 26-year-old Zach Zubia (1B, MIA), who maintained the same swing rate between the FSL and the Midwest League, most guys with a 45% or less swing rate in the FSL in 2022 saw a 5% to 10% increase in swing rate in my sample.

Blake Dunn (OF, CIN), who I scouted in Double-A in 2023, saw a 9% increase in swing rate. In the FSL in 2022, the data suggested he had a double-plus eye. I scouted his zone discipline as slightly above average in my looks in 2022. The data backed up my findings, with Dunn sporting a 44% swing rate between two levels (High-A and Double-A) in 2023. The ABS is utilized in 9 of the 10 FSL stadiums. The one stadium where it isn't in use is Jackie Robinson Field in Daytona, which happens to be the Reds FSL affiliate and was Dunn's home park in 2022. Jackie Robinson Field is not equipped with Hawkeye, the sophisticated ball tracking technology required to run the ABS. Dunn's increase in swing rate between the two seasons might have been greater if he had played most of his games in any other FSL park in 2022.

We'll continue to see this experiment push forward in the FSL in 2024. It will continue to skew results in this league. Eventually, every full-season level will have the ABS system in some form or fashion once Hawkeye replaces Trackman in every minor league park.

ABS Testing in Triple-A

In 2022, MLB began testing the ABS in 11 Triple-A stadiums. In 2023, they expanded the use of the ABS to all 30 Triple-A stadiums. The ABS in Triple-A is different than what is being used in the FSL. Like all levels of full-season minor league baseball, Triple-A plays six-game series. For the first three games of each series, Triple-A utilizes the same ABS as the FSL, where the Robo Umpires are calling balls and strikes. For the final three games of each series, umpires call balls and strikes but the teams can challenge calls, using the ABS for verification purposes. Players, coaches, and fans preferred the ABS verification system over the full ball and strikes ABS system. Tracking how the experiment is affecting evaluations is difficult, mostly because of variations in use.

For instance, at the start of the 2023 season, the ABS was only used in Pacific Coast League ballparks through April 23rd. On April 25th, the remaining Triple-A teams in the International League started using the ABS. Then, starting September 5th through the end of the season, the strike zone was altered.

Prior to September 5th, the system was programmed to call a two-dimensional zone based on where the ball crosses the midpoint of the plate. The system averaged batter heights, rather than accounting for stances and actual zones. On September 5th, the batter's actual zone was taken into consideration. Hawkeye was able to adjust the zone based on the individual's batting stance and strike zone, creating a batter-specific zone for each player.

At First Pitch Arizona in November 2023, The Athletic's Rates and Barrels Podcast, hosted by Derek VanRiper, Eno Sarris, and Chris Welsh, had Kyle Manzardo (1B, CLE) as their guest for a live recording. Welsh asked Manzardo about facing a high number of high fastballs during his Arizona Fall League (AFL) stint. Manzardo's answer broached the subject of the difference in going from a league utilizing ABS (Triple-A International League) to a league mostly without ABS (in the AFL, ABS is only used at Salt River Fields). He said the ABS zone was "really short up top." Manzardo continued, "In my head, I was eliminating anything up because the top of the zone was so short there. And out here (in the AFL), those pitches get called." VanRiper asked Manzardo if he liked using ABS and Manzardo chuckled and explained, "I loved it. The pitchers probably didn't like it."

Manzardo, a cerebral hitter, battled through some mid-season struggles while overcompensating for pull-side power by cutting off the outer half, which caused his BA to sag. He was mostly the same hitter in terms of swing rate, whiff rate, and chase rate as he was in High-A and Double-A during the 2022 season. However, I want to focus on Manzardo's last three weeks of action, utilizing his actual zone to gauge the ABS zone, even though it was a small sample size, to see if there were differences with Manzardo's swing rate, whiff rate, and chase rate. Manzardo is listed at 6-foot-0 and doesn't utilize an upright stance like most of today's hitters. His stance is slightly open with his knees bent, and he stays mostly compact throughout his swing, with just a toe tap and no stride, meaning his zone doesn't have a chance to expand. In other words, it's a smaller zone than the average six-foot hitter.

Rates	Overall (94 G)	After 9/5 (14 G)	Prior to 9/5 (14 G)
Swing Rate	41%	37%	42%
Whiff Rate	21%	18%	21%
Chase Rate	27%	26%	31%

It's hard to focus on 14-game samples, especially since the 14-game sample prior to 9/5 included an IL stint for a partially-dislocated shoulder, which he struggled with even before the IL stint. However, if anything, guys with injured extremities tend to swing less, preferring quality of swing with pain than quantity of swings, so the sample appears useful in the study. What we see here, with the shrinking of the zone, is that Manzardo swung at 5% fewer pitches than the previous 14-game sample and swung at 4% fewer pitches across the season overall.

While the September 5th change in ABS zone helped Manzardo and other hitters with compact stances, guys with upright stances swung at about the same percentage of pitches. I sampled 10 hitters with upright stances, the most prominent hitter being Colt Keith (3B, DET). In each instance, their swing rate and chase rate remained mostly unchanged after September 5th compared to their seasonal Triple-A rates. There were some variations in whiff rates, but that appeared mostly related to pitch mix and not zone-related changes, as hitters faced pitchers armed with better scouting reports on how to attack their weaknesses. It really goes from hitter to hitter on whether the change in the automated zone affected them or not.

Before finishing up, I wanted to look at Manzardo again, comparing his rates when it was full ABS versus when it was the challenge system. I also wanted to see how he fared when there was no ABS, especially given his comments on the Rates and Barrels Podcast. Unlike the sample with his real zone calculated, there was virtually no change. I also decided to look for another hitter from the International League with at-bats stretching throughout the entire season in Triple-A. I chose Connor Norby (2B, BAL), a less cerebral hitter.

Kyle Manzardo

Rates	Overall (94 G)	No ABS (17 G)	ABS Full Use (44 G)	ABS Challenge (33 G)
Swing Rate	41%	42%	41%	40%
Whiff Rate	21%	22%	22%	19%
Chase Rate	27%	28%	29%	26%

Connor Norby

Rates	Overall (94 G)	No ABS (17 G)	ABS Full Use (44 G)	ABS Challenge (33 G)
Swing Rate	50%	51%	49%	51%
Whiff Rate	24%	21%	23%	26%
Chase Rate	37%	39%	35%	38%

After crunching these numbers, I looked at several other International League players, mostly hitters who have exceeded MLB rookie eligibility. The increase in Norby's chase rate with no ABS system or when the ABS challenge system was in use, compared to full automation of the zone, was observed at a similar 3-to-4% increase with the 10 other hitters I observed.

Overall though, the Triple-A experiment with the automated zone has had little to no effect on swing, whiff, and chase rates, meaning the automated zone hasn't affected projections, such as MLE equivalencies. There is some evidence, even if it is from a shorter sample, where hitters with smaller zones benefited from the late-season change from averaged-height ABS strike zones to adjusted-height ABS zones.

Pre-tacked Baseball Experiment (Pitchers)

We are only a few seasons removed from MLB cracking down on pitchers using foreign substances to grip the baseball. The most well-known of these substances, Spider Tack, was the main pitch grip agent MLB wanted eliminated from the game. To regain an edge, pitchers have returned to the legal substance, Rosin, and have mixed it with other substances, which is illegal, even though this has been a normal operating procedure for pitchers throughout our lifetimes. To level the playing field, MLB partnered with Dow, formerly known as Dow Chemical, to come up with a new substance to help pitchers grip the baseball better. After experimenting with other pitch grip agents during the 2022 season in some Double-A and Triple-A leagues, MLB decided to test this new substance in the Southern League (Double-A) from the start of the season through June 11th.

Scouting the Southern League as part of my territory, I witnessed the experiment firsthand. I talked about it during numerous episodes of the Eyes Have It Podcast last season. I also wrote about the experiment in my April 20th Eyes Have It article on Andrew Abbott (LHP, CIN), who made his MLB debut six weeks later. Abbott dominated the Southern League in 3 starts, striking out 36 batters in 15.2 innings.

Abbott's pitch data in the Southern League was outrageous. His fastball's induced vertical break (IVB) was around 21 inches, which is 80-grade riding action. For a pitcher who was getting over 17 inches of IVB on his four-seam fastball in 2022, his 2023 Double-A numbers were insanity. In his MLB stint, Abbott IVB was under 17 inches of IVB, which is where he was in Triple-A prior to his MLB callup. Baseball Savant has his vertical break ranked as slightly above average in 2023.

It wasn't just the fastball getting a boost either. It also helped play up his curveball and sweeping slider. All three pitches operated as double-plus pitches in the Southern League.

Another pitcher who benefited greatly from the experimental pre-tacked ball was Coleman Crow (RHP, MIL). Crow made only four starts last season, all in the Southern League for the Angels affiliate in Rocket City, and all in the month of April. He was placed on the injured list in May, was traded to the Mets in June, underwent Tommy John surgery in August, and was traded to the Brewers in December.

Crow, like Abbott, was achieving 80-grade ride on his four-seam fastball. His IVB was over 19 inches in his four starts, which is significant, especially coming from a low 3/4s slot and a five-foot release height. He also has one of the flattest four-seam fastballs in the minors. Before this four-start stint, Crow was mostly viewed as a future middle reliever with a feel for spin. Since we don't have data from after the experiment to compare, it's impossible to know if he simply improved his fastball shape, efficiency, or break, or if it is an illusion. Given what we saw with Abbott and others, it's likely an illusion.

I mentioned Crow's feel for spin. His curveball IVB went from around 4 inches of IVB in 2022 to over 13 inches of IVB in 2023, and his horizontal movement went from nearly 12 inches in 2022 to over 21 inches in 2023.

So, what do we make of Coleman Crow? I handled Crow's write-up for this book, even though he was traded to the Brewers, an organization I'm not responsible for analyzing and writing about. In last year's book, Crow was rated a 6B pitcher with a future role of middle reliever. For this year's book, I increased his potential rating to a 7D pitcher with a future role of #4 starter. Admittedly, I hedged, in case this uptake in stuff was real. Obviously, I don't have much confidence in it being real. I would have gone much higher than a 7D potential rating if I thought the data was sustainable.

The moral of this analysis for pitching is to be mindful of future pre-tack baseball experiments when delving into their performances. Fantasy managers, some prospect media folks, and fans were declaring Andrew Abbott as a potential ace without considering the actual baseball was playing a big part in his performance. Pretty much every pitcher's fastball movement profile benefited from the grip enhancement during the experiment and dropped back to pre-experiment movement profiles once replaced with the normal baseballs. This experiment may not be repeated with this ball, but a similar pre-tack baseball will likely make its way to a Double-A League for testing again in 2024. The Southern League

and Texas League, given the similar climates and warmer weather throughout the season, are prime testing grounds for pre-tack baseballs.

Pre-tacked Baseball Experiment (Hitters)

While the experimental pre-tack baseball helped pitchers achieve improvements with their movement profiles, it caused younger hitters to struggle. I scouted Jackson Chourio (OF, MIL) for a few games in May. Chourio, who was the youngest player in the Southern League at the time, was a pop-up prospect in 2022 after slashing .288/.342/.538 with 20 HR across three different levels. Combined with his immense tool shed, we ranked Chourio in last offseason's HQ100 as our 4th overall prospect. The prospect I scouted in May of last year was a player struggling mightily. The Eyes Have It article I wrote on May 25th featuring Chourio was the most exciting Eyes Have It article I've written since writing up a Low-A prospect in 2016, Ronald Acuña.

At the time of my article, no one really wanted to talk about Chourio in the media space. We had all gone out on a limb about Chourio after his 2022 breakout. I live in this world where I bleed the lines of being a scouting analyst and being a scout for my prospect analysis. With Chourio struggling to start the season, I went into the Chourio series purely as a scout. What I found was a 19-year-old kid who was a mess mechanically because of MLB's experiment. Here are some quotes from the article.

Re: Chourio's Struggles

At the plate, Chourio is having issues with spin. Chourio ends up stepping into the bucket on nearly every pitch, especially against pitchers able to spin up a decent breaker.

Re: Diagnosing what's wrong with Chourio

Comparing my look with video looks last year and earlier in 2023, Chourio did not step in the bucket last year. In fact, he didn't utilize a leg lift at all to begin the season. He twisted his lead foot towards his back leg to transfer the energy to his back leg and then twisted the front foot forward, which kept Chourio on time and balanced throughout his swing. This was a much better operation than what it is now. Chourio likely went back to a leg lift, which he utilized last season, because of the spin at this level, which has been enhanced by the pre-tack baseballs being experimented on in the Southern League. When a young hitter makes this sort of change in season, the results aren't usually great. Chourio's best swings during the series were swings where he didn't step into the bucket. He hit a HR in game one and it was one of the few swings he took all series without stepping into the bucket.

How big were those issues? Here are the experimental baseball results, followed by the return of the regular baseball to the Southern League.

Experimental baseballs .262/.311/.422 (On identifiable pitches)

Rates	Overall	vs Fastball	vs Slider	vs Change-ups
Swing Rate	52%	54%	48%	51%
Whiff Rate	27%	19%	36%	55%
Chase Rate	33%	34%	26%	39%

Regular baseballs .302/.359/.516 (On identifiable pitches)

Rates	Overall	Versus Fastball	Versus Slider	Versus Change-ups
Swing Rate	47%	45%	48%	49%
Whiff Rate	20%	17%	27%	20%
Chase Rate	28%	26%	30%	33%

As you can see, there was a stark difference in patience, whiff rate, and overall production. While these percentages are estimates since 10% of the pitches tracked on this level are identified as unknown pitches, it's a great interpretation of what went on with Chourio during the experiment. When I scouted video of Chourio after the experiment, he was no longer stepping into the bucket. His operation was smooth, which helped Chourio rake at the level post-experiment. He looks to be a fantasy superstar in the not-too-distant future.

Most hitters I evaluated who were in the Southern League last year had similar issues with the enhanced spin and break from the experimental balls, specifically with whiff rates. Those players included Rece Hinds (OF, CIN) and Victor Mesa (OF, MIA). Owen Caissie (OF, CHC) was the same hitter regardless of the baseball, which isn't surprising given his advanced, discerning eye at the plate.

As I said with pitchers, it's likely the same experimental baseball will not be tested again. However, a similar pre-tack baseball will likely make its way back on the circuit in Double-A for 2024.

In conclusion, it's important to know what experiments are being conducted in the leagues your prospects are in. It makes it difficult, as a dynasty manager, to make quick decisions on prospects. Use your resources, like this book and BaseballHQ.com, and trust your gut. Experimenting in the minors will not go away, especially now that MLB has taken ownership of the minor leagues.

Major League Outcomes for High School vs. College Draftees

by Doug Otto

The three main ways that prospects enter MLB-affiliated pro ball are being drafted out of college, drafted out of high school, and signed as an international free agent. The way in which a player signs will have a large impact on their development path, in particular the difference between signing out of high school and signing out of college. College players have more experience at a more advanced level than high school, while high school players tend to be less developed. For this reason, college players are typically viewed as safer investments, while high school players are viewed as less proven upside plays. Given these differences and the implications they have for development paths, it sparks the question of whether or not one of these demographics is safer than the other or has better major league outcomes.

Data

For this analysis, we'll look at all college and high school draftees between 1990 and 2016. Cutting the sample off at 2016 helps ensure that draftees have had enough time to matriculate to the majors and accrue playing time. In addition, we'll include only those players who signed with their team following the draft. Due to limitations with the draft data lacking MLBID, all players who shared a name with another player were removed from analysis to ensure that draftees were matched with appropriate major league data. In total, there were 19,225 draftees. The table below shows a breakdown of the players by school type.

Position	College	High School	Total
C	1,322 (9.4%)	495 (9.6%)	1,817 (9.5%)
1B	739 (5.2%)	233 (4.5%)	972 (5.1%)
2B	739 (5.2%)	87 (1.7%)	826 (4.3%)
3B	692 (4.9%)	260 (5.1%)	952 (5.0%)
SS	1,106 (7.8%)	572 (11.1%)	1,678 (8.7%)
OF	2,233 (15.8%)	1,141 (22.2%)	3,374 (17.6%)
RHP	5,183 (36.8%)	1,702 (33.2%)	6,885 (35.8%)
LHP	2,080 (14.8%)	641 (12.5%)	2,721 (14.1%)
Total	14,094	5,131	19,225

Nearly three-fourths of draftees were college players (73.3%). A larger percentage of high school players were shortstops and outfielders, while a larger percentage of college players were second basemen and pitchers.

The table below shows the total number of draftees by pick range and school type. The results show that high schoolers made up a larger proportion of early draft picks compared to later draft picks. Accordingly, the mean draft position for high school draftees was 412 compared to 581 for college draftees. This could be a result of teams generally valuing high school players more than college players, but teams are also incentivized to use higher picks and more bonus pool money on high school players. This is because high school players have the option of going to college, which gives them more bargaining leverage than college players.

Position	College	High School	Total
Top 30	367 (51.5%)	345 (48.5%)	712
Top 100	1,152 (50.1%)	1,149 (49.9%)	2,301
Top 300	3,816 (66.7%)	2,583 (39.9%)	6,399

Next, we can look at major league outcomes for high schoolers and college players. Overall, 22.3% of all draftees made the major leagues. While 17.5% of all college draftees made the major leagues, 24.1% of all high schoolers made the major leagues. The following table shows the percentage of draftees who made the major leagues by school and position type. The demographic with the highest percentage reaching the major leagues was high school pitchers, while the demographic with the lowest percentage of players making the majors was college batters.

School Type	MLB	Debut Age	Total Draftees
College Batter	1,079 (15.8%)	25.7	6,831
College Pitcher	1,387 (19.1%)	25.8	7,263
High School Batter	611 (21.9%)	24.0	2,788
High School Pitcher	625 (26.7%)	24.0	2,343
Total	4,416 (22.3%)	25.2	19,225

High school players also tend to make their MLB debut younger than college players for both position types. On average, high schoolers were 24 at the time of their debut while college players were nearly 26 by the time of their debut. Of the 162 batters who reached the major leagues by the time they were 22, 138 (85.2%) were high school draftees. Of the 204 pitchers who reached the major leagues by 22, 145 were drafted out of high school (71.1%).

Finally, we can look at how productive draftees go on to be at the major league level. To measure major league production, we'll use FanGraphs.com's cumulative Offensive Runs Above Average (Off) for batters and Runs Above Average (RAR) for pitchers (the more the better). We'll set these stats to a rate of per 600 plate appearances (PA) for batters and per 180 IP for pitchers, or roughly a full season. The sample includes 793 batters with at least 600 career plate appearances between 1990 and 2016 and 831 pitchers with at least 180 career innings pitched between 1990 and 2016. The table below shows that for both pitchers and batters, high school draftees had slightly better average production than their college draftee counterparts.

School Type	Value Rate	Total
College Batter	-4.7	480
College Pitcher	14.8	531
High School Batter	-2.8	313
High School Pitcher	15.3	300

Regression Analysis

Based on these initial findings, it appears that high school players seem to have better marks across the board in terms of being drafted earlier, making the major leagues, and advancing to the major leagues at a younger age. High school draftees on average also appear to contribute slightly better production at the major league level than college draftees. While all of the results seem to paint a picture in favor of the high school demographic, there are other factors we haven't controlled for. For example, with changes to player development happening over time, there could be differences in outcomes based on the year in which a player was drafted. Also, given prior research on age as a predictor of major league outcomes, it's important to control for debut age. We can use regression analysis to accomplish this.

For the batter regression model, we'll set Off per 600 PA as the dependent variable of interest and draftee school type as the independent variable. The control variables will be debut age, pick number, draft year, and player position. Results for this model using major league batters with at least 600 PA between 1990 and 2016 show that the school type had no significant impact on major league production when controlling for other variables. However, debut age was found to be a significant predictor, as each 1-year increase in debut age was associated with a -2.8 decrease in Off per 600 PA.

For pitchers, the dependent variable is RAR per 180 IP, with school type as the independent variable and the same control variables as the batter model. Similar to the results from the batter regression model, school type was not found to have a significant effect on a pitcher's rate of production. Debut age was again found to have a significant effect on production, though to a lesser extent for pitchers. The regression results showed that every one-year increase in age was roughly associated with a 1.4 decrease in RAR per 180 IP.

To see whether or not high school draftees were more likely to make their debuts at a younger age than college draftees, we can run regression models with debut age as the dependent variable

and school type as the independent variable, with draft year, pick number, and position as the control variables for both batter and pitcher models. Results of the regression analysis showed that the school type was a significant predictor of debut age, when controlling for other variables. The results for both the batter and pitcher models showed that the average high school draftee batter is expected to be 1.7 years younger than the average college draftee batter at the time of debut, while high school pitcher draftees were expected to be 1.4 years younger than their college counterparts at the time of debut.

Conclusion

The results of this analysis showed that high school draftees generally have better major league outcomes than college draftees. The results of the regression analyses confirm the initial descriptive analyses, with one caveat. Specifically, the results showed that the effect of being a high school vs. college draftee was mediated by the age at which a player makes their major league debut. However, secondary analyses showed that high school draftees were significantly more likely to make the major leagues at a younger age than college draftees, among both batters and pitchers. In conclusion, the results of this analysis indicate that high school draft picks tend to be safer than college draft picks, all things being equal.

2023 Arizona Fall League Recap

by Shelly Verougstraete

The Arizona Fall League is seen as a finishing school for many top prospects. In 2023, Bryan Woo, Edouard Julien, Emmet Sheehan, and Mason Miller went from relatively unknown to baseball stars in less than a year's time. When rosters were announced for the 2023 AFL season, many felt a noticeable decrease in talent invited to the desert. While Jackson Jobe, Ricky Tiedemann, Chase DeLauter, and Kyle Manzardo got the initial buzz, several other prospects who weren't included on the HQ100 made some noise. Some have a shot to contribute to their big league club in 2024, while others will need another season or two in the minors before showcasing their skills in the big leagues. Here's a look at the next wave.

Jakob Marsee (OF, SD) seemed to come out of nowhere and put together an outstanding AFL performance. The 22-year-old hit .391/.509/.707 with 12 doubles, 5 homers, and 16 stolen bases. The center fielder was drafted by the Padres in the sixth round of the 2022 draft out of Central Michigan University. In his first full professional season, he hit .274/.413/.428 with 16 round-trippers across two levels. Known for his bat-to-ball skills, his power spike in the AFL is a bit suspect. While in High-A, he smashed six of his 15 homers at home, using Fort Wayne's Parkview Field's 318-foot right-field wall to his advantage. When he moved up to Double-A, he returned to his up-the-middle approach. Even if the power never materializes, Marsee's ability to make contact and play defense should carry him to a big-league role in a couple years.

Victor Scott II (OF, STL) was drafted in the fifth round of the 2022 draft by the Cardinals out of West Virginia University. He ran wild in his first full professional season, swiping 95 bags between two levels. He also hit over .300. Scott is a defensive wizard and will stick in center field. He kept up his running ways in the desert, swiping 18 bases across 99 plate appearances while hitting .286/.388/.417. Scott isn't your typical speed-only prospect. The 22-year-old has some sneaky pop. During his time in Double-A, he cranked seven of his nine homers. While he will never reach 20 homers, his ability to swipe bases and hit for non-zero power could propel him to fantasy baseball superstardom.

Jase Bowen (OF, PIT) has had an interesting career. A former two-sport star in high school, he was expected to continue playing football and baseball at Michigan State before the Pirates took him in the 11th round of the 2019 draft, offering him an over-slot deal. His first full professional season wasn't until 2021 due to the pandemic. Bowen struggled in his full season debut in 2021. However, he's come along since. In 2023, split between two levels, the 22-year-old hit .255/.327/.467 with 36 stolen bases and a career-high 23 home runs. Bowen continued to impress in the AFL, hitting .290/.355/.500 with 4 homers and 6 stolen bases. Bowen was left unprotected in the Rule 5 draft. He should begin the 2024 season in Double-A and could make his major league debut sometime this summer as the Pirates continue their rebuilding process.

While **Sterlin Thompson (2B, COL)** didn't put-up mind-blowing stats in the AFL, he is poised to become a solid player in the next couple of seasons. The Rockies selected him 31st overall during the 2022 draft out of the University of Florida. During his final year with the Gators, Thompson hit .354/.443/.563 with 11 homers and 10 stolen bases, and he has essentially done the same in professional ball. The Rockies assigned him to High-A Spokane out of spring training, and he thrived in the hitter's paradise known as Avista Stadium, where the RF fence is only 296 feet away. Thompson was on track for a quick promotion to Double-A Hartford before suffering an elbow injury, which caused him to miss a month of playing time. After returning, the 22-year-old hit .233/.325/.411 with seven homers and six stolen bases. Thompson hit .338/.460/.475 in the AFL, across 100 plate appearances. While he will never hit for much over-the-fence power, his innate ability to put the barrel on the ball should play well in Coors Field someday.

James Triantos (2B, CHC) was sent to the AFL to make up for lost playing time due to a torn meniscus in spring training and to build versatility by taking reps in the OF. The former 2021 second-round pick out of high school in Virginia finished with a .287/.364/.391 slash line across 363 plate appearances at 2023. At 20-years-old, Triantos was one of the youngest hitters in the AFL. He hit .417/.495/.679 with three homers and nine stolen bases. His 1.174 OPS was second to Jakob Marsee during the fall. While he didn't show much power in the desert, his ability to make hard contact should make him a solid contributor moving forward. He will likely begin the 2024 season in Double-A, where he should continue to tap into more over-the-fence power.

Damiano Palmegiani (3B, TOR) was drafted in the 14th round in the 2021 draft by Toronto out of the University of Southern Nevada. Palmegiani, nicknamed "Cheese" by his AFL teammates, hit .255/.365/.478 with 23 homers and 7 stolen bases across 557 plate appearances between upper-level affiliates. While in the AFL, the slugger slashed .263/.366/.575 with 6 homers and finished second in the Home Run Derby. He continues to show a patient eye at the plate, posting double-digit walk rates throughout his career, but he still needs to find a defensive home. Coming up through the minors, Palmegiani manned the hot corner but took a stab at first base this season.

Zach Penrod's (LHP, BOS) journey to the AFL seems more like a story from Hollywood than real life. Since 2021, he's pitched in independent ball and signed a minor league contract with the Red Sox this summer. He was assigned to High-A Greenville and posted a respectable 2.18 ERA, 1.30 WHIP, and 20/11 K/BB ratio across 4 starts. Penrod stepped up to the challenge in the AFL, posting a 1.29 ERA, 1.21 WHIP, and 14/8 K/BB ratio over 14 innings (4 starts). While he doesn't have overpowering stuff, the left-hander could soon play the role of a long reliever for the Red Sox.

Davis Daniel (RHP, LAA) heard his name called not once, not twice, but thrice during the June Amateur Draft process and finally put his name on the dotted line when the Angels selected him in the seventh round of the 2019 draft. The 6-1, 190 lb. right-hander was assigned to the AFL after missing most of the season with a shoulder strain. Even with the injury, he did make his MLB debut in September and posted a 2.19 ERA and 1.30 WHIP across three starts with Los Angeles. In the AFL, Daniel posted a 1.89 ERA, 0.79 WHIP, and 25/5 K/BB ratio across 4 starts. The Angels are poised to take a major step back next season and Daniel should be ready to compete for a role in the team's rotation during spring training.

Zach Maxwell (RHP, CIN), a gigantic 6-6, 275 lb. right-handed reliver, put an exclamation point on an otherwise fantastic season this fall. Maxwell is a late-inning reliever through and through. In the AFL, he posted a 2.19 ERA, 1.46 WHIP, and 22/9 K/BB ratio across 9 appearances. Like many relievers, Maxwell has plenty of stuff, but poor command has limited him from reaching his ceiling. The right-hander's fastball sits in the mid-nineties with elite movement, touching 100 MPH. He also throws a slider that has generated plenty of whiffs this fall. Maxwell finished the season with High-A, but he could enter the Reds bullpen mix this summer if his gains from the AFL carry over into the 2024 season.

Emiliano Teodo (RHP, TEX) made a name for himself while in the AFL. The flame-throwing right-hander transitioned to a reliever role and could be poised to take a late-inning role in the back of the Rangers bullpen soon. Teodo worked as a starter during the regular season, posting a 4.52 ERA, 1.39 WHIP, and 84/33 K/BB across 18 games (14 starts) In High-A. While in Arizona, the 6-1, 165 lb. right-hander posted a 0.00 ERA, 0.54 WHIP, and 19/3 K/BB ratio across eight appearances. As seen late in the season, the Rangers could use another flame-throwing reliever or two in their bullpen. Teodo looks to be a great internal candidate for the World Series Champions.

2023 MLB First-Year Player Draft Recap
by Rob Gordon (NL) and Jeremy Deloney (AL)

NATIONAL LEAGUE

ARIZONA DIAMONDBACKS

Picking at #12 the Diamondbacks added Stanford SS Tommy Troy to that young core with an under-slot deal. They then used some of the savings to ink Alabama RHP Grayson Hitt (4) to a $1.2 million bonus. Troy can do a bit of everything but also doesn't have any true plus tools. His .271/.374/.469 slash line in his pro debut is essentially his ceiling once he reaches the majors. Unlike previous years, the D-Backs went college-heavy throughout the draft. Troy, Hitt, and NC State 3B Gino Groover (2) all cracked the Diamondbacks Top 15 prospect list heading into the 2024 season. *Sleeper:* South Alabama RHP Sam Knowlton (12) is 6'8", 255 and owns an upper-90s heater. His secondaries need work and he's still figuring out how to sync his huge frame into a fluid delivery.
Grade: B+

ATLANTA BRAVES

After winning 101 games in 2022, the Braves had to wait to pick, but in typical Braves fashion, they were still able to land an exciting arm in Florida RHP Huston Waldrep. Waldrep struggled with control in college, blows hitters away with a plus 95-99 mph heater, a power slider, and a splitter that generates tons of swing-and-miss. The Braves then went over slot to sign Virginia Tech RHP Drue Hackenburg (2) and went college-heavy the rest of the draft, signing just one prep player—LHP Garrett Baumann (4). The Braves have done an excellent job turning throwers into pitchers and Waldrep has the potential to be a #2 or #3 starter if he can make the necessary adjustments. *Sleeper:* Cal State Northridge RHP Lucas Braun (6) doesn't have elite stuff, but he knows how to keep hitters off balance with a 4-pitch mix and ability to control the zone. He posted a 2.67 ERA with 5 BB/32 K in 27 IP in his pro debut.
Grade: A-

CHICAGO CUBS

For the second year in a row the Cubs were able to land an impact collegiate player who could move through the minors quickly. Last year it was RHP Cade Horton and this year it was Maryland SS Matt Shaw at #13. Shaw was widely viewed as one of the better pure hitters in the draft (.320/.413/.623 over three years), but because he played in the Big 10 and not one of the power conferences, skeptics questioned how quickly that would translate at the professional level. All Shaw did in his debut was hit .357/.400/.618 across three levels. The Cubs also added Arkansas RHP Jaxon Wiggins (2C) and Florida SS Josh Rivera (3). Rivera helped lead the Gators to within one game of the CWS title and has the tools to stick at short. Wiggins would have gone sooner but he's recovering from Tommy John surgery and will miss most of the 2024 season. If Wiggins pans out, this will be a solid haul for the Cubs. *Sleeper:* Wabash Valley Junior 3B College Brian Kalmer (18th) hit .357/.423/.667 with 10 HR between Rookie Ball and Low-A and could surprise.
Grade: A-

CINCINNATI REDS

The Reds didn't have much luck with the inaugural draft lottery; they fell to #7 but were able to land the 2nd best pitcher in the draft in Wake Forest ace Rhett Lowder. Lowder, who immediately becomes the Reds #2 prospect, has a plus 3-pitch mix highlighted by a mid-90s fastball and some of the best control and command in the draft. Given his extensive collegiate experience, Lowder enters pro ball with more polish than is typical. The Reds also added LSU RHP Ty Floyd (CB-A), prep SS Sammy Stafura (2), Arkansas LHP Hunter Hollan (3), and then went over slot to land high school RHP Cole Schoenwetter who was ranked in the top 50 of the draft class. Lowder and Floyd should both have long and productive careers, while the others have some intriguing upside. *Sleeper:* Texas A&M 1B Jack Moss (11) stands at 6'5", 215 with plus raw power, but he needs to tap into it more consistently. He does have good bat-to-ball skills so a tweak in swing path could allow him to reach that potential.
Grade: A-

COLORADO ROCKIES

For decades the Rockies have attempted to use the draft in their never-ending search for pitchers who can survive pitching in Coors Field. They did so again in 2023, taking Tennessee ace Chase Dollander with the 9th pick. Dollander was considered a likely top 5 pick coming into the year, but never really got on track despite having a plus fastball and an impressive 4-pitch mix. They took Wake Forest LHP Sean Sullivan (2), SD State C Cole Carrigg (CB-B), South Carolina RHP Jack Mahoney (3), and Ohio State LHP Isaiah Coupet (4). While Dollander has the highest upside, Carrigg is a unique prospect and is a plus defender at three positions: C, SS, and CF. *Sleeper:* Dallas Baptist LHP Bryson Hammer (12) has a nice three-pitch mix, highlighted by a 92-94 mph fastball and a potentially plus change-up. Hammer played just one year of DI baseball and needs to improve his mechanics.
Grade: B

LOS ANGELES DODGERS

The Dodgers forfeited their 1st round draft pick due to the luxury tax and had to wait until pick #36 to land high school OF Kendall George. George has double-plus speed and had a stellar pro debut, hitting .370/.458/.420 with 17 SB in 28 games between Rookie Ball and Low-A. They also added Virginia 3B Jake Gelof (the younger brother of A's 2B Zack) in the 2nd round, high school RHP Brady Smith (3), and FSU LHP Wyatt Crowell (4). Overall this was a pretty thin haul. Fortunately the Dodgers seemingly have unlimited resources and still have a top 10 farm system. *Sleeper:* LSU SS Jordan Thompson (15) doesn't have any standout tools and posted a slash line of just .260/.363/.419 in three years at LSU, but he's athletic, has good speed, and his defense could help him carve out a UT role.
Grade: C+

MIAMI MARLINS

The Marlins have an enviable track record of drafting and developing high school talent and in 2023 they stayed true to their roots, landing the best prep pitching prospect in Noble Meyer with the 8th overall pick. At 6'5", 185 the 18-year-old Meyer has a tall, projectable frame and possesses a plus mid-90s fastball that already tops out at 98. He also shows feel for spin with a mid-80s slider, a nascent change-up from a deceptive low ¾ arm slot. Then they added high school LHP Thomas White (CB-A) before going the collegiate route with their next 16 picks. Ole Miss OF Kemp Alderman (2) has the highest upside of any position player, though he struggled in his pro debut, while Nebraska LHP Emmett Olson (4) was one of the better pitchers in the Big 10 and cracks the Marlins Top 15.
Sleeper: North Carolina A&T RHP Xavier Meachem (10) has a good low-90s fastball and a high-spin slider, both of which he throws for strikes. He's only 21 and looked impressive in his pro debut, posting a 2.70 ERA with 12 BB/28 K in 20 innings between Rookie Ball and Low-A.
Grade: A

MILWAUKEE BREWERS

The Brewers snapped up Wake Forest 1B Brock Wilken with the 18th pick and inked him to a below-slot deal. They then used their extra draft capital to land four additional top 100 draft prospects in high school RHP Josh Knoth (CB-A), Nebraska-Omaha 3B Mike Boeve (2), high school SS Eric Bitonti (3), and high school SS Cooper Pratt (6). While there is too much swing-and-miss, Wilken has plus raw power and was 2nd in DI with 31 HR and had a solid debut, hitting a combined .285/.414/.473. Boeve put up even better numbers, hitting .324/.400/.529 between Rookie Ball and High-A. Wilkin is 1B-only on defense, but has the tools to hit 25+ HR on a regular basis.
Sleeper: High school RHP Bishop Letson (11) has a lean, projectable frame and owns a low-90s fastball that already features plus spin and late life up in the zone.
Grade: A-

NEW YORK METS

Coming into the draft the Mets were looking to follow up on their success in the 2022 draft and in 2023 mid-season trades, which netted them OF Drew Gilbert and 1B/OF Ryan Clifford. The club got off to a good start landing high school SS Colin Houck with the 32nd overall pick. Houck was considered a top 15 prospect but dropped due to signability concerns. The Mets went slightly over slot, giving Houck $2.75 million. They followed up by drafting Florida RHP Brandon Sproat (2), Oklahoma State 3B Nolan McLean (3), and Nevada RHP Kade Morris (3). Sproat has a plus FB/SL mix, but struggles with control. The past two drafts have helped the organization develop an underrated farm system and should infuse some much-needed youth to one of the older teams in the NL.
Sleeper: High school SS Boston Baro (8) has a lean, projectable frame with above-average speed, solid plate discipline, and some feel to hit. He showed those tools in an impressive pro debut, hitting .316/.458/.421 in 19 Rookie Ball AB.
Grade: A

PHILADELPHIA PHILLIES

Despite making the postseason the past two years and having the smallest draft budget in either league, the Phillies were still able to land a potential impact prospect in high school 3B Aidan Miller. Miller was considered a potential top 10 pick, but fell all the way to the Phillies at #27. Miller has 5 above-average tools highlighted by plus raw power and enough range and arm to stick at the hot corner. The club didn't have a 2nd round pick, but added high school SS Devin Saltiban (3), and IMG Academy OF Tjayy Walton (4), before picking their first college player in Minnesota RHP George Klassen (6). Miller is the crown jewel of this group and had a solid pro debut between Rookie Ball and Low-A.
Sleeper: TCU RHP Cam Brown (10) has a potentially above-average three-pitch mix, highlighted by a mid-90s fastball. Unfortunately, he struggles to find the strike zone and walked 40 in 55.1 IP for TCU.
Grade: B+

PITTSBURGH PIRATES

The perpetually rebuilding Pirates did exactly what they were supposed to do with a $16.2 million bonus budget and the 1st overall pick. They took the best player available in LSU ace Paul Skenes, who might have had the most dominant college season on record, posting video game numbers with a 1.69 ERA and 20 BB/209 K in 122.2 IP. He also led LSU to their first College World Series championship since 2009. After Skenes, the Bucs grabbed Michigan State SS Mitch Jebb (2) and RHP Zander Mueth (CB-B), the only high school player in their top 15 picks. Jebb had a solid pro debut, slashing .297/.382/.398 at Low-A and has an above-average hit tool, but needs to find a defensive home. The Pirates didn't leverage the rest of their bonus pool as effectively as they could have, but the addition of Skenes is a solid win.
Sleeper: Arizona State RHP Khristian Curtis (12) had ulnar transplant surgery and never really looked 100% healthy but in the past has shown a low-90s fastball with an above-average slider.
Grade: A-

SAN DIEGO PADRES

Because of the Padres on-field success they didn't pick until near the end of round one. With the 25th pick the Padres landed high school OF Dillon Head (1). While Head has plus speed, he stole just 4 bases in his pro debut and has below average power, though he should be able to stick in CF. The Padres didn't have a second round pick and again went the high school route with prep backstop J.D. Gonzalez (3) before adding Grand Canyon CF Homer Bush Jr (4) and Duke 2B Jay Beshears (6). Only Head and Bush cracked the Padres Top 15 for 2024 and neither profiles as an elite level prospect.
Sleeper: University of Mobile RHP Tucker Musgrove (7) was one of the better two-way players in the draft after a standout career in the NAIA. In three years, he hit .398/.505/.668 with 23 HR in 489 AB and posted a 4.70 ERA with 103 K in 99.2 IP.
Grade: C+

SAN FRANCISCO GIANTS

While the Giants didn't have a huge draft budget they did an excellent job of landing some high-upside prospects who slid in the draft. With the 16th overall pick the club took two-way high school OF/RHP Bryce Eldridge. At 6'7", 225 Eldridge has a huge frame and plus raw power. While his swing can get long, he had an impressive pro debut, hitting .294/.400/.505 between Rookie Ball and Low-A. He didn't pitch in his pro debut, but he does have a plus arm and topped 96 on the mound. The Giants also added high school SS Walker Martin (2), Kent State LHP Joe Whitman (2C), Auburn SS Cole Foster (3), and Tennessee SS Maui Ahuna (4). Ahuna is a true SS and has plus speed, but showed a lot of swing-and-miss in a somewhat disappointing junior year for the Volunteers. This was a solid draft and Eldridge could develop into an impact bat down the road.

Sleeper: Louisville C Jack Payton (11) isn't particularly athletic nor is he a sure thing to stick behind the plate, but he does know how to hit and has above-average power.

Grade: A-

ST. LOUIS CARDINALS

The Cardinals finished below .500 in 2023, but once again they had to wait until the back half of round one for their pick. With number 21 overall, the Cardinals added Arizona slugger Chase Davis. The 22-year-old Davis led the PAC 12 with 21 home runs and for now is a power-over-hit prospect. The Cardinals also added Boston College OF Travis Honey (3), Stanford LHP Quinn Matthews (4), and Miami OF Zach Levenson (5). Matthews created a sensation with his 156-pitch complete game win vs Texas in the Super Regionals, but his lack of velocity makes him more of a command and control lefty than a frontline starter. Overall this class lacks a top 100 prospect and the Cardinals have their work cut out for them to get younger and more talented.

Sleeper: Fresno State LHP Ixan Henderson (8) was the Bulldogs Friday night starter for much of the season and posted a 3.74 ERA with 100 K in 89 IP despite lacking elite velocity.

Grade: C

WASHINGTON NATIONALS

The Nationals had the good fortune of picking at #2 in a year where the draft was deep. They were thrilled to land LSU CF Dylan Crews and hand him the second-largest bonus in draft history—$9.0 million. All Crews did in his three years at LSU was hit .380/.498/.689 with more walks than strikeouts. Crews controls the strike zone, has a quick bat, makes consistent hard contact, and should be able to stick in CF. The Nationals followed up with a savvy second pick, landing Miami 3B Yohandy Morales (2). Morales was considered a likely late 1st rounder, but slid to the Nationals at #40. They also added high school RHP Travis Skora (3) and Alabama OF Andrew Pickney (4). When the dust had settled, the Nationals added three top 50 draft prospects and a generational talent in Crews.

Sleeper: Indian River State College RHP Gavin Adams (11) has a plus mid-90s fastball and an above-average power slider. Adams struck out 15/9 but struggles to throw strikes consistently. With some adjustments, he could turn into a decent MLB reliever.

Grade: A

AMERICAN LEAGUE

BALTIMORE ORIOLES

With five of the top 100 picks, the Orioles objective was to add to their already impressive farm system. They selected college players with their first 16 picks, led by 17th overall pick Enrique Bradfield (1), a speedster out of Vanderbilt. The obvious shortcoming is his lack of power, but he may be the best defensive CF as well as the fastest player in the draft. Their second-rounder was another college outfielder, Mac Horvath, who has some swing-and-miss concerns, but the overall game is quite solid. He hit .321/.455/.603 in his pro debut. The Orioles are also very high on college RHPs Jackson Baumeister (CB-B) and Kiefer Lord. The first six position players selected were all outfielders.

Sleeper: RHP Michael Forret (14) did not pitch upon signing, but he has excellent projection and the ability to miss bats with three average offerings. If he can add velocity and spin to his low-90s fastball, he could be an absolute steal.

Grade: B

BOSTON RED SOX

The Red Sox were overjoyed when C Kyle Teel (1) fell to them at #14. He already made it to Double-A in his pro debut, hitting .363/.483/.495 across multiple levels. Middle infielders were a priority as Boston nabbed two prep SS in Nazzan Zanetello (2) and Antonio Anderson (3). College SS Kristian Campbell and Justin Riemer were both compensatory picks in round 4. Clearly, some of these players will transition to other positions. Zanetello has the highest upside but it may take time for him to grow into his frame and get to above average pop. While the draft class may be absent prime-time stars, there were a few intriguing arms selected in RHP CJ Weins (6) and LHP Connelly Early (6).

Sleeper: OF Caden Rose (7) has outstanding speed and athleticism and should be able to be a sound defensive CF. The hope is he continues to develop a tad more power.

Grade: B-

CHICAGO WHITE SOX

This was a very college-heavy draft, headlined by SS Jacob Gonzalez (1) who is a natural hitter and has sound defensive attributes that should allow him to play SS long-term. Chicago handed out two additional $1 million+ signing bonuses: LSU RHP Grant Taylor (2), who has a big frame and strong arm to match but he underwent Tommy John surgery prior to the season; and high school OF George Wolkow (7), who is a development project but could evolve into a massive power hitter at his peak. This appears to be a fairly pedestrian draft class that lacks upside.

Sleeper: RHP Mathias LaCombe (12) was selected out of junior college in Arizona. He posted great numbers at junior college and has the fastball/slider combo that could work well as a pro.

Grade: C

CLEVELAND GUARDIANS

The Guardians generally like hitters who can control the strike zone and barrel while finding pitchers who have workable deliveries and command upside. With their top two picks, Cleveland opted for high school players, C Ralphy Velazquez (1) and LHP Alexander Clemmey (2). Velazquez has a very discerning eye and as much power upside as any hitter in the system. He likely will have to move off C at some point. Clemmey has significant projection and should be consistently in the high-90s upon maturity. The Guardians went well over slot to select SS Alex Mooney (7) out of Duke. These three prospects were signed to seven-figure bonuses. In the 3rd and 4th rounds, a pair of Miami teammates were selected: RHP Andrew Walters and OF C.J. Kayfus. The rest of the draft had a concerted focus on contact hitters. High school pitchers were selected in rounds 12 and 13.

Sleeper: LHP Jacob Bresnahan (13) was drafted out of a Washington high school and is a projectable arm that could produce mid-90s heat; the team is also excited about his potential plus change-up.

Grade: B+

DETROIT TIGERS

By selecting four HS players with their first five picks, it was clear that Detroit wanted to inject exciting youth into the system. With the 3rd overall pick, the Tigers selected OF Max Clark. There may not be a better pure hitter his age in the draft and he also complements the hit tool with incredible speed. He should be a long-term fixture in CF. SS Kevin McGonigle (CB-A) was the 37th overall pick and he could combine with Clark to be a terrific #1-2 combo at the top of a future big league lineup. In the 3rd and 4th rounds, Detroit took high school LHP Paul Wilson (3) and 3B Carson Rucker (4). In between was Nebraska 2B Max Anderson, who has excellent power and could move thru the minors fairly quickly. Some pundits will critique Detroit for the lack of pitching selections, but the hitters were too good to pass on.

Sleeper: RHP Jaden Hamm (5) has a legitimate three-pitch mix and a chance to earn his keep as a back-end starter, but he needs to reduce his walk rate. His fastball works well in the low-90s and drops in a solid curveball to give hitters fits.

Grade: A-

HOUSTON ASTROS

Many scouts were rather surprised by the Astros draft as their selections were mainly safe picks as compared to toolsy, projectable athletes. SS Brice Matthews (1) was a surprising pick at #28 as most projections had him going in round 2 or later. He is a disciplined hitter but doesn't make consistent or loud contact. Houston opted for college players with their top four picks and only selected one high school player in the first 10 rounds before opting for prepsters in rounds 11 and 12. RHP Alonzo Treadwell (2) out of UCLA has a history of injuries, including Tommy John surgery in high school. The Astros like high school SS Chase Jaworsky (5) a lot and that is mostly based off of his athleticism and speed. He could be a standout SS or possibly a CF down the road.

Sleeper: CF Nehomar Ochoa (11) is being discussed as a possible two-way player thanks to his raw power and big fastball. He only hit in his pro debut and he showcased several solid tools.

Grade: D

KANSAS CITY ROYALS

The Royals were in desperate need for a pop of excitement and this draft may have yielded it. They selected high school players with three of their top four picks and gave out seven-figure bonuses to all of them. They had a goal of adding to their catching depth and drafted two high school backstops in Blake Mitchell (1) and Stone Russell (18). Mitchell could make quite an impact with both the bat and glove. He is advanced defensively and has well above-average raw power from the left side. High school RHP Blake Wolters (2) has pure heat with the potential for more and has a slider that gives him another above average offering. RHP Hiro Wyatt (3) a high school hurler from Connecticut could have one of the better breaking balls in the entire system and will focus on developing his mechanics and durability. The Royals are excited about the upside in this class, but it likely won't pay dividends for several years.

Sleeper: RHP Logan Martin (12) didn't last through the entire season at Kentucky, but he's a relatively fresh arm who has a potential plus fastball that features both velocity and spin. If he throws strikes, he could have a chance as a mid-rotation starter.

Grade: B

LOS ANGELES ANGELS

The Angels may have put all of their draft capital into one prospect, though he's already gotten to the majors. 1B Nolan Schanuel (1) could be the Angels Opening Day 1B; the team would like to see him settle into his raw power by making harder contact. They went with college picks in the first seven rounds. Position players were in order after years of opting for arms in the draft. Stanford 3B Alberto Rios (3) and OF Joe Redfield (4) provide relatively safe picks. Rios has a decent all-around game while Redfield provides speed and defense. All in all, this was a middling class but the benefit, of course, is having a true big leaguer already among the bunch.

Sleeper: RHP Barrett Kent (8), a high school pick from Texas, has the tool set to be a quality starter in the system. There is a lot to work with here with a current average fastball and a potential above average slider.

Grade: B-

MINNESOTA TWINS

Likely no team benefited more from the new draft lottery than the Twins, who secured the #5 overall pick and then saw uber-talented high school OF Walker Jenkins (1) fall right into their lap. He offers immense upside and could advance relatively quickly for a prep star. They were also elated to select prep RHP Charlee Soto (CB-A), who brings a current plus fastball and could have to additional plus offerings if he reaches his ceiling. Four draftees earned seven-figure bonuses, including Arizona State 2B Luke Keaschall (2). After position players with four of the first seven picks, the Twins opted for pitchers in rounds 7 thru 18. HS RHP Dylan Questad (5) gives them another intriguing, fresh arm with plenty of current talent and projection.

Sleeper: RHP Jack Dougherty (9) pitched at Ole Miss and showed pose and a solid mix of offerings. The Twins believe they can remake his delivery to add a few ticks to his fastball while maintaining the effectiveness of his slider.

Grade: A-

NEW YORK YANKEES

The Yankees were without a 2nd or 5th round selection, but reserved their lone seven-figure bonus for high school SS George Lombard (1), who brings power potential and an exciting tool box to the table. He will need significant polish and development time but the Yankees can be patient. 2B Roc Riggio (4) is another quality bat who performed well in college. He is the type of player who could get to the high minors in short order. The Yankees opted to sit all of their drafted pitchers, giving them rest after their respective 2023 campaigns. LHP Kyle Carr (3) and RHP Cade Smith (6) have good arms with bat-missing ability. They are also very high on RHP Nicholas Judice (8) who has a devastating breaking ball that is tough to make contact against.

Sleeper: RHP Bryce Warrecker (20) may have been chosen in the last round but he has an intimidating and imposing frame (6'8", 245). He throws consistent strikes and has a chance to add velocity to an average fastball.

Grade: C

OAKLAND ATHLETICS

The A's surprised some by selecting Grand Canyon SS Jacob Wilson (1) at 6th overall. Many thought Oakland would snare a high-upside athlete, but they were confident in Wilson's ability to make consistent contact and play solid defense while exhibiting exceptional baseball intelligence. Then they lined up two other position players: 3B Myles Naylor (CB-A) and Rutgers OF Ryan Lasko (2), who both have good bats and have the potential to be MLB starters. Two high school arms followed: RHPs Steven Echavarria (3) and Cole Miller (4) both offer solid fastballs and plenty of projection. Miller needs to grow into his frame; Echavarria has a more promising upside. This is a very solid, well-rounded draft class.

Sleeper: OF/1B Will Simpson (15) was a senior sign but could be well on his way to doing professional damage as a hitter. The Athletics believe in his swing to produce above average pop to all fields.

Grade: A-

SEATTLE MARINERS

Early returns of the Mariners' draft look promising after Seattle selected three high school players, two of which are shortstops. Few can quibble with SS Colt Emerson's (1) pro debut; he hit .302/.436/.444 in 63 AB in Low-A ball. He makes very easy contact with a simple stroke and can play both middle infield spots. SS Tai Peete (CB-A) was taken with the 30th selection and is the most raw of the three, but he has immense upside with blazing speed. OF Jonny Farmelo was sandwiched between them and he exhibits plus bat speed with tremendous athleticism. For the rest of the draft, they continued to focus on upside and projection. Six of the first seven picks were hitters and they were able to sign 21 out of the 22 overall picks.

Sleeper: RHP Elijah Dale (13) lacks size and velocity but he's tough to square up with an arsenal that produces significant pitch movement and spin. He throws from a low release point to add to his effectiveness.

Grade: A

TAMPA BAY RAYS

Unsurprisingly, the Rays featured a strong mix of players with varying skills. 3B Brayden Taylor (1) is the gem of the class and has the offensive talent to be a middle-of-the-order run producer from the left side. The Rays are very high on Mississippi State OF Colton Ledbetter (2) who may have more power upside than Taylor but will need more work on his approach. In between, Tampa Bay took high school SS Adrian Santana who has excellent speed and sound defensive attributes. Most of the pitchers selected don't have great pedigrees, but the Rays really like RHP Trevor Harrison (5) and RHP Owen Wild (7). The best pro debut belonged to 1B Tre' Morgan (3) who is a dynamite defensive prospect who can put bat to ball.

Sleeper: RHP Garrett Edwards (11) has outstanding talent but was victimized by injury in the middle of his college season at LSU. He has a terrific fastball and slider and is only an offspeed pitch from being a capable mid-rotation guy.

Grade: B+

TEXAS RANGERS

The Rangers selected perhaps the best player in the draft in OF Wyatt Langford (1). Langford is already very close to making his major league debut after compiling a line of .360/.480/.677 with 10 HR and 12 SB in 161 AB across four levels. Though he didn't get the same amount of publicity as Paul Skenes or Dylan Crews, he might just become the better major leaguer. Texas didn't get a 2nd or 3rd round selection due to free agent signings. With their next four picks, they selected pitchers. The highest, RHP Skylar Hales (4), is a college reliever who may have been an overdraft. High school RHP Caden Scarborough (6) may have the highest upside of any arm selected, though he will need lots of professional instruction.

Sleeper: C Julian Brock (8) has good size and strength as a hitter and moves well enough behind the plate to project to become at least an average defender.

Grade: B

TORONTO BLUE JAYS

The Blue Jays focused on getting the best available player at their respective draft positions. SS Arjun Nimmala, a projectable high school hitter, was the 20th overall pick and he combines youth with a dazzling display of offensive tools. He has the frame to grow into and he should be able to stick at SS. They didn't have a 2nd round pick and opted for RHP Juaron Watts-Brown (3) whose stuff is much better than his production would indicate. Toronto is also intrigued with their next two pitchers selected, HS RHP Landen Maroudis (4) and Michigan LHP Connor O'Halloran. Maroudis increased his stock by adding velocity while O'Halloran is a savvy pitcher who can tantalize with an excellent slider. There were some shrewd position player picks here as well. OF Jace Bohrofen (6) and OF Braden Barry (8) have solid offensive talent.

Sleeper: OF Sam Shaw (9) is a high school talent from Canada who relies on instincts and a strong feel of hitting. He doesn't project to plus power but he should hit enough and play solid defense in a corner position.

Grade: B+

High School Players to Watch in 2024

by Chris Blessing

Here is our annual list of draft-eligible high school seniors who project as top MLB fantasy prospects heading into their prep season, beginning in mid-February in some states and extending into June in northern states. With the 2024 MLB Draft once again scheduled for All Star weekend in July, there are sure to be changes in rankings between now and then. This is merely a guideline for those managers who can roster anyone within the universe or those dynasty managers looking for a preview of their first-year player drafts in the summer and/or next off-season.

High school draft prospects have the most leverage among all prospects, meaning some of the best prep prospects on this list may decide to go to school if they believe they can improve their bonus earning potential by sticking with their college commitment. It's been a nice gamble for some prospects, including Cade Horton (RHP, CHC), a potential 2nd round pick in the 2020 draft who went undrafted, and Brooks Lee (SS, MIN), a potential 1st rounder in the 2019 draft who was taken in the 35th round as a courtesy pick, meaning a team likes a player but doesn't plan to sign them. However, sometimes it's not, like what took place with Mike Vasil (RHP, NYM), who was a potential 1st round pick in 2018 and chose to go to the University of Virginia. He was drafted in the 8th round of the 2021 draft, costing himself millions of dollars.

Nine prep position players, one prep pitcher and one two-way prep prospect were drafted in the 1st round of last year's draft. Additionally, four prep position players and two prep pitchers earned 1st round money signing outside of the 1st round. This year's prep class isn't deep, especially in the eastern time zone, including traditional strong states such as Georgia and North Carolina.

1. Konnor Griffin, OF – *Jackson Prep (MS), R/R 6-4, 210*
Griffin is a long-levered, athletic beast with multiple tools rated potential plus or better. Griffin did the most damage in the summer of 2023 playing for the Under-18 Team USA squad, showcasing his double-plus speed and raw plus power potential. A two-way player, who is up to 90 MPH on the mound, will likely be a CF prospect as a pro.

2. PJ Morlando, OF – *Summerville HS (SC), L/R 6-3, 200*
Morlando is a potential offensive powerhouse. During the summer showcase circuit and his time with the Under-18 Tean USA squad, Morlando consistently got to hard contact while also spraying the ball to the gaps. He adapted well to a variety of pitching and limited whiffs. There is potentially plus power to come and he projects as a future RF.

3. Cam Caminiti, LHP – *Saguaro HS (AZ), L/L 6-2, 205*
Caminiti, the son of former NL MVP Ken Caminiti, is the highest-rated pitcher on the list this year. He carried a better than 50% whiff rate throughout the summer. He sits 91-94 MPH with his fastball and also throws a potentially plus sweeper, along with two other pitches from an over-the-top slot. Caminiti hopes to throw more strikes this spring.

4. Noah Franco, OF/LHP – *IMG Academy (FL), L/L 6-3, 197*
Teams either really like Franco at the plate or they really like him on the mound. At the plate, he's more advanced than he is as a pitcher with power-driven hit tool and the potential to hit for above-average power at maturity. As a hurler, it's a LHP with a chance to get to elite velocity with strength gains and maturity.

5. Bryce Rainer, SS/RHP – *Harvard-Westlake HS (CA), L/R 6-3, 185*
Rainer's summer on the circuit wasn't as strong as others on the list. However, teams love the combination of power and athleticism in his profile. A two-way player, Rainer was much better in his limited action on the mound than with the bat. Most contacts still believe his future is at the plate, not on the mound.

6. Owen Paino, SS – *Roy C Ketcham HS (NY), L/R 6-3, 205*
Paino has one of the more refined prep approaches in the draft. His ability to get to hard contact while spraying the ball to all fields is only matched by the top two prospects on this list. Paino has plus power potential, especially with strength gains and swing adjustments. The body and arm fits best at 3B.

7. Derek Curiel, OF – *Orange Lutheran HS (CA), L/L 6-2, 175*
Curiel is noted for his athleticism. He had a solid summer, seemingly on the basepaths throughout the showcase circuit. It's a hit-over-power profile, working counts and spraying the ball, especially from the pull side to the gaps. A good defender, Curiel has the first step and the speed to patrol CF as a pro.

8. Caleb Bonemer, SS – *Okemos HS (MI), R/R 6-1, 195*
Bonemer is a power-over-hit prospect with a high fantasy ceiling due to his plus run tool. It was the tale of two summers for Bonemer, who struggled in the Prospect Pipeline Development (PDP) League with a whiff rate over 35% but dominated the showcase circuit as the summer wore on. It's raw plus-plus power potential if the profile makes enough contact.

9. Carter Johnson, SS – *Oxford HS (AL), L/R 6-2, 180*
Johnson is a contact-oriented hitter with a chance to get to above-average power potential. He struggled through periods of the summer with poor swing decisions. However, the player who started and ended the season were eerily similar. Evaluators are split whether Johnson can stick at SS long term.

10. Slade Caldwell, OF – *Valley View HS (AR), L/L 5-9, 172*
Caldwell is a short-statured hitter with a feel for hitting who had a solid summer circuit, leading to his draft season. It's a contact-oriented approach with spray tendencies. Power is depressed due to heavy groundball contact rate. A double-plus runner, Caldwell is a threat on the bases and has the reactions to stick in CF.

11. Charlie Bates, SS – *Palo Alto HS (CA), L/R 6-1, 185*
Bates has a contact, spray approach at the plate, featuring a short, compact swing and plus hand/eye skills. While he struggled piling up hits during the showcase circuit, Bates worked counts and got on base at a high rate, allowing for his plus speed to play as an SB threat. A pure SS, Bates will stick at the position long term.

12. Cade Arrambide, C – *Tomball HS (TX), R/R 6-3, 209*
Arrambide is the goods behind the plate with a chance at becoming an elite defender, which presently carries his profile. At the plate, it's a power-over-contact approach with a whiff rate over

40% on the showcase circuit. It's raw plus power to all fields; 40% of his hits were for extra bases during the summer.

More to Watch

Theodore Gillen, SS, *Westlake HS (TX)*

Owen Hall, RHP, *Edmond North HS (OK)*

Tegan Kuhns, RHP, *Gettysburg Area HS (PA)*

Brendan Lawson, SS, *Lawrence Pitts Collegiate HS (ON Canada)*

Joey Oakie, RHP, *Ankeny Centennial HS (IA)*

William Schmidt, RHP, *Catholic HS (LA)*

Anson Seibert, RHP, *Blue Valley Southwest HS (KS)*

Garrett Shull, OF, *Enid HS (OK)*

College Players to Watch in 2024

by Chris Lee

The 2024 MLB Amateur Draft will be held in Arlington, Texas, starting on July 14, with Cleveland picking first followed by Cincinnati, Colorado, Oakland and the White Sox. Here are the top college prospects to watch from a fantasy baseball perspective. It's a hitting-heavy class, with (as of fall 2023) a separation from the top three on the list to the next group.

1. JJ Wetherholt, 2B/SS— *West Virginia, L/R, 5-10, 190*
Wetherholt's only Division I offer was from WVU. Two years after arrival, he became the Division I batting champ after a .449/.517/.787 season, mashing 16 HR and adding 36 SB while earning Big 12 Player of the Year honors and frequently putting the ball in play (10 bb%, 8 k%). He's got gap-to-gap power and is widely is regarded by many as the best pure hitter in the draft. He might be a second baseman, which is where he played in high school and at WVU. But he's athletic and coordinated—an avid golfer, Wetherholt forced himself to do so right-handed, whereas he bats left-handed—and has also played third and in the outfield. He batted .263/.481/.579 with 2 HR in eight games with Team USA.

2. Travis Bazzana, 2B— *Oregon State, L/R, 6-0, 199*
Bazzanna, who hails from Sydney, Australia, hit .374/.500/.622 with 11 HR, 36 SB and a 1.3 Eye as a sophomore, then, hit .375 with 6 HR and 15 SB and a 1.3 Eye in 144 AB while earning Cape Cod League MVP honors. Bazzana's approach is cerebral—he's put together Power Point presentations about hitting to his teammates—and is heavily driven by analytics and time at Driveline, where he worked on his pull-side power (including adding backspin to his ability to drive the ball) and swing mechanics. That, and hitting with a wooden bat (which he started doing at 14, and credits for his ability to barrel the ball) helped him hit .382 with 6 HR, 16 SB and a 1.2 Eye in the Cape last summer.

3. Nick Kurtz, 1B— *Wake Forest, L/L, 6-5, 235*
A high-school basketball player who was a mostly-anonymous recruit, Kurtz turned his full attention to baseball, which resulted in a 15-HR freshman campaign in 2022. After off-season shoulder surgery, Kurtz then blossomed into one of the country's

best hitters last season with a .353/.527/.784, 24-HR sophomore season and a 1.3 Eye. He's a good defender who could play outfield and his swing draws comparisons to Matt Olson. Kurtz plays for one of the county's most data-driven programs at Wake Forest but describes his approach as, "I like to keep it as simple as possible and just hit."

4. Charlie Condon, 1B/OF— *Georgia, R/R, 6-6, 211*
Condon redshirted as freshman before exploding for a .386./484/.800 season (the latter led the Southeastern Conference) with 25 HR and an 0.7 Eye in 2023 and then hit 3 HR in 10 games for Team USA. While it is rare for a player to have that kind of breakout, Wyatt Langford (4 AB as a freshman for Florida) followed a similar path two seasons ago. The bat and raw power should get him there but where he plays is a question. With that limited skill set, there's a risk he's a right-handed platoon bat.

5. Jac Caglianone, 1B/LHP— *Florida, L/L, 6-5, 245*
Nicknamed "Jactani" due to his status as college baseball's top two-way star, Caglianone hit .323/.389/.738 with a BBCOR-bat-era-record 33 HR, adding a 10.5 Dom and a 1.6 Cmd in 74 2/3 IP as a left-handed starter inside the ultra-competitive Southeastern Conference. Caglianone's future appears to be as hitter thanks to mammoth power that's produced exit velocities up to 115 MPH and home-run distances of 488 feet, though selectivity and over-aggressiveness and chasing out of the zone (5 bb%, 18 k%) are concerns. Caglianone can touch 100 with his fastball and adds a change-up and a slider, but he's not been able to throw strikes or work deep into games with any consistency (though that reportedly got better in the fall).

6. Vance Honeycutt, OF— *North Carolina, R/R, 6-3, 205*
Honeycutt is a brilliant defender—he was the ACC Defensive Player of the Year—but there have been wild variations in his performance at the plate. As a freshman, he hit .296/.409/.672 with 25 HR but that came with a 14 bb% and a 30 k%. As a sophomore, those figures improved to 20 bb% and 20 k% but that came with 12 HR and a .257/.418/.492 line. But Honeycutt swiped 29 bases as a freshman and 19 as a sophomore, and with the right player development system, he could be a stat-stuffer in every category. The upside a potential plus-run guy with some power, but the downside is he's a fourth-outfielder valued more for defense than offense.

7. Hagen Smith, LHP— *Arkansas, L/L, 6-3, 215*
Smith, who posted a 13.7 Dom (but also a 5.8 bb%) last year, has size and the ability to touch 100 from the left side, and there aren't many of those. Throw in a slider that's got a chance to be special and the fact he won't turn 21 until August 2024 and there's a case he's the best college arm in the draft, with command and control obviously being the biggest concerns.

8. Brody Brecht, RHP— *Iowa, R/R, 6-4, 225*
Brecht's downside is obviously wildness (bb% of 10.0 as a freshman and 7.1 as a sophomore), but consider that Brecht also came to Iowa as a scholarship wide receiver on its football team. The fastball has exceeded 100, he's got an upper-80s slider as well as a curve and some think all can be elite pitches. As raw as Brecht

is, the 13.8 career Dom and a .143 average against in 2023 have everyone's attention.

9. Josh Hartle, LHP—*Wake Forest, L/L, 6-5, 200*
Hartle, easily the most refined pitcher on this list, posted a 12.3 Dom and a 2.1 bb% as junior, allowing 1.0 HR/9 pitching inside a bandbox of a home park. There's a low-90s fastball, a cutter and a curve and also consistency: he went five innings or more in 15 of his 18 starts last year. Reid Detmers or Jordan Montgomery might be reasonable comps.

10. Chase Burns, RHP—*Wake Forest, R/R, 6-4, 195*
When Burns is on, he's just about unhittable, as last year's 14.3 Dom suggests. The fact that Burns was demoted to the bullpen mid-season last year at Tennessee tells you something else. The fastball can hit 100-102 with a low-90s slider. He'll pitch his junior year at Wake Forest.

11. Tommy White, 3B—*LSU, R/R, 6-0, 236*
After a 27-HR freshman season at North Carolina State in 2022, "Tommy Tanks" bashed 24 HR with a .374/.432/.725 line last season in helping lead the Tigers to a national title. He puts the ball in play—a 7 bb% and 13 k%—but all his value is in the batter's box as he lacks athleticism and doesn't have other carrying tools, making him a potential high-risk selection.

12. Braden Montgomery, OF/RHP—*B/R, Texas A&M, 6-2, 217*
A switch-hitter with power, Montgomery showed improvements in his bat-to-ball skills from freshman year; although his home-run output dipped from 18 to 17, his slash line improved from .294/.361/.596 to .336/.461/.611 and as his bb% shot from 7 to 16 and his k% dipped from 27 to 21. Montgomery wasn't effective as a pitcher last year but does throw 96 and that may have played into his decision to transfer from Stanford to Texas A&M. More than likely, he's a corner-outfield bat with some pop.

Others to watch:

Kevin Bazzell, C, Texas Tech

Rodney Green Jr, OF, California

Seaver King, SS, Wake Forest

Mike Sirota, OF, Northeastern

Trey Yeseavage, RHP, East Carolina

Consider the Shallow Dynasty League
by Doug Otto

I was enticed by the notion of the dynasty format early on in my fantasy baseball experience. Because of the sheer volume of players, it seemed baseball was the best sport for the dynasty format, with a million different ways to craft a juggernaut. Stars frequently come out of nowhere, and I wanted to be the one scooping them up before anyone else. This desire led me to deep dynasty leagues from the get-go, first a 24-team league and then a 30-team league the following year. I was looking for the ultimate challenge and I believed I had found it. I wanted any and all players to be relevant, to have trade value, to be a step towards a well-oiled machine. I eventually built a contender, but it did not come without a few realizations about deep dynasty formats that have shaped a lot of what I now value in a dynasty baseball experience. Now in my ninth season of dynasty baseball, I've come to find shallow- to mid-sized leagues as my preferred format.

Owner Turnover
This is the first downside I came to resent in deep leagues. Dynasty leagues are often cobbled together by a group of strangers recruited on various web forums. The hope is always that you will get a group of 20-30 engaged, passionate owners who will stick around for years to come. This is unfortunately almost never the case. Every offseason invariably comes with owners dropping out, often orphaning teams that have not been actively managed. This makes them exceptionally hard to advertise to other people with whom you might have no personal connection. Trying to recruit managers for teams that have been mismanaged or left to rot with few, if any, enticing assets gets old quickly as a yearly exercise. There is still frequent owner turnover in shallower leagues, but the worst team in a 14-team league is an easier sell. There just aren't many people out there willing to take on a three- to four-year rebuilding project in a 30-team league.

Unresponsive Owners
Having active owners is important not only for limiting the work caused by owner turnover, but also for general league health. Every league has owners that just don't respond to trade offers, especially deep leagues. Deep-league dynasty baseball is a time-intensive hobby and can understandably become too much to keep up with. But it's frustrating to get non-responses in deep dynasty baseball where making moves is integral to success. There are unresponsive owners in leagues of all sizes, but it feels more

demoralizing in deep leagues where active participation is especially crucial to league health. Having owners you can work with determines your experience.

Trading is Everything

Much of the appeal of deep dynasty leagues is the added emphasis on trading. When seemingly every relevant player is rostered, the only realistic way to build a competitive team after the draft is over is to make trades, and plenty of them. If you love hashing out trades back and forth 365 days a year, then deep-league dynasty is for you. But when owners are unresponsive, or you can't get any of the players you want, or no one is interested in the players you have to offer, working out trades can get exhausting. And even in deep leagues, many owners are justifiably not interested in fringe players. In my experience, most trades involving fringe-type players end up being completely inconsequential anyway. Managers tend to understand this, as many trade discussions fail to get off the ground unless an exciting, impactful player is mentioned. Players that don't move the needle are naturally hard to get excited about, so most trades start with players that would be rostered in shallower leagues anyway.

When I first started playing in deep dynasty leagues, I loved engaging in days- or even weeks-long trade negotiations. But it's hard to keep up the level of dedication needed to continue making trades over time. One of the biggest benefits of playing in a shallower league is having viable free agents in the player pool to supplement your team, breaking up the monotony of trade negotiations.

Health Plays an Outsized Role

I first joined deep leagues with the desire to prove my mettle in the toughest fantasy baseball format. I assumed a 30-team dynasty league was the best format for this because it involved the deepest rosters with the most competitors. Don't get me wrong - winning one of these leagues is very difficult and requires plenty of diligent care and attention. As I mentioned before, you need to be an active manager willing to work through tricky trade negotiations and identify the right players to target year-round. While sustained success in deep dynasty leagues requires skill and dedication, it also requires plenty of luck. Never mind the luck that comes with having your team perform at the right times, deeper leagues mean thinner waiver wires, which in turn mean greater reliance on health.

Health is a fickle thing in all fantasy sports, and managing the inevitable blow of losing a key player to injury is what separates good fantasy players from great ones. But many winning fantasy squads need health to win, and having a healthy team requires plenty of luck. Some players are more injury-prone than others,

but it is nearly impossible to predict when and for how long players will be injured. And in deeper formats, it only takes a few key injuries to sink a team from contention. This, in combination with paper-thin free agent options, means getting lucky with good health is more important for success in deep leagues. In shallower leagues, owners are often challenged to work the waiver wire for injury replacements, which takes more skill to pull off than getting lucky with health.

Playing Time Disparities Are Heightened

This is the point that took me the longest to realize. In deep fantasy formats, there are naturally going to be more players in your lineup that have unstable playing time. You might have the talent to fill in for key injuries on your roster, but you don't get to decide if they actually play. A real-life GM might be able to weather the storm of losing their starting 2B for a month by calling up a prospect, but fantasy managers can't make that call. Thus, a player whose production level is rosterable only in deeper formats comes with variance in playing time that is entirely outside of the control of the fantasy manager. There is a greater proportion of players in deep leagues whose value is hampered by real-life roster construction, which isn't very fun to have to worry about when you have no control over it.

Conclusion

It must be reiterated that this is largely subjective. No one format is objectively the best, and everyone has their own unique preferences.

But after spending most of my dynasty playing time in deep leagues, I feel that they are no longer conducive to what I'm looking for in dynasty baseball. I want to feel like I can win a league by making the right moves, rather than lucking into a healthy team getting playing time. I want to play with managers who I know are active, and not bang my head against the wall replacing 5-10 of them every year. I want to play in leagues where I have options outside of making trades to improve my team. And maybe most importantly, I want to play in a format where I don't need to burn myself out just to stay on top of things.

It is totally understandable for prospect hounds to seek out 30-team leagues for the ultimate challenge and to put their prospect knowledge to the test. Deep leagues certainly are challenging, but I'm no longer of the opinion that they are the end-all-be-all format for flexing one's prospecting muscles. With that in mind, I now find 16-team leagues to feature the best combo of depth and flexibility for dynasty formats, allowing for deep prospect knowledge to yield competitive advantages while also relaxing the reliance on trading and good player health needed for success in deeper leagues.

2024's Top Fantasy Prospects

1	Jackson Holliday	SS	BAL		51	Drew Gilbert	OF	NYM
2	Jackson Chourio	OF	MIL		52	Emmanuel Rodriguez	OF	MIN
3	Wyatt Langford	OF	TEX		53	Mason Miller	RHP	OAK
4	Junior Caminero	3B	TAM		54	Jared Jones	RHP	PIT
5	Jordan Lawlar	SS	ARI		55	Luisangel Acuna	SS	NYM
6	Paul Skenes	RHP	PIT		56	Owen Caissie	OF	CHC
7	Dylan Crews	OF	WAS		57	Ronny Mauricio	SS	NYM
8	Evan Carter	OF	TEX		58	Jeferson Quero	C	MIL
9	Walker Jenkins	OF	MIN		59	Marco Luciano	SS	SF
10	James Wood	OF	WAS		60	Druw Jones	OF	ARI
11	Noelvi Marte	3B	CIN		61	Orelvis Martinez	SS	TOR
12	Coby Mayo	3B	BAL		62	Noble Meyer	RHP	MIA
13	Colt Keith	3B	DET		63	Rhett Lowder	RHP	CIN
14	Ethan Salas	C	SD		64	Hurston Waldrep	RHP	ATL
15	Pete Crow-Armstrong	OF	CHC		65	Noah Schultz	LHP	CHW
16	Jackson Merrill	SS	SD		66	Tink Hence	RHP	STL
17	Jasson Dominguez	OF	NYY		67	Sebastian Walcott	SS	TEX
18	Andrew Painter	RHP	PHI		68	Spencer Jones	OF	NYY
19	Cade Horton	RHP	CHC		69	Colt Emerson	SS	SEA
20	Ricky Tiedemann	LHP	TOR		70	Jace Jung	2B	DET
21	Jackson Jobe	RHP	DET		71	Max Meyer	RHP	MIA
22	Adael Amador	SS	COL		72	Mick Abel	RHP	PHI
23	Colson Montgomery	SS	CHW		73	Roderick Arias	SS	NYY
24	Marcelo Mayer	SS	BOS		74	Edwin Arroyo	SS	CIN
25	Kyle Harrison	LHP	SF		75	Yanquiel Fernandez	OF	COL
26	Colton Cowser	OF	BAL		76	Drew Thorpe	RHP	SD
27	Jett Williams	SS	NYM		77	Brayan Rocchio	SS	CLE
28	Curtis Mead	3B	TAM		78	Gavin Stone	RHP	LA
29	Matt Shaw	SS	CHC		79	Bryce Eldridge	OF	SF
30	Roman Anthony	OF	BOS		80	Justin Crawford	OF	PHI
31	Termarr Johnson	2B	PIT		81	Kyle Teel	C	BOS
32	Chase DeLauter	OF	CLE		82	Josue De Paula	OF	LA
33	Max Clark	OF	DET		83	Chase Hampton	RHP	NYY
34	Masyn Winn	SS	STL		84	Connor Norby	2B	BAL
35	Jacob Misiorowski	RHP	MIL		85	Nolan Schanuel	1B	LAA
36	AJ Smith-Shawver	RHP	ATL		86	Bubba Chandler	RHP	PIT
37	Cole Young	SS	SEA		87	Dalton Rushing	C	LA
38	Brady House	3B	WAS		88	Everson Pereira	OF	NYY
39	Ceddanne Rafaela	OF	BOS		89	Victor Scott	OF	STL
40	Kyle Manzardo	1B	CLE		90	Lazaro Montes	OF	SEA
41	Samuel Basallo	C	BAL		91	Connor Phillips	RHP	CIN
42	Heston Kjerstad	OF	BAL		92	Bryan Ramos	3B	CHW
43	Tyler Black	3B	MIL		93	Tekoah Roby	RHP	STL
44	Dylan Lesko	RHP	SD		94	Aidan Miller	3B	PHI
45	Michael Busch	2B	CHC		95	Brock Porter	RHP	TEX
46	Robby Snelling	LHP	SD		96	Daniel Espino	RHP	CLE
47	Harry Ford	C	SEA		97	Tommy Troy	SS	ARI
48	Brooks Lee	SS	MIN		98	Cade Cavalli	RHP	WAS
49	Carson Williams	SS	TAM		99	Chase Dollander	RHP	COL
50	Xavier Isaac	1B	TAM		100	Thomas Saggese	2B	STL

Sleepers Outside the HQ100

by Jeremy Deloney

Most who follow minor league baseball already know of the vast majority of top prospects. A cursory review of the HQ100 will likely result in debate over who should be ranked higher or lower. Such is life when putting together a cumulative list of votes from several minor league experts. Differences of opinion are what often make following prospects very exciting. One prospect may be highly touted by one but not highly regarded by another.

One of the more enjoyable aspects of assessing minor league prospects is identifying those players who have a credible shot at jumping into the HQ100 at some point – whether by midseason or the following season. These are players who should be on your radar for the future. It could be argued that some of these "sleepers" should currently be in the HQ100 as evidenced by their placements on individual Top 100 lists. Others may have the requisite skills to warrant a move in the near future. We highlight several of these players below.

AMERICAN LEAGUE

Though he hasn't spent much time in full season ball, **Luis Baez (OF, HOU)** has impressed with his variety of usable tools. The 19-year-old was signed out of the Dominican Republic in 2022 and made his stateside debut with 59 AB in Rookie ball before a promotion Low-A in July. Between the two levels, the right-handed hitter batted .248/.357/.481 with 11 HR in 214 AB. Those numbers may not jump off the page but he demonstrated sound hitting instincts along with massive power potential. Baez crushes fastballs with a simple stroke, though his aggressive swing tendencies could become more problematic as he climbs the minor league ladder. It is expected he will get better as he can read spin and hit breaking balls. He'll likely spend the entirety of 2024 in either Low-A or High-A and he could be one to watch, particularly in the power department.

Caden Dana (RHP, LAA) has quickly emerged as one of the Angels best prospects despite his 11th round selection in the 2022 draft. At 6'4" 215 pounds, he projects as a bulldog starter who could pitch near or at the top of the rotation. In his first full season of pro ball, the 20-year-old posted a 3.56 ERA, 11.7 K/9 and .206 oppBA in 68.1 innings between Low-A and High-A. To preserve his arm, the Angels shut him down in mid-July after a brief bout of arm fatigue. He generates easy velocity from a high ¾ delivery that he repeats effectively. Because of elite spin rates, his 91-96 mph fastball grades easily as a plus, if not double-plus, offering. He complements it with an improving, hard slider and a below average change-up. Dana has room to improve his control and command but both project well due to his ability to repeat his arm slot and speed.

The Tigers were thrilled to see the solid pro debut of **Kevin McGonigle (2B/SS, DET)** upon his selection in the 1st round of the 2023 draft out of a Pennsylvania high school. They have long known of his ability to hit but it was his advanced, professional at bats that really stood out. The 19-year-old hit .315/.452/.411 with 1 HR, 8 SB and an 18:10 BB to K ratio. The left-handed hitter has

a very clean, quick swing and a disciplined eye at the plate. He knows which pitches he can drive and he likes to go gap to gap. Most expect him to get to double-digit HR in the near-term, but he will likely be a doubles machine at any level. Though he is most likely to move over to 2B full-time due to a fringy arm, he profiles as an offensive-minded infielder with passable defense.

One would be hard pressed to find a more projectable prospect than **Arjun Nimmala (SS, TOR)**. Sure, he's very raw and will likely need several years of seasoning in the minors. However, the upside is incredible thanks to his lean frame, advanced instincts, and elite bat speed. The right-handed hitter was a first round selection out of a Florida high school in 2023 and he only had 25 AB in his pro debut in Rookie ball. Despite the limited game action, Nimmala did draw 14 walks against just 8 strikeouts. He flashed above average glovework at SS with excellent quickness and soft, clean hands. The right-handed hitter may take time to grow into his natural power but he makes good contact and has the natural loft in his stroke to reach the seats in the present.

The Mariners used one of their three first round selections on **Tai Peete (SS, SEA)** and are enthralled with the pick due to his youth and exciting upside. The left-handed hitter fared well in his debut despite being only age 17 and hit .283/.349/.404 with 2 HR and 6 SB in 99 AB. He was one of the youngest players in the high school class and possesses among the most athleticism of that group. The Mariners moved him around the infield to get him exposure to several positions and he held his own. While he can be pull happy and be a tad too aggressive with his swing decisions, he exhibits excellent bat speed and plus speed. He'll need to make more contact but with the combination of his strength and loft, he could provide well above average power down the line.

NATIONAL LEAGUE

With one of the more intriguing defensive profiles, **Cole Carrigg (C/SS/CF, COL)** saw his stock fall during his college season at San Diego State due to lingering effects of a shoulder issue. Many saw him as a first round talent prior to the campaign. The Rockies selected him with a compensation pick and saw him hit .350/.408/.600 with 5 HR and 13 SB in 140 AB between Rookie and Low-A ball. The switch-hitter offers well above average speed and an ability to hit for BA. He may only project to average power but he can impact the game with his wheels and defensive play. Not many prospects have the ability to play catcher, shortstop and CF, but Carrigg is a standout at all spots. If he can continue to get on base and use his speed, he could be a terrific fantasy option.

It has been well noted that **Cam Collier (3B, CIN)** didn't live up to expectations while in Low-A in 2023. He lost some of his athleticism and didn't exactly stand out with his shoddy glovework. Nevertheless, the 19-year-old has a high ceiling thanks to his immense power potential and ability to put bat to ball. The left-handed hitter was a first round selection in 2022 out of Chipola JC and hit .246/.349/.356 with 6 HR in Low-A ball in 2023. On the positive side, he was excellent over the last two months and he was one of the youngest players at that level. Collier has a very strong frame and can give the ball a ride with easy, hard contact. His swing mechanics and instincts also suggest that he can hit for a nice BA but he has hit far too many groundballs. The hope is he can improve his defensive acumen and stay at 3B as opposed to diminishing his value with a move to 1B.

He may only stand 5'7" 155 pounds, but **Luis Lara (OF, MIL)** is as exciting of a prospect as there is in the lower minors. He made his stateside debut as an 18-year-old in 2023 when he split the year between Low-A and High-A. The switch-hitter batted .286/.373/.359 with 2 HR and 30 SB while fanning only 61 times in 343 AB. He may only eventually get to average power at best but he wreaks havoc on the basepaths with plus speed and he has a solid understanding of the strike zone that allows him to work counts to get on base. Lara showcases a solid hit tool with impressive bat speed and an uncanny ability to make hard contact despite his smallish frame. If he can get to 15-20 HR down the line, he could be a top-notch CF at the major league level who can hit for BA, post a high OBP and steal 30+ bases.

Sal Stewart (3B, CIN) was often overlooked in a deep Reds system but his success in the 2023 campaign shot him up the prospect depth chart. He was a first round pick in 2022 and the 20-year-old hit .275/.396/.415 with 24 doubles, 12 HR, 15 SB and a 84:77 BB/K ratio between Low-A and High-A in 2023. He was initially drafted with the thought of a power-over-hit prospect but he has already exceeded expectations with his hitting instincts and ability to use the entire field. The raw power is already average and could grow into slightly more. The 6'3" right-handed hitter likes to use the middle of the field and would take a change in approach to reach the seats more consistently. He has stood out for his athleticism and defense at 3B as well. At his peak, Stewart could become a high BA/OBP hitter with at least 20 HR.

There isn't much in the way of minor league stats to support the inclusion of **Thomas White (LHP, MIA)** in this essay. However, few 19-year-old lefties have his bat-missing potential, size and velocity. He only pitched `4.1 innings upon his selection in the first round of the 2023 draft out of a Massachusetts high school but there is much excitement over his athletic, low ¾ delivery. He has the frame to add more strength which could lead to more velocity to his already-plus 92-96 mph fastball. He can dominate with his riding fastball all on its own. But he also has a curveball with great shape that also registers strikeouts and a change-up that has plus potential. All in all, White could eventually front a rotation with three above average to plus offerings and a durable frame.

POSITIONS: Up to four positions are listed for each batter and represent those for which he appeared in at least 15 games in 2021. Positions are shown with their numeric designation (2=CA, 3=1B, 7=LF, 0=DH, etc.)

BATS: Shows which side of the plate he bats from—right (R), left (L) or switch-hitter (S).

AGE: Player's age, as of April 1, 2024.

DRAFTED: The year, round, and school that the player performed at as an amateur if drafted, or where the player was signed from, if a free agent.

EXP MLB DEBUT: The year a player is expected to debut in the major leagues.

H/W: The player's height and weight.

FUT: The role that the batter is expected to have for the majority of his major league career, not necessarily his greatest upside.

SKILLS: Each skill a player possesses is graded and designated with a "+", indicating the quality of the skills, taking into context the batter's age and level played. An average skill will receive three "+" marks.

- **PWR:** Measures the player's ability to drive the ball and hit for power.
- **BAVG:** Measures the player's ability to hit for batting average and judge the strike zone.
- **SPD:** Measures the player's raw speed and base-running ability. When we've measured run times (point of bat-to-ball contact to foot hitting first base), we've included these next to the SPD box.
- **DEF:** Measures the player's overall defense, which includes arm strength, arm accuracy, range, agility, hands, and defensive instincts.

PLAYER STAT LINES: Player statistics for the last five teams that he played for (if applicable), including college and the major leagues.

TEAM DESIGNATIONS: Each team that the player performed for during a given year is included.

LEVEL DESIGNATIONS: The level for each team a player performed is included. "AAA" means Triple-A, "AA" means Double-A, "A+" means high Class-A, "A" means full-season low Class-A, and "Rk" means rookie level. Prior to 2020, an "A-" referred to short-season Class-A, a level between rookie level and full-season low-A. Starting in 2021, that level no longer exists.

SABERMETRIC CATEGORIES: Descriptions of all the sabermetric categories appear in the glossary.

CAPSULE COMMENTARIES: For each player, a brief analysis of their skills/statistics, and their future potential is provided.

ELIGIBILITY: Eligibility for inclusion is the standard for which Major League Baseball adheres to; less than 130 major league at-bats and less than 45 days on the 26-man MLB roster.

POTENTIAL RATINGS: The Potential Ratings are a two-part system in which a player is assigned a number rating based on his upside potential (1-10) and a letter rating based on the probability of reaching that potential (A-E).

Potential

10:	Hall of Famer	5:	MLB reserve
9:	Elite player	4:	Top minor leaguer
8:	Solid regular	3:	Average minor leaguer
7:	Average regular	2:	Minor league reserve
6:	Platoon player	1:	Minor league roster filler

Probability Rating

A: 90% probability of reaching potential
B: 70% probability of reaching potential
C: 50% probability of reaching potential
D: 30% probability of reaching potential
E: 10% probability of reaching potential

SKILLS: Scouts usually grade a player's skills on the 20-80 scale, and while most of the grades are subjective, there are grades that can be given to represent a certain hitting statistic or running speed. These are indicated on this chart:

Scout Grade	HR	BA	Speed (L)	Speed (R)
80	39+	.320+	3.9	4.0
70	32-38	.300-.319	4.0	4.1
60	25-31	.286-.299	4.1	4.2
50 (avg)	17-24	.270-.285	4.2	4.3
40	11-16	.250-.269	4.3	4.4
30	6-10	.220-.249	4.4	4.5
20	0-5	.219-	4.5	4.6

CATCHER POP TIMES: Catchers are timed (in seconds) from the moment the pitch reaches the catcher's mitt until the time that the middle infielder receives the baseball at second base. This number assists both teams in assessing whether a base-runner should steal second base or not.

1.85	+
1.95	MLB average
2.05	−

Abreu,Wilyer — 79 — Boston

EXP MLB DEBUT: 2023 | H/W: 5-10 215 | FUT: Starting OF | 7C

Bats L Age 24 — 2017 FA (VZ)

Pwr + + + | BAvg + + | Spd + + + | Def + + +

Year	Lev	Team	AB	R	H	HR	RBI	Avg	OB	Slg	OPS	bb%	ct%	Eye	SB	CS	x/h%	Iso	RC/G
2021	A+	Asheville	287	52	77	16	50	268	354	495	849	12	66	0.38	10	11	42	226	6.56
2022	AA	Corpus Christi	329	81	82	15	54	249	393	459	852	19	67	0.72	23	1	48	210	6.85
2022	AA	Portland	128	25	31	4	19	242	409	375	784	22	65	0.80	8	2	29	133	6.00
2023	AAA	Worcester	299	67	82	22	65	274	394	538	932	16	75	0.80	8	1	41	264	7.39
2023	MLB	Boston	76	10	24	2	14	316	388	474	862	11	70	0.39	3	1	33	158	6.65

Short, strong OF who improved across board in 2023. Set high in HR despite fewer AB and cut K rate. Exhibits both power and patience with honed instincts. Solid all-around player who can smash line drives to gaps and run well enough for SB or XBH. Lacks frontline tool and may struggle to hit for BA due to difficulty with spin.

Acevedo,Stiven — 789 — Baltimore

EXP MLB DEBUT: 2027 | H/W: 6-4 185 | FUT: Starting OF | 7E

Bats R Age 21 — 2019 FA (DR)

Pwr + + + | BAvg + + | Spd + + + | Def + +

Year	Lev	Team	AB	R	H	HR	RBI	Avg	OB	Slg	OPS	bb%	ct%	Eye	SB	CS	x/h%	Iso	RC/G
2021	Rk	FCL Orioles B	127	20	32	2	21	252	312	323	634	8	73	0.32	9	0	16	71	3.21
2021	Rk	FCL Orioles O	3	1	1	1	3	333	333	1333	1667	0	100		0	0	100	1000	12.52
2022	Rk	FCL Orioles B	52	8	14	2	10	269	387	481	868	16	75	0.77	5	1	50	212	6.77
2022	A	Delmarva	131	18	22	1	11	168	253	244	498	10	60	0.29	7	1	32	76	1.37
2023	A	Delmarva	394	52	94	14	52	239	301	411	712	8	67	0.27	33	11	38	173	4.41

A very big-bodied outfielder with power and speed at the plate. Acevedo's size jumps out, but so does his strikeout rate. He showed improvements during his second Single-A stint. There's upside, but the hit tool might hold him back. Typical high risk/high reward prospect.

Acosta,Max — 46 — Texas

EXP MLB DEBUT: 2025 | H/W: 6-1 187 | FUT: Utility player | 6C

Bats R Age 21 — 2019 FA (VZ)

Pwr + | BAvg + + | Spd + + | Def + +

Year	Lev	Team	AB	R	H	HR	RBI	Avg	OB	Slg	OPS	bb%	ct%	Eye	SB	CS	x/h%	Iso	RC/G
2021	Rk	ACL Rangers	61	11	15	1	5	246	281	393	675	5	75	0.20	7	2	33	148	3.73
2022	A	Down East	404	62	106	4	35	262	329	361	690	9	78	0.46	44	17	29	99	4.13
2023	A+	Hickory	431	69	112	11	60	260	313	390	702	7	77	0.33	26	8	29	130	4.08

Much of Acosta's value was predicated on SS future, as frame unlikely to get beyond 50-grade power. Thoracic outlet & average speed has complicated his SS future, but he looks solid at 2B. 50-grade hit tool projection remains but still theoretical he as poor splits against LHP. Plate discipline improved; closed year strong but trending towards a utility player.

Acosta,Victor — 6 — Cincinnati

EXP MLB DEBUT: 2025 | H/W: 5-11 170 | FUT: Reserve SS | 6C

Bats B Age 19 — 2021 FA (DR)

Pwr + | BAvg + + + | Spd + + + + | Def + + +

Year	Lev	Team	AB	R	H	HR	RBI	Avg	OB	Slg	OPS	bb%	ct%	Eye	SB	CS	x/h%	Iso	RC/G
2021	Rk	DSL Padres	186	45	53	5	31	285	406	484	890	17	76	0.84	26	7	42	199	7.19
2022	Rk	ACL Padres	111	17	27	2	11	243	339	360	699	13	73	0.53	5	7	26	117	4.37
2022	Rk	ACL Reds	28	5	6	0	1	214	333	357	690	15	75	0.71	0	0	67	143	4.58
2023	A	Daytona	347	41	87	2	31	251	330	354	684	11	76	0.48	12	2	31	104	4.17

Athletic, switch-hitting SS prospect made full-season debut in 2023. Short stature with athletic frame. Compact stance, somewhat upright, creating small zone. A small hitch in load. Linear swing plane produces a compact swing. Aggressive approach causes hit tool to play down. Minimal power in frame and swing. Plus runner. Solid defender with strong arm.

Acuna,Bryan — 46 — Minnesota

EXP MLB DEBUT: 2028 | H/W: 6-0 176 | FUT: Starting 2B | 8E

Bats R Age 18 — 2022 FA (VZ)

Pwr + + | BAvg + + | Spd + + | Def + + +

Year	Lev	Team	AB	R	H	HR	RBI	Avg	OB	Slg	OPS	bb%	ct%	Eye	SB	CS	x/h%	Iso	RC/G
2022	Rk	DSL Twins	145	33	45	0	16	310	394	393	787	12	75	0.56	9	4	27	83	5.65
2023	Rk	FCL Twins	119	8	22	1	14	185	326	227	553	17	67	0.64	4	4	14	42	2.35

Brother of Ronald with advanced feel for game and impressive defensive skills. Split time between 2B and SS with quick hands, plus arm. Not much current pop or projectable power. Should hit for nice BA given instincts and hitting mechanics. Knows how to control barrel and situationally hit. Works counts to get on base consistently.

Acuna,Luisangel — 46 — New York (N)

EXP MLB DEBUT: 2024 | H/W: 5-8 181 | FUT: Starting MIF | 8C

Bats R Age 22 — 2018 FA (VZ)

Pwr + + | BAvg + + + | Spd + + + + | Def + + + +

Year	Lev	Team	AB	R	H	HR	RBI	Avg	OB	Slg	OPS	bb%	ct%	Eye	SB	CS	x/h%	Iso	RC/G
2021	A	Down East	413	77	110	12	74	266	344	404	749	11	73	0.45	44	11	27	138	4.88
2022	A+	Hickory	205	45	65	8	29	317	414	483	897	14	71	0.57	28	6	28	166	7.17
2022	AA	Frisco	152	21	34	3	18	224	302	349	650	10	76	0.47	12	3	32	125	3.60
2023	AA	Binghamton	148	25	36	2	12	243	313	304	617	9	80	0.50	15	5	14	61	3.13
2023	AA	Frisco	362	68	114	7	51	315	378	453	831	9	79	0.49	42	5	30	138	5.90

Athletic, short-statured IF prospect with bloodlines was acquired in midseason trade with TEX. Swing is similar to his brother, though they are vastly different players. Aggressive approach mitigated by plus hand/eye. Gap hitter, will pile up XBH; HR power plays to pull side only. 14-20 HR at maturity. Plus runner with SB acumen.

Adams,Jordyn — 789 — Los Angeles (A)

EXP MLB DEBUT: 2023 | H/W: 6-2 181 | FUT: Reserve OF | 6B

Bats R Age 24 — 2018 (1) HS (NC)

Pwr + + | BAvg + | Spd + + + + + | Def + + + +

Year	Lev	Team	AB	R	H	HR	RBI	Avg	OB	Slg	OPS	bb%	ct%	Eye	SB	CS	x/h%	Iso	RC/G
2021	A+	Tri-City	277	37	60	5	27	217	289	310	599	9	58	0.24	18	4	23	94	3.03
2022	A+	Tri-City	219	31	50	0	22	228	296	306	602	9	75	0.39	18	3	28	78	3.00
2022	AA	Rocket City	209	33	52	4	20	249	317	359	676	9	67	0.30	15	0	25	110	3.98
2023	AAA	Salt Lake	415	74	111	15	67	267	350	465	815	11	68	0.40	44	5	41	198	6.07
2023	MLB	LA Angels	39	1	5	0	1	128	128	128	256	0	59	0.00	1	2	0	0	-2.79

Speedy, athletic OF prospect is a 4-tool player who got MLB taste in 2023. Former 2-sporter with a slight open stance and a bit of a hitch in his load. He struggles with swing path and length issues that compromise his hit tool. Raw plus power plays only when luck would have it. Exceptional speed is his only usable asset on bases and in the field.

Adams,Luke — 5 — Milwaukee

EXP MLB DEBUT: 2026 | H/W: 6-4 210 | FUT: Starting 1B | 7D

Bats R Age 19 — 2022 (12) HS (IL)

Pwr + + + | BAvg + + | Spd + + | Def + +

Year	Lev	Team	AB	R	H	HR	RBI	Avg	OB	Slg	OPS	bb%	ct%	Eye	SB	CS	x/h%	Iso	RC/G
2022	Rk	ACL Brewers G	32	9	12	1	7	375	487	563	1050	18	75	0.88	9	1	33	188	9.42
2023	A	Carolina	339	74	79	11	54	233	373	401	775	18	71	0.77	30	10	41	168	5.63

Large-framed 3B who has already exceeded expectations in 1st full season. Finished 2nd in CAR in OBP despite poor BA. Hits LHP well but struggles with RHP. Swing mechanics need work and can struggle to catch up to velocity. Steals bases despite fringy speed. Plays above tools with polished instincts. May eventually move to 1B.

Aguilar,Starlin — 45 — Seattle

EXP MLB DEBUT: 2027 | H/W: 5-11 170 | FUT: Starting 2B | 7E

Bats L Age 20 — 2021 FA (DR)

Pwr + | BAvg + + + | Spd + + | Def + +

Year	Lev	Team	AB	R	H	HR	RBI	Avg	OB	Slg	OPS	bb%	ct%	Eye	SB	CS	x/h%	Iso	RC/G
2021	Rk	DSL Mariners	183	38	45	2	21	246	349	361	710	14	78	0.71	0	2	36	115	4.63
2022	Rk	ACL Mariners	175	13	51	0	20	291	322	337	660	4	76	0.19	0	1	14	46	3.46
2023	Rk	ACL Mariners	60	11	18	1	10	300	373	467	840	10	72	0.41	0	0	39	167	6.36

Stout INF who has yet to appear in full season affiliate. Hits for high BA with short, quick lefty stroke and has excellent pitch recognition. Good situational hitter as well and can make contact against velocity and breakers. Not much power and hits lots of singles. Limited speed and athleticism and defense needs to be upgraded to stick.

Ahuna,Maui — 6 — San Francisco

EXP MLB DEBUT: 2026 | H/W: 6-1 170 | FUT: Starting SS | 7C

Bats L Age 22 — 2023 (4) Tennessee

Pwr + + | BAvg + + | Spd + + + + | Def + + + +

Year	Lev	Team	AB	R	H	HR	RBI	Avg	OB	Slg	OPS	bb%	ct%	Eye	SB	CS	x/h%	Iso	RC/G
2023	--	Did Not Play																	

All-around SS who was inconsistent in college but has the tools to be a contributor as pro. Plays game aggressively on both sides of ball. Plays solid SS with good body control and makes all routine plays. Often makes weak contact and approach may lead to high K totals. Offers upside with HR potential but will need to tame chasing.

Alcantara,Kevin — 89 — Chicago (N)

EXP MLB DEBUT: 2025 | H/W: 6-6 188 | FUT: Starting OF | 8D

Bats R Age 21 — 2018 FA (DR)

Pwr + + + | BAvg + + + | Spd + + + | Def + + +

Year	Lev	Team	AB	R	H	HR	RBI	Avg	OB	Slg	OPS	bb%	ct%	Eye	SB	CS	x/h%	Iso	RC/G
2021	Rk	ACL Cubs	92	27	31	4	21	337	419	609	1028	12	70	0.46	3	0	39	272	9.18
2022	A	Myrtle Beach	428	76	117	15	85	273	356	451	807	11	71	0.45	14	3	34	178	5.79
2023	Rk	ACL Cubs	4	2	1	0	1	250	500	250	750	33	75	2.00	0	0	0	0	6.01
2023	A+	South Bend	371	65	106	12	66	286	341	466	807	8	74	0.32	15	4	38	181	5.56
2023	AA	Tennessee	16	4	4	1	4	250	368	500	868	16	56	0.43	0	0	50	250	7.79

Toolsy athlete still growing into his huge frame. Easy raw power, but long levers and swing-and-miss issues limit present power. Covers ground well and should be able to stick in CF for now with enough arm to shift to RF down the road. Has been pushed aggressively and has responded well at every level. Huge upside if he can put it all together.

Alcantara,Marvin — 6 — Boston

EXP MLB DEBUT: 2028 | H/W: 5-10 157 | FUT: Starting SS | 8E

Bats R Age 19 | 2022 FA (VZ) | Pwr + | BAvg + + | Spd + + + | Def + + +

Year	Lev	Team	AB	R	H	HR	RBI	Avg	OB	Slg	OPS	bb%	ct%	Eye	SB	CS	x/h%	Iso	RC/G
2022	Rk	DSL Red Sox B	189	49	57	1	29	302	394	397	791	13	83	0.88	14	2	28	95	5.70
2023	Rk	FCL Red Sox	150	26	36	1	21	240	341	307	648	13	77	0.66	6	5	22	67	3.75
2023	A	Salem	74	9	15	1	7	203	272	257	528	9	64	0.26	6	0	13	54	1.70

Lean, athletic SS who spent 1st year in US. Focused more on contact and using whole field as opposed to pulling ball over fence. Mostly goes gap to gap and makes good contact. Has some projection but power not part of calculus. Strong defender with ample range to both sides and strong arm to be asset. Needs time to develop.

Alderman,Kemp — 79 — Miami

EXP MLB DEBUT: 2026 | H/W: 6-3 250 | FUT: Starting OF | 7D

Bats R Age 21 | 2023 (2) Mississippi | Pwr + + + + | BAvg + + | Spd + + | Def + + +

Year	Lev	Team	AB	R	H	HR	RBI	Avg	OB	Slg	OPS	bb%	ct%	Eye	SB	CS	x/h%	Iso	RC/G
2023	NCAA	Mississippi	213	44	80	19	61	376	444	709	1152	11	81	0.63	5	1	41	333	9.64
2023	A	Jupiter	117	13	24	1	15	205	250	316	566	6	67	0.18	4	0	42	111	2.36

Strong, power hitting prospect parlayed career year in college into 2nd round draft selection. Frame at physical projection. Mostly upright stance with hands back and low. Limited load. Aggressive at plate with ct% concerns. Pull-oriented approach but double-plus raw power plays to all fields. Could hit 25+ HR if hit tool allows.

Alexander,Blaze — 46 — Arizona

EXP MLB DEBUT: 2024 | H/W: 5-11 160 | FUT: Reserve IF | 6C

Bats R Age 24 | 2018 (11) HS (FL) | Pwr + | BAvg + + | Spd + | Def + + +

Year	Lev	Team	AB	R	H	HR	RBI	Avg	OB	Slg	OPS	bb%	ct%	Eye	SB	CS	x/h%	Iso	RC/G
2022	AA	Amarillo	317	48	97	17	54	306	371	539	911	9	71	0.36	10	6	38	233	7.08
2022	AAA	Reno	27	8	7	2	4	259	355	519	873	13	70	0.50	0	0	43	259	6.56
2023	Rk	ACL Dbacks	7	2	2	1	2	286	286	857	1143	0	86	0.00	0	0	100	571	8.51
2023	Rk	ACL DBacks R	15	2	4	1	4	267	267	533	800	0	73	0.00	0	0	50	267	4.92
2023	AAA	Reno	247	45	72	8	52	291	394	457	852	15	66	0.51	2	2	32	166	6.81

Infield prospect was productive despite April thumb injury. HR production cooled off following Amarillo outburst, but BABIP stayed strong. Contact limitations threaten BA long term. Lots of pre-swing movement, but doesn't seem to struggle with timing. Limited HR/SB upside. More of a backup type with on-base utility. Ready for majors.

Aliendo,Pablo — 2 — Chicago (N)

EXP MLB DEBUT: 2025 | H/W: 6-0 170 | FUT: Starting C | 6B

Bats R Age 22 | 2018 FA (VZ) | Pwr + + | BAvg + + | Spd + + + | Def + + + + +

Year	Lev	Team	AB	R	H	HR	RBI	Avg	OB	Slg	OPS	bb%	ct%	Eye	SB	CS	x/h%	Iso	RC/G
2021	A	Myrtle Beach	213	42	53	5	27	249	319	366	685	9	66	0.31	2	1	28	117	4.10
2021	A+	South Bend	51	7	6	0	3	118	167	118	284	6	73	0.21	0	1	0	0	-1.61
2022	A+	South Bend	318	34	85	7	35	267	323	390	713	8	76	0.34	3	1	28	123	4.26
2023	AA	Tennessee	321	49	74	16	61	231	318	458	776	11	64	0.36	5	0	54	227	5.55

Twitchy, athletic backstop uses a simple upright stance with short stride. Generates good torque and backspin with good balance, a quick bat, and strong upper half. Needs to be more selective at the plate, too often settling for weak contact. Plus defender behind the plate with good hands, blocks well, and the arm needed to stick at the position.

Allen II,Jay — 8 — Cincinnati

EXP MLB DEBUT: 2025 | H/W: 6-2 190 | FUT: Starting OF | 7E

Bats R Age 21 | 2021 (1) HS (FL) | Pwr + + | BAvg + + + | Spd + + + + | Def + + +

Year	Lev	Team	AB	R	H	HR	RBI	Avg	OB	Slg	OPS	bb%	ct%	Eye	SB	CS	x/h%	Iso	RC/G
2021	Rk	ACL Reds	61	20	20	3	11	328	406	557	963	12	80	0.67	14	1	35	230	7.55
2022	A	Daytona	241	48	54	3	21	224	335	332	666	14	70	0.55	31	6	33	108	4.03
2022	A+	Dayton	74	13	17	0	8	230	269	297	567	5	74	0.21	12	4	18	68	2.34
2023	Rk	ACL Reds	13	9	3	1	1	231	524	462	985	38	69	2.00	6	2	33	231	9.07
2023	A+	Dayton	91	15	14	1	3	154	222	220	442	8	56	0.20	10	3	29	66	0.38

Athletic OF prospect struggled with contact and thumb injury, contributing to lost season at High-A. Frame is at physical projection after adding strength prior to 2023 season. Plus run tool carries profile. However, hit tool issues have backed up profile considerably; mostly mechanical issues and protecting thumb. 2024 is make-or-break year.

Almeyda,Luis — 56 — Baltimore

EXP MLB DEBUT: 2028 | H/W: 6-2 180 | FUT: Starting SS | 7E

Bats R Age 17 | 2023 FA (DR) | Pwr + + + | BAvg + + | Spd + + + | Def + + +

Year	Lev	Team	AB	R	H	HR	RBI	Avg	OB	Slg	OPS	bb%	ct%	Eye	SB	CS	x/h%	Iso	RC/G
2023	Rk	DSL Orioles 2	58	6	11	2	14	190	288	310	598	12	76	0.57	2	2	27	121	2.84

As a not-even-18-year-old, he debuted in the DSL after receiving a $2.3 million signing bonus. His long, athletic frame means he could grow into some power. His DSL debut says there's still a long way to go. Will take lot of development time, but has good upside. Should be able to stick at SS with ample range and arm strength.

Almonte,Ariel — 79 — Cincinnati

EXP MLB DEBUT: 2026 | H/W: 6-1 170 | FUT: Starting OF | 7E

Bats L Age 20 | 2021 FA (DR) | Pwr + + + + | BAvg + + | Spd + + | Def + +

Year	Lev	Team	AB	R	H	HR	RBI	Avg	OB	Slg	OPS	bb%	ct%	Eye	SB	CS	x/h%	Iso	RC/G
2021	Rk	DSL Reds	162	35	45	5	33	278	378	438	816	14	68	0.50	15	6	33	160	6.17
2022	Rk	ACL Reds	140	28	40	6	24	286	379	493	872	13	65	0.43	1	0	43	207	7.11
2023	A	Daytona	335	35	68	5	33	203	292	299	590	11	60	0.32	4	0	31	96	2.87

Strong, powerful prospect struggled with contact in full-season debut. Sluggish frame has room for additional muscle, likely sapping remaining athleticism. Upright, slight open stance. Wraps bat into hit position, delaying swing from starting. Plus bat speed struggles to play due to several holes in zone. Plus raw power unlikely to materialize.

Alvarez,Ignacio — 6 — Atlanta

EXP MLB DEBUT: 2025 | H/W: 5-11 190 | FUT: Starting MIF | 7D

Bats R Age 20 | 2022 (5) Riverside CC | Pwr + + | BAvg + + + + | Spd + + | Def + + +

Year	Lev	Team	AB	R	H	HR	RBI	Avg	OB	Slg	OPS	bb%	ct%	Eye	SB	CS	x/h%	Iso	RC/G
2022	Rk	FCL Braves	43	11	12	1	5	279	380	419	799	14	86	1.17	4	0	25	140	5.76
2022	A	Augusta	51	14	15	0	6	294	486	373	858	27	82	2.11	4	1	20	78	7.39
2023	A+	Rome	419	62	119	7	66	284	381	391	773	14	79	0.76	16	5	26	107	5.39

Hit-first prospect had solid season in High-A. Bat was advanced for level but showed growth at SS on defense. Upright, open swing with short levers, producing flat, compact bat path. Spray approach with heavy groundball and top-spin heavy lined contact. Limited power upside in both frame and swing. High makeup likely carries him to MLB.

Amador,Adael — 46 — Colorado

EXP MLB DEBUT: 2024 | H/W: 6-0 200 | FUT: Starting SS | 9C

Bats B Age 20 | 2019 FA (DR) | Pwr + + + | BAvg + + + + + | Spd + + + | Def + + +

Year	Lev	Team	AB	R	H	HR	RBI	Avg	OB	Slg	OPS	bb%	ct%	Eye	SB	CS	x/h%	Iso	RC/G
2021	Rk	ACL Rockies	164	41	49	4	24	299	398	445	843	14	82	0.93	10	7	31	146	6.29
2022	A	Fresno	449	100	131	15	57	292	407	445	852	16	85	1.30	26	12	30	154	6.46
2023	Rk	ACL Rockies	18	6	7	2	9	389	500	778	1278	18	83	1.33	0	0	43	389	11.46
2023	A+	Spokane	222	46	67	9	35	302	387	514	901	12	88	1.19	12	4	39	212	6.81
2023	AA	Hartford	35	3	5	1	2	143	231	229	459	10	77	0.50	3	1	20	86	0.99

Struggled with injuries but still posted an .875 OPS at three levels. Holds his own from both sides of the plate with plus bat-to-ball skills and is willing to work counts and hunt pitches he can mash. Generates above-average power from his compact frame and should hit 20+ HR if he can add more loft to his swing. Fringe arm could bump him to 2B.

Amaya,Jacob — 46 — Miami

EXP MLB DEBUT: 2023 | H/W: 6-0 180 | FUT: Reserve SS | 6B

Bats R Age 25 | 2017 (11) HS (CA) | Pwr + + | BAvg + + | Spd + + + | Def + + + +

Year	Lev	Team	AB	R	H	HR	RBI	Avg	OB	Slg	OPS	bb%	ct%	Eye	SB	CS	x/h%	Iso	RC/G
2021	AA	Tulsa	417	60	90	12	47	216	303	343	646	11	75	0.50	5	0	31	127	3.49
2022	AA	Tulsa	182	39	48	9	26	264	374	500	874	15	84	1.10	3	1	46	236	6.61
2022	AAA	Oklahoma City	294	46	76	8	45	259	364	381	745	14	72	0.59	3	1	25	122	5.02
2023	AAA	Jacksonville	484	85	122	15	65	252	347	407	754	13	78	0.66	6	2	35	155	5.02
2023	MLB	Miami	9	1	2	0	2	222	222	222	444	0	89	0.00	1	0	0	0	0.93

Light-hitting, defensively skilled SS made MLB debut after solid MiLB season. Athletic frame. It's a contact-oriented bat that doesn't have much strength or the requisite bat speed to get to power. Struggles especially getting to velocity. Will work counts and eek out walks. Average runner with great first step defensively. Not a SB threat.

Anderson,Antonio — 56 — Boston

EXP MLB DEBUT: 2027 | H/W: 6-3 205 | FUT: Starting 3B | 8E

Bats B Age 18 | 2023 (3) HS (GA) | Pwr + + | BAvg + + | Spd + + | Def + +

Year	Lev	Team	AB	R	H	HR	RBI	Avg	OB	Slg	OPS	bb%	ct%	Eye	SB	CS	x/h%	Iso	RC/G
2023	Rk	FCL Red Sox	15	0	2	0	3	133	278	200	478	17	60	0.50	1	0	50	67	1.14
2023	A	Salem	27	2	5	0	1	185	214	222	437	4	67	0.11	0	1	20	37	0.31

Tall, strong INF who is all about the bat. Exhibits well above average bat speed though mechanics can get rough and choppy. Can differentiate between balls and strikes with ability to put charge into ball. Power is best projectable attribute and could get to BA due to eye. Not much athleticism in frame and likely to stick at 3B with plus arm.

Anderson,Max — 4 — Detroit

EXP MLB DEBUT: 2026 | H/W: 6-0 215 | FUT: Starting 2B | **7C**

Bats R Age 22
2023 (2) Nebraska
Pwr +++
BAvg +++
Spd +
Def +

Year	Lev	Team	AB	R	H	HR	RBI	Avg	OB	Slg	OPS	bb%	ct%	Eye	SB	CS	x/h%	Iso	RC/G
2023	NCAA	Nebraska	244	51	101	21	70	414	458	770	1229	8	88	0.69	0	0	43	357	10.01
2023	A	Lakeland	128	18	37	2	21	289	350	445	795	9	80	0.46	2	0	41	156	5.47

Professional hitter shows good balance, an all fields approach, and ability to find the barrel consistently. Slightly closed stance with a quick, compact stroke. Is rarely off-balance, but hit tool will have to click for him to carve out a starting role as lack of range and athleticism limit him to 2B and make him fairly one-dimensional.

Anthony,Roman — 8 — Boston

EXP MLB DEBUT: 2025 | H/W: 6-2 200 | FUT: Starting CF | **8B**

Bats L Age 19
2022 (2) HS (FL)
Pwr +++
BAvg +++
Spd +++
Def +++

Year	Lev	Team	AB	R	H	HR	RBI	Avg	OB	Slg	OPS	bb%	ct%	Eye	SB	CS	x/h%	Iso	RC/G
2022	Rk	FCL Red Sox	35	5	15	0	7	429	487	486	973	10	89	1.00	1	0	13	57	7.59
2022	A	Salem	37	2	7	0	5	189	286	243	529	12	89	1.25	0	0	29	54	2.70
2023	A	Salem	158	27	36	1	18	228	378	316	694	19	76	1.00	11	6	31	89	4.67
2023	A+	Greenville	204	41	60	12	38	294	410	569	978	16	63	0.53	2	1	48	275	9.02
2023	AA	Portland	35	10	12	1	8	343	465	543	1008	19	83	1.33	3	0	42	200	8.66

Fast-tracked OF who got better at each level upon promotions. High OBP guy who works counts and finds pitches to drive. Has more power than stats suggest as he can crush balls to all fields. Uses bat speed and strength to generate pop. Runs well for size and uses instincts on base and in CF. Can struggle with spin and high velocity.

Antico,Mike — 8 — St. Louis

EXP MLB DEBUT: 2024 | H/W: 5-10 200 | FUT: Reserve OF | **6C**

Bats L Age 26
2021 (8) Texas
Pwr ++
BAvg ++
Spd +++++
Def ++++

Year	Lev	Team	AB	R	H	HR	RBI	Avg	OB	Slg	OPS	bb%	ct%	Eye	SB	CS	x/h%	Iso	RC/G
2021	NCAA	Texas	231	69	63	10	47	273	429	489	918	21	81	1.47	41	5	44	216	7.57
2021	A	Palm Beach	143	21	38	6	19	266	327	490	816	8	77	0.39	8	1	45	224	5.63
2022	A+	Peoria	274	41	70	6	32	255	352	405	757	13	72	0.54	37	3	39	150	5.23
2022	AA	Springfield	240	44	56	8	31	233	319	383	702	11	72	0.45	30	4	36	150	4.25
2023	AA	Springfield	476	86	126	18	72	265	340	447	787	10	74	0.43	52	8	37	183	5.37

Short, athletic OF spreads out at the plate with short stride and quick stroke. Line drive, all-fields approach. Attempts to put the ball into play and utilize his plus speed, but contact issues - 24% K - undermine that approach. True CF, but arm is below average. Will draw walks and stole 119 bases over the past two seasons.

Areinamo,Jadher — 45 — Milwaukee

EXP MLB DEBUT: 2026 | H/W: 5-8 160 | FUT: Starting 2B | **7D**

Bats R Age 20
2021 FA (VZ)
Pwr +
BAvg +++
Spd +++
Def +++

Year	Lev	Team	AB	R	H	HR	RBI	Avg	OB	Slg	OPS	bb%	ct%	Eye	SB	CS	x/h%	Iso	RC/G
2021	Rk	DSL Brewers 2	152	32	42	0	10	276	349	349	698	10	86	0.77	5	4	21	72	4.42
2022	Rk	ACL Brewers G	127	31	41	1	21	323	411	472	883	13	85	1.00	4	4	34	150	6.85
2022	A	Carolina	97	16	29	0	11	299	358	320	678	8	86	0.64	2	1	7	21	4.01
2022	A+	Wisconsin	26	0	2	0	1	77	77	115	192	0	69	0.00	0	0	50	38	-3.11
2023	A	Carolina	396	52	121	4	52	306	334	407	741	4	87	0.33	16	5	26	101	4.50

Short, quick INF who was red hot over last 3 months and finished 2nd in CAR in BA. May not draw many walks but he controls bat and finds barrel consistently. Doesn't generate much pop but has been very difficult to strike out. Focuses on line drives to gaps and should get better as he adds strength. Provides average speed.

Arias,Leandro — 456 — Baltimore

EXP MLB DEBUT: 2027 | H/W: 6-1 155 | FUT: Starting MIF | **8E**

Bats B Age 19
2022 FA (DR)
Pwr ++
BAvg +++
Spd +++
Def +++

Year	Lev	Team	AB	R	H	HR	RBI	Avg	OB	Slg	OPS	bb%	ct%	Eye	SB	CS	x/h%	Iso	RC/G
2022	Rk	DSL Orioles 2	157	25	34	1	15	217	332	306	637	15	74	0.66	10	3	29	89	3.67
2023	Rk	FCL Orioles B	140	17	38	3	19	271	363	414	777	13	86	1.00	12	2	32	143	5.43

Has long levers with room to grow on the frame, which may indicate some future power. He showed great bat to ball skills on the complex, striking out at the same rate he walked: 12.3 percent. Right now it's a contact/speed profile. Monitoring his power output will be key for his potential fantasy impact.

Arias,Rayner — 8 — San Francisco

EXP MLB DEBUT: 2027 | H/W: 6-2 185 | FUT: Starting CF | **8D**

Bats R Age 17
2023 FA (DR)
Pwr +++
BAvg ++++
Spd ++
Def +++

Year	Lev	Team	AB	R	H	HR	RBI	Avg	OB	Slg	OPS	bb%	ct%	Eye	SB	CS	x/h%	Iso	RC/G
2023	Rk	DSL Giants O	58	19	24	4	21	414	534	793	1327	21	81	1.36	4	2	50	379	12.79

Advanced CF who was dynamite in pro debut in DSL. Plays well above years with disciplined eye and instinctual approach to hitting. Hits velocity and recognizes spin while putting charge into ball to all fields. Has frame to add more strength and may slow down with more weight. Could stick in CF long-term but needs to polish reads and routes.

Arias,Roderick — 6 — New York (A)

EXP MLB DEBUT: 2026 | H/W: 6-0 178 | FUT: Starting SS | **9E**

Bats B Age 19
2022 FA (DR)
Pwr ++++
BAvg +++
Spd ++++
Def ++++

Year	Lev	Team	AB	R	H	HR	RBI	Avg	OB	Slg	OPS	bb%	ct%	Eye	SB	CS	x/h%	Iso	RC/G
2022	Rk	DSL Yankees 2	108	25	21	3	11	194	360	370	731	21	57	0.61	10	2	52	176	5.52
2023	Rk	FCL Yankees	101	32	27	6	26	267	422	505	927	21	71	0.93	17	6	37	238	7.76

Switch-hitting, quick-twitch MIF prospect made successful US debut. Athletic frame with room to grow. Already generates lots of strength. Compact, slight uppercut swing. Gets to hard contact consistently despite young age. Power-driven hit tool, especially as LHH. 35+ HR power potential at maturity. Plus runner with developing instincts.

Arroyo,Edwin — 6 — Cincinnati

EXP MLB DEBUT: 2025 | H/W: 6-0 175 | FUT: Starting SS | **8C**

Bats B Age 20
2021 (2) HS (PR)
Pwr +++
BAvg +++
Spd ++++
Def ++++

Year	Lev	Team	AB	R	H	HR	RBI	Avg	OB	Slg	OPS	bb%	ct%	Eye	SB	CS	x/h%	Iso	RC/G
2022	Rk	ACL Reds	6	1	0	0	1	0	250	0	250	25	67	1.00	2	0		0	-2.42
2022	A	Daytona	97	16	22	1	16	227	292	381	674	8	68	0.29	4	2	45	155	4.08
2022	A	Modesto	364	76	115	13	67	316	376	514	890	9	75	0.39	21	4	34	198	6.67
2023	A+	Dayton	475	72	118	13	55	248	317	427	745	9	76	0.43	28	7	42	179	4.82
2023	AA	Chattanooga	17	2	6	0	5	353	389	588	977	6	65	0.17	1	0	50	235	8.99

Athletic, switch-hitting SS put together solid season at advanced levels. Lean build with room to grow. Wide open stance with hands back. Minimal load. More contact and better approach from LH side. From RH side, more power potential with better leverage for uppercut swing. Defensively skilled. Above-average run tool plays up due to headiness.

Arroyo,Michael — 6 — Seattle

EXP MLB DEBUT: 2026 | H/W: 5-8 160 | FUT: Starting 3B | **8D**

Bats R Age 19
2022 FA (CB)
Pwr ++
BAvg +++
Spd +++
Def +++

Year	Lev	Team	AB	R	H	HR	RBI	Avg	OB	Slg	OPS	bb%	ct%	Eye	SB	CS	x/h%	Iso	RC/G
2022	Rk	DSL Mariners	153	46	48	4	22	314	417	484	900	15	78	0.82	4	4	33	170	7.13
2023	Rk	ACL Mariners	11	3	7	1	5	636	667	909	1576	8	91	1.00	3	1	14	273	13.57
2023	A	Modesto	209	45	49	2	23	234	347	373	720	15	75	0.68	5	3	45	139	4.87

Short, powerful INF who impressed in first full pro season. Hasn't produced much power yet but has the natural strength and swing profile to get to average pop in time. Has advanced barrel control and pitch recognition to get on base and hit for BA. Has talent to be SS but may move to 3B with enough quickness, range and arm.

Arteaga,Aeverson — 6 — San Francisco

EXP MLB DEBUT: 2025 | H/W: 6-1 170 | FUT: Starting SS | **7C**

Bats R Age 21
2019 FA (VZ)
Pwr +++
BAvg ++
Spd +++
Def ++++

Year	Lev	Team	AB	R	H	HR	RBI	Avg	OB	Slg	OPS	bb%	ct%	Eye	SB	CS	x/h%	Iso	RC/G
2021	Rk	ACL Giants O	197	42	58	9	43	294	368	503	871	10	65	0.33	8	0	38	208	6.97
2021	A	San Jose	3	0	0	0	0	0	0	0	0	0	67	0.00	0	0		0	-6.12
2022	A	San Jose	503	87	136	14	84	270	335	431	767	9	69	0.32	11	6	38	161	5.22
2023	A+	Eugene	493	66	116	17	73	235	293	410	702	8	73	0.30	8	2	42	174	4.13

Lean, quick SS who set career-high in HR (5th in NWL) but finished with 3rd lowest OBP in league. Barrels balls, though production somewhat muted by chasing breaking balls out of zone. Swings early in count and often gets himself out. Good upside predicated on strength, speed and defense. Quick actions should keep him at SS.

Auer,Mason — 789 — Tampa Bay

EXP MLB DEBUT: 2025 | H/W: 6-1 210 | FUT: Starting OF | **7E**

Bats R Age 23
2021 (5) San Jacinto
Pwr +++
BAvg ++
Spd ++++
Def ++++

Year	Lev	Team	AB	R	H	HR	RBI	Avg	OB	Slg	OPS	bb%	ct%	Eye	SB	CS	x/h%	Iso	RC/G
2021	NJCAA	San Jacinto	204	60	76	11	56	373	526	627	1153	24	78	1.47	34	3	34	255	10.94
2021	Rk	FCL Rays	34	7	9	0	3	265	375	324	699	15	79	0.86	10	1	22	59	4.59
2022	A	Charleston	232	46	68	4	31	293	376	478	855	12	79	0.65	24	3	38	185	6.45
2022	A+	Bowling Green	226	38	65	11	31	288	356	496	852	10	73	0.39	24	4	34	208	6.19
2023	AA	Montgomery	454	59	93	11	51	205	282	348	630	10	59	0.27	47	11	39	143	3.55

Speedy OF prospect continues to struggle with whiffs, dampening potential. Strong, athletic built near projection. Plus runner and above-average power potential carries profile. Open stance with a bat wrap in load, delays swing. Flatter plane swing, depresses loft, contributing to high groundball rate. Double-plus arm. Plays all OF positions.

Baez,Jesus — 456 — New York (N)

EXP MLB DEBUT: 2026 | H/W: 5-9 180 | FUT: Starting SS | 7E

Bats R Age 19 — 2022 FA (DR)

Pwr +++ | BAvg ++ | Spd +++ | Def +++

Year	Lev	Team	AB	R	H	HR	RBI	Avg	OB	Slg	OPS	bb%	ct%	Eye	SB	CS	x/h%	Iso	RC/G
2022	Rk	DSL Mets	98	23	25	2	12	255	365	378	743	15	76	0.71	3	3	32	122	5.04
2022	Rk	DSL Mets 2	88	13	20	5	22	227	299	432	731	9	75	0.41	5	3	40	205	4.40
2023	Rk	FCL Mets	138	18	29	2	17	210	306	333	639	12	80	0.68	5	2	41	123	3.65

Strong, short-statured SS prospect did not fare well in US debut. Power-over-hit profile despite smaller frame. Struggled with timing and breaking pitches. Bat wrap was more pronounced and top-hand heavy swing didn't allow for adjustments in bat path. Struggled getting to barrels because of aggressive approach. Solid defender with average speed.

Baez,Joshua — 79 — St. Louis

EXP MLB DEBUT: 2026 | H/W: 6-3 220 | FUT: Reserve OF | 7E

Bats R Age 20 — 2021 (2) HS (MA)

Pwr ++++ | BAvg + | Spd ++ | Def +++

Year	Lev	Team	AB	R	H	HR	RBI	Avg	OB	Slg	OPS	bb%	ct%	Eye	SB	CS	x/h%	Iso	RC/G
2021	Rk	FCL Cardinals	76	18	12	2	8	158	289	303	592	16	63	0.50	5	0	50	145	2.86
2022	Rk	FCL Cardinals	38	4	9	1	5	237	326	395	720	12	63	0.36	6	1	44	158	4.89
2022	A	Palm Beach	63	11	18	3	16	286	392	540	932	15	52	0.37	4	3	50	254	9.78
2023	A	Palm Beach	298	54	65	7	36	218	321	383	703	13	59	0.37	30	2	48	164	4.91

Prospect status has plummeted due to injuries and poor performance. Above-average raw tools have failed to develop due aggressive approach and poor swing decisions - 34% K in repeat of Low-A . Does have a quick bat, strong frame, and hard contact, just doesn't do it often enough. Runs a tick above average with a plus arm but also spent time at DH.

Baez,Juan — 56 — Milwaukee

EXP MLB DEBUT: 2027 | H/W: 5-9 175 | FUT: Starting 3B | 8E

Bats R Age 18 — 2022 FA (DR)

Pwr ++ | BAvg +++ | Spd +++ | Def ++

Year	Lev	Team	AB	R	H	HR	RBI	Avg	OB	Slg	OPS	bb%	ct%	Eye	SB	CS	x/h%	Iso	RC/G
2022	Rk	DSL Brewers 2	198	33	53	3	22	268	326	359	684	8	84	0.55	17	6	23	91	4.00
2023	Rk	ACL Brewers G	192	39	71	4	42	370	395	557	952	4	88	0.35	17	2	34	188	6.91
2023	A	Carolina	30	7	7	0	6	233	281	333	615	6	87	0.50	2	0	43	100	3.31

Advanced hitter who finished 2nd in Arizona Complex League in BA in first year in US. Hits for high BA thanks to hand-eye coordination and level swing path. Rarely swings and misses and offers average power potential. Doesn't work counts and can swing aggressively early in count. Likely to move to 3B and will need to polish glove due to too many errors.

Baez,Luis — 789 — Houston

EXP MLB DEBUT: 2027 | H/W: 6-1 205 | FUT: Reserve OF | 7E

Bats R Age 20 — 2022 FA (DR)

Pwr +++ | BAvg ++ | Spd ++ | Def ++

Year	Lev	Team	AB	R	H	HR	RBI	Avg	OB	Slg	OPS	bb%	ct%	Eye	SB	CS	x/h%	Iso	RC/G
2022	Rk	DSL Houston O	203	40	62	9	43	305	350	552	902	6	72	0.25	10	7	48	246	6.85
2023	Rk	FCL Astros	59	10	16	7	15	271	427	661	1088	21	76	1.14	1	1	56	390	9.42
2023	A	Fayetteville	155	20	37	4	23	239	314	413	727	10	69	0.35	0	0	49	174	4.74

International signing projects for power, decent hit tool. First taste of full season ball went OK, though aggressive approach and swing-and-miss indicate work ahead. Swing plane generates loft, but indiscriminate pitch selection results in easy FB outs. Has arm for RF but lacks speed, may be better fit for LF.

Balcazar,Leonardo — 56 — Cincinnati

EXP MLB DEBUT: 2026 | H/W: 5-10 190 | FUT: Starting SS | 8E

Bats R Age 19 — 2021 FA (VZ)

Pwr ++ | BAvg ++++ | Spd +++ | Def +++

Year	Lev	Team	AB	R	H	HR	RBI	Avg	OB	Slg	OPS	bb%	ct%	Eye	SB	CS	x/h%	Iso	RC/G
2021	Rk	DSL Reds	112	26	29	6	15	259	336	536	872	10	74	0.45	8	4	52	277	6.53
2022	Rk	ACL Reds	143	25	46	4	26	322	398	476	873	11	71	0.43	13	1	26	154	6.77
2023	A	Daytona	68	11	22	1	11	324	432	471	903	16	68	0.59	2	2	32	147	7.75

Athletic SS prospect was on verge of breakout season when a torn ACL ended season prematurely. Short-statured with room to grow. Upright stance with simple load and hitting mechanics. Spray approach with linear swing, producing hard contact on the ground and on a line. Approach isn't conducive for power development. Above-average runner.

Baldwin,Drake — 2 — Atlanta

EXP MLB DEBUT: 2024 | H/W: 6-0 210 | FUT: Starting C | 7C

Bats L Age 23 — 2022 (3) Missouri State

Pwr +++ | BAvg +++ | Spd + | Def +++

Year	Lev	Team	AB	R	H	HR	RBI	Avg	OB	Slg	OPS	bb%	ct%	Eye	SB	CS	x/h%	Iso	RC/G
2022	Rk	FCL Braves	8	2	3	0	3	375	444	625	1069	11	63	0.33	0	0	67	250	11.04
2022	A	Augusta	81	13	20	0	6	247	384	284	668	18	73	0.82	1	0	15	37	4.23
2023	A+	Rome	335	57	87	14	54	260	374	466	839	15	75	0.73	0	0	46	206	6.30
2023	AA	Mississippi	53	4	17	1	5	321	390	396	786	10	79	0.55	0	0	12	75	5.28
2023	AAA	Gwinnett	12	2	4	1	2	333	333	583	917	0	75	0.00	0	0	25	250	6.13

Strong catcher-only profile who enjoyed strong 2023 season. Hit-first bat with some OBP upside. Upright, slight open stance with a lot of body movement to get to contact. Seemingly stays balanced and on-time despite hitting mechanics. Flatter swing plane doesn't allow plus power in frame and EVs to play. Solid receiver behind the dish.

Ballesteros,Moises — 2 — Chicago (N)

EXP MLB DEBUT: 2026 | H/W: 5-7 195 | FUT: Starting C | 7D

Bats L Age 20 — 2021 FA (VZ)

Pwr +++ | BAvg ++++ | Spd ++ | Def ++

Year	Lev	Team	AB	R	H	HR	RBI	Avg	OB	Slg	OPS	bb%	ct%	Eye	SB	CS	x/h%	Iso	RC/G
2022	Rk	ACL Cubs	97	12	26	7	18	268	355	536	891	12	80	0.68	0	0	46	268	6.50
2022	A	Myrtle Beach	109	17	27	3	15	248	354	394	749	14	74	0.64	0	1	37	147	5.07
2023	A	Myrtle Beach	197	28	54	8	32	274	397	457	853	17	85	1.33	5	0	37	183	6.49
2023	A+	South Bend	203	33	61	6	31	300	369	463	832	10	78	0.49	2	0	34	163	5.91
2023	AA	Tennessee	21	3	5	0	1	238	273	238	511	5	86	0.33	0	0	0	0	1.80

Short, stocky backstop lacks athleticism and will need to work hard on conditioning with bottom of the scale speed. At the plate, it's a different story and he continues to rake despite his youth and a tough home park environment. Advanced understanding of the strike zone with near elite bat-to-ball skills (63 BB/78 K) and surprising pop for size.

Banfield,Will — 2 — Miami

EXP MLB DEBUT: 2024 | H/W: 6-0 215 | FUT: Reserve C | 6C

Bats R Age 24 — 2018 (2) HS (GA)

Pwr ++++ | BAvg ++ | Spd ++ | Def +++

Year	Lev	Team	AB	R	H	HR	RBI	Avg	OB	Slg	OPS	bb%	ct%	Eye	SB	CS	x/h%	Iso	RC/G
2019	A	Clinton	397	44	79	9	55	199	246	310	556	6	70	0.21	0	0	30	111	2.05
2021	A+	Beloit	266	30	48	6	42	180	251	308	559	9	64	0.26	1	0	44	128	2.23
2022	A+	Beloit	269	29	55	8	36	204	236	349	585	4	75	0.16	1	1	40	145	2.40
2022	AA	Pensacola	116	14	31	3	16	267	298	405	703	4	78	0.20	0	0	29	138	3.93
2023	AA	Pensacola	458	70	118	23	76	258	296	472	768	5	73	0.20	3	0	42	214	4.81

Strong-bodied backstop had best season as pro in Double-A. Open, mostly upright stance. Slight load gets hands to hit position, leg lift squares up lower half. Uppercut swing with moderate length. Geared towards driving ball out to LF. It's plus power-dependent on hit tool to play. Pull-oriented approach overall. Fringe receiving skills.

Barber,Colin — 79 — Houston

EXP MLB DEBUT: 2025 | H/W: 5-11 200 | FUT: Starting OF | 7C

Bats L Age 23 — 2019 (4) HS (CA)

Pwr ++ | BAvg +++ | Spd ++ | Def +++

Year	Lev	Team	AB	R	H	HR	RBI	Avg	OB	Slg	OPS	bb%	ct%	Eye	SB	CS	x/h%	Iso	RC/G
2021	A+	Asheville	42	10	9	3	7	214	353	452	805	18	48	0.41	1	1	44	238	7.61
2022	Rk	FCL Astros	3	0	0	0	0	0	0	0	0	0	100		0	0		0	-2.66
2022	Rk	FCL Astros O	7	0	2	0	0	286	286	286	571	0	86	0.00	0	0	0	0	2.18
2022	A+	Asheville	218	35	65	7	33	298	383	450	833	12	74	0.53	7	4	28	151	6.08
2023	AA	Corpus Christi	270	42	66	11	40	244	352	433	786	14	73	0.62	5	2	42	189	5.53

OF prospect shows potential for above average hit tool, modest power. Quiet setup from left side with easy, direct swing. Rarely chases outside pitches, forces pitchers into the zone. Good contact overall, knows which pitches to attack. Gets to most of below-average raw power in game. Inefficient base-stealer, likely to lose a step at next level.

Barger,Addison — 569 — Toronto

EXP MLB DEBUT: 2024 | H/W: 6-0 210 | FUT: Starting 3B | 7B

Bats L Age 24 — 2018 (6) HS (FL)

Pwr ++ | BAvg +++ | Spd ++ | Def +++

Year	Lev	Team	AB	R	H	HR	RBI	Avg	OB	Slg	OPS	bb%	ct%	Eye	SB	CS	x/h%	Iso	RC/G
2022	AA	New Hampshire	176	26	55	9	29	313	376	528	905	9	72	0.36	2	2	36	216	6.94
2022	AAA	Buffalo	31	8	11	3	9	355	444	677	1122	14	84	1.00	0	1	36	323	9.26
2023	Rk	FCL Blue Jays	6	0	0	0	0	0	250	0	250	25	83	2.00	0	0		0	-0.69
2023	A	Dunedin	11	3	3	0	1	273	429	273	701	21	73	1.00	0	0	0	0	4.80
2023	AAA	Buffalo	340	53	85	9	46	250	349	403	752	13	75	0.60	5	3	40	153	5.09

All-around LHH who had big drop in HR and BA but likely result of modified swing and approach. Closed holes but improved exit velo, plate discipline and walk rate. Has more of line drive stroke but knows when to elevate. Not a great runner. Steals bases more on jumps and instincts. Plays multiple positions, including RF.

Barrosa,Jorge — 78 — Arizona

EXP MLB DEBUT: 2024 | H/W: 5-5 165 | FUT: Starting OF | 7B

Bats B Age 23 — 2017 FA (VZ)

Pwr ++ | BAvg +++ | Spd ++ | Def ++++

Year	Lev	Team	AB	R	H	HR	RBI	Avg	OB	Slg	OPS	bb%	ct%	Eye	SB	CS	x/h%	Iso	RC/G
2021	A	Visalia	147	30	49	3	16	333	364	449	813	5	79	0.23	9	4	22	116	5.31
2021	A+	Hillsboro	242	41	62	4	21	256	318	405	723	8	80	0.46	20	7	40	149	4.54
2022	A+	Hillsboro	40	5	12	1	6	300	333	450	783	5	88	0.40	4	1	33	150	4.99
2022	AA	Amarillo	434	85	120	12	51	276	371	438	809	13	82	0.81	22	11	37	161	5.78
2023	AAA	Reno	412	91	113	13	65	274	392	456	849	16	80	0.98	15	7	36	182	6.47

Short-statured young OF prospect excels at making contact, defensive plays. Has superb batting eye, though tendency to get passive on zone pitches. Limited power projection but has steadily ticked up over the years. Could unlock more power with some measured aggression on heaters. Defensive asset in CF, could bounce around INF in a pinch.

Basallo,Samuel — 23 — Baltimore

EXP MLB DEBUT: 2025 | H/W: 6-3 180 | FUT: Starting 1B | 9D

Bats L Age 19 — 2021 FA (DR)

Pwr ++++ / BAvg +++ / Spd ++ / Def +++

Year	Lev	Team	AB	R	H	HR	RBI	Avg	OB	Slg	OPS	bb%	ct%	Eye	SB	CS	x/h%	Iso	RC/G
2021	Rk	DSL Orioles	134	18	32	5	19	239	333	410	744	12	76	0.59	1	0	41	172	4.85
2022	Rk	FCL Orioles B	158	22	44	6	32	278	341	424	765	9	77	0.41	1	0	25	146	4.88
2023	A	Delmarva	308	52	92	12	60	299	381	503	884	12	76	0.56	7	3	38	205	6.72
2023	A+	Aberdeen	96	21	32	8	24	333	443	688	1131	17	79	0.95	5	2	50	354	9.91
2023	AA	Bowie	15	2	7	0	2	467	500	667	1167	6	93	1.00	0	0	29	200	9.50

The Orioles have another primary catcher with massive upside at the plate. Just turned 19 years old and won CAR MVP en route to AA. Has potential to be significant offensive producer. Combines size, strength and batting eye. Has work to do with pitch recognition. Likely to move to 1B unless receiving improves but has plus arm strength.

Beavers,Dylan — 789 — Baltimore

EXP MLB DEBUT: 2025 | H/W: 6-4 206 | FUT: Starting OF | 8D

Bats L Age 22 — 2022 (1) California

Pwr +++ / BAvg +++ / Spd +++ / Def +++

Year	Lev	Team	AB	R	H	HR	RBI	Avg	OB	Slg	OPS	bb%	ct%	Eye	SB	CS	x/h%	Iso	RC/G
2022	Rk	FCL Orioles B	9	1	1	0	0	111	273	222	495	18	78	1.00	0	0	100	111	2.06
2022	A	Delmarva	64	13	23	0	13	359	461	531	992	16	83	1.09	6	1	39	172	8.49
2022	A+	Aberdeen	14	0	4	0	2	286	375	286	661	13	64	0.40	0	0	0	0	3.92
2023	A+	Aberdeen	311	46	85	9	48	273	374	463	837	14	73	0.60	22	6	45	190	6.35
2023	AA	Bowie	134	29	43	2	12	321	409	478	887	13	76	0.63	5	4	33	157	6.98

At present, speed is best asset. However there's a lot of untapped game power left in his quick, physical swing. Hit tool may cap the power output, though strides have been shown in that department in the short time since being drafted. Much improved pitch recognition and more consistent, hard contact have elevated profile. Will need to improve against LHP.

Beck,Jordan — 79 — Colorado

EXP MLB DEBUT: 2024 | H/W: 6-3 225 | FUT: Starting OF | 8C

Bats R Age 22 — 2022 (1) Tennessee

Pwr ++++ / BAvg ++ / Spd +++ / Def +++

Year	Lev	Team	AB	R	H	HR	RBI	Avg	OB	Slg	OPS	bb%	ct%	Eye	SB	CS	x/h%	Iso	RC/G
2022	NCAA	Tennessee	252	70	75	18	61	298	388	595	983	13	75	0.60	6	4	48	298	7.95
2022	Rk	ACL Rockies	49	9	15	1	10	306	404	469	873	14	78	0.73	0	0	40	163	6.78
2022	A	Fresno	39	11	11	2	9	282	462	487	949	25	77	1.44	0	0	36	205	8.14
2023	A+	Spokane	295	62	86	20	72	292	382	566	948	13	76	0.61	11	3	47	275	7.45
2023	AA	Hartford	192	22	46	5	19	240	342	406	749	14	63	0.42	9	2	46	167	5.42

Tall, athletic OF has easy pull-side power, but is willing to drive the ball to all fields. Stands tall at the plate with hands close to chest and generates a quick stroke and plus exit velo. Can be patient at the plate, but can be induced to expand the zone and he does have some in-zone swing-and-miss. Profiles as a corner OF.

Beltre,Manuel — 46 — Toronto

EXP MLB DEBUT: 2026 | H/W: 5-10 155 | FUT: Starting 2B | 7D

Bats R Age 19 — 2021 FA (DR)

Pwr ++ / BAvg ++ / Spd +++ / Def +++

Year	Lev	Team	AB	R	H	HR	RBI	Avg	OB	Slg	OPS	bb%	ct%	Eye	SB	CS	x/h%	Iso	RC/G
2021	Rk	DSL Blue Jays	182	39	41	2	29	225	371	346	717	19	82	1.27	10	4	37	121	5.04
2022	Rk	FCL Blue Jays	171	25	40	1	23	234	321	310	631	11	76	0.54	9	4	25	76	3.46
2022	A	Dunedin	21	3	8	1	3	381	409	571	981	5	86	0.33	0	0	25	190	7.07
2023	A	Dunedin	368	67	85	6	50	231	320	340	659	12	77	0.58	12	2	33	109	3.81

Fundamentally-sound INF who has nice tools, though production hasn't matched. Starting to drive ball more by focusing on pulling. Added muscle to lean frame but likely never getting to average power. Uses discerning eye to get on base. Runs well and can steal bases. Plays both 2B and SS well due to quick, soft hands and strong arm.

Bergolla,William — 46 — Philadelphia

EXP MLB DEBUT: 2027 | H/W: 5-11 165 | FUT: Starting SS | 7D

Bats L Age 19 — 2022 FA (VZ)

Pwr + / BAvg +++ / Spd ++ / Def ++++

Year	Lev	Team	AB	R	H	HR	RBI	Avg	OB	Slg	OPS	bb%	ct%	Eye	SB	CS	x/h%	Iso	RC/G
2022	Rk	DSL Phillies W	71	18	27	0	14	380	463	423	886	13	96	3.67	2	3	11	42	6.93
2023	A	Clearwater	192	26	49	0	20	255	356	286	642	14	91	1.76	2	5	8	31	4.13

Uber-patient hitter whose BB/K ratio in 55 low-A games stands out. He backs the walks with an extreme contact profile; rarely swings and misses. Good speed has yet to show up in SB column. Is not overly physical and will need to add strength. Has shortstop actions and is reliable on defense; could move to 2B later if necessary.

Bericoto,Victor — 379 — San Francisco

EXP MLB DEBUT: 2025 | H/W: 6-1 155 | FUT: Starting OF | 7E

Bats R Age 22 — 2018 FA (VZ)

Pwr +++ / BAvg +++ / Spd ++ / Def ++

Year	Lev	Team	AB	R	H	HR	RBI	Avg	OB	Slg	OPS	bb%	ct%	Eye	SB	CS	x/h%	Iso	RC/G
2021	Rk	ACL Giants B	17	4	5	2	6	294	333	647	980	6	65	0.17	0	0	40	353	7.96
2021	Rk	ACL Giants O	1	1	1	0	1	1000	###	###	3000	0	100		0	0	100	1000	27.71
2022	A	San Jose	423	63	112	12	68	265	352	395	747	12	74	0.53	3	4	28	130	4.90
2023	A+	Eugene	270	47	80	16	55	296	365	533	898	10	78	0.48	1	0	38	237	6.59
2023	AA	Richmond	186	29	44	11	31	237	290	478	768	7	71	0.26	0	1	50	242	4.94

Under the radar prospect who led org in HR and RBI in breakout season. Struggled in AA at end of season. More than doubled previous high in HR and played multiple positions to increase versatility. Has strong build and good pop to all fields. Can be beaten with high FB and has unpolished pitch recognition.

Bernabel,Warming — 5 — Colorado

EXP MLB DEBUT: 2024 | H/W: 6-1 180 | FUT: Starting 3B | 7D

Bats R Age 21 — 2018 FA (DR)

Pwr ++ / BAvg +++ / Spd ++ / Def +++

Year	Lev	Team	AB	R	H	HR	RBI	Avg	OB	Slg	OPS	bb%	ct%	Eye	SB	CS	x/h%	Iso	RC/G
2021	A	Fresno	83	9	17	1	7	205	267	313	580	8	83	0.50	4	1	41	108	2.79
2022	A	Fresno	262	52	83	10	54	317	385	504	889	10	85	0.74	21	6	35	187	6.50
2022	A+	Spokane	105	18	32	4	17	305	318	486	803	2	84	0.12	2	2	34	181	4.95
2023	Rk	ACL Rockies	33	9	11	2	8	333	353	636	989	3	82	0.17	0	0	55	303	7.28
2023	AA	Hartford	302	30	68	6	28	225	262	338	600	5	77	0.22	2	0	31	113	2.68

Slow start and back injury derailed season. Aggressive approach and always seems to be in swing mode but also doesn't whiff much. Looks for pitches to drive to the pull side, but has eye-hand coordination to make consistent contact, even on balls out of the zone. Big leg kick, and drifts into the zone leaving him in between.

Bernal,Leonardo — 2 — St. Louis

EXP MLB DEBUT: 2026 | H/W: 6-0 200 | FUT: Starting C | 7D

Bats B Age 20 — 2021 FA (PN)

Pwr ++ / BAvg ++ / Spd + / Def +++

Year	Lev	Team	AB	R	H	HR	RBI	Avg	OB	Slg	OPS	bb%	ct%	Eye	SB	CS	x/h%	Iso	RC/G
2021	Rk	DSL Cardinals B	158	23	33	5	29	209	286	373	659	10	82	0.61	3	1	45	165	3.74
2022	A	Palm Beach	156	22	40	7	29	256	310	455	765	7	79	0.38	1	1	40	199	4.81
2023	A	Palm Beach	268	45	71	3	44	265	379	362	740	15	79	0.89	4	1	27	97	5.11

Glove-first backstop continues to make steady progress and despite repeat of Low-A was young for this level. Switch-hitter has a thick frame with below average speed, but moves well behind the plate with a strong, accurate arm and showed improved plate discipline - 49 BB/55 K. Swing path and lack of bat speed results in limited power upside.

Bernard,Derek — 64 — Colorado

EXP MLB DEBUT: 2028 | H/W: 6-0 190 | FUT: Starting 2B | 7D

Bats L Age 18 — 2022 FA (DR)

Pwr +++ / BAvg +++ / Spd +++ / Def ++

Year	Lev	Team	AB	R	H	HR	RBI	Avg	OB	Slg	OPS	bb%	ct%	Eye	SB	CS	x/h%	Iso	RC/G
2022	Rk	DSL Rockies	214	49	66	4	25	308	370	439	809	9	69	0.32	11	4	27	131	5.88
2023	Rk	DSL Colorado	12	2	2	0	1	167	333	417	750	20	92	3.00	1	0	100	250	5.99
2023	Rk	DSL Rockies	139	30	45	7	39	324	420	576	995	14	78	0.74	16	3	42	252	8.23

Dominican infielder moves well with good range at short, but will likely settle in at 2B Upright, closed stance and needs to incorporate his lower half to tap into his above-average raw power, but does find the barrel and gets the ball in the air consistently. Still a teenagers, posted solid offensive numbers with the Rockies DSL squad.

Berry,Jacob — 35 — Miami

EXP MLB DEBUT: 2024 | H/W: 6-0 212 | FUT: Starting 1B | 7D

Bats B Age 22 — 2022 (1) LSU

Pwr +++ / BAvg +++ / Spd ++ / Def ++

Year	Lev	Team	AB	R	H	HR	RBI	Avg	OB	Slg	OPS	bb%	ct%	Eye	SB	CS	x/h%	Iso	RC/G
2022	NCAA	LSU	208	47	77	15	48	370	443	630	1072	11	89	1.23	0	0	31	260	8.49
2022	Rk	FCL Marlins	16	1	2	0	2	125	176	125	301	6	63	0.17	0	0	0	0	-1.89
2022	A	Jupiter	125	19	33	3	24	264	333	392	725	9	82	0.57	1	1	30	128	4.53
2023	A+	Beloit	317	28	72	4	37	227	264	369	633	5	78	0.23	5	1	42	142	3.24
2023	AA	Pensacola	113	22	28	5	22	248	303	442	746	7	77	0.35	5	0	39	195	4.60

Switch-hitting former 1st round pick struggled with bat throughout 2023. Pros: Plus bat speed from both sides and creates solid loft from RH side. Cons: Struggles against off-speed pitches, sweepy swing plane and doesn't incorporate lower half from LH side, and looks to be moving in quicksand at 3B. Likely 1B-only outcome if the bat can carry.

Beshears,Jay — 345 — San Diego

EXP MLB DEBUT: 2026 | H/W: 6-4 215 | FUT: Starting 2B | 7D

Bats R Age 21 — 2023 (6) Duke

Pwr +++ / BAvg ++ / Spd ++ / Def +++

Year	Lev	Team	AB	R	H	HR	RBI	Avg	OB	Slg	OPS	bb%	ct%	Eye	SB	CS	x/h%	Iso	RC/G
2023	NCAA	Duke	237	58	79	15	56	333	410	586	997	12	81	0.69	5	0	38	253	7.86
2023	Rk	ACL Padres	4	4	1	0	0	250	500	250	750	33	50	1.00	0	0	0	0	6.58
2023	A	Lake Elsinore	105	10	24	1	13	229	264	314	578	5	69	0.15	1	0	25	86	2.40

Tall, strong INF who can play variety of positions on diamond. Not a master at any one spot but arm could play anywhere. Lack of quickness likely to lead to 2B. Mostly pull power at present and has generally good plate discipline to go with slight uppercut stroke. Too much swing and miss but swing revision could lead to better contact.

Bigbie,Justice — 79 — Detroit

EXP MLB DEBUT: 2024 | H/W: 6-2 200 | FUT: Starting OF | 7D

Bats R Age 25 — 2021 (19) Western Carolina

Pwr +++ | BAvg +++ | Spd ++ | Def ++

Year	Lev	Team	AB	R	H	HR	RBI	Avg	OB	Slg	OPS	bb%	ct%	Eye	SB	CS	x/h%	Iso	RC/G
2022	A	Lakeland	330	37	85	2	41	258	316	358	673	8	73	0.31	4	2	28	100	3.89
2022	A+	West Michigan	31	6	12	1	7	387	424	613	1037	6	81	0.33	0	1	42	226	8.22
2023	A+	West Michigan	138	25	46	6	27	333	399	543	942	10	80	0.54	1	1	35	210	7.21
2023	AA	Erie	243	51	88	12	43	362	415	564	979	8	86	0.65	5	1	28	202	7.34
2023	AAA	Toledo	51	5	14	1	8	275	339	392	731	9	71	0.33	0	0	29	118	4.68

19th rounder slugged his way across three levels. Posted an 8% BB rate and 12.5% K rate at AA and bought into organizational philosophy of owning the strike zone. Strong frame, solid bat-to-ball skills, and willingness to shoot balls to the opposite field allow him to hit for average and power. Below average defense limits his upside.

Bitonti,Eric — 56 — Milwaukee

EXP MLB DEBUT: 2028 | H/W: 6-4 218 | FUT: Starting 3B | 8D

Bats L Age 18 — 2023 (3) HS (CA)

Pwr +++ | BAvg ++ | Spd +++ | Def +++

Year	Lev	Team	AB	R	H	HR	RBI	Avg	OB	Slg	OPS	bb%	ct%	Eye	SB	CS	x/h%	Iso	RC/G
2023	Rk	ACL Brewers G	39	8	7	2	9	179	333	410	744	19	62	0.60	0	0	57	231	5.30

Tall, projectable INF with massive upside as hitter. Offers significant raw power but will take time to develop in-game pop. Has inconsistent swing and has room to add strength. Long arms have led to exploitable holds in stroke. Quite agile and nimble for size with average speed. Has played both SS and 3B with the latter more likely long-term.

Black,Tyler — 5 — Milwaukee

EXP MLB DEBUT: 2024 | H/W: 5-10 204 | FUT: Starting 3B | 8C

Bats L Age 23 — 2021 (1) Wright State

Pwr +++ | BAvg ++++ | Spd +++ | Def ++

Year	Lev	Team	AB	R	H	HR	RBI	Avg	OB	Slg	OPS	bb%	ct%	Eye	SB	CS	x/h%	Iso	RC/G
2021	Rk	ACL Brewers B	6	4	3	1	2	500	750	1000	1750	50	67	3.00	2	0	33	500	22.16
2021	A	Carolina	81	11	18	0	6	222	376	272	648	20	64	0.69	3	2	22	49	4.00
2022	A+	Wisconsin	231	45	65	4	35	281	399	424	823	16	81	1.02	13	6	32	143	6.22
2023	AA	Biloxi	308	70	84	14	48	273	393	513	906	17	75	0.79	47	9	45	240	7.28
2023	AAA	Nashville	142	35	44	4	25	310	420	514	934	16	84	1.17	8	3	39	204	7.56

Natural-hitting INF who moved to 3B after previous stints in CF and 2B. Led org in SB and 2nd in SL in OBP. Uses short, quick stroke to make easy contact and has exceptional eye to work counts. Hand-eye coordination is plus and can make adjustments in swing. Set easy high in HR and could hit in middle of lineup. Defense still in question.

Blanco,Tony — 3 — Pittsburgh

EXP MLB DEBUT: 2027 | H/W: 6-6 243 | FUT: Starting 1B | 8E

Bats R Age 18 — 2022 FA (DR)

Pwr +++ | BAvg ++ | Spd ++ | Def ++

Year	Lev	Team	AB	R	H	HR	RBI	Avg	OB	Slg	OPS	bb%	ct%	Eye	SB	CS	x/h%	Iso	RC/G
2022	Rk	DSL Pirates G	19	1	4	1	4	211	211	368	579	0	47	0.00	0	0	25	158	3.26
2023	Rk	DSL Pirates G	136	21	32	5	25	235	320	397	717	11	57	0.29	0	1	38	162	5.13

Gigantic 1B who makes hard contact and has significant power projection. Lot of swing and miss and hits too many gb for profile. Swing can get choppy. Destroys LHP and can catch up to any velocity. Has tendency to expand zone and long arms have led to long swing and Ks. Relegated to 1B but profiles as decent defender with strong arm.

Bleis,Miguel — 89 — Boston

EXP MLB DEBUT: 2026 | H/W: 6-0 170 | FUT: Starting OF | 8D

Bats R Age 20 — 2021 FA (DR)

Pwr ++ | BAvg +++ | Spd +++ | Def +++

Year	Lev	Team	AB	R	H	HR	RBI	Avg	OB	Slg	OPS	bb%	ct%	Eye	SB	CS	x/h%	Iso	RC/G
2021	Rk	DSL Red Sox R	119	17	30	4	17	252	321	420	741	9	79	0.48	7	4	37	168	4.67
2022	Rk	FCL Red Sox	153	28	46	5	27	301	344	542	886	6	71	0.22	18	3	50	242	6.83
2023	A	Salem	126	18	29	1	16	230	287	325	612	7	70	0.26	11	4	24	95	3.02

Missed most of season from shoulder surgery after being injured while swinging. Tooled-up OF with strength, leverage and projection. Can be pull happy and can chase outside of zone. Has big-time potential with power and will need to mute approach to find better pitches. Runs well now but may slow down as he grows.

Bliss,Ryan — 46 — Seattle

EXP MLB DEBUT: 2024 | H/W: 5-6 165 | FUT: Starting 2B | 7B

Bats R Age 24 — 2021 (2) Auburn

Pwr +++ | BAvg +++ | Spd +++ | Def +++

Year	Lev	Team	AB	R	H	HR	RBI	Avg	OB	Slg	OPS	bb%	ct%	Eye	SB	CS	x/h%	Iso	RC/G
2021	A	Visalia	158	22	41	6	23	259	316	443	759	8	75	0.33	11	4	39	184	4.85
2022	A+	Hillsboro	426	68	91	10	37	214	286	343	628	9	72	0.36	31	12	35	129	3.22
2023	AA	Amarillo	293	67	105	12	47	358	407	594	1001	8	81	0.44	30	8	39	235	7.81
2023	AAA	Reno	56	6	11	1	4	196	262	357	619	8	79	0.42	5	3	45	161	3.23
2023	AAA	Tacoma	191	37	48	10	35	251	350	466	816	13	73	0.56	20	4	40	215	5.83

Short and spry, he struggled a bit in AAA after hot start in AA. Finished 5th in MiLB in hits and 3rd in runs. Set easy career-highs with both HR and SB. Showcased improving power and projects to hit ton of doubles with line drive approach. Can bury ball in ground too often but uses speed well. Fits more of utility profile but was terrific SS in A.

Boeve,Mike — 4 — Milwaukee

EXP MLB DEBUT: 2025 | H/W: 6-2 210 | FUT: Starting 2B | 7C

Bats L Age 21 — 2023 (2) Nebraska-Omaha

Pwr ++ | BAvg ++++ | Spd + | Def ++

Year	Lev	Team	AB	R	H	HR	RBI	Avg	OB	Slg	OPS	bb%	ct%	Eye	SB	CS	x/h%	Iso	RC/G
2023	NCAA	Nebraska-Omaha	167	37	67	4	32	401	497	563	1060	16	95	3.56	6	0	28	162	8.96
2023	Rk	ACL Brewers G	30	8	15	4	12	500	559	###	1559	12	80	0.67	0	0	47	500	14.72
2023	A+	Wisconsin	72	11	18	1	18	250	341	333	675	12	74	0.53	1	0	22	83	4.00

Natural-hitting INF who sprays ball to all fields in disciplined approach. Doesn't fan much with quick, short stroke. Power is muted by swing mechanics and may only get to average power at peak. Hits lot of GB and weak contact. Will work to modify stroke to get to harder contact. Doesn't run well and is limited defensively at 2B.

Bohrofen,Jace — 9 — Toronto

EXP MLB DEBUT: 2026 | H/W: 6-2 205 | FUT: Starting OF | 7D

Bats L Age 22 — 2023 (6) Arkansas

Pwr ++ | BAvg +++ | Spd ++ | Def +++

Year	Lev	Team	AB	R	H	HR	RBI	Avg	OB	Slg	OPS	bb%	ct%	Eye	SB	CS	x/h%	Iso	RC/G
2023	NCAA	Arkansas	214	54	68	16	52	318	407	612	1019	13	71	0.51	7	3	46	294	8.70
2023	Rk	FCL Blue Jays	15	3	4	1	2	267	421	467	888	21	60	0.67	1	0	25	200	7.69
2023	A	Dunedin	62	17	19	6	16	306	442	677	1119	19	71	0.83	0	0	58	371	10.32

Strong OF who has flown under radar. Drives ball consistently and leverages natural strength and bat speed to produce pull power. Can be too pull-conscious but can catch up to good velo. Struggles with spin and will swing and miss. Not a SB threat though exhibits good range and arm in RF. Lot of work to do, but interesting guy.

Bolte,Henry — 89 — Oakland

EXP MLB DEBUT: 2026 | H/W: 6-3 195 | FUT: Starting CF | 8D

Bats R Age 20 — 2022 (2) HS (CA)

Pwr +++ | BAvg ++ | Spd +++++ | Def ++++

Year	Lev	Team	AB	R	H	HR	RBI	Avg	OB	Slg	OPS	bb%	ct%	Eye	SB	CS	x/h%	Iso	RC/G
2022	Rk	ACL Athletics	33	5	7	0	2	212	316	212	528	13	42	0.26	0	1	0	0	2.80
2023	A	Stockton	420	77	108	14	68	257	353	421	774	13	61	0.38	32	9	33	164	5.85

High-upside OF with great tools but struggles with contact. Led CAL in Ks, though 5th in HR and 3rd in SB. Brings elite speed to basepaths and CF where he profiles as plus defender. Swing mechanics far too erratic and will need to pull ball more. Struck out in 33% of plate appearances. Will take time to develop but exciting potential.

Bonaci,Brainer — 46 — Boston

EXP MLB DEBUT: 2025 | H/W: 5-10 164 | FUT: Starting 2B | 7D

Bats B Age 21 — 2018 FA (VZ)

Pwr ++ | BAvg +++ | Spd ++ | Def +++

Year	Lev	Team	AB	R	H	HR	RBI	Avg	OB	Slg	OPS	bb%	ct%	Eye	SB	CS	x/h%	Iso	RC/G
2021	Rk	FCL Red Sox	139	27	35	2	17	252	350	403	753	13	73	0.57	12	0	46	151	5.23
2021	A	Salem	49	5	11	0	8	224	269	327	596	6	84	0.38	0	0	36	102	2.98
2022	A	Salem	397	86	104	6	50	262	397	385	783	18	78	1.00	28	6	30	123	5.80
2023	A+	Greenville	256	34	77	9	38	301	354	473	826	8	75	0.33	6	3	32	172	5.72
2023	AA	Portland	61	10	17	2	7	279	371	426	798	13	72	0.53	1	1	29	148	5.67

Quick, versatile INF who is improving with bat and growing into short frame. Reached AA after career high in HR and showed more aggression with swing decisions. SB fell off cliff and could stand to get on base more. Very good defender with quick glovework and soft hands. Fits utility profile, but future in doubt after club suspension.

Bonilla,Enmanuel — 8 — Toronto

EXP MLB DEBUT: 2027 | H/W: 6-1 180 | FUT: Starting CF | 8E

Bats R Age 18 — 2023 FA (DR)

Pwr +++ | BAvg +++ | Spd +++ | Def +++

Year	Lev	Team	AB	R	H	HR	RBI	Avg	OB	Slg	OPS	bb%	ct%	Eye	SB	CS	x/h%	Iso	RC/G
2023	Rk	DSL Blue Jays	189	41	58	3	22	307	394	429	822	13	71	0.49	5	5	24	122	6.17

Big international signee who impressed in DSL. Lot of raw ability in physical frame. Possesses all tools in arsenal. Aggressive hitter who extends arms in hopes of pop. Exhibits above average bat speed and is in need of more strength to hit for consistent power. Has speed and ranges well in CF. Will need time to improve reads.

Bowman,Cooper — 4 — Oakland

EXP MLB DEBUT: 2025 | H/W: 6-0 205 | FUT: Starting 2B | 7D

Bats R Age 24	Year	Lev	Team	AB	R	H	HR	RBI	Avg	OB	Slg	OPS	bb%	ct%	Eye	SB	CS	x/h%	Iso	RC/G
2021 (4) Louisville	2021	A	Tampa	93	17	22	3	22	237	317	441	758	11	72	0.42	11	1	55	204	5.13
Pwr ++	2022	A+	Hudson Valley	299	54	65	8	35	217	339	355	693	16	68	0.57	35	6	37	137	4.39
BAvg ++	2022	A+	Lansing	115	12	24	3	12	209	266	304	570	7	67	0.24	12	0	21	96	2.23
Spd ++++	2023	Rk	ACL Athletics	12	4	3	0	2	250	308	333	641	8	67	0.25	3	0	33	83	3.56
Def +++	2023	AA	Midland	271	49	71	8	38	262	349	435	784	12	75	0.53	35	3	39	173	5.45

Speedy 2B who finished 3rd in org in SB despite only 68 games due to injury. Returned in July and was impressive. Game all about legs as double-plus speed is best attribute. Started to hit for more power but expanded zone and K rate increased. Has sufficient strength and bat speed. Owns fringe-average arm and is adequate defender.

Boyd,Emaarion — 789 — Philadelphia

EXP MLB DEBUT: 2027 | H/W: 5-11 177 | FUT: Starting CF | 7C

Bats R Age 20	Year	Lev	Team	AB	R	H	HR	RBI	Avg	OB	Slg	OPS	bb%	ct%	Eye	SB	CS	x/h%	Iso	RC/G
2022 (11) HS (MS)																				
Pwr ++																				
BAvg ++	2022	Rk	FCL Phillies	29	6	10	0	2	345	441	379	820	15	83	1.00	7	2	10	34	6.11
Spd +++++	2022	A	Clearwater	7	1	3	0	0	429	429	429	857	0	100		1	0	0	0	5.47
Def ++++	2023	A	Clearwater	343	68	90	1	36	262	331	324	654	9	83	0.58	56	18	16	61	3.75

Fantastic CF defender and baserunner who the new MLB rules seem made for. But getting on base at higher levels given the lack of impact with the bat will be his main challenge. Showed patience in first full season, and is a small-ball dasher with top-scale speed. Would benefit from getting stronger; but not much projection left in his frame.

Bradfield Jr.,Enrique — 78 — Baltimore

EXP MLB DEBUT: 2025 | H/W: 6-1 170 | FUT: Starting CF | 7A

Bats L Age 22	Year	Lev	Team	AB	R	H	HR	RBI	Avg	OB	Slg	OPS	bb%	ct%	Eye	SB	CS	x/h%	Iso	RC/G
2023 (1) Vanderbilt																				
Pwr ++	2023	NCAA	Vanderbilt	233	69	65	6	34	279	396	429	825	16	83	1.13	37	7	32	150	6.18
BAvg +++	2023	Rk	FCL Orioles B	9	4	5	0	0	556	667	667	1333	25	67	1.00	1	0	20	111	15.30
Spd +++++	2023	A	Delmarva	53	15	16	0	6	302	486	340	826	26	83	2.11	20	2	13	38	6.91
Def ++++	2023	A+	Aberdeen	17	3	2	0	0	118	286	118	403	19	76	1.00	4	0	0	0	0.64

Well known collegiate commodity who gets credited as more of an old school player because of elite speed and defensive CF abilities. Hit tool will have to make up for the fact that there isn't a lot of power projection. More BB than K in college career and rarely strikes out. Could be more of an impact in real life than fantasy with exception of SB potential.

Bradley,Tucker — 79 — Kansas City

EXP MLB DEBUT: 2024 | H/W: 5-9 206 | FUT: Reserve OF | 6B

Bats L Age 25	Year	Lev	Team	AB	R	H	HR	RBI	Avg	OB	Slg	OPS	bb%	ct%	Eye	SB	CS	x/h%	Iso	RC/G
2020 FA (Georgia)	2021	A	Columbia	23	2	8	0	3	348	444	391	836	15	87	1.33	3	1	13	43	6.34
Pwr ++	2021	A+	Quad Cities	307	53	86	6	42	280	367	430	797	12	75	0.55	9	1	34	150	5.70
BAvg ++	2022	AA	NW Arkansas	396	73	116	12	53	293	379	455	834	12	79	0.65	19	6	32	162	6.04
Spd +++	2023	AA	NW Arkansas	93	12	28	3	19	301	369	473	842	10	74	0.42	1	0	32	172	6.11
Def +++	2023	AAA	Omaha	210	37	56	4	36	267	366	433	800	14	75	0.63	10	4	43	167	5.84

Former undrafted free agent has played way up to AAA. Solid organizational soldier who has produced above tools. Grinds out at bats with passive approach and has enough strength and bat speed to pull ball out of park on occasion. Has skill set of extra outfielder who can provide quality at bats.

Brannigan,Jack — 56 — Pittsburgh

EXP MLB DEBUT: 2025 | H/W: 6-0 190 | FUT: Starting 3B | 7C

Bats R Age 23	Year	Lev	Team	AB	R	H	HR	RBI	Avg	OB	Slg	OPS	bb%	ct%	Eye	SB	CS	x/h%	Iso	RC/G
2022 (3) Notre Dame	2022	NCAA	Notre Dame	206	46	61	11	45	296	356	539	894	8	77	0.40	10	4	44	243	6.57
Pwr +++	2022	Rk	FCL Pirates B	5	0	1	0	0	200	333	200	533	17	60	0.50	0	0	0	0	1.98
BAvg +++	2022	A	Bradenton	95	14	20	3	14	211	318	337	655	14	71	0.54	6	3	30	126	3.67
Spd +++	2023	A	Bradenton	162	38	41	7	17	253	376	451	827	16	67	0.59	17	2	39	198	6.41
Def +++	2023	A+	Greensboro	147	26	44	12	37	299	387	605	992	13	61	0.36	7	1	45	306	9.21

Burgeoning INF who fared better in High-A upon promotion. Hit for more power and higher BA as he got comfortable with swing. Owns good raw power and started to pull more for HR. Draws walks with discerning eye and making harder, more consistent contact. Arm strength is best tool and is good defender on left side of infield.

Brannon,Brooks — 2 — Boston

EXP MLB DEBUT: 2026 | H/W: 5-11 210 | FUT: Starting C | 8E

Bats R Age 19	Year	Lev	Team	AB	R	H	HR	RBI	Avg	OB	Slg	OPS	bb%	ct%	Eye	SB	CS	x/h%	Iso	RC/G
2022 (9) HS (NC)																				
Pwr ++++																				
BAvg +	2022	Rk	FCL Red Sox	13	6	6	0	5	462	533	846	1379	13	62	0.40	0	0	50	385	16.67
Spd +	2023	Rk	FCL Red Sox	48	8	12	3	14	250	294	542	836	6	75	0.25	0	0	58	292	5.74
Def ++	2023	A	Salem	24	4	7	3	9	292	320	667	987	4	67	0.13	0	0	43	375	7.76

Missed most of season with freak hand injury and also suffered sore shoulder. Has impressive bat speed and plus strength to get balls a long way. Has the typical C frame (short, stocky) with plus arm strength. Very raw receiver but has improved throwing mechanics. Has high upside but will need to find consistency in plate approach.

Brito,Juan — 45 — Cleveland

EXP MLB DEBUT: 2025 | H/W: 5-11 202 | FUT: Starting 2B | 7B

Bats B Age 22	Year	Lev	Team	AB	R	H	HR	RBI	Avg	OB	Slg	OPS	bb%	ct%	Eye	SB	CS	x/h%	Iso	RC/G
2018 FA (DR)	2021	Rk	ACL Rockies	88	20	26	3	11	295	398	432	830	15	76	0.71	5	4	23	136	6.08
Pwr ++	2022	A	Fresno	402	91	115	11	72	286	402	470	872	16	82	1.10	17	9	40	184	6.80
BAvg +++	2023	A+	Lake County	132	29	35	4	14	265	378	424	802	15	84	1.14	3	1	37	159	5.83
Spd ++	2023	AA	Akron	315	46	87	10	60	276	372	444	816	13	80	0.76	3	7	37	168	5.87
Def ++	2023	AAA	Columbus	14	1	3	0	1	214	450	286	736	30	71	1.50	1	0	33	71	5.65

Versatile INF who played at 3 levels and finished 3rd in EL in BA and led org in BB. Has exceptional feel for strike zone and posts high OBP by drawing walks and making contact. Revised swing for more lift and more pop. Added strength helps. Hits better from left side. Passable defender with fringy speed and quickness.

Brown, Jr.,Eric — 6 — Milwaukee

EXP MLB DEBUT: 2025 | H/W: 5-10 190 | FUT: Starting SS | 7B

Bats R Age 23	Year	Lev	Team	AB	R	H	HR	RBI	Avg	OB	Slg	OPS	bb%	ct%	Eye	SB	CS	x/h%	Iso	RC/G
2022 (1) Coastal Carolina	2022	Rk	ACL Brewers G	13	7	4	0	1	308	471	538	1009	24	69	1.00	4	0	75	231	9.86
Pwr ++	2022	A	Carolina	84	16	22	3	7	262	347	440	788	12	80	0.65	15	2	36	179	5.40
BAvg +++	2023	Rk	ACL Brewers G	11	5	2	2	2	182	357	727	1084	21	73	1.00	1	0	100	545	9.07
Spd +++	2023	A+	Wisconsin	245	48	65	4	25	265	350	347	697	12	80	0.67	37	5	18	82	4.28
Def +++	2023	AA	Biloxi	7	1	0	0	0	0	125	0	125	13	57	0.33	1	0		0	-5.26

Quick, athletic SS who suffered thru awful start to season and missed time with injury. All in all, had solid season that saw him end in AA. Has impressive tools and all but power has appeared. Runs very well and has hand-eye coordination and pitch recognition to produce with stick. Finds barrels and can ddrive to gaps. May eventually move to 2B.

Brown,Dasan — 8 — Toronto

EXP MLB DEBUT: 2025 | H/W: 5-11 185 | FUT: Reserve OF | 6B

Bats R Age 22	Year	Lev	Team	AB	R	H	HR	RBI	Avg	OB	Slg	OPS	bb%	ct%	Eye	SB	CS	x/h%	Iso	RC/G
2019 (3) HS (ON)	2021	A	Dunedin	198	33	42	4	16	212	284	323	608	9	63	0.27	22	6	31	111	3.02
Pwr +	2022	Rk	FCL Blue Jays	16	5	3	0	1	188	278	250	528	11	56	0.29	2	1	33	63	2.04
BAvg ++	2022	A	Dunedin	140	35	39	4	12	279	357	450	807	11	68	0.38	11	6	36	171	5.96
Spd +++++	2022	A+	Vancouver	151	25	45	2	11	298	358	411	768	8	67	0.28	11	3	29	113	5.38
Def ++++	2023	A+	Vancouver	403	59	88	7	39	218	291	315	606	9	71	0.35	26	11	25	97	2.90

Elite speed, exceptional CF range ... and not much else. Has BA concerns due to inability to catch up to good velocity and weak contact continues to mute production. At best when keeps ball on ground and uses legs to get infield hits. Able to work counts but lack of bat speed hurts. Outstanding defender with sound reads and routes.

Brown,Vaun — 8 — San Francisco

EXP MLB DEBUT: 2024 | H/W: 6-0 215 | FUT: Starting CF | 7C

Bats R Age 25	Year	Lev	Team	AB	R	H	HR	RBI	Avg	OB	Slg	OPS	bb%	ct%	Eye	SB	CS	x/h%	Iso	RC/G
2021 (10) Florida Southern	2022	A+	Eugene	157	50	55	9	34	350	430	611	1042	12	67	0.42	21	3	38	261	9.46
Pwr +++	2022	AA	Richmond	2	0	0	0	0	0	0	0	0	0	100		0	0		0	-2.66
BAvg ++	2023	A	San Jose	17	4	7	0	1	412	474	529	1003	11	71	0.40	3	0	29	118	8.82
Spd ++++	2023	A+	Eugene	20	2	6	1	3	300	364	550	914	9	75	0.40	2	0	50	250	6.97
Def +++	2023	AA	Richmond	190	27	42	8	34	221	271	421	692	6	59	0.17	15	0	48	200	4.47

Toolsy OF who looks and plays the part but struggled with injuries all throughout 2023. Ended season in early August with knee issues. Power/speed combo could lead to 30/30 seasons but K rate may make it a moot point. Holes in swing exploited, particularly with breaking balls, and BA in question. Runs bases aggressively and plays mean CF.

Buelvas,Brayan — 8 — Oakland

EXP MLB DEBUT: 2025 | H/W: 5-11 155 | FUT: Starting CF | 7D

Bats R Age 21	Year	Lev	Team	AB	R	H	HR	RBI	Avg	OB	Slg	OPS	bb%	ct%	Eye	SB	CS	x/h%	Iso	RC/G
2018 FA (CB)	2022	Rk	ACL Athletics	23	4	6	1	4	261	370	522	892	15	74	0.67	4	0	50	261	7.10
Pwr ++	2022	A+	Lansing	236	28	46	7	26	195	249	352	601	7	76	0.30	7	4	48	157	2.76
BAvg ++	2023	A	Stockton	200	36	58	9	33	290	385	515	900	13	75	0.61	23	2	41	225	7.05
Spd ++++	2023	A+	Lansing	111	6	15	2	10	135	200	243	443	8	66	0.24	8	2	47	108	0.46
Def +++	2023	AA	Midland	75	13	14	1	19	187	238	293	531	6	72	0.24	0	0	36	107	1.83

Wiry strong OF who looks the part and has nice tools but can't put them all together to produce. Really struggled in High-A and AA despite solid plate approach. Plays a solid defensive CF with a strong arm and plenty of range. Has bat speed for power and runs very well. Set personal best in SB and needs to hit to advance.

Burke,Jacob — 8 — Chicago (A)

EXP MLB DEBUT: 2025 | H/W: 6-1 208 | FUT: Reserve OF | 6B

Bats R Age 23 — 2022 (11) Miami — Pwr +++ | BAvg +++ | Spd +++ | Def +++

Year	Lev	Team	AB	R	H	HR	RBI	Avg	OB	Slg	OPS	bb%	ct%	Eye	SB	CS	x/h%	Iso	RC/G
2022	NCAA	Miami	222	59	77	13	58	347	408	599	1007	9	78	0.48	10	2	36	252	7.98
2022	Rk	ACL White Sox	18	2	6	1	2	333	429	556	984	14	78	0.75	0	0	33	222	7.99
2022	A	Kannapolis	78	13	21	1	12	269	321	410	732	7	74	0.30	4	2	38	141	4.64
2023	A	Kannapolis	127	23	40	4	22	315	387	512	899	11	74	0.45	9	3	40	197	6.99
2023	A+	Winston Salem	203	40	57	2	18	281	348	394	742	9	74	0.40	10	4	30	113	4.87

Strong, hard nosed OF prospect had solid season split between multiple levels. Pros: Calmed approach, sprayed the ball better while still maintaining pull tendencies and improved route running in CF. Cons: Still chases out of the zone, still whiffs those pitches out of the zone and doesn't generate loft despite hard hit tendencies. 4th OF.

Burrowes,Ryan — 46 — Chicago (A)

EXP MLB DEBUT: 2027 | H/W: 6-2 170 | FUT: Starting MIF | 7E

Bats R Age 19 — 2022 FA (PN) — Pwr +++ | BAvg +++ | Spd +++ | Def +++

Year	Lev	Team	AB	R	H	HR	RBI	Avg	OB	Slg	OPS	bb%	ct%	Eye	SB	CS	x/h%	Iso	RC/G
2022	Rk	DSL White Sox	158	38	42	3	18	266	366	392	759	14	78	0.74	12	0	31	127	5.21
2023	Rk	ACL White Sox	158	24	41	2	15	259	312	386	698	7	68	0.24	12	5	32	127	4.29

Slim, athletic MIF prospect had solid US debut. Room to grow into frame but will always be on light side. Upright, slight open stance with hitch in load. Lacking flexibility in swing, struggles getting to balls up in zone. Doesn't have feel for spin at present. Below-average power projected. Could stick at either MIF position.

Busch,Michael — 54 — Chicago (N)

EXP MLB DEBUT: 2023 | H/W: 6-1 210 | FUT: Starting 2B | 8B

Bats L Age 26 — 2019 (1) North Carolina — Pwr ++++ | BAvg ++ | Spd ++ | Def ++

Year	Lev	Team	AB	R	H	HR	RBI	Avg	OB	Slg	OPS	bb%	ct%	Eye	SB	CS	x/h%	Iso	RC/G
2021	AA	Tulsa	409	84	109	20	67	267	374	484	858	15	68	0.54	2	3	44	218	6.70
2022	AA	Tulsa	108	31	33	11	29	306	432	667	1098	18	67	0.67	1	0	52	361	10.28
2022	AAA	Oklahoma City	444	87	118	21	79	266	340	480	820	10	70	0.38	3	2	45	214	5.88
2023	AAA	Oklahoma City	390	85	126	27	90	323	420	618	1038	14	77	0.74	4	0	45	295	8.69
2023	MLB	Los Angeles	72	9	12	2	7	167	250	292	542	10	63	0.30	1	0	42	125	1.93

Continued dominance in the high minors has yet to translate to the major league level. Strong, thick frame with above-average to plus all-fields power. Plus eye at the plate; looks for balls he can punish without expanding the zone and posted a .431 OBP at AAA. Below average speed and a fringe-average defender without a clear defensive home.

Bush,Homer — 78 — San Diego

EXP MLB DEBUT: 2026 | H/W: 6-3 200 | FUT: Starting CF | 7C

Bats R Age 22 — 2023 (4) Grand Canyon — Pwr ++ | BAvg +++ | Spd ++++ | Def +++

Year	Lev	Team	AB	R	H	HR	RBI	Avg	OB	Slg	OPS	bb%	ct%	Eye	SB	CS	x/h%	Iso	RC/G
2023	NCAA	Grand Canyon	238	69	88	2	41	370	457	500	957	14	89	1.41	25	6	27	130	7.72
2023	Rk	ACL Padres	44	16	18	2	4	409	490	614	1104	14	84	1.00	10	0	28	205	9.31
2023	A	Lake Elsinore	85	16	21	1	10	247	340	341	681	12	82	0.80	11	1	29	94	4.23
2023	AA	San Antonio	28	2	12	0	3	429	448	464	913	3	93	0.50	1	1	8	36	6.31

Tall, athletic OF with dazzling pro debut on three levels. Speed is best present tool and should steal loads of bases. Nifty defender at any OF spot with plus range and strong arm. Profiles more as a BA guy due to level swing path and situational hitting. Should add strength to lean frame for harder contact. Will get on base consistently.

Caba,Starlyn — 6 — Philadelphia

EXP MLB DEBUT: 2027 | H/W: 5-10 160 | FUT: Starting SS | 8E

Bats B Age 18 — 2023 FA (DR) — Pwr ++ | BAvg +++ | Spd ++++ | Def ++++

Year	Lev	Team	AB	R	H	HR	RBI	Avg	OB	Slg	OPS	bb%	ct%	Eye	SB	CS	x/h%	Iso	RC/G
2023	Rk	DSL Phillies W	133	29	40	0	17	301	422	346	768	17	88	1.75	16	6	10	45	5.74

Teenage switch-hitter with great contact skills and advanced eye, at least in limited DSL stint. Frame is not really projectable for more strength/power, but high-BA, gap-to-gap spray hitter is among realm of outcomes. Is advanced defensively with outstanding quickness and projects to stay at SS. Should also chip in some SB.

Cabbage,Trey — 379 — Los Angeles (A)

EXP MLB DEBUT: 2023 | H/W: 6-2 204 | FUT: Starting 1B | 7E

Bats L Age 26 — 2015 (4) HS (TN) — Pwr +++ | BAvg ++ | Spd ++ | Def ++

Year	Lev	Team	AB	R	H	HR	RBI	Avg	OB	Slg	OPS	bb%	ct%	Eye	SB	CS	x/h%	Iso	RC/G
2021	A+	Cedar Rapids	143	21	38	9	33	266	340	538	878	10	65	0.32	4	0	53	273	7.00
2021	AA	Wichita	244	40	64	18	49	262	345	533	878	11	55	0.28	2	0	45	270	7.98
2022	AA	Rocket City	113	21	37	10	32	327	429	664	1092	15	58	0.43	10	2	46	336	11.30
2023	AAA	Salt Lake	418	83	128	30	89	306	374	596	969	10	66	0.32	32	3	45	289	8.22
2023	MLB	LA Angels	53	5	11	1	7	208	236	321	557	4	51	0.08	1	1	36	113	2.77

Older 1B-only prospect put up huge Triple-A numbers to earn MLB callup in 2023. Open, mostly upright stance. Wraps bat on load, slowing reactions. Uber-aggressive approach with chase rate on wrong side of 40%. Add in whiff rate just shy of 40% and is flirting with not enough hit for plus power to play. When he connects, high EV darling.

Cabrera,Ricardo — 56 — Cincinnati

EXP MLB DEBUT: 2026 | H/W: 5-11 178 | FUT: Starting SS | 8E

Bats R Age 19 — 2022 FA (VZ) — Pwr +++ | BAvg +++ | Spd ++++ | Def +++

Year	Lev	Team	AB	R	H	HR	RBI	Avg	OB	Slg	OPS	bb%	ct%	Eye	SB	CS	x/h%	Iso	RC/G
2022	Rk	DSL Reds	150	30	38	1	19	253	313	380	693	8	73	0.33	5	4	32	127	4.21
2023	Rk	ACL Reds	143	41	50	5	21	350	433	559	992	13	76	0.60	21	2	32	210	8.29
2023	A	Daytona	19	7	6	0	2	316	458	316	774	21	74	1.00	3	0	0	0	5.83

Toolsy, athletic SS prospect had exceptional stateside debut. Short-statured with athletic frame. Upright, slightly open stance with easy swing mechanics. Up-the-middle approach is terrific hitting foundation. Strong despite lean frame. Power could come with strength gains and getting to lofted contact consistently. Plus runner. Should stick at SS.

Cabrera,Yeremi — 789 — Texas

EXP MLB DEBUT: 2027 | H/W: 5-11 155 | FUT: Reserve OF | 6C

Bats L Age 18 — 2022 FA (DR) — Pwr ++ | BAvg ++ | Spd ++ | Def ++

Year	Lev	Team	AB	R	H	HR	RBI	Avg	OB	Slg	OPS	bb%	ct%	Eye	SB	CS	x/h%	Iso	RC/G
2022	Rk	DSL Rangers 2	140	22	25	2	12	179	307	286	593	16	79	0.90	11	3	32	107	3.19
2023	Rk	DSL Rangers 2	56	16	18	2	6	321	415	500	915	14	80	0.82	3	1	28	179	7.14
2023	Rk	DSL Rangers	114	33	38	5	23	333	449	588	1037	17	85	1.41	6	5	37	254	8.82

DSL repeat went much better contact-wise but deferred CF to more RF starts. Still no carrying tool in profile, sum-of-parts guy so will need to push power if he's a RF. No splits, solid contact, 25/32/43 LD/GB/FB, though heavy pull (54%). Should open stateside at 18 years old, needs to add weight & trending in right direction.

Caissie,Owen — 79 — Chicago (N)

EXP MLB DEBUT: 2024 | H/W: 6-3 190 | FUT: Starting OF | 8D

Bats L Age 21 — 2020 (2) HS (ON) — Pwr +++++ | BAvg +++ | Spd ++ | Def ++

Year	Lev	Team	AB	R	H	HR	RBI	Avg	OB	Slg	OPS	bb%	ct%	Eye	SB	CS	x/h%	Iso	RC/G
2021	Rk	ACL Cubs	109	20	38	6	20	349	474	596	1070	19	64	0.67	1	2	37	248	10.52
2021	A	Myrtle Beach	73	15	17	1	9	233	371	329	700	18	62	0.57	0	0	29	96	4.79
2022	A+	South Bend	378	57	96	11	58	254	341	402	743	12	67	0.40	11	6	34	148	5.02
2023	AA	Tennessee	439	77	127	22	84	289	394	519	914	15	63	0.46	7	9	43	230	7.99

Breakout campaign by Canadian-born masher. Has plus raw power and gets to it more frequently. Good bat speed as he hunts for pitches he can punish, but long levers and an aggressive approach results in plenty of swing and miss. Did post career highs in walks and OBP. Improved bat to ball skills give him a chance to hit for average and power.

Calaz,Robert — 8 — Colorado

EXP MLB DEBUT: 2027 | H/W: 6-2 202 | FUT: Starting OF | 8D

Bats R Age 18 — 2023 FA (DR) — Pwr +++++ | BAvg +++ | Spd ++ | Def ++

Year	Lev	Team	AB	R	H	HR	RBI	Avg	OB	Slg	OPS	bb%	ct%	Eye	SB	CS	x/h%	Iso	RC/G
2023	Rk	DSL Colorado	157	38	51	7	29	325	408	561	968	12	73	0.51	6	0	41	236	8.04

Tall, projectable frame with plus raw power. Drifts into the hitting zone, sapping hard contact, but can be fixed and has plus bat speed and exit velo when he finds the barrel. Impressed in DSL and will make state-side debut in 2024. Has the tools to carve out FT role in Coors.

Callihan,Tyler — 4 — Cincinnati

EXP MLB DEBUT: 2024 | H/W: 6-1 205 | FUT: Reserve IF | 6C

Bats L Age 23 — 2019 (3) HS (FL) — Pwr ++ | BAvg +++ | Spd +++ | Def ++

Year	Lev	Team	AB	R	H	HR	RBI	Avg	OB	Slg	OPS	bb%	ct%	Eye	SB	CS	x/h%	Iso	RC/G
2021	A	Daytona	87	14	26	2	10	299	358	437	795	8	85	0.62	5	1	31	138	5.35
2022	A	Daytona	117	18	33	3	13	282	339	419	757	8	84	0.53	9	1	30	137	4.84
2022	A+	Dayton	211	27	49	4	20	232	289	384	673	7	71	0.28	6	2	41	152	3.87
2023	A+	Dayton	399	44	94	8	47	236	300	373	674	8	74	0.36	25	4	36	138	3.86
2023	AA	Chattanooga	87	11	27	1	11	310	400	460	860	13	77	0.65	4	1	41	149	6.62

Hit-first IF prospect steadily improved as season wore on, earning Double-A callup. Upright, open stance with short trigger. Loosen top hand up in swing, providing for swing flexibility. Hit over power. Aggressiveness results in low BA. Hits the ball hard with linear swing. Average speed, good at picking spots on bases. Below average defender.

Caminero,Junior

56 | Tampa Bay | EXP MLB DEBUT: 2023 | H/W: 6-1 157 | FUT: Starting 3B | 9B

Bats R Age 20 — 2019 FA (DR)
Pwr ++++ / BAvg ++++ / Spd +++ / Def +++

Year	Lev	Team	AB	R	H	HR	RBI	Avg	OB	Slg	OPS	bb%	ct%	Eye	SB	CS	x/h%	Iso	RC/G
2022	Rk	FCL Rays	132	18	43	5	31	326	395	492	887	10	84	0.71	7	1	26	167	6.47
2022	A	Charleston	107	19	32	6	20	299	348	505	852	7	79	0.36	5	0	28	206	5.79
2023	A+	Bowling Green	146	30	52	11	32	356	397	685	1082	6	73	0.25	2	1	44	329	9.13
2023	AA	Montgomery	314	55	97	20	62	309	373	548	921	9	81	0.53	3	4	33	239	6.74
2023	MLB	Tampa Bay	34	4	8	1	7	235	278	353	631	6	76	0.25	0	0	25	118	3.02

Quick-twitch hitter busted it between two MiLB levels to make MLB debut in 2023. Stocky, athletic frame, near physical projection. Open stance with big leg lift and easy trigger. Exceptional bat speed fuels profile. Utilizes entire field, peppering line drives. Exceptional power potential to all fields. Swing achieves natural loft. Average runner.

Campos,Roberto

79 | Detroit | EXP MLB DEBUT: 2025 | H/W: 6-3 200 | FUT: Starting OF | 8E

Bats R Age 20 — 2019 FA (CU)
Pwr ++++ / BAvg ++ / Spd +++ / Def +++

Year	Lev	Team	AB	R	H	HR	RBI	Avg	OB	Slg	OPS	bb%	ct%	Eye	SB	CS	x/h%	Iso	RC/G
2021	Rk	FCL Tigers West	136	20	31	8	19	228	314	441	755	11	70	0.41	3	0	42	213	4.89
2022	A	Lakeland	403	52	104	5	50	258	325	385	710	9	76	0.41	7	3	35	127	4.40
2023	A+	West Michigan	339	34	87	5	53	257	313	395	709	8	76	0.35	4	2	37	139	4.32

Strong, powerful frame with above average raw power, but has failed to live up to the hype after receiving franchise-record $2.85 million international bonus. Shows power to all fields and willing to go the other way, but struggles to control the zone and find the barrel consistently, often making weak contact and has just 18 HR over three seasons.

Canario,Alexander

89 | Chicago (N) | EXP MLB DEBUT: 2023 | H/W: 5-11 165 | FUT: Starting OF | 7D

Bats R Age 23 — 2016 FA (DR)
Pwr ++++ / BAvg ++ / Spd +++ / Def ++

Year	Lev	Team	AB	R	H	HR	RBI	Avg	OB	Slg	OPS	bb%	ct%	Eye	SB	CS	x/h%	Iso	RC/G
2022	AAA	Iowa	65	16	15	6	14	231	359	538	897	17	68	0.62	3	0	53	308	7.07
2023	Rk	ACL Cubs	21	6	6	1	5	286	400	619	1019	16	76	0.80	0	0	67	333	8.86
2023	A+	South Bend	39	4	10	0	7	256	356	282	638	13	64	0.43	0	0	10	26	3.64
2023	AAA	Iowa	145	23	40	8	35	276	344	524	868	9	69	0.33	2	0	50	248	6.59
2023	MLB	Chicago (N)	17	1	5	1	6	294	294	647	941	0	53	0.00	0	0	60	353	9.75

Short, but physically strong OF has plus raw power. Upright, slightly open stance with an aggressive approach looking for mistakes over the plate, mostly to the pull side. Late start to the season after dealing with ankle and shoulder injuries. Average speed, but runs the bases well. Will need to make more consistent contact and profiles best in RF.

Cappe,Yidde

46 | Miami | EXP MLB DEBUT: 2025 | H/W: 6-3 175 | FUT: Starting 2B | 7D

Bats R Age 21 — 2021 FA (CU)
Pwr +++ / BAvg +++ / Spd ++ / Def +++

Year	Lev	Team	AB	R	H	HR	RBI	Avg	OB	Slg	OPS	bb%	ct%	Eye	SB	CS	x/h%	Iso	RC/G
2021	Rk	DSL Marlins	189	31	51	2	27	270	337	402	739	9	81	0.54	9	8	39	132	4.81
2022	Rk	FCL Marlins	118	23	36	6	25	305	354	517	871	7	84	0.47	6	4	36	212	6.04
2022	A	Jupiter	158	18	44	3	15	278	305	380	685	4	86	0.27	7	1	20	101	3.75
2023	A+	Beloit	509	53	112	5	53	220	247	308	555	3	80	0.18	18	9	29	88	2.15

Twitchy athletic MIF prospect struggled with spin in aggressive assignment. High-waisted build with room to grow. Potential above-average power present with strength gains and swing adjustments. Aggressive approach, will chase, especially off-speed pitches. Gap power now, will transition soon to over-the-fence power. Below-average runner.

Cardenas,Noah

2 | Minnesota | EXP MLB DEBUT: 2025 | H/W: 5-11 195 | FUT: Starting C | 7D

Bats R Age 24 — 2021 (8) UCLA
Pwr ++ / BAvg ++ / Spd ++ / Def ++++

Year	Lev	Team	AB	R	H	HR	RBI	Avg	OB	Slg	OPS	bb%	ct%	Eye	SB	CS	x/h%	Iso	RC/G
2020	NCAA	UCLA	38	6	9	0	10	237	341	289	630	14	76	0.67	0	0	22	53	3.58
2021	NCAA	UCLA	213	42	57	5	32	268	336	404	740	9	80	0.51	2	0	32	136	4.71
2021	Rk	FCL Twins	20	3	6	1	4	300	391	500	891	13	85	1.00	0	0	33	200	6.65
2022	A	Fort Myers	310	42	81	9	43	261	402	413	815	19	77	1.04	11	5	35	152	6.17
2023	A+	Cedar Rapids	309	44	84	3	38	272	382	382	764	15	75	0.71	9	5	32	110	5.43

Above average defensive C who finished 4th in MWL in OBP. Advancing one level per year and has chance due to plus receiving and blocking. Throws very well with quick release. Has feel for strike zone and doesn't swing and miss much. Has limited offensive upside with below average power and bat speed.

Carrigg,Cole

268 | Colorado | EXP MLB DEBUT: 2025 | H/W: 6-3 200 | FUT: Starting C | 9E

Bats B Age 21 — 2023 (2) San Diego State
Pwr +++ / BAvg +++ / Spd ++++ / Def ++++

Year	Lev	Team	AB	R	H	HR	RBI	Avg	OB	Slg	OPS	bb%	ct%	Eye	SB	CS	x/h%	Iso	RC/G
2023	NCAA	San Diego St	155	30	47	2	27	303	341	458	800	5	86	0.41	17	7	32	155	5.33
2023	Rk	ACL Rockies	48	13	19	2	13	396	463	688	1150	11	73	0.46	7	2	47	292	10.60
2023	A	Fresno	92	19	30	3	16	326	374	554	928	7	78	0.35	6	1	37	228	7.04

Switch-hitter had impressive pro debut posting a 1.008 OPS at two levels. Unique skill set of plus speed and positional versatility at SS, CF, and C with a double-plus arm. Aggressive approach and long swing could leave him in-between, raising concerns about ability to hit for both average and power. He did make adjustments in debut.

Cartaya,Diego

2 | Los Angeles (N) | EXP MLB DEBUT: 2024 | H/W: 6-3 219 | FUT: Starting C | 8D

Bats R Age 22 — 2018 FA (VZ)
Pwr +++ / BAvg + / Spd ++ / Def +++

Year	Lev	Team	AB	R	H	HR	RBI	Avg	OB	Slg	OPS	bb%	ct%	Eye	SB	CS	x/h%	Iso	RC/G
2019	Rk	AZL Dodgers M	135	25	40	3	13	296	349	437	786	8	77	0.35	1	0	33	141	5.23
2021	A	Rancho Cuca	114	31	34	10	31	298	394	614	1008	14	68	0.49	0	0	47	316	8.71
2022	A	Rancho Cuca	131	31	34	9	31	260	370	550	920	15	66	0.52	0	0	56	290	7.67
2022	A+	Great Lakes	231	43	58	13	41	251	362	476	838	15	68	0.53	1	0	45	225	6.38
2023	AA	Tulsa	354	51	67	19	57	189	266	379	645	9	67	0.32	0	0	43	189	3.29

Struggled all season with a K rate at AA. Strong frame with a quick bat, plus raw power, and some of the best exit velo in the system. Will chase breaking balls out of the zone due to an overly aggressive approach. Regressed defensively as he's matured and filled out his frame, but has the tools to be at least an average defender.

Carter,Evan

789 | Texas | EXP MLB DEBUT: 2023 | H/W: 6-2 190 | FUT: Starting CF | 9C

Bats L Age 21 — 2020 (2) HS (TN)
Pwr ++ / BAvg +++ / Spd +++ / Def +++

Year	Lev	Team	AB	R	H	HR	RBI	Avg	OB	Slg	OPS	bb%	ct%	Eye	SB	CS	x/h%	Iso	RC/G
2022	AA	Frisco	21	8	9	1	7	429	538	714	1253	19	71	0.83	2	1	44	286	12.66
2023	Rk	ACL Rangers	9	3	2	1	2	222	417	667	1083	25	78	1.50	1	0	100	444	9.58
2023	AA	Frisco	377	68	107	12	62	284	401	451	852	16	73	0.72	22	10	31	167	6.63
2023	AAA	Round Rock	34	8	12	0	3	353	421	382	803	11	82	0.67	3	1	8	29	5.61
2023	MLB	Texas	62	15	19	5	12	306	419	645	1064	16	61	0.50	3	0	53	339	10.51

Coalesced into starting LF and 3-hole hitter on World Series Champ with all of 75 MLB PA. 60-grade hit and plus tools with knack for impact contact and avoiding chase. Just turned 21 and way more power can be hung on his frame. Not even close to a finished product. Arm says he'll defer to others in CF but solid otherwise.

Castanon,Marcos

45 | San Diego | EXP MLB DEBUT: 2025 | H/W: 6-0 195 | FUT: Starting 3B | 7D

Bats R Age 25 — 2021 (12) UC Santa Barbara
Pwr +++ / BAvg +++ / Spd + / Def ++

Year	Lev	Team	AB	R	H	HR	RBI	Avg	OB	Slg	OPS	bb%	ct%	Eye	SB	CS	x/h%	Iso	RC/G
2021	NCAA	UC Santa Barbara	109	31	44	8	40	404	476	716	1191	12	80	0.68	3	0	41	312	10.39
2021	Rk	ACL Padres	51	4	7	2	12	137	170	333	503	4	69	0.13	0	0	86	196	1.26
2022	A	Lake Elsinore	421	82	110	23	85	261	379	485	864	16	71	0.66	0	3	44	223	6.68
2023	A+	Fort Wayne	289	47	83	13	58	287	352	491	844	9	76	0.41	1	0	40	204	5.99
2023	AA	San Antonio	211	24	59	4	26	280	336	436	772	8	77	0.37	0	0	41	156	5.14

Natural hitter who made better contact with smooth stroke. Can hit velocity and spin but can often sell out for power. Led org in doubles and likes to work to gaps. Very tough on LHP and could be ideal platoon guy. Lacks secondary skills. Well below average speed and sub-par arm mute defensive ability. Good on two levels in 2023.

Castillo,Neyfy

3789 | Arizona | EXP MLB DEBUT: 2025 | H/W: 6-1 175 | FUT: Utility player | 7D

Bats R Age 23 — 2017 FA (DR)
Pwr ++ / BAvg + / Spd ++ / Def +++

Year	Lev	Team	AB	R	H	HR	RBI	Avg	OB	Slg	OPS	bb%	ct%	Eye	SB	CS	x/h%	Iso	RC/G
2019	Rk	AZL Dbacks	169	23	44	1	29	260	324	391	715	9	73	0.35	7	1	34	130	4.56
2021	A	Visalia	382	74	88	21	72	230	332	453	785	13	55	0.34	26	9	44	223	6.37
2022	Rk	ACL Dbacks	6	0	2	0	0	333	333	333	667	0	33	0.00	0	0	0	0	9.40
2022	A+	Hillsboro	309	35	77	11	29	249	318	411	729	9	63	0.27	15	9	34	162	4.87
2023	AA	Amarillo	348	61	83	17	63	239	308	448	756	9	63	0.27	19	6	43	210	5.23

Versatile defender shows solid approach, production. Tall, physically mature with slightly open stance and lots of movement in hands. Benefitted from Amarillo park power boost. Has some OBP upside despite lackluster hit tool, subpar contact skills. Needs to refine SB decisions.

Castro,Allan

78 | Boston | EXP MLB DEBUT: 2025 | H/W: 6-0 170 | FUT: Reserve OF | 6B

Bats B Age 20 — 2019 FA (DR)
Pwr + / BAvg +++ / Spd +++ / Def +++

Year	Lev	Team	AB	R	H	HR	RBI	Avg	OB	Slg	OPS	bb%	ct%	Eye	SB	CS	x/h%	Iso	RC/G
2021	Rk	DSL Red Sox R	164	24	38	3	19	232	319	421	740	11	74	0.49	3	2	47	189	4.99
2022	Rk	FCL Red Sox	122	19	34	3	17	279	348	451	799	10	74	0.41	8	2	32	172	5.62
2022	A	Salem	32	7	6	0	4	188	316	344	660	16	66	0.55	0	0	50	156	4.24
2023	A	Salem	251	39	62	3	29	247	374	378	753	17	78	0.94	15	5	40	131	5.37
2023	A+	Greenville	166	23	47	4	17	283	350	446	796	9	78	0.47	4	1	36	163	5.46

Switch-hitting OF who finished 2nd in org in doubles and set highs in HR and SB. Benefitted from being more patient at plate and more consistent, hard contact. Knows strike zone well. Hasn't mastered LHP and has limited power projection. Better hitter from left side. Doesn't have overwhelming tools and profiles as 4th OF at best.

Cauley,Cameron — 46 — Texas

EXP MLB DEBUT: 2026 | H/W: 5-10 170 | FUT: Starting CF | 7E

Bats R Age 21
2021 (3) HS (TX)
Pwr ++
BAvg ++
Spd ++++
Def ++

Year	Lev	Team	AB	R	H	HR	RBI	Avg	OB	Slg	OPS	bb%	ct%	Eye	SB	CS	x/h%	Iso	RC/G
2021	Rk	ACL Rangers	94	20	24	0	17	255	314	383	697	8	67	0.26	10	1	33	128	4.48
2022	A	Down East	287	36	60	2	21	209	302	289	591	12	68	0.42	38	5	27	80	2.85
2023	A	Down East	242	43	59	7	35	244	327	405	732	11	63	0.34	22	3	37	161	5.03
2023	A+	Hickory	125	25	31	5	24	248	338	424	762	12	65	0.39	14	2	39	176	5.35

Plus-plus burner whose aggressive, pull-heavy approach struggled in low minors. Lots of chase and zone contact issues kept BA low though did inch the power up. Defense predicated on huge range but average arm may ultimately push off dirt out to CF. Upside remains and elite speed will buoy him but without contact gains a utility/pinch runner.

Ceballos,Sabin — 5 — Atlanta

EXP MLB DEBUT: 2026 | H/W: 6-3 225 | FUT: Starting 3B | 7E

Bats R Age 21
2023 (3) Oregon
Pwr +++
BAvg ++
Spd +
Def ++++

Year	Lev	Team	AB	R	H	HR	RBI	Avg	OB	Slg	OPS	bb%	ct%	Eye	SB	CS	x/h%	Iso	RC/G
2023	NCAA	Oregon	213	48	71	18	70	333	425	643	1068	14	83	0.94	0	1	41	310	8.71
2023	Rk	FCL Braves	8	4	3	0	2	375	643	375	1018	43	63	2.00	2	0	0	0	11.18
2023	A	Augusta	32	3	9	1	6	281	343	375	718	9	66	0.27	0	0	11	94	4.44

Hard hitting 3B prospect parlayed big junior season at Oregon into a 3rd round pick. Average build, close to physical projection. Slightly open stance with significant bat wrap at trigger. Plus bat speed once it gets going with above-average power potential if hit tool allows. Gold-Glove 3B in college but also has experience behind the plate.

Celesten,Felnin — 6 — Seattle

EXP MLB DEBUT: 2028 | H/W: 6-1 175 | FUT: Starting SS | 9E

Bats B Age 18
2023 FA (DR)
Pwr +++
BAvg +++
Spd ++++
Def +++

Year	Lev	Team	AB	R	H	HR	RBI	Avg	OB	Slg	OPS	bb%	ct%	Eye	SB	CS	x/h%	Iso	RC/G
2023	--	Did Not Play																	

High-profile international signing with extraordinary upside predicated on plus tools across board. Athletic frame oozes projection. Swings aggressively but makes good contact and flashes well above average raw power to all fields. Has 30/30 talent with speed and instincts. Arm and quickness suitable for any INF spot.

Cerda,Christian — 2 — Arizona

EXP MLB DEBUT: 2026 | H/W: 6-0 190 | FUT: Reserve C | 6C

Bats R Age 21
2019 FA (NY)
Pwr +++
BAvg +
Spd +
Def ++

Year	Lev	Team	AB	R	H	HR	RBI	Avg	OB	Slg	OPS	bb%	ct%	Eye	SB	CS	x/h%	Iso	RC/G
2021	Rk	DSL Rays	133	18	29	1	18	218	342	338	680	16	81	1.00	5	3	41	120	4.45
2022	Rk	ACL Dbacks	34	5	7	0	1	206	357	294	651	19	79	1.14	0	0	43	88	4.21
2022	Rk	FCL Rays	54	15	17	2	12	315	464	519	982	22	78	1.25	5	0	41	204	8.56
2023	A	Visalia	238	35	60	5	32	252	392	382	775	19	74	0.90	1	0	33	130	5.67
2023	A+	Hillsboro	127	24	30	6	21	236	412	425	837	23	72	1.09	0	0	40	189	6.55

Catching prospect showed plate discipline, interesting power in full-season debut. Mixes patience at plate with keen understanding of strike zone. Unique setup with front leg turned in, helps generate swing torque. Projects as high-OBP/average power backup C.

Cermak,Ryan — 89 — Tampa Bay

EXP MLB DEBUT: 2026 | H/W: 6-0 205 | FUT: Starting OF | 7D

Bats R Age 22
2022 (2) Illinois State
Pwr +++
BAvg ++
Spd ++++
Def +++

Year	Lev	Team	AB	R	H	HR	RBI	Avg	OB	Slg	OPS	bb%	ct%	Eye	SB	CS	x/h%	Iso	RC/G
2022	NCAA	Illinois St	194	45	66	19	43	340	429	696	1124	13	77	0.68	8	1	47	356	9.60
2022	Rk	FCL Rays	22	5	6	2	5	273	304	636	941	4	59	0.11	3	0	50	364	8.34
2023	Rk	FCL Rays	13	2	3	0	0	231	286	308	593	7	92	1.00	0	0	33	77	3.29
2023	A	Charleston	142	20	38	6	28	268	333	465	798	9	75	0.39	8	2	39	197	5.42

Power/speed profile struggled with pro pitching and injuries in first full season. Short-statured with athletic frame. Upright, slight open stance with hitchy load and lot of pre-swing movement. Aggressive approach with significant chase and whiff tendencies. Raw above-average power, mostly to pull field. Plus runner with chance to stick in CF.

Cespedes,Yoeilin — 6 — Boston

EXP MLB DEBUT: 2028 | H/W: 5-9 181 | FUT: Starting SS | 8D

Bats R Age 18
2023 FA (DR)
Pwr +++
BAvg +++
Spd +++
Def ++

Year	Lev	Team	AB	R	H	HR	RBI	Avg	OB	Slg	OPS	bb%	ct%	Eye	SB	CS	x/h%	Iso	RC/G
2023	Rk	DSL Red Sox B	191	37	66	6	38	346	390	560	950	7	87	0.58	1	2	38	215	7.07

Young, talented SS who has yet to play in US but has been consistently good in DSL. Has high offensive upside with keen knowledge of strike zone and loud, hard contact. Should get to 25+ HR when mature but can be too passive with stick. May need to move off SS as range could be a tad short. Runs well now but doesn't steal bases.

Charles,Austin — 56 — Kansas City

EXP MLB DEBUT: 2027 | H/W: 6-4 215 | FUT: Starting MIF | 7D

Bats R Age 20
2022 (20) HS (CA)
Pwr +++
BAvg ++
Spd +++
Def +++

Year	Lev	Team	AB	R	H	HR	RBI	Avg	OB	Slg	OPS	bb%	ct%	Eye	SB	CS	x/h%	Iso	RC/G
2022	Rk	ACL Royals B	11	1	3	0	0	273	273	273	545	0	64	0.00	0	0	0	0	1.70
2023	Rk	ACL Royals B	11	5	5	1	3	455	455	###	1455	0	73	0.00	0	0	60	545	13.96
2023	A	Columbia	261	29	60	3	31	230	290	356	646	8	72	0.30	12	3	40	126	3.52

The talent and athleticism is apparent, but there's still quite a bit of seasoning left. Best present asset is defense, but the hope is that he can develop into some big power. His frame alone suggests it's there. With his speed he has multi-category potential. May be one of better athletes in system. May be too big for SS, but 3B would be ideal with strong arm.

Cheng,Tsung Che — 46 — Pittsburgh

EXP MLB DEBUT: 2025 | H/W: 5-7 173 | FUT: Starting 2B | 7B

Bats L Age 22
2019 FA (TW)
Pwr ++
BAvg +++
Spd ++++
Def +++

Year	Lev	Team	AB	R	H	HR	RBI	Avg	OB	Slg	OPS	bb%	ct%	Eye	SB	CS	x/h%	Iso	RC/G
2021	Rk	FCL Pirates G	122	32	38	4	31	311	447	492	939	20	89	2.14	16	6	34	180	7.79
2022	A	Bradenton	385	79	104	6	52	270	373	418	791	14	75	0.66	33	6	37	148	5.75
2023	A+	Greensboro	214	45	66	9	31	308	406	575	980	14	78	0.74	13	9	45	266	8.12
2023	AA	Altoona	247	35	62	4	25	251	299	352	651	6	79	0.32	13	3	26	101	3.44

Short, quick INF who struggled at AA but was solid in High-A. 2nd in org in hits with above average ability to make contact with short stroke. Sees pitches and has advanced two-strike approach. Doesn't have much pop, as he likes to focus on line drives but did set personal high in HR. Uses plus speed well on base for SB. Good defender in MIF.

Cho,Won Bin — 789 — St. Louis

EXP MLB DEBUT: 2026 | H/W: 6-1 200 | FUT: Starting OF | 7D

Bats L Age 20
2022 FA (KR)
Pwr +++
BAvg +++
Spd +++
Def ++

Year	Lev	Team	AB	R	H	HR	RBI	Avg	OB	Slg	OPS	bb%	ct%	Eye	SB	CS	x/h%	Iso	RC/G
2022	Rk	FCL Cardinals	76	10	16	1	3	211	375	316	691	21	64	0.74	6	4	31	105	4.64
2023	A	Palm Beach	378	64	102	7	52	270	376	389	764	14	74	0.65	32	11	25	119	5.35

Korean-born OF has average tools across the board, but none that stand out as plus. Professional approach at the plate with a quick bat and willing to take walks. Line-drive, gap-to-gap approach and now owns a career .380 OBP. Above-average speed, but not a true burner. CF for now, but not likely to stick there as he matures.

Chourio,Jackson — 8 — Milwaukee

EXP MLB DEBUT: 2024 | H/W: 5-11 165 | FUT: Starting CF | 9A

Bats R Age 20
2021 FA (VZ)
Pwr ++++
BAvg +++
Spd ++++
Def +++

Year	Lev	Team	AB	R	H	HR	RBI	Avg	OB	Slg	OPS	bb%	ct%	Eye	SB	CS	x/h%	Iso	RC/G
2022	A	Carolina	250	51	81	12	47	324	372	600	972	7	70	0.25	10	2	49	276	8.06
2022	A+	Wisconsin	127	24	32	8	24	252	312	488	800	8	76	0.35	4	1	44	236	5.24
2022	AA	Biloxi	23	0	2	0	4	87	160	130	290	8	52	0.18	2	1	50	43	-2.33
2023	AA	Biloxi	510	84	143	22	89	280	334	467	801	7	80	0.40	43	9	34	186	5.26
2023	AAA	Nashville	21	4	7	0	2	333	391	476	867	9	95	2.00	1	0	43	143	6.48

Elite prospect who does everything well. Progressing quickly and likely will be star. Only plate discipline could be an obstacle. Crushes balls to all fields with sweet swing and can reach seats in any park. Consistently produces pop and profiles to hit for above average BA. Big jump in SB with double plus speed and ranges well in CF.

Chourio,Jaison — 8 — Cleveland

EXP MLB DEBUT: 2027 | H/W: 6-1 162 | FUT: Starting CF | 8D

Bats B Age 18
2022 FA (VZ)
Pwr ++
BAvg ++++
Spd +++
Def +++

Year	Lev	Team	AB	R	H	HR	RBI	Avg	OB	Slg	OPS	bb%	ct%	Eye	SB	CS	x/h%	Iso	RC/G
2022	Rk	DSL Indians 2	132	32	37	1	28	280	448	402	849	23	83	1.82	14	4	30	121	7.03
2023	Rk	ACL Indians	149	40	52	1	25	349	481	463	944	20	75	1.03	19	2	27	114	8.24
2023	A	Lynchburg	35	7	7	0	3	200	317	229	546	15	57	0.40	1	0	14	29	2.27

Advanced hitter who controls strike zone and puts ball in play. Swing may need adjustments as he hits fair amount of GB. Focuses on contact and using all fields. Some power projection but needs strength on very lean frame. Exhibits solid eye at plate and can recognize spin. Has above average speed and has chance for 20/20 seasons.

Clark,Max

8 | Detroit | EXP MLB DEBUT: 2026 | H/W: 6-1 205 | FUT: Starting CF | 9D

Bats L Age 19	Year	Lev	Team	AB	R	H	HR	RBI	Avg	OB	Slg	OPS	bb%	ct%	Eye	SB	CS	x/h%	Iso	RC/G
2023 (1) HS (IN)																				
Pwr +++																				
BAvg ++++																				
Spd +++++	2023	Rk	FCL Tigers East	46	13	13	2	12	283	400	543	943	16	78	0.90	4	1	54	261	7.74
Def +++++	2023	A	Lakeland	39	5	6	0	7	154	353	179	532	24	62	0.80	1	0	17	26	2.05

Legit 5-tool prospect with plus speed and potential GG defense. Strong lower half and simple LH stroke with the ability to get the ball in the air should result in at least average or above power. Fared well on the showcase circuit but did not face elite HS competition and currently struggles with velo. Good strike zone awareness and willing to draw walks.

Clarke,Denzel

89 | Oakland | EXP MLB DEBUT: 2024 | H/W: 6-5 220 | FUT: Starting OF | 8C

Bats R Age 23	Year	Lev	Team	AB	R	H	HR	RBI	Avg	OB	Slg	OPS	bb%	ct%	Eye	SB	CS	x/h%	Iso	RC/G
2021 (4) Cal State Northridge	2021	NCAA	CSUN	142	30	46	8	25	324	429	570	999	15	72	0.65	15	2	41	246	8.58
Pwr ++++	2021	Rk	ACL Athletics	19	2	6	1	1	316	409	579	988	14	68	0.50	1	2	50	263	8.64
BAvg ++	2022	A	Stockton	156	37	46	7	26	295	402	545	947	15	64	0.50	14	2	50	250	8.51
Spd ++++	2022	A+	Lansing	187	30	39	8	21	209	312	406	718	13	58	0.35	16	1	49	198	5.08
Def ++++	2023	AA	Midland	234	54	61	12	43	261	362	496	857	14	64	0.44	11	1	44	235	6.95

Elite athlete with incredible tools and just starting to realize potential. Despite large frame, runs as well as any in org. All fields approach and hits hard line drives but long arms and swing can be exploited by good breaking balls. Stroke getting better. Massive power potential but needs to add more loft. Terrific OF with plus range.

Clarke,Wes

23 | Milwaukee | EXP MLB DEBUT: 2024 | H/W: 6-0 228 | FUT: Starting 1B | 7D

Bats R Age 24	Year	Lev	Team	AB	R	H	HR	RBI	Avg	OB	Slg	OPS	bb%	ct%	Eye	SB	CS	x/h%	Iso	RC/G
2021 (10) South Carolina	2021	Rk	ACL Brewers B	8	1	2	1	2	250	250	625	875	0	100		0	0	50	375	5.41
Pwr ++++	2021	A	Carolina	68	13	14	4	19	206	393	426	820	24	69	1.00	0	1	50	221	6.27
BAvg ++	2022	A+	Wisconsin	273	27	61	9	52	223	358	392	750	17	70	0.69	0	1	46	168	5.23
Spd +	2022	AA	Biloxi	59	9	15	5	9	254	333	542	876	11	64	0.33	0	0	47	288	6.80
Def ++	2023	AA	Biloxi	398	68	96	26	80	241	380	497	877	18	63	0.61	6	1	52	256	7.31

Power-hitting prospect who gives ball a ride. Led SL in HR but also most K in org. Doesn't hit for BA because of poor contact and expansion of strike zone. Obliterates LHP with massive power to pull side. Has patience to draw walks but can be pitched to up in zone. Has very poor foot speed. Adds value by playing catcher.

Clase,Jonatan

8 | Seattle | EXP MLB DEBUT: 2025 | H/W: 5-9 150 | FUT: Starting OF | 8D

Bats B Age 21	Year	Lev	Team	AB	R	H	HR	RBI	Avg	OB	Slg	OPS	bb%	ct%	Eye	SB	CS	x/h%	Iso	RC/G
2018 FA (DR)																				
Pwr +++	2021	Rk	ACL Mariners	49	12	12	2	10	245	327	388	715	11	69	0.40	16	0	25	143	4.37
BAvg +++	2022	A	Modesto	423	91	113	13	49	267	365	463	828	13	69	0.49	55	10	41	196	6.36
Spd +++++	2023	A+	Everett	87	23	29	7	17	333	448	701	1149	17	68	0.64	17	4	59	368	11.14
Def ++	2023	AA	Arkansas	414	79	92	13	51	222	326	396	722	13	67	0.47	62	11	42	174	4.80

Short, speedy CF who finished 3rd in minors in SB, yet had 4th lowest BA in TL and had 2nd most Ks in org. Lot of plusses and minuses in tool box. Draws lots of walks for quality OBP but struggles to make contact despite bat speed and level bat path. Injuries have plagued in career and hasn't developed CF defense. Power will determine future.

Clifford,Ryan

379 | New York (N) | EXP MLB DEBUT: 2025 | H/W: 6-3 200 | FUT: Starting 1B | 8D

Bats L Age 20	Year	Lev	Team	AB	R	H	HR	RBI	Avg	OB	Slg	OPS	bb%	ct%	Eye	SB	CS	x/h%	Iso	RC/G
2022 (11) HS (NC)	2022	Rk	FCL Astros O	36	8	8	1	5	222	417	389	806	25	56	0.75	2	0	50	167	7.06
Pwr ++++	2022	A	Fayetteville	41	5	11	1	5	268	412	390	802	20	63	0.67	0	0	27	122	6.37
BAvg +++	2023	A	Fayetteville	92	22	31	2	15	337	479	457	935	21	71	0.93	3	1	23	120	8.20
Spd +	2023	A+	Asheville	214	35	58	16	46	271	336	547	883	9	71	0.34	1	1	47	276	6.52
Def ++	2023	A+	Brooklyn	117	13	22	6	20	188	296	376	672	13	56	0.35	1	0	45	188	4.22

Strong, power-hitting prospect acquired at trade deadline from HOU. Muscular frame with below average athleticism. Upright stance with slight bat wrap in load. Uppercut swing with double-plus bat speed propels power profile, which is plus-plus raw. Patient approach should aid in OBP if BA backtracks to due ct%. Double-plus arm. Struggles in OF.

Coffey,Cutter

56 | Boston | EXP MLB DEBUT: 2026 | H/W: 6-1 190 | FUT: Starting 3B | 7D

Bats R Age 19	Year	Lev	Team	AB	R	H	HR	RBI	Avg	OB	Slg	OPS	bb%	ct%	Eye	SB	CS	x/h%	Iso	RC/G
2022 (2) HS (CA)																				
Pwr ++																				
BAvg ++	2022	Rk	FCL Red Sox	32	7	4	0	0	125	282	156	438	18	66	0.64	1	0	25	31	0.59
Spd ++	2023	A	Salem	296	51	67	6	30	226	328	348	676	13	73	0.57	18	6	33	122	4.06
Def +++	2023	A+	Greenville	66	8	9	0	5	136	260	167	426	14	68	0.52	1	1	22	30	0.46

Gifted INF who got off to slow start but still showed good athleticism and power potential. Draws walks in passive approach but can often lengthen swing and get himself out. Struggles with velocity up in zone. Raw power is best attribute. Has brute strength and bat speed. Possesses good feet in field and could be above average 3B with plus arm.

Collier,Cam

5 | Cincinnati | EXP MLB DEBUT: 2026 | H/W: 6-2 210 | FUT: Starting 1B | 8D

Bats L Age 19	Year	Lev	Team	AB	R	H	HR	RBI	Avg	OB	Slg	OPS	bb%	ct%	Eye	SB	CS	x/h%	Iso	RC/G
2022 (1) Chipola JC																				
Pwr +++																				
BAvg +++	2022	NJCAA	Chipola	177	35	59	8	47	333	416	537	953	12	81	0.76	5	0	34	203	7.44
Spd ++	2022	Rk	ACL Reds	27	7	10	2	4	370	500	630	1130	21	78	1.17	0	2	30	259	10.19
Def ++	2023	A	Daytona	390	40	96	6	68	246	342	356	699	13	73	0.54	5	1	30	110	4.39

Strong-bodied teenaged CIF prospect backed up physically, struggling in first full season as pro. Strong body with risk of XXL frame. Open stance at plate. Lots of movement to get to load. Long linear swing produced loads of groundball contact. Plus bat speed remains. With swing adjustments, can get back to above-average power/hit projections.

Colmenarez,Carlos

6 | Tampa Bay | EXP MLB DEBUT: 2026 | H/W: 5-9 170 | FUT: Reserve IF | 6C

Bats L Age 20	Year	Lev	Team	AB	R	H	HR	RBI	Avg	OB	Slg	OPS	bb%	ct%	Eye	SB	CS	x/h%	Iso	RC/G
2021 FA (VZ)																				
Pwr ++	2021	Rk	DSL Rays	97	7	24	0	12	247	305	289	593	8	69	0.27	7	6	13	41	2.74
BAvg ++	2022	Rk	FCL Rays	126	36	32	1	19	254	343	381	724	12	67	0.41	13	2	34	127	4.92
Spd +++	2023	Rk	FCL Rays	21	4	7	0	5	333	417	429	845	13	71	0.50	0	0	29	95	6.60
Def +++	2023	A	Charleston	283	42	57	6	28	201	325	304	629	16	53	0.39	10	11	28	102	3.85

Athletic, former bonus baby struggled significantly in full season debut. Wiry frame with strength growth expected. Upright, slight open stance. Doesn't put hands in good position to hit. Top hand heavy, no flexibility in bat path. 40%+ whiff rate. Struggled in and out of zone. Defensive shortcomings continued at SS, where glove was expected to carry profile.

Conticello,Gavin

35 | Arizona | EXP MLB DEBUT: 2025 | H/W: 6-4 195 | FUT: Starting 1B | 7E

Bats L Age 20	Year	Lev	Team	AB	R	H	HR	RBI	Avg	OB	Slg	OPS	bb%	ct%	Eye	SB	CS	x/h%	Iso	RC/G
2021 (8) HS (FL)	2021	Rk	ACL Dbacks	45	6	13	0	3	289	319	356	675	4	76	0.18	2	1	23	67	3.69
Pwr +++	2022	Rk	ACL DBacks Reds	126	17	31	2	19	246	326	381	707	11	63	0.32	3	1	35	135	4.75
BAvg ++	2022	A	Visalia	105	16	22	1	12	210	303	305	607	12	64	0.37	1	1	27	95	3.14
Spd +	2023	A	Visalia	370	50	80	15	49	216	301	408	709	11	74	0.47	12	5	48	192	4.33
Def ++	2023	A+	Hillsboro	38	4	10	2	9	263	282	500	782	3	71	0.09	0	0	50	237	4.98

Corner INF prospect with some pop, bat-to-ball skills. Likely limited to 1B going forward. Sees the ball well, good strike zone awareness. Left-handed swing has uppercut motion, leads to healthy FB%. Strong arms, sleek frame with room to add on to lower half. Pressure on bat given defensive limitations.

Cook,Billy

34789 | Baltimore | EXP MLB DEBUT: 2025 | H/W: 6-1 200 | FUT: Utility player | 7D

Bats R Age 25	Year	Lev	Team	AB	R	H	HR	RBI	Avg	OB	Slg	OPS	bb%	ct%	Eye	SB	CS	x/h%	Iso	RC/G
2021 (10) Pepperdine	2021	NCAA	Pepperdine	131	36	39	17	42	298	357	725	1082	8	67	0.28	5	1	54	427	9.37
Pwr +++	2021	Rk	FCL Orioles O	21	3	6	0	4	286	318	381	699	5	62	0.13	3	0	33	95	4.57
BAvg +++	2021	A	Delmarva	93	17	24	6	25	258	317	516	833	8	65	0.24	7	1	50	258	6.22
Spd +++	2022	A+	Aberdeen	389	49	86	15	65	221	284	422	705	8	64	0.24	25	4	49	201	4.45
Def +++	2023	AA	Bowie	447	64	112	24	81	251	315	456	771	9	72	0.34	30	3	38	206	5.00

Coming off of a great HR/SB season in AA. That'll make some noise to go along with the lowest strikeout rate of his career. If the Orioles just unlocked this from their 2021 10th rounder, then his defensive versatility becomes even more interesting. Power more from sitting on FB rather than bat speed or strength.

Corona,Kenedy

789 | Houston | EXP MLB DEBUT: 2025 | H/W: 5-10 184 | FUT: Reserve OF | 6B

Bats R Age 24	Year	Lev	Team	AB	R	H	HR	RBI	Avg	OB	Slg	OPS	bb%	ct%	Eye	SB	CS	x/h%	Iso	RC/G
2019 FA (VZ)	2021	A	Fayetteville	201	30	49	2	22	244	293	343	636	7	74	0.26	19	7	31	100	3.29
Pwr +++	2022	A	Fayetteville	165	32	43	9	30	261	344	491	835	11	74	0.49	8	2	44	230	5.98
BAvg ++	2022	A+	Asheville	245	56	71	10	37	290	363	498	861	10	74	0.44	20	6	39	208	6.37
Spd ++	2023	A+	Asheville	25	7	9	2	4	360	448	600	1048	14	64	0.44	1	1	22	240	9.64
Def ++++	2023	AA	Corpus Christi	434	63	106	20	61	244	320	449	769	10	71	0.38	31	9	42	205	5.14

OF prospect enjoyed productive season at Double-A, adding to power/speed track record. However, hit tool limitations continued with persistent swing and miss. Good eye at plate, but holes in swing limit contact skills. Pull-heavy approach works for now, but may have trouble keeping up production going forward.

Cova,Ricardo
4 | **Seattle** | EXP MLB DEBUT: 2027 | H/W: 5-9 145 | FUT: Starting 2B | **7D**

Bats R Age 19 — 2021 FA (VZ)

Skill	Year	Lev	Team	AB	R	H	HR	RBI	Avg	OB	Slg	OPS	bb%	ct%	Eye	SB	CS	x/h%	Iso	RC/G
Pwr +																				
BAvg +++	2021	Rk	DSL Mariners	77	8	19	1	9	247	326	312	637	10	83	0.69	4	2	16	65	3.54
Spd +++	2022	Rk	DSL Mariners	140	16	43	3	28	307	349	450	799	6	69	0.20	7	1	28	143	5.61
Def ++	2023	Rk	ACL Mariners	91	26	30	1	11	330	419	440	859	13	64	0.42	17	3	27	110	7.20

Short, versatile INF who performed well in first stint in US. Offers high BA potential with feel for barrel and using entire field. Can be a bit aggressive early in count and put himself into bad spots but has sneaky quick wrists to put ball in play. Could develop average power with added size and strength. Uses average speed and quickness well.

Cowser,Colton
789 | **Baltimore** | EXP MLB DEBUT: 2023 | H/W: 6-2 220 | FUT: Starting OF | **8C**

Bats L Age 24 — 2021 (1) Sam Houston State

Skill	Year	Lev	Team	AB	R	H	HR	RBI	Avg	OB	Slg	OPS	bb%	ct%	Eye	SB	CS	x/h%	Iso	RC/G
	2022	A+	Aberdeen	229	42	59	4	22	258	380	410	790	16	66	0.57	16	1	42	153	6.11
Pwr +++	2022	AA	Bowie	176	49	60	10	33	341	453	568	1021	17	68	0.63	2	2	33	227	9.25
BAvg +++	2022	AAA	Norfolk Tides	105	23	23	5	11	219	305	429	734	11	64	0.34	0	0	52	210	4.90
Spd +++	2023	AAA	Norfolk Tides	323	72	97	17	62	300	416	520	936	17	67	0.60	9	3	37	220	8.02
Def +++	2023	MLB	Baltimore	61	15	7	0	4	115	270	148	418	18	64	0.59	1	0	29	33	0.19

A jack-of-all-trades kind of profile. Struggled in limited time in BAL but hit tool stands out from the pack. Owns a simple operation at the plate with a smooth stroke that is repeatable. Likes to swing hard and aggressively to give ball a ride. Ability to play all OF positions gives him value. Instincts allow tools to play up.

Cox,Jonah
8 | **Oakland** | EXP MLB DEBUT: 2025 | H/W: 6-3 200 | FUT: Starting OF | **7C**

Bats R Age 22 — 2023 (6) Oral Roberts

Skill	Year	Lev	Team	AB	R	H	HR	RBI	Avg	OB	Slg	OPS	bb%	ct%	Eye	SB	CS	x/h%	Iso	RC/G
Pwr ++																				
BAvg ++++	2023	NCAA	Oral Roberts	277	69	114	11	68	412	469	646	1115	10	81	0.57	28	4	31	235	9.39
Spd ++++	2023	Rk	ACL Athletics	19	6	8	0	5	421	522	579	1101	17	95	4.00	6	0	25	158	9.70
Def ++	2023	A	Stockton	110	16	29	2	10	264	296	373	668	4	64	0.13	14	2	21	109	3.81

Natural-hitting OF who knows value of working counts and getting on base. Power not part of calculus and lacks strength. Makes easy contact with short stroke and brings above average speed to beat out grounders. Has skill set to hit at top of order. Spent all of pro debut in CF and needs to take better routes. Below average arm.

Crawford,Justin
8 | **Philadelphia** | EXP MLB DEBUT: 2026 | H/W: 6-1 175 | FUT: Starting CF | **8C**

Bats L Age 20 — 2022 (1) HS (NV)

Skill	Year	Lev	Team	AB	R	H	HR	RBI	Avg	OB	Slg	OPS	bb%	ct%	Eye	SB	CS	x/h%	Iso	RC/G
Pwr ++	2022	Rk	FCL Phillies	37	6	11	0	5	297	381	351	732	12	84	0.83	8	3	9	54	4.89
BAvg +++	2022	A	Clearwater	21	2	3	0	0	143	217	143	360	9	57	0.22	2	1	0	0	-1.08
Spd ++++	2023	A	Clearwater	276	51	95	3	60	344	399	478	877	8	81	0.47	40	7	26	134	6.45
Def ++++	2023	A+	Jersey Shore	73	20	21	0	4	288	350	425	775	9	78	0.44	7	1	38	137	5.35

Had a surprisingly good first full pro season, led by outstanding contact rate and passable patience. The problem: quality of contact. His swing is in need of some loft, even though his GB-heavy approach meshes well with his excellent footspeed. Will be a big base-stealer, is a plus centerfielder, but extra pop would take game to the next level.

Crews,Dylan
8 | **Washington** | EXP MLB DEBUT: 2024 | H/W: 6-0 205 | FUT: Starting CF | **9C**

Bats R Age 22 — 2023 (1) LSU

Skill	Year	Lev	Team	AB	R	H	HR	RBI	Avg	OB	Slg	OPS	bb%	ct%	Eye	SB	CS	x/h%	Iso	RC/G
Pwr ++++	2023	NCAA	LSU	258	100	110	18	70	426	550	713	1263	22	82	1.54	6	0	33	287	11.86
BAvg ++++	2023	Rk	FCL Nationals	3	3	3	0	0	1000	###	###	2333	0	100		0	0	33	333	20.12
Spd +++	2023	A	Fredericksburg	62	16	22	5	24	355	412	645	1057	9	69	0.32	1	3	36	290	9.06
Def +++	2023	AA	Harrisburg	72	7	15	0	5	208	288	278	565	10	74	0.42	3	3	33	69	2.53

With natural strength and leverage coming from a strong upper body, he punishes pitches he can handle and has shown a strong batting eye throughout college and in his early pro stops. Makes good contact. On defense, athletic enough to handle center field with speed and good instincts also should translate to the base paths.

Crooks,Jimmy
2 | **St. Louis** | EXP MLB DEBUT: 2025 | H/W: 6-1 210 | FUT: Starting C | **7D**

Bats L Age 22 — 2022 (4) Oklahoma

Skill	Year	Lev	Team	AB	R	H	HR	RBI	Avg	OB	Slg	OPS	bb%	ct%	Eye	SB	CS	x/h%	Iso	RC/G
Pwr ++																				
BAvg ++	2022	NCAA	Oklahoma	249	49	76	9	51	305	408	506	914	15	77	0.75	10	4	41	201	7.27
Spd ++	2022	A	Palm Beach	79	12	21	3	7	266	363	468	831	13	72	0.55	0	0	38	203	6.19
Def +++	2023	A+	Peoria	413	71	112	12	73	271	353	433	786	11	76	0.51	2	1	38	162	5.42

Overcame a slow start to put up solid season of production. Big leg kick to start swing, but quick LH stroke and improved plate discipline allow for average and a bit of pull-side power. Steady improvements on D with a strong, accurate arm should enable him to stick behind the plate. Will need to tap into raw power more often as he moves up.

Cross,Gavin
8 | **Kansas City** | EXP MLB DEBUT: 2025 | H/W: 6-1 210 | FUT: Starting OF | **8E**

Bats L Age 23 — 2022 (1) Virginia Tech

Skill	Year	Lev	Team	AB	R	H	HR	RBI	Avg	OB	Slg	OPS	bb%	ct%	Eye	SB	CS	x/h%	Iso	RC/G
	2022	NCAA	Virginia Tech	244	70	80	17	50	328	401	660	1061	11	83	0.73	12	0	49	332	8.61
Pwr +++	2022	Rk	ACL Royals B	10	4	5	1	3	500	583	###	1583	17	80	1.00	0	0	60	500	15.76
BAvg ++	2022	A	Columbia	99	20	29	7	22	293	421	596	1017	18	69	0.71	4	2	48	303	9.12
Spd +++	2023	A+	Quad Cities	355	49	73	12	58	206	290	383	673	11	68	0.37	23	3	49	177	3.92
Def +++	2023	AA	NW Arkansas	5	0	0	0	0	0	167	0	167	17	60	0.50	0	0		0	-4.34

First full season and he barely hit over the Mendoza Line in High-A. Given patience and eye at plate, the low BA is a bit surprising. Modified swing mechanics may be to blame. Struggles continued in AFL. Still walked a lot. A good defender with a solid arm, so might wind up in right field. Steals bases despite fringe-avg speed.

Crow Armstrong,Pete
8 | **Chicago (N)** | EXP MLB DEBUT: 2023 | H/W: 5-11 184 | FUT: Starting CF | **9C**

Bats L Age 21 — 2020 (1) HS (CA)

Skill	Year	Lev	Team	AB	R	H	HR	RBI	Avg	OB	Slg	OPS	bb%	ct%	Eye	SB	CS	x/h%	Iso	RC/G
	2022	A	Myrtle Beach	158	39	56	7	27	354	433	557	990	12	79	0.67	13	4	27	203	7.98
Pwr +++	2022	A+	South Bend	265	50	76	9	34	287	323	498	821	5	74	0.20	19	7	41	211	5.65
BAvg ++++	2023	AA	Tennessee	298	68	86	14	60	289	356	527	882	9	72	0.38	27	8	44	238	6.69
Spd ++++	2023	AAA	Iowa	140	30	38	6	22	271	342	479	821	10	66	0.32	10	2	39	207	6.11
Def +++++	2023	MLB	Chicago (N)	14	3	0	0	1	0	176	0	176	18	50	0.43	2	2		0	-5.24

Blasted through Double and Triple-A but struggled in limited MLB debut. 5 above-average to plus tools with plus defense in CF. Crowds the plate with an upright stance, almost no stride, and quick LH stroke. Approach is geared towards contact, spraying line drives to all fields, but there is more power than anticipated. Smart, confident, fearless.

Cruz,Armando
46 | **Washington** | EXP MLB DEBUT: 2026 | H/W: 5-10 160 | FUT: Starting SS | **7E**

Bats R Age 20 — 2021 FA (DR)

Skill	Year	Lev	Team	AB	R	H	HR	RBI	Avg	OB	Slg	OPS	bb%	ct%	Eye	SB	CS	x/h%	Iso	RC/G
Pwr +	2021	Rk	DSL Nationals	177	22	41	1	17	232	295	305	600	8	85	0.59	11	4	24	73	3.11
BAvg ++	2022	Rk	FCL Nationals	207	41	57	2	20	275	312	362	674	5	81	0.28	6	5	21	87	3.70
Spd ++	2022	A	Fredericksburg	15	3	4	0	2	267	353	333	686	12	87	1.00	0	0	25	67	4.41
Def +++++	2023	A	Fredericksburg	331	44	63	3	33	190	260	251	510	9	80	0.46	7	7	21	60	1.81

Vaunted for his elite SS defense, has plus hands, range, actions and arm. But bat is another story; though he makes enough contact, he doesn't impact the ball enough to have any thing other than a bottom-of-the-order profile. Smallish frame even calls "putting on good weight" into question. Could end up as defense-first bench piece.

Cruz,John
789 | **New York (A)** | EXP MLB DEBUT: 2026 | H/W: 6-3 171 | FUT: Starting OF | **8E**

Bats L Age 18 — 2022 FA (DR)

Skill	Year	Lev	Team	AB	R	H	HR	RBI	Avg	OB	Slg	OPS	bb%	ct%	Eye	SB	CS	x/h%	Iso	RC/G
Pwr ++++																				
BAvg +++																				
Spd +++	2022	Rk	DSL Yankees	169	38	38	5	24	225	396	396	793	22	63	0.77	10	5	42	172	6.28
Def +++	2023	Rk	FCL Yankees	177	28	52	10	47	294	372	531	903	11	75	0.50	9	4	37	237	6.84

Powerful OF prospect flexed muscles hitting 10 HR at complex in 2023. Strong, athletic build. Should put on lots of muscle before maturity. Upright stance with a hitch and bat wrap on trigger. Plus-plus bat speed. Mostly pull-oriented power but strength likely plays to all fields. 30+ HR if hit tool cooperates. Average runner, likely ends up in an OF corner.

Cuevas,Yohairo
379 | **New York (N)** | EXP MLB DEBUT: 2026 | H/W: 6-3 172 | FUT: Starting 1B | **7E**

Bats L Age 20 — 2021 FA (NY)

Skill	Year	Lev	Team	AB	R	H	HR	RBI	Avg	OB	Slg	OPS	bb%	ct%	Eye	SB	CS	x/h%	Iso	RC/G
Pwr ++++	2021	Rk	DSL Mets	103	15	16	0	8	155	310	214	523	18	60	0.56	5	0	38	58	1.91
BAvg ++	2022	Rk	DSL Mets	166	29	46	2	31	277	378	398	776	14	74	0.63	7	3	33	120	5.55
Spd ++	2023	Rk	FCL Mets	71	13	22	4	15	310	449	577	1027	20	70	0.86	7	1	41	268	9.34
Def +++	2023	A	St. Lucie	79	11	17	2	13	215	295	354	650	10	70	0.38	6	1	35	139	3.57

Strong, long-levered 1B/OF prospect struggled after promotion to Low-A. Long body with room to grow into more muscle. Upright, open stance with a slight lean to the plate and easy actions to hit position. Hit tool suffers from several holes in plate coverage and remedial feel for spin. Plus power is raw and could develop if hit tool allows it.

Cunningham,Jake | 789 | Baltimore

EXP MLB DEBUT: 2026 | H/W: 6-4 205 | FUT: Utility player | 7D

Bats R Age 21	Year	Lev	Team	AB	R	H	HR	RBI	Avg	OB	Slg	OPS	bb%	ct%	Eye	SB	CS	x/h%	Iso	RC/G
2023 (5) Charlotte																				
Pwr ++																				
BAvg +++	2023	NCAA	Charlotte	187	40	50	11	41	267	354	519	872	12	70	0.45	1	0	50	251	6.67
Spd +++	2023	Rk	FCL Orioles B	6	3	3	0	2	500	667	500	1167	33	67	1.50	1	0	0	0	13.05
Def ++	2023	A	Delmarva	35	7	8	1	10	229	386	343	729	20	71	0.90	3	1	25	114	5.00

Athletic OF who showed excellent patience and a very good eye at the plate. Also puts the ball in play. He may be a slow burn, but if the tools come around there's a lot to like. Fits profile of recent BAL draftees who can hit, run and provide versatility. No plus tools in repertoire but not a liability in any phase of game.

Davidson,Logan | 345 | Oakland

EXP MLB DEBUT: 2024 | H/W: 6-3 185 | FUT: Utility player | 6B

Bats B Age 26	Year	Lev	Team	AB	R	H	HR	RBI	Avg	OB	Slg	OPS	bb%	ct%	Eye	SB	CS	x/h%	Iso	RC/G
2019 (1) Clemson	2019	A-	Vermont	205	42	49	4	12	239	339	332	671	13	73	0.56	5	0	22	93	3.94
Pwr ++	2021	AA	Midland	448	53	95	7	48	212	308	313	620	12	65	0.40	4	3	32	100	3.27
BAvg ++	2022	AA	Midland	424	72	107	14	56	252	335	406	741	11	68	0.40	4	1	34	153	4.89
Spd +++	2023	AA	Midland	182	26	54	7	28	297	373	484	856	11	69	0.39	2	2	35	187	6.53
Def +++	2023	AAA	Las Vegas	208	24	55	3	31	264	332	375	707	9	75	0.41	4	1	29	111	4.33

Returned to AA for 3rd year before promotion to AAA in July. Moved to 1B and still saw action at 2B and 3B but no longer a SS. Can be selective hitter but swing and miss can be problematic. Struggles from right side and with pitches in lower half. Has good talent that could be leveraged in utility role. Runs well and flashes power.

Davis,Brennen | 8 | Chicago (N)

EXP MLB DEBUT: 2024 | H/W: 6-0 210 | FUT: Starting OF | 7D

Bats R Age 24	Year	Lev	Team	AB	R	H	HR	RBI	Avg	OB	Slg	OPS	bb%	ct%	Eye	SB	CS	x/h%	Iso	RC/G
2018 (2) HS (AZ)	2022	A+	South Bend	23	0	3	0	2	130	130	130	261	0	65	0.00	0	0	0	0	-2.47
Pwr +++	2022	AAA	Iowa	141	16	27	4	13	191	305	319	624	14	63	0.44	0	1	37	128	3.31
BAvg +	2023	Rk	ACL Cubs	11	0	5	0	1	455	500	636	1136	8	73	0.33	0	0	40	182	10.45
Spd +++	2023	A+	South Bend	24	3	5	1	3	208	208	417	625	0	50	0.00	0	0	60	208	4.17
Def +++	2023	AAA	Iowa	219	27	41	4	26	187	261	279	540	9	74	0.38	9	3	29	91	2.00

Prospect status has plummeted after two injury-plagued seasons. Still has above-average speed and power, but aggressive approach, long levers, and a lack of plate discipline have resulted in weak contact and too much swing and miss. A return to health could revive his career, but at 24 that will need to happen now, making 2024 a pivotal season.

Davis,Chase | 8 | St. Louis

EXP MLB DEBUT: 2026 | H/W: 6-1 216 | FUT: Starting OF | 8D

Bats L Age 22	Year	Lev	Team	AB	R	H	HR	RBI	Avg	OB	Slg	OPS	bb%	ct%	Eye	SB	CS	x/h%	Iso	RC/G
2023 (1) Arizona																				
Pwr ++++																				
BAvg ++																				
Spd +++	2023	NCAA	Arizona	221	71	80	21	74	362	466	742	1208	16	82	1.08	0	0	50	380	10.67
Def +++	2023	A	Palm Beach	104	15	22	0	23	212	364	269	634	19	67	0.74	3	0	27	58	3.76

Strong, athletic frame generates easy power. Improvements in swing decisions and better plate discipline helped post a 1.231 OPS with 43 BB/40 K. Concerns about hit tool vs LHP and ability to handle elite velocity re-emerged in pro debut. Runs well and will get an extended look in CF. Needs to make more contact to fully tap into plus power.

De Andrade,Danny | 6 | Minnesota

EXP MLB DEBUT: 2026 | H/W: 5-11 190 | FUT: Starting 2B | 8D

Bats R Age 19	Year	Lev	Team	AB	R	H	HR	RBI	Avg	OB	Slg	OPS	bb%	ct%	Eye	SB	CS	x/h%	Iso	RC/G
2021 FA (VZ)																				
Pwr ++																				
BAvg ++	2021	Rk	DSL Twins	178	16	47	0	16	264	321	348	670	8	85	0.56	6	2	30	84	3.96
Spd +++	2022	Rk	FCL Twins	178	27	43	4	23	242	315	371	686	10	81	0.56	4	2	33	129	4.06
Def +++	2023	A	Fort Myers	394	72	96	11	67	244	341	396	737	13	74	0.56	20	4	36	152	4.85

Underrated SS who impressed in first full season as pro. Showcased surprising pop and good speed. Made better contact as season progressed and showed advanced feel for game. Average defender now but could become plus with quickness and excellent arm. Knows value of working counts. Pitch recognition could be better.

De Jesus,Alex | 56 | Toronto

EXP MLB DEBUT: 2026 | H/W: 6-1 170 | FUT: Starting 3B | 7D

Bats R Age 22	Year	Lev	Team	AB	R	H	HR	RBI	Avg	OB	Slg	OPS	bb%	ct%	Eye	SB	CS	x/h%	Iso	RC/G
2018 FA (DR)	2022	Rk	FCL Blue Jays	6	2	3	1	3	500	571	###	1738	14	100		0	0	67	667	15.27
Pwr +++	2022	A	Rancho Cuca	143	34	37	7	22	259	394	483	877	18	65	0.64	2	0	46	224	7.32
BAvg ++	2022	A+	Great Lakes	195	27	55	4	26	282	372	421	793	13	67	0.43	0	1	31	138	5.90
Spd ++	2022	A+	Vancouver	90	10	19	2	13	211	304	333	637	12	60	0.33	0	0	37	122	3.65
Def ++	2023	A+	Vancouver	294	56	73	11	59	248	338	466	804	12	69	0.44	5	4	48	218	5.91

Growing, versatile INF who spent all season in High-A and split time between SS and 3B. Led NWL in triples and is emerging as flyball hitter. Lot of Ks despite average power profile. Hits LHP. Clean swing with quick hands and could stand to take advantage of greater strength. Fringy defender with plus arm.

De La Cruz,Carlos | 3789 | Philadelphia

EXP MLB DEBUT: 2024 | H/W: 6-8 210 | FUT: Starting OF | 8D

Bats R Age 24	Year	Lev	Team	AB	R	H	HR	RBI	Avg	OB	Slg	OPS	bb%	ct%	Eye	SB	CS	x/h%	Iso	RC/G
2017 FA (NY)	2021	A	Clearwater	122	10	18	2	11	148	230	238	467	10	54	0.23	2	0	39	90	0.85
Pwr ++++	2021	A+	Jersey Shore	62	10	15	3	14	242	299	452	750	7	63	0.22	0	0	47	210	5.11
BAvg ++	2022	A+	Jersey Shore	214	29	57	10	24	266	326	463	789	8	65	0.25	5	2	37	196	5.59
Spd ++	2022	AA	Reading	151	21	42	7	23	278	314	510	824	5	70	0.18	1	0	48	232	5.77
Def +++	2023	AA	Reading	509	80	132	24	67	259	330	454	784	10	69	0.34	3	0	38	194	5.38

Returned to AA and polished up selectivity from his half-season there in 2022. Held contact gains which aren't superior, but with his frame and natural strength that produce high EVs and HR, every little bit helps. Still vulnerable to good pitching; solid enough defensively to hold down COR OF or 1B which helps finding an MLB spot.

de la Rosa,Jeremy | 8 | Washington

EXP MLB DEBUT: 2026 | H/W: 6-0 215 | FUT: Starting OF | 7D

Bats L Age 22	Year	Lev	Team	AB	R	H	HR	RBI	Avg	OB	Slg	OPS	bb%	ct%	Eye	SB	CS	x/h%	Iso	RC/G
2018 FA (DR)	2019	Rk	GCL Nationals	82	14	19	2	10	232	330	366	696	13	65	0.41	3	2	26	134	4.44
Pwr ++	2021	A	Fredericksburg	326	34	68	5	22	209	275	316	591	8	63	0.25	7	8	31	107	2.80
BAvg ++	2022	A	Fredericksburg	279	56	88	10	57	315	394	505	899	11	72	0.46	26	5	35	190	7.07
Spd ++	2022	A+	Wilmington	118	10	23	1	10	195	269	271	540	9	69	0.32	13	2	26	76	2.01
Def +++	2023	A+	Wilmington	338	44	81	7	42	240	322	361	683	11	62	0.32	13	7	31	121	4.32

Collection of mid-range range tools, but none that really stand out. After big strides in 2022, fell back both in terms of contact rate and batted ball quality. Will likely head to Double-A, but is time to produce. Still has some speed and athleticism along with occasional power but was taken off the 40-man roster. Important year ahead.

De Los Santos,Deyvison | 35 | Cleveland

EXP MLB DEBUT: 2025 | H/W: 5-11 185 | FUT: Starting 1B | 8E

Bats R Age 20	Year	Lev	Team	AB	R	H	HR	RBI	Avg	OB	Slg	OPS	bb%	ct%	Eye	SB	CS	x/h%	Iso	RC/G
2019 FA (DR)	2021	A	Visalia	145	26	40	3	20	276	335	421	756	8	70	0.30	2	0	38	145	5.04
Pwr ++++	2022	A	Visalia	316	43	104	12	67	329	373	513	885	7	73	0.26	4	1	31	184	6.51
BAvg ++	2022	A+	Hillsboro	158	24	44	9	33	278	309	506	815	4	66	0.13	1	0	41	228	5.74
Spd +	2022	AA	Amarillo	39	5	9	1	6	231	318	359	677	11	77	0.56	0	0	33	128	3.97
Def +	2023	AA	Amarillo	452	73	115	20	61	254	294	431	725	5	72	0.20	4	1	33	177	4.24

Rule 5 pick from ARI. Corner prospect known for big power handled first extended AA run well. Big-time hyper-aggressive approach, particularly against zone pitches. Struggles with breaking balls but showing improvement picking up spin. Decent at 3B, shift to 1B feels imminent. Plate approach continues to hold back huge power.

De Paula,Josue | 79 | Los Angeles (N)

EXP MLB DEBUT: 2026 | H/W: 6-3 185 | FUT: Starting OF | 8D

Bats L Age 18	Year	Lev	Team	AB	R	H	HR	RBI	Avg	OB	Slg	OPS	bb%	ct%	Eye	SB	CS	x/h%	Iso	RC/G
2022 FA (NY)																				
Pwr +++																				
BAvg ++++																				
Spd +++	2022	Rk	DSL Dodgers B	186	42	65	5	30	349	445	522	966	15	83	1.03	16	6	31	172	7.85
Def +	2023	A	Rancho Cuca	282	55	80	2	40	284	384	372	756	14	78	0.75	14	3	24	89	5.26

Lean, athletic frame with exciting tools. Slightly open stance with a quick LH stroke that should result in more power as he matures. Controls the strike zone with excellent bat-to-ball skills and has the tools to hit for average and power. Average speed and range will move him to a corner OF slot where his defense is a work in progress.

Del Castillo,Adrian | 2 | Arizona

EXP MLB DEBUT: 2024 | H/W: 5-11 208 | FUT: Reserve C | 6D

Bats L Age 24	Year	Lev	Team	AB	R	H	HR	RBI	Avg	OB	Slg	OPS	bb%	ct%	Eye	SB	CS	x/h%	Iso	RC/G
2021 (2) Miami	2022	Rk	ACL Dbacks	11	0	3	0	0	273	333	364	697	8	64	0.25	0	0	33	91	4.56
Pwr +++	2022	A	Visalia	18	2	6	0	1	333	429	444	873	14	67	0.50	0	0	33	111	7.38
BAvg ++	2022	A+	Hillsboro	286	30	57	7	30	199	278	346	624	10	76	0.44	5	0	46	147	3.22
Spd +	2023	AA	Amarillo	220	36	60	12	45	273	385	505	889	15	70	0.60	2	2	43	232	7.10
Def +++	2023	AAA	Reno	137	18	34	2	23	248	344	350	694	13	66	0.43	0	0	26	102	4.42

Catching prospect had slight bounce back season after rough 2022. Struggles with breaking ball contact. Slightly hunched posture at plate with pronounced leg kick and busy hands that may complicate timing. Playable power, Double-A outburst partially fueled by Amarillo elevation given Reno comedown. Best current skills are behind plate.

DeLauter,Chase

89 | Cleveland | EXP MLB DEBUT: 2025 | H/W: 6-4 235 | FUT: Starting OF | 8A

Bats L Age 22	Year	Lev	Team	AB	R	H	HR	RBI	Avg	OB	Slg	OPS	bb%	ct%	Eye	SB	CS	x/h%	Iso	RC/G
2022 (1) James Madison																				
Pwr ++++																				
BAvg +++	2023	Rk	ACL Indians	28	8	8	1	4	286	444	500	944	22	82	1.60	3	0	50	214	8.02
Spd +++	2023	A+	Lake County	164	24	60	4	31	366	402	549	951	6	87	0.45	3	3	37	183	7.01
Def +++	2023	AA	Akron	22	3	8	0	4	364	481	409	891	19	86	1.67	0	0	13	45	7.26

Do-it-all OF with fantastic pro debut after missing time with broken foot. Exhibits plus plate discipline and professional swing to make easy contact. Offers leverage and loft to project to plus power to all fields. Runs very well which adds to CF range and has strong arm. Obliterates RHP. Can lengthen swing at times and be too passive.

Delgado,Keiner

46 | New York (A) | EXP MLB DEBUT: 2026 | H/W: 5-7 145 | FUT: Starting MIF | 7D

Bats B Age 20	Year	Lev	Team	AB	R	H	HR	RBI	Avg	OB	Slg	OPS	bb%	ct%	Eye	SB	CS	x/h%	Iso	RC/G
2021 FA (VZ)																				
Pwr ++																				
BAvg +++																				
Spd ++++	2022	Rk	DSL Yankees 2	168	50	52	3	28	310	487	506	993	26	83	2.07	34	8	44	196	8.98
Def +++	2023	Rk	FCL Yankees	198	54	58	8	31	293	402	485	887	15	84	1.16	36	7	36	192	6.81

Short-statured, switch-hitting MIF prospect enjoyed successful US debut. Adding strength is a must to maintain offensive upside. Hitterish contact bat. Passive to an extreme at the plate. Lots of movement to get to swing, especially big leg lift. It's a linear swing plane with pull tendencies from LH side. More complete hitter from RH side.

DeLoach,Zach

9 | Seattle | EXP MLB DEBUT: 2024 | H/W: 6-0 205 | FUT: Starting OF | 7C

Bats L Age 25	Year	Lev	Team	AB	R	H	HR	RBI	Avg	OB	Slg	OPS	bb%	ct%	Eye	SB	CS	x/h%	Iso	RC/G
2020 (2) Texas A&M	2020	NCAA	Texas A&M	57	25	24	6	17	421	535	789	1325	20	95	4.67	6	0	38	368	11.73
Pwr +++	2021	A+	Everett	249	56	78	9	37	313	391	530	922	11	75	0.51	6	3	44	217	7.30
BAvg +++	2021	AA	Arkansas	185	28	42	5	22	227	329	384	712	13	69	0.48	1	2	40	157	4.61
Spd ++	2022	AA	Arkansas	418	79	108	14	73	258	366	409	775	15	72	0.60	4	1	30	151	5.43
Def ++	2023	AAA	Tacoma	528	90	151	23	88	286	383	481	864	14	67	0.48	8	3	36	195	6.84

Set career-highs in HR, 2B and BB in another solid offensive campaign. Has advanced one level per year and continues to impress in multiple ways. No plus tools in arsenal but has fundamental swing with quick wrists. K rate jumped (led org in Ks) due to sub-par hand-eye coordination. Hits LHP well. Lacks speed and relegated to OF corner.

Dezenzo,Zach

345 | Houston | EXP MLB DEBUT: 2025 | H/W: 6-4 220 | FUT: Starting 1B | 7D

Bats R Age 23	Year	Lev	Team	AB	R	H	HR	RBI	Avg	OB	Slg	OPS	bb%	ct%	Eye	SB	CS	x/h%	Iso	RC/G
2022 (12) Ohio State																				
Pwr ++++	2022	NCAA	Ohio St	207	54	66	19	56	319	400	700	1100	12	76	0.56	0	0	59	382	9.39
BAvg +	2022	A	Fayetteville	102	13	26	4	15	255	333	402	735	11	64	0.32	4	0	27	147	4.89
Spd ++++	2023	A+	Asheville	113	38	46	4	20	407	481	628	1109	12	76	0.59	6	2	35	221	9.81
Def ++	2023	AA	Corpus Christi	245	42	63	14	41	257	328	486	814	10	68	0.33	16	0	43	229	5.82

IF prospect stormed through A+ to reach AA in 2023. Corner profile headlined by huge raw power, impact speed. Engaged stance at plate, with hands held high in bat wag. Grooved swing is geared toward loft. Showed tendency to swing over breaking balls at AA. Must develop more discerning approach, better barrel control for MLB success.

Di Turi,Filippo

6 | Milwaukee | EXP MLB DEBUT: 2028 | H/W: 5-11 165 | FUT: Starting SS | 7D

Bats B Age 18	Year	Lev	Team	AB	R	H	HR	RBI	Avg	OB	Slg	OPS	bb%	ct%	Eye	SB	CS	x/h%	Iso	RC/G
2023 FA (VZ)																				
Pwr +																				
BAvg +++																				
Spd ++																				
Def +++	2023	Rk	DSL Brewers 2	181	35	51	0	27	282	406	354	760	17	82	1.19	12	8	22	72	5.56

Spent all of 2023 in DSL and flashed several advanced skills. Doesn't exhibit much power yet and has some projection in lean frame. Has advanced swing and approach that results in more walks than Ks. Can hit velocity and spin. Has quality defensive tools, especially strong arm. May eventually move to 2B or 3B but will stick at SS for now.

Dingler,Dillon

2 | Detroit | EXP MLB DEBUT: 2024 | H/W: 6-3 210 | FUT: Starting C | 7D

Bats R Age 25	Year	Lev	Team	AB	R	H	HR	RBI	Avg	OB	Slg	OPS	bb%	ct%	Eye	SB	CS	x/h%	Iso	RC/G
2020 (2) Ohio State	2021	AA	Erie	188	24	38	4	20	202	239	314	552	5	67	0.15	1	0	26	112	1.97
Pwr +++	2022	AA	Erie	387	56	92	14	58	238	317	419	736	10	63	0.31	1	0	42	181	5.04
BAvg +	2023	A	Lakeland	43	9	17	4	8	395	480	767	1247	14	81	0.88	3	0	47	372	11.04
Spd +++	2023	AA	Erie	182	35	46	9	41	253	349	462	811	13	65	0.43	3	1	43	209	6.06
Def ++++	2023	AAA	Toledo	99	14	20	3	9	202	262	384	646	7	66	0.24	0	0	55	182	3.53

Knee surgery cost him a month of action, but upon return set career highs in most offensive categories. Stiff, upright stance and short toe-tap to start swing, but good raw power should result in at least average power for the position. Lack of elite bat speed and swing-and-miss, limit offensive upside. Agile behind the dish with a strong arm.

Dominguez,Jasson

78 | New York (A) | EXP MLB DEBUT: 2023 | H/W: 5-9 190 | FUT: Starting CF | 8C

Bats B Age 21	Year	Lev	Team	AB	R	H	HR	RBI	Avg	OB	Slg	OPS	bb%	ct%	Eye	SB	CS	x/h%	Iso	RC/G
2019 FA (DR)	2022	A+	Hudson Valley	157	33	48	6	22	306	394	510	904	13	78	0.68	17	1	33	204	6.98
Pwr ++++	2022	AA	Somerset	19	5	2	1	1	105	227	368	596	14	74	0.60	1	0	100	263	2.86
BAvg +++	2023	AA	Somerset	425	83	108	15	66	254	369	414	783	15	69	0.59	37	7	33	160	5.62
Spd +++	2023	AAA	Scranton/WB	31	6	13	0	10	419	514	581	1094	16	90	2.00	3	1	31	161	9.58
Def +++	2023	MLB	New York (A)	31	6	8	4	7	258	303	677	980	6	74	0.25	1	0	63	419	7.28

Short-statured, powerful switch-hitter made MLB debut after strange MiLB season. Started ice cold then got super hot for a four-week period, coinciding with MLB debut. Frame is at physical projection. Better hitter from LH side. Patient approach, sprays the ball a good bit. Sold out for power during late-season run, piling HR. Above-average runner.

Doncon,Rayne

46 | Los Angeles (N) | EXP MLB DEBUT: 2026 | H/W: 6-2 176 | FUT: Starting 2B | 8E

Bats R Age 20	Year	Lev	Team	AB	R	H	HR	RBI	Avg	OB	Slg	OPS	bb%	ct%	Eye	SB	CS	x/h%	Iso	RC/G
2021 FA (DR)																				
Pwr ++++	2021	Rk	DSL Dodgers B	99	20	28	3	15	283	383	455	837	14	72	0.57	7	1	32	172	6.36
BAvg ++	2022	Rk	ACL Dodgers	199	28	51	9	38	256	308	482	791	7	81	0.39	6	2	51	226	5.17
Spd ++	2022	A	Rancho Cuca	40	6	10	3	8	250	302	475	777	7	88	0.60	0	0	30	225	4.78
Def ++	2023	A	Rancho Cuca	427	62	92	14	52	215	276	368	644	8	76	0.35	3	2	39	152	3.33

Dominican infielder has above-average to plus raw power, but approach is all to the pull side and was overmatched in his full season debut where he was one of the younger players in the CAL. Athletic frame and quick bat should lead to double digit HR. Moves well on D with good speed, range, and a strong arm, but long-term profiles better at 2B.

Doughty,Cade

45 | Toronto | EXP MLB DEBUT: 2025 | H/W: 6-1 195 | FUT: Starting 3B | 7C

Bats R Age 23	Year	Lev	Team	AB	R	H	HR	RBI	Avg	OB	Slg	OPS	bb%	ct%	Eye	SB	CS	x/h%	Iso	RC/G
2022 (2) LSU																				
Pwr +++																				
BAvg ++	2022	NCAA	LSU	238	56	71	15	57	298	375	567	942	11	79	0.59	4	1	48	269	7.20
Spd +++	2022	A	Dunedin	103	21	28	6	24	272	336	495	831	9	72	0.34	3	2	39	223	5.83
Def +++	2023	A+	Vancouver	375	61	99	18	68	264	327	459	785	9	66	0.28	4	2	37	195	5.45

Emerging INF who finished 3rd in NWL in HR. Producing more pop due to better use of lower half. Possesses good wrist action and clean swing mechanics. Likes to swing and will chase out of zone. Draws very few walks and lots of Ks. Spent most of time at 3B but also some action at 2B. Potential to be above average defender.

Drake,Isaiah

8 | Atlanta | EXP MLB DEBUT: 2027 | H/W: 6-0 180 | FUT: Starting CF | 8E

Bats L Age 18	Year	Lev	Team	AB	R	H	HR	RBI	Avg	OB	Slg	OPS	bb%	ct%	Eye	SB	CS	x/h%	Iso	RC/G
2023 (5) HS (GA)																				
Pwr +++																				
BAvg ++																				
Spd +++++																				
Def ++++	2023	Rk	FCL Braves	68	9	15	0	8	221	303	279	582	11	57	0.28	9	2	13	59	2.94

Raw, athletic CF prospect struggled in pro debut after gaining prospect helium running up to the draft. Slim, athletic frame with room for strength. 80-grade run is premium tool. Aggressive approach, will expand the zone. Short, compact swing cuts off outer half with pull-dominant profile. Plus strength in frame. Power plays only to RF.

Dunn,Blake

789 | Cincinnati | EXP MLB DEBUT: 2024 | H/W: 6-0 210 | FUT: Starting CF | 8D

Bats R Age 25	Year	Lev	Team	AB	R	H	HR	RBI	Avg	OB	Slg	OPS	bb%	ct%	Eye	SB	CS	x/h%	Iso	RC/G
2021 (15) Western Michigan	2021	A	Daytona	14	1	5	1	5	357	357	643	1000	0	64	0.00	0	0	40	286	8.40
Pwr +++	2022	Rk	ACL Reds	13	0	1	0	1	77	143	77	220	7	77	0.33	2	0	0	0	-2.10
BAvg +++	2022	A	Daytona	93	22	27	4	16	290	436	495	931	21	69	0.83	18	1	37	204	8.05
Spd ++++	2023	A+	Dayton	163	32	45	8	27	276	359	460	819	11	72	0.46	19	3	29	184	5.80
Def +++	2023	AA	Chattanooga	295	75	98	15	52	332	414	556	970	12	72	0.49	35	4	33	224	8.03

Older prospect, finally healthy, had true breakout campaign in 2023. Premium athlete, near physical projection. Plus-plus runner with great first step. Simple batting setup with minimal load, works counts. Above-average bat speed propels uppercut swing to loft. Pull-oriented approach, plays up average power. Potential 20 HR/30 SB bat.

Duno, Alfredo — 2 — Cincinnati

| | | | EXP MLB DEBUT: | 2027 | H/W: | 6-2 | 210 | FUT: | Starting C | | 9E |

Bats R Age 18
2023 FA (VZ)

Pwr ++++
BAvg +++
Spd ++
Def +++

Year	Lev	Team	AB	R	H	HR	RBI	Avg	OB	Slg	OPS	bb%	ct%	Eye	SB	CS	x/h%	Iso	RC/G
2023	Rk	DSL Reds	152	36	46	6	41	303	442	493	936	20	73	0.93	6	0	35	191	7.93

Strong, teenaged C prospect succeeded expectations during pro debut. Has a developed frame with minimal room for growth. Solid athlete with good agility and a foundational, power-driven hit tool. Will need to sharpen up pre-swing movement. Uppercut trajectory swing with solid angles for lofted contact. Should stick behind plate.

Eldridge, Bryce — 9 — San Francisco

| | | | EXP MLB DEBUT: | 2026 | H/W: | 6-7 | 223 | FUT: | Starting OF | | 9D |

Bats L Age 19
2023 (1) HS (VA)

Pwr ++++
BAvg +++
Spd ++
Def +++

Year	Lev	Team	AB	R	H	HR	RBI	Avg	OB	Slg	OPS	bb%	ct%	Eye	SB	CS	x/h%	Iso	RC/G
2023	Rk	ACL Giants O	51	8	15	5	13	294	400	647	1047	15	69	0.56	0	0	53	353	9.21
2023	A	San Jose	58	7	17	1	5	293	406	379	785	16	69	0.61	1	0	18	86	5.78

Two-way player with slightly more upside as a hitter. Has the size, strength and leveraged stroke to potentially produce massive power. Currently uses all fields with compact swing and leverages bat speed and natural hitting ability to make hard contact. Doesn't run well and likely slots in at RF due to plus arm.

Elliott, Clark — 7 — Oakland

| | | | EXP MLB DEBUT: | 2025 | H/W: | 6-0 | 183 | FUT: | Starting OF | | 7E |

Bats L Age 23
2022 (2) Michigan

Pwr ++
BAvg ++
Spd +++
Def +++

Year	Lev	Team	AB	R	H	HR	RBI	Avg	OB	Slg	OPS	bb%	ct%	Eye	SB	CS	x/h%	Iso	RC/G
2022	NCAA	Michigan	243	73	82	16	69	337	449	630	1078	17	77	0.88	19	4	44	292	9.43
2022	Rk	ACL Athletics	1	1	0	0	0	0	500	0	500	50	100		0	0		0	4.75
2023	A	Stockton	93	16	25	1	12	269	404	344	748	18	78	1.05	5	3	16	75	5.32
2023	A+	Lansing	215	31	42	1	16	195	288	247	535	12	78	0.60	8	0	19	51	2.22

Toolsy OF who began year in Low-A before atrocious performance in High-A. Works counts but can be detrimental as he gets behind and expands zone with two strikes. Made too weak contact and showed little XBH power. Still has talent in tank. Was pure hitter in college with sweet lefty swing and ability to crush FB. Athletic with good speed.

Emerson, Colt — 6 — Seattle

| | | | EXP MLB DEBUT: | 2026 | H/W: | 6-1 | 195 | FUT: | Starting SS | | 8C |

Bats L Age 18
2023 (1) HS (OH)

Pwr +++
BAvg ++++
Spd +++
Def +++

Year	Lev	Team	AB	R	H	HR	RBI	Avg	OB	Slg	OPS	bb%	ct%	Eye	SB	CS	x/h%	Iso	RC/G
2023	Rk	ACL Mariners	28	10	15	1	5	536	618	786	1403	18	79	1.00	4	0	33	250	13.95
2023	A	Modesto	63	17	19	1	8	302	405	444	850	15	78	0.79	4	0	37	143	6.53

Advanced INF who set rookie ball ablaze in debut. Has chance to be exceptional hitter due to clean swing and easy, hard contact. Knows strike zone and controls barrel. Should get to at least average power at maturity, maybe more. Runs well and enhanced by high baserunning IQ. Consistent, steady defender who may eventually move to 2B.

Ewing, AJ — 478 — New York (N)

| | | | EXP MLB DEBUT: | 2027 | H/W: | 6-0 | 160 | FUT: | Starting OF | | 7E |

Bats L Age 19
2023 (4) HS (OH)

Pwr ++
BAvg +++
Spd ++++
Def +++

Year	Lev	Team	AB	R	H	HR	RBI	Avg	OB	Slg	OPS	bb%	ct%	Eye	SB	CS	x/h%	Iso	RC/G
2023	Rk	FCL Mets	14	3	4	0	3	286	474	357	831	26	57	0.83	1	0	25	71	7.70

Projectable UT prospect was taken in 4th round of 2023 draft. Skinny frame but strong. There is room to grow additional strength. Mostly upright stance with smooth trigger and short leg lift. Pull-oriented approach with flat-plane swing. Gets to hard barreled contact but not with a lot of loft. Natural IF, likely moves to OF full time.

Fabian, Jud — 789 — Baltimore

| | | | EXP MLB DEBUT: | 2025 | H/W: | 6-1 | 195 | FUT: | Starting OF | | 8E |

Bats R Age 23
2022 (2) Florida

Pwr ++++
BAvg ++
Spd +++
Def ++++

Year	Lev	Team	AB	R	H	HR	RBI	Avg	OB	Slg	OPS	bb%	ct%	Eye	SB	CS	x/h%	Iso	RC/G
2022	Rk	FCL Orioles B	10	2	5	0	3	500	688	600	1288	38	60	1.50	1	0	20	100	16.46
2022	A	Delmarva	44	16	17	3	9	386	481	841	1322	15	80	0.89	0	0	71	455	12.57
2022	A+	Aberdeen	24	1	4	0	4	167	310	208	519	17	67	0.63	0	2	25	42	1.89
2023	A+	Aberdeen	192	35	54	9	43	281	397	490	887	16	68	0.61	19	6	41	208	7.21
2023	AA	Bowie	238	36	42	15	31	176	305	399	704	16	55	0.41	12	2	52	223	4.84

Toolsy OF with offensive upside due to above average power and speed. THitit tool has some questions, as seen with the move to AA. He can draw walks, but his K rates are extremely high. Massive SB total from 2023 something to watch. Can play CF with outstanding reads and routes with enough arm to succeed in corner spot.

Farmelo, Jonny — 8 — Seattle

| | | | EXP MLB DEBUT: | 2027 | H/W: | 6-2 | 205 | FUT: | Starting CF | | 8D |

Bats L Age 19
2023 (1) HS (VA)

Pwr +++
BAvg +++
Spd ++++
Def +++

Year	Lev	Team	AB	R	H	HR	RBI	Avg	OB	Slg	OPS	bb%	ct%	Eye	SB	CS	x/h%	Iso	RC/G
2023	--	Did Not Play																	

Strong, young OF who projects well with both bat and speed. Has raw swing and instincts, though underlying tools are well above average. Bat speed enhances profile and will need time to master swing decisions and batting eye. Hits velocity and spin. Has speed for CF and could play in OF corner with strong arm.

Feduccia, Hunter — 2 — Los Angeles (N)

| | | | EXP MLB DEBUT: | 2024 | H/W: | 6-0 | 215 | FUT: | Reserve C | | 6C |

Bats L Age 26
2018 (12) LSU

Pwr ++
BAvg +++
Spd +
Def +++

Year	Lev	Team	AB	R	H	HR	RBI	Avg	OB	Slg	OPS	bb%	ct%	Eye	SB	CS	x/h%	Iso	RC/G
2019	A+	Rancho Cuca	71	8	17	0	12	239	325	282	607	11	73	0.47	1	2	12	42	3.09
2021	AA	Tulsa	284	44	72	10	45	254	344	398	742	12	78	0.63	0	0	28	144	4.78
2022	AA	Tulsa	144	21	34	8	26	236	345	458	804	14	74	0.63	0	0	44	222	5.67
2022	AAA	Oklahoma City	150	25	36	7	25	240	317	473	791	10	70	0.38	0	0	58	233	5.53
2023	AAA	Oklahoma City	319	61	89	11	57	279	390	451	841	15	75	0.73	0	0	35	172	6.35

Older organizational player has the potential to develop into a reliable backup receiver. Shows good receiving and block skills but a fringe arm and pop times keeps him from being a plus defender. Contact-orientated approach with good plate discipline results in career .363 OBP. Power is a tick below average and will keep him from a starting role.

Fernandez, Yanquiel — 79 — Colorado

| | | | EXP MLB DEBUT: | 2024 | H/W: | 6-2 | 198 | FUT: | Starting OF | | 9D |

Bats L Age 21
2019 FA (CU)

Pwr ++++
BAvg ++
Spd ++
Def +++

Year	Lev	Team	AB	R	H	HR	RBI	Avg	OB	Slg	OPS	bb%	ct%	Eye	SB	CS	x/h%	Iso	RC/G
2021	Rk	DSL Rockies	177	29	59	6	34	333	407	531	938	11	85	0.85	0	0	39	198	7.21
2022	A	Fresno	475	76	135	21	109	284	339	507	846	8	76	0.34	5	1	44	223	5.97
2023	A	Fresno	13	3	3	0	3	231	375	308	683	19	54	0.50	0	0	33	77	5.09
2023	A+	Spokane	248	47	79	17	64	319	355	605	960	5	81	0.29	1	1	43	286	7.02
2023	AA	Hartford	218	20	45	8	25	206	258	362	620	6	64	0.19	0	0	40	156	3.01

Cuban-born slugger has the best raw power in the system and blasted 25 HR across three levels along with some feel hit. Strong hands, quick bat and an aggressive all-or-nothing swing results in all-fields power, but also tons of swing and miss. The Ks piled up once he moved up to AA and faced advanced pitching.

Fernandez, Yeiner — 24 — Los Angeles (N)

| | | | EXP MLB DEBUT: | 2025 | H/W: | 5-9 | 170 | FUT: | Reserve C | | 6B |

Bats R Age 21
2019 FA (VZ)

Pwr +
BAvg +++
Spd ++
Def ++

Year	Lev	Team	AB	R	H	HR	RBI	Avg	OB	Slg	OPS	bb%	ct%	Eye	SB	CS	x/h%	Iso	RC/G
2021	Rk	ACL Dodgers	141	24	45	2	15	319	364	454	818	7	81	0.37	1	3	31	135	5.59
2021	A	Rancho Cuca	31	4	16	1	10	516	545	645	1191	6	90	0.67	0	0	13	129	9.43
2022	A	Rancho Cuca	363	76	106	10	68	292	372	430	801	11	85	0.84	3	2	26	138	5.57
2023	A+	Great Lakes	373	47	102	6	50	273	355	375	730	11	85	0.84	4	2	23	102	4.77

Short, athletic backstop out of Venezuela has done nothing but hit since signing for $700,000. Advanced bat-to-ball skills and hand-eye coordination with a closed, upright stance with hands high as he looks to spray line drives to all fields. Approach and size limit power profile, but he owns a career .379 OBP, a 16% K rate, and can also play 2B.

Figuereo, Gleider — 5 — Texas

| | | | EXP MLB DEBUT: | 2027 | H/W: | 6-0 | 165 | FUT: | Reserve OF | | 6C |

Bats L Age 19
2020 FA (DR)

Pwr ++
BAvg +++
Spd ++
Def +

Year	Lev	Team	AB	R	H	HR	RBI	Avg	OB	Slg	OPS	bb%	ct%	Eye	SB	CS	x/h%	Iso	RC/G
2021	Rk	DSL Rangers	156	23	36	2	28	231	348	359	707	15	80	0.90	3	2	33	128	4.70
2022	Rk	ACL Rangers	125	29	35	9	31	280	357	616	973	11	74	0.45	7	1	54	336	7.86
2022	A	Down East	24	0	5	0	1	208	269	208	478	8	67	0.25	0	0	40	0	0.95
2023	A	Down East	396	51	87	9	51	220	295	323	618	10	67	0.32	8	3	26	104	3.06

Pull-heavy approach remained with heavy GB tilt and whiffs, below avg contact, and bad LHP splits. Sub-.400 SLG in 107 games, and was gassed in July with 28 errors at 3B. A future COF move weighs profile down. Only 19 years old so there's time, but likely to slow down so needs to hit and get in the air. Arm is strong but but inaccurate, though will fit in RF.

Figueroa,Derlin | 37 | Kansas City | EXP MLB DEBUT: 2027 | H/W: 6-0 163 | FUT: Reserve IF | 6C

Bats L Age 20	Year	Lev	Team	AB	R	H	HR	RBI	Avg	OB	Slg	OPS	bb%	ct%	Eye	SB	CS	x/h%	Iso	RC/G
2021 FA (DR)	2021	Rk	DSL Dodgers B	134	14	22	0	14	164	304	216	521	17	70	0.68	2	4	23	52	2.02
Pwr +++	2022	Rk	DSL Dodgers B	43	4	10	2	10	233	298	488	786	9	79	0.44	4	2	60	256	5.25
BAvg ++	2022	Rk	DSL Dodgers S	99	27	32	7	28	323	422	556	978	15	74	0.65	4	2	28	232	7.96
Spd +++	2023	Rk	ACL Dodgers	93	16	22	3	21	237	366	376	742	17	73	0.76	5	1	32	140	5.04
Def ++	2023	Rk	ACL Royals B	35	14	20	2	8	571	659	###	1688	20	89	2.25	1	2	60	457	16.82

Came to the Royals at the deadline in the Ryan Yarbrough trade. He had quite the impressive streak immediately following joining his new organization. He's a patient hitter with some power upside, though it's time to test the waters outside of Rookie ball.

Fisher,Cam | 79 | Houston | EXP MLB DEBUT: 2026 | H/W: 6-2 210 | FUT: Reserve OF | 6E

Bats L Age 22	Year	Lev	Team	AB	R	H	HR	RBI	Avg	OB	Slg	OPS	bb%	ct%	Eye	SB	CS	x/h%	Iso	RC/G
2023 (4) Charlotte																				
Pwr ++++																				
BAvg +	2023	NCAA	Charlotte	224	72	78	30	66	348	493	813	1306	22	72	1.02	10	0	56	464	12.85
Spd ++	2023	Rk	FCL Astros	3	0	0	0	0	0	0	0	0	0	67	0.00	0	0		0	-6.12
Def ++	2023	A	Fayetteville	110	16	30	5	15	273	394	500	894	17	60	0.50	5	0	43	227	8.02

College draftee selected on merit of big time raw power. One-note plate approach geared toward attacking pitches he can pull in the air, trying to lay off everything else. Holes in swing make him vulnerable, whiff-prone. Lack of range limits defensive outlook to corner OF. Has power to be game-changer, though hit tool could stall out High-A.

Ford,Harry | 2 | Seattle | EXP MLB DEBUT: 2025 | H/W: 5-10 200 | FUT: Starting C | 7B

Bats R Age 21	Year	Lev	Team	AB	R	H	HR	RBI	Avg	OB	Slg	OPS	bb%	ct%	Eye	SB	CS	x/h%	Iso	RC/G
2021 (1) HS (GA)																				
Pwr +++																				
BAvg +++	2021	Rk	ACL Mariners	55	12	16	3	10	291	391	582	972	14	75	0.64	3	0	63	291	8.08
Spd +++	2022	A	Modesto	390	89	107	11	65	274	408	438	846	18	71	0.77	23	5	36	164	6.74
Def +++	2023	A+	Everett	444	89	114	15	67	257	397	430	827	19	75	0.94	24	8	38	173	6.32

Very athletic, fast C who started well and ended strong. Led NWL in walks and OBP and has stolen at least 23 bases in each of past 2 years. Set career best in HR and profiles well with both BA and HR. Drives ball to all fields and recognizes pitches like veteran. Solid overall backstop with strong arm and will need polish with framing and blocking.

Forrester,Garrett | 5 | Pittsburgh | EXP MLB DEBUT: 2025 | H/W: 6-1 208 | FUT: Starting 1B | 7D

Bats R Age 22	Year	Lev	Team	AB	R	H	HR	RBI	Avg	OB	Slg	OPS	bb%	ct%	Eye	SB	CS	x/h%	Iso	RC/G
2023 (3) Oregon State																				
Pwr ++																				
BAvg +++																				
Spd +	2023	NCAA	Oregon State	232	50	79	10	52	341	474	522	996	20	78	1.16	3	3	28	181	8.57
Def ++	2023	A	Bradenton	18	4	5	0	3	278	536	278	813	36	61	1.43	0	0	0	0	7.22

Fundamentally-sound hitter with bat speed, pitch recognition and bat-to-ball skills. May not have the typical power for 3B but has level swing with enough strength for line drives to gaps. Draws walks for nice OBP due to keen eye. Secondary skills are lacking - speed and defense are below average. May have to move to 1B.

Foscue,Justin | 345 | Texas | EXP MLB DEBUT: 2024 | H/W: 5-11 205 | FUT: Starting OF | 7C

Bats R Age 25	Year	Lev	Team	AB	R	H	HR	RBI	Avg	OB	Slg	OPS	bb%	ct%	Eye	SB	CS	x/h%	Iso	RC/G
2020 (1) Mississippi State	2021	Rk	ACL Rangers	11	4	3	1	3	273	333	636	970	8	64	0.25	1	0	67	364	8.36
Pwr +++	2021	A+	Hickory	125	34	37	14	35	296	376	736	1112	11	69	0.41	1	1	70	440	9.99
BAvg +++	2021	AA	Frisco	93	14	23	2	13	247	307	387	694	8	69	0.28	0	1	39	140	4.17
Spd ++	2022	AA	Frisco	400	60	115	15	81	288	360	483	842	10	84	0.68	3	4	41	195	5.98
Def ++	2023	AAA	Round Rock	462	94	123	18	84	266	380	468	848	16	85	1.21	14	7	43	201	6.38

Consistently outkicks tool grades with single carrying tool (hit) which may be enough to project as starter. Muscular with excellent swing decisions and approach but slow and slowing down with enough doubt on him staying on the dirt. Projects better in LF or even 1B; swing adjustments mid-season helped unlock more power.

Foster,Cole | 6 | San Francisco | EXP MLB DEBUT: 2026 | H/W: 6-1 193 | FUT: Starting SS | 7D

Bats B Age 22	Year	Lev	Team	AB	R	H	HR	RBI	Avg	OB	Slg	OPS	bb%	ct%	Eye	SB	CS	x/h%	Iso	RC/G
2023 (3) Auburn																				
Pwr ++																				
BAvg +++	2023	NCAA	Auburn	223	57	75	13	49	336	415	570	985	12	78	0.60	5	2	35	233	7.85
Spd +++	2023	Rk	ACL Giants B	30	8	10	3	8	333	355	700	1055	3	67	0.10	0	0	50	367	8.97
Def +++	2023	A	San Jose	100	14	23	4	15	230	287	390	677	7	65	0.23	2	1	35	160	3.86

Fundamentally-sound INF who likes to swing the bat aggressively. Has fair share of Ks with lengthy stroke and can sell out for power. Only has average pop at best and may need to tone down swing. Uses entire field and will draw walks. Runs fairly well and has quickness to be asset at SS. Has some upside if he makes adjustments.

Fox,Jake | 8 | Cleveland | EXP MLB DEBUT: 2026 | H/W: 5-11 185 | FUT: Reserve OF | 6B

Bats L Age 21	Year	Lev	Team	AB	R	H	HR	RBI	Avg	OB	Slg	OPS	bb%	ct%	Eye	SB	CS	x/h%	Iso	RC/G
2021 (3) HS (FL)																				
Pwr +																				
BAvg ++	2021	Rk	ACL Indians	42	10	17	0	6	405	479	429	908	13	79	0.67	7	0	6	24	7.09
Spd ++++	2022	A	Lynchburg	380	74	94	5	44	247	370	374	744	16	76	0.82	21	3	36	126	5.20
Def +++	2023	A+	Lake County	402	61	103	8	53	256	331	398	729	10	74	0.44	9	5	35	142	4.68

Steady OF who got off to slow start but recovered by midseason. Advancing one level per year and has usable tools. Not huge producer but gets on base consistently and can put ball in play with simple lefty stroke. Shows proficiency in CF with good range. Plus speed accentuates defense. Not much pop in profile and can expand zone.

Francisca,Welbyn | 6 | Cleveland | EXP MLB DEBUT: 2028 | H/W: 5-8 148 | FUT: Starting 3B | 7C

Bats B Age 17	Year	Lev	Team	AB	R	H	HR	RBI	Avg	OB	Slg	OPS	bb%	ct%	Eye	SB	CS	x/h%	Iso	RC/G
2023 FA (DR)																				
Pwr ++																				
BAvg +++																				
Spd +++																				
Def +++	2023	Rk	DSL Guardians	152	34	48	3	24	316	409	500	909	14	77	0.69	11	7	33	184	7.29

Young, aggressive INF with potential to be solid offensive contributor. Solid production in DSL as he hits velocity well and makes loud contact to gaps. Impressive bat speed for age and lack of size. Power will take time as pitch recognition improves. Spent most of time at SS with good range and also saw action at 2B and 3B. Impressive arm strength.

Franklin,Christian | 789 | Chicago (N) | EXP MLB DEBUT: 2025 | H/W: 5-8 195 | FUT: Reserve OF | 6C

Bats R Age 24	Year	Lev	Team	AB	R	H	HR	RBI	Avg	OB	Slg	OPS	bb%	ct%	Eye	SB	CS	x/h%	Iso	RC/G
2021 (4) Arkansas	2021	A	Myrtle Beach	65	13	13	1	5	200	366	292	658	21	65	0.74	1	4	31	92	4.06
Pwr +++	2023	Rk	ACL Cubs	25	10	9	2	11	360	467	800	1267	17	80	1.00	0	1	56	440	11.78
BAvg ++	2023	A	Myrtle Beach	42	8	10	1	7	238	319	429	748	11	67	0.36	4	0	50	190	5.22
Spd +++	2023	A+	South Bend	234	46	58	9	36	248	362	410	773	15	68	0.57	9	6	34	162	5.47
Def +++	2023	AA	Tennessee	10	3	2	0	2	200	333	400	733	17	80	1.00	1	0	50	200	5.32

Was back in action after missing two seasons following knee surgery. Short, powerful frame and understands the strike zone well, but has plenty of swing-and-miss (both in and out of the zone) as he hunts for mistakes he can drive over the fence. Speed is a tick above-average, but understands how to run the bases and get the most out of his skills.

Franklin,Jesse | 789 | Atlanta | EXP MLB DEBUT: 2024 | H/W: 6-1 215 | FUT: Reserve OF | 6C

Bats L Age 25	Year	Lev	Team	AB	R	H	HR	RBI	Avg	OB	Slg	OPS	bb%	ct%	Eye	SB	CS	x/h%	Iso	RC/G
2020 (3) Michigan																				
Pwr +++																				
BAvg ++	2021	A+	Rome	360	55	88	24	61	244	310	522	832	9	68	0.30	19	4	57	278	6.02
Spd +++	2022	AA	Mississippi	55	6	13	2	9	236	311	400	711	10	67	0.33	2	0	31	164	4.43
Def +++	2023	AA	Mississippi	341	55	79	15	46	232	298	419	717	9	66	0.28	21	4	42	188	4.47

Athletic, strong OF prospect came back after recovery from 2022 Tommy John surgery. Upright, open stance. Doesn't cover entire zone. Combined with aggressive approach, makes for lots of whiffs. Recovery from surgery zapped some bat speed. It's average bat speed at present. Above-average power potential. Near-plus runner.

Frias,Dayan | 5 | Cleveland | EXP MLB DEBUT: 2026 | H/W: 5-9 140 | FUT: Starting 3B | 7D

Bats B Age 21	Year	Lev	Team	AB	R	H	HR	RBI	Avg	OB	Slg	OPS	bb%	ct%	Eye	SB	CS	x/h%	Iso	RC/G
2018 FA (CB)																				
Pwr ++																				
BAvg ++	2021	Rk	ACL Indians	152	32	49	4	24	322	425	520	944	15	75	0.71	3	2	39	197	7.87
Spd +++	2022	A	Lynchburg	443	64	106	6	46	239	337	330	666	13	71	0.50	8	5	25	90	3.93
Def ++++	2023	A+	Lake County	338	43	88	11	49	260	357	426	783	13	75	0.61	8	3	36	166	5.46

Short, stout INF who saw big jump in SLG with high in HR. Increased walk rate and put himself on map with added pop. Showed better ability to use all fields and improved glovework ups prospect status. Struggles with LHP and likely to slow down as he gets older, putting more pressure on bat. Very good 3B with smooth actions.

Garcia,Johanfran | 2 | Boston | EXP MLB DEBUT: 2027 | H/W: 5-10 196 | FUT: Starting C | 7D

Bats R Age 19	Year	Lev	Team	AB	R	H	HR	RBI	Avg	OB	Slg	OPS	bb%	ct%	Eye	SB	CS	x/h%	Iso	RC/G
2022 FA (VZ)																				
Pwr ++																				
BAvg ++	2022	Rk	DSL Red Sox R	138	26	37	0	23	268	365	333	698	13	82	0.84	0	1	22	65	4.54
Spd +	2023	Rk	FCL Red Sox	149	21	45	5	32	302	381	497	878	11	75	0.51	3	1	38	195	6.67
Def ++	2023	A	Salem	59	8	12	1	5	203	266	305	571	8	59	0.21	3	0	33	102	2.52

Talented backstop who got off to hot start in 1st year in US but faded down stretch. Has potential to be average defender as receiving and blocking need attention. Throws well and mutes running game. Drives ball to gaps as flyball hitter and has above average power potential. Can hit breaking balls, though looks lost at times.

Gauthier,Austin | 79 | Los Angeles (N) | EXP MLB DEBUT: 2024 | H/W: 6-0 188 | FUT: Utility player | 6B

Bats R Age 24	Year	Lev	Team	AB	R	H	HR	RBI	Avg	OB	Slg	OPS	bb%	ct%	Eye	SB	CS	x/h%	Iso	RC/G
2021 FA (Hofstra)	2021	Rk	ACL Dodgers	98	22	25	0	17	255	397	327	723	19	61	0.61	5	1	20	71	5.37
Pwr ++	2022	A	Rancho Cuca	300	81	86	6	49	287	448	433	882	23	73	1.09	10	1	33	147	7.43
BAvg ++++	2022	A+	Great Lakes	62	9	11	1	5	177	338	274	612	19	71	0.83	2	2	36	97	3.34
Spd +++	2023	A+	Great Lakes	148	39	54	6	25	365	489	568	1057	20	80	1.20	4	0	31	203	9.33
Def ++	2023	AA	Tulsa	321	72	94	6	34	293	410	433	843	17	83	1.19	15	6	31	140	6.49

Went undrafted but had a monster season, posting a .910 OPS between High-A and Double-A with the best plate discipline in the system. Line-drive, contact-over-power approach results in plenty of hard contact, but below-average pop. Can play 2B, SS, and both corner OF spots, but is defense is average at best.

Gelof,Jake | 5 | Los Angeles (N) | EXP MLB DEBUT: 2026 | H/W: 6-1 195 | FUT: Starting 3B | 7C

Bats R Age 22	Year	Lev	Team	AB	R	H	HR	RBI	Avg	OB	Slg	OPS	bb%	ct%	Eye	SB	CS	x/h%	Iso	RC/G
2023 (2) Virginia																				
Pwr ++++																				
BAvg +++	2023	NCAA	Virginia	252	71	81	23	90	321	430	710	1140	16	80	0.96	3	2	60	389	9.92
Spd +	2023	Rk	ACL Dodgers	13	6	3	1	4	231	412	692	1104	24	62	0.80	2	0	100	462	11.54
Def ++	2023	A	Rancho Cuca	120	23	27	5	23	225	316	433	750	12	66	0.39	2	1	52	208	5.15

Younger brother of Zack, he posted a 1.113 OPS over 3 years at UVA. Uses strong lower half along with quick bat, hip rotation, and small leg kick to find easy power, but will chase and can be beat up in the zone. Pitchers exploited aggressiveness in pro debut. Played 3B and DH at Low-A, but will likely move him to a corner OF slot.

Genao,Angel | 56 | Cleveland | EXP MLB DEBUT: 2026 | H/W: 5-9 150 | FUT: Starting 3B | 7D

Bats B Age 19	Year	Lev	Team	AB	R	H	HR	RBI	Avg	OB	Slg	OPS	bb%	ct%	Eye	SB	CS	x/h%	Iso	RC/G
2021 FA (DR)																				
Pwr +	2021	Rk	DSL Indians B	151	36	40	1	14	265	416	364	780	21	81	1.34	16	0	23	99	5.95
BAvg +++	2022	Rk	ACL Indians	149	22	48	2	18	322	388	416	804	10	73	0.40	6	3	19	94	5.67
Spd +++	2022	A	Lynchburg	28	3	5	0	3	179	281	214	496	13	82	0.80	0	1	20	36	1.96
Def +++	2023	A	Lynchburg	278	44	73	4	32	263	343	385	728	11	82	0.69	6	3	34	122	4.73

Smart, savvy INF who maximizes average tools. Impressed with more XBHs including high in doubles. Uses quick stroke and exhibits good feel for hitting. Uses all fields in approach but may hit too many GB, particularly with average speed. May not get to average pop and will need to up defensive work, though still good at present.

Gentry,Tyler | 9 | Kansas City | EXP MLB DEBUT: 2024 | H/W: 6-0 210 | FUT: Starting OF | 7B

Bats R Age 25	Year	Lev	Team	AB	R	H	HR	RBI	Avg	OB	Slg	OPS	bb%	ct%	Eye	SB	CS	x/h%	Iso	RC/G
2020 (3) Alabama	2020	NCAA	Alabama	56	19	24	4	21	429	515	750	1265	15	82	1.00	2	2	42	321	11.43
Pwr +++	2021	A+	Quad Cities	147	29	38	6	28	259	381	449	830	16	63	0.53	4	0	42	190	6.71
BAvg +++	2022	A+	Quad Cities	128	22	43	5	23	336	426	516	941	14	70	0.51	2	2	28	180	7.87
Spd +++	2022	AA	NW Arkansas	274	57	88	16	63	321	408	555	962	13	76	0.61	8	4	36	234	7.68
Def +++	2023	AAA	Omaha	475	69	120	16	71	253	362	421	783	15	73	0.64	14	3	38	168	5.54

Came back down to earth a little bit against AAA arms after breakout 2022. Big and physical, still commanded zone and put bat to ball well with simple and repeatable operation at plate. Gets on base and has chance to reach average power potential. He's likely to find a home in a corner outfield spot.

George,Kendall | 8 | Los Angeles (N) | EXP MLB DEBUT: 2027 | H/W: 5-10 170 | FUT: Starting CF | 8E

Bats L Age 19	Year	Lev	Team	AB	R	H	HR	RBI	Avg	OB	Slg	OPS	bb%	ct%	Eye	SB	CS	x/h%	Iso	RC/G
2023 (1) HS (TX)																				
Pwr +																				
BAvg +++																				
Spd +++++	2023	Rk	ACL Dodgers	58	11	21	0	7	362	464	414	878	16	81	1.00	11	4	14	52	6.94
Def ++++	2023	A	Rancho Cuca	42	13	16	0	3	381	458	429	887	13	79	0.67	6	2	13	48	6.86

36th pick in 2023 draft has elite speed with sub-4.00 times to 1B and should be able to stick in CF. Excellent pro debut and showed good contact skills while swiping 17 bases in just 28 games. He doesn't have the size or physicality to hit for power and had just 5 extra base hits in 100 AB.

Gerardo,Jose | 89 | Miami | EXP MLB DEBUT: 2027 | H/W: 6-0 179 | FUT: Starting OF | 7E

Bats R Age 18	Year	Lev	Team	AB	R	H	HR	RBI	Avg	OB	Slg	OPS	bb%	ct%	Eye	SB	CS	x/h%	Iso	RC/G
2022 FA (DR)																				
Pwr ++++																				
BAvg ++																				
Spd +++	2022	Rk	DSL Marlins	176	44	50	11	31	284	397	551	948	16	63	0.50	18	1	48	267	8.52
Def ++++	2023	Rk	FCL Marlins	182	40	35	5	29	192	329	319	647	17	47	0.39	17	5	34	126	4.70

Promising power bat misfired in US debut after slugging 11 HR in DSL during summer of 2022. Lots of swing and miss in profile with limited flexibility in bat path. Also, struggles with spin significantly. Raw plus power plays to all fields but hampered by hit tool. Exceptional arm, likely transition to mound candidate if hit tool is a bust.

Gilbert,Drew | 789 | New York (N) | EXP MLB DEBUT: 2024 | H/W: 5-9 195 | FUT: Starting OF | 8C

Bats L Age 23	Year	Lev	Team	AB	R	H	HR	RBI	Avg	OB	Slg	OPS	bb%	ct%	Eye	SB	CS	x/h%	Iso	RC/G
2022 (1) Tennessee	2022	Rk	FCL Astros O	11	5	5	1	4	455	571	818	1390	21	82	1.50	3	0	40	364	13.39
Pwr +++	2022	A	Fayetteville	21	4	5	1	2	238	273	381	654	5	100		3	1	20	143	3.80
BAvg +++	2023	A+	Asheville	86	21	31	6	18	360	402	686	1088	7	76	0.29	4	0	48	326	9.03
Spd +++	2023	AA	Binghamton	123	22	40	6	21	325	415	561	976	13	76	0.63	2	2	38	236	8.01
Def +++	2023	AA	Corpus Christi	224	36	54	6	20	241	339	371	709	13	79	0.72	6	3	31	129	4.47

Strong, short-statured OF prospect acquired mid-season from HOU. Athletic, muscular frame. Open stance, closes up before pitch is released. Patient approach. Plus bat speed with uppercut trajectory swing. Sells out for pull power but will spray in pitchers counts. Above-average power potential in frame and swing. Average runner; not a SB source.

Gold,Luke | 45 | Detroit | EXP MLB DEBUT: 2025 | H/W: 6-0 220 | FUT: Utility player | 6C

Bats R Age 23	Year	Lev	Team	AB	R	H	HR	RBI	Avg	OB	Slg	OPS	bb%	ct%	Eye	SB	CS	x/h%	Iso	RC/G
2022 (5) Boston College	2022	NCAA	Boston Col	201	38	62	9	37	308	382	557	939	11	86	0.86	3	1	50	249	7.17
Pwr ++	2022	Rk	FCL Tigers E	10	0	2	0	0	200	273	200	473	9	80	0.50	0	0	0	0	1.36
BAvg +++	2022	A	Lakeland	55	5	11	0	11	200	313	236	549	14	69	0.53	0	0	18	36	2.31
Spd ++	2023	A	Lakeland	208	32	56	6	37	269	348	428	776	11	74	0.46	11	1	36	159	5.28
Def ++	2023	A+	West Michigan	136	27	34	6	22	250	320	456	776	9	80	0.52	1	0	44	206	5.09

Slow-developing player had a solid full-season debut. Uses a short, compact stroke to shoot line drives to all fields that limits power upside, though he did hit a career high 12 HR between Low and High-A. Fringe defender split time between 3B and 2B and will be hard-pressed to carve out a starting role given the organization depth at the position.

Gomez,Kenni | 8 | Houston | EXP MLB DEBUT: 2027 | H/W: 5-11 185 | FUT: Reserve OF | 7E

Bats L Age 18	Year	Lev	Team	AB	R	H	HR	RBI	Avg	OB	Slg	OPS	bb%	ct%	Eye	SB	CS	x/h%	Iso	RC/G
2022 FA (CU)																				
Pwr +++																				
BAvg ++																				
Spd ++	2022	Rk	DSL Astros	102	20	30	4	24	294	400	500	900	15	73	0.64	10	5	37	206	7.23
Def ++	2023	Rk	FCL Astros	53	8	11	2	12	208	288	321	609	10	77	0.50	8	3	18	113	2.88

Young bat made stateside debut in 2023. Polished swing from left side on level plane, tendency to hit GBs. Makes solid contact despite aggressive approach. Has power to all fields but takes heavy pull-side approach. Holistic approach with more loft could do wonders for this profile, depending on how contact holds up in full-season ball.

Gomez,Moises | 79 | St. Louis | EXP MLB DEBUT: 2024 | H/W: 5-11 200 | FUT: Reserve OF | 7E

Bats R Age 25	Year	Lev	Team	AB	R	H	HR	RBI	Avg	OB	Slg	OPS	bb%	ct%	Eye	SB	CS	x/h%	Iso	RC/G
2015 FA (VZ)	2019	A+	Charlotte	428	55	94	16	66	220	298	402	700	10	62	0.29	3	3	47	182	4.52
Pwr +++++	2021	AA	Montgomery	269	34	46	8	23	171	247	309	555	9	57	0.23	5	3	46	138	2.26
BAvg +	2022	AA	Springfield	224	53	72	23	54	321	394	705	1100	11	60	0.30	7	3	56	384	10.97
Spd ++	2022	AAA	Memphis	218	36	58	16	40	266	342	541	883	10	61	0.30	3	0	45	275	7.27
Def ++	2023	AAA	Memphis	514	77	119	30	79	232	286	457	743	7	65	0.22	5	1	45	226	4.78

Hands close to the chest with a big, slow leg kick. Dead red hitter drifts into zone making swing long, but has plus-plus power and ball explodes off of bat when he makes contact. Aggressive approach and struggles to lay off or square up breaking balls resulting in 32% K rate. Below average speed and defense leaving him with just one plus tool.

Gonzalez,Gabriel | 9 | Seattle | EXP MLB DEBUT: 2025 | H/W: 5-10 165 | FUT: Starting OF | 8D

Bats R Age 20	Year	Lev	Team	AB	R	H	HR	RBI	Avg	OB	Slg	OPS	bb%	ct%	Eye	SB	CS	x/h%	Iso	RC/G
2021 FA (VZ)	2021	Rk	DSL Mariners	188	39	54	7	36	287	359	521	880	10	81	0.60	9	3	48	234	6.52
Pwr +++	2022	Rk	ACL Mariners	126	20	45	5	17	357	396	548	943	6	83	0.38	5	3	31	190	6.87
BAvg ++++	2022	A	Modesto	126	31	36	2	17	286	353	389	741	9	83	0.62	4	1	22	103	4.77
Spd +++	2023	A	Modesto	296	51	103	9	54	348	395	530	925	7	84	0.50	8	0	31	182	6.80
Def ++	2023	A+	Everett	181	27	39	9	30	215	268	387	655	7	76	0.30	2	0	33	171	3.29

Led CAL in BA by 50 points but struggled in High-A upon promotion. Rarely draws walks due to fringy swing decisions early in count. Makes hard, loud contact and has power to hit to all fields. Uses quick wrists to generate pop and rarely fans. Set highs in HR and 2B. Relegated to corner OF as he has average speed and poor arm.

Gonzalez,J.D. | 2 | San Diego | EXP MLB DEBUT: 2028 | H/W: 6-0 182 | FUT: Starting C | 8E

Bats L Age 18	Year	Lev	Team	AB	R	H	HR	RBI	Avg	OB	Slg	OPS	bb%	ct%	Eye	SB	CS	x/h%	Iso	RC/G
2023 (3) HS (PR)																				
Pwr +++																				
BAvg ++																				
Spd +																				
Def +++	2023	--	Did Not Play																	

Young, high-upside C with massive raw power but long ways away from realizing potential. Impressive defensive tools highlighted by plus arm. Moves well laterally and is average blocker and receiver. Swing mechanics a bit disjointed and will need to smooth out to hit pro pitching. Hits ball hard though can be too pull-heavy.

Gonzalez,Jacob | 6 | Chicago (A) | EXP MLB DEBUT: 2025 | H/W: 6-2 200 | FUT: Starting MIF | 7C

Bats L Age 21	Year	Lev	Team	AB	R	H	HR	RBI	Avg	OB	Slg	OPS	bb%	ct%	Eye	SB	CS	x/h%	Iso	RC/G
2023 (1) Mississippi																				
Pwr +++																				
BAvg +++	2023	NCAA	Mississippi	202	46	66	10	51	327	426	564	991	15	86	1.25	0	2	42	238	7.99
Spd ++	2023	Rk	ACL White Sox	12	2	3	0	4	250	400	250	650	20	83	1.50	0	0	0	0	4.27
Def +++	2023	A	Kannapolis	111	16	23	1	13	207	328	261	590	15	79	0.87	1	1	17	54	3.10

2023 1st round pick struggled in pro debut. Open stance with solid bat-to-ball skills. High walk rate from college continued into pros. Contact-oriented swing with spray tendency. At best, it's a line drive, ground ball producing bat. Above-average power in frame, approach doesn't let it play in game. Slower runner. Likely 2B as MLB player.

Gonzalez,Martin | 5 | Seattle | EXP MLB DEBUT: 2027 | H/W: 5-10 165 | FUT: Starting 3B | 7E

Bats R Age 19	Year	Lev	Team	AB	R	H	HR	RBI	Avg	OB	Slg	OPS	bb%	ct%	Eye	SB	CS	x/h%	Iso	RC/G
2022 FA (DR)																				
Pwr ++																				
BAvg ++																				
Spd +++	2022	Rk	DSL Mariners	172	28	40	3	24	233	353	326	679	16	50	0.37	2	4	25	93	5.15
Def +++	2023	Rk	DSL Mariners	129	17	25	1	15	194	325	264	588	16	56	0.44	1	0	28	70	3.07

Athletic 3B with raw tools and attributes. Hits lots of flyballs but without much pop at present. Can be pull happy and get beaten on outer half. Has yet to demonstrate BA ability. Has potential to grow into average power. Strong present defense in first year at 3B. Moved from SS where he kept nimble feet and soft, quick hands.

Gonzalez,Tres | 789 | Pittsburgh | EXP MLB DEBUT: 2025 | H/W: 5-11 185 | FUT: Reserve OF | 6B

Bats L Age 23	Year	Lev	Team	AB	R	H	HR	RBI	Avg	OB	Slg	OPS	bb%	ct%	Eye	SB	CS	x/h%	Iso	RC/G
2022 (5) Georgia Tech	2022	NCAA	Georgia Tech	230	57	78	5	57	339	447	474	921	16	88	1.67	6	2	26	135	7.39
Pwr ++	2022	Rk	FCL Pirates B	2	1	0	0	0	0	0	0	0	0	100		0	0		0	-2.66
BAvg +++	2022	A	Bradenton	80	12	26	0	12	325	393	400	793	10	85	0.75	7	1	19	75	5.54
Spd +++	2023	A	Bradenton	67	15	20	1	12	299	427	403	830	18	84	1.36	6	0	25	104	6.41
Def ++	2023	A+	Greensboro	366	73	105	8	46	287	394	402	796	15	77	0.77	22	8	25	115	5.74

Versatile OF who finished 2nd in SAL in OBP in first full pro season. Does not have any plus or frontline tool and is more of a tweener than future regular. Runs well and steals bases more on instincts than speed. Gets on base consistently by seeing lot of pitches. Doesn't hit many flyballs or HR. Poor arm limits OF defense.

Goodman,Hunter | 23 | Colorado | EXP MLB DEBUT: 2023 | H/W: 5-11 210 | FUT: Starting 1B | 7D

Bats R Age 24	Year	Lev	Team	AB	R	H	HR	RBI	Avg	OB	Slg	OPS	bb%	ct%	Eye	SB	CS	x/h%	Iso	RC/G
2021 (4) Memphis	2022	A+	Spokane	197	39	62	12	34	315	351	589	940	5	69	0.18	1	0	47	274	7.41
Pwr ++++	2022	AA	Hartford	44	5	10	2	4	227	277	364	640	6	73	0.25	1	0	20	136	3.05
BAvg ++	2023	AA	Hartford	348	53	83	25	78	239	319	523	842	11	72	0.42	0	0	59	284	6.03
Spd +	2023	AAA	Albuquerque	62	15	23	9	33	371	409	903	1312	6	73	0.24	0	1	65	532	11.93
Def +	2023	MLB	Colorado	70	6	14	1	17	200	253	386	639	7	66	0.21	1	0	57	186	3.60

Strong, compact frame with an aggressive approach that generates above-average to plus power. Small leg kick to start swing and keeps weight back well as he seeks to launch. Has worked to use more of the field, but power remains mostly to the pull side. Swing can get long, leaving him vulnerable to elite velocity and breaking balls out of the zone.

Gorski,Matt | 38 | Pittsburgh | EXP MLB DEBUT: 2024 | H/W: 6-2 198 | FUT: Starting OF | 7C

Bats R Age 26	Year	Lev	Team	AB	R	H	HR	RBI	Avg	OB	Slg	OPS	bb%	ct%	Eye	SB	CS	x/h%	Iso	RC/G
2019 (2) Indiana	2022	A+	Greensboro	126	34	37	17	37	294	378	754	1132	12	69	0.44	9	1	59	460	10.07
Pwr +++	2022	AA	Altoona	141	27	39	6	28	277	346	489	836	10	67	0.32	10	2	41	213	6.33
BAvg ++	2022	AAA	Indianapolis	2	0	1	0	0	500	500	500	1000	0	50	0.00	1	0	0	0	11.13
Spd +++	2023	AA	Altoona	357	56	85	17	54	238	292	437	729	7	72	0.27	19	4	41	199	4.40
Def +++	2023	AAA	Indianapolis	58	9	11	3	7	190	266	414	679	9	74	0.40	4	0	64	224	3.81

Athletic, strong RHH who had 2nd straight 20/20 season and finished 2nd in org in HR. Has long hit for low BA as he chases breaking balls and cheats on FB. Hasn't been able to maintain health. Good power and speed combo and plays both CF and 1B. Possesses range in CF with above average speed and exhibits solid instincts.

Graham,Peyton | 65 | Detroit | EXP MLB DEBUT: 2025 | H/W: 6-3 185 | FUT: Starting SS | 7D

Bats R Age 23	Year	Lev	Team	AB	R	H	HR	RBI	Avg	OB	Slg	OPS	bb%	ct%	Eye	SB	CS	x/h%	Iso	RC/G
2022 (2) Oklahoma																				
Pwr ++	2022	NCAA	Oklahoma	278	75	93	20	71	335	395	640	1036	9	75	0.41	34	2	44	306	8.47
BAvg ++	2022	A	Lakeland	100	19	27	1	13	270	336	370	706	9	71	0.34	7	1	26	100	4.39
Spd ++++	2023	Rk	FCL Tigers E	4	0	1	0	0	250	250	500	750	0	75	0.00	1	0	100	250	4.87
Def +++	2023	A	Lakeland	203	38	47	4	29	232	325	355	679	12	74	0.53	15	3	34	123	4.07

Lean, projectable frame but needs to get stronger and overmatched at Low-A, though nagging injuries did hinder production. Long swing and can be beat by elite velocity. Now owns a career .362 SLG. Line-drive swing and all fields approach, but needs to be more selective and improve hard hit rate. Plus speed and should be able to stick at shortstop.

Green,Elijah | 8 | Washington | EXP MLB DEBUT: 2026 | H/W: 6-3 225 | FUT: Starting OF | 9E

Bats R Age 20	Year	Lev	Team	AB	R	H	HR	RBI	Avg	OB	Slg	OPS	bb%	ct%	Eye	SB	CS	x/h%	Iso	RC/G
2022 (1) HS (FL)																				
Pwr ++++																				
BAvg ++	2022	Rk	FCL Nationals	43	9	13	2	9	302	388	535	923	12	51	0.29	1	0	46	233	9.79
Spd ++++	2023	Rk	FCL Nationals	22	9	7	1	3	318	483	591	1074	24	50	0.64	1	0	43	273	13.32
Def +++	2023	A	Fredericksburg	281	36	59	4	36	210	319	306	625	14	51	0.32	30	5	31	96	4.09

One of the toolsiest players in all of MiLB, but huge swing and miss threatens to derail him. When he makes contact, the HR are majestic and the liners are rockets. Present strength, speed and can handle CF with a RF arm. Has shown patience so far, but his K% was over 40% in 2023. There's time, but the range of outcomes are extreme.

Groover,Gino | 5 | Arizona | EXP MLB DEBUT: 2025 | H/W: 6-2 212 | FUT: Starting 3B | 7C

Bats R Age 21	Year	Lev	Team	AB	R	H	HR	RBI	Avg	OB	Slg	OPS	bb%	ct%	Eye	SB	CS	x/h%	Iso	RC/G
2023 (2) NC State																				
Pwr ++																				
BAvg ++++	2023	Rk	ACL DBacks R	4	1	1	0	1	250	250	250	500	0	100		0	0	0	0	2.09
Spd ++	2023	Rk	ACL DBacks	8	1	4	0	1	500	500	625	1125	0	88	0.00	0	0	25	125	8.52
Def ++	2023	A+	Hillsboro	87	13	23	1	14	264	326	379	706	8	90	0.89	1	1	30	115	4.47

College draftee has potentially best pure hit tool in D-Backs system. Smooth, confident swing from right side of plate with controlled pre-swing movements. Swing geared more towards line drives than loft. Showed some power development in 2023 but may stall out given body, swing mechanics. Playable at 3B.

Guanipa,Luis | 8 | Atlanta | EXP MLB DEBUT: 2027 | H/W: 5-11 188 | FUT: Starting OF | 8E

Bats R Age 18	Year	Lev	Team	AB	R	H	HR	RBI	Avg	OB	Slg	OPS	bb%	ct%	Eye	SB	CS	x/h%	Iso	RC/G
2023 FA (VZ)																				
Pwr +++																				
BAvg +++																				
Spd ++++																				
Def ++++	2023	Rk	DSL Braves	172	34	41	4	17	238	328	384	712	12	76	0.55	20	6	39	145	4.49

Short-statured prospect had solid pro debut despite lacking BA. Athletic frame with room to grow. Solid approach, willing to work counts with average chase% tendencies. Struggled to get to consistent hard contact. Solid launch angles with growth could get to an average power outcome. Plus speed aided SB totals. Could be plus defender in CF.

Guerrero,Brailer

9 | **Tampa Bay** | EXP MLB DEBUT: 2027 | H/W: 6-1 215 | FUT: Starting OF | **8E**

Bats L Age 17
2023 FA (DR)
- Pwr ++++
- BAvg +++
- Spd ++
- Def ++

Year	Lev	Team	AB	R	H	HR	RBI	Avg	OB	Slg	OPS	bb%	ct%	Eye	SB	CS	x/h%	Iso	RC/G
2023	Rk	DSL Rays	23	3	6	0	5	261	370	391	762	15	74	0.67	0	1	50	130	5.53

Offensively-skilled OF prospect signed for $3.7 million in January 2023 but suffered shoulder injury in pro debut. Limited to only 7 games. Power is the calling card; raw double-plus in frame, which is already near maturity. Said to also have advanced feel for hitting. Not a speedster; likely future LF.

Guerrero,Juan

79 | **Colorado** | EXP MLB DEBUT: 2026 | H/W: 6-1 160 | FUT: Starting OF | **8E**

Bats R Age 22
2019 FA (DR)
- Pwr +++
- BAvg ++
- Spd +++
- Def +++

Year	Lev	Team	AB	R	H	HR	RBI	Avg	OB	Slg	OPS	bb%	ct%	Eye	SB	CS	x/h%	Iso	RC/G
2021	Rk	ACL Rockies	148	32	47	4	26	318	384	500	884	10	80	0.55	9	5	38	182	6.58
2022	A	Fresno	453	89	124	14	89	274	331	437	768	8	81	0.46	18	8	34	163	4.96
2023	A+	Spokane	441	62	113	6	59	256	307	374	681	7	84	0.46	14	7	30	118	3.95

Dominican OF has a projectable frame and should continue to add power as he matures. Solid bat-to-ball skills with an upright stance with a big leg kick as he looks to get the ball in the air. Swing can get long, leaving him vulnerable to high heat and breaking balls, but limits chase out of the zone. Runs well with a plus arm and RF profile.

Guilarte,Daniel

46 | **Milwaukee** | EXP MLB DEBUT: 2027 | H/W: 5-11 160 | FUT: Starting 2B | **7C**

Bats R Age 20
2021 FA (VZ)
- Pwr +
- BAvg +++
- Spd ++++
- Def +++

Year	Lev	Team	AB	R	H	HR	RBI	Avg	OB	Slg	OPS	bb%	ct%	Eye	SB	CS	x/h%	Iso	RC/G
2022	Rk	ACL Brewers B	124	17	38	0	20	306	399	371	770	13	75	0.61	8	3	21	65	5.45
2023	Rk	ACL Brewers G	20	9	9	0	2	450	476	450	926	5	90	0.50	5	0	0	0	6.50
2023	A	Carolina	223	35	60	0	31	269	368	314	682	14	70	0.53	26	8	13	45	4.26

Athletic, lithe INF with productive first full season despite litany of injuries. Can be a tough out with ability to put bat to ball. Controls barrel and can go to opposite field. Has found success against LHP. No power at present but the hope is he adds strength to keep defense honest. Has enough range and arm for SS and has seen time at 2B.

Guillemette,Garret

23 | **Houston** | EXP MLB DEBUT: 2027 | H/W: 6-1 210 | FUT: Reserve C | **6D**

Bats R Age 22
2023 (15) Texas
- Pwr ++
- BAvg ++
- Spd +
- Def ++

Year	Lev	Team	AB	R	H	HR	RBI	Avg	OB	Slg	OPS	bb%	ct%	Eye	SB	CS	x/h%	Iso	RC/G
2023	NCAA	Texas	218	43	65	11	60	298	393	541	934	13	76	0.65	0	1	46	243	7.43
2023	Rk	FCL Astros	3	0	0	0	0	0	0	0	0	0	100		0	0		0	-2.66
2023	A	Fayetteville	102	15	24	3	17	235	297	382	680	8	82	0.50	0	0	38	147	3.89

College catcher drafted in 15th round of 2023 draft. Made pro debut with intriguing pull-side power, OBP skills. Puts ball in air with steep swing plane. Patience at plate bleeds into passivity on hittable pitches. Solid offensive profile and skills behind plate combine for reserve catcher outlook.

Gutierrez,Anthony

8 | **Texas** | EXP MLB DEBUT: 2026 | H/W: 6-3 180 | FUT: Starting OF | **8D**

Bats R Age 19
2022 FA (VZ)
- Pwr ++
- BAvg ++
- Spd ++
- Def +++

Year	Lev	Team	AB	R	H	HR	RBI	Avg	OB	Slg	OPS	bb%	ct%	Eye	SB	CS	x/h%	Iso	RC/G
2022	Rk	DSL Rangers 2	91	22	32	3	16	352	404	538	943	8	80	0.44	5	3	34	187	7.14
2022	Rk	ACL Rangers	81	13	21	1	8	259	286	407	693	4	80	0.19	6	3	38	148	3.94
2023	Rk	ACL Rangers	20	4	7	0	2	350	381	550	931	5	70	0.17	2	1	29	200	7.67
2023	A	Down East	293	39	76	2	34	259	318	338	655	8	75	0.35	30	10	21	78	3.60

Enigmatic upside bet showing impressive tools with some red flags on the hit. Originally projected for RF, turned in full season stateside in CF showing good speed, but body may still push him to RF where arm plays up. Shortened up long swing some but still a hyper-aggressive approach with little BB and lots of GB begs caution.

Gutierrez,Daiverson

2 | **New York (N)** | EXP MLB DEBUT: 2027 | H/W: 5-11 206 | FUT: Starting C | **7E**

Bats R Age 18
2023 FA (VZ)
- Pwr +++
- BAvg ++
- Spd ++
- Def +++

Year	Lev	Team	AB	R	H	HR	RBI	Avg	OB	Slg	OPS	bb%	ct%	Eye	SB	CS	x/h%	Iso	RC/G
2023	Rk	DSL Mets	105	23	23	2	16	219	305	286	591	11	80	0.62	1	0	13	67	2.86
2023	Rk	DSL Mets 2	67	4	9	0	6	134	237	179	416	12	78	0.60	1	0	33	45	0.71

Hit-first catching prospect struggled with hit tool in pro debut. Stocky frame with some room to grow. Hit tool struggles at start with exaggerated hitch in load to get to hit position. Inconsistent swing path and aggressiveness also play in role. Plus raw power but doesn't play due to hit tool.

Guzman,Denzer

6 | **Los Angeles (A)** | EXP MLB DEBUT: 2026 | H/W: 6-1 180 | FUT: Starting 3B | **7E**

Bats R Age 20
2021 FA (DR)
- Pwr +++
- BAvg ++
- Spd ++
- Def +++

Year	Lev	Team	AB	R	H	HR	RBI	Avg	OB	Slg	OPS	bb%	ct%	Eye	SB	CS	x/h%	Iso	RC/G
2021	Rk	DSL Angels	141	21	30	3	27	213	311	362	672	12	83	0.83	11	7	47	149	4.13
2022	Rk	ACL Angels	192	38	55	3	33	286	338	422	760	7	77	0.34	3	1	31	135	4.93
2022	A	Inland Empire	17	2	3	0	2	176	391	176	568	26	41	0.60	1	0	0	0	3.23
2023	A	Inland Empire	426	62	102	7	52	239	308	371	679	9	69	0.32	8	4	34	131	4.02

MIF prospect took a step back and hurt his prospect stock. Athletic frame with room to grow muscle. Projects as a power-over-hit bat. Upright stance with hitch and arm bar in load. Struggled to get consistent hard contact due to swing length. Plus raw power, still working to bring to game. Likely future 3B if power carries.

Hackenberg,Adam

2 | **Chicago (A)** | EXP MLB DEBUT: 2024 | H/W: 6-1 225 | FUT: Reserve C | **6C**

Bats R Age 24
2021 (18) Clemson
- Pwr ++
- BAvg +++
- Spd ++
- Def ++++

Year	Lev	Team	AB	R	H	HR	RBI	Avg	OB	Slg	OPS	bb%	ct%	Eye	SB	CS	x/h%	Iso	RC/G
2021	A	Kannapolis	81	8	28	1	11	346	376	457	833	5	80	0.25	0	0	21	111	5.62
2022	A+	Winston-Salem	277	32	64	7	28	231	311	343	654	10	75	0.46	1	1	27	112	3.57
2022	AA	Birmingham	42	3	7	1	2	167	222	262	484	7	67	0.21	0	0	29	95	0.97
2023	AA	Birmingham	228	38	63	5	25	276	363	386	749	12	74	0.53	2	0	24	110	4.96
2023	AAA	Charlotte	112	12	29	3	13	259	325	393	718	9	73	0.37	1	0	31	134	4.40

Defensively skilled catching prospect saw offensive gains and solidified future path to big leagues. Starts upright in stance but becomes compact as the pitch is delivered. Sprayed the ball around the diamond, mostly finding holes with lighter contact. Does not generate loft for HR power despite present strength. Glove carries profile to reserve role.

Halpin,Petey

8 | **Cleveland** | EXP MLB DEBUT: 2025 | H/W: 6-0 200 | FUT: Starting CF | **7C**

Bats L Age 21
2020 (3) HS (CA)
- Pwr ++
- BAvg +++
- Spd ++++
- Def +++

Year	Lev	Team	AB	R	H	HR	RBI	Avg	OB	Slg	OPS	bb%	ct%	Eye	SB	CS	x/h%	Iso	RC/G
2021	A	Lynchburg	221	34	65	1	18	294	355	425	781	9	77	0.42	11	9	32	131	5.38
2022	A+	Lake County	382	68	100	6	36	262	340	385	724	11	76	0.49	16	7	31	123	4.63
2023	AA	Akron	452	55	110	9	38	243	315	372	686	9	72	0.37	12	2	33	128	4.06

Instinctual, fundamental OF with quick stroke and ability to discern balls from strikes. K rate rose as he tried to sell out for power but pop isn't his game. Recognizes pitches well and can hit velocity. Struggles to make hard contact against LHP and could stand to pull ball more. Possesses plus speed and range in CF with solid to plus arm.

Hamilton,David

6 | **Boston** | EXP MLB DEBUT: 2023 | H/W: 5-10 188 | FUT: Utility player | **6A**

Bats L Age 26
2019 (8) Texas
- Pwr ++
- BAvg ++
- Spd ++++
- Def +++

Year	Lev	Team	AB	R	H	HR	RBI	Avg	OB	Slg	OPS	bb%	ct%	Eye	SB	CS	x/h%	Iso	RC/G
2021	A+	Wisconsin	270	50	71	5	31	263	348	422	770	11	79	0.60	41	6	37	159	5.30
2021	AA	Biloxi	133	16	33	3	12	248	324	414	738	10	76	0.47	11	3	36	165	4.80
2022	AA	Portland	463	81	116	12	42	251	331	402	733	11	74	0.47	70	8	32	151	4.72
2023	AAA	Worcester	393	74	97	17	54	247	362	438	800	15	72	0.65	57	14	38	191	5.76
2023	MLB	Boston	33	2	4	0	0	121	256	182	438	15	70	0.60	2	1	50	61	0.76

Speedy INF who led org in SB. Was org's defensive player of year at SS, though not flashy defender. Makes routine plays and has fringy arm strength. Set high in HR despite limited bat speed and strength. Increased walk rate which enhances plus speed. Could serve valuable role of utility infielder who can get on base and steal bags.

Hardman,Tyler

5 | **New York (A)** | EXP MLB DEBUT: 2025 | H/W: 6-2 230 | FUT: Starting 3B | **7D**

Bats R Age 25
2021 (5) Oklahoma
- Pwr ++++
- BAvg ++
- Spd ++
- Def +++

Year	Lev	Team	AB	R	H	HR	RBI	Avg	OB	Slg	OPS	bb%	ct%	Eye	SB	CS	x/h%	Iso	RC/G
2021	Rk	FCL Yankees	6	2	2	0	2	333	429	667	1095	14	100		0	0	100	333	9.58
2021	A	Tampa	101	18	24	4	17	238	300	406	706	8	55	0.20	4	1	38	168	4.98
2022	A+	Hudson Valley	397	53	104	22	79	262	330	479	808	9	66	0.29	14	4	38	217	5.82
2022	AA	Somerset	15	0	1	0	2	67	67	67	133	0	60	0.00	0	0	0	0	-4.70
2023	AA	Somerset	283	56	67	26	56	237	331	558	890	12	61	0.36	9	3	55	322	7.34

Strong-bodied power prospect struggled to make contact in 2023. Frame is at physical projection. Power is loud and to all fields. HR power alley is to LF but will take outside FB the other way over the fence. Doesn't cover the plate well with lots of in-zone whiffs. Will also chase breakers out of zone. Solid defender, agile for size.

Harris,Brett

5 | Oakland | EXP MLB DEBUT: 2024 | H/W: 6-1 208 | FUT: Starting 3B | 7C

Bats R Age 25	Year	Lev	Team	AB	R	H	HR	RBI	Avg	OB	Slg	OPS	bb%	ct%	Eye	SB	CS	x/h%	Iso	RC/G
2021 (7) Gonzaga	2021	A+	Lansing	81	14	18	3	11	222	292	370	663	9	75	0.40	3	1	33	148	3.58
Pwr ++	2022	A+	Lansing	102	22	31	7	18	304	413	578	992	16	79	0.90	0	0	45	275	8.07
BAvg +++	2022	AA	Midland	315	51	90	10	45	286	350	441	791	9	80	0.50	11	5	30	156	5.28
Spd +++	2023	AA	Midland	258	44	73	5	48	283	379	426	806	13	84	0.95	6	1	33	143	5.83
Def +++	2023	AAA	Las Vegas	129	19	35	4	14	271	324	419	742	7	79	0.37	4	0	31	147	4.57

Fundamentally-sound 3B who reached AAA on basis of improving approach and ease of contact. No major shortcoming in game. Has strength and bat speed but focuses more on line drives to gaps. Impresses with pitch recognition and hand-eye coordination. Runs OK and has potential to be above average defender.

Harris,Dustin

37 | Texas | EXP MLB DEBUT: 2024 | H/W: 6-3 185 | FUT: Starting OF | 7C

Bats L Age 24	Year	Lev	Team	AB	R	H	HR	RBI	Avg	OB	Slg	OPS	bb%	ct%	Eye	SB	CS	x/h%	Iso	RC/G
2019 (11) St. Petersburg JC	2021	A	Down East	259	54	78	10	53	301	382	483	865	12	81	0.71	20	1	31	181	6.33
Pwr ++	2021	A+	Hickory	145	32	54	10	32	372	424	648	1072	8	83	0.52	5	1	37	276	8.47
BAvg ++	2022	AA	Frisco	331	58	85	17	66	257	340	471	812	11	78	0.57	19	5	41	215	5.61
Spd ++	2023	AA	Frisco	229	42	56	5	29	245	366	406	772	16	72	0.68	24	2	41	162	5.60
Def +	2023	AAA	Round Rock	242	47	66	9	31	273	376	455	830	14	74	0.63	17	3	35	182	6.15

Frustrating 2023 saw power and hit regress, though took to speed changes and ran wild despite 1B/LF defensive projection. Got better in AAA though noteworthy that when Rangers needed bats he was passed over. Splits were good and ended solid down stretch so you can still see average hit, power, and speed projection in here, just needs more reps.

Haskin,Hudson

78 | Baltimore | EXP MLB DEBUT: 2024 | H/W: 6-0 200 | FUT: Reserve OF | 6C

Bats R Age 24	Year	Lev	Team	AB	R	H	HR	RBI	Avg	OB	Slg	OPS	bb%	ct%	Eye	SB	CS	x/h%	Iso	RC/G
2020 (2) Tulane	2021	A+	Aberdeen	91	15	25	0	9	275	347	385	731	10	80	0.56	5	2	32	110	4.81
Pwr ++	2022	AA	Bowie	387	58	102	15	56	264	337	455	792	10	74	0.43	5	3	40	191	5.43
BAvg ++	2023	A+	Aberdeen	12	3	4	0	5	333	500	417	917	25	67	1.00	2	0	25	83	8.50
Spd +++	2023	AA	Bowie	21	3	7	0	2	333	333	381	714	0	71	0.00	1	0	14	48	3.99
Def +++	2023	AAA	Norfolk Tides	82	14	22	3	13	268	318	463	782	7	59	0.18	5	1	41	195	6.07

2023 ended early, as he underwent hip surgery in mid-July. He's shown the ability to hit for some power along with a little speed. The former 2nd rounder is going to have to make more contact and prove his speed is still there after injury.

Hassell III,Robert

789 | Washington | EXP MLB DEBUT: 2024 | H/W: 6-1 195 | FUT: Starting OF | 7C

Bats L Age 22	Year	Lev	Team	AB	R	H	HR	RBI	Avg	OB	Slg	OPS	bb%	ct%	Eye	SB	CS	x/h%	Iso	RC/G
2020 (1) HS (TN)	2022	A+	Fort Wayne	304	49	91	10	55	299	377	467	844	11	78	0.58	20	3	33	168	6.11
Pwr ++	2022	A+	Wilmington	38	9	8	0	3	211	318	237	555	14	68	0.50	3	0	13	26	2.36
BAvg ++	2022	AA	Harrisburg	108	9	24	1	12	222	306	296	602	11	68	0.37	1	0	25	74	2.95
Spd +++	2023	A	Fredericksburg	53	12	10	1	4	189	377	302	679	23	83	1.78	2	0	30	113	4.71
Def ++	2023	AA	Harrisburg	414	54	93	8	37	225	311	324	635	11	63	0.34	13	5	26	99	3.47

Stock has fallen since he was one of the principles in the Soto trade; has not hit since the deal. Has not yet added strength to his thin frame, and power production has suffered. Owns a keen eye that results in walks, but doesn't impact the baseball. Good speed, but likely a COR outfielder, and jury is still out on the hit tool.

Head,Dillon

8 | San Diego | EXP MLB DEBUT: 2027 | H/W: 6-0 185 | FUT: Starting CF | 8C

Bats L Age 19	Year	Lev	Team	AB	R	H	HR	RBI	Avg	OB	Slg	OPS	bb%	ct%	Eye	SB	CS	x/h%	Iso	RC/G
2023 (1) HS (IL)																				
Pwr ++																				
BAvg +++																				
Spd +++++	2023	Rk	ACL Padres	51	15	15	1	8	294	419	471	890	18	82	1.22	3	1	40	176	7.17
Def ++++	2023	A	Lake Elsinore	54	3	13	0	3	241	293	333	626	7	81	0.40	1	2	23	93	3.34

Elite athlete with exceptional speed who can impact game with legs and CF range. Has Gold Glove potential with above average arm and can chase down balls to gaps. Uses speed effectively, including with beating out GB, though SB totals have been light so far. Raw hitter and will take time to develop power; mostly a spray gap-to-gap buy at present.

Helman,Michael

4567 | Minnesota | EXP MLB DEBUT: 2024 | H/W: 5-11 195 | FUT: Utility player | 6A

Bats R Age 27	Year	Lev	Team	AB	R	H	HR	RBI	Avg	OB	Slg	OPS	bb%	ct%	Eye	SB	CS	x/h%	Iso	RC/G
2018 (11) Texas A&M	2022	AA	Wichita	144	34	40	6	20	278	370	472	842	13	78	0.66	10	0	35	194	6.14
Pwr +++	2022	AAA	St. Paul	368	67	92	14	40	250	324	416	739	10	78	0.50	30	5	35	166	4.64
BAvg +++	2023	A	Fort Myers	19	7	8	0	4	421	500	684	1184	14	84	1.00	3	0	50	263	10.77
Spd +++	2023	AA	Wichita	22	2	5	1	5	227	261	409	670	4	77	0.20	0	0	40	182	3.44
Def ++	2023	AAA	St. Paul	108	22	32	6	31	296	339	546	885	6	85	0.44	5	1	44	250	6.15

Versatile, underrated prospect who missed time with injuries but performed admirably when healthy. Power starting to emerge and has always run well with above average speed. Walk rate tends to fall on lower side but knows how to hit and use whole field. Highs of 20 HR and 40 SB, both in 2022. Should fill utility role.

Heredia,Raylin

89 | Philadelphia | EXP MLB DEBUT: 2027 | H/W: 6-0 174 | FUT: Starting OF | 7C

Bats R Age 20	Year	Lev	Team	AB	R	H	HR	RBI	Avg	OB	Slg	OPS	bb%	ct%	Eye	SB	CS	x/h%	Iso	RC/G
2021 FA (DR)																				
Pwr +++	2021	Rk	DSL Phillies R	4	0	2	0	1	500	500	500	1000	0	75	0.00	0	0	0	0	7.40
BAvg +++	2022	Rk	DSL Phillies W	172	27	47	2	33	273	324	459	784	7	72	0.27	7	1	49	186	5.52
Spd ++	2023	Rk	FCL Phillies	141	30	46	4	25	326	399	532	931	11	70	0.40	7	3	37	206	7.69
Def +++	2023	A	Clearwater	66	9	19	1	9	288	347	409	756	8	65	0.26	4	0	26	121	5.29

Strikeouts can be a problem, but held much of his own at Low-A after hitting a ton in complex ball. Solid athletic frame, good hitter with some pop when needed. Stays on-time at the plate. Plus runner who currently mans center, but could move as his arm could handle RF. One to watch in A-ball in 2024.

Hernaiz,Darell

6 | Oakland | EXP MLB DEBUT: 2024 | H/W: 5-11 190 | FUT: Starting 2B | 7C

Bats R Age 22	Year	Lev	Team	AB	R	H	HR	RBI	Avg	OB	Slg	OPS	bb%	ct%	Eye	SB	CS	x/h%	Iso	RC/G
2019 (5) HS (TX)	2022	A	Delmarva	127	25	36	6	25	283	326	512	838	6	83	0.36	9	0	42	228	5.64
Pwr ++	2022	A+	Aberdeen	226	41	69	5	29	305	367	456	823	9	81	0.51	22	3	30	150	5.74
BAvg +++	2022	AA	Bowie	53	6	6	1	8	113	190	189	378	9	70	0.31	1	1	33	75	-0.41
Spd +++	2023	AA	Midland	278	43	94	5	43	338	395	486	880	9	83	0.54	7	3	30	147	6.44
Def ++	2023	AAA	Las Vegas	220	44	66	4	28	300	369	418	787	10	88	0.89	6	2	26	118	5.39

Hit over .300 at both AA and AAA in consistent campaign. Led org in hits and 3rd in doubles as he focused on level swing and hard contact. Starting to realize bit more pop but not much power potential. Tough to fan, though will need to improve against LHP. Likely to move to 2B or 3B due to fringy range. SB dropped from 32 to 13.

Hernandez,Cristian

6 | Chicago (N) | EXP MLB DEBUT: 2026 | H/W: 6-1 175 | FUT: Starting SS | 8E

Bats R Age 20	Year	Lev	Team	AB	R	H	HR	RBI	Avg	OB	Slg	OPS	bb%	ct%	Eye	SB	CS	x/h%	Iso	RC/G
2021 FA (DR)																				
Pwr +++																				
BAvg ++	2021	Rk	DSL Cubs B	158	38	45	5	22	285	399	424	823	16	75	0.77	21	3	24	139	6.10
Spd ++++	2022	Rk	ACL Cubs	157	21	41	3	21	261	318	357	674	8	66	0.25	6	3	20	96	3.87
Def ++++	2023	A	Myrtle Beach	385	46	86	4	40	223	295	301	596	9	69	0.33	27	5	22	78	2.80

Has yet to follow up on his impressive DSL debut, posting a .603 OPS and a 27% K rate. Quick bat and above-average speed and power give him exciting tools, but too much swing-and-miss up in the zone and can be induced to expand. Plus range, arm, and defense make him a sure fire SS at the next level, but will need to show more at the plate.

Hernandez,Heriberto

79 | Tampa Bay | EXP MLB DEBUT: 2024 | H/W: 5-11 195 | FUT: Starting OF | 7D

Bats R Age 24	Year	Lev	Team	AB	R	H	HR	RBI	Avg	OB	Slg	OPS	bb%	ct%	Eye	SB	CS	x/h%	Iso	RC/G
2017 FA (DR)	2019	Rk	AZL Rangers	192	42	66	11	48	344	425	646	1070	12	70	0.47	3	3	48	302	9.64
Pwr ++++	2019	A-	Spokane	8	4	3	0	1	375	500	375	875	20	63	0.67	3	0	0	0	7.80
BAvg ++	2021	A	Charleston	254	57	64	12	44	252	373	453	826	16	65	0.54	7	4	42	201	6.45
Spd ++	2022	A+	Bowling Green	419	70	107	24	89	255	358	499	857	14	63	0.43	6	2	50	243	6.94
Def ++	2023	AA	Montgomery	389	64	97	13	60	249	372	411	783	16	66	0.57	7	2	35	162	5.83

Strong, defensively limited OF prospect suffered power drop off as swing mechanics backed up, attempting to cash in on more contact. Wide open stance with a bat wrap in load. Dips back shoulder, unleashing awkward swing. Power plays to all fields when ball is lofted. Too many grounders in 2023. Patient approach with high whiff%. Slow runner.

Hernandez,Ronald

2 | New York (N) | EXP MLB DEBUT: 2026 | H/W: 5-11 155 | FUT: Starting C | 7E

Bats B Age 20	Year	Lev	Team	AB	R	H	HR	RBI	Avg	OB	Slg	OPS	bb%	ct%	Eye	SB	CS	x/h%	Iso	RC/G
2021 FA (VZ)	2021	Rk	DSL Marlins	134	30	28	3	26	209	358	358	716	19	76	0.97	3	1	39	149	4.86
Pwr ++	2022	Rk	FCL Marlins	140	14	33	2	22	236	305	321	627	9	77	0.44	2	1	21	86	3.24
BAvg +++	2023	Rk	FCL Marlins	104	27	31	3	25	298	463	452	915	24	74	1.19	3	0	29	154	7.84
Spd ++	2023	Rk	FCL Mets	35	6	10	1	11	286	500	486	986	30	71	1.50	1	1	50	200	9.29
Def +++	2023	A	St. Lucie	29	3	5	0	7	172	314	241	556	17	55	0.46	0	0	40	69	2.58

Switch-hitting catching prospect, acquired in mid-season trade with MIA, had big offensive season, mostly at complex. Slight open stance with easy load. Patient approach, will work up-the-middle and to pull field. Linear swing plane reduces loft but there is power in frame with swing adjustments. Solid backstop with strong arm behind plate.

Hernandez,Ronny — 2 — Chicago (A)
EXP MLB DEBUT: 2026 | H/W: 6-1 200 | FUT: Starting C | 7C

Bats L Age 19
2022 FA (VZ)
Pwr +++
BAvg +++
Spd ++
Def +++

Year	Lev	Team	AB	R	H	HR	RBI	Avg	OB	Slg	OPS	bb%	ct%	Eye	SB	CS	x/h%	Iso	RC/G
2022	Rk	DSL White Sox	97	20	26	6	22	268	383	526	908	16	78	0.86	0	0	50	258	7.05
2023	Rk	ACL White Sox	148	20	50	3	36	338	424	493	917	13	76	0.63	1	0	32	155	7.32

Contact-oriented, LHH catching prospect had splendid US debut in Arizona Complex League. Stocky frame with room for more strength. Utilizes open stance with simple load. Flat-angled swing generates solid contact and he shows ability to spray the ball around. Power is on the lighter side but could play up with swing adjustments.

Hickey,Nathan — 2 — Boston
EXP MLB DEBUT: 2025 | H/W: 5-11 210 | FUT: Starting C | 7C

Bats L Age 24
2021 (5) Florida
Pwr ++++
BAvg ++
Spd +
Def ++

Year	Lev	Team	AB	R	H	HR	RBI	Avg	OB	Slg	OPS	bb%	ct%	Eye	SB	CS	x/h%	Iso	RC/G
2021	A	Salem	8	1	1	0	1	125	364	125	489	27	75	1.50	0	0	0	0	1.95
2022	A	Salem	140	31	38	7	39	271	430	507	937	22	72	1.00	0	1	50	236	8.01
2022	A+	Greenville	115	19	29	9	23	252	381	539	920	17	66	0.62	0	0	52	287	7.67
2023	A+	Greenville	68	13	20	4	9	294	400	588	988	15	71	0.60	0	0	55	294	8.53
2023	AA	Portland	291	49	75	15	56	258	347	474	822	12	69	0.44	3	0	44	216	6.02

Strong, stout C had a breakout year offensively. Set personal high in HR and has as much raw power as any in system. Leverages natural strength and loft in swing to hit extreme amount of flyballs. Will whiff a lot due to long, uppercut stroke. Needs to improve receiving and blocking to be starting C. Has enough arm strength.

Hicks,Liam — 2 — Texas
EXP MLB DEBUT: 2025 | H/W: 5-11 185 | FUT: Reserve C | 6C

Bats L Age 24
2021 Arkansas State
Pwr +
BAvg ++
Spd ++
Def ++

Year	Lev	Team	AB	R	H	HR	RBI	Avg	OB	Slg	OPS	bb%	ct%	Eye	SB	CS	x/h%	Iso	RC/G
2022	Rk	ACL Rangers	46	10	22	1	11	478	547	652	1199	13	87	1.17	0	0	23	174	10.47
2022	A	Down East	88	11	24	2	17	273	439	409	848	23	88	2.36	5	1	33	136	6.91
2022	A+	Hickory	16	2	3	0	4	188	316	188	503	16	69	0.60	0	0	0	0	1.61
2023	A+	Hickory	45	5	14	1	5	311	436	400	836	18	76	0.91	3	0	14	89	6.43
2023	AA	Frisco	253	30	68	3	40	269	387	368	755	16	79	0.94	4	0	26	99	5.33

Paced AFL with .449 BA & .553 OBP, with more walks than Ks. Sacrifices power for contact, though hit more FB than GB in '23. No speed, few errors behind dish, but lateral movement slow (one-knee C), arm a liability - just 15% CS in AA, Contact-only offensive 2nd C used against slow teams.

Hinds,Rece — 79 — Cincinnati
EXP MLB DEBUT: 2024 | H/W: 6-4 215 | FUT: Starting OF | 7C

Bats R Age 23
2019 (2) HS (FL)
Pwr ++++
BAvg ++
Spd +++
Def +++

Year	Lev	Team	AB	R	H	HR	RBI	Avg	OB	Slg	OPS	bb%	ct%	Eye	SB	CS	x/h%	Iso	RC/G
2021	A	Daytona	167	33	42	10	27	251	306	515	821	7	69	0.25	6	2	52	263	5.81
2022	Rk	ACL Reds	16	2	1	0	0	63	167	63	229	11	63	0.33	2	2	0	0	-3.01
2022	A+	Dayton	247	33	58	10	26	235	300	425	725	9	57	0.21	13	5	40	190	5.25
2022	AA	Chattanooga	29	3	9	2	4	310	310	655	966	0	59	0.00	0	1	56	345	8.90
2023	AA	Chattanooga	412	63	111	23	98	269	325	536	862	8	63	0.23	20	6	52	267	6.87

Athletic, power-hitting prospect had season filled with hard contact for first time in career. Long, athletic frame with present strength. Upright, slightly open stance, has improved directness of hands to load. Uppercut trajectory swing generates significant loft, 30 HR potential in bat. Struggles mightily against spin, which dampens profile.

Hiraldo,Miguel — 4 — Toronto
EXP MLB DEBUT: 2025 | H/W: 5-9 197 | FUT: Starting 2B | 7E

Bats R Age 23
2017 FA (DR)
Pwr +++
BAvg +++
Spd ++
Def ++

Year	Lev	Team	AB	R	H	HR	RBI	Avg	OB	Slg	OPS	bb%	ct%	Eye	SB	CS	x/h%	Iso	RC/G
2019	Rk	Bluefield	237	43	71	7	37	300	339	481	820	6	85	0.39	11	3	39	181	5.47
2019	A	Lansing	4	0	1	0	0	250	250	750	1000	0	100		0	0	100	500	7.78
2021	A	Dunedin	390	66	97	7	52	249	336	390	725	12	72	0.46	29	5	38	141	4.75
2022	A+	Vancouver	398	47	92	11	55	231	280	382	662	6	68	0.21	28	5	37	151	3.62
2023	AA	New Hampshire	320	41	88	12	54	275	329	453	783	8	65	0.23	16	5	38	178	5.51

Short, stout INF who set career high in HR. Has advanced one level per year and has good tools. Almost exclusively 2B where arm works well. Exhibits decent range and hands. Strikes out in bunches due to swing-happy approach. OBP a big question if he's not hitting. Bat profile looks acceptable with average BA and power.

Holliday,Jackson — 46 — Baltimore
EXP MLB DEBUT: 2024 | H/W: 6-0 185 | FUT: Starting SS | 9A

Bats L Age 20
2022 (1) HS (OK)
Pwr +++
BAvg ++++
Spd ++++
Def ++++

Year	Lev	Team	AB	R	H	HR	RBI	Avg	OB	Slg	OPS	bb%	ct%	Eye	SB	CS	x/h%	Iso	RC/G
2022	A	Delmarva	42	8	10	0	6	238	439	333	772	26	76	1.50	1	1	40	95	6.12
2023	A	Delmarva	53	15	21	2	16	396	522	660	1183	21	75	1.08	3	0	43	264	11.46
2023	A+	Aberdeen	207	52	65	5	35	314	447	488	935	19	74	0.93	17	7	32	174	8.01
2023	AA	Bowie	142	28	48	3	15	338	423	507	930	13	76	0.62	3	1	31	169	7.52
2023	AAA	Norfolk Tides	75	18	20	2	9	267	396	400	796	18	77	0.94	1	1	30	133	5.84

It took him no time to go from first overall pick to knocking on Baltimore's doorstep. He has a great eye and patience at the plate, resulting in a lot of walks, and he makes plenty of contact. He's been young at every level, but still showing near elite hit tool ability, with signs of impending power and speed to go along with it. Has immense, impact game.

Honeyman,Travis — 79 — St. Louis
EXP MLB DEBUT: 2026 | H/W: 6-2 190 | FUT: Starting OF | 7D

Bats R Age 22
2023 (3) Boston College
Pwr ++
BAvg +++
Spd +++
Def +++

Year	Lev	Team	AB	R	H	HR	RBI	Avg	OB	Slg	OPS	bb%	ct%	Eye	SB	CS	x/h%	Iso	RC/G
2023	--	Did Not Play																	

3rd round pick out has average across the board tools, but has yet to make his pro debut. Slightly open stance with big leg kick as he attacks. Good bat speed and excellent plate discipline and bat-to-ball skills, but power is more gap than over the fence. Runs well with an above-average arm, but not likely to stick in CF.

Hood,Josh — 45 — Seattle
EXP MLB DEBUT: 2025 | H/W: 6-2 202 | FUT: Utility player | 6B

Bats R Age 23
2022 (6) NC State
Pwr ++
BAvg +++
Spd +++
Def +++

Year	Lev	Team	AB	R	H	HR	RBI	Avg	OB	Slg	OPS	bb%	ct%	Eye	SB	CS	x/h%	Iso	RC/G
2022	NCAA	NC St	231	42	62	13	52	268	355	498	853	12	75	0.54	4	1	44	229	6.20
2022	Rk	ACL Mariners	20	2	3	0	2	150	292	150	442	17	65	0.57	2	0	0	0	0.56
2023	A	Modesto	391	71	109	11	61	279	359	422	781	11	77	0.54	18	3	29	143	5.31
2023	A+	Everett	60	7	14	2	8	233	313	383	697	10	70	0.39	0	1	29	150	4.18

Very athletic INF who plays variety of positions with plus arm but no other above average tools. Plays game aggressively and with instincts. Not much offensive upside but can hit for BA due to level swing path and knowledge of strike zone. Makes loud contact against LHP. Runs well enough to be effective on base.

Horvath,Mac — 45 — Baltimore
EXP MLB DEBUT: 2026 | H/W: 6-1 195 | FUT: Utility player | 7C

Bats R Age 22
2023 (2) North Carolina
Pwr +++
BAvg ++
Spd +++
Def +++

Year	Lev	Team	AB	R	H	HR	RBI	Avg	OB	Slg	OPS	bb%	ct%	Eye	SB	CS	x/h%	Iso	RC/G
2023	NCAA	North Carolina	239	73	73	24	66	305	411	711	1123	15	74	0.70	25	4	64	406	9.92
2023	Rk	FCL Orioles B	9	6	5	1	3	556	667	###	1778	25	67	1.00	0	1	60	556	21.62
2023	A	Delmarva	52	11	16	2	5	308	419	500	919	16	67	0.59	9	0	38	192	7.83
2023	A+	Aberdeen	17	9	4	2	3	235	435	647	1082	26	65	1.00	5	0	75	412	10.31

Intriguing INF with power and speed upside. Has been very pull-heavy; selling out for power. Played several positions in both the infield and outfield at UNC and in his pro debut. Bat will determine future value. Likes to swing; has ample bat speed and strength to thrive and reads spin well. Hit tool lacks, as inconsistent stroke harms BA.

Horwitz,Spencer — 37 — Toronto
EXP MLB DEBUT: 2023 | H/W: 5-10 190 | FUT: Starting 1B | 7C

Bats L Age 26
2019 (24) Radford
Pwr ++
BAvg ++++
Spd ++
Def ++

Year	Lev	Team	AB	R	H	HR	RBI	Avg	OB	Slg	OPS	bb%	ct%	Eye	SB	CS	x/h%	Iso	RC/G
2021	AA	New Hampshire	16	3	6	2	4	375	375	875	1250	0	88	0.00	0	0	67	500	9.60
2022	AA	New Hampshire	232	46	69	10	39	297	407	517	925	16	77	0.80	3	1	43	220	7.43
2022	AAA	Buffalo	171	31	42	2	12	246	358	363	721	15	76	0.73	4	1	38	117	4.83
2023	AAA	Buffalo	392	61	132	10	72	337	447	495	942	17	82	1.08	9	2	31	158	7.69
2023	MLB	Toronto	39	5	10	1	7	256	326	385	710	9	69	0.33	0	0	30	128	4.38

Disciplined LHH who finished 3rd in minors in OBP. Walked more than fanned with exceptional eye and solid barrel control. Makes good contact but big concern is power. Lacks ideal pop for 1B/LF type. Career high in HR of 12 in 21 and 22. Shortens swing with 2 strikes and hits line drives to gaps. Below average speed and defense.

Houck,Colin — 6 — New York (N)
EXP MLB DEBUT: 2026 | H/W: 6-2 190 | FUT: Starting SS | 8D

Bats R Age 19
2023 (1) HS (GA)
Pwr +++
BAvg +++
Spd +++
Def +++

Year	Lev	Team	AB	R	H	HR	RBI	Avg	OB	Slg	OPS	bb%	ct%	Eye	SB	CS	x/h%	Iso	RC/G
2023	Rk	FCL Mets	29	6	7	0	4	241	389	310	699	19	72	0.88	0	1	14	69	4.77

Former 2-sport prep star moved up draft boards after focusing on baseball. Above-average tools across the board. Short, compact swing from an upright, closed stance. Mostly pull oriented, contact hitter, though above-average power plays to CF and to the pull gap. With strength gains, could get to plus power. Sticks on left side of IF defensively.

House,Brady

5 | **Washington** | EXP MLB DEBUT: 2025 | H/W: 6-4 215 | FUT: Starting 3B | **8C**

Bats R Age 20	Year	Lev	Team	AB	R	H	HR	RBI	Avg	OB	Slg	OPS	bb%	ct%	Eye	SB	CS	x/h%	Iso	RC/G
2021 (1) HS (GA)	2021	Rk	FCL Nationals	59	14	19	4	12	322	394	576	970	11	78	0.54	0	0	37	254	7.52
Pwr ++++	2022	A	Fredericksburg	176	24	49	3	31	278	324	375	699	6	66	0.20	1	0	22	97	4.21
BAvg +++	2023	A	Fredericksburg	138	22	41	6	22	297	370	500	870	10	75	0.47	5	1	37	203	6.43
Spd ++	2023	A+	Wilmington	63	11	20	3	13	317	348	540	888	5	79	0.23	3	0	40	222	6.20
Def +++	2023	AA	Harrisburg	139	19	45	3	12	324	356	475	831	5	70	0.17	1	1	29	151	5.95

Stayed healthy all year after lost most of 2022 to a back injury. With a classic power hitter's build, he consistently registers high exit velocities that bode well for future HR. Chases too much and swing can get long; massively high BABIP resulted in inflated .312 combined BA. Now a 3B with the range/arm to stay there. Solid regular; not a star.

Hunt,Blake

2 | **Seattle** | EXP MLB DEBUT: 2024 | H/W: 6-3 215 | FUT: Reserve C | **6B**

Bats R Age 25	Year	Lev	Team	AB	R	H	HR	RBI	Avg	OB	Slg	OPS	bb%	ct%	Eye	SB	CS	x/h%	Iso	RC/G
2017 (2) HS (CA)	2021	A+	Bowling Green	227	41	51	9	41	225	304	427	732	10	65	0.33	1	0	51	203	4.87
Pwr +++	2021	AA	Montgomery	56	5	7	0	0	125	210	161	370	10	55	0.24	0	0	29	36	-0.84
BAvg +	2022	AA	Montgomery	273	31	67	5	39	245	299	363	662	7	74	0.30	2	0	31	117	3.61
Spd +	2023	AA	Montgomery	132	22	33	6	18	250	322	455	776	10	71	0.37	2	1	45	205	5.22
Def ++++	2023	AAA	Durham	114	18	30	6	23	263	311	518	829	7	80	0.35	0	1	57	254	5.60

Defensive-oriented backstop, flirted with offensive upside once again during successful 2023 season. Strong, physical physique. Plus power potential remains in frame. Closed, upright stance with hands extended over plate. Long load limits plate reactions. Upper-cut oriented swing, sells out to power sometimes. Power plays to CF and the pull side.

Hunter,Cade

2 | **Cincinnati** | EXP MLB DEBUT: 2025 | H/W: 6-2 200 | FUT: Reserve C | **6C**

Bats L Age 23	Year	Lev	Team	AB	R	H	HR	RBI	Avg	OB	Slg	OPS	bb%	ct%	Eye	SB	CS	x/h%	Iso	RC/G
2022 (5) Virginia Tech	2022	Rk	ACL Reds	15	5	6	1	5	400	550	867	1417	25	73	1.25	0	0	67	467	15.18
Pwr +++	2022	A	Daytona	26	5	8	2	8	308	357	577	934	7	73	0.29	3	0	38	269	6.99
BAvg ++	2023	A	Daytona	212	34	52	10	34	245	336	410	746	12	65	0.39	5	3	29	165	5.01
Spd +++	2023	A+	Dayton	149	26	34	5	18	228	331	356	687	13	72	0.55	0	1	26	128	4.09
Def +++	2023	AA	Chattanooga	9	1	2	0	0	222	417	222	639	25	67	1.00	0	0	0	0	3.91

Defensive-minded catching prospect found ways to get on base and drive the ball in 2023. Body is at physical projection. Slight open stance with bat wrap in load. Uppercut swing, maximizes over-the-fence power potential. Think 10-15 HR with playing time. Pull-oriented approach, doesn't expand zone. Solid receiver with strong arm.

Hurley,Jack

8 | **Arizona** | EXP MLB DEBUT: 2026 | H/W: 6-0 185 | FUT: Reserve OF | **6C**

Bats L Age 22	Year	Lev	Team	AB	R	H	HR	RBI	Avg	OB	Slg	OPS	bb%	ct%	Eye	SB	CS	x/h%	Iso	RC/G
2023 (3) Virginia Tech																				
Pwr ++	2023	NCAA	Virginia Tech	178	46	57	17	49	320	389	713	1102	10	78	0.50	4	2	60	393	9.18
BAvg +	2023	Rk	ACL DBacks R	11	6	2	0	0	182	400	182	582	27	45	0.67	1	0	0	0	3.22
Spd +++	2023	A	Visalia	34	3	9	1	5	265	390	471	861	17	62	0.54	3	0	56	206	7.47
Def +++	2023	A+	Hillsboro	82	12	24	1	6	293	333	415	748	6	70	0.20	6	1	29	122	4.88

Toolsy CF prospect selected in 3rd round of 2023 draft. Employs pronounced leg kick, takes aggressive swings. Generates power with tight wind-up and above-average bat speed. Prone to chasing, swinging over breaking balls. All-fields approach. Best present tool is plus speed and can handle all OF spots. Needs to clean up hit tool, plate approach.

Ingle,Cooper

2 | **Cleveland** | EXP MLB DEBUT: 2025 | H/W: 5-10 190 | FUT: Reserve C | **6B**

Bats L Age 22	Year	Lev	Team	AB	R	H	HR	RBI	Avg	OB	Slg	OPS	bb%	ct%	Eye	SB	CS	x/h%	Iso	RC/G
2023 (4) Clemson																				
Pwr +																				
BAvg +++																				
Spd ++	2023	NCAA	Clemson	256	60	84	6	34	328	417	461	878	13	89	1.34	1	2	26	133	6.65
Def +++	2023	A+	Lake County	52	8	15	0	10	288	464	385	848	25	85	2.13	2	1	33	96	7.16

Assigned to High-A immediately upon signing and validated trust with solid pro debut. Exhibits strong on-base skills and ability to use short stroke to advantage. Rarely strikes out and has disciplined eye to get on base consistently. Lacks projectable power and has backup profile. Arm strength a bit short, but receives and blocks well.

Isaac,Xavier

3 | **Tampa Bay** | EXP MLB DEBUT: 2026 | H/W: 6-3 240 | FUT: Starting 1B | **9C**

Bats L Age 20	Year	Lev	Team	AB	R	H	HR	RBI	Avg	OB	Slg	OPS	bb%	ct%	Eye	SB	CS	x/h%	Iso	RC/G
2022 (1) HS (NC)																				
Pwr ++++																				
BAvg +++	2022	Rk	FCL Rays	19	4	4	0	5	211	286	368	654	10	84	0.67	0	0	75	158	3.99
Spd ++	2023	A	Charleston	312	58	83	13	56	266	378	462	839	15	74	0.70	10	0	39	196	6.29
Def +++	2023	A+	Bowling Green	49	13	20	6	16	408	491	898	1389	14	76	0.67	2	0	55	490	13.29

Power-driven 1B only prospect slimmed down and improved prospect stock with big 2023 season in lower minors. Raw double-plus power potential in frame and swing. Open stance with easy swing mechanics. Improved bat path, shortening swing significantly. Patient hitter. Cashed in on over-the-fence power as season wore on with power to all fields.

Jackson,Jeremiah

4567 | **New York (N)** | EXP MLB DEBUT: 2024 | H/W: 6-0 165 | FUT: Utility player | **6C**

Bats R Age 24	Year	Lev	Team	AB	R	H	HR	RBI	Avg	OB	Slg	OPS	bb%	ct%	Eye	SB	CS	x/h%	Iso	RC/G
2018 (2) HS (AL)	2021	Rk	ACL Angels	21	5	8	2	4	381	409	714	1123	5	67	0.14	2	0	38	333	10.01
Pwr +++	2021	A	Inland Empire	167	29	44	8	46	263	356	527	883	13	61	0.37	11	3	57	263	7.67
BAvg ++	2022	AA	Rocket City	307	44	66	14	44	215	301	404	705	11	75	0.49	7	4	45	189	4.22
Spd +++	2023	AA	Binghamton	129	15	34	7	24	264	340	457	798	10	61	0.30	6	2	32	194	5.96
Def +++	2023	AA	Rocket City	311	46	77	15	56	248	320	447	767	10	70	0.35	21	7	40	199	5.09

Athletic UT player, acquired from LAA in mid-season trade, continues to be plagued by swing-and-miss. Aggressive approach, struggles to adjust to opponents pitch patterns. Single plane swing with top hand heaviness. Strong with above-average power, mostly to pull side. Athletic frame. Above-average speed and asset on the bases.

Jaworsky,Chase

6 | **Houston** | EXP MLB DEBUT: 2027 | H/W: 6-1 170 | FUT: Starting OF | **7C**

Bats L Age 19	Year	Lev	Team	AB	R	H	HR	RBI	Avg	OB	Slg	OPS	bb%	ct%	Eye	SB	CS	x/h%	Iso	RC/G
2023 (5) HS (CO)																				
Pwr ++																				
BAvg ++																				
Spd +++																				
Def +++	2023	Rk	FCL Astros	32	4	9	0	2	281	395	281	676	16	81	1.00	0	0	0	0	4.30

2023 draftee features solid tools, plate approach. Pretty left-handed swing, controls barrel well through zone. Stays on time and direct to ball despite pre-swing movements. Power likely below average but could get to more with added muscle. At SS currenlty, but good enough defender to move to OF, with arm for RF. Potential to be SB producer as well.

Jebb,Mitch

46 | **Pittsburgh** | EXP MLB DEBUT: 2025 | H/W: 6-1 185 | FUT: Starting 2B | **7B**

Bats L Age 21	Year	Lev	Team	AB	R	H	HR	RBI	Avg	OB	Slg	OPS	bb%	ct%	Eye	SB	CS	x/h%	Iso	RC/G
2023 (2) Michigan State																				
Pwr ++																				
BAvg +++																				
Spd ++++	2023	NCAA	Michigan St	202	41	68	1	36	337	427	495	922	14	86	1.14	14	4	34	158	7.39
Def +++	2023	A	Bradenton	128	26	38	1	13	297	379	398	778	12	91	1.55	11	1	24	102	5.55

Contact-oriented INF who makes exceptional barrels with level swing path and pitch recognition. Very tough to fan and able to spray line drives to all fields. Compact stroke with some raw power present. Hits a lot of GB to use plus speed on base. Profiles as top of order hitter with OBP and SB. Lacks arm strength but passable defender at SS/2B.

Jenkins,Walker

8 | **Minnesota** | EXP MLB DEBUT: 2026 | H/W: 6-3 210 | FUT: Starting CF | **9C**

Bats L Age 19	Year	Lev	Team	AB	R	H	HR	RBI	Avg	OB	Slg	OPS	bb%	ct%	Eye	SB	CS	x/h%	Iso	RC/G
2023 (1) HS (NC)																				
Pwr ++++																				
BAvg ++++																				
Spd +++	2023	Rk	FCL Twins	54	6	18	2	12	333	390	537	927	8	85	0.63	4	2	33	204	6.88
Def +++	2023	A	Fort Myers	51	10	20	1	10	392	436	608	1044	7	88	0.67	2	1	30	216	8.25

Multi-tooled OF who was excellent at two levels in pro debut. No apparent shortcoming and projects to hit for plus power and BA. Hits velocity and spin and can use whole field. Pull power is immense with sweet lefty stroke. Patrols CF well with routes, reads and instincts. Accentuated by above average speed. Plus arm would be playable in RF.

Jensen,Carter

2 | **Kansas City** | EXP MLB DEBUT: 2026 | H/W: 6-1 210 | FUT: Starting C | **7E**

Bats L Age 20	Year	Lev	Team	AB	R	H	HR	RBI	Avg	OB	Slg	OPS	bb%	ct%	Eye	SB	CS	x/h%	Iso	RC/G
2021 (3) HS (MO)																				
Pwr +++	2021	Rk	ACL Royals G	55	8	15	1	7	273	385	382	766	15	65	0.53	4	0	20	109	5.63
BAvg ++	2021	Rk	ACL Royals B	2	1	1	0	0	500	500	###	1500	0	50	0.00	0	0	100	500	22.52
Spd ++	2022	A	Columbia	393	66	89	11	50	226	361	382	743	17	74	0.81	8	6	42	155	5.13
Def +++	2023	A+	Quad Cities	399	61	84	11	45	211	358	363	722	19	70	0.77	11	1	42	153	4.90

Might have one of the smoothest swings in baseball. The results haven't obliged, however, particularly with BA. A solid defender, won't need to hit a ton to be useful in real life, but for fantasy the bat will need to take a step forward. There's some power, but he just doesn't hit enough right now. Benefits from keen eye to get on base. One to keep an eye on.

Jimenez,Leo — 46 — Toronto

EXP MLB DEBUT: 2024 | H/W: 5-10 215 | FUT: Starting 2B | 7B

Bats R Age 22 | 2017 FA (PN) | Pwr + + | BAvg + + + | Spd + + | Def + + +

Year	Lev	Team	AB	R	H	HR	RBI	Avg	OB	Slg	OPS	bb%	ct%	Eye	SB	CS	x/h%	Iso	RC/G
2021	Rk	FCL Blue Jays	13	6	5	0	2	385	500	538	1038	19	92	3.00	1	0	40	154	9.12
2021	A	Dunedin	168	35	53	1	19	315	475	381	856	23	79	1.46	4	1	17	65	7.07
2022	A+	Vancouver	244	45	56	6	40	230	306	385	692	10	76	0.47	7	3	41	156	4.14
2023	AA	New Hampshire	289	54	83	8	44	287	358	436	794	10	82	0.60	8	2	30	149	5.41
2023	AAA	Buffalo	63	8	12	0	3	190	292	238	530	13	76	0.60	0	0	25	48	2.18

Instinctual INF who is advancing quickly and on verge of majors. Struggled a bit in AAA. Rarely swings and misses and can use all fields with simple swing. Not much of power stroke but adding muscle. Works counts to get on base, though with fringy speed, there's not much SB benefit. Solid defender overall and can play both MIF spots.

Johnson,Termarr — 4 — Pittsburgh

EXP MLB DEBUT: 2025 | H/W: 5-8 175 | FUT: Starting 2B | 8A

Bats L Age 19 | 2022 (1) HS (GA) | Pwr + + + | BAvg + + + | Spd + + + | Def + + +

Year	Lev	Team	AB	R	H	HR	RBI	Avg	OB	Slg	OPS	bb%	ct%	Eye	SB	CS	x/h%	Iso	RC/G
2022	Rk	FCL Pirates B	23	0	3	0	0	130	310	217	528	21	65	0.75	2	0	67	87	2.11
2022	A	Bradenton	40	7	11	1	6	275	420	450	870	20	68	0.77	4	1	45	175	7.33
2023	A	Bradenton	250	57	61	13	44	244	413	448	861	22	65	0.82	7	2	39	204	7.12
2023	A+	Greensboro	99	26	24	5	15	242	414	414	828	23	68	0.91	3	0	29	172	6.46

Pure-hitting 2B who has all offensive attributes in tool box despite low BA in 2023. Possesses elite bat speed and hand-eye coordination and makes hard contact to all fields. Hits FB and breaking balls with fast hands. Posts high OBP due to disciplined eye and led to 100+ BB. Power should come next and profiles well. Average speed and glove.

Jones,Brock — 78 — Tampa Bay

EXP MLB DEBUT: 2025 | H/W: 5-11 197 | FUT: Starting CF | 7E

Bats L Age 23 | 2022 (2) Stanford | Pwr + + + | BAvg + + | Spd + + + + | Def + + +

Year	Lev	Team	AB	R	H	HR	RBI	Avg	OB	Slg	OPS	bb%	ct%	Eye	SB	CS	x/h%	Iso	RC/G
2022	Rk	FCL Rays	19	4	4	0	2	211	375	211	586	21	68	0.83	2	2	0	0	2.99
2022	A	Charleston	49	15	14	4	12	286	426	653	1079	20	57	0.57	9	3	64	367	11.53
2023	A+	Bowling Green	318	49	64	15	49	201	306	412	718	13	61	0.39	10	7	52	211	4.83

Former collegiate two-sport athlete struggled with contact in first full pro season. Played safety at Stanford. Muscular build with raw plus power in frame and plus speed. Open stance with slight bat wrap in load. Top hand heavy swing, struggles getting to velocity up in zone while also cutting off the plate. 20/20 potential if hit tool verifies.

Jones,Druw — 8 — Arizona

EXP MLB DEBUT: 2025 | H/W: 6-4 180 | FUT: Starting CF | 9E

Bats R Age 20 | 2022 (1) HS (GA) | Pwr + + + | BAvg + + + | Spd + + + | Def + + + +

Year	Lev	Team	AB	R	H	HR	RBI	Avg	OB	Slg	OPS	bb%	ct%	Eye	SB	CS	x/h%	Iso	RC/G
2023	Rk	ACL DBacks R	9	3	2	0	2	222	417	222	639	25	67	1.00	2	0	0	0	3.91
2023	Rk	ACL Dbacks	27	6	5	0	1	185	267	259	526	10	70	0.38	1	1	20	74	1.94
2023	A	Visalia	111	19	28	2	9	252	366	351	718	15	69	0.59	6	2	21	99	4.75

Second pick in 2022 draft has had rocky start to pro career due to shoulder, hamstring injuries. Boasted sky-high 5-tool potential in draft year, has struggled to regain offense since. Great zone recognition, BB%. Extreme GB% needs correction. Excellent defense in CF with true Gold Glove upside. SB production should rebound with more health.

Jones,Greg — 68 — Tampa Bay

EXP MLB DEBUT: 2024 | H/W: 6-2 175 | FUT: Reserve IF | 6C

Bats B Age 26 | 2019 (1) UNC Wilmington | Pwr + + + | BAvg + + | Spd + + + + | Def + + +

Year	Lev	Team	AB	R	H	HR	RBI	Avg	OB	Slg	OPS	bb%	ct%	Eye	SB	CS	x/h%	Iso	RC/G
2021	A+	Bowling Green	220	48	64	13	38	291	373	527	901	12	66	0.39	27	2	36	236	7.31
2021	AA	Montgomery	54	8	10	1	2	185	241	296	538	7	61	0.19	7	0	30	111	1.92
2022	AA	Montgomery	319	54	76	8	40	238	298	392	690	8	60	0.21	37	5	39	154	4.49
2023	AA	Montgomery	81	11	14	3	9	173	256	358	614	10	56	0.25	12	0	50	185	3.40
2023	AAA	Durham	169	32	47	7	26	278	337	467	804	8	57	0.21	12	4	36	189	6.60

Athletic, switch-hitting MIF prospect recovered from slow start to post respectable numbers at Triple-A. Missed time due to hamstring injury. Former 1st round pick hasn't lived up to potential due to whiffs and inconsistent hard contact rates. Average power potential remains and a plus runner. Likely not enough hit tool to carry to regular reps.

Jones,Spencer — 8 — New York (A)

EXP MLB DEBUT: 2025 | H/W: 6-6 235 | FUT: Starting CF | 8C

Bats L Age 22 | 2022 (1) Vanderbilt | Pwr + + + + | BAvg + + | Spd + + + | Def + + +

Year	Lev	Team	AB	R	H	HR	RBI	Avg	OB	Slg	OPS	bb%	ct%	Eye	SB	CS	x/h%	Iso	RC/G
2022	NCAA	Vanderbilt	230	62	85	12	60	370	447	643	1090	12	72	0.50	14	1	42	274	9.75
2022	Rk	FCL Yankees	10	3	5	1	4	500	545	900	1445	9	80	0.50	2	0	40	400	13.22
2022	A	Tampa	83	18	27	3	8	325	398	494	892	11	78	0.56	10	0	30	169	6.67
2023	A+	Hudson Valley	411	62	110	13	56	268	336	450	786	9	68	0.32	35	9	41	182	5.58
2023	AA	Somerset	69	9	18	3	10	261	329	406	735	9	68	0.32	8	3	22	145	4.60

Long limbed, athletic CF prospect struggled with whiffs in 2023. Muscular frame with slight room for additional development. Upright, open stance with toe tap and easy trigger to hit position. Aggressive approach. Uppercut trajectory swing geared towards lofted contact. Raw plus-plus power struggles to play due to hit tool. Above-average runner.

Jordan,Blaze — 35 — Boston

EXP MLB DEBUT: 2025 | H/W: 6-2 220 | FUT: Starting 1B | 7C

Bats R Age 21 | 2020 (3) HS (MS) | Pwr + + + + | BAvg + + | Spd + | Def + +

Year	Lev	Team	AB	R	H	HR	RBI	Avg	OB	Slg	OPS	bb%	ct%	Eye	SB	CS	x/h%	Iso	RC/G
2021	A	Salem	36	7	9	2	7	250	289	444	734	5	78	0.25	0	0	33	194	4.22
2022	A	Salem	370	48	106	8	57	286	351	446	797	9	82	0.55	4	1	38	159	5.46
2022	A+	Greenville	93	12	28	4	11	301	375	441	816	11	71	0.41	1	0	18	140	5.73
2023	A+	Greenville	287	48	93	12	55	324	384	533	917	9	84	0.60	2	0	38	209	6.78
2023	AA	Portland	189	19	48	6	31	254	299	402	701	6	85	0.43	0	0	33	148	4.04

Bat-only prospect who set career highs in HR and 2B while posting high BA. Demolishes LHP with aggressive approach and hard contact to all fields. Exhibits plus bat speed with improving pitch recognition. Lacks foot speed and quickness. Not much of asset defensively and likely to move to 1B full time where he has to hit.

Jorge,Carlos — 48 — Cincinnati

EXP MLB DEBUT: 2025 | H/W: 5-10 160 | FUT: Starting CF | 8D

Bats L Age 20 | 2021 FA (DR) | Pwr + + | BAvg + + + + | Spd + + + + | Def + + +

Year	Lev	Team	AB	R	H	HR	RBI	Avg	OB	Slg	OPS	bb%	ct%	Eye	SB	CS	x/h%	Iso	RC/G
2021	Rk	DSL Reds	159	38	55	3	33	346	432	579	1010	13	80	0.75	27	5	38	233	8.55
2022	Rk	ACL Reds	119	32	31	7	21	261	389	529	918	17	66	0.61	27	4	52	269	7.87
2023	A	Daytona	298	70	88	9	36	295	391	483	875	14	77	0.67	31	7	33	188	6.74
2023	A+	Dayton	88	8	21	3	14	239	280	398	677	5	66	0.17	1	2	33	159	3.83

Athletic on-base machine was one of the best hitters in Low-A. Twitchy, short-statured frame. Upright, open stance with minimal load to hit position. Short levers allow for compact swing. Aggressive approach but ends up in deep counts due to plus hand/eye skills. Below-average power in bat and swing but shoots gaps for XBH. Plus runner.

Jorge,Dyan — 6 — Colorado

EXP MLB DEBUT: 2026 | H/W: 6-3 170 | FUT: Starting SS | 8E

Bats R Age 21 | 2022 FA (CU) | Pwr + + | BAvg + + + | Spd + + + + | Def + + + +

Year	Lev	Team	AB	R	H	HR	RBI	Avg	OB	Slg	OPS	bb%	ct%	Eye	SB	CS	x/h%	Iso	RC/G
2022	Rk	DSL Rockies	15	2	5	0	5	333	375	467	842	6	73	0.25	0	0	40	133	6.20
2022	Rk	DSL Colorado	191	35	61	4	20	319	393	450	843	11	84	0.74	13	10	26	131	6.07
2023	Rk	ACL Rockies	73	31	27	3	18	370	500	644	1144	21	84	1.58	9	0	41	274	10.45
2023	A	Fresno	198	29	56	0	22	283	327	338	665	6	82	0.37	10	2	20	56	3.71

Signed for $2.8 million in 2022. Large, athletic, projectable frame with above-average to plus speed and should be able to stick at SS. Plus bat speed with projectable power and a patient approach at the plate. Solid stateside debut in rookie ball, but was less dangerous once he moved up to Low-A.

Jung,Jace — 4 — Detroit

EXP MLB DEBUT: 2024 | H/W: 6-0 205 | FUT: Starting 3B | 9D

Bats L Age 23 | 2022 (1) Texas Tech | Pwr + + + + | BAvg + + + + | Spd + + | Def + + +

Year	Lev	Team	AB	R	H	HR	RBI	Avg	OB	Slg	OPS	bb%	ct%	Eye	SB	CS	x/h%	Iso	RC/G
2022	NCAA	Texas Tech	224	68	75	14	57	335	473	612	1085	21	81	1.40	5	0	44	277	9.60
2022	A+	West Michigan	108	16	25	1	13	231	376	333	709	19	74	0.89	1	0	32	102	4.83
2023	A+	West Michigan	303	46	77	14	43	254	370	465	836	16	73	0.67	5	1	44	211	6.28
2023	AA	Erie	183	28	52	14	39	284	364	563	927	11	69	0.41	0	0	44	279	7.32

Breakout season and is on track for a 2024 debut. A plus defender at 2B - he won the MiLB Gold Glove - but could move to 3B upon reaching Detroit. Worked hard to refine his approach at the plate and tap into plus raw power and launched 28 long balls while posting a .376 OBP. Concerns about funky pre-pitch set up have faded after he dominated at AA.

Karros,Kyle — 5 — Colorado

EXP MLB DEBUT: 2026 | H/W: 6-5 220 | FUT: Starting 3B | 7D

Bats R Age 21 | 2023 (5) UCLA | Pwr + + | BAvg + + + | Spd + + | Def + + +

Year	Lev	Team	AB	R	H	HR	RBI	Avg	OB	Slg	OPS	bb%	ct%	Eye	SB	CS	x/h%	Iso	RC/G
2023	NCAA	UCLA	169	30	48	5	34	284	366	420	787	12	79	0.63	3	1	27	136	5.37
2023	Rk	ACL Rockies	49	15	16	0	11	327	441	408	849	17	84	1.25	3	0	19	82	6.67
2023	A	Fresno	81	15	21	0	6	259	355	284	639	13	79	0.71	0	0	10	25	3.66

Son of big leaguer Eric Karros had a pedestrian career at UCLA but the Rockies took a chance on him in the 5th round. Tall frame with an upright stance and long levers. Raw power is a tick above average, but he's hit-over-power for now. Lack of plus bat speed leaves him in between and failed to homer in debut. Should stick at 3B with a plus arm.

Kasevich,Josh — 6 — Toronto

EXP MLB DEBUT: 2025 | H/W: 6-1 200 | FUT: Utility player | 6B

Bats R Age 23 — 2022 (2) Oregon

Pwr + + / BAvg + + + / Spd + + + / Def + + +

Year	Lev	Team	AB	R	H	HR	RBI	Avg	OB	Slg	OPS	bb%	ct%	Eye	SB	CS	x/h%	Iso	RC/G
2022	NCAA	Oregon	245	53	76	7	44	310	372	445	817	9	93	1.50	6	0	24	135	5.69
2022	A	Dunedin	107	18	28	0	7	262	331	336	667	9	92	1.22	0	2	29	75	4.20
2023	A+	Vancouver	334	46	95	4	50	284	358	365	723	10	88	0.93	11	2	20	81	4.68

Finished 2nd in NWL in BA. Low K%; has eye for contact with flat, simple stroke. Making harder contact as he gains confidence in natural bat speed and strength. Not much of a power profile. Likes to go to opposite field and use average speed and instincts to leg out hits. Likely to stick at SS long-term with strong arm.

Kayfus,C.J. — 3 — Cleveland

EXP MLB DEBUT: 2025 | H/W: 6-0 192 | FUT: Starting 1B | 7D

Bats L Age 22 — 2023 (3) Miami

Pwr + + / BAvg + + + / Spd + + / Def + +

Year	Lev	Team	AB	R	H	HR	RBI	Avg	OB	Slg	OPS	bb%	ct%	Eye	SB	CS	x/h%	Iso	RC/G
2023	NCAA	Miami	236	61	82	13	41	347	454	581	1034	16	81	1.05	8	4	34	233	8.67
2023	A	Lynchburg	59	13	16	4	19	271	419	542	961	20	80	1.25	5	2	50	271	7.92

Fundamentally-sound 1B who may lack ideal power for position but plays game aggressively with sound hitting mechanics. Walks more than fans with keen eye. Uses all fields and focuses on hard line drives. Lacks ideal speed but can steal occasional base. Not much of a defender so he will have to hit. Could get to average pop down the line.

Keaschall,Luke — 4 — Minnesota

EXP MLB DEBUT: 2025 | H/W: 6-1 190 | FUT: Starting 2B | 7C

Bats R Age 21 — 2023 (2) Arizona State

Pwr + + / BAvg + + + / Spd + + + / Def + + +

Year	Lev	Team	AB	R	H	HR	RBI	Avg	OB	Slg	OPS	bb%	ct%	Eye	SB	CS	x/h%	Iso	RC/G
2023	NCAA	Arizona St	218	55	77	18	58	353	413	725	1137	9	87	0.79	18	2	57	372	9.19
2023	Rk	FCL Twins	7	4	1	0	0	143	333	143	476	22	71	1.00	2	0	0	0	1.46
2023	A	Fort Myers	72	20	21	1	9	292	414	472	886	17	72	0.75	8	0	48	181	7.38
2023	A+	Cedar Rapids	32	5	10	2	6	313	353	563	915	6	91	0.67	1	0	40	250	6.40

Pure hitter who does little things well - gets on base, shortens stroke with two strikes and puts ball in play. Projects as top-of-order hitter with above average speed and instincts. Can drive ball to gaps and get to occasional pull power. Spent time at 3 levels upon signing. Likely to be full-time 2B due to limited SS range. Good footwork.

Keegan,Dominic — 23 — Tampa Bay

EXP MLB DEBUT: 2025 | H/W: 6-0 210 | FUT: Starting 1B | 7C

Bats R Age 23 — 2022 (4) Vanderbilt

Pwr + + + / BAvg + + + / Spd + + / Def + +

Year	Lev	Team	AB	R	H	HR	RBI	Avg	OB	Slg	OPS	bb%	ct%	Eye	SB	CS	x/h%	Iso	RC/G
2022	NCAA	Vanderbilt	229	47	85	14	67	371	463	646	1109	15	78	0.76	2	0	39	275	9.68
2022	Rk	FCL Rays	17	2	7	0	5	412	500	647	1147	15	76	0.75	1	0	57	235	10.84
2022	A	Charleston	23	4	6	2	6	261	320	522	842	8	74	0.33	0	0	33	261	5.64
2023	A	Charleston	200	34	63	5	35	315	407	475	882	13	76	0.65	2	0	29	160	6.85
2023	A+	Bowling Green	173	26	44	8	30	254	358	457	815	14	76	0.67	0	1	43	202	5.84

Hit-first catcher continued to progress as hitter in lower minors. Upright, closed stance with slight trigger and advanced hit skills. It's a compact swing with slight uppercut trajectory. Works counts into favorable hitting situations. Sprays ball well. Power mostly plays to pull side. 25+ HR potential at projection. Struggles behind the dish.

Keirsey,DaShawn — 8 — Minnesota

EXP MLB DEBUT: 2024 | H/W: 6-0 195 | FUT: Reserve OF | 6B

Bats L Age 26 — 2018 (4) Utah

Pwr + + / BAvg + + / Spd + + + + / Def + + + +

Year	Lev	Team	AB	R	H	HR	RBI	Avg	OB	Slg	OPS	bb%	ct%	Eye	SB	CS	x/h%	Iso	RC/G
2021	Rk	FCL Twins	11	4	4	0	0	364	364	364	727	0	91	0.00	1	0	0	0	3.99
2021	A+	Cedar Rapids	141	17	28	7	24	199	289	433	722	11	65	0.36	10	3	54	234	4.72
2022	AA	Wichita	425	61	115	7	48	271	322	395	717	7	75	0.30	42	7	31	125	4.36
2023	AA	Wichita	361	59	110	13	48	305	360	488	847	8	74	0.33	31	5	32	183	6.06
2023	AAA	St. Paul	129	20	34	2	13	264	358	364	722	13	76	0.61	8	0	18	101	4.69

Speedy, defensive-oriented CF with best pro season to date. Finished 4th in TL in BA before promotion to AAA. Led org in hits. Hits lots of GB but has speed to get infield hits. Enough punch to go gap to gap and leg out doubles. Not much of a power threat but can get to double digits. May have best speed in org and ranges very well in CF.

Keith,Colt — 5 — Detroit

EXP MLB DEBUT: 2024 | H/W: 6-2 211 | FUT: Starting 2B | 9D

Bats L Age 22 — 2020 (5) HS (MS)

Pwr + + + + + / BAvg + + + + / Spd + + / Def + +

Year	Lev	Team	AB	R	H	HR	RBI	Avg	OB	Slg	OPS	bb%	ct%	Eye	SB	CS	x/h%	Iso	RC/G
2021	A	Lakeland	147	32	47	1	21	320	435	422	857	17	73	0.77	4	1	21	102	6.87
2021	A+	West Michigan	68	7	11	1	6	162	250	250	500	11	60	0.30	0	0	27	88	1.35
2022	A+	West Michigan	193	38	58	9	31	301	372	544	916	10	78	0.52	4	0	45	244	6.98
2023	AA	Erie	246	43	80	14	50	325	387	585	973	9	74	0.40	2	1	43	260	7.75
2023	AAA	Toledo	261	45	75	13	51	287	372	521	893	12	78	0.60	1	1	45	234	6.73

Monster season has him on the verge of MLB debut. Quick bat, plus raw power, and improved command of the strike zone fueled the breakout. Does a better job of keeping his weight back and then exploding into the zone and is significantly stronger. Defensive limitations prevented a late-season callup and bring into question his future defensive home.

King, Jr.,Lamar — 2 — San Diego

EXP MLB DEBUT: 2027 | H/W: 6-3 215 | FUT: Starting C | 8E

Bats R Age 20 — 2022 (4) HS (MD)

Pwr + + + / BAvg + + / Spd + + / Def + + +

Year	Lev	Team	AB	R	H	HR	RBI	Avg	OB	Slg	OPS	bb%	ct%	Eye	SB	CS	x/h%	Iso	RC/G
2022	Rk	ACL Padres	9	1	1	0	1	111	200	111	311	10	78	0.50	0	0	0	0	-0.77
2023	Rk	ACL Padres	68	14	22	0	10	324	432	397	829	16	66	0.57	5	1	14	74	6.75

Very raw prospect with limited pro time since 2022 draft. Has struggled with injuries, but nothing major. Has size and strength to be power-hitting backstop while defensive abilities give him even more upside. Agile and mobile, also has strong arm. Has showcased solid swing mechanics that lead to hard contact, but can be beaten with breaking balls.

Kjerstad,Heston — 379 — Baltimore

EXP MLB DEBUT: 2023 | H/W: 6-3 205 | FUT: Starting OF | 8C

Bats L Age 25 — 2020 (1) Arkansas

Pwr + + + + / BAvg + + + / Spd + + + / Def + + +

Year	Lev	Team	AB	R	H	HR	RBI	Avg	OB	Slg	OPS	bb%	ct%	Eye	SB	CS	x/h%	Iso	RC/G
2022	A	Delmarva	80	17	37	2	17	463	538	650	1188	14	79	0.76	0	0	30	188	10.82
2022	A+	Aberdeen	163	28	38	3	20	233	302	362	664	9	71	0.34	1	0	34	129	3.75
2023	AA	Bowie	184	30	57	11	23	310	362	576	938	8	83	0.48	3	3	42	266	6.88
2023	AAA	Norfolk Tides	295	57	88	10	32	298	357	498	855	8	77	0.39	2	1	39	200	6.18
2023	MLB	Baltimore	30	3	7	2	3	233	281	467	748	6	67	0.20	0	0	43	233	4.68

Proved health and made way to BAL. A quick bat allows him to flash power to all fields. He's skilled at getting the barrel to all parts of the zone, too. In a much smaller sample size than the rest of the team, he posted the highest average EV at 92.3 MPH in 21 batted ball events. Stellar approach is highlight and has even more power in tank.

Langford,Wyatt — 7 — Texas

EXP MLB DEBUT: 2024 | H/W: 6-1 225 | FUT: Starting OF | 9B

Bats R Age 22 — 2023 (1) Florida

Pwr + + + + / BAvg + + + + / Spd + + + / Def + +

Year	Lev	Team	AB	R	H	HR	RBI	Avg	OB	Slg	OPS	bb%	ct%	Eye	SB	CS	x/h%	Iso	RC/G
2023	NCAA	Florida	236	83	88	21	57	373	493	784	1277	19	81	1.27	9	1	59	411	11.87
2023	Rk	ACL Rangers	13	3	5	1	4	385	429	846	1275	7	77	0.33	1	0	80	462	11.57
2023	A+	Hickory	87	22	29	5	15	333	448	644	1091	17	79	1.00	7	1	52	310	9.61
2023	AA	Frisco	42	7	17	4	10	405	528	762	1290	21	83	1.57	1	2	41	357	11.92
2023	AAA	Round Rock	19	4	7	0	1	368	520	526	1046	24	68	1.00	3	0	43	158	10.46

Not unknown but still exploded into pro ball with white hot impact tools. Plus hit, plus power, plus run blankets profile and materialized consistently in-game. Ended debut year in Triple-A with more BB than K and a .677 SLG. Underlying data on EV, LA, SwK, ct, chase and flat platoon splits say he's a prohibitive top 3 prospect in MLB.

Lara,Luis — 8 — Milwaukee

EXP MLB DEBUT: 2026 | H/W: 5-7 155 | FUT: Starting CF | 8D

Bats B Age 19 — 2022 FA (VZ)

Pwr + + / BAvg + + + / Spd + + + + / Def + + +

Year	Lev	Team	AB	R	H	HR	RBI	Avg	OB	Slg	OPS	bb%	ct%	Eye	SB	CS	x/h%	Iso	RC/G
2022	Rk	DSL Brewers 1	200	39	52	2	21	260	330	385	715	10	86	0.75	7	7	33	125	4.60
2023	A	Carolina	274	55	78	2	21	285	374	354	728	12	83	0.85	22	9	18	69	4.82
2023	A+	Wisconsin	69	13	20	0	8	290	338	377	715	7	78	0.33	8	1	20	87	4.38

Enjoyed 1st year in US and made it to High-A late in season. Among fastest players in org and leverages it well on base and in CF. Has advanced knowledge of strike zone and should hit for BA due to ability to make loud contact. Questions remain on power development. Has bat speed but uses more of level swing path at present.

Lasko,Ryan — 8 — Oakland

EXP MLB DEBUT: 2025 | H/W: 6-0 190 | FUT: Starting OF | 7D

Bats R Age 21 — 2023 (2) Rutgers

Pwr + + / BAvg + + / Spd + + + + / Def + + +

Year	Lev	Team	AB	R	H	HR	RBI	Avg	OB	Slg	OPS	bb%	ct%	Eye	SB	CS	x/h%	Iso	RC/G
2023	NCAA	Rutgers	227	60	75	11	54	330	424	581	1006	14	85	1.09	18	2	43	251	8.17
2023	Rk	ACL Athletics	26	3	4	0	3	154	241	231	472	10	81	0.60	1	0	50	77	1.58

Fast, rangy CF who plays a professional game. Produces above tools with nifty plate approach and solid swing mechanics. Lack of bat speed hinders power production and can be victimized by velocity. Has outstanding speed and above average arm strength that leads to solid CF defense. Puts ball in play.

Laverde,Dario — 2 — Los Angeles (A)

EXP MLB DEBUT: 2026 | H/W: 5-10 160 | FUT: Starting C | 7E

Bats L Age 19
2022 FA (VZ)
Pwr ++
BAvg +++
Spd ++
Def +++

Year	Lev	Team	AB	R	H	HR	RBI	Avg	OB	Slg	OPS	bb%	ct%	Eye	SB	CS	x/h%	Iso	RC/G
2022	Rk	DSL Angels	151	35	45	0	28	298	384	404	788	12	87	1.11	9	4	22	106	5.69
2023	Rk	ACL Angels	134	23	41	1	32	306	426	455	881	17	77	0.90	7	3	34	149	7.19

Hit-first catching prospect hit for high BA in US debut at complex. Stocky frame at physical project. Patient approach with advanced zone discipline drove complex performance. Hitch in load will need to be worked out prior to upper minors. Power is limited based on present swing dynamics but could get to power with adjustments.

Lawlar,Jordan — 6 — Arizona

EXP MLB DEBUT: 2023 | H/W: 6-1 190 | FUT: Starting SS | 9C

Bats R Age 21
2021 (1) HS (TX)
Pwr +++
BAvg +++
Spd ++++
Def ++++

Year	Lev	Team	AB	R	H	HR	RBI	Avg	OB	Slg	OPS	bb%	ct%	Eye	SB	CS	x/h%	Iso	RC/G
2022	A+	Hillsboro	111	31	32	3	17	288	378	477	855	13	70	0.48	13	1	41	189	6.68
2022	AA	Amarillo	85	18	18	4	11	212	295	353	648	11	67	0.36	2	1	22	141	3.34
2023	AA	Amarillo	350	77	92	15	48	263	350	474	824	12	75	0.53	33	4	45	211	5.94
2023	AAA	Reno	67	18	24	5	19	358	434	612	1046	12	82	0.75	3	1	25	254	8.35
2023	MLB	Arizona	31	2	4	0	0	129	182	129	311	6	65	0.18	1	1	0	0	-1.65

Prized SS prospect barreled through upper minors, made major league debut. Terrific defense at short with great reactions, range, arm. Prolific base stealer. Disciplined batter with feel for strike zone, knows which pitches to drive, maximizes game power. Prone to bite on inside breaking balls. Pitch selection props up BA despite average contact%.

Ledbetter,Colton — 89 — Tampa Bay

EXP MLB DEBUT: 2026 | H/W: 6-2 205 | FUT: Starting OF | 7C

Bats L Age 22
2023 (2) Mississippi State
Pwr +++
BAvg +++
Spd +++
Def +++

Year	Lev	Team	AB	R	H	HR	RBI	Avg	OB	Slg	OPS	bb%	ct%	Eye	SB	CS	x/h%	Iso	RC/G
2023	NCAA	Mississippi St	197	52	63	12	52	320	451	574	1024	19	82	1.31	17	1	40	254	8.69
2023	Rk	FCL Rays	10	4	4	1	4	400	500	700	1200	17	90	2.00	1	0	25	300	10.16
2023	A	Charleston	63	11	16	1	8	254	356	397	753	14	75	0.63	2	2	44	143	5.21

Solid OF prospect played way up to 2nd round selection in 2023 draft. Average-to-above-average tools across the board, plays up due to baseball IQ. Upright, closed stance with easy trigger to hit position. Compact, slight uppercut swing. Not afraid to take what pitchers give and drive to opposite field. Could stick in CF long term.

Lee,Brooks — 6 — Minnesota

EXP MLB DEBUT: 2024 | H/W: 5-11 205 | FUT: Starting SS | 8A

Bats B Age 22
2022 (1) Cal Poly
Pwr +++
BAvg ++++
Spd ++
Def +++

Year	Lev	Team	AB	R	H	HR	RBI	Avg	OB	Slg	OPS	bb%	ct%	Eye	SB	CS	x/h%	Iso	RC/G
2022	Rk	FCL Twins	17	2	6	0	3	353	353	471	824	0	100		0	0	33	118	5.38
2022	A+	Cedar Rapids	97	14	28	4	12	289	389	454	843	14	81	0.89	0	2	29	165	6.16
2022	AA	Wichita	8	1	3	0	0	375	375	375	750	0	75	0.00	0	0	0	0	4.24
2023	AA	Wichita	349	63	102	11	61	292	367	476	842	11	82	0.65	6	4	41	183	6.05
2023	AAA	St. Paul	152	20	36	5	23	237	305	428	733	9	82	0.54	1	0	44	191	4.63

Fundamentally-sound INF who was promoted to AAA in August. Uses contact-oriented approach to complement ability to use all fields. Hits lots of doubles and adding strength to potentially get to above average power. Simply knows how to hit with keen pitch recognition. Not much of a runner and has range and hands for SS or 3B.

Lee,Hao Yu — 4 — Detroit

EXP MLB DEBUT: 2025 | H/W: 5-9 190 | FUT: Starting 2B | 7C

Bats R Age 21
2021 FA (TW)
Pwr ++
BAvg ++++
Spd ++
Def ++

Year	Lev	Team	AB	R	H	HR	RBI	Avg	OB	Slg	OPS	bb%	ct%	Eye	SB	CS	x/h%	Iso	RC/G
2022	A	Clearwater	258	37	73	7	50	283	371	415	785	12	78	0.63	10	7	26	132	5.42
2022	A+	Jersey Shore	35	5	9	1	2	257	350	486	836	13	74	0.56	3	0	56	229	6.30
2023	Rk	FCL Phillies	11	1	2	0	3	182	250	273	523	8	73	0.33	0	0	50	91	1.91
2023	A+	Jersey Shore	247	35	70	5	26	283	359	401	760	11	79	0.55	14	3	26	117	5.02
2023	A+	West Michigan	28	4	6	1	3	214	290	429	719	10	68	0.33	2	2	50	214	4.63

Acquired at the deadline for Michael Lorenzen. Strong bat-to-ball skills with good strike zone awareness. Crowds the plate with a simple leg kick and line-drive approach. Short, stocky frame results in below-average speed and range, limiting him to 2B. Size and fringe bat speed limit power upside, but there is more in the tank than many realize.

Leon,Pedro — 489 — Houston

EXP MLB DEBUT: 2024 | H/W: 5-8 170 | FUT: Reserve OF | 6C

Bats R Age 25
2021 FA (CU)
Pwr +++
BAvg +
Spd +++
Def +++

Year	Lev	Team	AB	R	H	HR	RBI	Avg	OB	Slg	OPS	bb%	ct%	Eye	SB	CS	x/h%	Iso	RC/G
2021	Rk	FCL Astros	9	0	2	0	1	222	222	222	444	0	78	0.00	1	0	0	0	0.46
2021	AA	Corpus Christi	185	29	46	9	33	249	338	443	781	12	64	0.37	13	8	37	195	5.64
2021	AAA	Sugar Land	61	11	8	0	2	131	293	164	457	19	62	0.61	4	2	25	33	0.79
2022	AAA	Sugar Land	413	71	94	17	63	228	341	431	772	15	65	0.49	38	18	50	203	5.61
2023	AAA	Sugar Land	483	74	118	21	72	244	332	435	766	12	67	0.39	21	7	40	190	5.29

2021 signee out of Cuba spent 2nd straight season at AAA. Has impressive raw power for size. Pull-oriented approach helps power output but makes him predictable. Susceptible to chasing breaking balls, struggles with contact%. SB volume took step backward, but made big improvements in efficiency. Solid speed, arm play well in OF.

Leonard,Eddys — 6 — Detroit

EXP MLB DEBUT: 2024 | H/W: 5-11 195 | FUT: Reserve SS | 6C

Bats R Age 23
2017 FA (DR)
Pwr +++
BAvg ++
Spd ++
Def +++

Year	Lev	Team	AB	R	H	HR	RBI	Avg	OB	Slg	OPS	bb%	ct%	Eye	SB	CS	x/h%	Iso	RC/G
2021	A	Rancho Cuca	261	59	77	14	57	295	376	544	920	12	72	0.46	6	2	45	249	7.31
2021	A+	Great Lakes	164	30	49	8	24	299	365	530	895	9	74	0.40	3	1	41	232	6.75
2022	A+	Great Lakes	496	80	131	15	61	264	325	435	761	8	76	0.38	4	4	39	171	4.94
2023	AA	Tulsa	350	37	89	11	44	254	311	411	723	8	76	0.34	3	3	36	157	4.38
2023	AAA	Toledo	149	30	45	8	31	302	373	530	904	10	75	0.46	2	1	40	228	6.82

Acquired from LA for cash after the Eduardo Rodriguez deal fell through. Plus bat speed and barrel awareness give him a chance to hit at the major league level. Not a true burner but runs well with enough range and arm to play SS, 3B, and 2B. Surprising pop from his frame and profiles as a super UT type.

Lile,Daylen — 78 — Washington

EXP MLB DEBUT: 2026 | H/W: 5-11 195 | FUT: Starting OF | 7C

Bats L Age 21
2021 (2) HS (KY)
Pwr ++
BAvg +++
Spd +++
Def ++

Year	Lev	Team	AB	R	H	HR	RBI	Avg	OB	Slg	OPS	bb%	ct%	Eye	SB	CS	x/h%	Iso	RC/G
2021	Rk	FCL Nationals	64	16	14	0	10	219	367	250	617	19	69	0.75	2	1	14	31	3.47
2023	A	Fredericksburg	251	49	73	7	48	291	380	510	890	13	77	0.62	21	3	47	219	6.95
2023	A+	Wilmington	154	16	36	2	18	234	306	357	663	9	73	0.39	2	3	33	123	3.80

Split seasons between A-ball levels with some success. Hit tool that made him a 2nd-rounder in 2021 came back after 2022 Tommy John surgery. How much power will develop is the question; showed it early but struggled at higher level. Sweet lefty swing, some base running ability but only marginal defender, so pop must come to reach everyday ceiling.

Lin,Sheng En — 68 — Cincinnati

EXP MLB DEBUT: 2027 | H/W: 5-11 185 | FUT: Starting OF | 8E

Bats L Age 18
2023 FA (TW)
Pwr ++
BAvg +++
Spd ++++
Def +++

Year	Lev	Team	AB	R	H	HR	RBI	Avg	OB	Slg	OPS	bb%	ct%	Eye	SB	CS	x/h%	Iso	RC/G

Two-way player signed for $1.2 million in last year's international class. Hasn't made pro debut. Bat appears ahead of arm. Hit over power approach, reportedly with good zone discipline and spray approach. A plus runner with solid range at SS and CF. Fits best in CF. Slim frame has room to grow into. Throws low 90s on mound with feel for spin.

Lipscomb,Trey — 3456 — Washington

EXP MLB DEBUT: 2024 | H/W: 6-2 200 | FUT: Utility player | 7C

Bats R Age 23
2022 (3) Tennessee
Pwr ++
BAvg +++
Spd +++
Def +++

Year	Lev	Team	AB	R	H	HR	RBI	Avg	OB	Slg	OPS	bb%	ct%	Eye	SB	CS	x/h%	Iso	RC/G
2022	NCAA	Tennessee	251	68	89	22	84	355	415	717	1132	9	85	0.70	4	1	49	363	9.16
2022	A	Fredericksburg	97	15	29	1	13	299	327	392	718	4	80	0.21	12	1	21	93	4.17
2023	A+	Wilmington	191	19	48	4	27	251	306	387	693	7	78	0.36	6	3	38	136	4.03
2023	AA	Harrisburg	320	40	91	10	45	284	310	438	748	4	81	0.20	4	3	30	153	4.43

Versatile, he played every infield position in first full pro season. Whippy swing from an upright stance that doesn't really engage his lower half, which limits his HR output. Makes good contact, but swing can get stiff. Runs a little, but calling card will be play-anywhere defense that is likely to manifest in a valuable utility player in MLB.

Liranzo,Thayron — 2 — Los Angeles (N)

EXP MLB DEBUT: 2026 | H/W: 6-3 195 | FUT: Starting C | 8D

Bats B Age 20
2020 FA (DR)
Pwr +++
BAvg ++
Spd +
Def +++

Year	Lev	Team	AB	R	H	HR	RBI	Avg	OB	Slg	OPS	bb%	ct%	Eye	SB	CS	x/h%	Iso	RC/G
2021	Rk	DSL Dodgers S	68	11	17	1	9	250	378	353	731	17	71	0.70	3	1	29	103	5.04
2022	Rk	ACL Dodgers	148	23	35	8	30	236	331	486	818	12	72	0.50	0	0	57	250	5.90
2023	A	Rancho Cuca	345	81	94	24	70	272	395	562	957	17	68	0.63	2	1	53	290	8.23

Teen backstop had a breakout campaign, mashing home runs and posting a .962 OPS. Switch-hitter has good bat speed and plus raw power, but there is some chase and swing-and-miss especially vs LHP (30% K rate). Moves well behind the plate with a large, athletic frame, sub-2.00 pop time, and a strong arm. Still raw, but tons of upside.

Locklear,Tyler

3	Seattle	EXP MLB DEBUT: 2025	H/W: 6-1 210	FUT: Starting 1B	7C

Bats R Age 23	Year	Lev	Team	AB	R	H	HR	RBI	Avg	OB	Slg	OPS	bb%	ct%	Eye	SB	CS	x/h%	Iso	RC/G
2022 (2) VCU	2022	Rk	ACL Mariners	6	0	2	0	2	333	429	500	929	14	83	1.00	0	0	50	167	7.60
Pwr ++++	2022	A	Modesto	117	19	33	7	29	282	323	504	827	6	75	0.24	0	0	36	222	5.48
BAvg +++	2023	Rk	ACL Mariners	6	0	0	0	0	0	0	0	0	0	67	0.00	0	0		0	-6.12
Spd ++	2023	A+	Everett	226	40	69	12	44	305	401	549	949	14	73	0.60	10	0	45	243	7.73
Def ++	2023	AA	Arkansas	77	11	20	1	8	260	352	403	755	13	82	0.79	2	0	40	143	5.20

Moved to 1B full-time and had breakout season with bat. Makes easy, hard contact and has bat speed and strength to project to plus power. Could hit 30 HR in time but will need to close holes in swing. Pitch recognition a little short but has quick stroke to make up for mistakes. Not much speed and relies on instincts. Poor defender with strong arm.

Loftin,Nick

345	Kansas City	EXP MLB DEBUT: 2023	H/W: 5-11 180	FUT: Utility player	7A

Bats R Age 25	Year	Lev	Team	AB	R	H	HR	RBI	Avg	OB	Slg	OPS	bb%	ct%	Eye	SB	CS	x/h%	Iso	RC/G
2020 (1) Baylor	2022	AA	NW Arkansas	363	78	98	12	47	270	350	421	772	11	84	0.79	24	4	31	152	5.17
Pwr +++	2022	AAA	Omaha	153	26	33	5	19	216	264	359	623	6	73	0.24	5	2	36	144	2.96
BAvg +++	2023	Rk	ACL Royals B	17	10	8	1	5	471	609	706	1315	26	76	1.50	1	0	25	235	13.36
Spd +++	2023	AAA	Omaha	315	41	85	14	56	270	341	444	785	10	85	0.72	6	4	32	175	5.19
Def +++	2023	MLB	Kansas City	62	10	20	0	10	323	364	435	799	6	81	0.33	2	0	30	113	5.41

Short, fundamentally-sound INF who debuted in majors in 2023. His defensive versatility means that as long a his strong hit tool continues to play, he'll keep finding AB. There's some pop, but not a big power threat. Best as a utility option. Puts bat to ball with ease and leverages polished instincts to exceed tools. Runs bases aggressively with average speed.

Lombard Jr.,George

6	New York (A)	EXP MLB DEBUT: 2026	H/W: 6-3 190	FUT: Starting SS	8D

Bats R Age 18	Year	Lev	Team	AB	R	H	HR	RBI	Avg	OB	Slg	OPS	bb%	ct%	Eye	SB	CS	x/h%	Iso	RC/G
2023 (1) HS (FL)																				
Pwr +++																				
BAvg +++																				
Spd +++	2023	Rk	FCL Yankees	12	3	5	0	2	417	588	500	1088	29	83	2.50	3	0	20	83	10.59
Def +++	2023	A	Tampa	33	6	9	0	4	273	415	303	718	20	70	0.80	1	2	11	30	5.01

Athletic, 2nd generation SS prospect made pro debut after ascent up draft boards. High waisted frame with room to grow. Above-average raw tools across the board. Upright stance with easy trigger. Utilizes lower half well, achieving leverage in swing. Gap-to-gap approach with advanced eye. Works counts. Power will come with adjustments. Sticks at SS.

Loperfido,Joey

34789	Houston	EXP MLB DEBUT: 2024	H/W: 6-3 220	FUT: Utility player	7E

Bats L Age 25	Year	Lev	Team	AB	R	H	HR	RBI	Avg	OB	Slg	OPS	bb%	ct%	Eye	SB	CS	x/h%	Iso	RC/G
2021 (7) Duke	2022	A	Fayetteville	296	51	90	9	45	304	387	473	860	12	74	0.53	30	9	32	169	6.48
Pwr +++	2022	A+	Asheville	96	19	34	3	24	354	431	552	983	12	74	0.52	2	2	35	198	8.22
BAvg +	2023	A+	Asheville	34	4	9	1	5	265	306	529	835	6	76	0.25	3	0	56	265	5.94
Spd +++	2023	AA	Corpus Christi	314	60	93	19	57	296	388	548	936	13	74	0.58	20	3	43	252	7.41
Def +++	2023	AAA	Sugar Land	119	15	28	5	16	235	326	403	729	12	62	0.36	4	1	36	168	4.92

Versatile prospect with impact power, impressive speed. Altered swing at Double-A to get more loft, with encouraging results. However, plate discipline took step backward at Triple-A, with more chase, less contact. Returned to GB tilt as a result, needs to regain discipline against more advanced stuff.

Lopez,Dariel

56	San Francisco	EXP MLB DEBUT: 2025	H/W: 6-1 183	FUT: Starting 3B	7C

Bats R Age 22	Year	Lev	Team	AB	R	H	HR	RBI	Avg	OB	Slg	OPS	bb%	ct%	Eye	SB	CS	x/h%	Iso	RC/G
2018 FA (DR)																				
Pwr +++																				
BAvg ++	2021	A	Bradenton	361	52	93	10	64	258	333	393	727	10	71	0.40	1	2	30	136	4.60
Spd +	2022	A+	Greensboro	391	58	112	19	58	286	323	476	799	5	73	0.20	6	4	31	189	5.20
Def +++	2023	--	Did Not Play																	

Missed all of 2023 with dislocated right knee. Chosen from PIT in minor league Rule 5. Has tremendous raw power with quick wrists in handsy swing. Has pop to opp field. Lacks disciplined approach and can be free swinger. Doesn't run particularly well and not much of threat on base. Likely to move off SS to 3B full-time with good arm.

Lopez,Fabian

6	Miami	EXP MLB DEBUT: 2027	H/W: 6-0 165	FUT: Starting SS	7E

Bats B Age 18	Year	Lev	Team	AB	R	H	HR	RBI	Avg	OB	Slg	OPS	bb%	ct%	Eye	SB	CS	x/h%	Iso	RC/G
2023 FA (DR)																				
Pwr +++																				
BAvg +++																				
Spd +++																				
Def ++++	2023	Rk	DSL Miami	200	28	53	4	22	265	319	405	724	7	74	0.30	15	5	34	140	4.49

Defensively skilled SS flashed above-average power potential in pro debut. Athletic, twitchy frame with lots of body maturing yet to do. Open stance with some mechanical issues to work out in load. Utilizes leverage well in lower half, getting to lofted contact. Aggressive approach, struggled with spin recognition. Above-average runner.

Lopez,Jesus

2	Texas	EXP MLB DEBUT: 2027	H/W: 6-1 180	FUT: Starting C	7E

Bats L Age 18	Year	Lev	Team	AB	R	H	HR	RBI	Avg	OB	Slg	OPS	bb%	ct%	Eye	SB	CS	x/h%	Iso	RC/G
2022 FA (VZ)																				
Pwr +++																				
BAvg +++	2022	Rk	DSL Rangers	1	0	1	0	1	1000	###	###	2000	0	100		0	0	0	0	16.32
Spd ++	2022	Rk	DSL Rangers 2	109	13	25	3	16	229	359	385	744	17	84	1.29	4	3	44	156	5.22
Def ++	2023	Rk	ACL Rangers	45	8	13	3	8	289	360	644	1004	10	71	0.38	0	0	62	356	8.52

In stateside debut, showcased huge plus raw and ability to hit premium velo & spin. Hit and receiving quite raw, meaning floor is non-C stuck in A+, but moves well behind dish for bottom-of-barrel speed with 60-grade arm & barrel manipulating ability. Yes, teenage catchers, but profile could explode if he hits in A-ball.

Lopez,Otto

46	Toronto	EXP MLB DEBUT: 2021	H/W: 5-10 185	FUT: Utility player	6B

Bats R Age 25	Year	Lev	Team	AB	R	H	HR	RBI	Avg	OB	Slg	OPS	bb%	ct%	Eye	SB	CS	x/h%	Iso	RC/G
2016 FA (DR)	2021	MLB	Toronto	1	0	0	0	0	0	0	0	0	0	0	0.00	0	0		0	
Pwr +	2022	A	Dunedin	20	0	1	0	2	50	136	50	186	9	80	0.50	0	0	0	0	-2.20
BAvg +++	2022	AAA	Buffalo	340	53	101	3	34	297	373	415	787	11	82	0.67	14	5	28	118	5.49
Spd +++	2022	MLB	Toronto	9	0	6	0	3	667	700	667	1367	10	89	1.00	0	1	0	0	11.90
Def +++	2023	AAA	Buffalo	318	48	82	2	35	258	308	343	651	7	83	0.42	13	4	21	85	3.57

Contact-oriented INF who spent time in majors in 2021 and 2022 but not in 2023. Oblique strain ended season in August. Very versatile with ability to play multiple positions. Makes very easy contact with short swing and hits a lot of groundballs in order to use speed. Severe lack of pop but gets on base to use speed.

Luciano,Marco

6	San Francisco	EXP MLB DEBUT: 2023	H/W: 6-1 178	FUT: Starting SS	8B

Bats R Age 22	Year	Lev	Team	AB	R	H	HR	RBI	Avg	OB	Slg	OPS	bb%	ct%	Eye	SB	CS	x/h%	Iso	RC/G
2018 FA (DR)	2022	Rk	ACL Giants B	22	6	7	1	6	318	423	545	969	15	68	0.57	0	0	43	227	8.46
Pwr ++++	2022	A+	Eugene	205	27	54	10	30	263	335	459	793	10	75	0.43	0	0	37	195	5.31
BAvg +++	2023	AA	Richmond	202	32	46	11	32	228	345	450	795	15	64	0.50	6	0	50	223	5.90
Spd ++	2023	AAA	Sacramento	67	10	14	4	8	209	312	418	730	13	58	0.36	0	0	43	209	5.05
Def ++	2023	MLB	San Francisco	39	4	9	0	0	231	333	308	641	13	56	0.35	1	0	33	77	4.11

High-upside prospect who reached majors and struggled but can be building block for future. Exhibits exceptional bat speed and outstanding power potential. Uses entire field, though BA may be in question due to overly aggressive approach and K rate. Has slowed down and may have to move off SS due to fringy range.

Luis,Jansel

46	Arizona	EXP MLB DEBUT: 2026	H/W: 6-0 170	FUT: Starting 2B	8D

Bats B Age 19	Year	Lev	Team	AB	R	H	HR	RBI	Avg	OB	Slg	OPS	bb%	ct%	Eye	SB	CS	x/h%	Iso	RC/G
2022 FA (DR)	2022	Rk	DSL Dbacks	13	2	6	0	4	462	462	538	1000	0	85	0.00	1	0	17	77	7.13
Pwr +++	2022	Rk	DSL Dbacks 2	161	33	54	1	14	335	382	404	785	7	87	0.57	8	3	15	68	5.17
BAvg +++	2023	Rk	ACL Dbacks	2	1	1	0	0	500	667	###	1667	33	100		1	0	100	500	17.46
Spd ++	2023	Rk	ACL DBacks R	92	17	26	3	12	283	340	467	807	8	83	0.50	8	2	38	185	5.46
Def ++	2023	A	Visalia	144	19	37	4	15	257	296	417	713	5	76	0.23	7	2	32	160	4.16

18-year-old INF prospect earned 36 A-ball games. Results out-paced underlying plate manners given so-so contact, aggressive approach. Drives pitches to all fields, lefty swing generates loft. Room to add to frame, could reach plus power. Has athleticism to stay up the middle. On encouraging trajectory with intriguing upside.

Mack,Joe

2	Miami	EXP MLB DEBUT: 2025	H/W: 6-1 210	FUT: Reserve C	6C

Bats L Age 21	Year	Lev	Team	AB	R	H	HR	RBI	Avg	OB	Slg	OPS	bb%	ct%	Eye	SB	CS	x/h%	Iso	RC/G
2021 (1) HS (NY)																				
Pwr ++	2021	Rk	FCL Marlins	53	9	7	1	2	132	370	208	577	27	58	0.91	0	1	29	75	2.60
BAvg ++	2022	Rk	FCL Marlins	27	2	8	2	3	296	387	519	906	13	74	0.57	0	0	25	222	6.81
Spd ++	2022	A	Jupiter	121	18	28	3	12	231	380	355	735	19	67	0.73	0	0	29	124	5.16
Def +++	2023	A+	Beloit	449	46	98	6	36	218	285	287	572	9	74	0.36	0	0	19	69	2.43

Once promising catching prospect has struggled to hit as pro. Long, athletic frame for catcher. Defense currently carries profile. At plate, upright, open stance with hands high, which produces linear swing plane. Bat struggles to get to hard contact and has swing and miss issues despite a quicker swing. Above-average power in frame doesn't play.

Made,Kevin | 456 | Washington

EXP MLB DEBUT: 2024 | H/W: 5-9 160 | FUT: Utility player | 7C

Bats R Age 21	Year	Lev	Team	AB	R	H	HR	RBI	Avg	OB	Slg	OPS	bb%	ct%	Eye	SB	CS	x/h%	Iso	RC/G
2019 FA (DR)	2021	A	Myrtle Beach	235	19	64	1	20	272	290	366	656	2	76	0.11	2	0	27	94	3.38
Pwr +++	2022	A	Myrtle Beach	222	41	59	9	30	266	345	450	796	11	78	0.55	0	1	39	185	5.43
BAvg ++	2022	A+	South Bend	130	14	21	1	14	162	268	246	515	13	76	0.61	3	0	38	85	1.97
Spd +++	2023	A+	South Bend	262	39	63	3	25	240	318	355	673	10	79	0.56	3	4	35	115	4.00
Def +++	2023	A+	Wilmington	73	5	10	0	5	137	232	192	423	11	75	0.50	1	0	40	55	0.69

Very good defender who played all over the infield, but who struggled with the bat after coming to WAS in the Jeimer Candelario trade. Needs to make better use of his solid bat-to-ball skills and power that could get him to double digit HR in the majors. Good eye, runs well but not a base stealer. Could well end up a play-all-over utility guy.

Malloy,Justyn Henry | 57 | Detroit

EXP MLB DEBUT: 2024 | H/W: 6-1 212 | FUT: Starting OF | 7C

Bats R Age 24	Year	Lev	Team	AB	R	H	HR	RBI	Avg	OB	Slg	OPS	bb%	ct%	Eye	SB	CS	x/h%	Iso	RC/G
2021 (6) Georgia Tech	2021	A	Augusta	122	23	33	5	21	270	390	434	825	16	75	0.80	4	2	30	164	6.09
Pwr ++++	2022	A+	Rome	263	51	80	10	44	304	410	479	889	15	72	0.64	3	0	33	175	7.05
BAvg +++	2022	AA	Mississippi	190	35	51	6	31	268	403	421	824	18	68	0.72	0	0	33	153	6.43
Spd +	2022	AAA	Gwinnett	25	5	7	1	6	280	438	440	878	22	80	1.40	2	0	29	160	7.04
Def +	2023	AAA	Toledo	487	89	135	23	83	277	410	474	885	18	69	0.72	5	1	36	197	7.22

Led all minor leaguers with 110 walks and 2,654 pitches seen and owns a career .411 OBP. Will not expand the zone, instead hunting for mistakes he can drive to the pull side. Bails a bit on swing resulting in too many GB, but has plus power when he gets the ball in the air. Well below average defense leaves him without a clear path to FT AB.

Manzardo,Kyle | 3 | Cleveland

EXP MLB DEBUT: 2024 | H/W: 6-0 205 | FUT: Starting 1B | 7A

Bats L Age 23	Year	Lev	Team	AB	R	H	HR	RBI	Avg	OB	Slg	OPS	bb%	ct%	Eye	SB	CS	x/h%	Iso	RC/G
2021 (2) Washington State	2022	A+	Bowling Green	225	53	74	17	55	329	441	636	1076	17	80	0.98	0	0	46	307	9.20
Pwr +++	2022	AA	Montgomery	99	18	32	5	26	323	407	576	983	12	81	0.74	1	1	47	253	7.86
BAvg ++++	2023	Rk	ACL Indians	8	1	0	0	1	0	111	0	111	11	88	1.00	0	0		0	-2.31
Spd +	2023	AAA	Columbus	78	16	20	6	16	256	356	590	945	13	82	0.86	0	0	70	333	7.30
Def ++	2023	AAA	Durham	265	33	63	11	38	238	342	442	784	14	75	0.65	1	1	49	204	5.46

Offensive 1B who had big struggle in BA due to shoulder injury. Acquired from TAM in July, had issues with LHP. Still, combines disciplined approach with quick stroke to profile well with BA and power. Secondary skills are well below average. Has no foot speed and stuck at 1B with below average arm. Draws lot of walks and makes contact.

Marsee,Jakob | 8 | San Diego

EXP MLB DEBUT: 2024 | H/W: 6-0 180 | FUT: Starting CF | 7B

Bats L Age 22	Year	Lev	Team	AB	R	H	HR	RBI	Avg	OB	Slg	OPS	bb%	ct%	Eye	SB	CS	x/h%	Iso	RC/G
2022 (6) Central Michigan	2022	NCAA	Central Michigan	229	60	79	7	66	345	457	550	1007	17	86	1.42	18	3	34	205	8.48
Pwr ++	2022	Rk	ACL Padres	33	13	7	0	3	212	447	303	750	30	70	1.40	3	0	29	91	5.87
BAvg +++	2022	A	Lake Elsinore	67	18	17	2	8	254	398	463	860	19	78	1.07	12	1	53	209	6.85
Spd +++	2023	A+	Fort Wayne	400	91	109	13	41	273	402	425	827	18	80	1.06	41	9	29	153	6.24
Def +++	2023	AA	San Antonio	56	12	16	3	5	286	403	446	849	16	73	0.73	5	0	19	161	6.34

Emerging OF who was MVP of AFL after leading MWL in OBP. Led org in SB with aggressive game. Sees lot of pitches with discerning eye and has plus understanding of strike zone. Starting to hit for pop with tweaked swing mechanics, though more about contact and hitting gaps. Plays sound defense in CF with average range and arm.

Marte,Noelvi | 56 | Cincinnati

EXP MLB DEBUT: 2023 | H/W: 6-0 216 | FUT: Starting 3B | 9C

Bats R Age 22	Year	Lev	Team	AB	R	H	HR	RBI	Avg	OB	Slg	OPS	bb%	ct%	Eye	SB	CS	x/h%	Iso	RC/G
2018 FA (DR)	2022	A+	Dayton	106	12	31	4	13	292	390	443	834	14	78	0.74	10	3	26	151	6.05
Pwr ++++	2023	Rk	ACL Reds	9	1	2	0	0	222	300	222	522	10	89	1.00	0	0	0	0	2.41
BAvg +++	2023	AA	Chattanooga	196	37	55	8	25	281	353	464	817	10	81	0.58	10	2	35	184	5.64
Spd ++++	2023	AAA	Louisville	143	31	40	3	20	280	368	455	823	12	78	0.65	8	2	40	175	6.02
Def +++	2023	MLB	Cincinnati	114	15	36	3	15	316	361	456	817	7	78	0.32	6	2	28	140	5.50

Muscular IF elevated prospect stock by improving frequency of hard contact, earning MLB debut. Developed physique, near physical projection. Open stance with bat wiggle and minimal load. Unleashes swing with plus-plus bat speed on linear swing plane. EV rates and frame suggest plus power. Presently, too much topspin-heavy contact. Plus runner.

Martin,Austin | 4 | Minnesota

EXP MLB DEBUT: 2024 | H/W: 6-0 185 | FUT: Starting 2B | 7C

Bats R Age 25	Year	Lev	Team	AB	R	H	HR	RBI	Avg	OB	Slg	OPS	bb%	ct%	Eye	SB	CS	x/h%	Iso	RC/G
2020 (1) Vanderbilt	2022	Rk	FCL Twins	8	1	2	0	3	250	400	375	775	20	88	2.00	1	1	50	125	6.05
Pwr ++	2022	AA	Wichita	336	59	81	2	32	241	334	315	650	12	84	0.87	34	5	22	74	3.90
BAvg +++	2023	Rk	FCL Twins	7	2	3	1	1	429	556	857	1413	22	86	2.00	2	0	33	429	13.07
Spd ++++	2023	A	Fort Myers	19	0	3	0	1	158	200	158	358	5	89	0.50	1	0	0	0	0.34
Def +++	2023	AAA	St. Paul	205	33	54	6	28	263	373	405	778	15	79	0.84	16	4	31	141	5.46

Continues to miss time with various injuries but had solid season upon returning in July. Makes elite contact with simple stroke and starting to add to power arsenal. Set high in HR despite limited AB. Walks at very high level and has plus speed on base. Played mostly 2B in 23 and may see time in CF going forward. Versatile utility type.

Martin,Walker | 6 | San Francisco

EXP MLB DEBUT: 2027 | H/W: 6-2 188 | FUT: Starting 3B | 8D

Bats L Age 20	Year	Lev	Team	AB	R	H	HR	RBI	Avg	OB	Slg	OPS	bb%	ct%	Eye	SB	CS	x/h%	Iso	RC/G
2023 (2) HS (CO)																				
Pwr ++																				
BAvg +++																				
Spd +++																				
Def +++	2023	--	Did Not Play																	

Projectable athlete with good nose for game, yet current present ability to succeed. May not have a plus tool at disposal but has solid hitting mechanics with clean defensive actions. Level swing path and gap approach mute power upside, but more leverage could change that outlook. Likely to move to 3B long-term with good range and arm.

Martinez,Angel | 456 | Cleveland

EXP MLB DEBUT: 2024 | H/W: 6-0 200 | FUT: Starting 2B | 7B

Bats B Age 22	Year	Lev	Team	AB	R	H	HR	RBI	Avg	OB	Slg	OPS	bb%	ct%	Eye	SB	CS	x/h%	Iso	RC/G
2018 FA (DR)	2021	A	Lynchburg	377	62	91	7	46	241	319	382	701	10	77	0.49	13	6	36	141	4.31
Pwr ++	2022	A+	Lake County	281	46	81	10	27	288	377	477	854	12	79	0.69	10	6	37	189	6.30
BAvg +++	2022	AA	Akron	82	10	20	3	17	244	340	451	792	13	78	0.67	2	1	50	207	5.55
Spd +++	2023	AA	Akron	383	55	94	11	60	245	312	392	704	9	78	0.45	10	3	32	146	4.19
Def +++	2023	AAA	Columbus	142	17	38	3	19	268	316	401	717	7	75	0.28	1	0	32	134	4.31

Instinctual, quick INF who does everything well except hit for power. Has some pop in game, though makes easy contact from both sides with quick hands/wrists. Set high in HR but also expanded strike zone and raised K rate. Could stand to drive ball more. Possesses good speed and is solid defender at any INF spot.

Martinez,Gabriel | 79 | Toronto

EXP MLB DEBUT: 2025 | H/W: 5-9 170 | FUT: Starting OF | 7E

Bats R Age 21	Year	Lev	Team	AB	R	H	HR	RBI	Avg	OB	Slg	OPS	bb%	ct%	Eye	SB	CS	x/h%	Iso	RC/G
2018 FA (VZ)	2021	A	Dunedin	12	1	4	0	1	333	385	417	801	8	67	0.25	0	1	25	83	5.93
Pwr ++	2022	Rk	FCL Blue Jays	10	1	1	0	0	100	182	200	382	9	80	0.50	1	0	100	100	0.41
BAvg +++	2022	A	Dunedin	240	46	69	11	46	288	347	483	831	8	81	0.49	3	1	36	196	5.67
Spd ++	2022	A+	Vancouver	102	11	33	3	13	324	378	490	869	8	83	0.53	0	0	33	167	6.19
Def ++	2023	A+	Vancouver	409	58	99	12	49	242	295	374	670	7	82	0.42	2	2	28	132	3.68

Burgeoning OF who spent all year in High-A and showed enough to stay a prospect. Tinkered with swing to take advantage of added strength. Impressive athlete and has feel for contact in simple approach. Doesn't have plus tool in arsenal. Because contact is solid, he won't draw many walks. Getting to average power would help.

Martinez,Orelvis | 456 | Toronto

EXP MLB DEBUT: 2024 | H/W: 5-11 200 | FUT: Starting 3B | 8D

Bats R Age 22	Year	Lev	Team	AB	R	H	HR	RBI	Avg	OB	Slg	OPS	bb%	ct%	Eye	SB	CS	x/h%	Iso	RC/G
2018 FA (DR)	2021	A	Dunedin	283	49	79	19	68	279	354	572	927	10	70	0.39	4	1	54	293	7.39
Pwr ++++	2021	A+	Vancouver	112	17	24	9	19	214	279	491	770	8	75	0.36	0	1	54	277	4.77
BAvg ++	2022	AA	New Hampshire	433	57	88	30	76	203	271	446	716	8	68	0.29	6	3	51	242	4.24
Spd ++	2023	AA	New Hampshire	239	33	54	17	46	226	339	485	825	15	75	0.68	0	0	50	259	5.85
Def ++	2023	AAA	Buffalo	209	37	55	11	48	263	345	507	852	11	68	0.39	2	0	51	244	6.48

Slugger who got off to very slow start and ended in AAA. Led org in HR and RBI and continues to show massive power to all fields. Exhibits patient approach to find ideal pitches and then turns on them for hard contact. Lot of swing and miss. Has hit at least 28 HR in each of last 3 seasons. Continues to play SS but likely to go to 3B or 2B.

Martinez,Orlando | 79 | Los Angeles (A)

EXP MLB DEBUT: 2024 | H/W: 6-0 185 | FUT: Reserve OF | 6C

Bats L Age 26	Year	Lev	Team	AB	R	H	HR	RBI	Avg	OB	Slg	OPS	bb%	ct%	Eye	SB	CS	x/h%	Iso	RC/G
2017 FA (CU)	2022	Rk	ACL Angels	11	4	5	0	2	455	500	727	1227	8	64	0.25	0	0	60	273	13.24
Pwr ++	2022	AA	Rocket City	141	25	43	4	33	305	384	454	838	11	77	0.55	6	4	28	149	6.08
BAvg +++	2022	AAA	Salt Lake	244	27	61	5	34	250	304	393	698	7	76	0.32	3	3	34	143	4.11
Spd +++	2023	AA	Rocket City	292	33	78	9	55	267	323	445	768	8	78	0.38	6	3	38	178	4.98
Def +++	2023	AAA	Salt Lake	147	20	36	3	15	245	311	374	685	9	80	0.47	2	1	36	129	4.00

Older prospect running out of time to develop into regular contributor. Open stance with moderate leg kick and direct load to hit position. It's a linear swing with groundball and line drive tendencies. There's above-average strength in frame, hasn't brought it to the game. Aggressive approach, will expand the zone. Limited to COF defensively.

Martorella,Nathan — 37 — San Diego

EXP MLB DEBUT: 2025 | H/W: 6-1 224 | FUT: Starting 1B | 7C

Bats L Age 23
2022 (5) California
Pwr +++
BAvg +++
Spd +
Def ++

Year	Lev	Team	AB	R	H	HR	RBI	Avg	OB	Slg	OPS	bb%	ct%	Eye	SB	CS	x/h%	Iso	RC/G
2022	NCAA	California	228	47	76	11	46	333	420	553	972	13	87	1.17	1	0	36	219	7.63
2022	Rk	ACL Padres	31	4	12	1	10	387	457	613	1070	11	81	0.67	0	0	42	226	9.02
2022	A	Lake Elsinore	59	10	17	2	11	288	408	458	866	17	75	0.80	0	0	35	169	6.78
2023	A+	Fort Wayne	398	71	103	16	73	259	374	450	823	15	78	0.84	5	3	42	191	6.04
2023	AA	San Antonio	89	12	21	3	15	236	306	382	688	9	84	0.64	0	0	33	146	4.05

Big and strong, he was 2nd in org in HR. Fits profile of LHH masher with high OBP ability. Can also hit LHP with advanced swing and instincts. Bat speed is fringe-average; he draws tons of walks with patient approach and rarely chases out of zone. Secondary skills are lacking and likely to end up at 1B full-time.

Matthews,Brice — 6 — Houston

EXP MLB DEBUT: 2025 | H/W: 6-0 190 | FUT: Starting SS | 8D

Bats R Age 22
2023 (1) Nebraska
Pwr ++++
BAvg ++
Spd +++
Def +++

Year	Lev	Team	AB	R	H	HR	RBI	Avg	OB	Slg	OPS	bb%	ct%	Eye	SB	CS	x/h%	Iso	RC/G
2023	NCAA	Nebraska	206	61	74	20	67	359	478	723	1202	19	74	0.89	20	7	45	364	11.19
2023	Rk	FCL Astros	5	0	0	0	0	0	167	0	167	17	80	1.00	2	1		0	-2.27
2023	A	Fayetteville	120	22	26	4	11	217	347	367	714	17	67	0.60	16	3	38	150	4.70

Burst onto radar with improved hit, power output. Excellent athlete with swift bat speed, has plus raw power to all fields. Strong pitch zone recognition. Quiet setup but contact skills took step back in pro ball, hit tool likely average. Rangy defender capable of big plays, though fielding is occasionally sloppy. Potent basestealer.

Mauricio,Ronny — 4567 — New York (N)

EXP MLB DEBUT: 2023 | H/W: 6-3 166 | FUT: Starting MIF | 8C

Bats B Age 23
2017 FA (DR)
Pwr ++++
BAvg ++
Spd +++
Def +++

Year	Lev	Team	AB	R	H	HR	RBI	Avg	OB	Slg	OPS	bb%	ct%	Eye	SB	CS	x/h%	Iso	RC/G
2021	A+	Brooklyn	392	55	95	19	63	242	286	449	735	6	74	0.24	9	7	40	207	4.39
2021	AA	Binghamton	31	3	10	1	1	323	364	452	815	6	65	0.18	2	0	20	129	5.94
2022	AA	Binghamton	509	71	132	26	89	259	293	472	764	5	75	0.19	20	11	41	212	4.67
2023	AAA	Syracuse	490	76	143	23	71	292	339	506	845	7	80	0.36	24	7	39	214	5.78
2023	MLB	New York (N)	101	11	25	2	9	248	296	347	643	6	69	0.23	7	0	24	99	3.30

Switch-hitting power prospect had okay showing during MLB callup. Aggressive approach with tendency to chase. Open, upright stance from both sides of plate has moderate leg kick prior to swing, squaring up lower half. Linear swing but hits snot out of ball upon contact; it's plus power if ct% allows it. Reactions play up speed on bases.

Mayea,Brando — 8 — New York (A)

EXP MLB DEBUT: 2027 | H/W: 5-11 175 | FUT: Starting OF | 8E

Bats R Age 18
2023 FA (CU)
Pwr +++
BAvg +++
Spd ++++
Def +++

Year	Lev	Team	AB	R	H	HR	RBI	Avg	OB	Slg	OPS	bb%	ct%	Eye	SB	CS	x/h%	Iso	RC/G
2023	Rk	DSL Yankees 2	145	27	40	3	18	276	371	400	771	13	81	0.81	22	7	28	124	5.34

Quick twitch, toolsy OF prospect made pro debut in the Dominican Summer League. Shorter frame with lean build. Will grow into strength. Upright, open stance with slight bat wrap on trigger. Aggressive approach with linear swing plane. Lots of groundball contact present but above-average power should come. Double-plus runner with raw SB attributes.

Mayer,Marcelo — 6 — Boston

EXP MLB DEBUT: 2025 | H/W: 6-2 188 | FUT: Starting SS | 9C

Bats L Age 21
2021 (1) HS (CA)
Pwr +++
BAvg +++
Spd ++
Def +++

Year	Lev	Team	AB	R	H	HR	RBI	Avg	OB	Slg	OPS	bb%	ct%	Eye	SB	CS	x/h%	Iso	RC/G
2021	Rk	FCL Red Sox	91	25	25	3	17	275	377	440	817	14	70	0.56	7	1	32	165	6.08
2022	A	Salem	252	46	72	9	40	286	406	504	910	17	69	0.65	16	0	50	218	7.68
2022	A+	Greenville	98	15	26	4	13	265	374	449	823	15	70	0.59	1	0	35	184	6.14
2023	A+	Greenville	145	23	42	7	34	290	364	524	888	10	74	0.46	5	2	45	234	6.72
2023	AA	Portland	169	20	32	6	20	189	255	355	610	8	71	0.31	4	3	47	166	2.88

Dynamic, multi-tooled SS with advanced skills and penchant for making impact with bat and glove. Very smart hitter with quick stroke and plus power potential. Can focus too much on contact and take weak hack. Recognizes spin and has frame to add strength. Leverages natural quickness and plus arm to be solid SS.

Mayo,Coby — 35 — Baltimore

EXP MLB DEBUT: 2024 | H/W: 6-5 230 | FUT: Starting 3B | 9D

Bats R Age 22
2020 (4) HS (FL)
Pwr ++++
BAvg +++
Spd ++
Def +++

Year	Lev	Team	AB	R	H	HR	RBI	Avg	OB	Slg	OPS	bb%	ct%	Eye	SB	CS	x/h%	Iso	RC/G
2022	Rk	FCL Orioles B	5	1	0	0	0	0	167	0	167	17	60	0.50	0	0		0	-4.34
2022	A+	Aberdeen	255	50	64	14	49	251	323	494	817	10	76	0.44	5	1	50	243	5.64
2022	AA	Bowie	128	21	32	5	20	250	314	398	713	9	61	0.24	0	0	28	148	4.63
2023	AA	Bowie	287	48	88	17	44	307	411	603	1014	15	70	0.59	4	1	56	296	8.95
2023	AAA	Norfolk Tides	217	36	58	12	55	267	386	512	898	16	71	0.68	1	0	48	244	7.18

EL MVP with improved plate patience. Power is the name of the game here. He can hit the ball a very long way, which, when coupled with his penchant for drawing walks at a high rate, give him the upside of a power hitting asset. His defensive home will be in question thanks to a crowded and youthful Orioles infield.

McCabe,David — 5 — Atlanta

EXP MLB DEBUT: 2025 | H/W: 6-3 230 | FUT: Starting OF | 7D

Bats B Age 24
2022 (4) Charlotte
Pwr +++
BAvg +++
Spd +
Def ++

Year	Lev	Team	AB	R	H	HR	RBI	Avg	OB	Slg	OPS	bb%	ct%	Eye	SB	CS	x/h%	Iso	RC/G
2022	NCAA	Charlotte	153	47	59	16	52	386	513	784	1297	21	82	1.43	4	0	49	399	12.05
2022	Rk	FCL Braves	6	1	0	0	0	0	143	0	143	14	100		0	0		0	-0.54
2022	A	Augusta	100	14	26	1	23	260	357	350	707	13	73	0.56	0	2	27	90	4.53
2023	A	Augusta	146	26	39	8	25	267	382	493	875	16	68	0.57	1	1	41	226	6.97
2023	A+	Rome	292	37	82	9	50	281	391	428	819	15	77	0.80	9	1	30	147	6.02

XXL frame CIF prospect showed ability with bat between in lower minors. Switch-hitter with distinct stances from each side but similar approach. Spray-oriented with above-average bat control. Flatter plane swing produces lined and groundball contact. Plus power potential in frame and max EVs, lacks loft in swing. Limited defensively.

McCray,Grant — 8 — San Francisco

EXP MLB DEBUT: 2025 | H/W: 6-2 190 | FUT: Starting OF | 7C

Bats L Age 23
2019 (3) HS (FL)
Pwr +++
BAvg ++
Spd ++++
Def +++

Year	Lev	Team	AB	R	H	HR	RBI	Avg	OB	Slg	OPS	bb%	ct%	Eye	SB	CS	x/h%	Iso	RC/G
2021	Rk	ACL Giants O	55	16	17	1	6	309	406	455	861	14	64	0.45	3	1	29	145	7.25
2021	A	San Jose	80	8	20	2	12	250	302	400	702	7	63	0.20	4	1	30	150	4.50
2022	A	San Jose	436	92	127	21	69	291	374	525	900	12	66	0.39	35	10	40	234	7.40
2022	A+	Eugene	52	12	14	2	10	269	377	423	800	15	58	0.41	8	0	29	154	6.52
2023	A+	Eugene	494	101	126	14	66	255	350	417	767	13	65	0.42	52	10	37	162	5.53

Quick, athletic OF who led org in SB, but also in Ks. Has stolen at least 43 bases in each of past two seasons and should continue to accumulate due to plentiful walk rate. Improved swing (more loft) has helped production but struggles with spin and too patient approach have led to Ks. Showed ability to hit LHP and has improved defensively.

McGeary,Haydn — 3 — Chicago (N)

EXP MLB DEBUT: 2024 | H/W: 6-4 235 | FUT: Starting 1B | 7D

Bats R Age 24
2022 (15) Mesa State
Pwr ++++
BAvg +++
Spd +
Def +

Year	Lev	Team	AB	R	H	HR	RBI	Avg	OB	Slg	OPS	bb%	ct%	Eye	SB	CS	x/h%	Iso	RC/G
2022	NCAA	Mesa St.	214	86	103	35	79	481	568	###	1629	17	81	1.08	3	1	51	579	15.70
2022	Rk	ACL Cubs	18	1	4	0	3	222	333	278	611	14	67	0.50	0	0	25	56	3.27
2022	A	Myrtle Beach	48	5	14	1	8	292	346	458	804	8	75	0.33	0	0	43	167	5.59
2023	A+	South Bend	76	9	28	3	13	368	461	592	1053	15	79	0.81	3	0	39	224	9.02
2023	AA	Tennessee	361	56	92	16	75	255	371	435	806	16	71	0.64	4	3	35	180	5.88

Large-framed 1B has plus raw strength and launched a career-high 19 HR while drawing 80 walks. Sets up with hands high and spread out stance. Slight leg kick, but gets leg down early with good balance. Plus bat speed and raw power make him worth watching. Can be beat by soft stuff down and away and below average speed limits him to 1B.

McGonigle,Kevin — 64 — Detroit

EXP MLB DEBUT: 2027 | H/W: 5-10 187 | FUT: Starting 2B | 8D

Bats L Age 19
2023 (1) HS (PA)
Pwr +++
BAvg ++++
Spd +++
Def +++

Year	Lev	Team	AB	R	H	HR	RBI	Avg	OB	Slg	OPS	bb%	ct%	Eye	SB	CS	x/h%	Iso	RC/G
2023	Rk	FCL Tigers East	33	11	9	0	1	273	455	333	788	25	85	2.20	6	3	22	61	6.38
2023	A	Lakeland	40	7	14	1	5	350	447	475	922	15	88	1.40	2	2	21	125	7.25

CB-A pick out of high school has intriguing upside and performed well on the showcase circuit. Slight crouch at the plate with weight back, but drifts into the hitting zone, which could limit power upside if not corrected. Does show a knack for finding the barrel consistently and rarely expands. Solid if not spectacular defender with upside.

Mead,Curtis — 45 — Tampa Bay

EXP MLB DEBUT: 2023 | H/W: 6-0 171 | FUT: Starting 2B | 9C

Bats R Age 23
2018 FA (AU)
Pwr ++++
BAvg ++++
Spd ++
Def +++

Year	Lev	Team	AB	R	H	HR	RBI	Avg	OB	Slg	OPS	bb%	ct%	Eye	SB	CS	x/h%	Iso	RC/G
2022	AA	Montgomery	210	35	64	10	36	305	379	548	926	11	79	0.56	6	2	48	243	7.11
2022	AAA	Durham	72	8	20	3	14	278	373	486	860	13	76	0.65	1	0	45	208	6.45
2023	Rk	FCL Rays	12	0	2	0	4	167	231	250	481	8	92	1.00	0	0	50	83	2.10
2023	AAA	Durham	235	41	69	9	45	294	385	515	900	13	80	0.73	4	2	46	221	6.94
2023	MLB	Tampa Bay	83	12	21	1	5	253	311	349	661	8	75	0.33	0	0	24	96	3.64

Offensively skilled IF prospect had big second half, fueling successful MLB debut. Missed time due to wrist injury. Showed no rust. Upright, slight open stance with smooth swing mechanics. Stays compact with ability to spray the ball to the gaps. Above-average power plays up due to plus hit tool. 30+ HR likely at projection. Below-average runner.

Meadows,Parker

8 | Detroit | EXP MLB DEBUT: 2023 | H/W: 6-5 205 | FUT: Starting CF | 7C

Bats L Age 24
2018 (2) HS (GA)
Pwr + + +
BAvg + +
4.00 Spd + + + +
Def + + + +

Year	Lev	Team	AB	R	H	HR	RBI	Avg	OB	Slg	OPS	bb%	ct%	Eye	SB	CS	x/h%	Iso	RC/G
2021	A+	West Michigan	355	50	74	8	44	208	283	330	613	9	72	0.37	9	8	34	121	3.01
2022	A+	West Michigan	61	16	14	4	7	230	277	525	802	6	70	0.22	0	0	64	295	5.43
2022	AA	Erie	425	64	117	16	51	275	354	466	820	11	79	0.58	17	2	37	191	5.78
2023	AAA	Toledo	449	78	115	19	65	256	340	474	814	11	73	0.46	19	2	46	218	5.84
2023	MLB	Detroit	125	19	30	3	13	240	331	376	707	12	70	0.46	8	1	30	136	4.45

Athletic OF had a solid season at AAA and looked at home in MLB debut. Enough speed and range to stick in CF. Still lots of swing and miss with length to swing, but doing a better job of keeping his weight back and making hard contact. Is not going to be a high average guy, but has plus speed and defense and has the tools to go 20/20.

Meckler,Wade

789 | San Francisco | EXP MLB DEBUT: 2023 | H/W: 5-10 178 | FUT: Starting OF | 7B

Bats L Age 23
2022 (8) Oregon State
Pwr + +
BAvg + + + +
Spd + + + +
Def + + +

Year	Lev	Team	AB	R	H	HR	RBI	Avg	OB	Slg	OPS	bb%	ct%	Eye	SB	CS	x/h%	Iso	RC/G
2022	A	San Jose	41	9	18	1	8	439	540	683	1223	18	80	1.13	1	0	44	244	11.55
2023	A+	Eugene	79	14	36	2	17	456	494	633	1127	7	89	0.67	2	1	25	177	9.02
2023	AA	Richmond	149	36	50	2	23	336	431	450	881	14	81	0.86	4	3	22	114	6.84
2023	AAA	Sacramento	82	12	29	2	10	354	470	500	970	18	76	0.90	7	0	24	146	8.31
2023	MLB	San Francisco	56	6	13	0	4	232	306	250	556	10	55	0.24	0	0	8	18	2.47

Short, rangy OF who reached majors quickly in first full pro season. Hit at least .336 at each level of ball and showcased good defensive ability with plus speed. Doesn't profile well in power department due to groundball tendencies and swing mechanics. Goes to opp field a lot. Split time at all OF spots and uses speed well to offset fringy arm.

Meidroth,Chase

45 | Boston | EXP MLB DEBUT: 2025 | H/W: 5-9 170 | FUT: Utility player | 6B

Bats R Age 22
2022 (4) San Diego
Pwr + +
BAvg + + +
Spd + +
Def + +

Year	Lev	Team	AB	R	H	HR	RBI	Avg	OB	Slg	OPS	bb%	ct%	Eye	SB	CS	x/h%	Iso	RC/G
2022	NCAA-1	San Diego	228	53	75	10	47	329	429	544	973	15	89	1.60	6	3	39	215	7.80
2022	Rk	FCL Red Sox	8	4	3	0	3	375	500	375	875	20	75	1.00	0	0	0	0	7.20
2022	A	Salem	68	15	21	4	12	309	413	559	971	15	87	1.33	4	2	43	250	7.71
2023	A+	Greenville	74	19	25	2	14	338	484	459	944	22	73	1.05	4	0	20	122	8.21
2023	AA	Portland	325	59	83	7	43	255	370	375	745	15	76	0.76	9	1	29	120	5.09

Short INF with limited athleticism but gets on base consistently and leverages instincts well. Solid hitter with keen eye at plate and ability to lace balls to gaps. Uses entire field in approach. Lacks bat speed and power while exit velo a little short. Limited defensive utility with sub-par range and poor arm. Needs to hit to reach majors.

Mejia,Jonathan

6 | St. Louis | EXP MLB DEBUT: 2027 | H/W: 5-11 185 | FUT: Reserve IF | 6D

Bats B Age 18
2022 FA (DR)
Pwr +
BAvg + + +
Spd + +
Def + + +

Year	Lev	Team	AB	R	H	HR	RBI	Avg	OB	Slg	OPS	bb%	ct%	Eye	SB	CS	x/h%	Iso	RC/G
2022	Rk	DSL Cardinals B	165	33	44	5	34	267	389	479	868	17	71	0.69	3	2	50	212	7.01
2023	Rk	FCL Cardinals	104	16	18	2	8	173	328	288	617	19	64	0.65	7	1	28	115	3.34
2023	A	Palm Beach	28	3	3	0	2	107	219	143	362	13	64	0.40	1	0	33	36	-0.72

Switch-hitting Dominican infielder signed for $2 million. Quick bat and willing to work counts, but too much in zone swing-and-miss. Gets the ball in the air and could add power at maturity, but will be fringe at best. Reliable defender with strong arm, but lack of range will likely push him to 2B. Was over-matched in state-side debut.

Melendez,Ivan

35 | Arizona | EXP MLB DEBUT: 2025 | H/W: 6-3 225 | FUT: Reserve 1B | 7E

Bats R Age 24
2022 (2) Texas
Pwr + + + +
BAvg + +
Spd +
Def +

Year	Lev	Team	AB	R	H	HR	RBI	Avg	OB	Slg	OPS	bb%	ct%	Eye	SB	CS	x/h%	Iso	RC/G
2022	Rk	ACL Dbacks	1	1	0	0	0	0	667	0	667	67	100		0	0		0	7.21
2022	Rk	ACL DBacks R	9	1	2	0	0	222	300	222	522	10	44	0.20	0	0	0	0	2.54
2022	A	Visalia	87	11	18	3	8	207	289	368	656	10	77	0.50	0	0	39	161	3.62
2023	A+	Hillsboro	226	36	61	18	43	270	332	593	925	9	62	0.24	4	0	59	323	7.88
2023	AA	Amarillo	153	29	42	12	33	275	319	556	875	6	61	0.17	0	2	43	281	7.04

2022 NCAA star reached Double-A in second pro season. The good: undeniable light tower power. Uses thick, muscular lower half to generate all-fields power. The bad: Undisciplined approach results in poor contact, plenty of Ks. Not a good fit for 3B, most likely 1B/DH at next level. Hit tool woes cap ceiling.

Melton,Jacob

789 | Houston | EXP MLB DEBUT: 2025 | H/W: 6-3 208 | FUT: Starting OF | 7C

Bats L Age 23
2022 (2) Oregon State
Pwr + + +
BAvg + +
Spd + + + +
Def + +

Year	Lev	Team	AB	R	H	HR	RBI	Avg	OB	Slg	OPS	bb%	ct%	Eye	SB	CS	x/h%	Iso	RC/G
2022	NCAA	Oregon State	261	66	94	17	83	360	418	670	1089	9	80	0.51	21	1	46	310	8.93
2022	Rk	FCL Astros	17	0	0	0	0	0	0	0	0	0	65	0.00	1	0		0	-6.32
2022	A	Fayetteville	71	11	23	4	13	324	415	577	992	13	72	0.55	4	2	43	254	8.39
2023	A+	Asheville	344	73	84	18	42	244	337	453	790	12	76	0.58	41	7	42	209	5.38
2023	AA	Corpus Christi	52	10	13	5	13	250	304	558	861	7	69	0.25	5	0	46	308	6.06

Lefty prospect shows intriguing power/speed profile. Power boosted by Asheville, but continued to produce at AA. Wide, open stance at plate with leg kick. Uses lower half to generate torque, but prone to chasing outside pitches. Plus speed is best asset. Capable of legging out infield hits, could be perennial 30-SB producer in today's environment.

Mendez,Hendry

9 | Philadelphia | EXP MLB DEBUT: 2027 | H/W: 6-2 175 | FUT: Starting OF | 7D

Bats L Age 20
2021 FA (DR)
Pwr + +
BAvg + +
Spd + + +
Def + + +

Year	Lev	Team	AB	R	H	HR	RBI	Avg	OB	Slg	OPS	bb%	ct%	Eye	SB	CS	x/h%	Iso	RC/G
2021	Rk	ACL Brewers B	63	6	21	0	10	333	425	460	885	14	84	1.00	3	1	29	127	6.96
2021	Rk	DSL Brewers 1	54	10	16	1	9	296	377	481	859	11	96	3.50	0	0	44	185	6.54
2022	A	Carolina	377	47	92	5	39	244	351	318	669	14	81	0.89	7	8	18	74	4.11
2023	Rk	ACL Brewers G	15	5	9	0	5	600	600	800	1400	0	100		0	1	33	200	11.01
2023	A+	Wisconsin	233	29	55	3	25	236	305	326	631	9	83	0.58	0	1	24	90	3.42

Talented OF who was acquired from MIL after season. Makes easy contact with short stroke and hand-eye coordination. Hits far too many groundballs and hasn't produced much pop despite bat speed. Choppy swing needs work. Has some physical projection. Only 8 HR in last 2 seasons. Owns average arm and speed.

Mercedes,Yasser

89 | Minnesota | EXP MLB DEBUT: 2027 | H/W: 6-2 175 | FUT: Starting OF | 8D

Bats R Age 19
2022 FA (PR)
Pwr + + +
BAvg + +
Spd + + + +
Def + + +

Year	Lev	Team	AB	R	H	HR	RBI	Avg	OB	Slg	OPS	bb%	ct%	Eye	SB	CS	x/h%	Iso	RC/G
2022	Rk	DSL Twins	155	34	55	4	20	355	422	555	977	10	77	0.51	30	5	36	200	7.93
2023	Rk	FCL Twins	97	14	19	4	17	196	243	381	624	6	76	0.26	6	1	47	186	2.97

Tall, projectable OF who spent 1st year in US. Very raw tools but has good barrel control for age. Has as much raw pop as any in org but may take awhile to get to it during games. Knows strike zone and makes decent swing decisions. Will add muscle and likely to reduce above average speed. Plays CF and RF with good arm strength.

Merrill,Jackson

6 | San Diego | EXP MLB DEBUT: 2024 | H/W: 6-3 195 | FUT: Starting SS | 8B

Bats L Age 20
2021 (1) HS (MD)
Pwr + +
BAvg + + + +
Spd + + +
Def + + +

Year	Lev	Team	AB	R	H	HR	RBI	Avg	OB	Slg	OPS	bb%	ct%	Eye	SB	CS	x/h%	Iso	RC/G
2021	Rk	ACL Padres	107	19	30	0	10	280	342	383	725	9	75	0.37	5	1	30	103	4.67
2022	Rk	ACL Padres	30	5	13	1	6	433	452	700	1152	3	93	0.50	3	0	38	267	8.92
2022	A	Lake Elsinore	197	33	64	5	34	325	384	482	866	9	79	0.45	8	5	28	157	6.30
2023	A+	Fort Wayne	279	50	78	10	33	280	321	444	765	6	87	0.46	10	3	31	165	4.78
2023	AA	San Antonio	187	26	51	5	31	273	337	444	780	9	87	0.72	5	1	39	171	5.24

Tall, advanced INF who is ascending ladder quickly. Reached AA in August and continues to shine with bat and glove. Puts bat to ball with ease while demonstrating keen plate discipline. Hits too many GB but has power potential with strength gains. Increased HR from 6 to 15. Focuses on all-fields hitting. Solid SS with strong arm and saw time at 2B.

Mervis,Matt

3 | Chicago (N) | EXP MLB DEBUT: 2023 | H/W: 6-2 225 | FUT: Starting 1B | 7C

Bats L Age 25
2020 FA (Duke)
Pwr + + + +
BAvg + +
Spd +
Def + +

Year	Lev	Team	AB	R	H	HR	RBI	Avg	OB	Slg	OPS	bb%	ct%	Eye	SB	CS	x/h%	Iso	RC/G
2022	A+	South Bend	100	17	35	7	29	350	381	650	1031	5	74	0.19	0	0	46	300	8.22
2022	AA	Tennessee	203	34	61	14	51	300	363	596	959	9	77	0.43	2	0	51	296	7.37
2022	AAA	Iowa	209	41	62	15	39	297	372	593	965	11	83	0.71	0	0	50	297	7.35
2023	AAA	Iowa	362	77	102	22	78	282	394	533	927	16	72	0.67	2	1	45	251	7.49
2023	MLB	Chicago (N)	90	8	15	3	11	167	235	289	524	8	64	0.25	0	0	33	122	1.53

Failed to duplicate breakout and floundered in MLB debut. Was unable to get to plus raw power due to poor swing decisions and an aggressive approach. Too much swing-and-miss (both in and out of zone). Power is to all fields with a short, compact stroke that should yield better results. Below average speed and defense means has to SLG to have value.

Mesa Jr,Victor

89 | Miami | EXP MLB DEBUT: 2024 | H/W: 6-0 195 | FUT: Starting CF | 7C

Bats L Age 22
2018 FA (CU)
Pwr + + + +
BAvg + +
Spd + + +
Def + + +

Year	Lev	Team	AB	R	H	HR	RBI	Avg	OB	Slg	OPS	bb%	ct%	Eye	SB	CS	x/h%	Iso	RC/G
2021	A	Jupiter	428	66	114	5	71	266	319	402	721	7	76	0.32	12	5	32	136	4.47
2022	A+	Beloit	460	53	112	5	50	243	322	346	667	10	78	0.53	10	4	30	102	3.90
2023	AA	Pensacola	483	73	117	18	76	242	302	412	714	8	75	0.34	16	3	38	170	4.24

Strong OF prospect began to show power prowess in 2023. Lean muscular build close to projection. Upright, slightly open stance with a moderate leg kick and bat wrap that loads hands at hit position. Creates leverage with lower half to power uppercut trajectory swing. Best working up-the-middle approach. Plus power potential. Solid defender in CF.

Millas,Drew — 2 — Washington

EXP MLB DEBUT: 2023 | H/W: 6-2 198 | FUT: Reserve C | 7C

Bats B Age 26
2019 (7) Missouri State
Pwr ++
BAvg ++
Spd +++
Def ++++

Year	Lev	Team	AB	R	H	HR	RBI	Avg	OB	Slg	OPS	bb%	ct%	Eye	SB	CS	x/h%	Iso	RC/G
2022	A+	Wilmington	76	13	18	1	10	237	408	434	842	22	74	1.10	1	0	61	197	6.95
2022	AA	Harrisburg	152	12	32	3	16	211	281	296	577	9	65	0.28	1	1	22	86	2.45
2023	AA	Harrisburg	82	14	28	4	19	341	449	537	986	16	80	1.00	2	1	29	195	8.09
2023	AAA	Rochester	196	26	53	3	24	270	356	403	759	12	83	0.79	4	1	32	133	5.18
2023	MLB	Washington	28	1	8	1	6	286	375	464	839	13	82	0.80	0	0	38	179	6.08

Interesting profile where his contact rates have improved at the higher levels and results have followed. Stable double-digit walk rates pushed career-best BA/OBP numbers, and carries enough pop to stay viable. Still likely a backup profile, but a very good defender with a solid arm and blocking/receiving skills. Ready to stick in the majors.

Miller,Aidan — 6 — Philadelphia

EXP MLB DEBUT: 2027 | H/W: 6-2 205 | FUT: Starting 3B | 8D

Bats R Age 19
2023 (1) HS (FL)
Pwr ++++
BAvg +++
Spd ++
Def +++

Year	Lev	Team	AB	R	H	HR	RBI	Avg	OB	Slg	OPS	bb%	ct%	Eye	SB	CS	x/h%	Iso	RC/G
2023	Rk	FCL Phillies	29	6	12	0	2	414	514	483	997	17	83	1.20	0	0	17	69	8.53
2023	A	Clearwater	37	4	8	0	0	216	326	297	623	14	73	0.60	4	1	25	81	3.49

Seen as one of the best hit-plus-power in the 2023 prep class, he showed off his elite bat speed and knack for hitting in short stints in complex and low-A. Shows advanced ball-strike approach and has the solid build to project as an MLB power hitter. Most feel he'll end up at 3B; he has the arm and reactions for the position.

Miller,Noah — 6 — Minnesota

EXP MLB DEBUT: 2026 | H/W: 5-11 190 | FUT: Starting SS | 7C

Bats B Age 21
2021 (1) HS (WI)
Pwr +
BAvg ++
Spd +++
Def +++

Year	Lev	Team	AB	R	H	HR	RBI	Avg	OB	Slg	OPS	bb%	ct%	Eye	SB	CS	x/h%	Iso	RC/G
2021	Rk	FCL Twins	84	11	20	2	14	238	312	369	681	10	69	0.35	1	1	30	131	4.00
2022	A	Fort Myers	383	62	81	2	24	211	342	279	621	17	71	0.69	23	7	22	68	3.47
2023	A+	Cedar Rapids	462	71	103	8	60	223	310	340	649	11	77	0.54	12	3	32	117	3.65

Instinctual SS who was better in last two months of year after very slow start. Set high in HR and SLG, though OBP took step back. Controls strike zone and will draw walks but has fanned over 100 times in each of last 2 years. Doubles jumped but makes weak contact foo frequently. Plays solid SS with strong, accurate arm.

Misner,Kameron — 89 — Tampa Bay

EXP MLB DEBUT: 2024 | H/W: 6-4 218 | FUT: Starting OF | 7D

Bats L Age 26
2019 (1) Missouri
Pwr +++
BAvg ++
Spd ++++
Def +++

Year	Lev	Team	AB	R	H	HR	RBI	Avg	OB	Slg	OPS	bb%	ct%	Eye	SB	CS	x/h%	Iso	RC/G
2019	A	Clinton	134	25	37	2	20	276	374	373	747	14	74	0.60	8	0	24	97	5.07
2021	A+	Beloit	340	58	83	11	56	244	341	424	765	13	65	0.42	24	2	43	179	5.50
2021	AA	Pensacola	55	12	17	1	3	309	387	491	878	11	69	0.41	2	2	47	182	7.09
2022	AA	Montgomery	415	80	104	16	62	251	379	431	811	17	63	0.55	32	7	40	181	6.42
2023	AAA	Durham	421	85	95	21	58	226	363	458	822	18	56	0.49	21	6	54	233	7.13

Power/speed OF prospect continues to be limited by swing and miss in profile. Patient approach, will work into favorable counts and take walks. Struggles with in-zone whiff rate. Power plays to all field. It's raw plus power but plays as average due to the hit tool. Plus runner, has feel for base stealing. Enticing profile if not for BA issues.

Mitchell,Blake — 2 — Kansas City

EXP MLB DEBUT: 2027 | H/W: 6-1 202 | FUT: Starting C | 9D

Bats L Age 19
2023 (1) HS (TX)
Pwr +++
BAvg +++
Spd ++
Def ++++

Year	Lev	Team	AB	R	H	HR	RBI	Avg	OB	Slg	OPS	bb%	ct%	Eye	SB	CS	x/h%	Iso	RC/G
2023	Rk	ACL Royals B	34	8	5	0	3	147	431	176	608	33	59	1.21	1	0	20	29	3.32

The Royals took him 8th overall despite the risk behind first round prep catchers. Still, with a huge arm behind the plate and plus raw power to tap into there's reason to be excited about the pick. Combines a solid batting eye with exemplary bat speed to project to quality offensive backstop. Has some holes in swing to clean up.

Mogollon,Javier — 46 — Chicago (A)

EXP MLB DEBUT: 2027 | H/W: 5-8 160 | FUT: Starting 2B | 8E

Bats R Age 18
2023 FA (VZ)
Pwr +++
BAvg +++
Spd +++
Def +++

Year	Lev	Team	AB	R	H	HR	RBI	Avg	OB	Slg	OPS	bb%	ct%	Eye	SB	CS	x/h%	Iso	RC/G
2023	Rk	DSL White Sox	165	41	52	10	42	315	411	582	993	14	83	0.96	11	2	42	267	7.97

Short-statured MIF prospect burst onto scene with big Dominican Summer League performance. Strong, athletic body. Slight open stance with easy trigger and slight uppercut swing trajectory. Showed patience and contact skills while posting high exit velocities. Hit and power tool project to be above-average. Above-average runner, range taxed at SS.

Montes,Lazaro — 9 — Seattle

EXP MLB DEBUT: 2026 | H/W: 6-3 210 | FUT: Starting OF | 8D

Bats L Age 19
2022 FA (CU)
Pwr ++++
BAvg +++
Spd +++
Def ++

Year	Lev	Team	AB	R	H	HR	RBI	Avg	OB	Slg	OPS	bb%	ct%	Eye	SB	CS	x/h%	Iso	RC/G
2022	Rk	DSL Mariners	176	34	50	10	41	284	403	585	988	17	58	0.47	3	1	56	301	9.91
2023	Rk	ACL Mariners	110	31	31	6	31	282	448	555	1002	23	66	0.89	1	2	55	273	9.38
2023	A	Modesto	131	27	42	7	30	321	414	565	979	14	70	0.54	1	0	40	244	8.34

Physical behemoth with immense power upside. Was good in rookie ball and Low-A as he hits well against LHP and RHP. Posts high OBP due to discerning eye but will be too aggressive at times and get himself out when lengthening stroke. Improving RF but needs more time with range and routes. Average hit tool and speed.

Montgomery,Benny — 8 — Colorado

EXP MLB DEBUT: 2025 | H/W: 6-4 200 | FUT: Starting CF | 8D

Bats R Age 21
2021 (1) HS (PA)
Pwr +++
BAvg ++
Spd ++++
Def ++++

Year	Lev	Team	AB	R	H	HR	RBI	Avg	OB	Slg	OPS	bb%	ct%	Eye	SB	CS	x/h%	Iso	RC/G
2021	Rk	ACL Rockies	47	7	16	0	6	340	404	383	787	10	81	0.56	5	1	6	43	5.37
2022	Rk	ACL Rockies	22	3	6	0	2	273	273	409	682	0	73	0.00	0	0	33	136	3.76
2022	A	Fresno	233	48	73	6	42	313	370	502	872	8	70	0.30	9	1	40	189	6.77
2023	A+	Spokane	438	62	110	10	51	251	331	370	700	11	69	0.39	18	5	27	119	4.31

Quick-twitch athlete with plus speed and the chops to stick in CF. Busy approach at the plate with pre-pitch movement in his hands, but does have a quick bat and a good understanding of the strike zone. Needs to add muscle to generate power and swing is more of a slash-and-dash right now. He's young for this level, but needs to make adjustments.

Montgomery,Colson — 6 — Chicago (A)

EXP MLB DEBUT: 2024 | H/W: 6-3 205 | FUT: Starting SS | 9C

Bats L Age 22
2021 (1) HS (IN)
Pwr ++++
BAvg +++
Spd +++
Def +++

Year	Lev	Team	AB	R	H	HR	RBI	Avg	OB	Slg	OPS	bb%	ct%	Eye	SB	CS	x/h%	Iso	RC/G
2022	A+	Winston-Salem	132	22	34	5	14	258	380	417	796	16	80	1.00	1	0	29	159	5.72
2022	AA	Birmingham	48	5	7	2	7	146	180	292	472	4	69	0.13	0	0	43	146	0.67
2023	Rk	ACL White Sox	34	9	12	1	6	353	511	588	1099	24	85	2.20	2	0	42	235	10.17
2023	A+	Winston Salem	58	15	20	3	10	345	513	552	1065	26	74	1.33	0	2	30	207	9.93
2023	AA	Birmingham	131	27	32	4	21	244	365	427	793	16	73	0.69	0	1	44	183	5.81

Offensively skilled SS prospect struggled with core injury for much of 2023. Long frame with present athleticism. Open stance with little trigger getting hands to hit position. Powerful hit rotation powers high EV rates. Patient approach, works counts. Power driven hit tool, mostly to pull side. Average runner with plus IQ. Should stick at SS.

Montgomery,Torin — 3 — Miami

EXP MLB DEBUT: 2025 | H/W: 6-3 230 | FUT: Reserve 1B | 6C

Bats R Age 22
2022 (14) Missouri
Pwr +++
BAvg ++
Spd ++
Def +++

Year	Lev	Team	AB	R	H	HR	RBI	Avg	OB	Slg	OPS	bb%	ct%	Eye	SB	CS	x/h%	Iso	RC/G
2022	NCAA	Missouri	181	44	66	7	49	365	431	547	978	10	80	0.57	4	0	29	182	7.70
2022	Rk	FCL Marlins	16	4	6	1	3	375	412	625	1037	6	75	0.25	0	0	33	250	8.27
2022	A	Jupiter	108	17	27	3	16	250	314	398	712	8	70	0.31	0	0	37	148	4.36
2023	A	Jupiter	185	36	63	3	32	341	463	486	949	19	75	0.89	4	3	30	146	8.17
2023	A+	Beloit	131	11	28	1	12	214	299	282	582	11	73	0.46	1	0	25	69	2.70

Older, lower minors prospect had big first half in Low-A but couldn't carry success to High-A. XL frame at physical projection. Strong but struggles with high groundball rate due to linear swing plane. Struggles with plate coverage and in-zone swing decisions. Raw plus power in frame. Not enough present power to carry bat to 1B reps in MLB.

Mooney,Alex — 56 — Cleveland

EXP MLB DEBUT: 2025 | H/W: 6-1 195 | FUT: Starting 3B | 7D

Bats R Age 21
2023 (7) Duke
Pwr +
BAvg +++
Spd +++
Def +++

Year	Lev	Team	AB	R	H	HR	RBI	Avg	OB	Slg	OPS	bb%	ct%	Eye	SB	CS	x/h%	Iso	RC/G
2023	NCAA	Duke	254	68	80	8	38	315	400	504	904	12	83	0.84	21	5	38	189	6.92
2023	A	Lynchburg	66	8	10	0	4	152	233	212	445	10	80	0.54	4	0	40	61	1.16

Instinctual INF who plays above tools. Power may never be part of equation but is more hit over pop with good contact from short stroke. Swing modifications could bring some pop in time. Can chase and make weak contact. Uses speed well on base and in field. Makes some highlight-reel plays but seems destined for 2B or 3B as he lacks frontline range.

Moore,Robert — 46 — Philadelphia

EXP MLB DEBUT: 2025 | H/W: 5-9 170 | FUT: Starting 2B | 7C

Bats B Age 22
2022 (2) Arkansas
Pwr ++
BAvg ++
Spd +++
Def +++

Year	Lev	Team	AB	R	H	HR	RBI	Avg	OB	Slg	OPS	bb%	ct%	Eye	SB	CS	x/h%	Iso	RC/G
2022	NCAA	Arkansas	241	48	56	8	44	232	346	427	774	15	81	0.91	5	2	52	195	5.44
2022	Rk	ACL Brewers B	11	1	1	0	1	91	167	182	348	8	91	1.00	0	0	100	91	0.67
2022	Rk	ACL Brewers G	4	2	1	0	1	250	400	250	650	20	75	1.00	1	0	0	0	4.03
2022	A	Carolina	110	14	29	3	14	264	341	418	760	11	75	0.46	6	2	38	155	5.06
2023	A+	Wisconsin	490	68	114	8	62	233	310	361	671	10	78	0.51	26	13	39	129	3.93

Short, instinctual INF who finished 2nd in MWL in doubles in first full season as pro. Tools may lack but makes up for with savvy. Strikes out far too much for little pop, though has double-digit HR projection. Better hitter from left side and swings aggressively but doesn't chase. Lack of arm strength likely keeps him at 2B and makes routine plays.

Morabito,Nick — 8 — New York (N)

EXP MLB DEBUT: 2026 | H/W: 5-11 185 | FUT: Starting OF | 7E

Bats R Age 20
2022 (2) HS (VA)
Pwr ++
BAvg +++
Spd ++++
Def +++

Year	Lev	Team	AB	R	H	HR	RBI	Avg	OB	Slg	OPS	bb%	ct%	Eye	SB	CS	x/h%	Iso	RC/G
2022	Rk	FCL Mets	22	1	2	0	2	91	167	136	303	8	36	0.14	1	0	50	45	-1.86
2023	Rk	FCL Mets	111	22	36	1	18	324	427	432	860	15	80	0.91	11	1	22	108	6.67
2023	A	St. Lucie	98	14	28	1	7	286	375	378	753	13	72	0.52	10	3	21	92	5.15

Short-statured, athletic OF prospect enjoyed solid season split between two lower levels. Compact frame, near physical projection. Crouched stance with slightest trigger to hit position. Short levers contribute to contact-centric swing. Has feel for hitter, works all fields. Doesn't possess much power. Plus-plus runner. Could stick in CF

Morales,Yohandy — 5 — Washington

EXP MLB DEBUT: 2025 | H/W: 6-4 225 | FUT: Starting 3B | 8D

Bats R Age 22
2023 (2) Miami
Pwr ++++
BAvg +++
Spd ++
Def ++

Year	Lev	Team	AB	R	H	HR	RBI	Avg	OB	Slg	OPS	bb%	ct%	Eye	SB	CS	x/h%	Iso	RC/G
2023	NCAA	Miami	240	58	98	20	70	408	474	713	1187	11	77	0.55	7	3	34	304	10.33
2023	Rk	FCL Nationals	5	0	2	0	1	400	400	400	800	0	100		0	0	0	0	4.93
2023	A	Fredericksburg	77	18	30	0	17	390	447	571	1018	9	77	0.44	1	1	40	182	8.66
2023	A+	Wilmington	70	12	22	0	14	314	385	443	827	10	77	0.50	0	0	32	129	6.12
2023	AA	Harrisburg	14	0	4	0	0	286	412	357	769	18	86	1.50	0	0	25	71	5.75

Powerful corner IF with plus exit velocity and strength to be a HR force, though did not hit a long ball in first partial season. Can tend to chase; swing can get long and create strikeout problems. Average hit tool with a strong arm and athleticism that fits at 3B, but could slow down some and end up at 1B. SB not part of the package.

Morel,Braylin — 9 — Texas

EXP MLB DEBUT: 2027 | H/W: 6-2 180 | FUT: Starting OF | 7D

Bats R Age 18
2023 FA (DR)
Pwr +++
BAvg +
Spd +
Def ++

Year	Lev	Team	AB	R	H	HR	RBI	Avg	OB	Slg	OPS	bb%	ct%	Eye	SB	CS	x/h%	Iso	RC/G
2023	Rk	DSL Rangers 2	180	40	62	7	43	344	413	644	1057	10	72	0.42	2	2	52	300	9.38

2nd in DSL SLG, he made big splash in debut but came with significant contact concerns. Athletic, good arm, future RF. No splits but less thump vs LHP with good LA and lots of FB give future plus raw projection and impact bat upside, but spin an issue. Stateside debut could rocket up lists but until then big risk.

Morgan,Tre' — 37 — Tampa Bay

EXP MLB DEBUT: 2026 | H/W: 6-1 215 | FUT: Starting OF | 7E

Bats L Age 21
2023 (3) LSU
Pwr ++
BAvg +++
Spd ++
Def +++

Year	Lev	Team	AB	R	H	HR	RBI	Avg	OB	Slg	OPS	bb%	ct%	Eye	SB	CS	x/h%	Iso	RC/G
2023	NCAA	LSU	269	66	85	9	53	316	395	502	897	12	88	1.06	0	1	33	186	6.73
2023	Rk	FCL Rays	12	1	5	1	4	417	417	750	1167	0	92	0.00	0	0	40	333	8.55
2023	A	Charleston	36	7	14	0	2	389	500	472	972	18	94	4.00	4	1	14	83	8.28

Contact-oriented 1B prospect enjoyed successful pro debut despite limited hard contact. Plus bat-to-ball skill carries profile. Doesn't get to barreled contact often, relying on punching the ball between the gaps. Power doesn't carry profile at first and likely a tweener prospect in the COF. Excellent defender at 1B. Below-average runner.

Morrobel,Yeison — 89 — Texas

EXP MLB DEBUT: 2026 | H/W: 6-2 170 | FUT: Reserve OF | 6C

Bats L Age 20
2021 FA (DR)
Pwr +
BAvg ++
Spd ++
Def ++

Year	Lev	Team	AB	R	H	HR	RBI	Avg	OB	Slg	OPS	bb%	ct%	Eye	SB	CS	x/h%	Iso	RC/G
2021	Rk	DSL Rangers	185	33	50	1	30	270	372	411	783	14	86	1.20	8	4	36	141	5.74
2022	Rk	ACL Rangers	152	31	50	3	21	329	396	487	883	10	78	0.50	5	5	34	158	6.67
2022	A	Down East	26	3	6	0	3	231	310	269	580	10	77	0.50	2	1	17	38	2.74
2023	A	Down East	128	16	35	1	13	273	380	313	693	15	73	0.65	12	3	9	39	4.35

Another year of "not bad" but still south of "good," season was getting better but shut down with June shoulder surgery. Trending 4th OF rather than starter & sliding more RF than CF, Morrobel will need to lift the ball to project there and 54% GB% won't cut it. Contact \not ideal for this profile with speed likely to tick down. Cusp starter.

Muncy,Max — 6 — Oakland

EXP MLB DEBUT: 2025 | H/W: 6-1 180 | FUT: Starting SS | 8C

Bats R Age 21
2021 (1) HS (CA)
Pwr +++
BAvg +++
Spd +++
Def +++

Year	Lev	Team	AB	R	H	HR	RBI	Avg	OB	Slg	OPS	bb%	ct%	Eye	SB	CS	x/h%	Iso	RC/G
2021	Rk	ACL Athletics	31	3	4	0	4	129	206	129	335	9	61	0.25	1	0	0	0	-1.38
2022	A	Stockton	304	50	70	16	51	230	341	447	788	14	64	0.47	6	5	47	217	5.79
2022	A+	Lansing	168	19	38	3	19	226	301	375	676	10	64	0.30	13	1	45	149	4.17
2023	A+	Lansing	275	36	70	6	31	255	330	385	716	10	67	0.34	9	3	34	131	4.62
2023	AA	Midland	202	40	61	4	31	302	368	446	813	9	73	0.39	4	0	34	144	5.81

Advanced INF who hit over .300 after promotion to AA; 2nd in org in doubles and 5th in Ks. Drives ball to all fields with improving approach and has bat speed and strength to reach seats. Cut K rate but still chases breakers out of zone. Has all tools to be solid overall player. Runs well with fundamental SS skills. Has 20/20 potential.

Munoz,Samuel — 79 — Los Angeles (N)

EXP MLB DEBUT: 2027 | H/W: 6-3 190 | FUT: Starting OF | 7D

Bats L Age 19
2022 FA (DR)
Pwr +++
BAvg ++
Spd +++
Def +++

Year	Lev	Team	AB	R	H	HR	RBI	Avg	OB	Slg	OPS	bb%	ct%	Eye	SB	CS	x/h%	Iso	RC/G
2022	Rk	DSL Dodgers S	173	39	60	1	42	347	432	491	923	13	80	0.76	4	5	30	145	7.42
2023	Rk	ACL Dodgers	216	35	59	2	32	273	338	412	750	9	81	0.51	9	2	32	139	4.95

Dominican OF signed for $767,500. Upright stance then shifts weight back with leg kick and drifts into the zone. Has good hand-eye coordination and barrel control, but swing is geared towards contact and will need to keep weight back better to generate more loft and power. Speed is a tick above-average, but frame projects to slow as he matures.

Murray,BJ — 35 — Chicago (N)

EXP MLB DEBUT: 2024 | H/W: 5-10 205 | FUT: Starting 3B | 7D

Bats B Age 24
2021 (15) Florida Atlantic
Pwr +++
BAvg +++
Spd +
Def ++

Year	Lev	Team	AB	R	H	HR	RBI	Avg	OB	Slg	OPS	bb%	ct%	Eye	SB	CS	x/h%	Iso	RC/G
2021	NCAA	Fl Atlantic	209	49	65	14	52	311	424	584	1008	16	74	0.75	0	2	42	273	8.57
2021	Rk	ACL Cubs	56	12	16	2	8	286	344	482	826	8	75	0.36	2	0	38	196	5.81
2022	A	Myrtle Beach	128	31	39	3	25	305	422	461	883	17	76	0.84	0	0	36	156	7.07
2022	A+	South Bend	187	22	51	5	28	273	390	406	797	16	75	0.78	8	4	27	134	5.79
2023	AA	Tennessee	452	71	119	16	74	263	376	462	839	15	71	0.64	14	3	45	199	6.44

Set career highs in most categories. Short, compact frame with strong legs and some of the best plate discipline in the system. Keeps weight back with an all fields approach and above average power - 15% BB and .199 ISO rate at Double-A. Speed is below average with a fringe arm and will need to work hard to stick at 3B.

Muzziotti,Simon — 8 — Philadelphia

EXP MLB DEBUT: 2022 | H/W: 6-0 175 | FUT: Reserve OF | 7D

Bats L Age 25
2015 FA (VZ)
Pwr ++
BAvg +++
Spd ++++
Def ++++

Year	Lev	Team	AB	R	H	HR	RBI	Avg	OB	Slg	OPS	bb%	ct%	Eye	SB	CS	x/h%	Iso	RC/G
2022	A	Clearwater	8	0	0	0	0	0	111	0	111	11	50	0.25	0	0		0	-6.20
2022	AA	Reading	143	23	37	5	20	259	346	455	800	12	78	0.61	7	3	38	196	5.61
2022	AAA	Lehigh Valley	16	2	5	0	0	313	389	313	701	11	81	0.67	1	0	0	0	4.34
2022	MLB	Philadelphia	7	0	1	0	0	143	143	143	286	0	71	0.00	1	0	0	0	-1.83
2023	AAA	Lehigh Valley	473	67	140	7	61	296	357	404	761	9	83	0.56	26	12	24	108	4.97

Stayed healthy and got full-time AB at Triple-A, but got passed over when big club needed an extra OFer. Bit of old-school approach of high contact, solid on-base skills player who can run. Has seen the fruits of bulking up some over the years and hit a career high 7 HR. Can handle CF well which makes his an MLB-quality backup package.

Myers,Dane — 789 — Miami

EXP MLB DEBUT: 2023 | H/W: 6-0 205 | FUT: Starting CF | 7D

Bats R Age 28
2017 (6) Rice
Pwr ++
BAvg +++
Spd ++++
Def ++++

Year	Lev	Team	AB	R	H	HR	RBI	Avg	OB	Slg	OPS	bb%	ct%	Eye	SB	CS	x/h%	Iso	RC/G
2022	AA	Erie	407	59	109	25	72	268	307	506	813	5	71	0.19	20	4	41	238	5.45
2022	AAA	Toledo	43	5	11	0	5	256	273	326	598	2	65	0.07	1	1	27	70	2.73
2023	AA	Pensacola	182	34	53	7	25	291	383	462	844	13	80	0.73	14	1	28	170	6.15
2023	AAA	Jacksonville	192	43	65	8	37	339	409	516	925	11	78	0.53	6	2	26	177	7.07
2023	MLB	Miami	67	9	18	1	9	269	290	358	648	3	72	0.11	1	1	22	90	3.21

Former MiLB Rule 5 pick enjoyed breakout season in upper minors, including MLB callup. Older prospect with athletic frame. Slightly open, upright stance with strange hand setup and load. Aggressive approach: chases, but hand/eye bails him out. Below-average power due to linear swing plane. Plus runner with defensive chops in CF.

Naylor,Myles — 56 — Oakland

EXP MLB DEBUT: 2026 | H/W: 6-2 195 | FUT: Starting 3B | 8D

Bats R Age 18
2023 (1) HS (ON)

- Pwr +++
- BAvg ++
- Spd ++
- Def +++

Year	Lev	Team	AB	R	H	HR	RBI	Avg	OB	Slg	OPS	bb%	ct%	Eye	SB	CS	x/h%	Iso	RC/G
2023	Rk	ACL Athletics	6	2	2	0	0	333	429	500	929	14	50	0.33	0	0	50	167	10.72
2023	A	Stockton	120	16	25	6	17	208	275	375	650	8	57	0.21	2	0	32	167	3.74

Strong INF who impressed with solid tools in pro debut. Clean swing mechanics and raw power stand out and provide hitting upside. Struggles to recognize pitches and can flail at breaking balls. Owns natural strength and quick bat and has potential to hit for BA and power. Fringy runner and likely to slow down. Profiles better at 3B with average arm.

Newell,Chris — 789 — Los Angeles (N)

EXP MLB DEBUT: 2025 | H/W: 6-3 200 | FUT: Starting OF | 7D

Bats L Age 22
2022 (13) Virginia

- Pwr ++++
- BAvg ++
- Spd +++
- Def +++

Year	Lev	Team	AB	R	H	HR	RBI	Avg	OB	Slg	OPS	bb%	ct%	Eye	SB	CS	x/h%	Iso	RC/G
2022	NCAA	Virginia	190	51	49	12	32	258	368	468	836	15	65	0.50	16	2	33	211	6.36
2022	Rk	ACL Dodgers	41	5	9	1	2	220	238	366	604	2	73	0.09	3	3	44	146	2.63
2023	A	Rancho Cuca	154	41	48	14	38	312	430	662	1092	17	66	0.62	7	2	50	351	10.30
2023	A+	Great Lakes	158	24	35	7	22	222	324	424	748	13	63	0.41	8	5	49	203	5.24

Toolsy OF has plus bat speed and above-average power, but aggressive approach results in plenty of swing-and-miss. Looks for pitches he can mash to the pull side. Did crush 21 HR in just 312 AB and notched 15 SB to boot. Draws plenty of walks, but needs to make better swing decisions to avoid being a three true outcomes player.

Nimmala,Arjun — 6 — Toronto

EXP MLB DEBUT: 2027 | H/W: 6-1 170 | FUT: Starting SS | 8C

Bats R Age 18
2023 (1) HS (FL)

- Pwr +++
- BAvg +++
- Spd +++
- Def +++

Year	Lev	Team	AB	R	H	HR	RBI	Avg	OB	Slg	OPS	bb%	ct%	Eye	SB	CS	x/h%	Iso	RC/G
2023	Rk	FCL Blue Jays	25	7	5	0	3	200	487	320	807	36	68	1.75	1	0	40	120	6.93

Projectable young SS with plentiful tools and significant upside on both sides of ball. Should continue to grow into lean frame to provide above average power in time. Has quick, simple swing with loft and can identify pitches well. Possesses good speed and quickness to be asset at SS. Owns above average arm strength and instincts.

Nivens,Spencer — 78 — Kansas City

EXP MLB DEBUT: 2025 | H/W: 5-11 185 | FUT: Starting OF | 7D

Bats L Age 22
2023 (5) Missouri State

- Pwr ++
- BAvg +++
- Spd +++
- Def +++

Year	Lev	Team	AB	R	H	HR	RBI	Avg	OB	Slg	OPS	bb%	ct%	Eye	SB	CS	x/h%	Iso	RC/G
2023	NCAA	Missouri St	226	55	77	14	45	341	427	650	1077	13	81	0.77	7	1	47	310	9.08
2023	Rk	ACL Royals B	16	3	5	0	1	313	353	563	915	6	88	0.50	1	1	80	250	6.95
2023	A	Columbia	98	12	18	2	7	184	339	276	614	19	80	1.15	7	3	28	92	3.54

Short, speedy OF who was a data darling on draft night. He doesn't chase much and makes good swing decisions. The eye test is kinder to him than his statistical output in Low-A. Enjoys patient approach at plate with clean swing, though power upside a bit limited without better pitch recognition.

Noel,Jhonkensy — 359 — Cleveland

EXP MLB DEBUT: 2024 | H/W: 6-3 250 | FUT: Starting 1B | 7D

Bats R Age 22
2017 FA (DR)

- Pwr ++++
- BAvg +
- Spd +
- Def ++

Year	Lev	Team	AB	R	H	HR	RBI	Avg	OB	Slg	OPS	bb%	ct%	Eye	SB	CS	x/h%	Iso	RC/G
2021	A+	Lake County	100	13	28	8	25	280	339	550	889	8	69	0.29	3	1	39	270	6.62
2022	A+	Lake County	228	35	50	19	42	219	276	509	785	7	65	0.23	1	0	56	289	5.30
2022	AA	Akron	240	43	58	13	42	242	326	488	813	11	74	0.48	2	0	53	246	5.72
2022	AAA	Columbus	17	2	3	0	0	176	222	235	458	6	59	0.14	0	0	33	59	0.72
2023	AAA	Columbus	519	81	114	27	85	220	287	420	707	9	72	0.34	1	3	44	200	4.12

Spent all 23 in AA and finished 2nd in org in HR but 3rd in Ks. Has best raw power in system and possibly the minors. Takes vicious hacks and combines brute strength with bat speed. Very pull happy and can be pitched to. Doesn't hit for BA and struggles with two strikes. Power is the calling card here. No speed. No defense.

Norby,Connor — 479 — Baltimore

EXP MLB DEBUT: 2024 | H/W: 5-9 180 | FUT: Starting 2B | 8D

Bats R Age 23
2021 (2) East Carolina

- Pwr +++
- BAvg ++++
- Spd +++
- Def ++

Year	Lev	Team	AB	R	H	HR	RBI	Avg	OB	Slg	OPS	bb%	ct%	Eye	SB	CS	x/h%	Iso	RC/G
2021	A	Delmarva	99	17	28	3	17	283	408	434	843	18	72	0.75	5	3	29	152	6.57
2022	A+	Aberdeen	186	27	44	8	20	237	304	425	729	9	73	0.36	6	3	39	188	4.48
2022	AA	Bowie	252	58	75	17	46	298	381	571	953	12	77	0.58	10	2	44	274	7.45
2022	AAA	Norfolk Tides	39	7	14	4	7	359	405	718	1123	7	87	0.60	0	1	43	359	8.68
2023	AAA	Norfolk Tides	565	104	164	21	92	290	355	483	838	9	76	0.42	10	4	39	193	5.98

Broke out with huge 2nd half in AAA. He can hit the ball, and that's his thing. He's boasts an above average hit tool with average to potentially above average power. Makes hard contact with simple approach and should hit for high BA with ability to go to opp field. Below average arm limits defensive upside.

Nunez,Abraham — 89 — Chicago (A)

EXP MLB DEBUT: 2027 | H/W: 6-2 175 | FUT: Starting CF | 7E

Bats L Age 18
2023 FA (DR)

- Pwr ++
- BAvg +++
- Spd ++++
- Def +++

Year	Lev	Team	AB	R	H	HR	RBI	Avg	OB	Slg	OPS	bb%	ct%	Eye	SB	CS	x/h%	Iso	RC/G
2023	Rk	DSL White Sox	147	28	44	3	29	299	428	442	870	18	85	1.50	12	7	30	143	6.91

Athletic OF prospect with MLB bloodlines made professional debut in Dominican Summer League. Son of Abraham, former OF for MIA and KC in early 00s, son is more athletic than father. Solid bat-to-ball skills carry offensive profile with slasher approach. Also, plus speed is there, which is a plus on the bases and defensively in CF.

Nunez,Malcom — 35 — Pittsburgh

EXP MLB DEBUT: 2024 | H/W: 6-0 205 | FUT: Starting 1B | 7C

Bats R Age 23
2018 FA (CU)

- Pwr ++++
- BAvg ++
- Spd +
- Def ++

Year	Lev	Team	AB	R	H	HR	RBI	Avg	OB	Slg	OPS	bb%	ct%	Eye	SB	CS	x/h%	Iso	RC/G
2022	AAA	Indianapolis	13	1	3	1	1	231	412	462	873	24	62	0.80	0	0	33	231	7.27
2023	Rk	FCL Pirates B	5	1	2	0	2	400	625	600	1225	38	100		0	0	50	200	12.76
2023	A	Bradenton	15	2	5	0	2	333	444	400	844	17	87	1.50	0	0	20	67	6.60
2023	A+	Greensboro	16	3	5	1	7	313	421	625	1046	16	75	0.75	0	0	60	313	9.10
2023	AAA	Indianapolis	241	30	57	7	34	237	292	357	649	7	73	0.30	0	2	26	120	3.34

Strong, stout INF who missed time with shoulder issue and struggled to match HR production from 2022. Has to hit to stick. Makes consistent contact and has plus bat speed with quick, strong wrists. Can give the ball a ride, particularly to pull side. Struggles to recognize breaking balls and hits too many GB. No speed and not a sound defender.

Nunez,Nasim — 46 — Washington

EXP MLB DEBUT: 2024 | H/W: 5-9 168 | FUT: Starting MIF | 7D

Bats B Age 23
2019 (2) HS (GA)

- Pwr +
- BAvg ++
- Spd ++++
- Def ++++

Year	Lev	Team	AB	R	H	HR	RBI	Avg	OB	Slg	OPS	bb%	ct%	Eye	SB	CS	x/h%	Iso	RC/G
2021	A	Jupiter	189	33	46	0	10	243	362	265	626	16	76	0.76	33	10	7	21	3.55
2022	A+	Beloit	300	53	74	2	27	247	391	323	714	19	66	0.69	49	11	22	77	4.99
2022	AA	Pensacola	142	22	37	0	14	261	367	303	670	14	75	0.67	21	5	16	42	4.12
2023	AA	Pensacola	490	84	110	5	43	224	341	286	627	15	78	0.81	52	7	16	61	3.55

Super athletic, contact-oriented switch-hitter was 2023 Futures Game MVP. Defensively gifted with quick reactions, soft hands and strong arm. Spray approach at the plate, especially from LH side. Loads of ground ball contact, taking advantage of double-plus foot speed. Discerning eye, will work counts. Struggles versus breakers, depressing BA.

Nunez,Rainer — 3 — Toronto

EXP MLB DEBUT: 2026 | H/W: 6-2 180 | FUT: Starting 1B | 8E

Bats R Age 23
2017 FA (DR)

- Pwr ++++
- BAvg ++
- Spd +
- Def ++

Year	Lev	Team	AB	R	H	HR	RBI	Avg	OB	Slg	OPS	bb%	ct%	Eye	SB	CS	x/h%	Iso	RC/G
2021	A	Dunedin	19	4	5	1	3	263	364	421	785	14	79	0.75	0	0	20	158	5.27
2022	A	Dunedin	361	50	108	15	63	299	325	482	807	4	77	0.17	0	0	32	183	5.17
2022	A+	Vancouver	106	15	34	4	19	321	379	491	870	9	75	0.37	0	0	29	170	6.35
2023	A+	Vancouver	139	27	43	3	26	309	381	446	827	10	78	0.53	0	0	28	137	5.89
2023	AA	New Hampshire	304	26	68	10	42	224	274	352	626	6	71	0.24	0	0	28	128	2.97

Tall, physical 1B who is power-only prospect at present. Very little secondary skills in tool box but can drive ball to all fields with vicious uppercut stroke. Pitch recognition a bit lacking but improving. Has struggled to get to game power due to moving parts in swing. Makes better contact than expected. Poor speed and limited with glove.

O Rae,Dylan — 48 — Milwaukee

EXP MLB DEBUT: 2026 | H/W: 5-7 160 | FUT: Starting 2B | 8D

Bats L Age 20
2022 (3) HS (ON)

- Pwr +
- BAvg ++++
- Spd +++++
- Def +++

Year	Lev	Team	AB	R	H	HR	RBI	Avg	OB	Slg	OPS	bb%	ct%	Eye	SB	CS	x/h%	Iso	RC/G
2022	Rk	ACL Brewers G	26	6	8	0	3	308	438	308	745	19	73	0.86	4	1	0	0	5.31
2023	Rk	ACL Brewers G	130	44	47	0	15	362	512	408	919	24	82	1.74	28	2	11	46	7.96
2023	A	Carolina	88	14	29	0	8	330	438	375	813	16	84	1.21	16	4	14	45	6.14

Advanced hitter with ability to use all fields and leverage knowledge of strike zone and barrel control. Led ACL in OBP and 2nd in SB. Walked more than struck out. Very little power in short frame and hits ton of GB where he can use double-plus speed. Very smart player who maximizes quickness in field. Plays both 2B and CF.

Ochoa Jr.,Nehomar — 9 — Houston

EXP MLB DEBUT: 2027 | H/W: 6-4 210 | FUT: Starting OF | 9E

Bats R Age 18
2023 (11) HS (TX)
Pwr ++++
BAvg +++
Spd +++
Def +++

Year	Lev	Team	AB	R	H	HR	RBI	Avg	OB	Slg	OPS	bb%	ct%	Eye	SB	CS	x/h%	Iso	RC/G
2023	Rk	FCL Astros	36	10	8	3	9	222	282	528	810	8	81	0.43	1	0	63	306	5.23

Young OF prospect with raw power to all fields, knows how to lift and pull pitches out of the park. Somewhat aggressive at plate, but recognizes pitches well, makes good contact. Strong, physically mature build. Good runner, potential to be SB threat. Strong arm aids OF projection. Significant upside.

Ogans,Keshawn — 456 — Atlanta

EXP MLB DEBUT: 2024 | H/W: 5-8 180 | FUT: Reserve IF | 6B

Bats R Age 22
2022 (20) California
Pwr ++
BAvg +++
Spd +++
Def +++

Year	Lev	Team	AB	R	H	HR	RBI	Avg	OB	Slg	OPS	bb%	ct%	Eye	SB	CS	x/h%	Iso	RC/G
2022	NCAA	California	219	36	69	3	30	315	372	420	792	8	87	0.71	4	3	23	105	5.36
2022	Rk	FCL Braves	7	2	1	0	0	143	250	143	393	13	43	0.25	0	0	0	0	-0.41
2022	A	Augusta	77	13	22	1	9	286	329	351	680	6	84	0.42	9	0	14	65	3.81
2022	A+	Rome	24	3	4	0	1	167	259	208	468	11	71	0.43	0	0	25	42	1.09
2023	A+	Rome	388	43	103	9	67	265	343	397	740	11	78	0.53	10	8	31	131	4.78

Short-statured, UT infielder improved steadily during 2023 season in High-A. Strength gains during the off-season and tweaks to swing in-season helped bat come alive late. Short levers aid contact bat profile. Works counts and will spray the ball. Surprising pop to the pull side but likely caps HR production at 10-15 HR. Fringe average runner.

Olivar,Ricardo — 27 — Minnesota

EXP MLB DEBUT: 2026 | H/W: 5-10 176 | FUT: Starting OF | 7D

Bats R Age 22
2019 FA (VZ)
Pwr ++
BAvg +++
Spd ++
Def ++

Year	Lev	Team	AB	R	H	HR	RBI	Avg	OB	Slg	OPS	bb%	ct%	Eye	SB	CS	x/h%	Iso	RC/G
2021	Rk	FCL Twins	49	5	10	1	5	204	316	347	663	14	65	0.47	3	0	40	143	4.00
2022	Rk	FCL Twins	129	16	45	5	23	349	429	605	1033	12	74	0.55	5	5	44	256	8.91
2022	A	Fort Myers	9	0	2	0	1	222	300	222	522	10	67	0.33	0	0	0	0	1.69
2023	A	Fort Myers	372	75	106	10	58	285	383	452	834	14	75	0.63	12	1	38	167	6.24

Intriguing prospect who finished 4th in BA and 2nd in OBP in first full year in minors. Plays both C and LF, though not above average at either spot. Shows athleticism and mobility behind plate. Not a great arm but sufficient. Did better job of controlling strike zone and hitting spin. Making harder contact with smoother swing.

Ornelas,Jonathan — 468 — Texas

EXP MLB DEBUT: 2023 | H/W: 6-0 196 | FUT: Utility player | 6B

Bats R Age 23
2018 (3) HS (AZ)
Pwr ++
BAvg ++
Spd +++
Def +++

Year	Lev	Team	AB	R	H	HR	RBI	Avg	OB	Slg	OPS	bb%	ct%	Eye	SB	CS	x/h%	Iso	RC/G
2019	A	Hickory	413	61	106	6	38	257	325	373	698	9	75	0.41	13	4	31	116	4.22
2021	A+	Hickory	376	71	98	8	38	261	300	394	693	5	77	0.24	9	5	31	133	3.92
2022	AA	Frisco	525	84	157	14	64	299	354	425	779	8	77	0.37	14	6	23	126	5.09
2023	AAA	Round Rock	434	78	110	8	52	253	362	359	722	15	72	0.61	15	1	25	106	4.75
2023	MLB	Texas	7	2	1	0	0	143	143	143	286	0	43	0.00	0	0	0	0	-2.26

Aggressive approach with negligible power, raw swing decisions, & slow load. Tons of GB contact, though doubled BB% in AAA. 114 max EV is surprising on 85 mph avg EV, but 15% SwK on offspeed tempers otherwise okay contact skills. Good speed & average glove with reps in both IF and OF says super utility projection without more pop.

Ornelas,Tirso — 79 — San Diego

EXP MLB DEBUT: 2024 | H/W: 6-2 200 | FUT: Reserve OF | 6B

Bats L Age 24
2017 FA (MX)
Pwr +++
BAvg +++
Spd ++
Def ++

Year	Lev	Team	AB	R	H	HR	RBI	Avg	OB	Slg	OPS	bb%	ct%	Eye	SB	CS	x/h%	Iso	RC/G
2021	A+	Fort Wayne	383	57	95	7	55	248	338	389	727	12	74	0.53	3	1	41	141	4.75
2022	AA	San Antonio	441	62	127	7	51	288	351	408	759	9	81	0.51	7	2	29	120	4.97
2022	AAA	El Paso	14	2	3	0	2	214	267	286	552	7	86	0.50	0	0	33	71	2.54
2023	AA	San Antonio	264	38	75	11	51	284	386	473	860	14	78	0.75	4	4	37	189	6.45
2023	AAA	El Paso	214	34	61	4	24	285	354	425	780	10	78	0.49	4	2	33	140	5.29

Consistent OF who returned to AA to begin 23 but later promoted to AAA mid-season. Set personal best in HR while also improving contact rate. No plus tools in arsenal but gets on base and uses instincts well. Hits lot of GB and has been befuddled by LHP. Limited speed impacts OF range. Likely has platoon upside if not 4th OF.

Ortiz,Abimelec — 39 — Texas

EXP MLB DEBUT: 2026 | H/W: 6-0 230 | FUT: Starting 1B | 7D

Bats L Age 22
2021 FA (FL SW State JC)
Pwr ++++
BAvg ++
Spd +
Def +

Year	Lev	Team	AB	R	H	HR	RBI	Avg	OB	Slg	OPS	bb%	ct%	Eye	SB	CS	x/h%	Iso	RC/G
2021	Rk	DSL Rangers	129	33	30	11	33	233	389	581	970	20	76	1.06	5	1	73	349	8.05
2022	A	Down East	292	37	66	11	39	226	302	380	683	10	68	0.34	6	7	32	154	3.95
2023	A	Down East	101	19	31	7	20	307	402	604	1006	14	64	0.44	0	1	48	297	9.16
2023	A+	Hickory	290	59	84	26	81	290	362	624	986	10	69	0.37	1	0	50	334	8.14

A-ball repeat breakout held huge power gains in high-A though value is predicated entirely on bat. Is a 1B/LF defensive profile sliding wrong way towards DH. Will take walks and contact quality improved over year with elite EVs alongside, but will always be swing-and-miss due to nature of aggressive approach. Splits, though, do look okay.

Ortiz,Joey — 456 — Baltimore

EXP MLB DEBUT: 2023 | H/W: 5-9 190 | FUT: Utility player | 7B

Bats R Age 25
2019 (4) New Mexico St
Pwr ++
BAvg +++
Spd +++
Def ++++

Year	Lev	Team	AB	R	H	HR	RBI	Avg	OB	Slg	OPS	bb%	ct%	Eye	SB	CS	x/h%	Iso	RC/G
2021	AA	Bowie	60	11	14	4	9	233	303	467	770	9	77	0.43	1	0	43	233	4.85
2022	AA	Bowie	435	69	117	15	71	269	332	455	787	9	81	0.51	2	1	40	186	5.24
2022	AAA	Norfolk Tides	104	22	36	4	14	346	398	567	966	8	84	0.53	6	1	36	221	7.34
2023	AAA	Norfolk Tides	349	66	112	9	58	321	378	507	885	8	80	0.46	11	4	38	186	6.52
2023	MLB	Baltimore	33	4	7	0	4	212	212	242	455	0	73	0.00	0	0	14	30	0.52

Short, strong INF with standout defensive attributes. True SS with elite range and strong arm. While he's shown some power in recent seasons, he's not a slam dunk double digit HR hitter year in and year out. A lot of his value will live with his defensive versatility. Makes very easy contact and has enough speed and instincts to beat out grounders and leg out xbh.

Osuna,Alejandro — 89 — Texas

EXP MLB DEBUT: 2025 | H/W: 6-0 185 | FUT: Reserve OF | 6C

Bats L Age 21
2020 FA (MX)
Pwr ++
BAvg +++
Spd +++
Def ++

Year	Lev	Team	AB	R	H	HR	RBI	Avg	OB	Slg	OPS	bb%	ct%	Eye	SB	CS	x/h%	Iso	RC/G
2021	A	Down East	201	36	45	6	36	224	336	383	719	14	63	0.46	17	5	44	159	4.90
2022	A	Down East	273	54	84	8	44	308	388	451	839	12	81	0.71	32	15	26	143	6.03
2022	A+	Hickory	78	14	22	1	10	282	333	346	679	7	78	0.35	2	3	14	64	3.79
2023	A+	Hickory	247	56	64	5	35	259	375	385	760	16	73	0.69	16	5	31	126	5.35

Uses whole field, takes a walk, no splits, 4th OF floor, but K rate akin to someone with much more power. His hit tool could be above-average in time, but everything else looks a tick below, with that 2022 speed more a mirage that should tick down to single digits. Unless more pop develops, the floor is also the ceiling.

Packard,Spencer — 7 — Seattle

EXP MLB DEBUT: 2024 | H/W: 5-10 210 | FUT: Reserve OF | 6B

Bats L Age 26
2021 (9) Campbell
Pwr +++
BAvg +++
Spd +
Def ++

Year	Lev	Team	AB	R	H	HR	RBI	Avg	OB	Slg	OPS	bb%	ct%	Eye	SB	CS	x/h%	Iso	RC/G
2021	Rk	ACL Mariners	4	3	2	0	1	500	714	500	1214	43	75	3.00	1	0	0	0	13.75
2021	A	Modesto	120	20	30	3	18	250	323	375	698	10	84	0.68	1	0	27	125	4.25
2022	Rk	ACL Mariners	12	1	5	0	4	417	462	500	962	8	83	0.50	0	0	20	83	7.38
2022	A+	Everett	255	43	72	12	37	282	382	490	872	14	82	0.87	5	1	39	208	6.51
2023	AA	Arkansas	466	66	136	14	82	292	382	448	831	13	82	0.79	1	1	32	157	6.01

Short, strong LF with unique profile. Rarely swings and misses and draws tons of walks with discerning eye. Can tap into average power by identifying pitches to drive. Bat speed may be a tad slow for projection purposes and has zero secondary skills. Not a good athlete and has limited speed. Has to hit to get to majors.

Pages,Andy — 789 — Los Angeles (N)

EXP MLB DEBUT: 2024 | H/W: 6-1 212 | FUT: Starting OF | 8C

Bats R Age 23
2018 FA (CU)
Pwr ++++
BAvg ++
Spd ++
Def +++

Year	Lev	Team	AB	R	H	HR	RBI	Avg	OB	Slg	OPS	bb%	ct%	Eye	SB	CS	x/h%	Iso	RC/G
2019	Rk	Ogden	235	57	70	19	55	298	368	651	1019	10	66	0.33	7	6	61	353	8.98
2021	A+	Great Lakes	438	96	116	31	88	265	375	539	914	15	70	0.58	6	3	49	274	7.32
2022	AA	Tulsa	487	69	115	26	80	236	322	468	791	11	71	0.44	6	3	50	232	5.46
2023	AA	Tulsa	109	23	31	3	25	284	418	495	913	19	71	0.78	7	3	52	211	7.80
2023	AAA	Oklahoma City	3	0	0	0	0	0	250	0	250	25	33	0.50	0	0		0	-5.88

Cuban-born masher missed most of 2023 with a torn labrum that required surgery. Strong, muscular frame has thickened since turning pro, but was leaner and quicker in 2023. Plus bat speed and upper-cut swing results in above-average to plus power, but leaves him vulnerable to high heat. Lack of speed and a plus arm point to RF as his future home.

Pages,Pedro — 2 — St. Louis

EXP MLB DEBUT: 2024 | H/W: 6-1 234 | FUT: Reserve C | 6C

Bats R Age 25
2019 (6) Florida Atlantic
Pwr +++
BAvg ++
Spd ++
Def +++

Year	Lev	Team	AB	R	H	HR	RBI	Avg	OB	Slg	OPS	bb%	ct%	Eye	SB	CS	x/h%	Iso	RC/G
2019	A-	State College	179	29	52	2	21	291	386	430	817	14	78	0.72	1	0	38	140	6.06
2021	A+	Peoria	301	28	75	9	39	249	325	385	711	10	73	0.41	1	2	29	136	4.34
2022	AA	Springfield	138	22	32	6	28	232	346	413	759	15	59	0.43	1	0	41	181	5.65
2022	AAA	Memphis	153	16	34	4	16	222	287	353	640	8	70	0.30	0	0	35	131	3.34
2023	AA	Springfield	424	63	113	16	72	267	356	443	800	12	77	0.61	3	0	36	177	5.57

Thick-framed backstop showed improved plate discipline, cutting down on swing-and-miss while maintaining moderate power. Bottom of the scale speed, but moves well behind the plate with good blocking and receiving skills and a plus arm. Will need to hit to carve out a backup C role and at 25 the clock is ticking.

Palma,Miguel — 23 — Houston

EXP MLB DEBUT: 2026 | H/W: 5-8 170 | FUT: Reserve C | 6D

Bats R Age 22 — 2018 FA (VZ)
- Pwr ++
- BAvg ++
- Spd +
- Def +++

Year	Lev	Team	AB	R	H	HR	RBI	Avg	OB	Slg	OPS	bb%	ct%	Eye	SB	CS	x/h%	Iso	RC/G
2021	A	Fayetteville	39	8	12	0	8	308	426	410	836	17	67	0.62	2	0	33	103	6.91
2022	A	Fayetteville	205	28	46	6	29	224	312	366	678	11	80	0.65	0	0	37	141	4.00
2022	A+	Asheville	104	15	34	7	29	327	369	587	956	6	79	0.32	0	0	35	260	7.05
2023	Rk	FCL Astros	26	5	10	1	8	385	385	577	962	0	85	0.00	0	0	30	192	6.61
2023	A+	Asheville	230	29	63	6	38	274	340	409	749	9	78	0.45	3	1	30	135	4.78

Catching prospect shows average offensive/defensive tools. Relaxed setup at plate, discerning approach. Struggles against breaking balls but lays off outside pitches. Swing can be flat, leading to high GB%. Improved launch angle could unlock more raw power.

Palmegiani,Damiano — 35 — Toronto

EXP MLB DEBUT: 2024 | H/W: 6-1 188 | FUT: Starting 3B | 7C

Bats R Age 24 — 2021 (14) Coll of So NV
- Pwr +++
- BAvg ++
- Spd ++
- Def ++

Year	Lev	Team	AB	R	H	HR	RBI	Avg	OB	Slg	OPS	bb%	ct%	Eye	SB	CS	x/h%	Iso	RC/G
2021	Rk	FCL Blue Jays	39	11	13	2	9	333	435	538	973	15	77	0.78	1	0	31	205	7.95
2022	A	Dunedin	195	30	50	11	37	256	335	508	843	11	76	0.49	2	0	52	251	6.02
2022	A+	Vancouver	228	44	51	13	46	224	317	443	760	12	74	0.52	3	0	47	219	4.94
2023	AA	New Hampshire	393	57	98	19	71	249	346	463	809	13	68	0.46	6	0	46	214	5.91
2023	AAA	Buffalo	74	13	21	4	22	284	404	554	959	17	62	0.54	1	0	57	270	8.86

Power-hitting INF who is advancing quickly and impressed in AFL. 2nd most HR and most K in org. Racks up XBH due to pure strength and leveraged stroke. Mostly pull hitter and can chase on outer half. K rate a concern as he struggles to read spin, bringing BA into question. Improving defender but below average at 1B/3B.

Parada,Kevin — 2 — New York (N)

EXP MLB DEBUT: 2025 | H/W: 5-11 197 | FUT: Starting C | 7C

Bats R Age 22 — 2022 (1) Georgia Tech
- Pwr +++
- BAvg +++
- Spd ++
- Def ++

Year	Lev	Team	AB	R	H	HR	RBI	Avg	OB	Slg	OPS	bb%	ct%	Eye	SB	CS	x/h%	Iso	RC/G
2022	Rk	FCL Mets	11	1	3	0	3	273	385	455	839	15	91	2.00	0	0	67	182	6.65
2022	A	St. Lucie	29	5	8	1	5	276	462	414	875	26	59	0.83	0	1	25	138	8.01
2023	A	St. Lucie	13	2	1	0	1	77	200	77	277	13	46	0.29	0	0	0	0	-3.11
2023	A+	Brooklyn	340	44	90	11	42	265	324	447	771	8	72	0.31	1	2	40	182	5.16
2023	AA	Binghamton	54	4	10	3	11	185	241	389	630	7	57	0.17	0	0	50	204	3.37

Former 1st round pick saw offensive profile crash and burn in dreadful 2023 season. Strong-bodied and at physical projection. Unusual stance with problematic load. Struggles to get bat moving forward. Plus bat speed remains though and plus pull-side power. Defensively challenged, HR will need to carry the profile.

Paris,Kyren — 468 — Los Angeles (A)

EXP MLB DEBUT: 2023 | H/W: 6-0 180 | FUT: Starting 2B | 7C

Bats R Age 22 — 2019 (2) HS (CA)
- Pwr +++
- BAvg ++
- Spd ++++
- Def +++

Year	Lev	Team	AB	R	H	HR	RBI	Avg	OB	Slg	OPS	bb%	ct%	Eye	SB	CS	x/h%	Iso	RC/G
2022	Rk	ACL Angels	7	1	1	1	2	143	333	571	905	22	57	0.67	0	0	100	429	7.57
2022	A+	Tri-City	328	58	75	8	32	229	329	387	716	13	64	0.42	28	4	41	159	4.83
2022	AA	Rocket City	39	11	14	3	8	359	490	641	1131	20	64	0.71	5	0	36	282	11.36
2023	AA	Rocket City	415	79	106	14	45	255	386	417	803	17	64	0.58	44	5	36	161	6.26
2023	MLB	LA Angels	40	4	4	0	1	100	182	100	282	9	58	0.24	3	0	0	0	-2.42

Athletic MIF prospect did enough in Double-A to earn MLB promotion. Upright, slightly open swing with a small hitch in load. Swing has lengthened to extend hands and drive the ball, compromising once-promising hit tool. Power gains have been minimal, and pop projects only average at maturity. Speedy runner with SB acumen; either 2B or UT future.

Pauley,Graham — 5 — San Diego

EXP MLB DEBUT: 2025 | H/W: 6-1 200 | FUT: Starting 3B | 7C

Bats L Age 23 — 2022 (13) Duke
- Pwr +++
- BAvg +++
- Spd ++
- Def +++

Year	Lev	Team	AB	R	H	HR	RBI	Avg	OB	Slg	OPS	bb%	ct%	Eye	SB	CS	x/h%	Iso	RC/G
2022	Rk	ACL Padres	47	9	10	2	12	213	339	447	786	16	85	1.29	0	0	60	234	5.67
2022	A	Lake Elsinore	58	14	19	2	13	328	443	500	943	17	83	1.20	6	3	32	172	7.66
2023	A	Lake Elsinore	230	50	71	4	36	309	411	465	876	15	83	1.00	12	3	32	157	6.82
2023	A+	Fort Wayne	170	33	51	16	46	300	350	629	979	7	76	0.32	8	2	47	329	7.39
2023	AA	San Antonio	81	15	26	3	12	321	375	556	931	8	85	0.58	2	0	50	235	6.94

Sleeper prospect who hit .300 at 3 levels in first full pro season. Led org in hits, HR and RBI with simple approach. Leverages short stroke to make contact and makes good swing decisions to find pitches to drive. Could stand to use all fields more consistently and may have utility profile due to lack of plus tool. Passable defender.

Paulino,Eddinson — 456 — Boston

EXP MLB DEBUT: 2025 | H/W: 5-10 155 | FUT: Starting 2B | 7C

Bats L Age 21 — 2018 FA (DR)
- Pwr ++
- BAvg +++
- Spd +++
- Def +++

Year	Lev	Team	AB	R	H	HR	RBI	Avg	OB	Slg	OPS	bb%	ct%	Eye	SB	CS	x/h%	Iso	RC/G
2021	Rk	FCL Red Sox	113	25	38	0	13	336	414	549	963	12	81	0.71	5	2	53	212	7.96
2022	A	Salem	463	96	123	13	66	266	355	469	824	12	77	0.61	27	5	47	203	6.02
2023	A+	Greenville	440	68	113	12	58	257	333	420	753	10	74	0.44	26	8	39	164	4.97

Sweet-swinging INF who has advanced one level per year and hit over .300 in last 2 months of 2023. Exhibits plus hand-eye coordination and puts bat to ball with ease. Lacks ideal pop but could add strength and be more aggressive. Runs bases well and has quickness and arm to stick at any infield spot. Tends to expand zone at times.

Peete,Tai — 56 — Seattle

EXP MLB DEBUT: 2027 | H/W: 6-2 193 | FUT: Starting SS | 8D

Bats L Age 18 — 2023 (1) HS (GA)
- Pwr +++
- BAvg ++
- Spd ++++
- Def +++

Year	Lev	Team	AB	R	H	HR	RBI	Avg	OB	Slg	OPS	bb%	ct%	Eye	SB	CS	x/h%	Iso	RC/G
2023	Rk	ACL Mariners	37	4	13	0	6	351	429	432	861	12	70	0.45	3	1	15	81	6.82
2023	A	Modesto	62	7	15	2	14	242	299	387	686	7	69	0.26	3	0	33	145	3.92

Young, projectable INF who ranks among top athletes in system. May take time to develop plate discipline and pitch recognition. Shows high upside with natural swing and quick wrists. Swings very fast bat and shows ability to barrel balls to pull side. Split time between SS and 3B and has range for either. Plus arm strength an asset.

Peguero,Antony — 78 — Miami

EXP MLB DEBUT: 2027 | H/W: 6-0 175 | FUT: Starting OF | 7E

Bats R Age 18 — 2022 FA (DR)
- Pwr ++
- BAvg +++
- Spd +++
- Def +++

Year	Lev	Team	AB	R	H	HR	RBI	Avg	OB	Slg	OPS	bb%	ct%	Eye	SB	CS	x/h%	Iso	RC/G
2022	Rk	DSL Miami	196	24	56	5	33	286	330	423	754	6	82	0.37	7	6	29	138	4.68
2023	Rk	FCL Marlins	156	24	35	0	21	224	301	282	583	10	73	0.40	6	3	20	58	2.73

Promising hitting prospect struggled mightily in US debut. Lean, athletic frame. Overmatched by complex pitching. Closed stance with lots of movement to get hands to hit position. Linear swing with average swing speed. Struggles getting to hard contact. Aggressive approach. Average runner. Taxed as CF but lacks power carry for corner OF.

Pena,Manuel — 46 — Arizona

EXP MLB DEBUT: 2025 | H/W: 6-1 170 | FUT: Reserve IF | 7E

Bats L Age 20 — 2021 FA (DR)
- Pwr ++
- BAvg ++
- Spd ++
- Def +++

Year	Lev	Team	AB	R	H	HR	RBI	Avg	OB	Slg	OPS	bb%	ct%	Eye	SB	CS	x/h%	Iso	RC/G
2021	Rk	DSL Dbacks	194	30	49	4	30	253	341	361	702	12	76	0.57	17	7	22	108	4.32
2022	Rk	ACL DBacks R	116	25	33	4	28	284	341	466	807	8	74	0.33	4	1	30	181	5.54
2022	A	Visalia	137	17	34	0	17	248	344	314	658	13	70	0.49	1	3	24	66	3.91
2023	A	Visalia	206	22	51	1	24	248	311	345	656	8	72	0.33	8	5	27	97	3.70
2023	A+	Hillsboro	215	25	52	4	24	242	297	381	679	7	73	0.29	5	5	35	140	3.90

Teenager split season between Low and High-A, with vanilla offensive results across the board. Physically mature. Plate approach, pitch selection need refinement. Necessary adjustments could unlock raw power. Defensively limited at 2B, struggles with routine plays. Will need to step up offense to survive shift down defensive ladder.

Pereira,Everson — 789 — New York (A)

EXP MLB DEBUT: 2023 | H/W: 5-11 191 | FUT: Starting OF | 8D

Bats R Age 22 — 2017 FA (VZ)
- Pwr ++++
- BAvg ++
- Spd ++++
- Def +++

Year	Lev	Team	AB	R	H	HR	RBI	Avg	OB	Slg	OPS	bb%	ct%	Eye	SB	CS	x/h%	Iso	RC/G
2022	A+	Hudson Valley	288	55	79	9	43	274	351	455	806	11	70	0.39	19	5	35	181	5.83
2022	AA	Somerset	113	21	32	5	13	283	336	504	840	7	67	0.24	2	2	38	221	6.27
2023	AA	Somerset	165	24	48	10	31	291	364	545	910	10	67	0.35	7	2	44	255	7.30
2023	AAA	Scranton/WB	138	29	43	8	33	312	371	551	922	9	68	0.30	4	0	37	239	7.34
2023	MLB	New York (A)	93	6	14	0	10	151	218	194	411	8	57	0.20	4	0	29	43	-0.08

Powerful CF prospect known for max EV earned MLB stint late in season. Athletic build at physical projection with visible muscle mass. Upright stance with a slight trigger and dynamic hip rotation on the swing. It's plus-plus bat speed with inconsistent bat path. Struggles with whiffs and aggressiveness. Plus power plays to all fields. Plus runner.

Perez, Jr.,Robert — 79 — Seattle

EXP MLB DEBUT: 2024 | H/W: 6-0 170 | FUT: Reserve OF | 6B

Bats R Age 23 — 2016 FA (VZ)
- Pwr ++++
- BAvg +
- Spd +
- Def +

Year	Lev	Team	AB	R	H	HR	RBI	Avg	OB	Slg	OPS	bb%	ct%	Eye	SB	CS	x/h%	Iso	RC/G
2021	A	Modesto	401	62	113	15	77	282	338	456	794	8	69	0.30	0	0	34	175	5.40
2022	A	Modesto	345	78	93	20	87	270	359	501	860	12	69	0.44	5	0	42	232	6.55
2022	A+	Everett	120	22	41	7	27	342	448	583	1031	16	72	0.68	1	1	34	242	9.05
2023	Rk	ACL Mariners	10	2	3	1	1	300	417	600	1017	17	70	0.67	0	0	33	300	8.62
2023	AA	Arkansas	450	56	109	16	62	242	301	416	717	8	66	0.25	2	2	39	173	4.53

Very strong OF with significant power to pull side. Prospect with pop and very little else. Could provide offensive jolt in limited situations. Makes very loud contact when bat meets ball. Tough against LHP. Rarely draws walks and will strike out at very high levels. Struggles with FB up in zone. Probable 1B/DH long-term with poor foot speed.

Perez,Onil — 2 — San Francisco

EXP MLB DEBUT: 2026 | H/W: 6-1 187 | FUT: Starting C | **7E**

Bats R Age 21
2019 FA (DR)

- Pwr +
- BAvg + + +
- Spd +
- Def + +

Year	Lev	Team	AB	R	H	HR	RBI	Avg	OB	Sig	OPS	bb%	ct%	Eye	SB	CS	x/h%	Iso	RC/G
2021	Rk	DSL Giants B	103	24	30	2	15	291	451	398	849	23	85	2.00	6	4	23	107	6.89
2022	Rk	ACL Giants B	149	18	41	0	20	275	345	383	728	10	80	0.53	3	2	32	107	4.76
2023	A	San Jose	253	46	76	2	36	300	359	403	762	8	88	0.74	21	2	24	103	5.07
2023	A+	Eugene	45	4	13	0	1	289	333	333	667	6	84	0.43	2	2	8	44	3.74

Solid all-around backstop who has unique profile with contact-making abilities and good hit tool. Has work to do behind plate but will be given time to develop. Receives well and has strong arm with quick release. Mostly line drives and groundballs at present but it has worked. Very rarely swings and misses. Well below average power and lacks projection.

Perez,Wenceel — 4 — Detroit

EXP MLB DEBUT: 2024 | H/W: 5-11 203 | FUT: Utility player | **6B**

Bats B Age 24
2016 FA (DR)

- Pwr +
- BAvg + + +
- Spd + + + +
- Def + + +

Year	Lev	Team	AB	R	H	HR	RBI	Avg	OB	Sig	OPS	bb%	ct%	Eye	SB	CS	x/h%	Iso	RC/G
2022	A+	West Michigan	206	35	59	9	38	286	369	529	898	12	82	0.71	13	1	46	243	6.79
2022	AA	Erie	150	28	46	5	28	307	370	540	910	9	85	0.65	5	4	43	233	6.81
2023	A	Lakeland	21	4	8	0	1	381	409	524	933	5	76	0.20	1	0	38	143	7.17
2023	AA	Erie	299	56	81	6	28	271	347	375	722	10	83	0.67	19	2	21	104	4.56
2023	AAA	Toledo	129	29	34	3	19	264	391	496	887	17	78	0.93	6	5	59	233	7.21

Switch-hitting infield prospect has a quick bat and rarely chases out of the zone. Athletic frame with above-average speed and range to stick at 2B. Keeps weight on front foot with a discerning eye at the plate, but short, quick stroke and flat bat path leads to line drives and GB and makes him a contact over power hitter. Destined for a UT role.

Perlaza,Yonathan — 7 — Chicago (N)

EXP MLB DEBUT: 2024 | H/W: 5-9 170 | FUT: Reserve OF | **6C**

Bats B Age 25
2015 FA (VZ)

- Pwr + + + +
- BAvg + + +
- Spd + +
- Def +

Year	Lev	Team	AB	R	H	HR	RBI	Avg	OB	Sig	OPS	bb%	ct%	Eye	SB	CS	x/h%	Iso	RC/G
2019	A-	Eugene	99	11	29	1	9	293	340	434	774	7	73	0.26	5	1	38	141	5.24
2019	A	South Bend	84	11	20	1	11	238	333	333	667	13	69	0.46	0	1	30	95	3.96
2021	A+	South Bend	357	54	100	15	64	280	349	479	828	10	73	0.40	6	4	40	199	5.90
2022	AA	Tennessee	470	81	120	23	73	255	354	491	846	13	73	0.57	15	6	52	236	6.32
2023	AAA	Iowa	461	100	131	23	85	284	385	534	919	14	74	0.64	13	5	50	249	7.35

Switch-hitting prospect continues to put up impressive offensive numbers. Short, stocky frame with above-average pull-side power. Gets foot down early with a strong lower half with grooved swing, but draws plenty of walks with lots of hard contact (66 XBH), though he sometimes cheats to get to it. Below average speed and defense limit him to LF.

Pineda,Esmith — 9 — Cincinnati

EXP MLB DEBUT: 2026 | H/W: 5-10 183 | FUT: Starting OF | **7E**

Bats R Age 19
2022 FA (PN)

- Pwr + + +
- BAvg + + +
- Spd + + +
- Def + + +

Year	Lev	Team	AB	R	H	HR	RBI	Avg	OB	Sig	OPS	bb%	ct%	Eye	SB	CS	x/h%	Iso	RC/G
2022	Rk	DSL Reds	49	10	18	3	13	367	446	592	1038	13	82	0.78	2	1	28	224	8.39
2023	Rk	ACL Reds	165	30	45	1	36	273	368	400	768	13	75	0.61	5	2	38	127	5.46

Raw, offensively skilled prospect had solid US debut. Strong, compact frame with solid power projection. Open stance with bat wrap in load. Plus bat speed with uppercut trajectory swing. Creates good loft but not enough leverage presently to hit ball over fence. Gap-to-gap hitter. Above-average raw power in frame. Strong arm, likely COF long term.

Pineda,Israel — 2 — Washington

EXP MLB DEBUT: 2022 | H/W: 5-11 217 | FUT: Starting C | **7C**

Bats R Age 24
2016 FA (VZ)

- Pwr + + +
- BAvg + +
- Spd +
- Def + +

Year	Lev	Team	AB	R	H	HR	RBI	Avg	OB	Sig	OPS	bb%	ct%	Eye	SB	CS	x/h%	Iso	RC/G
2022	AAA	Rochester	21	3	2	1	5	95	269	286	555	19	67	0.71	0	0	100	190	2.15
2022	MLB	Washington	13	1	1	0	0	77	143	77	220	7	46	0.14	0	0	0	0	-4.03
2023	Rk	FCL Nationals	5	3	2	1	1	400	500	###	1500	17	80	1.00	0	0	50	600	13.87
2023	A+	Wilmington	39	3	8	1	4	205	225	308	533	3	74	0.10	0	0	25	103	1.59
2023	AA	Harrisburg	98	6	15	1	9	153	210	214	424	7	65	0.21	0	0	27	61	0.12

Injury-riddled season again that took a bite out the upside of this power-over-hit catcher. Has the raw pop to sit in the mid-teens HR range, but has to stay on the field, and a questionable hit tool could cap his playing time. Defensive only average. Still young enough to improve and present strength, but trend is heading towards a backup role.

Placencia,Adrian — 46 — Los Angeles (A)

EXP MLB DEBUT: 2024 | H/W: 5-11 173 | FUT: Reserve SS | **6C**

Bats B Age 20
2019 FA (DR)

- Pwr + +
- BAvg + +
- Spd + + +
- Def + + + +

Year	Lev	Team	AB	R	H	HR	RBI	Avg	OB	Sig	OPS	bb%	ct%	Eye	SB	CS	x/h%	Iso	RC/G
2021	Rk	ACL Angels	143	29	25	5	19	175	310	343	653	16	66	0.57	4	2	44	168	3.76
2022	A	Inland Empire	382	83	97	13	64	254	378	427	804	17	63	0.54	21	8	39	173	6.33
2023	A+	Tri City	390	59	85	9	46	218	354	336	690	17	66	0.62	24	11	31	118	4.42
2023	AA	Rocket City	53	5	9	1	4	170	228	226	454	7	55	0.17	0	0	11	57	0.49

Short-statured MIF prospect struggled to hit in 2023. Aggressive approach with chase and whiff tendencies. Slightly open, upright stance with lots of unnecessary moving parts in lower half prior to unleashing swing. High leg kick is comical given profile. MIF defense carries profile to an up/down outcome.

Polanco,Shalin — 8 — Pittsburgh

EXP MLB DEBUT: 2027 | H/W: 6-0 168 | FUT: Starting OF | **8E**

Bats L Age 20
2021 FA (DR)

- Pwr + + +
- BAvg + + +
- Spd + + +
- Def + + +

Year	Lev	Team	AB	R	H	HR	RBI	Avg	OB	Sig	OPS	bb%	ct%	Eye	SB	CS	x/h%	Iso	RC/G
2021	Rk	DSL Pirates B	157	16	32	3	22	204	286	338	623	10	72	0.41	6	2	38	134	3.24
2022	Rk	FCL Pirates B	132	24	33	3	17	250	313	371	684	8	70	0.30	7	4	30	121	3.97
2023	A	Bradenton	264	38	64	12	45	242	317	439	757	10	67	0.33	17	7	44	197	5.08

High-profile international signee with raw tools but significant projection. Has frame to add weight. Quick bat produces hard line drives and has potential to hit for plus power. Speed is solid and runs bases well. Plays game aggressively and can lead to expansion of strike zone. Strong arm highlights CF defense and needs work on reads.

Pollard,Chandler — 456 — Texas

EXP MLB DEBUT: 2027 | H/W: 6-2 173 | FUT: Utility player | **7E**

Bats R Age 19
2022 (5) HS (GA)

- Pwr + +
- BAvg + +
- Spd + + + +
- Def + +

Year	Lev	Team	AB	R	H	HR	RBI	Avg	OB	Sig	OPS	bb%	ct%	Eye	SB	CS	x/h%	Iso	RC/G
2022	Rk	ACL Rangers	5	0	0	0	0	0	167	0	167	17	60	0.50	0	1		0	-4.34
2023	Rk	ACL Rangers	183	43	43	3	23	235	324	388	712	12	57	0.30	20	2	40	153	5.27
2023	A	Down East	5	1	1	0	0	200	429	400	829	29	60	1.00	1	0	100	200	7.54

Tooled up but sushi raw upside bet struck out 36% at complex while struggling at SS defensively. Pull-heavy, hyper aggressive approach stumbled across board even if development path was already long. Geared for power with flyball lean, and easy plus speed but LHP splits bottom-of-barrel point to utility ceiling.

Pomares,Jairo — 79 — San Francisco

EXP MLB DEBUT: 2025 | H/W: 6-0 185 | FUT: Starting OF | **8E**

Bats L Age 23
2018 FA (CU)

- Pwr + + + +
- BAvg + +
- Spd + +
- Def + +

Year	Lev	Team	AB	R	H	HR	RBI	Avg	OB	Sig	OPS	bb%	ct%	Eye	SB	CS	x/h%	Iso	RC/G
2021	A	San Jose	199	45	74	14	44	372	416	693	1109	7	73	0.28	0	0	49	322	9.54
2021	A+	Eugene	103	13	27	6	15	262	269	505	774	1	68	0.03	1	0	44	243	4.89
2022	Rk	ACL Giants	15	5	8	3	7	533	563	###	1896	6	87	0.50	0	0	75	800	17.32
2022	A+	Eugene	338	49	86	14	59	254	326	438	764	10	62	0.28	0	0	40	183	5.44
2023	Rk	ACL Giants O	26	4	8	0	3	308	419	385	804	16	65	0.56	0	0	25	77	6.41

Power-hitting OF who was mired with injuries (quad, back) in 23. May have best pure power in org with elite bat speed and massive strength. Plate approach needs work. Swings aggressively and chases out of zone. Sells out for power which can impact BA. Has actually hit for BA but will likely fall at upper levels. All other tools below average.

Pouaka-Grego,Nikau — 6 — Philadelphia

EXP MLB DEBUT: 2027 | H/W: 5-10 175 | FUT: Starting 2B | **8E**

Bats L Age 19
2022 FA (NZ)

- Pwr + + +
- BAvg + +
- Spd + +
- Def + +

Year	Lev	Team	AB	R	H	HR	RBI	Avg	OB	Sig	OPS	bb%	ct%	Eye	SB	CS	x/h%	Iso	RC/G
2022	Rk	FCL Phillies	103	20	31	3	16	301	395	466	861	13	84	1.00	2	2	32	165	6.45
2023	--	Did Not Play																	

Torn ACL in winter Australian league wiped out his 2023. Popped on radar in 2022 with a hit-over-power profile that featured a patient eye at the plate and some developing pop. Still just 19, he played both MIF positions in complex league ball when we last saw him, but range and arm likely work best at 2B. Sleeper potential here due to the injury.

Pratt,Cooper — 6 — Milwaukee

EXP MLB DEBUT: 2027 | H/W: 6-4 195 | FUT: Starting 3B | **8D**

Bats R Age 19
2023 (6) HS (MS)

- Pwr + +
- BAvg + + +
- Spd + + +
- Def + + +

Year	Lev	Team	AB	R	H	HR	RBI	Avg	OB	Sig	OPS	bb%	ct%	Eye	SB	CS	x/h%	Iso	RC/G
2023	Rk	ACL Brewers Gold	45	9	16	0	8	356	420	444	864	10	76	0.45	4	0	19	89	6.56

Projectable INF who has outstanding hitting profile. Plenty of room to grow into long, lean frame. Already has strong batting eye and ability to read spin. Relies on instincts which should only enhance existing tools. Makes easy contact and drives ball to all fields. Should get to at least average power if not more. Likely to move to 3B or OF.

Prieto,Cesar — 456 — St. Louis

EXP MLB DEBUT: 2024 | H/W: 5-9 175 | FUT: Utility player | **7D**

Bats L Age 24 — 2022 FA (CU) — Pwr ++ | BAvg ++++ | Spd ++ | Def ++

Year	Lev	Team	AB	R	H	HR	RBI	Avg	OB	Slg	OPS	bb%	ct%	Eye	SB	CS	x/h%	Iso	RC/G
2022	A+	Aberdeen	97	13	33	7	20	340	373	619	991	5	84	0.31	3	1	39	278	7.23
2022	AA	Bowie	368	44	94	4	37	255	285	348	632	4	84	0.26	2	5	28	92	3.19
2023	AA	Bowie	231	33	84	4	29	364	402	476	879	6	93	0.88	5	6	20	113	6.17
2023	AAA	Memphis	163	24	44	4	20	270	300	387	687	4	85	0.28	2	0	23	117	3.76
2023	AAA	Norfolk Tides	104	16	33	2	20	317	366	471	837	7	90	0.80	2	1	33	154	5.84

Cuban-born infielder was acquired in the Jack Flaherty trade. Plus bat-to-ball skills and a quick, compact stroke result in a plus hit tool - 30 BB/52 K. Short frame and line-drive approach result in fringe power without much upside. Lack of range and speed leave him without a clear defensive home and is likely a UT player who can hit.

Quero,Edgar — 2 — Chicago (A)

EXP MLB DEBUT: 2024 | H/W: 5-11 170 | FUT: Starting C | **7B**

Bats B Age 21 — 2021 FA (CU) — Pwr ++ | BAvg +++ | Spd ++ | Def +++

Year	Lev	Team	AB	R	H	HR	RBI	Avg	OB	Slg	OPS	bb%	ct%	Eye	SB	CS	x/h%	Iso	RC/G
2021	Rk	ACL Angels	87	21	22	4	24	253	409	506	915	21	68	0.82	1	1	59	253	7.90
2021	A	Inland Empire	34	2	7	1	6	206	308	353	661	13	53	0.31	1	0	43	147	4.48
2022	A	Inland Empire	413	86	129	17	75	312	416	530	946	15	78	0.80	12	5	42	218	7.66
2023	AA	Birmingham	112	12	31	3	22	277	372	393	765	13	79	0.74	0	0	23	116	5.18
2023	AA	Rocket City	256	40	63	3	35	246	379	332	711	18	79	1.04	1	2	25	86	4.82

Short, stocky contact-oriented C prospect was traded mid-season by LAA. Switch-hitter, completely different type of hitter from either side. From LH side, employs spray approach with patience and contact at premium. From RH side, greater slugging, more likely to drive ball to gaps. Overall, above-average hit tool. Fringe defender behind the dish.

Quero,Jeferson — 2 — Milwaukee

EXP MLB DEBUT: 2024 | H/W: 5-11 215 | FUT: Starting C | **7B**

Bats R Age 21 — 2019 FA (VZ) — Pwr +++ | BAvg +++ | Spd ++ | Def ++++

Year	Lev	Team	AB	R	H	HR	RBI	Avg	OB	Slg	OPS	bb%	ct%	Eye	SB	CS	x/h%	Iso	RC/G
2021	Rk	ACL Brewers B	68	15	21	2	8	309	413	500	913	15	85	1.20	4	3	38	191	7.20
2022	A	Carolina	284	44	79	6	43	278	343	412	755	9	79	0.46	10	2	32	134	4.90
2022	A+	Wisconsin	83	10	26	4	14	313	329	530	860	2	82	0.13	0	0	35	217	5.64
2023	AA	Biloxi	336	47	88	16	49	262	337	440	777	10	80	0.56	5	0	32	179	5.07

Short, strong C who enjoyed consistent campaign with both bat and glove. Learning to draw more walks and using natural strength to hit high in HR. Showcases plus arm strength behind plate. Moves well and is adept at blocking and receiving. May not have plus offensive tool but can hit spin and understands value of putting ball in play.

Quintana,Roismar — 37 — Washington

EXP MLB DEBUT: 2026 | H/W: 6-1 175 | FUT: Starting OF | **7D**

Bats R Age 21 — 2020 FA (VZ) — Pwr ++++ | BAvg +++ | Spd ++ | Def ++

Year	Lev	Team	AB	R	H	HR	RBI	Avg	OB	Slg	OPS	bb%	ct%	Eye	SB	CS	x/h%	Iso	RC/G
2021	Rk	FCL Nationals	13	3	4	1	5	308	526	692	1219	32	62	1.20	0	0	75	385	13.68
2022	Rk	FCL Nationals	180	41	52	5	28	289	323	439	762	5	74	0.20	3	1	31	150	4.77
2023	A	Fredericksburg	321	38	82	4	41	255	345	346	691	12	68	0.42	0	0	22	90	4.32

Big, strong right-handed OF who also saw some time at first base, which may be his long-term home. Has all-fields pop, but hasn't translated into HR, and strikeouts piled up in his first full-season league. With very little speed, the power will need to come to carry the profile, especially if he's in OF/1B mode.

Quintero,Geraldo — 457 — Atlanta

EXP MLB DEBUT: 2026 | H/W: 5-5 155 | FUT: Reserve IF | **6C**

Bats B Age 22 — 2019 FA (VZ) — Pwr + | BAvg +++ | Spd ++++ | Def ++

Year	Lev	Team	AB	R	H	HR	RBI	Avg	OB	Slg	OPS	bb%	ct%	Eye	SB	CS	x/h%	Iso	RC/G
2021	Rk	FCL Braves	121	23	25	0	6	207	304	273	577	12	79	0.65	12	5	20	66	2.89
2022	A	Augusta	362	61	95	6	47	262	349	423	771	12	81	0.70	26	8	39	160	5.35
2022	A+	Rome	80	12	19	2	12	238	322	363	685	11	73	0.45	8	3	32	125	4.05
2023	A+	Rome	406	54	102	3	41	251	341	325	666	12	78	0.63	29	13	19	74	3.95

Tiny, switch-hitting IF was one dimensional hitter in High-A. Aggressive approach with solid bat-to-ball skills. Slasher profile, struggles to drive the ball with flat, linear swing. Any power comes from RH side. Plus runner with raw base stealing skills. Mostly outruns throws, high caught rate. Played mostly IF with some OF reps late in season.

Rada,Nelson — 8 — Los Angeles (A)

EXP MLB DEBUT: 2026 | H/W: 5-10 160 | FUT: Starting OF | **8D**

Bats L Age 18 — 2022 FA (VZ) — Pwr +++ | BAvg +++ | Spd ++++ | Def +++

Year	Lev	Team	AB	R	H	HR	RBI	Avg	OB	Slg	OPS	bb%	ct%	Eye	SB	CS	x/h%	Iso	RC/G
2022	Rk	DSL Angels	164	50	51	1	26	311	405	439	844	14	84	1.00	27	6	31	128	6.41
2023	A	Inland Empire	439	94	121	2	48	276	379	346	725	14	78	0.74	55	11	17	71	4.86

Athletic, teenaged OF prospect handled aggressive full-season assignment well. Slim build with room to grow. Short-levered swing promotes contact over power. With swing modifications and strength gains, has the capacity to hit for average power. Works counts and sprays hits around. Plus runner with SB and bunting capabilities. Will stick in CF.

Rafaela,Ceddanne — 8 — Boston

EXP MLB DEBUT: 2023 | H/W: 5-9 165 | FUT: Starting CF | **8A**

Bats R Age 23 — 2017 FA (CC) — Pwr ++++ | BAvg +++ | Spd ++++ | Def +++++

Year	Lev	Team	AB	R	H	HR	RBI	Avg	OB	Slg	OPS	bb%	ct%	Eye	SB	CS	x/h%	Iso	RC/G
2022	A+	Greenville	197	37	65	9	36	330	362	594	956	5	74	0.20	14	2	46	264	7.41
2022	AA	Portland	284	45	79	12	50	278	317	500	817	5	78	0.26	14	5	42	222	5.44
2023	AA	Portland	245	40	72	6	37	294	332	441	773	5	78	0.25	30	8	33	147	4.92
2023	AAA	Worcester	199	40	62	14	42	312	351	618	969	6	76	0.25	6	5	48	307	7.37
2023	MLB	Boston	83	11	20	2	5	241	276	386	661	5	66	0.14	3	1	40	145	3.63

Toolsy, versatile prospect who finished 4th in org in HR en route to majors. May be best defender in minors with ability to play both CF and SS. Very aggressive hitter who chases breaking balls. Won't draw many walks. Hits for high BA by using all fields approach with hard line drives. Lot of speed for SB and plus CF range.

Ramirez,Agustin — 2 — New York (A)

EXP MLB DEBUT: 2025 | H/W: 6-0 210 | FUT: Reserve C | **6C**

Bats R Age 22 — 2018 FA (DR) — Pwr +++ | BAvg +++ | Spd + | Def ++

Year	Lev	Team	AB	R	H	HR	RBI	Avg	OB	Slg	OPS	bb%	ct%	Eye	SB	CS	x/h%	Iso	RC/G
2021	Rk	FCL Yankees	91	19	20	4	15	220	330	462	792	14	64	0.45	0	1	70	242	6.01
2022	Rk	FCL Yankees	168	34	51	6	51	304	387	506	893	12	82	0.74	13	2	41	202	6.77
2023	A	Tampa	184	35	45	7	35	245	388	397	784	19	78	1.05	7	4	31	152	5.66
2023	A+	Hudson Valley	112	21	43	9	23	384	425	714	1139	7	85	0.47	2	0	44	330	9.06
2023	AA	Somerset	128	17	27	2	11	211	268	313	581	7	79	0.37	3	0	33	102	2.61

Offensively skilled catching prospect enjoyed solid season across 3 levels. Strong, stocky frame is at physical projection. Upright, slight open stance with simple load. Aggressive approach, will chase breakers out of zone. Linear swing plane conducive for solid average but limits power to under 20 HR. Fringe defender. Catcher-only outcome.

Ramirez,Alex — 78 — New York (N)

EXP MLB DEBUT: 2025 | H/W: 6-3 170 | FUT: Starting CF | **7D**

Bats R Age 21 — 2019 FA (DR) — Pwr +++ | BAvg ++ | Spd ++++ | Def +++

Year	Lev	Team	AB	R	H	HR	RBI	Avg	OB	Slg	OPS	bb%	ct%	Eye	SB	CS	x/h%	Iso	RC/G
2021	A	St. Lucie	302	41	78	5	35	258	311	384	695	7	66	0.22	16	7	31	126	4.28
2022	A	St. Lucie	271	40	77	6	37	284	351	443	794	9	75	0.41	17	9	32	159	5.51
2022	A+	Brooklyn	227	22	63	5	34	278	325	427	752	7	76	0.30	4	7	37	150	4.78
2023	A+	Brooklyn	457	66	101	7	53	221	306	317	623	11	75	0.49	21	6	29	96	3.26

Toolsy, athletic prospect struggled mightily with second chance at High-A. Quality of contact regressed. Upright stance with hitchy load. Struggles getting bat started from hit position, especially against velocity. Only positive was cut down on chase rate. Above-average power in profile. Plus runner with improved SB%.

Ramirez,Ramon — 2 — Kansas City

EXP MLB DEBUT: 2028 | H/W: 6-0 180 | FUT: Starting C | **7E**

Bats R Age 18 — 2023 FA (VZ) — Pwr +++ | BAvg +++ | Spd ++ | Def +++

Year	Lev	Team	AB	R	H	HR	RBI	Avg	OB	Slg	OPS	bb%	ct%	Eye	SB	CS	x/h%	Iso	RC/G
2023	Rk	DSL Royals	122	26	42	8	27	344	441	615	1055	15	85	1.17	6	4	40	270	8.68

A teenage catcher with seemingly high upside. Reports from the DSL have been very impressive. He crushed the level showing the ability to hit for average and power. He also gets high marks for defensive ability. Quick release enhances arm strength. Will need plenty of development time with swing mechanics and defensive nuances.

Ramos,Bryan — 5 — Chicago (A)

EXP MLB DEBUT: 2024 | H/W: 6-2 190 | FUT: Starting 3B | **8D**

Bats R Age 22 — 2018 FA (CU) — Pwr +++ | BAvg +++ | Spd ++ | Def +++

Year	Lev	Team	AB	R	H	HR	RBI	Avg	OB	Slg	OPS	bb%	ct%	Eye	SB	CS	x/h%	Iso	RC/G
2021	A	Kannapolis	431	64	105	13	57	244	324	415	739	11	74	0.46	13	4	40	172	4.78
2022	A+	Winston-Salem	382	64	105	19	74	275	344	471	815	9	81	0.56	1	0	34	196	5.51
2022	AA	Birmingham	80	8	18	3	12	225	271	375	646	6	81	0.33	0	1	33	150	3.27
2023	A	Kannapolis	16	3	2	1	2	125	125	313	438	0	75	0.00	0	0	50	188	0.12
2023	AA	Birmingham	291	46	79	14	48	271	356	457	813	12	74	0.51	4	3	32	186	5.67

Strong, CIF prospect struggled early with hamstring injury but came on late, bringing power potential to games. Muscular build, at physical projection. Upright, slightly closed stance with easy trigger to hit position. Improved lower body work has opened up loft in profile. 25+ HR at projection. Improved defender, should stick at 3B.

Ramos,Heliot

9 | **San Francisco** | EXP MLB DEBUT: 2022 | H/W: 6-0 195 | FUT: Starting OF | **7D**

Bats R | Age 24 | 2017 (1) HS (PR)

Pwr + + + | BAvg + + + | Spd + + | Def + +

Year	Lev	Team	AB	R	H	HR	RBI	Avg	OB	Sig	OPS	bb%	ct%	Eye	SB	CS	x/h%	Iso	RC/G
2022	AAA	Sacramento	427	61	97	11	45	227	295	349	644	9	74	0.37	6	6	30	122	3.37
2022	MLB	San Francisco	20	4	2	0	0	100	182	100	282	9	70	0.33	0	0	0	0	-1.72
2023	A	San Jose	17	2	6	2	6	353	421	882	1303	11	76	0.50	0	1	83	529	11.93
2023	AAA	Sacramento	227	44	68	12	45	300	374	546	920	11	71	0.41	9	4	43	247	7.31
2023	MLB	San Francisco	56	5	10	1	2	179	233	304	537	7	64	0.20	0	0	50	125	1.90

Thick OF who has shuttled back and forth between AAA and majors. Had strong season in minors with big increase in BA and jump in HR despite limited AB. Hits ball hard with good bat speed and quick wrists. Hits too many balls on ground, though getting better. Has slowed down as he's grown but is passable defender in RF.

Ramos,Jose

78 | **Los Angeles (N)** | EXP MLB DEBUT: 2025 | H/W: 6-1 200 | FUT: Starting OF | **8E**

Bats R | Age 23 | 2018 FA (PN)

Pwr + + + + | BAvg + | Spd + + | Def + +

Year	Lev	Team	AB	R	H	HR	RBI	Avg	OB	Sig	OPS	bb%	ct%	Eye	SB	CS	x/h%	Iso	RC/G
2021	Rk	ACL Dodgers	60	13	23	3	15	383	448	633	1081	10	77	0.50	1	0	39	250	9.17
2021	A	Rancho Cuca	195	30	61	8	44	313	365	559	924	8	71	0.28	1	4	48	246	7.34
2022	A	Rancho Cuca	112	20	31	6	23	277	377	518	895	14	68	0.50	2	0	39	241	7.24
2022	A+	Great Lakes	362	63	87	19	74	240	314	467	781	10	63	0.29	2	0	47	227	5.63
2023	AA	Tulsa	416	55	100	19	68	240	328	409	736	11	66	0.39	7	2	32	168	4.79

Added bulk and muscle and now features plus raw power. All-or-nothing approach as he seeks to tap into that power results in plenty of swing-and-miss (29% K) and tends to chase breaking balls out of the zone. Average speed with a plus arm profiles well in RF. Is willing to take a free pass, but needs to tone down his approach to reach his potential.

Redfield,Joe

8 | **Los Angeles (A)** | EXP MLB DEBUT: 2025 | H/W: 6-2 200 | FUT: Starting OF | **7C**

Bats R | Age 22 | 2023 (4) Sam Houston St

Pwr + + | BAvg + + + | Spd + + + | Def + + +

Year	Lev	Team	AB	R	H	HR	RBI	Avg	OB	Sig	OPS	bb%	ct%	Eye	SB	CS	x/h%	Iso	RC/G
2023	NCAA	Sam Houston St.	244	79	98	14	54	402	475	676	1151	12	86	1.03	15	4	37	275	9.68
2023	Rk	ACL Angels	10	1	2	0	1	200	273	300	573	9	90	1.00	1	1	50	100	3.13
2023	A+	Tri City	47	8	12	1	8	255	327	426	752	10	79	0.50	2	1	42	170	4.97

Contact-oriented 4th round pick had solid small sample pro debut. Open, crouched stance with wide base and minimal load to hit position. Compact, flat swing maximizes contact over power. Heavy groundball tendencies in profile, matches current spray approach. Has strength in frame to be more. Average defender in CF, could stick there.

Reimer,Jacob

35 | **New York (N)** | EXP MLB DEBUT: 2026 | H/W: 6-2 205 | FUT: Starting 3B | **7D**

Bats R | Age 20 | 2022 (4) HS (CA)

Pwr + + + | BAvg + + + | Spd + + | Def + +

Year	Lev	Team	AB	R	H	HR	RBI	Avg	OB	Sig	OPS	bb%	ct%	Eye	SB	CS	x/h%	Iso	RC/G
2022	Rk	FCL Mets	23	5	6	1	7	261	414	478	892	21	87	2.00	0	0	33	217	7.21
2023	Rk	FCL Mets	7	2	3	1	4	429	500	857	1357	13	86	1.00	0	0	33	429	11.63
2023	A	St. Lucie	250	48	70	6	37	280	388	392	780	15	76	0.72	3	1	23	112	5.50
2023	A+	Brooklyn	79	13	16	1	8	203	344	278	622	18	72	0.77	0	1	25	76	3.47

Strong CIF prospect started strong in Low-A but struggled in High-A. At physical projection with no room to grow. Open stance. Bars hand at trigger. Solid bat speed with linear swing plane. Swing is too groundball prone and can get long. Solid approach, will work counts, spray the ball. Power in frame has yet to show up as pro. Poor defender.

Rhodes,John

79 | **Baltimore** | EXP MLB DEBUT: 2026 | H/W: 6-0 200 | FUT: Reserve OF | **6B**

Bats R | Age 23 | 2021 (3) Kentucky

Pwr + + + | BAvg + + | Spd + + + | Def + +

Year	Lev	Team	AB	R	H	HR	RBI	Avg	OB	Sig	OPS	bb%	ct%	Eye	SB	CS	x/h%	Iso	RC/G
2021	Rk	FCL Orioles B	1	0	1	0	2	1000		###	2000	0	100		0	0	0	0	16.32
2021	A	Delmarva	94	20	25	2	18	266	330	372	702	9	83	0.56	6	0	24	106	4.22
2022	A+	Aberdeen	201	43	52	5	35	259	369	428	797	15	75	0.70	16	0	42	169	5.80
2022	AA	Bowie	90	12	17	0	9	189	284	267	551	12	76	0.55	0	0	29	78	2.46
2023	AA	Bowie	408	60	93	17	69	228	317	422	738	11	70	0.43	8	1	45	194	4.81

Saw a power surge this past year putting up 10 more homeruns in 2023 than he had combined the two years prior. Add that to some stolen bases and a good eye at the plate, there's the makings of a corner outfield profile. If the hit tool allows.

Rice,Ben

2 | **New York (A)** | EXP MLB DEBUT: 2024 | H/W: 6-1 215 | FUT: Starting C | **7B**

Bats L | Age 25 | 2021 (12) Dartmouth

Pwr + + + | BAvg + + + + | Spd + + | Def + +

Year	Lev	Team	AB	R	H	HR	RBI	Avg	OB	Sig	OPS	bb%	ct%	Eye	SB	CS	x/h%	Iso	RC/G
2021	A	Tampa	62	8	13	3	12	210	338	387	725	16	71	0.67	1	0	38	177	4.67
2022	A	Tampa	206	32	55	9	36	267	355	442	796	12	80	0.68	4	1	33	175	5.44
2023	A	Tampa	35	7	10	2	10	286	375	543	918	13	71	0.50	1	0	50	257	7.31
2023	A+	Hudson Valley	44	15	15	2	10	341	532	523	1055	29	77	1.80	3	0	27	182	9.89
2023	AA	Somerset	196	40	64	16	48	327	392	648	1040	10	79	0.50	7	3	47	321	8.31

Ivy educated hit-first catcher enjoyed dynamic season across multiple levels. Older prospect at projection. Slight open stance with hands trigger smoothly to hit position. Stays balanced throughout swing with compact, slight uppercut trajectory. Sprays ball to all fields with power from CF to pull side. Struggles controlling run game behind plate.

Ricketts,Caleb

2 | **Philadelphia** | EXP MLB DEBUT: 2027 | H/W: 6-3 225 | FUT: Reserve C | **7D**

Bats L | Age 23 | 2022 (7) San Diego

Pwr + + | BAvg + + + | Spd + | Def + +

Year	Lev	Team	AB	R	H	HR	RBI	Avg	OB	Sig	OPS	bb%	ct%	Eye	SB	CS	x/h%	Iso	RC/G
2022	NCAA	San Diego	228	46	85	16	55	373	409	658	1067	6	87	0.48	0	4	36	285	8.09
2022	A	Clearwater	81	13	21	3	10	259	348	370	718	12	63	0.37	0	0	14	111	4.64
2023	Rk	FCL Phillies	9	0	2	0	2	222	364	333	697	18	89	2.00	0	0	50	111	5.05
2023	A	Clearwater	95	16	35	1	23	368	388	547	935	3	86	0.23	2	2	37	179	6.74
2023	A+	Jersey Shore	170	21	37	3	25	218	281	300	581	8	79	0.43	4	2	16	82	2.62

Lefty-hitting catcher who has fought off some injuries, he has shown a strong eye at the plate and solid bat-to-ball skills. He has not hit for the power he showed in his final NCAA season, but he has the frame to put on some strength. Adequate defensively but is definitely a bat-first backstop. There's no speed to speak of here.

Riggio,Roc

4 | **New York (A)** | EXP MLB DEBUT: 2026 | H/W: 5-9 180 | FUT: Starting 2B | **7D**

Bats L | Age 21 | 2023 (4) Oklahoma State

Pwr + + + | BAvg + + + | Spd + + | Def + +

Year	Lev	Team	AB	R	H	HR	RBI	Avg	OB	Sig	OPS	bb%	ct%	Eye	SB	CS	x/h%	Iso	RC/G
2023	NCAA	Oklahoma St	224	66	75	18	61	335	448	679	1127	17	79	0.96	7	0	51	344	9.93
2023	Rk	FCL Yankees	16	2	3	0	0	188	350	188	538	20	63	0.67	0	0	0	0	2.10
2023	A	Tampa	57	11	11	0	9	193	387	228	615	24	68	1.00	3	1	18	35	3.55

Offensively-skilled 2B prospect struggled mightily in short-sample pro-debut. Shorty stature, stocky frame. Maxed out physically. Patient approach, works counts. Open stance with longer load. Short levers produce compact, uppercut swing. Does well to get to loft but average power at best. Offensive skill set must carry profile to playing time.

Rincon,Bryan

6 | **Philadelphia** | EXP MLB DEBUT: 2026 | H/W: 5-10 185 | FUT: Starting SS | **7C**

Bats B | Age 20 | 2022 (14) HS (PA)

Pwr + + | BAvg + + | Spd + + + | Def + + + +

Year	Lev	Team	AB	R	H	HR	RBI	Avg	OB	Sig	OPS	bb%	ct%	Eye	SB	CS	x/h%	Iso	RC/G
2022	Rk	FCL Phillies	34	7	6	2	9	176	300	412	712	15	79	0.86	4	0	67	235	4.45
2023	A	Clearwater	276	49	63	8	45	228	364	370	734	18	77	0.94	23	10	35	141	4.99
2023	A+	Jersey Shore	62	13	16	0	7	258	352	323	675	13	79	0.69	4	4	25	65	4.17

Defense-first player whose range, hands, footwork, arm all grade out as a plus middle infielder. Bat prioritizes contact and pitch selectivity beyond his years, though showing game power at the higher levels will be key. Great natural timing in the box, and has shown some speed so far. Tools are there.

Rincones Jr,Gabriel

79 | **Philadelphia** | EXP MLB DEBUT: 2026 | H/W: 6-3 225 | FUT: Starting OF | **8D**

Bats L | Age 23 | 2022 (3) Florida Atlantic

Pwr + + + | BAvg + + + | Spd + + | Def + +

Year	Lev	Team	AB	R	H	HR	RBI	Avg	OB	Sig	OPS	bb%	ct%	Eye	SB	CS	x/h%	Iso	RC/G
2023	A	Clearwater	178	31	47	5	21	264	364	444	808	14	69	0.51	24	3	43	180	6.05
2023	A+	Jersey Shore	281	50	67	10	39	238	318	416	735	11	72	0.42	8	3	43	178	4.72

Great size and powerful left-handed swing is the draw. Hit tool is a bit behind, especially vs. LHP, which will limit his BA upside for as long as it remains. Despite 32 SB, speed not seen as a part of his future game. Currently gets by on defense in a corner, but could end up at first base. Has the slugger's build and exit velocity for it.

Rios,Alberto

27 | **Los Angeles (A)** | EXP MLB DEBUT: 2025 | H/W: 6-0 203 | FUT: Starting OF | **8D**

Bats R | Age 22 | 2023 (3) Stanford

Pwr + + + | BAvg + + + + | Spd + + | Def + +

Year	Lev	Team	AB	R	H	HR	RBI	Avg	OB	Sig	OPS	bb%	ct%	Eye	SB	CS	x/h%	Iso	RC/G
2023	NCAA	Stanford	242	69	93	18	73	384	468	707	1174	14	83	0.90	5	1	45	322	10.13
2023	Rk	ACL Angels	10	3	2	0	1	200	333	200	533	17	100		1	0	0	0	3.60
2023	A	Inland Empire	127	19	23	3	18	181	262	315	577	10	71	0.38	7	2	39	134	2.53

Unheralded college player forced Stanford to play him with weekday performances, earned Pac-12 player of the year award by year's end. Simple approach with present hit tool. Struggled in pro debut when swing slowed and lengthened, though instincts & mechanics stayed intact. Above-average raw power. Picks spots for lift but mostly linear swing.

Ritter,Ryan | 64 | Colorado | EXP MLB DEBUT: 2025 | H/W: 6-2 200 | FUT: Starting SS | 7D

Bats R Age 23 — 2022 (4) Kentucky — Pwr +++ | BAvg ++ | Spd +++ | Def ++++

Year	Lev	Team	AB	R	H	HR	RBI	Avg	OB	Slg	OPS	bb%	ct%	Eye	SB	CS	x/h%	Iso	RC/G
2022	NCAA	Kentucky	226	43	64	8	36	283	344	469	813	9	70	0.31	15	0	38	186	5.81
2022	Rk	ACL Rockies	25	9	8	1	4	320	370	680	1050	7	88	0.67	2	0	75	360	8.41
2023	A	Fresno	246	53	75	18	58	305	396	606	1001	13	71	0.51	6	3	47	301	8.48
2023	A+	Spokane	170	33	45	6	26	265	349	441	790	11	59	0.32	12	2	38	176	6.21
2023	AA	Hartford	25	4	4	0	1	160	250	200	450	11	56	0.27	2	0	25	40	0.60

Breakout season for 4th rounder. Athletic frame, spreads out at the plate with a quick bat and above-average power. Did a better job of getting the ball in the air, launching 24 HR across three levels. Plus defender has the range, hands, and arm to stick at short and is a prospect on the rise. Will need to prove the spike in power wasn't a fluke.

Rivera,Josh | 645 | Chicago (N) | EXP MLB DEBUT: 2025 | H/W: 6-2 215 | FUT: Starting 2B | 7C

Bats R Age 23 — 2023 (3) Florida — Pwr +++ | BAvg +++ | Spd +++ | Def +++

Year	Lev	Team	AB	R	H	HR	RBI	Avg	OB	Slg	OPS	bb%	ct%	Eye	SB	CS	x/h%	Iso	RC/G
2023	NCAA	Florida	256	70	89	19	72	348	447	617	1064	15	86	1.31	18	4	34	270	8.72
2023	Rk	ACL Cubs	11	3	4	1	4	364	364	818	1182	0	82	0.00	0	0	50	455	9.37
2023	A+	South Bend	92	18	23	2	12	250	317	402	719	9	72	0.35	1	1	43	152	4.53

Posted a monster season in College World Series run, highlighted by a career-high 19 HR. Slightly closed stance with a quick bat and average power. Does make hard contact, but handsy swing lacks natural loft. Solid average tools on defense, but range might move him from SS to 2B. High baseball IQ and work ethic give him a solid floor, but lacks a true plus tool.

Robinson,Kristian | 79 | Arizona | EXP MLB DEBUT: 2025 | H/W: 6-3 190 | FUT: Starting OF | 8E

Bats R Age 23 — 2017 FA (BM) — Pwr +++ | BAvg + | Spd +++ | Def +++

Year	Lev	Team	AB	R	H	HR	RBI	Avg	OB	Slg	OPS	bb%	ct%	Eye	SB	CS	x/h%	Iso	RC/G
2022	--	Did Not Play																	
2023	Rk	ACL DBacks R	27	3	8	1	4	296	296	519	815	0	70	0.00	1	0	38	222	5.45
2023	A	Visalia	156	29	45	9	26	288	383	538	922	13	63	0.41	20	3	40	250	8.01
2023	A+	Hillsboro	34	6	9	2	6	265	342	441	783	11	62	0.31	2	3	22	176	5.60
2023	AA	Amarillo	16	4	4	2	6	250	294	688	982	6	56	0.14	0	1	75	438	9.28

Former highly-ranked player returned to game action after 4-year layoff due to personal/legal issues. Exceptional athlete, potent combo of raw strength/speed in lean, muscular frame. Knows which pitches to attack, but swing results in way too many whiffs, GB. Deserves some slack, but don't ignore red flags.

Roccaforte,Carson | 8 | Kansas City | EXP MLB DEBUT: 2026 | H/W: 6-1 195 | FUT: Starting OF | 8E

Bats L Age 22 — 2023 (2) La-Lafayette — Pwr ++ | BAvg +++ | Spd +++ | Def ++++

Year	Lev	Team	AB	R	H	HR	RBI	Avg	OB	Slg	OPS	bb%	ct%	Eye	SB	CS	x/h%	Iso	RC/G
2023	NCAA	La-Lafayette	236	64	75	8	55	318	408	538	946	13	77	0.67	22	12	47	220	7.67
2023	Rk	ACL Royals B	15	3	8	0	3	533	533	600	1133	0	80	0.00	5	0	13	67	8.87
2023	A	Columbia	101	19	26	0	12	257	375	356	731	16	69	0.61	11	3	31	99	5.18

Quick, athletic CF who should be able to play any position on the grass. He has enough speed to steal bases and is good at putting bat to ball. Focuses on line drives with level swing path and didn't reach seats as pro. Owns some raw pop but game more about speed, defense and hit tool. Has swing and natural strength to get to power, however.

Rocchio,Brayan | 6 | Cleveland | EXP MLB DEBUT: 2023 | H/W: 5-10 170 | FUT: Starting SS | 8C

Bats B Age 23 — 2017 FA (VZ) — Pwr +++ | BAvg +++ | Spd +++ | Def +++

Year	Lev	Team	AB	R	H	HR	RBI	Avg	OB	Slg	OPS	bb%	ct%	Eye	SB	CS	x/h%	Iso	RC/G
2021	AA	Akron	184	34	54	6	30	293	340	505	846	7	78	0.32	7	4	43	212	5.96
2022	AA	Akron	373	62	99	13	48	265	340	432	771	10	78	0.52	12	6	35	166	5.10
2022	AAA	Columbus	137	21	32	5	16	234	295	387	682	8	85	0.57	2	3	34	153	3.91
2023	AAA	Columbus	468	81	131	7	65	280	362	421	783	11	86	0.91	25	7	35	141	5.48
2023	MLB	Cleveland	81	9	20	0	8	247	282	321	603	5	67	0.15	0	0	30	74	2.87

Natural-hitting INF who reached majors and led org in 2B. Better hitter from left side as he recognizes pitches and posts very low K rate. Ton of bat speed and offers at least average power potential. HR output dropped but may be a byproduct of seeing more spin. Very fast on base but too many CS. Sound defender with quickness.

Roden,Alan | 79 | Toronto | EXP MLB DEBUT: 2025 | H/W: 5-11 215 | FUT: Starting OF | 7B

Bats L Age 24 — 2022 (3) Creighton — Pwr ++ | BAvg ++++ | Spd +++ | Def +++

Year	Lev	Team	AB	R	H	HR	RBI	Avg	OB	Slg	OPS	bb%	ct%	Eye	SB	CS	x/h%	Iso	RC/G
2022	NCAA	Creighton	194	48	75	4	45	387	466	598	1064	13	96	3.63	9	4	41	211	8.84
2022	A	Dunedin	90	17	21	1	9	233	355	311	666	16	86	1.31	5	1	24	78	4.31
2023	A+	Vancouver	268	57	86	4	41	321	413	459	872	14	88	1.31	15	2	33	138	6.68
2023	AA	New Hampshire	174	35	54	6	27	310	400	460	860	13	82	0.81	9	2	24	149	6.34

Pure-hitting OF who led NWL in BA and had only one month under .300. Performed admirably on two levels and showcased keen eye to draw more walks than Ks. Focuses on hard contact to gaps but can jerk ball out of park, particularly to pull side. Uses all fields with elite contact. Runs well and owns average range and arm in corners.

Rodriguez,Alberto | 9 | Seattle | EXP MLB DEBUT: 2025 | H/W: 5-10 227 | FUT: Starting OF | 7C

Bats L Age 23 — 2017 FA (DR) — Pwr ++ | BAvg +++ | Spd ++ | Def ++

Year	Lev	Team	AB	R	H	HR	RBI	Avg	OB	Slg	OPS	bb%	ct%	Eye	SB	CS	x/h%	Iso	RC/G
2021	A	Modesto	370	75	109	10	63	295	380	484	864	12	74	0.54	13	7	41	189	6.61
2021	A+	Everett	24	5	5	0	2	208	269	250	519	8	71	0.29	2	0	20	42	1.70
2022	A+	Everett	472	59	123	10	46	261	331	396	728	10	71	0.36	6	4	33	136	4.67
2023	A+	Everett	281	61	86	11	58	306	375	580	955	10	75	0.45	3	1	56	274	7.70
2023	AA	Arkansas	179	17	52	3	27	291	362	385	747	10	72	0.39	5	2	21	95	4.92

Stout OF who hit 14 HR in High-A, but 0 in AA upon promotion in August. Very strong swing and uses entire field in simple approach. Has fanned over 100 times in each of last 3 seasons and odd stroke can be exploited. Chases breaking balls out of zone. Led NWL in doubles and triples and set high in HR. Has ability to hit LHP.

Rodriguez,Emmanuel | 8 | Minnesota | EXP MLB DEBUT: 2025 | H/W: 5-10 210 | FUT: Starting OF | 8C

Bats L Age 21 — 2019 FA (DR) — Pwr ++++ | BAvg ++ | Spd +++ | Def +++

Year	Lev	Team	AB	R	H	HR	RBI	Avg	OB	Slg	OPS	bb%	ct%	Eye	SB	CS	x/h%	Iso	RC/G
2021	Rk	FCL Twins	126	31	27	10	23	214	336	524	859	15	56	0.41	9	4	63	310	7.59
2022	A	Fort Myers	136	35	37	9	25	272	487	551	1039	30	62	1.10	11	5	46	279	10.44
2023	A+	Cedar Rapids	354	87	85	16	55	240	397	463	860	21	62	0.69	20	5	45	223	7.34

High-OBP OF who hit well under .200 until June and turned up the heat. Led MWL in OPS and walks. Generates significant power to all fields with exemplary bat speed and swing path. Makes loud, hard contact but can expand zone when selling out for pop. Can be too passive. Also has above average speed for SB. Likely RF long-term.

Rodriguez,Hector | 78 | Cincinnati | EXP MLB DEBUT: 2025 | H/W: 5-8 186 | FUT: Starting OF | 8D

Bats L Age 20 — 2020 FA (DR) — Pwr +++ | BAvg ++++ | Spd ++++ | Def ++

Year	Lev	Team	AB	R	H	HR	RBI	Avg	OB	Slg	OPS	bb%	ct%	Eye	SB	CS	x/h%	Iso	RC/G
2022	Rk	ACL Reds	25	7	10	0	4	400	464	720	1184	11	100		3	2	60	320	10.16
2022	A	Daytona	45	7	13	0	6	289	319	467	786	4	78	0.20	1	1	46	178	5.32
2022	A	St. Lucie	7	1	1	0	0	143	250	143	393	13	100		0	0	0	0	1.90
2023	A	Daytona	410	85	120	16	56	293	336	510	846	6	80	0.32	18	5	40	217	5.85
2023	A+	Dayton	51	6	15	0	5	294	308	373	680	2	80	0.10	0	1	20	78	3.64

Twitchy and athletic, has hitting instincts and flashed power out of nowhere in 2023. Lean build with surprising strength. Has simple, flat swing with minimal wasted movement that gets to hard contact frequently. Power entirely to pull-side. Will spray the ball to the gaps. Plus runner but doesn't get good reads. Struggles with routes in CF.

Rodriguez,Jeremy | 6 | New York (N) | EXP MLB DEBUT: 2026 | H/W: 6-0 170 | FUT: Starting SS | 8E

Bats L Age 17 — 2023 FA (DR) — Pwr +++ | BAvg +++ | Spd ++++ | Def +++

Year	Lev	Team	AB	R	H	HR	RBI	Avg	OB	Slg	OPS	bb%	ct%	Eye	SB	CS	x/h%	Iso	RC/G
2023	Rk	DSL Mets 2	45	13	19	1	15	422	536	711	1247	20	91	2.75	7	1	42	289	11.55
2023	Rk	DSL Dbacks	122	24	30	2	18	246	361	377	738	15	78	0.81	12	5	33	131	5.06

Raw SS prospect acquired by NYM in Tommy Pham trade with Arizona. Lean build with room to grow. Upright, open stance with slight load. Spray approach with solid plate discipline. Data suggests plus bat speed, which could aid in future power development. Plus runner with 20+ SB potential. Solid at SS but likely body gains move profile to 3B.

Rodriguez,Johnathan | 79 | Cleveland | EXP MLB DEBUT: 2024 | H/W: 6-0 224 | FUT: Starting OF | 7C

Bats R Age 24 — 2017 (3) HS (PR) — Pwr ++++ | BAvg ++ | Spd + | Def ++

Year	Lev	Team	AB	R	H	HR	RBI	Avg	OB	Slg	OPS	bb%	ct%	Eye	SB	CS	x/h%	Iso	RC/G
2021	A+	Lake County	79	9	17	2	11	215	295	342	637	10	72	0.41	2	1	35	127	3.36
2022	A+	Lake County	295	48	86	21	59	292	341	573	914	7	69	0.24	2	0	45	281	7.04
2022	AA	Akron	107	10	22	5	15	206	241	449	690	4	60	0.12	0	1	64	243	4.39
2023	AA	Akron	322	42	93	18	55	289	357	512	869	10	70	0.35	3	2	37	224	6.51
2023	AAA	Columbus	175	32	49	11	33	280	370	560	930	13	62	0.38	0	0	51	280	8.16

Bat-only OF who was equally good at AA and AAA. Led org in hits, HR and RBI and has strong frame to continue to produce with bat. Makes good swing decisions but has holes that lead to Ks. Can be beaten upstairs and with good breaking balls. Fits profile of high HR, low BA guy. No speed in tool box and stuck in corner OF with poor range.

Rodriguez,Jose E. — 79 — Minnesota

EXP MLB DEBUT: 2027 | H/W: 6-2 196 | FUT: Starting OF | 8E

Bats R Age 18
2022 FA (DR)
Pwr + + +
BAvg + +
Spd + +
Def + +

Year	Lev	Team	AB	R	H	HR	RBI	Avg	OB	Slg	OPS	bb%	ct%	Eye	SB	CS	x/h%	Iso	RC/G
2022	Rk	DSL Twins	190	39	55	13	49	289	360	605	965	10	73	0.40	5	0	56	316	7.77
2023	Rk	FCL Twins	187	28	49	6	23	262	327	412	739	9	78	0.44	0	2	33	150	4.61

Physical OF who showed off plus power potential in first year in US. Hits ton of flyballs with uppercut swing, though comes with lot of swing and miss. Struggles to read spin and loves to swing bat. Power is the carrying tool and could grow to double plus. Owns large frame and a tad on the slow side with limited athleticism.

Rodriguez,Jose G. — 456 — Chicago (A)

EXP MLB DEBUT: 2023 | H/W: 5-11 175 | FUT: Starting MIF | 7C

Bats R Age 22
2018 FA (DR)
Pwr + + +
BAvg + + +
Spd + + +
Def + + +

Year	Lev	Team	AB	R	H	HR	RBI	Avg	OB	Slg	OPS	bb%	ct%	Eye	SB	CS	x/h%	Iso	RC/G
2021	AA	Birmingham	14	2	3	0	0	214	214	286	500	0	86	0.00	0	1	33	71	1.55
2022	AA	Birmingham	440	75	123	11	68	280	337	430	766	8	85	0.58	40	10	31	150	4.99
2023	AA	Birmingham	382	63	101	18	54	264	298	450	748	5	75	0.19	28	6	35	186	4.45
2023	AAA	Charlotte	87	11	22	3	8	253	270	379	649	2	85	0.15	3	3	23	126	3.15
2023	MLB	Chicago (A)	0	1	0	0	0												

Short-statured, hit-first MIF improved getting to barreled contact in 2023. Solid athlete at physical projection. Utilized lower half better generating torque and creating leverage to get to higher exit velocities. Mostly pull approach, especially with power but takes what is given to CF. Solid runner, taxed defensively at SS. Likely 2B long term.

Rodriguez,Yophery — 8 — Milwaukee

EXP MLB DEBUT: 2028 | H/W: 6-1 185 | FUT: Starting CF | 8E

Bats L Age 18
2023 FA (DR)
Pwr + + +
BAvg + + +
Spd + + +
Def + + +

Year	Lev	Team	AB	R	H	HR	RBI	Avg	OB	Slg	OPS	bb%	ct%	Eye	SB	CS	x/h%	Iso	RC/G
2023	Rk	DSL Brewers 1	178	34	45	6	36	253	393	449	842	19	78	1.03	12	7	47	197	6.53

Long-term project with nice ingredients with which to work. Erratic approach but more in unusual way. Draws more walks than Ks but can be too aggressive one AB and too passive in the next. Still a lot of development time ahead. Makes good contact, has good speed and has intriguing power potential. Plays solid CF.

Rojas,Anderdson — 478 — Arizona

EXP MLB DEBUT: 2027 | H/W: 5-10 150 | FUT: Starting 2B | 7E

Bats L Age 20
2021 FA (DR)
Pwr + +
BAvg + + +
Spd + +
Def + +

Year	Lev	Team	AB	R	H	HR	RBI	Avg	OB	Slg	OPS	bb%	ct%	Eye	SB	CS	x/h%	Iso	RC/G
2021	Rk	DSL Dbacks	148	20	31	1	20	209	273	277	550	8	78	0.39	10	4	19	68	2.26
2022	Rk	DSL Dbacks 2	116	24	41	1	23	353	385	509	894	5	89	0.46	6	4	29	155	6.38
2022	Rk	ACL DBacks R	39	1	7	0	3	179	220	231	450	5	77	0.22	3	0	29	51	0.85
2023	A	Visalia	393	45	98	2	51	249	273	346	619	3	82	0.19	12	5	29	97	3.02

Teenager at Single-A showed intriguing bat-to-ball, pitch recognition skills. Quiet setup with smooth lefty swing, keeps bat in zone. Ultra-aggressive approach sapped OBP, but contact% helps offset. Could reach average power with more discerning approach, muscle. Has raw speed to be productive on base paths, needs to pick better spots.

Rojas,Jefferson — 6 — Chicago (N)

EXP MLB DEBUT: 2026 | H/W: 5-10 150 | FUT: Starting SS | 8D

Bats R Age 18
2022 FA (DR)
Pwr + + +
BAvg + + +
Spd + + +
Def + + +

Year	Lev	Team	AB	R	H	HR	RBI	Avg	OB	Slg	OPS	bb%	ct%	Eye	SB	CS	x/h%	Iso	RC/G
2022	Rk	DSL Cubs B	145	27	44	1	19	303	373	407	780	10	88	0.89	15	2	23	103	5.38
2023	Rk	ACL Cubs	3	0	0	0	0	0	0	0	0	0	67	0.00	0	0		0	-6.12
2023	A	Myrtle Beach	272	48	73	7	31	268	325	404	730	8	78	0.38	13	4	30	136	4.48

Signed out of Dominican for $1 million and showed well in state-side debut. Works from a strong base with hands high and a short stride, generating loft with slight uppercut swing. Makes good swing decisions and should continue to add power as he matures, but smallish stature limits upside. Solid range with good hands and enough arm to stick at SS.

Romero,Mikey — 46 — Boston

EXP MLB DEBUT: 2026 | H/W: 5-11 175 | FUT: Starting 2B | 7D

Bats L Age 20
2022 (1) HS (CA)
Pwr +
BAvg + +
Spd + +
Def + + +

Year	Lev	Team	AB	R	H	HR	RBI	Avg	OB	Slg	OPS	bb%	ct%	Eye	SB	CS	x/h%	Iso	RC/G
2022	Rk	FCL Red Sox	36	5	9	1	6	250	372	417	789	16	89	1.75	1	0	44	167	5.83
2022	A	Salem	43	6	15	0	11	349	364	581	945	2	74	0.09	1	0	47	233	7.48
2023	Rk	FCL Red Sox	24	4	6	0	4	250	379	292	671	17	83	1.25	0	0	17	42	4.43
2023	A	Salem	92	11	20	0	9	217	287	304	591	9	82	0.53	2	3	30	87	3.02
2023	A+	Greenville	10	0	1	0	0	100	100	100	200	0	60	0.00	0	0	0	0	-3.65

Missed lot of time with injuries and never got going in poor campaign. Has natural tools and IQ to be solid player but no one tool stands out. Weak contact and low exit velo hampered production. Knows how to read spin and shorten stroke when needed. Puts ball in play consistently. Likely to move to 2B where hands and arm work best.

Romo,Drew — 2 — Colorado

EXP MLB DEBUT: 2024 | H/W: 5-11 205 | FUT: Starting C | 7B

Bats B Age 22
2020 (1) HS (TX)
Pwr + + +
BAvg + +
Spd + +
Def + + + + +

Year	Lev	Team	AB	R	H	HR	RBI	Avg	OB	Slg	OPS	bb%	ct%	Eye	SB	CS	x/h%	Iso	RC/G
2021	A	Fresno	312	48	98	6	47	314	353	439	793	6	84	0.38	23	6	26	125	5.15
2022	A+	Spokane	374	52	95	5	58	254	318	372	690	9	78	0.43	18	3	31	118	4.09
2023	AA	Hartford	327	45	83	13	48	254	315	440	755	8	80	0.43	6	7	40	187	4.77
2023	AAA	Albuquerque	17	2	6	0	3	353	353	529	882	0	76	0.00	0	0	33	176	6.29

Plus defender with good blocking and receiving skills and a strong arm. Started slow at AA, but posted an .891 OPS in the second half and finished the year at AAA. Aggressive approach at the plate and can be induced to chase. Power is average, but the glove will get him to the majors and give him plenty of runway.

Rosario,Eguy — 456 — San Diego

EXP MLB DEBUT: 2022 | H/W: 5-7 150 | FUT: Utility player | 6A

Bats R Age 24
2015 FA (DR)
Pwr + + +
BAvg + +
Spd + +
Def + + +

Year	Lev	Team	AB	R	H	HR	RBI	Avg	OB	Slg	OPS	bb%	ct%	Eye	SB	CS	x/h%	Iso	RC/G
2022	AAA	El Paso	490	98	141	22	81	288	364	508	872	11	78	0.54	21	8	43	220	6.44
2022	MLB	San Diego	5	0	1	0	0	200	333	200	533	17	60	0.50	0	0	0	0	1.98
2023	Rk	ACL Padres	7	3	5	1	4	714	750	###	2179	13	86	1.00	0	1	60	714	21.75
2023	AAA	El Paso	166	24	44	5	28	265	344	422	766	11	77	0.51	4	4	34	157	5.10
2023	MLB	San Diego	36	6	9	2	6	250	270	500	770	3	67	0.08	0	0	44	250	5.04

Versatile, short INF who repeated AAA and saw big league action after beginning season late due to recovery from broken ankle. Fits utility bill with ability to play multiple positions. Takes advantage of instincts on base and in field when healthy and has solid understanding of strike zone. Can put charge in ball, but power not in his game.

Rosario,Kala'i — 9 — Minnesota

EXP MLB DEBUT: 2025 | H/W: 6-0 205 | FUT: Starting OF | 8D

Bats R Age 21
2020 (5) HS (HI)
Pwr + + +
BAvg + + +
Spd + +
Def + +

Year	Lev	Team	AB	R	H	HR	RBI	Avg	OB	Slg	OPS	bb%	ct%	Eye	SB	CS	x/h%	Iso	RC/G
2021	Rk	FCL Twins	188	32	52	5	40	277	343	452	795	9	65	0.29	4	0	37	176	5.91
2022	A	Fort Myers	373	53	89	12	46	239	302	408	710	8	64	0.25	7	2	40	169	4.56
2023	A+	Cedar Rapids	445	71	112	21	94	252	360	467	827	14	65	0.48	2	2	46	216	6.44

Emerging OF who led MWL in HR and RBI but also 3rd in K. Struggles to read spin but has worked to value drawing walks. Dramatically increased BB% with improved approach. Still has holes in swing that need to be closed. Has plus raw power and starting to show more opposite field pop. Lacks frontline speed and is sub-par defender.

Rucker,Carson — 5 — Detroit

EXP MLB DEBUT: 2027 | H/W: 6-2 195 | FUT: Starting 3B | 7D

Bats R Age 19
2023 (4) HS (TN)
Pwr + + +
BAvg + + +
Spd + + +
Def + + +

Year	Lev	Team	AB	R	H	HR	RBI	Avg	OB	Slg	OPS	bb%	ct%	Eye	SB	CS	x/h%	Iso	RC/G
2023	Rk	FCL Tigers E	33	5	8	1	9	242	359	364	723	15	73	0.67	4	1	25	121	4.70

4th round pick out of HS is already physically mature and features some of the best exit velo in the draft class. Plus bat speed and a quick RH stroke give him above-average to plus raw power, though mostly to the pull side for now. Speed is a tick above average, but not enough to stick at short and split time between SS and 3B in solid pro debut.

Rudick,Matt — 79 — New York (N)

EXP MLB DEBUT: 2024 | H/W: 5-6 170 | FUT: Reserve OF | 6C

Bats L Age 25
2021 (13) San Diego St.
Pwr + +
BAvg + + +
Spd + + +
Def + + +

Year	Lev	Team	AB	R	H	HR	RBI	Avg	OB	Slg	OPS	bb%	ct%	Eye	SB	CS	x/h%	Iso	RC/G
2022	Rk	FCL Mets	3	0	0	0	0	0	250	0	250	25	33	0.50	0	0		0	-5.88
2022	A+	Brooklyn	300	50	73	3	28	243	342	360	702	13	81	0.78	17	5	34	117	4.54
2022	AAA	Syracuse	15	3	2	0	0	133	235	200	435	12	80	0.67	0	0	50	67	1.12
2023	Rk	FCL Mets	17	2	4	0	2	235	316	353	669	11	88	1.00	0	0	50	118	4.26
2023	AA	Binghamton	214	45	58	9	31	271	400	449	849	18	80	1.10	12	1	34	178	6.44

Tiny OF prospect utilizes patience and leverage to produce career season at Double-A. Solid athletic build at physical projection. Closed stance with simple trigger. Works counts, takes advantage of small zone to pile walks. Pull-oriented approach with linear swing, lots of liners and groundballs. Has potential to hit for 10+ HR with reps.

Ruiz,Jorge | 789 | Los Angeles (A) | EXP MLB DEBUT: 2025 | H/W: 5-10 164 | FUT: Starting OF | 7E

Bats L Age 19	Year	Lev	Team	AB	R	H	HR	RBI	Avg	OB	Slg	OPS	bb%	ct%	Eye	SB	CS	x/h%	Iso	RC/G
2021 FA (VZ)																				
Pwr +																				
BAvg ++++	2021	Rk	DSL Angels	174	32	47	1	14	270	352	362	714	11	86	0.88	19	6	26	92	4.67
Spd +++	2022	Rk	ACL Angels	203	36	68	0	23	335	372	414	786	6	90	0.60	8	2	21	79	5.19
Def +++	2023	A	Inland Empire	296	49	90	3	52	304	364	419	783	9	82	0.52	13	4	28	115	5.29

Lean, athletic OF slapped way through Low-A. 2022 Arizona Complex League MVP, continued to hit for high BA. Contact-oriented hitter with aggressive approach. Short levers and compact, flat swing help enable spray approach. Hand/eye skills limit whiffs despite high chase rate. Average runner out of the box. Can play CF but lacks instincts.

Rumfield,TJ | 3 | New York (A) | EXP MLB DEBUT: 2024 | H/W: 6-4 225 | FUT: Reserve 1B | 6C

Bats L Age 23	Year	Lev	Team	AB	R	H	HR	RBI	Avg	OB	Slg	OPS	bb%	ct%	Eye	SB	CS	x/h%	Iso	RC/G
2021 (12) Virginia Tech	2022	Rk	FCL Yankees	2	0	0	0	0	0	0	0	0	0	100		0	0		0	-2.66
Pwr ++++	2022	A	Tampa	10	0	1	0	1	100	100	100	200	0	80	0.00	0	0	0	0	-2.36
BAvg ++	2022	A+	Hudson Valley	197	27	56	4	34	284	376	411	787	13	77	0.64	4	2	30	127	5.54
Spd ++	2023	A+	Hudson Valley	14	2	4	0	3	286	333	429	762	7	86	0.50	0	0	50	143	5.07
Def +++	2023	AA	Somerset	297	43	65	17	55	219	310	438	747	12	75	0.52	8	3	48	219	4.75

1B-only, struggled through injury and performance woes in lost 2023 season. Strong frame, at physical projection. Open, mostly upright stance with awkward high leg lift and slight load. Despite longer levers, has feel for contact. Struggled getting to hard contact often, mostly due to present approach. Plus power in profile plays despite low BA.

Rushing,Dalton | 23 | Los Angeles (N) | EXP MLB DEBUT: 2025 | H/W: 6-1 220 | FUT: Starting C | 8C

Bats L Age 23	Year	Lev	Team	AB	R	H	HR	RBI	Avg	OB	Slg	OPS	bb%	ct%	Eye	SB	CS	x/h%	Iso	RC/G
2022 (2) Louisville																				
Pwr ++++	2022	NCAA	Louisville	226	68	70	23	62	310	435	686	1121	18	74	0.86	4	0	56	376	9.99
BAvg ++	2022	Rk	ACL Dodgers	5	0	0	0	0	0	167	0	167	17	80	1.00	0	0		0	-2.27
Spd ++	2022	A	Rancho Cuca	99	27	42	8	30	424	525	778	1303	18	79	1.00	1	0	45	354	12.28
Def ++	2023	A+	Great Lakes	290	55	66	15	53	228	381	452	833	20	68	0.77	1	0	52	224	6.50

Strong, thick frame and good bat speed results in above-average to plus power, and he has some of the best plate discipline in the system. Slight crouch, open stance with all fields power. Split time between C/1B/DH with two stints on the IL with concussions. Has a plus arm, but isn't likely to stick at catcher.

Saggese,Thomas | 456 | St. Louis | EXP MLB DEBUT: 2024 | H/W: 5-11 175 | FUT: Starting 2B | 7C

Bats R Age 21	Year	Lev	Team	AB	R	H	HR	RBI	Avg	OB	Slg	OPS	bb%	ct%	Eye	SB	CS	x/h%	Iso	RC/G
2020 (5) HS (CA)	2022	A+	Hickory	380	56	117	14	61	308	357	487	844	7	75	0.31	11	3	32	179	5.92
Pwr +++	2022	AA	Frisco	21	5	8	1	9	381	409	857	1266	5	86	0.33	1	0	75	476	10.87
BAvg +++	2023	AA	Frisco	367	67	115	15	78	313	372	512	884	8	74	0.35	8	2	35	199	6.58
Spd ++	2023	AA	Springfield	130	25	43	10	29	331	400	662	1062	10	74	0.44	3	0	47	331	8.97
Def ++	2023	AAA	Memphis	58	9	12	1	4	207	246	345	591	5	76	0.21	1	0	50	138	2.64

Concerns about aggressive approach at the plate have largely abated due to breakout season that saw him rip 34 doubles and 26 HR across three levels. And while there will be plenty of swing-and-miss, his ability to play multiple positions and to make consistent hard contact give him plenty of pathways to regular playing time.

Salas,Ethan | 2 | San Diego | EXP MLB DEBUT: 2025 | H/W: 6-2 185 | FUT: Starting C | 9D

Bats L Age 17	Year	Lev	Team	AB	R	H	HR	RBI	Avg	OB	Slg	OPS	bb%	ct%	Eye	SB	CS	x/h%	Iso	RC/G
2022 FA (VZ)																				
Pwr +++																				
BAvg +++	2023	A	Lake Elsinore	191	35	51	9	35	267	349	487	836	11	70	0.42	5	2	43	220	6.18
Spd ++	2023	A+	Fort Wayne	35	3	7	0	3	200	243	229	472	5	71	0.20	0	0	14	29	0.94
Def ++	2023	AA	San Antonio	28	2	5	0	3	179	281	214	496	13	71	0.50	0	1	20	36	1.54

Young backstop who reached AA at age 17. Owns all requisite tools to be standout in short order. Swings quick bat with above average pop and shows instincts to shorten stroke to put ball in play. Can be beaten up in zone with velocity. Makes good contact and doesn't chase often. Raw defender, however, has strong arm and blocking skills.

Salas,Jose | 45 | Minnesota | EXP MLB DEBUT: 2026 | H/W: 6-0 191 | FUT: Starting 3B | 8E

Bats B Age 20	Year	Lev	Team	AB	R	H	HR	RBI	Avg	OB	Slg	OPS	bb%	ct%	Eye	SB	CS	x/h%	Iso	RC/G
2019 FA (VZ)	2021	A	Jupiter	108	12	27	1	8	250	319	315	634	9	74	0.39	6	0	19	65	3.33
Pwr ++	2022	A	Jupiter	221	40	59	5	24	267	336	421	757	9	76	0.43	15	1	36	154	5.00
BAvg ++	2022	A+	Beloit	191	29	44	4	17	230	303	340	644	9	79	0.49	18	0	27	110	3.47
Spd ++++	2023	Rk	FCL Twins	9	2	1	0	0	111	200	111	311	10	78	0.50	0	0	0	0	-0.77
Def +++	2023	A+	Cedar Rapids	331	36	63	4	33	190	251	272	523	8	71	0.28	22	9	29	82	1.71

Returned to High-A and regressed across board. Hit under .200 in all months of season but two. Rarely draws walks and saw both HR and SB production drop. Seemed to press too much. Moved of SS to 2B. Tools and underlying skills suggest some upside. Has above average bat speed and plus speed. Capable of being outstanding defender.

Saltiban,Devin | 6 | Philadelphia | EXP MLB DEBUT: 2027 | H/W: 5-10 180 | FUT: Starting SS | 8D

Bats R Age 19	Year	Lev	Team	AB	R	H	HR	RBI	Avg	OB	Slg	OPS	bb%	ct%	Eye	SB	CS	x/h%	Iso	RC/G
2023 (3) HS (HI)																				
Pwr +++																				
BAvg ++																				
Spd +++																				
Def +++	2023	Rk	FCL Phillies	42	10	14	1	7	333	378	452	830	7	83	0.43	5	1	21	119	5.60

A bit under the radar in his draft class, he impressed in the MLB Draft League with solid hit and power tools with enough speed and athleticism to move his stock up. Good bat speed from compact RH swing; energetic, has the defensive tools (arm, hands) to play in the middle of the diamond.

Sanchez,Carlos | 56 | Cincinnati | EXP MLB DEBUT: 2026 | H/W: 6-0 177 | FUT: Starting MIF | 7E

Bats L Age 19	Year	Lev	Team	AB	R	H	HR	RBI	Avg	OB	Slg	OPS	bb%	ct%	Eye	SB	CS	x/h%	Iso	RC/G
2022 FA (DR)																				
Pwr ++																				
BAvg +++	2022	Rk	DSL Reds	138	42	49	2	26	355	500	442	942	22	80	1.43	14	4	14	87	8.12
Spd +++	2023	Rk	ACL Reds	128	42	36	1	26	281	465	445	910	26	66	1.00	9	4	44	164	8.45
Def +++	2023	A	Daytona	16	2	3	0	3	188	316	313	628	16	50	0.38	0	0	67	125	4.45

Athletic MIF prospect continued strong 2022 debut in DSL at the Arizona complex. Hit over power profile with spray approach. Open stance with direct trigger and linear swing. Does well to guide hands through zone and get to solid contact. Will need to create leverage in lower half and add strength to get to power. Fringe range for SS.

Sanchez,Jadiel | 79 | Los Angeles (A) | EXP MLB DEBUT: 2025 | H/W: 6-2 185 | FUT: Reserve OF | 6C

Bats B Age 22	Year	Lev	Team	AB	R	H	HR	RBI	Avg	OB	Slg	OPS	bb%	ct%	Eye	SB	CS	x/h%	Iso	RC/G
2019 (12) HS (PR)	2021	A	Clearwater	74	13	22	2	6	297	366	446	812	10	81	0.57	0	2	27	149	5.62
Pwr ++	2022	Rk	FCL Phillies	2	0	1	0	0	500	500	###	1500	0	100		0	0	100	500	12.52
BAvg +++	2022	A	Clearwater	140	13	33	6	19	236	287	429	715	7	81	0.37	2	2	39	193	4.19
Spd +++	2022	A	Inland Empire	55	7	17	0	6	309	356	400	756	7	80	0.36	0	1	24	91	4.90
Def +++	2023	A	Inland Empire	381	59	113	11	66	297	374	475	849	11	83	0.73	7	4	32	178	6.17

Switch hitting OF prospect performed well at older age in Low-A. Lean build near projection. Open stance, hands direct to hit position, stays balanced and simple to the ball with a contact approach. Will expand the zone, trusting hand/eye, but often results in soft contact. Below-average power; tweener COR profile as such.

Sanoja,Javier | 468 | Miami | EXP MLB DEBUT: 2025 | H/W: 5-7 150 | FUT: Utility player | 6C

Bats R Age 21	Year	Lev	Team	AB	R	H	HR	RBI	Avg	OB	Slg	OPS	bb%	ct%	Eye	SB	CS	x/h%	Iso	RC/G
2019 FA (VZ)	2021	Rk	DSL Marlins	219	43	51	3	26	233	291	333	624	8	95	1.64	11	5	29	100	3.69
Pwr +	2022	Rk	FCL Marlins	107	27	34	3	19	318	392	514	906	11	94	2.17	9	3	41	196	6.89
BAvg +++	2022	A	Jupiter	268	37	64	3	25	239	274	325	599	5	85	0.32	9	6	20	86	2.84
Spd +++	2023	A	Jupiter	400	51	123	1	57	308	357	400	757	7	92	0.97	31	16	22	93	5.04
Def +++	2023	A+	Beloit	131	10	35	3	10	267	319	351	670	7	92	1.00	6	6	14	84	3.94

Contact-oriented MIF prospect enjoyed best season between lower minor affiliates. Shorter with some strength gains possible. Open stance with simple load. Average bat speed and linear swing path geared towards singles approach. Small levers help maintain high ct%. Weak power in profile. Will be hard to get to 10 HR. Above-average runner.

Santana,Adrian | 6 | Tampa Bay | EXP MLB DEBUT: 2027 | H/W: 5-11 155 | FUT: Starting SS | 7C

Bats B Age 18	Year	Lev	Team	AB	R	H	HR	RBI	Avg	OB	Slg	OPS	bb%	ct%	Eye	SB	CS	x/h%	Iso	RC/G
2023 (1) HS (FL)																				
Pwr ++																				
BAvg +++																				
Spd ++++																				
Def ++++	2023	Rk	FCL Rays	39	6	8	0	3	205	326	256	582	15	77	0.78	3	0	25	51	3.02

Switch-hitting, quick twitch player was drafted with 31st overall pick in last year's draft. Wiry frame with strength gains needed. Better hitter from LH side than RH side. Slasher approach but can create loft in trajectory from LH side. Double-plus run tool fuels fantasy profile. Defensive skills at SS likely carry profile overall.

Santana,Cristian — 6 — Detroit

EXP MLB DEBUT: 2026 | H/W: 5-11 165 | FUT: Utility player | 6D

Bats R Age 20
2021 FA (DR)
Pwr ++
BAvg ++
Spd +++
Def ++

Year	Lev	Team	AB	R	H	HR	RBI	Avg	OB	Slg	OPS	bb%	ct%	Eye	SB	CS	x/h%	Iso	RC/G
2021	Rk	DSL Tigers	171	40	46	9	27	269	378	520	899	15	73	0.65	12	7	50	251	7.11
2022	Rk	FCL Tigers East	5	3	1	1	2	200	556	800	1356	44	40	1.33	0	1	100	600	20.47
2022	A	Lakeland	265	52	57	9	30	215	348	366	714	17	67	0.61	10	5	39	151	4.70
2023	A	Lakeland	308	68	48	12	42	156	348	312	660	23	62	0.78	6	5	50	156	3.93

Signed out of D.R. for club record $2.9 million, but has been overmatched in two stints at Low-A. Slow leg kick, lack of power, and inability to identify spin. Odd ability to draw walks while simultaneously failing to make contact - 22% BB/28% K. Shows range and positional flexibility on D, but will need to make an adjustment to remain relevant.

Sasaki,Shane — 89 — Tampa Bay

EXP MLB DEBUT: 2025 | H/W: 5-11 165 | FUT: Starting OF | 7C

Bats R Age 23
2019 (3) HS (HI)
Pwr ++
BAvg +++
Spd ++++
Def +++

Year	Lev	Team	AB	R	H	HR	RBI	Avg	OB	Slg	OPS	bb%	ct%	Eye	SB	CS	x/h%	Iso	RC/G
2021	Rk	FCL Rays	124	33	36	2	16	290	380	403	784	13	70	0.49	22	2	22	113	5.63
2022	A	Charleston	346	71	112	9	57	324	408	497	905	12	73	0.53	47	4	35	173	7.21
2023	Rk	FCL Rays	12	2	3	0	0	250	438	417	854	25	67	1.00	4	0	33	167	7.55
2023	A+	Bowling Green	256	53	77	7	39	301	374	465	839	10	75	0.46	12	4	32	164	6.14

Short, athletic OF missed half the season with injury, enjoyed success in limited action. Upright, slight open stance with easy trigger and toe tap. Contact oriented bat with flatter swing plane. Sprays the ball to all fields with average patience. Below-average power plays to LCF gap. Double-plus runner. 13 for 13 in SB in AFL.

Schanuel,Nolan — 3 — Los Angeles (A)

EXP MLB DEBUT: 2023 | H/W: 6-4 220 | FUT: Starting 1B | 7A

Bats L Age 22
2023 (1) Florida Atlantic
Pwr +++
BAvg ++++
Spd ++
Def +++

Year	Lev	Team	AB	R	H	HR	RBI	Avg	OB	Slg	OPS	bb%	ct%	Eye	SB	CS	x/h%	Iso	RC/G
2023	NCAA	Fl Atlantic	197	70	88	19	64	447	593	868	1461	26	93	5.07	14	1	47	421	14.03
2023	Rk	ACL Angels	8	3	2	0	1	250	500	375	875	33	88	4.00	1	0	50	125	8.03
2023	A	Inland Empire	6	2	5	0	2	833	857	833	1690	14	100		0	0	0	0	15.27
2023	AA	Rocket City	60	15	20	1	12	333	474	467	940	21	85	1.78	1	0	25	133	7.98
2023	MLB	LA Angels	109	19	30	1	6	275	388	330	718	16	83	1.05	0	0	13	55	4.83

2023 1st rounder made it to MLB after month in pro ball. Held own against MLB pitching, posting exceptionally high BB% and ct%. Spray approach peppers all fields with groundballs and liners. Unorthodox stance with hands high over head. Incorporates moderate leg lift with swing, never appearing off-balanced. Power limited with approach and swing.

Schobel,Tanner — 45 — Minnesota

EXP MLB DEBUT: 2025 | H/W: 5-9 170 | FUT: Starting 3B | 7C

Bats R Age 22
2022 (2) Virginia Tech
Pwr +++
BAvg +++
Spd +++
Def +++

Year	Lev	Team	AB	R	H	HR	RBI	Avg	OB	Slg	OPS	bb%	ct%	Eye	SB	CS	x/h%	Iso	RC/G
2022	NCAA	Virginia Tech	235	68	85	19	74	362	444	689	1134	13	83	0.88	7	1	45	328	9.52
2022	Rk	FCL Twins	15	3	3	0	1	200	250	267	517	6	80	0.33	1	0	33	67	1.88
2022	A	Fort Myers	99	11	24	1	10	242	359	303	662	15	77	0.78	6	1	17	61	4.00
2023	A+	Cedar Rapids	302	53	87	14	61	288	364	493	857	11	79	0.56	9	1	33	205	6.18
2023	AA	Wichita	177	19	40	2	18	226	322	305	627	12	77	0.63	3	1	23	79	3.42

All-around solid INF who got off to slow start but heated up midseason. Rarely swings and misses and puts ball in play, including to opp field. May not have plus tool in arsenal but no glaring weakness either. Big power spike in 2023 as he added more leverage to righty stroke. Also hitting breaking balls better. Split time between 2B and 3B.

Schunk,Aaron — 54 — Colorado

EXP MLB DEBUT: 2024 | H/W: 6-1 205 | FUT: Utility player | 6C

Bats R Age 26
2019 (2) Georgia
Pwr +++
BAvg ++
Spd +
Def +++

Year	Lev	Team	AB	R	H	HR	RBI	Avg	OB	Slg	OPS	bb%	ct%	Eye	SB	CS	x/h%	Iso	RC/G
2019	NCAA	Georgia	230	49	78	15	58	339	377	604	981	6	87	0.48	3	1	37	265	7.14
2019	A-	Boise	173	31	53	6	23	306	358	503	861	7	86	0.56	4	1	38	197	6.05
2021	A+	Spokane	358	57	80	8	45	223	274	346	621	7	69	0.23	13	5	30	123	3.02
2022	AA	Hartford	450	62	116	14	77	258	313	427	739	7	74	0.31	6	2	41	169	4.62
2023	AAA	Albuquerque	458	71	133	14	77	290	353	461	813	9	73	0.36	12	7	33	170	5.71

Athletic OF had a solid season, but lacks a standout tool needed to thrive at the next level and could end up a Quad-A player. Good bat speed, but struggles to make contact against better velocity. Makes hard contact when he finds the barrel, but lacks natural loft needed for HR power. Split time between 3B/2B giving him positional flexibility.

Scott,Victor — 8 — St. Louis

EXP MLB DEBUT: 2025 | H/W: 5-10 190 | FUT: Starting CF | 8D

Bats L Age 23
2022 (5) West Virginia
Pwr +
BAvg +++
Spd +++++
Def ++++

Year	Lev	Team	AB	R	H	HR	RBI	Avg	OB	Slg	OPS	bb%	ct%	Eye	SB	CS	x/h%	Iso	RC/G
2022	NCAA	West Virginia	194	44	54	6	47	278	389	454	842	15	73	0.66	38	7	37	175	6.46
2022	A	Palm Beach	108	20	24	2	12	222	364	389	753	18	76	0.92	13	3	42	167	5.40
2023	A+	Peoria	266	44	75	2	29	282	350	398	749	10	80	0.54	50	7	25	117	4.95
2023	AA	Springfield	282	51	91	7	34	323	363	450	814	6	84	0.40	44	7	22	128	5.37

5th round pick has some of the best speed in the minors and swiped a minor league leading 94 bags while showing impressive bat-to-ball skills. Quiet, balanced approach at the plate with quick hands, a compact stroke, and surprising pop for size. Plus defender in CF and speed will get him to the show in '24 after an impressive showing in the AFL.

Sequera,Manuel — 6 — Detroit

EXP MLB DEBUT: 2025 | H/W: 6-1 170 | FUT: Utility player | 7E

Bats R Age 21
2019 FA (VZ)
Pwr ++
BAvg ++
Spd ++
Def ++

Year	Lev	Team	AB	R	H	HR	RBI	Avg	OB	Slg	OPS	bb%	ct%	Eye	SB	CS	x/h%	Iso	RC/G
2021	Rk	FCL Tigers East	171	31	42	11	40	246	306	509	815	8	67	0.26	1	1	55	263	5.83
2022	A	Lakeland	457	59	106	19	64	232	264	422	686	4	76	0.18	4	5	45	190	3.70
2023	Rk	FCL Tigers East	22	8	10	2	6	455	520	773	1293	12	82	0.75	0	0	30	318	11.36
2023	A	Lakeland	213	30	44	7	35	207	268	357	625	8	70	0.29	3	1	41	150	3.07

Signed out of Venezuela for $750,000, but has failed to adjust as a hitter and now owns a career line of .234/.294/.396. Overly aggressive at the plate hunting for pitches he can drive to the pull side, but too often expands and chases balls out of the zone. Put up pedestrian numbers in a repeat of Low-A and will need more to remain relevant.

Serna,Jared — 46 — New York (A)

EXP MLB DEBUT: 2025 | H/W: 5-6 168 | FUT: Reserve IF | 6C

Bats R Age 21
2019 FA (MX)
Pwr ++
BAvg +++
Spd +++
Def +++

Year	Lev	Team	AB	R	H	HR	RBI	Avg	OB	Slg	OPS	bb%	ct%	Eye	SB	CS	x/h%	Iso	RC/G
2021	Rk	DSL Yankees	151	34	36	3	16	238	378	384	762	18	82	1.26	24	4	39	146	5.55
2022	Rk	FCL Yankees	129	40	39	6	28	302	416	527	943	16	81	1.04	16	4	41	225	7.57
2022	A	Tampa	39	6	7	0	2	179	238	231	469	7	62	0.20	1	1	29	51	0.89
2023	A	Tampa	400	72	113	19	71	283	348	483	830	9	81	0.53	19	6	36	200	5.70
2023	A+	Hudson Valley	108	18	31	0	8	287	342	389	731	8	86	0.60	10	2	29	102	4.71

Contact-oriented, MIF prospect enjoyed solid 2023 season in lower minors. Short statured, near physical projection. Utilizes open stance with leg lift and smooth trigger. Opposite field approach, hitting line drives and groundballs. Flat-angled swing. Surprised with 19 HR but not sustainable power. Average runner with range for 2B.

Serretti,Danny — 564 — Detroit

EXP MLB DEBUT: 2025 | H/W: 6-0 195 | FUT: Utility player | 6C

Bats B Age 23
2022 (6) North Carolina
Pwr +++
BAvg ++
Spd ++
Def ++

Year	Lev	Team	AB	R	H	HR	RBI	Avg	OB	Slg	OPS	bb%	ct%	Eye	SB	CS	x/h%	Iso	RC/G
2022	A	Lakeland	32	11	12	2	7	375	565	688	1253	30	81	2.33	4	1	50	313	12.46
2022	A+	West Michigan	38	9	11	0	4	289	386	395	781	14	71	0.55	1	1	36	105	5.77
2022	AA	Erie	19	6	5	0	2	263	391	263	654	17	79	1.00	2	0	0	0	4.06
2023	A+	West Michigan	204	35	58	5	24	284	365	441	806	11	78	0.58	2	4	34	157	5.70
2023	AA	Erie	156	15	32	1	15	205	315	269	584	14	77	0.69	1	1	25	64	2.94

Has a unique set up; holds hands above head preload with a small leg kick to start swing. Uses a line drive, all-fields approach that limits power upside. Does have a good understanding of the zone and won't chase. Below average speed with solid instincts and good hands. Split time between SS, 2B, and 3B and upside is as a UT player.

Severino,Jhonny — 56 — Pittsburgh

EXP MLB DEBUT: 2027 | H/W: 6-1 185 | FUT: Starting 3B | 8E

Bats R Age 19
2022 FA (DR)
Pwr +++
BAvg ++
Spd ++
Def ++

Year	Lev	Team	AB	R	H	HR	RBI	Avg	OB	Slg	OPS	bb%	ct%	Eye	SB	CS	x/h%	Iso	RC/G
2022	Rk	DSL Brewers 1	179	26	48	3	25	268	321	391	712	7	69	0.25	10	1	31	123	4.41
2023	Rk	ACL Brewers G	48	12	12	4	10	250	265	583	849	2	79	0.10	5	0	58	333	5.47
2023	Rk	FCL Pirates B	10	3	3	1	2	300	364	600	964	9	90	1.00	2	0	33	300	6.93

Acquired from MIL in July and spent all year in Rookie ball. Free swinger who will need to tone down approach to realize potential for average hit tool. Has nice, clean swing and could develop into middle of order run producer. Rarely draws walks. Signed as SS but has seen more action at 3B. Young, raw, projectable.

Severino,Yunior — 45 — Minnesota

EXP MLB DEBUT: 2024 | H/W: 6-0 189 | FUT: Starting 2B | 7D

Bats B Age 24
2016 FA (DR)
Pwr ++++
BAvg ++
Spd ++
Def +

Year	Lev	Team	AB	R	H	HR	RBI	Avg	OB	Slg	OPS	bb%	ct%	Eye	SB	CS	x/h%	Iso	RC/G
2021	A+	Cedar Rapids	134	19	43	3	17	321	409	493	902	13	63	0.40	1	0	37	172	7.95
2022	A+	Cedar Rapids	159	30	45	11	40	283	380	572	953	14	73	0.58	0	0	49	289	7.70
2022	AA	Wichita	143	19	39	8	25	273	338	497	834	9	66	0.29	0	1	41	224	6.16
2023	AA	Wichita	334	56	96	24	62	287	357	560	917	10	65	0.31	3	4	43	272	7.48
2023	AAA	St. Paul	133	24	31	11	22	233	311	511	822	10	58	0.27	0	0	45	278	6.50

Led all minor leagues in HR but also led org in Ks. First time in career he hit 20+ HR as he impacted ball from both sides of plate. Impressive exit velo but has trouble putting bat to ball. Chases balls out of zone and aggressive swing decisions mute BA. Power only prospect as he has limited speed and poor defense at 2B and 3B.

Shaw,Matt | 64 | Chicago (N) | EXP MLB DEBUT: 2025 | H/W: 5-11 185 | FUT: Starting 2B | 8D

Bats R Age 22
2023 (1) Maryland
Pwr +++
BAvg ++++
Spd +++
Def ++

Year	Lev	Team	AB	R	H	HR	RBI	Avg	OB	Slg	OPS	bb%	ct%	Eye	SB	CS	x/h%	Iso	RC/G
2023	NCAA	Maryland	264	80	90	24	69	341	433	697	1130	14	84	1.02	18	1	50	356	9.46
2023	Rk	ACL Cubs	8	3	4	1	1	500	600	###	1600	20	88	2.00	2	1	50	500	15.27
2023	A+	South Bend	84	14	33	4	18	393	420	655	1075	5	86	0.33	7	1	33	262	8.29
2023	AA	Tennessee	65	10	19	3	9	292	324	523	847	4	82	0.25	6	1	42	231	5.67

Hard worker with a high baseball IQ. Slashed .320/.413/.623 in Big 10 play and uses a simple stroke with above average bat speed and makes consistent, hard contact. Played SS for Maryland but split time at 2B in pro debut where fringe arm and quickness fit better. Above-average runner with the potential to steal 20+ bases with 20 HR in MLB.

Shenton,Austin | 35 | Tampa Bay | EXP MLB DEBUT: 2024 | H/W: 6-0 205 | FUT: Starting 3B | 8C

Bats L Age 26
2019 (5) Florida Intl
Pwr ++++
BAvg +++
Spd ++
Def ++

Year	Lev	Team	AB	R	H	HR	RBI	Avg	OB	Slg	OPS	bb%	ct%	Eye	SB	CS	x/h%	Iso	RC/G
2021	AA	Arkansas	43	6	14	1	8	326	383	512	895	9	77	0.40	0	0	43	186	6.77
2021	AA	Montgomery	48	5	13	2	9	271	300	458	758	4	69	0.13	0	0	38	188	4.81
2022	AA	Montgomery	195	28	46	8	29	236	332	415	747	13	64	0.40	0	0	39	179	5.16
2023	AA	Montgomery	254	45	78	15	49	307	413	567	980	15	69	0.58	0	0	46	260	8.49
2023	AAA	Durham	219	57	66	14	50	301	427	603	1030	18	66	0.64	0	0	58	301	9.63

Strong-bodied CIF prospect rebounded from injury riddled 2022 to post career numbers in 2023. Open, upright stance with bat wrap on trigger. Whiff rate increased as batted ball profile and EV rates expanded. Patient hitter with natural spray tendencies. Plus power plays to CF and RF. Power carries profile to playing time, especially if at 1B.

Shewmake,Braden | 46 | Chicago (A) | EXP MLB DEBUT: 2023 | H/W: 6-3 190 | FUT: Reserve IF | 6B

Bats L Age 26
2019 (1) Texas A&M
Pwr +++
BAvg ++
Spd +++
Def +++

Year	Lev	Team	AB	R	H	HR	RBI	Avg	OB	Slg	OPS	bb%	ct%	Eye	SB	CS	x/h%	Iso	RC/G
2019	AA	Mississippi	46	7	10	0	1	217	280	217	497	8	76	0.36	2	0	0	0	1.47
2021	AA	Mississippi	324	40	74	12	40	228	267	401	668	5	77	0.23	4	2	39	173	3.51
2022	AAA	Gwinnett	278	37	72	7	25	259	316	399	715	8	79	0.40	9	0	32	140	4.30
2023	AAA	Gwinnett	474	79	111	16	69	234	292	407	700	8	78	0.38	27	1	42	173	4.08
2023	MLB	Atlanta	4	0	0	0	0	0	0	0	0	0	75	0.00	0	0		0	-5.26

Former 1st round pick struggled to get to consistent hard contact once again in 2023. Made MLB debut and was traded this off-season by ATL. Upright, open stance. Has sold out for average pull power at expense of hit tool. Average runner with good baserunning instincts. 27 for 28 in SB attempts. Average defender at SS.

Siani,Michael | 8 | St. Louis | EXP MLB DEBUT: 2022 | H/W: 6-1 188 | FUT: Reserve OF | 6C

Bats L Age 24
2018 (4) HS (PA)
Pwr +
BAvg ++
Spd ++++
Def ++++

Year	Lev	Team	AB	R	H	HR	RBI	Avg	OB	Slg	OPS	bb%	ct%	Eye	SB	CS	x/h%	Iso	RC/G
2022	MLB	Cincinnati	24	1	4	0	0	167	167	167	333	0	71	0.00	0	1	0	0	-1.22
2023	AAA	Louisville	378	63	86	9	47	228	347	354	701	15	71	0.63	22	4	31	127	4.48
2023	AAA	Memphis	31	6	7	0	1	226	368	290	659	18	74	0.88	1	0	29	65	4.16
2023	MLB	Cincinnati	0	1	0	0	0					100			0	1			
2023	MLB	St. Louis	5	0	0	0	0	0	0	0	0	0	80	0.00	1	0		0	-4.74

OF was claimed off waivers when released by the Reds after an inauspicious MLB debut. Uses a line-drive, all-fields approach and is willing to draw walks, but can be induced to expand and power is a tick below average. Plus speed and ability to get on base give him a chance to be a 4th OF, but at 24 the clock is ticking.

Simpson,Chandler | 789 | Tampa Bay | EXP MLB DEBUT: 2025 | H/W: 6-2 170 | FUT: Reserve OF | 6C

Bats L Age 23
2022 (2) Georgia Tech
Pwr +
BAvg ++++
Spd +++++
Def +++

Year	Lev	Team	AB	R	H	HR	RBI	Avg	OB	Slg	OPS	bb%	ct%	Eye	SB	CS	x/h%	Iso	RC/G
2022	NCAA	Georgia Tech	203	64	88	1	25	433	509	517	1026	13	92	1.94	27	4	14	84	8.41
2022	Rk	FCL Rays	27	5	10	0	3	370	485	481	966	18	85	1.50	8	0	30	111	8.23
2023	A	Charleston	354	66	101	0	24	285	355	333	688	10	90	1.09	81	12	13	48	4.37
2023	A+	Bowling Green	89	22	29	0	7	326	429	393	822	15	90	1.78	13	3	17	67	6.28

Wiry, athletic OF prospect continues to be an on-base magnet despite providing no power upside. Contact, slasher bat. Walks more than strikes out. Whiff rate extremely low, around 10%. Exceptional speed and bat-to-ball skills carry profile. Was 94 for 109 in SB attempts, split between levels. Likely not enough bat for regular MLB playing time.

Smith Njigba,Canaan | 79 | Pittsburgh | EXP MLB DEBUT: 2022 | H/W: 6-0 230 | FUT: Reserve OF | 6B

Bats L Age 24
2017 (4) HS (TX)
Pwr +++
BAvg +++
Spd ++
Def ++

Year	Lev	Team	AB	R	H	HR	RBI	Avg	OB	Slg	OPS	bb%	ct%	Eye	SB	CS	x/h%	Iso	RC/G
2021	AAA	Indianapolis	21	1	2	0	2	95	174	95	269	9	57	0.22	0	0	0	0	-2.66
2022	AAA	Indianapolis	184	31	51	1	19	277	387	408	795	15	72	0.63	8	3	37	130	6.00
2022	MLB	Pittsburgh	5	1	1	0	0	200	333	400	733	17	100		0	0	100	200	5.88
2023	AAA	Indianapolis	389	57	109	15	74	280	367	473	840	12	70	0.45	21	5	40	193	6.33
2023	MLB	Pittsburgh	32	3	4	0	5	125	222	219	441	11	50	0.25	1	0	50	94	0.68

Strong OF who set career bests in HR and SB. Displays disciplined eye at plate and has bat speed and leverage to produce good pop. Makes hard contact when contact made. Expands zone and long swing can be exploited. Steals bases despite fringy speed and lacks ideal range for corner OF. Projects as reserve OF.

Smith,Aidan | 8 | Seattle | EXP MLB DEBUT: 2027 | H/W: 6-3 190 | FUT: Starting CF | 8D

Bats R Age 19
2023 (4) HS (TX)
Pwr +++
BAvg +++
Spd ++++
Def +++

Year	Lev	Team	AB	R	H	HR	RBI	Avg	OB	Slg	OPS	bb%	ct%	Eye	SB	CS	x/h%	Iso	RC/G
2023	Rk	ACL Mariners	23	7	6	0	3	261	414	435	849	21	65	0.75	6	1	33	174	7.42
2023	A	Modesto	49	11	9	1	5	184	245	327	572	8	67	0.25	0	0	44	143	2.43

Athletic, toolsy OF who has projectable frame and good nose for game. Played mostly CF in pro debut and has plus arm for RF. Plenty of room to add muscle and realize at least average power potential. Can struggle with swing and miss but more a byproduct of aggressive approach. Runs very well underway and has 20/20 potential.

Soto,Livan | 456 | Los Angeles (A) | EXP MLB DEBUT: 2022 | H/W: 5-10 160 | FUT: Reserve IF | 6C

Bats L Age 23
2016 FA (VZ)
Pwr +
BAvg ++
Spd +++
Def ++++

Year	Lev	Team	AB	R	H	HR	RBI	Avg	OB	Slg	OPS	bb%	ct%	Eye	SB	CS	x/h%	Iso	RC/G
2022	AA	Rocket City	456	69	128	6	57	281	378	362	739	13	78	0.70	18	8	19	81	4.94
2022	MLB	LA Angels	55	9	22	1	9	400	421	582	1003	4	76	0.15	1	1	32	182	7.88
2023	AA	Rocket City	107	18	22	1	5	206	325	271	596	15	68	0.56	1	1	23	65	2.98
2023	AAA	Salt Lake	298	48	74	8	42	248	345	389	734	13	72	0.53	0	0	32	141	4.83
2023	MLB	LA Angels	9	2	2	0	0	222	417	222	639	25	78	1.50	0	0	0	0	4.16

Defensive-oriented IF finally got past Double-A en route to late season MLB callup. Upright, open stance with hands hanging over the plate. Slight load and linear swing. Doesn't generate leverage for power in lower half. Lots of groundball contact. Patient approach with solid contact skills. Mostly pull oriented approach. Average runner.

Squires,Brett | 37 | Kansas City | EXP MLB DEBUT: 2026 | H/W: 6-2 210 | FUT: Reserve 1B | 6B

Bats L Age 24
2022 FA (Oklahoma)
Pwr +++
BAvg ++
Spd +++
Def +++

Year	Lev	Team	AB	R	H	HR	RBI	Avg	OB	Slg	OPS	bb%	ct%	Eye	SB	CS	x/h%	Iso	RC/G
2023	A	Columbia	419	65	110	15	69	263	363	430	792	14	65	0.45	32	8	35	167	5.89

Went undrafted in 2022 out of Oklahoma in part thanks to a hand injury. The Royals scooped him up and the lefty swinger responded by putting up impressive numbers in Colombia. If he keeps it up, one to put on watchlists.

Stafura,Sammy | 6 | Cincinnati | EXP MLB DEBUT: 2026 | H/W: 6-0 188 | FUT: Starting MIF | 8E

Bats R Age 19
2023 (2) HS (NY)
Pwr +++
BAvg +++
Spd ++++
Def +++

Year	Lev	Team	AB	R	H	HR	RBI	Avg	OB	Slg	OPS	bb%	ct%	Eye	SB	CS	x/h%	Iso	RC/G
2023	Rk	ACL Reds	42	7	3	1	6	71	220	190	410	16	45	0.35	0	0	100	119	-0.38

Cold-weather prep prospect drafted by Reds in 2nd round had horrible pro debut with bat. Athletic frame with lean muscular build. Had rep in HS for being contact bat but struck out in nearly half of his ABs in ACL. Hit over power profile with chance at above-average hit and average power outcome. Plus runner who is an average defender at SS.

Stewart,Sal | 45 | Cincinnati | EXP MLB DEBUT: 2025 | H/W: 6-3 215 | FUT: Starting 3B | 8D

Bats R Age 20
2022 (1) HS (FL)
Pwr +++
BAvg ++++
Spd ++
Def ++

Year	Lev	Team	AB	R	H	HR	RBI	Avg	OB	Slg	OPS	bb%	ct%	Eye	SB	CS	x/h%	Iso	RC/G
2022	Rk	ACL Reds	24	5	7	0	5	292	393	458	851	14	79	0.80	0	0	57	167	6.68
2023	A	Daytona	316	55	85	10	60	269	395	424	819	17	81	1.12	10	4	34	155	6.11
2023	A+	Dayton	110	16	32	2	11	291	391	391	782	14	84	1.00	5	0	22	100	5.52

Hitability 3B prospect enjoyed solid season in lower minors. Strong build, close to physical projection. Upright, slight open stance. Minimal load and easy swing mechanics lead to high ct%. Opposite field gap approach. Linear swing plane with above-average bat speed. Could get to average power with more pull contact and continued high EV rates.

Suero,Estuar — 8 — Pittsburgh

EXP MLB DEBUT: 2027 | H/W: 6-5 180 | FUT: Starting OF | 8E

Bats B Age 18 — 2022 FA (DR)

Pwr +++ | BAvg ++ | Spd +++ | Def ++

Year	Lev	Team	AB	R	H	HR	RBI	Avg	OB	Slg	OPS	bb%	ct%	Eye	SB	CS	x/h%	Iso	RC/G
2022	Rk	DSL Padres	152	33	38	3	21	250	341	395	736	12	66	0.40	14	4	34	145	5.08
2023	Rk	ACL Padres	139	22	30	4	23	216	297	345	642	10	65	0.33	7	3	30	129	3.48
2023	Rk	FCL Pirates B	46	7	10	1	6	217	379	326	705	21	74	1.00	2	2	20	109	4.73

Young, exciting OF who was acquired from SD at deadline. Very raw skills and erratic swing mechanics but upside is huge. Very tall, lean frame with incredible projection and athleticism. Runs very well and could be dynamic CF who hits in middle of lineup. Lot of swing and miss and gets questionable jumps in OF. Long-term development plan.

Sugastey,Adrian — 2 — San Francisco

EXP MLB DEBUT: 2025 | H/W: 6-1 210 | FUT: Starting C | 7D

Bats R Age 21 — 2019 FA (PN)

Pwr + | BAvg +++ | Spd + | Def +++

Year	Lev	Team	AB	R	H	HR	RBI	Avg	OB	Slg	OPS	bb%	ct%	Eye	SB	CS	x/h%	Iso	RC/G
2021	Rk	ACL Giants O	148	23	53	2	25	358	406	439	845	8	82	0.46	1	0	15	81	5.87
2022	Rk	ACL Giants O	26	4	6	0	2	231	333	346	679	13	81	0.80	0	0	33	115	4.37
2022	A	San Jose	300	41	72	5	32	240	309	333	642	9	82	0.57	1	0	24	93	3.52
2023	A+	Eugene	248	23	74	4	40	298	333	423	757	5	85	0.35	1	0	28	125	4.71

Contact-oriented C with good hit tool. Could stand to be more selective at plate but makes such easy contact that he can thrive despite aggression. Hasn't yet developed much pop and likely won't without swing change. Possesses electric arm strength with quick release. Has improved receiving and will just need more time.

Susac,Daniel — 2 — Oakland

EXP MLB DEBUT: 2025 | H/W: 6-4 218 | FUT: Starting C | 8B

Bats R Age 22 — 2022 (1) Arizona

Pwr +++ | BAvg ++++ | Spd ++ | Def +++

Year	Lev	Team	AB	R	H	HR	RBI	Avg	OB	Slg	OPS	bb%	ct%	Eye	SB	CS	x/h%	Iso	RC/G
2022	NCAA	Arizona	273	50	100	12	61	366	416	582	998	8	81	0.44	0	0	33	216	7.73
2022	Rk	ACL Athletics	6	1	3	0	2	500	500	667	1167	0	100		0	0	33	167	8.73
2022	A	Stockton	98	14	28	1	13	286	333	388	721	7	74	0.28	0	0	29	102	4.42
2023	A+	Lansing	366	47	111	7	54	303	370	437	808	10	76	0.44	8	0	27	134	5.66
2023	AA	Midland	50	2	14	1	8	280	308	360	668	4	72	0.14	1	0	14	80	3.44

Tall, athletic backstop with polished hitting skills and exquisite ability to put bat to ball. Hits far too many grounders but gives ball a ride when swinging with more leverage. Potential to develop plus power and can crush LHP with pretty swing. Needs to pull ball more. Led MWL in BA. Will need to improve receiving.

Sweeney,Trey — 6 — Los Angeles (N)

EXP MLB DEBUT: 2024 | H/W: 6-2 212 | FUT: Starting MIF | 7C

Bats L Age 23 — 2021 (1) Eastern Illinois

Pwr +++ | BAvg +++ | Spd +++ | Def +++

Year	Lev	Team	AB	R	H	HR	RBI	Avg	OB	Slg	OPS	bb%	ct%	Eye	SB	CS	x/h%	Iso	RC/G
2021	Rk	FCL Yankees	5	4	3	1	1	600	778	###	1978	44	60	2.00	1	0	33	600	27.61
2021	A	Tampa	110	26	27	6	13	245	352	518	870	14	74	0.62	3	1	52	273	6.67
2022	A+	Hudson Valley	390	70	94	14	51	241	341	415	756	13	72	0.55	29	2	38	174	5.11
2022	AA	Somerset	43	6	10	2	5	233	340	395	735	14	77	0.70	2	1	30	163	4.71
2023	AA	Somerset	397	67	100	13	49	252	357	411	768	14	77	0.72	20	7	35	159	5.27

Former 1st round pick continues to struggle against pro pitching. Respectable slash line. However, hit tool plays fringe without power carry to make up for it. Patient approach, works counts. Long swing operation limits frequency of hard contact. Average power, almost entirely to pull field. 20 HR max potential. Average runner. Likely 2B.

Tait,Eduardo — 2 — Philadelphia

EXP MLB DEBUT: 2027 | H/W: 6-0 175 | FUT: Starting C | 8E

Bats L Age 17 — 2023 FA (PN)

Pwr +++ | BAvg +++ | Spd ++ | Def ++

Year	Lev	Team	AB	R	H	HR	RBI	Avg	OB	Slg	OPS	bb%	ct%	Eye	SB	CS	x/h%	Iso	RC/G
2023	Rk	DSL Phillies W	26	3	9	0	9	346	414	346	760	10	73	0.43	1	0	0	0	5.07
2023	Rk	DSL Phillies R	121	25	40	3	27	331	377	554	931	7	80	0.38	3	2	45	223	7.07

Teenage hard-hit machine in the Dominican Summer League that has the team excited. Balanced LH swing, good contact rate with some loft. Consistently high exit velocities that stand out for his age; a hit-plus-power profile. Adequate defense with a plus arm; should stay behind the plate. A long ways off, but altogether positive first impression.

Tatum,Terrell — 78 — Chicago (A)

EXP MLB DEBUT: 2025 | H/W: 5-9 167 | FUT: Starting CF | 7E

Bats L Age 24 — 2021 (16) NC State

Pwr + | BAvg +++ | Spd ++++ | Def +++

Year	Lev	Team	AB	R	H	HR	RBI	Avg	OB	Slg	OPS	bb%	ct%	Eye	SB	CS	x/h%	Iso	RC/G
2021	A+	Salem	10	4	2	0	2	200	429	200	629	29	40	0.67	4	0	0	0	4.83
2022	A	Kannapolis	25	6	8	0	1	320	528	400	928	31	56	1.00	6	1	25	80	9.77
2022	A+	Winston-Salem	110	18	28	3	20	255	369	418	787	15	65	0.53	10	3	39	164	5.94
2023	A+	Winston Salem	209	54	56	4	29	268	427	421	848	22	67	0.84	32	9	38	153	7.11
2023	AA	Birmingham	222	35	51	2	22	230	352	315	668	16	64	0.53	15	0	25	86	4.19

Athletic OBP magnet made it up to Double-A in 2023. Slight build with little room to grow. Slasher type with solid spray tendencies but present contact issues, flawing the profile. Contact issues are related to a heavy top hand, which creates susceptibility to hard stuff up. Doesn't chase, works walks. Plus runner who sticks in CF.

Tavera,Braylin — 8 — Baltimore

EXP MLB DEBUT: 2027 | H/W: 6-2 175 | FUT: Starting OF | 8E

Bats R Age 19 — 2022 FA (DR)

Pwr +++ | BAvg +++ | Spd +++ | Def +++

Year	Lev	Team	AB	R	H	HR	RBI	Avg	OB	Slg	OPS	bb%	ct%	Eye	SB	CS	x/h%	Iso	RC/G
2022	Rk	DSL Orioles 2	144	24	35	2	14	243	394	319	714	20	67	0.77	7	4	20	76	4.90
2023	Rk	FCL Orioles B	107	15	28	4	20	262	388	421	808	17	79	0.96	13	5	32	159	5.90

Signed for $1.7 million in 2022. Made his stateside debut, showing he was ready for competition on the Complex. Scouts have been very positive, making him a buy-low option before his potential breakout. Works counts to get on base and leverages above average speed for SB and CF range. Needs to add muscle to lean frame.

Taylor,Brayden — 5 — Tampa Bay

EXP MLB DEBUT: 2025 | H/W: 6-1 180 | FUT: Starting 2B | 8D

Bats L Age 21 — 2023 (1) TCU

Pwr +++ | BAvg +++ | Spd +++ | Def +++

Year	Lev	Team	AB	R	H	HR	RBI	Avg	OB	Slg	OPS	bb%	ct%	Eye	SB	CS	x/h%	Iso	RC/G
2023	NCAA	TCU	260	77	80	23	70	308	427	631	1058	17	77	0.90	14	0	48	323	8.99
2023	Rk	FCL Rays	9	4	2	0	0	222	417	556	972	25	67	1.00	2	0	100	333	9.60
2023	A	Charleston	82	15	20	5	15	244	354	512	866	15	62	0.45	9	0	50	268	7.19

Hitability IF prospect struggled with breaking balls in pro debut. Parlayed power driven spring into 1st round selection. Average build with strong lower half. Hit 31 HR between college and pro ball. Still, hit over power prospect. Simple trigger with compact, slight uppercut swing. Works counts, sprays hits to CF and RF. Average runner.

Taylor,Samad — 478 — Kansas City

EXP MLB DEBUT: 2023 | H/W: 5-8 160 | FUT: Utility player | 6A

Bats R Age 25 — 2016 (10) HS (CA)

Pwr ++ | BAvg +++ | Spd ++++ | Def +++

Year	Lev	Team	AB	R	H	HR	RBI	Avg	OB	Slg	OPS	bb%	ct%	Eye	SB	CS	x/h%	Iso	RC/G
2019	A+	Dunedin	319	48	69	7	38	216	321	364	684	13	66	0.46	26	10	43	147	4.28
2021	AA	New Hampshire	320	69	94	16	52	294	376	503	879	12	66	0.38	30	8	36	209	7.04
2022	AAA	Buffalo	244	41	63	9	45	258	335	426	761	10	75	0.45	23	5	33	168	4.99
2023	AAA	Omaha	335	65	101	8	55	301	416	466	882	16	75	0.78	43	10	35	164	7.07
2023	MLB	Kansas City	60	11	12	0	4	200	284	267	550	10	63	0.32	8	0	25	67	2.27

Acquired in an offseason trade, his speed plays for steals. The interesting part is his average jumped way up in AAA during his first year with the organization. He was able to make his MLB debut in 2023 and play several different positions defensively.

Teel,Kyle — 2 — Boston

EXP MLB DEBUT: 2025 | H/W: 6-1 190 | FUT: Starting C | 8C

Bats L Age 22 — 2023 (1) Virginia

Pwr +++ | BAvg +++ | Spd +++ | Def ++

Year	Lev	Team	AB	R	H	HR	RBI	Avg	OB	Slg	OPS	bb%	ct%	Eye	SB	CS	x/h%	Iso	RC/G
2023	NCAA	Virginia	258	67	105	13	69	407	472	655	1127	11	86	0.89	5	1	36	248	9.34
2023	Rk	FCL Red Sox	7	2	3	1	2	429	556	857	1413	22	100		0	0	33	429	12.56
2023	A+	Greenville	53	10	20	0	9	377	484	453	937	17	79	1.00	1	0	20	75	7.85
2023	AA	Portland	31	3	10	1	11	323	462	484	945	21	65	0.73	2	0	30	161	8.65

Athletic, mobile catcher who made it to AA in first season. Could be frontline backstop due to hitting and defensive abilities. Makes easy contact and can shoot ball to gaps. Should continue to grow into above average power with swing adjustments. Knows strike zone and isn't fooled by spin. Will focus on improving receiving.

Tejeda,Enmanuel — 6 — New York (A)

EXP MLB DEBUT: 2027 | H/W: 5-11 158 | FUT: Starting 2B | 7E

Bats R Age 19 — 2022 FA (DR)

Pwr +++ | BAvg +++ | Spd +++ | Def +++

Year	Lev	Team	AB	R	H	HR	RBI	Avg	OB	Slg	OPS	bb%	ct%	Eye	SB	CS	x/h%	Iso	RC/G
2022	Rk	DSL Yankees	142	35	41	3	22	289	448	493	941	22	82	1.64	11	6	39	204	8.11
2023	Rk	FCL Yankees	166	37	51	5	30	307	452	458	910	21	73	1.00	24	6	24	151	7.65

Short-statured MIF enjoyed big 2024 offensive season at the complex. Strong with room to grow into build. Average-to-above tools across the board. Despite success, lots of rawness. Slight, open stance with hands close to body. On trigger, hitches hands and also arm bars his lead arm, delaying bat from moving forward. Refinement needed.

Tena,Jose
6 | **Cleveland** | EXP MLB DEBUT: 2023 | H/W: 5-11 195 | FUT: Utility player | **6A**

Bats L Age 23 · 2017 FA (DR) · Pwr ++ · BAvg +++ · Spd +++ · Def +++

Year	Lev	Team	AB	R	H	HR	RBI	Avg	OB	Slg	OPS	bb%	ct%	Eye	SB	CS	x/h%	Iso	RC/G
2022	AA	Akron	516	74	136	13	66	264	298	411	708	5	73	0.18	8	5	32	147	4.11
2022	AAA	Columbus	19	7	7	1	2	368	478	632	1110	17	79	1.00	0	0	43	263	9.88
2023	AA	Akron	308	44	80	4	37	260	347	370	717	12	66	0.39	16	7	31	110	4.77
2023	AAA	Columbus	60	9	21	4	11	350	391	667	1057	6	72	0.24	0	1	48	317	8.92
2023	MLB	Cleveland	31	2	7	0	3	226	294	290	584	9	58	0.23	0	0	29	65	2.94

Reliable, consistent INF with no plus ability but is contributor with both bat and glove. Puts bat to ball with quick stroke and ideal hand-eye coordination. More hitter over power yet can turn on pitch and make loud contact. Mostly doubles power at present. Mostly SS as pro and can play multiple positions. Offers quickness and soft hands.

Thomas,Colby
79 | **Oakland** | EXP MLB DEBUT: 2025 | H/W: 6-0 190 | FUT: Starting OF | **7B**

Bats R Age 23 · 2022 (3) Mercer · Pwr +++ · BAvg +++ · Spd +++ · Def +++

Year	Lev	Team	AB	R	H	HR	RBI	Avg	OB	Slg	OPS	bb%	ct%	Eye	SB	CS	x/h%	Iso	RC/G
2023	A	Stockton	290	49	82	8	49	283	342	476	818	8	74	0.34	14	4	44	193	5.81
2023	A+	Lansing	217	38	63	10	33	290	325	516	841	5	68	0.16	11	2	43	226	6.12

Instinctual, consistent OF who was promoted to High-A mid-year in first pro season. Does everything well but nothing plus. Can be too aggressive with bat early in count and will need to close holes in swing. Solid power/speed combo and uses IQ well on base. Has strength and stroke to make hard contact to gaps. Doubles machine.

Thompson,Sterlin
4579 | **Colorado** | EXP MLB DEBUT: 2025 | H/W: 6-4 200 | FUT: Utility player | **7C**

Bats L Age 22 · 2022 (1) Florida · Pwr +++ · BAvg ++++ · Spd +++ · Def ++

Year	Lev	Team	AB	R	H	HR	RBI	Avg	OB	Slg	OPS	bb%	ct%	Eye	SB	CS	x/h%	Iso	RC/G
2022	NCAA	Florida	254	59	90	11	51	354	436	563	999	13	81	0.79	10	3	32	209	8.07
2022	Rk	ACL Rockies	55	9	15	1	6	273	298	382	680	4	71	0.13	1	0	27	109	3.70
2022	A	Fresno	46	9	16	1	4	348	388	500	888	6	74	0.25	2	0	31	152	6.59
2023	A+	Spokane	229	42	74	7	39	323	385	520	905	9	82	0.55	14	2	41	197	6.75
2023	AA	Hartford	126	14	30	7	17	238	319	429	748	11	75	0.47	3	1	33	190	4.68

Keeps weight back well with a balanced swing and slight pre-launch leg kick. Contact-oriented; he shoots line drives to all fields. Elbow injury limited him to 94 games but did finish the season in the AFL. Fringe-average speed with positional flexibility but lack of power or other elite tools could keep him in a UT role.

Tolbert,Tyler
689 | **Kansas City** | EXP MLB DEBUT: 2025 | H/W: 6-0 160 | FUT: Reserve OF | **6B**

Bats R Age 26 · 2019 (13) UAB · Pwr ++ · BAvg ++ · Spd +++++ · Def +++

Year	Lev	Team	AB	R	H	HR	RBI	Avg	OB	Slg	OPS	bb%	ct%	Eye	SB	CS	x/h%	Iso	RC/G
2021	Rk	ACL Royals B	11	5	5	0	0	455	500	455	955	8	64	0.25	2	0	0	0	8.36
2021	A	Columbia	283	56	62	5	32	219	338	357	695	15	66	0.54	49	2	35	138	4.54
2021	A+	Quad Cities	16	4	3	1	4	188	316	438	753	16	63	0.50	4	0	67	250	5.28
2022	A+	Quad Cities	447	79	100	4	36	224	309	340	649	11	72	0.44	60	0	34	116	3.70
2023	AA	NW Arkansas	518	95	143	10	50	276	328	419	747	7	75	0.31	50	8	31	143	4.76

Over the last two seasons Tolbert has stolen 110 bases. His first season at AA was also his best hitting season. Hitting double digit home runs for the first time and adding a significant amount to his batting average. Defensive versatility may get him to majors. Likely to be quality reserve OF and SS.

Tolentino,Milan
6 | **Cleveland** | EXP MLB DEBUT: 2025 | H/W: 6-1 185 | FUT: Starting SS | **7D**

Bats L Age 22 · 2020 (4) HS (CA) · Pwr + · BAvg ++ · Spd +++ · Def ++++

Year	Lev	Team	AB	R	H	HR	RBI	Avg	OB	Slg	OPS	bb%	ct%	Eye	SB	CS	x/h%	Iso	RC/G
2021	A	Lynchburg	63	6	13	1	9	206	275	286	561	9	65	0.27	0	0	23	79	2.22
2022	A	Lynchburg	168	33	56	1	26	333	440	423	863	16	74	0.73	8	1	23	89	6.88
2022	A+	Lake County	244	39	54	3	28	221	340	332	672	15	62	0.48	21	2	39	111	4.30
2023	A+	Lake County	254	38	66	5	25	260	336	406	741	10	70	0.38	12	0	36	146	4.95
2023	AA	Akron	116	15	24	0	6	207	298	241	539	11	69	0.42	2	0	17	34	2.08

Talented defensive SS who ranges well to both sides and leverages quick hands and strong arm to stick at position long-term. Promoted to AA in September but not because of bat. Struggles to make hard contact and at best when going gap to gap. No more than 7 HR in any one season. Could stand to make more contact and use speed.

Toman,Tucker
56 | **Toronto** | EXP MLB DEBUT: 2026 | H/W: 5-11 190 | FUT: Starting 3B | **8E**

Bats B Age 20 · 2022 (2) HS (SC) · Pwr +++ · BAvg ++ · Spd ++ · Def ++

Year	Lev	Team	AB	R	H	HR	RBI	Avg	OB	Slg	OPS	bb%	ct%	Eye	SB	CS	x/h%	Iso	RC/G
2022	Rk	FCL Blue Jays	38	4	11	0	5	289	400	368	768	16	68	0.58	0	0	27	79	5.71
2023	A	Dunedin	428	59	89	5	51	208	310	313	623	13	68	0.47	7	1	36	105	3.35

Young, versatile INF who really struggled in Low-A and was 2nd in Ks in FSL. Has as much power potential as any in org but inconsistent swing path hampers production. Recognizes pitches well and willing to find his pitch. Hasn't translated to BA or HR. Not fleet of foot but exhibits quickness and range at SS and 3B.

Torin,Cristofer
46 | **Arizona** | EXP MLB DEBUT: 2026 | H/W: 5-10 155 | FUT: Starting 2B | **8E**

Bats R Age 18 · 2022 FA (VZ) · Pwr + · BAvg ++++ · Spd ++ · Def +++

Year	Lev	Team	AB	R	H	HR	RBI	Avg	OB	Slg	OPS	bb%	ct%	Eye	SB	CS	x/h%	Iso	RC/G
2022	Rk	DSL Dbacks	159	45	53	0	26	333	459	434	893	19	87	1.85	21	6	26	101	7.38
2023	Rk	ACL DBacks R	103	31	33	2	13	320	435	427	863	17	91	2.33	15	0	18	107	6.78
2023	A	Visalia	140	16	33	2	11	236	305	300	605	9	79	0.47	6	4	12	64	2.95

Young INF prospect made full season debut. Patient batter with bat-to-ball skills beyond his years. Already showing ability to use whole field. Busy setup but does not struggle with timing. Has shown ability to turn on pitches, could get to more power eventually. Offers some SB upside as well. Likely stays up the middle.

Torres,Marcos
379 | **Texas** | EXP MLB DEBUT: 2026 | H/W: 6-3 163 | FUT: Reserve OF | **6C**

Bats L Age 19 · 2022 FA (VZ) · Pwr ++ · BAvg ++ · Spd +++ · Def ++

Year	Lev	Team	AB	R	H	HR	RBI	Avg	OB	Slg	OPS	bb%	ct%	Eye	SB	CS	x/h%	Iso	RC/G
2022	Rk	DSL Rangers	181	34	51	6	33	282	372	464	836	13	76	0.60	13	6	35	182	6.14
2023	Rk	ACL Rangers	164	33	41	7	32	250	356	494	850	14	71	0.56	23	3	49	244	6.57
2023	A	Down East	37	2	4	0	1	108	175	108	283	8	51	0.17	0	3	0	0	-2.60

Held own in stateside ACL debut though 10-game A-ball dip was bad. Projectable power though .244 ACL ISO was solid with a 43% FB%. Surprising speed could, though played 1B as much as RF in 2023 and should get thicker. Strong hands, takes BB and can lay off so hit tool could be average in time.

Town,River
79 | **Kansas City** | EXP MLB DEBUT: 2025 | H/W: 5-9 181 | FUT: Reserve OF | **6C**

Bats L Age 24 · 2021 (15) Dallas Baptist · Pwr ++ · BAvg ++ · Spd +++ · Def +++

Year	Lev	Team	AB	R	H	HR	RBI	Avg	OB	Slg	OPS	bb%	ct%	Eye	SB	CS	x/h%	Iso	RC/G
2022	A	Columbia	282	47	70	12	45	248	365	461	826	16	77	0.81	18	3	47	213	6.10
2022	A+	Quad Cities	100	15	25	2	14	250	312	350	662	8	83	0.53	4	0	20	100	3.70
2023	Rk	ACL Royals B	8	2	1	1	2	125	364	500	864	27	88	3.00	1	0	100	375	6.59
2023	A+	Quad Cities	301	44	81	6	38	269	357	365	722	12	82	0.75	20	4	20	96	4.63
2023	AA	NW Arkansas	9	1	1	0	1	111	385	111	496	31	67	1.33	1	0	0	0	1.60

He can draw walks and put bat to ball well. He'll steal his share of bases, too. There's not too much power, so there's a lot of pressure on the hit tool for offensive productivity. Short, strong frame could lead to fringy pop with swing adjustments. Focuses more on contact and line drives to gaps.

Triantos,James
458 | **Chicago (N)** | EXP MLB DEBUT: 2025 | H/W: 6-1 195 | FUT: Starting 2B | **7C**

Bats R Age 21 · 2021 (2) HS (VA) · Pwr +++ · BAvg ++++ · Spd ++ · Def ++

Year	Lev	Team	AB	R	H	HR	RBI	Avg	OB	Slg	OPS	bb%	ct%	Eye	SB	CS	x/h%	Iso	RC/G
2021	Rk	ACL Cubs	101	27	33	6	19	327	370	594	964	6	82	0.39	3	3	42	267	7.15
2022	A	Myrtle Beach	456	74	124	7	50	272	329	386	715	8	82	0.48	20	3	26	114	4.38
2023	A+	South Bend	305	43	87	4	46	285	357	390	747	10	88	0.92	16	4	24	105	4.97
2023	AA	Tennessee	12	2	4	0	2	333	385	417	801	8	83	0.50	0	0	25	83	5.48

Offensive minded infielder had a bounce-back season. Slight crouch at the plate with advanced bat-to-ball skills, a lightning quick bat, and rarely chases out of the zone (34 BB/37 K at AA). Line drive swing and all fields approach limits over-the-fence power but it should develop as average once he matures. Below speed and range limit him to 2B.

Troy,Tommy
6 | **Arizona** | EXP MLB DEBUT: 2025 | H/W: 5-10 197 | FUT: Starting SS | **8E**

Bats R Age 22 · 2023 (1) Stanford · Pwr +++ · BAvg ++ · Spd +++ · Def ++++

Year	Lev	Team	AB	R	H	HR	RBI	Avg	OB	Slg	OPS	bb%	ct%	Eye	SB	CS	x/h%	Iso	RC/G
2023	NCAA	Stanford	249	76	98	17	58	394	468	699	1167	12	83	0.83	17	3	39	305	9.96
2023	Rk	ACL DBacks R	11	4	5	0	5	455	600	636	1236	27	82	2.00	1	0	20	182	12.48
2023	A+	Hillsboro	85	13	21	4	16	247	340	447	787	12	69	0.46	8	0	43	200	5.52

2023 first-rounder boasts well-rounded game, with potential to do a little bit of everything. Polished defender who figures to stick at short, he has speed and efficiency as a base stealer. Filled-out frame, muscles pitches out to all fields. Aggressive yet effective approach against fastballs, needs to improve against breaking balls.

Valdes,Javier | 23 | Atlanta | EXP MLB DEBUT: 2025 | H/W: 5-10 205 | FUT: Reserve C | 6C

Bats R Age 25	Year	Lev	Team	AB	R	H	HR	RBI	Avg	OB	Slg	OPS	bb%	ct%	Eye	SB	CS	x/h%	Iso	RC/G
2019 (21) Florida Intl	2021	A	Augusta	76	7	20	0	11	263	333	329	662	10	74	0.40	3	0	25	66	3.81
Pwr ++	2021	A+	Rome	16	6	4	0	1	250	333	313	646	11	81	0.67	0	0	25	63	3.76
BAvg +++	2022	A+	Rome	186	32	49	11	34	263	338	478	817	10	82	0.64	0	0	37	215	5.51
Spd +	2022	AA	Mississippi	78	13	18	2	11	231	368	372	740	18	73	0.81	1	0	33	141	5.12
Def ++	2023	AA	Mississippi	239	33	56	8	26	234	358	402	760	16	74	0.73	1	2	41	167	5.28

Older, hit-first catching prospect had solid season in Double-A. Patient approach, works counts and takes walks. OBP and gap XBH power carry profile. Open stance with long load and moderate leg lift. Gap-to-gap spray chart with HR power exclusively to pull side. Fringe average defensive backstop with below-average arm. Slow runner.

Valdez,Derniche | 6 | Chicago (N) | EXP MLB DEBUT: 2028 | H/W: 5-11 150 | FUT: Starting SS | 7D

Bats R Age 18	Year	Lev	Team	AB	R	H	HR	RBI	Avg	OB	Slg	OPS	bb%	ct%	Eye	SB	CS	x/h%	Iso	RC/G
2023 FA (DR)																				
Pwr ++																				
BAvg +++																				
Spd +++																				
Def +++	2023	Rk	DSL Cubs Blue	107	17	25	6	20	234	328	477	805	12	52	0.29	4	4	48	243	7.16

Projectable Dominican teen signed for $2.8 million and had solid DSL debut. Quick bat with surprising pop, but free-swinging, aggressive approach resulted in an alarming 40% K. Runs well with good range, instincts, and a enough arm to stick at SS. Shows some feel for hit, but will need to refine approach and make more contact to realize potential.

Valenzuela,Brandon | 2 | San Diego | EXP MLB DEBUT: 2025 | H/W: 6-0 225 | FUT: Reserve C | 6B

Bats B Age 23	Year	Lev	Team	AB	R	H	HR	RBI	Avg	OB	Slg	OPS	bb%	ct%	Eye	SB	CS	x/h%	Iso	RC/G
2017 FA (MX)	2021	A	Lake Elsinore	329	50	101	6	62	307	389	444	833	12	76	0.55	3	2	30	137	6.14
Pwr ++	2021	A+	Fort Wayne	49	4	12	1	7	245	422	327	748	23	59	0.75	1	0	17	82	5.74
BAvg ++	2022	A+	Fort Wayne	345	39	72	10	47	209	331	348	679	15	72	0.66	0	1	36	139	4.12
Spd +	2023	A+	Fort Wayne	136	22	38	4	15	279	359	456	815	11	73	0.46	0	0	39	176	5.90
Def ++++	2023	AA	San Antonio	94	10	17	1	6	181	280	255	536	12	69	0.45	2	0	29	74	2.01

Standout defensive C who does everything well behind plate. Not much of a producer with bat. Draws walks with patient approach and has enough bat speed to make occasional hard contact. Not much of a power threat due to swing path. Showcases plus agility and blocking ability. Coupled with strong arm, he's a deterrent to would-be basestealers.

Valera,George | 78 | Cleveland | EXP MLB DEBUT: 2024 | H/W: 6-0 195 | FUT: Starting OF | 8D

Bats L Age 23	Year	Lev	Team	AB	R	H	HR	RBI	Avg	OB	Slg	OPS	bb%	ct%	Eye	SB	CS	x/h%	Iso	RC/G
2017 FA (DR)	2021	AA	Akron	86	6	23	3	22	267	351	407	757	11	65	0.37	1	0	26	140	5.23
Pwr +++	2022	AA	Akron	330	64	87	15	59	264	364	470	834	14	70	0.52	2	4	40	206	6.26
BAvg ++	2022	AAA	Columbus	154	25	34	9	23	221	318	448	766	13	71	0.49	0	0	50	227	5.11
Spd +++	2023	Rk	ACL Indians	21	5	7	1	3	333	440	667	1107	16	76	0.80	2	0	71	333	10.05
Def +++	2023	AAA	Columbus	256	40	54	10	35	211	340	375	715	16	67	0.59	1	2	39	164	4.66

Toolsy OF who missed time due to suspension and injuries. Spent all year in AAA and turning more into slugger than BA guy. Lot of pull power from vicious lefty stroke and produces high exit velo. Middling production against LHP and lot of swing and miss. Has good speed but not many SB and helps defense in LF.

Valor,Andres | 789 | Miami | EXP MLB DEBUT: 2027 | H/W: 6-3 180 | FUT: Starting OF | 7E

Bats R Age 18	Year	Lev	Team	AB	R	H	HR	RBI	Avg	OB	Slg	OPS	bb%	ct%	Eye	SB	CS	x/h%	Iso	RC/G
2023 FA (VZ)																				
Pwr +++																				
BAvg +++																				
Spd +++																				
Def +++	2023	Rk	DSL Miami	204	39	60	5	25	294	360	466	826	9	73	0.38	21	7	38	172	5.99

Tall, projectable OF prospect was organizational MVP on Dominican Summer League squad. Athletic frame with room to grow. Power over hit profile. Upright stance with slight bat wrap. Explodes bat head with plus bat speed. Uppercut trajectory swing with heavy top hand, causing struggles with stuff up in zone. Above-average runner, likely corner OF.

Vaquero,Cristhian | 89 | Washington | EXP MLB DEBUT: 2027 | H/W: 6-3 180 | FUT: Starting CF | 8E

Bats B Age 19	Year	Lev	Team	AB	R	H	HR	RBI	Avg	OB	Slg	OPS	bb%	ct%	Eye	SB	CS	x/h%	Iso	RC/G
2022 FA (CU)																				
Pwr ++																				
BAvg +++	2022	Rk	DSL Nationals	176	33	45	1	22	256	373	341	714	16	78	0.87	17	7	20	85	4.81
Spd ++++	2023	Rk	FCL Nationals	140	34	39	1	16	279	402	393	795	17	75	0.83	15	8	31	114	6.00
Def +++	2023	A	Fredericksburg	66	10	13	1	9	197	321	288	608	15	73	0.67	7	0	23	91	3.19

Bonus baby from 2022, he'll play most of 2024 at 19 years old. Lean and athletic but exceedingly raw, he has high ceiling, but it will take time. Good approach, patient at the plate, but doesn't make enough hard contact at present. Excellent runner who should get steals, but defense could use some shoring up. A project but tools are here.

Vargas,Echedry | 456 | Texas | EXP MLB DEBUT: 2026 | H/W: 5-11 170 | FUT: Starting 2B | 7C

Bats R Age 19	Year	Lev	Team	AB	R	H	HR	RBI	Avg	OB	Slg	OPS	bb%	ct%	Eye	SB	CS	x/h%	Iso	RC/G
2022 FA (DR)																				
Pwr ++																				
BAvg +++	2022	Rk	DSL Rangers	196	40	59	4	27	301	344	510	855	6	86	0.48	13	5	47	209	6.04
Spd +++	2023	Rk	ACL Rangers	197	46	62	11	39	315	381	569	949	10	73	0.39	17	3	44	254	7.55
Def ++	2023	A	Down East	2	1	1	0	0	500	500	500	1000	0	50	0.00	0	0	0	0	11.13

While not the most athletic nor with a standout tool, has exceeded expectations and moved utility projection to potential starter. Aggressive, pull-oriented approach tempered by quality zone contact, though this may be his undoing at higher levels. Led ACL in HR so there's potential here that he outkicks mild frame projection into average power.

Vargas,Joendry | 6 | Los Angeles (N) | EXP MLB DEBUT: 2028 | H/W: 6-4 175 | FUT: Starting SS | 8D

Bats R Age 18	Year	Lev	Team	AB	R	H	HR	RBI	Avg	OB	Slg	OPS	bb%	ct%	Eye	SB	CS	x/h%	Iso	RC/G
2023 FA (DR)																				
Pwr +++																				
BAvg +++																				
Spd +++																				
Def +++	2023	Rk	DSL Dodgers B	174	47	57	7	31	328	426	529	955	15	82	0.97	19	5	35	201	7.65

Large, athletic teen signed for $2 million and had an impressive pro debut. Will need to work hard to stick at short, but shows good range and footwork with a plus arm. Spreads out at the plate with big leg kick to start swing, but shows good bat-to-ball skills with the potential for above-average to plus power. He's raw, but lots to like.

Vargas,Marco | 46 | New York (N) | EXP MLB DEBUT: 2026 | H/W: 6-0 170 | FUT: Starting 2B | 7C

Bats L Age 18	Year	Lev	Team	AB	R	H	HR	RBI	Avg	OB	Slg	OPS	bb%	ct%	Eye	SB	CS	x/h%	Iso	RC/G
2022 FA (MX)																				
Pwr ++	2022	Rk	DSL Miami	182	30	58	2	38	319	429	456	885	16	82	1.09	14	6	31	137	7.04
BAvg +++	2023	Rk	FCL Mets	47	9	11	0	5	234	368	298	666	18	81	1.11	2	0	27	64	4.34
Spd +++	2023	Rk	FCL Marlins	120	32	34	2	19	283	456	442	897	24	82	1.73	8	2	41	158	7.64
Def +++	2023	A	St. Lucie	26	5	8	0	4	308	419	308	727	16	73	0.71	3	2	0	0	4.93

Pop-up complex league bat was acquired mid-season from MIA. Slight build with some room to grow. Upright, slight open stance with direct load to hit position. Contact-oriented bat with spray approach. Works counts, more BB than K. Spray approach and swing trajectory cuts off power potential. Average runner with limited range. Likely long-term 2B.

Vasquez,Willy | 456 | Tampa Bay | EXP MLB DEBUT: 2025 | H/W: 6-2 191 | FUT: Starting 3B | 7C

Bats R Age 22	Year	Lev	Team	AB	R	H	HR	RBI	Avg	OB	Slg	OPS	bb%	ct%	Eye	SB	CS	x/h%	Iso	RC/G
2019 FA (DR)																				
Pwr +++																				
BAvg ++	2021	Rk	FCL Rays	146	26	42	2	31	288	373	411	784	12	82	0.74	14	6	26	123	5.50
Spd +++	2022	A	Charleston	449	78	115	10	73	256	311	410	721	7	72	0.29	25	3	35	154	4.48
Def +++	2023	A+	Bowling Green	420	53	98	16	62	233	309	393	702	10	74	0.42	17	9	32	160	4.15

IF prospect made strength gains while hit tool regressed in lackluster 2023 season. High-waisted athlete has sculpted muscular frame. Upright, closed stance with moderate leg lift and hitchy load, reducing reaction time. Plus bat speed with slight uppercut trajectory swing. Aggressive approach will chase. Above-average power projected.

Vaz,Javier | 4678 | Kansas City | EXP MLB DEBUT: 2025 | H/W: 5-9 151 | FUT: Utility player | 7D

Bats L Age 21	Year	Lev	Team	AB	R	H	HR	RBI	Avg	OB	Slg	OPS	bb%	ct%	Eye	SB	CS	x/h%	Iso	RC/G
2022 (15) Vanderbilt	2022	NCAA	Vanderbilt	157	24	44	5	30	280	392	490	883	16	89	1.71	11	2	48	210	6.90
Pwr ++	2022	Rk	ACL Royals B	8	2	2	0	0	250	333	375	708	11	63	0.33	1	0	50	125	4.96
BAvg +++	2022	A	Columbia	100	14	26	1	12	260	383	370	753	17	86	1.43	4	3	31	110	5.46
Spd ++++	2023	A+	Quad Cities	333	49	90	6	39	270	364	390	754	13	90	1.53	26	2	27	120	5.28
Def +++	2023	AA	NW Arkansas	112	17	34	2	12	304	386	429	814	12	84	0.83	4	1	24	125	5.82

Short, versatile INF with quick, compact swing and incredible bat-to-ball skills. Has plus speed, and his eye and patience stand out. There isn't much power and he can play almost anywhere defensively. Lacks loft to hit for pop and settles for weak contact. Arm strength a bit short, but quickness in abundance.

Vazquez,Daniel

6 | Kansas City | EXP MLB DEBUT: 2027 | H/W: 6-1 150 | FUT: Reserve IF | 6E

Bats R Age 20	Year	Lev	Team	AB	R	H	HR	RBI	Avg	OB	Slg	OPS	bb%	ct%	Eye	SB	CS	x/h%	Iso	RC/G
2021 FA (DR)																				
Pwr ++																				
BAvg +	2021	Rk	DSL Royals Blue	102	17	19	1	10	186	284	265	549	12	70	0.45	4	0	26	78	2.23
Spd +++	2022	A	Columbia	293	25	57	0	31	195	265	229	493	9	71	0.33	10	5	18	34	1.36
Def +++	2023	A	Columbia	400	57	89	3	43	223	327	288	614	13	73	0.58	32	10	21	65	3.25

Signed for $1.5 million in 2021. Things haven't panned out to this point. He has long levers on his frame. Speed his is best asset right now. The bat hasn't come around. Struggles with spin and can swing passively, thus leading to weak contact. Can be pitched to, particularly up in zone and inside. Still has hope, but will need to take step forward after two years in Low-A.

Vazquez,Luis

654 | Chicago (N) | EXP MLB DEBUT: 2024 | H/W: 6-0 165 | FUT: Utility player | 6C

Bats R Age 24	Year	Lev	Team	AB	R	H	HR	RBI	Avg	OB	Slg	OPS	bb%	ct%	Eye	SB	CS	x/h%	Iso	RC/G
2017 (14) HS (PR)	2021	AA	Tennessee	29	2	7	0	1	241	267	276	543	3	72	0.13	0	0	14	34	1.84
Pwr +++	2022	AA	Tennessee	325	43	77	8	36	237	287	366	654	7	76	0.29	7	7	31	129	3.43
BAvg ++	2022	AAA	Iowa	84	7	15	1	7	179	216	262	478	5	75	0.19	2	0	33	83	1.08
Spd ++	2023	AA	Tennessee	232	38	66	11	40	284	331	483	813	6	72	0.25	4	7	36	198	5.53
Def ++	2023	AAA	Iowa	222	34	57	9	40	257	365	428	793	15	75	0.68	6	3	35	171	5.60

Upright stance with big leg kick and can get out on front foot. Worked hard to add weight and is noticeably stronger. Had best season as pro. Aggressive approach results in swing-and-miss but also uptick in power. Average runner with a strong arm could move to 2B or 3B in the majors. At 24, the clock is ticking, but there is some upside here.

Veen,Zac

89 | Colorado | EXP MLB DEBUT: 2024 | H/W: 6-3 190 | FUT: Starting CF | 8D

Bats L Age 22	Year	Lev	Team	AB	R	H	HR	RBI	Avg	OB	Slg	OPS	bb%	ct%	Eye	SB	CS	x/h%	Iso	RC/G
2020 (1) HS (FL)																				
Pwr +++	2021	A	Fresno	399	83	120	15	75	301	397	501	899	14	68	0.51	36	17	38	201	7.37
BAvg ++++	2022	A+	Spokane	342	72	92	11	60	269	362	439	801	13	74	0.56	50	4	36	170	5.72
Spd ++++	2022	AA	Hartford	124	12	22	1	7	177	261	234	495	10	66	0.33	5	5	23	56	1.30
Def +++	2023	AA	Hartford	172	15	36	2	24	209	303	308	611	12	75	0.53	22	2	31	99	3.17

9th pick in 2020 struggled all season with a wrist injury. Attempted to play through it before having surgery in June. Lean frame, but has yet to develop the kind of raw power many anticipated though remains a potential 5-tool player. For now, he's more speed and contact over power and does have 113 minor league SB in just 278 games.

Velasquez,Diego

46 | San Francisco | EXP MLB DEBUT: 2026 | H/W: 6-1 150 | FUT: Starting 2B | 7D

Bats B Age 20	Year	Lev	Team	AB	R	H	HR	RBI	Avg	OB	Slg	OPS	bb%	ct%	Eye	SB	CS	x/h%	Iso	RC/G
2021 FA (VZ)																				
Pwr ++	2021	Rk	ACL Giants B	160	19	34	0	10	213	272	231	503	8	84	0.52	2	1	9	19	1.86
BAvg +++	2022	Rk	ACL Giants O	159	18	44	1	20	277	361	352	713	12	81	0.68	7	1	18	75	4.58
Spd +++	2022	A	San Jose	44	6	7	0	0	159	213	182	395	6	80	0.33	0	0	14	23	0.28
Def +++	2023	A	San Jose	426	76	127	8	69	298	380	434	814	12	81	0.68	23	6	32	136	5.81

Switch-hitting INF who had terrific season, all in Low-A. Led CAL in hits and doubles and 2nd in BA. Proficient from both sides of plate and uses quick stroke to spray ball to all fields. Has minimal projectable power. Has frame to add muscle but game all about contact. Ranges well at 2B and saw time at SS. Arm works well for both.

Velazquez,Ralphy

23 | Cleveland | EXP MLB DEBUT: 2027 | H/W: 6-3 215 | FUT: Starting C | 8E

Bats L Age 18	Year	Lev	Team	AB	R	H	HR	RBI	Avg	OB	Slg	OPS	bb%	ct%	Eye	SB	CS	x/h%	Iso	RC/G
2023 (1) HS (CA)																				
Pwr +++																				
BAvg +++																				
Spd +																				
Def +	2023	Rk	ACL Indians	23	7	8	2	8	348	423	739	1162	12	78	0.60	1	0	63	391	10.08

Disciplined hitter with potential for high BA and plus pop. Uses all fields and has bat speed to catch up to velocity. Very strong swing with loft and has good eye for spin. Possesses strong arm behind plate, but lacks mobility and agility. Too soon to move off C but can go to 1B where bat would play. Offers little to no speed.

Vera,Arol

46 | Los Angeles (A) | EXP MLB DEBUT: 2024 | H/W: 6-2 213 | FUT: Reserve IF | 6C

Bats B Age 21	Year	Lev	Team	AB	R	H	HR	RBI	Avg	OB	Slg	OPS	bb%	ct%	Eye	SB	CS	x/h%	Iso	RC/G
2019 FA (VZ)	2021	Rk	ACL Angels	145	24	46	0	17	317	369	469	838	8	73	0.31	2	2	41	152	6.28
Pwr ++	2021	A	Inland Empire	82	10	23	0	5	280	330	280	610	7	76	0.30	9	2	0	0	2.86
BAvg ++	2022	A	Inland Empire	487	71	101	4	59	207	285	281	566	10	69	0.36	19	7	24	74	2.41
Spd +++	2023	A+	Tri City	438	54	101	3	60	231	286	297	583	7	71	0.27	10	5	21	66	2.55
Def +++	2023	AA	Rocket City	56	8	16	2	8	286	298	411	709	2	82	0.10	2	0	19	125	3.75

Switch-hitting MIF with high chase rate has never known a pitch not worthy of swinging at. Upright, slight open stance with direct trigger. Decent hitting foundation if aggression was calmed. Stays compact within swing, especially from LH side. Just can't lay off anything. Below-average power. Average runner and average defender.

Veras,Wilfred

79 | Chicago (A) | EXP MLB DEBUT: 2025 | H/W: 6-2 180 | FUT: Starting OF | 7E

Bats R Age 21	Year	Lev	Team	AB	R	H	HR	RBI	Avg	OB	Slg	OPS	bb%	ct%	Eye	SB	CS	x/h%	Iso	RC/G
2019 FA (DR)	2021	Rk	ACL White Sox	152	25	49	4	26	322	405	533	938	12	72	0.50	3	1	45	211	7.76
Pwr +++	2022	A	Kannapolis	394	58	105	17	67	266	314	454	768	6	70	0.23	5	0	36	188	4.99
BAvg +++	2022	AA	Birmingham	45	5	12	3	5	267	313	533	846	6	69	0.21	0	0	50	267	6.06
Spd ++	2023	A+	Winston Salem	372	52	103	11	63	277	314	438	752	5	73	0.20	18	7	36	161	4.70
Def +++	2023	AA	Birmingham	152	23	47	6	30	309	344	533	877	5	71	0.18	6	0	45	224	6.50

Uber-aggressive COF prospect enjoyed BA fueled solid 2023 season. Strong frame with present power. Piled up XBH but lacked big HR total, mostly due to timing in swing. Power was mostly gap-to-gap. Uber-aggressive is understatement. Swung at nearly 60% of the pitches faced. Lost a step in the OF and on the bases. Likely LF only.

Verdugo,Rosman

6 | San Diego | EXP MLB DEBUT: 2027 | H/W: 6-0 180 | FUT: Starting 2B | 7D

Bats R Age 19	Year	Lev	Team	AB	R	H	HR	RBI	Avg	OB	Slg	OPS	bb%	ct%	Eye	SB	CS	x/h%	Iso	RC/G
2022 FA (MX)																				
Pwr ++																				
BAvg ++																				
Spd ++	2022	Rk	ACL Padres	167	26	42	7	35	251	339	467	806	12	59	0.32	3	4	43	216	6.55
Def ++	2023	A	Lake Elsinore	410	44	90	3	53	220	298	332	630	10	70	0.37	15	8	41	112	3.42

Intriguing SS who had cold end to campaign in first full pro season. Finished 2nd in CAL in doubles, but 3rd most K in org. Lot of potential in bat and showed more consistent contact as season progressed. Has pull power and could get to average overall with more time. Footwork issues may lead to 3B, but has enough arm and quickness.

Viars,Jordan

79 | Philadelphia | EXP MLB DEBUT: 2026 | H/W: 6-2 215 | FUT: Starting OF | 7D

Bats L Age 20	Year	Lev	Team	AB	R	H	HR	RBI	Avg	OB	Slg	OPS	bb%	ct%	Eye	SB	CS	x/h%	Iso	RC/G
2021 (3) HS (TX)																				
Pwr ++++	2021	Rk	FCL Phillies	47	13	12	3	18	255	397	468	865	19	74	0.92	2	0	33	213	6.61
BAvg ++	2022	Rk	FCL Phillies	154	28	37	2	20	240	316	331	647	10	74	0.43	5	0	24	91	3.54
Spd +++	2022	A	Clearwater	24	2	5	0	3	208	269	208	478	8	63	0.22	0	0	0	0	0.91
Def ++	2023	A	Clearwater	280	43	60	6	29	214	283	343	626	9	69	0.31	6	3	38	129	3.21

High pick from 2021 entered org with some promise and power buzz, but time has been marred by lots of swing and miss and too many ground balls. Physical LH hitter with raw strength and athleticism to play in an outfield corner, but the bat has fallen short so far. Young enough to improve, but the time is now as he moves to High-A.

Vivas,Jorbit

45 | New York (A) | EXP MLB DEBUT: 2024 | H/W: 5-10 171 | FUT: Utility player | 7D

Bats L Age 23	Year	Lev	Team	AB	R	H	HR	RBI	Avg	OB	Slg	OPS	bb%	ct%	Eye	SB	CS	x/h%	Iso	RC/G
2017 FA (VZ)	2021	A	Rancho Cuca	328	73	102	13	73	311	363	515	879	8	87	0.64	5	3	36	204	6.23
Pwr +++	2021	A+	Great Lakes	85	12	27	1	14	318	408	424	832	13	85	1.00	3	1	26	106	6.15
BAvg +++	2022	A+	Great Lakes	479	73	129	10	66	269	354	401	755	12	88	1.09	2	1	28	132	5.14
Spd ++	2023	AA	Tulsa	404	82	113	12	54	280	365	436	800	12	87	1.04	21	4	33	156	5.62
Def ++	2023	AAA	Oklahoma City	102	16	23	1	9	225	325	294	619	13	81	0.79	4	1	17	69	3.43

Superlative bat-to-ball skills. Short, compact frame and uses a slow leg-kick to start his stroke. Quick path through the zone and rarely chases. Has surprising pop for his size, but over the fence power is limited and now owns a career .422 SLG, but also a .383 OBP. Lack of plus range and speed make 2B his future home. Dealt to Yankees during the offseason.

Vradenburg,Brock

3 | Miami | EXP MLB DEBUT: 2026 | H/W: 6-7 230 | FUT: Starting 1B | 7D

Bats L Age 22	Year	Lev	Team	AB	R	H	HR	RBI	Avg	OB	Slg	OPS	bb%	ct%	Eye	SB	CS	x/h%	Iso	RC/G
2023 (3) Michigan State																				
Pwr +++																				
BAvg +++																				
Spd ++	2023	NCAA	Michigan St	215	62	86	13	69	400	486	721	1207	14	84	1.06	1	0	45	321	10.64
Def +++	2023	NCAA	Jupiter	110	15	26	1	10	236	364	291	655	17	66	0.59	3	1	15	55	3.91

Long, strong 1B-only prospect enjoyed breakout season with bat in draft year. Upright, slight open stance with hands direct to hit position on load. Plus bat speed produces hard contact with linear swing. Patient hitter with contact skills despite height. Will spray ball more than overpower with hard contact. Will try to get to more loft for HR.

Vukovich,A.J.
35678 | **Arizona** | EXP MLB DEBUT: 2024 | H/W: 6-2 210 | FUT: Reserve OF | **7C**

Bats R Age 22	Year	Lev	Team	AB	R	H	HR	RBI	Avg	OB	Slg	OPS	bb%	ct%	Eye	SB	CS	x/h%	Iso	RC/G
2020 (4) HS (WI)	2021	A	Visalia	247	42	64	10	42	259	312	449	761	7	69	0.25	10	1	41	190	5.01
Pwr ++	2021	A+	Hillsboro	121	13	36	3	20	298	315	438	753	2	77	0.11	6	3	25	140	4.48
BAvg +	2022	A+	Hillsboro	424	55	116	15	69	274	303	450	754	4	75	0.17	35	4	37	177	4.59
Spd ++	2022	AA	Amarillo	44	6	13	2	9	295	311	432	743	2	70	0.08	1	0	15	136	4.28
Def +++	2023	AA	Amarillo	456	84	120	24	96	263	331	485	815	9	68	0.32	20	9	40	221	5.82

Slightly crouched batting stance, almost on tip toes. Short swing, willing to choke up in 2-strike counts. Penchant for swing and miss limits hit tool. Showed plate patience development, though K% stubbornly high. HR results likely aided by Amarillo elevation in spite of GB%. Inefficient base stealer. Handled rare transition from 3B to CF well.

Wagner,Max
45 | **Baltimore** | EXP MLB DEBUT: 2025 | H/W: 6-0 215 | FUT: Utility player | **7D**

Bats R Age 22	Year	Lev	Team	AB	R	H	HR	RBI	Avg	OB	Slg	OPS	bb%	ct%	Eye	SB	CS	x/h%	Iso	RC/G
2022 (2) Clemson	2022	Rk	FCL Orioles B	4	0	2	0	2	500	500	750	1250	0	100		1	0	50	250	9.68
Pwr ++	2022	A	Delmarva	48	9	12	1	8	250	368	438	806	16	73	0.69	0	0	42	188	6.09
BAvg +++	2022	A+	Aberdeen	18	3	3	0	1	167	167	167	333	0	72	0.00	1	0	0	0	-1.16
Spd +++	2023	A+	Aberdeen	299	60	70	10	36	234	346	401	747	15	70	0.57	26	5	39	167	5.09
Def +++	2023	AA	Bowie	111	16	28	3	18	252	297	414	711	6	69	0.21	1	1	39	162	4.31

Former 2nd round pick who has already found way to AA. Wasn't able to showcase it in his first stint at level, but has shown in the past he can draw a lot of walks. Between A+ and AA he posted 27 steals. Limited bat speed mutes power and BA upside but can give ball ride when running into fastball. Possesses good defensive ability at multiple spots.

Wagner,Will
45 | **Houston** | EXP MLB DEBUT: 2024 | H/W: 5-11 210 | FUT: Reserve 3B | **6C**

Bats L Age 24	Year	Lev	Team	AB	R	H	HR	RBI	Avg	OB	Slg	OPS	bb%	ct%	Eye	SB	CS	x/h%	Iso	RC/G
2021 (18) Liberty	2022	A+	Asheville	163	22	45	4	25	276	395	405	800	16	75	0.78	3	1	27	129	5.87
Pwr ++	2022	AA	Corpus Christi	251	40	63	6	28	251	343	386	729	12	77	0.61	5	1	32	135	4.72
BAvg ++	2023	Rk	FCL Astros	16	5	5	0	2	313	522	375	897	30	94	7.00	1	0	20	63	8.28
Spd +	2023	AA	Corpus Christi	207	36	64	7	32	309	386	507	894	11	77	0.55	3	2	39	198	6.81
Def +++	2023	AAA	Sugar Land	26	3	15	0	4	577	607	692	1299	7	92	1.00	2	0	20	115	10.89

Older IF prospect spent most of season in AA before reaching AAA. Showed impressive plate discipline, contact skills. Bats from left side, has good timing and swing keeps bat in zone for long time. Below-average power, more of GB hitter who uses all fields. Took to 3B well, though lack of power limits future role.

Walcott,Sebastian
6 | **Texas** | EXP MLB DEBUT: 2026 | H/W: 6-4 190 | FUT: Starting SS | **9D**

Bats R Age 18	Year	Lev	Team	AB	R	H	HR	RBI	Avg	OB	Slg	OPS	bb%	ct%	Eye	SB	CS	x/h%	Iso	RC/G
2023 FA (BM)																				
Pwr ++++																				
BAvg ++	2023	Rk	ACL Rangers	143	26	39	7	19	273	320	524	845	7	64	0.20	9	5	49	252	6.53
Spd ++	2023	Rk	DSL Rangers	31	4	5	0	3	161	366	323	688	24	74	1.25	3	0	80	161	4.88
Def +++	2023	A+	Hickory	13	2	2	0	2	154	313	231	543	19	62	0.60	0	1	50	77	2.29

$3.2M Bahamian may have most explosive tools in system long term. Athletic, power-over-hit profile, potentially plus-plus raw projection on premium frame that should initially stick at SS. Ample swing-and-miss with longitudinal concerns there but there's hit projection and very its early in the process. Size projection may move him to 3B.

Wallace,Cayden
5 | **Kansas City** | EXP MLB DEBUT: 2025 | H/W: 5-10 205 | FUT: Starting 3B | **8C**

Bats R Age 22	Year	Lev	Team	AB	R	H	HR	RBI	Avg	OB	Slg	OPS	bb%	ct%	Eye	SB	CS	x/h%	Iso	RC/G
2022 (2) Arkansas	2022	NCAA	Arkansas	275	62	82	16	60	298	383	553	936	12	80	0.68	12	1	45	255	7.22
Pwr +++	2022	Rk	ACL Royals B	7	3	2	0	1	286	500	429	929	30	86	3.00	0	0	50	143	8.52
BAvg +++	2022	A	Columbia	109	15	32	2	16	294	364	468	832	10	80	0.55	8	1	38	174	6.01
Spd +++	2023	A+	Quad Cities	376	56	98	10	64	261	335	431	766	10	75	0.45	15	6	39	170	5.14
Def +++	2023	AA	NW Arkansas	127	19	30	3	20	236	302	362	664	9	82	0.52	3	0	30	126	3.75

Able to generate power from a quick, compact, simple swing. Shows the patience at the plate to wait for pitches to drive. Doesn't just wait passively and focuses on quality contact to all fields. Should be able to add more power with continued loft improvement. Crazy arm strength with natural actions.

Walton,TJayy
7 | **Philadelphia** | EXP MLB DEBUT: 2027 | H/W: 6-3 225 | FUT: Starting OF | **8D**

Bats R Age 19	Year	Lev	Team	AB	R	H	HR	RBI	Avg	OB	Slg	OPS	bb%	ct%	Eye	SB	CS	x/h%	Iso	RC/G
2023 (4) HS (FL)																				
Pwr ++++																				
BAvg +++																				
Spd ++																				
Def ++	2023	Rk	FCL Phillies	13	4	5	0	4	385	500	692	1192	19	54	0.50	0	1	60	308	15.39

Tall, muscular teenager with excellent bat speed and elite hard-hit rates. Makes good contact but hits a few too many grounders; getting him to lift the ball more to use his outstanding strength will be a priority. Likely to end up in a COR OF spot due to a fringy arm; runs well now but likely to slow down as he matures. Impact power potential.

Watson,Kahlil
46 | **Cleveland** | EXP MLB DEBUT: 2025 | H/W: 5-10 178 | FUT: Starting 2B | **8E**

Bats L Age 20	Year	Lev	Team	AB	R	H	HR	RBI	Avg	OB	Slg	OPS	bb%	ct%	Eye	SB	CS	x/h%	Iso	RC/G
2021 (1) HS (NC)	2022	Rk	FCL Marlins	11	4	3	1	3	273	500	727	1227	31	55	1.00	0	0	100	455	14.96
Pwr +++	2022	A	Jupiter	324	50	75	9	44	231	291	395	686	8	61	0.21	16	3	40	164	4.35
BAvg ++	2023	Rk	FCL Marlins	6	2	2	2	2	333	333	###	1667	0	83	0.00	0	0	100	1000	13.83
Spd ++++	2023	A+	Beloit	199	26	41	7	22	206	325	362	687	15	66	0.51	14	2	41	156	4.24
Def +++	2023	A+	Lake County	86	15	20	5	16	233	298	442	740	9	72	0.33	11	1	40	209	4.52

Toolsy athlete who was acquired from MIA at deadline. Few can match physical gifts and ability. Exhibits sweet, short stroke with plus bat speed and wiry strength. Has plus speed on base and ample quickness to be potential dynamo at SS. Big struggles against LHP and makes poor swing decisions to get himself out. Careless errors in field.

Wells,Austin
2 | **New York (A)** | EXP MLB DEBUT: 2023 | H/W: 6-2 220 | FUT: Starting C | **7B**

Bats L Age 24	Year	Lev	Team	AB	R	H	HR	RBI	Avg	OB	Slg	OPS	bb%	ct%	Eye	SB	CS	x/h%	Iso	RC/G
2020 (1) Arizona	2022	AA	Somerset	211	34	55	12	43	261	350	479	829	12	73	0.50	7	0	38	218	5.93
Pwr +++	2023	A	Tampa	17	2	3	1	2	176	300	353	653	15	82	1.00	0	0	33	176	3.69
BAvg +++	2023	AA	Somerset	228	28	54	11	50	237	323	443	766	11	74	0.48	5	0	46	206	5.07
Spd +	2023	AAA	Scranton/WB	126	16	32	5	20	254	338	452	790	11	73	0.47	2	1	47	198	5.49
Def +++	2023	MLB	New York (A)	70	8	16	4	13	229	260	486	746	4	80	0.21	0	0	63	257	4.41

Power-first backstop improved significantly behind the plate, earning MLB debut late in 2023. Catcher frame, at physical projection. Upright, open stance with quick trigger. Reduced bat drag, improved hard hit rate. Struggles with aggressiveness, especially expanding zone. Short, uppercut swing geared towards hard contact. 25+ HR potential.

Wendzel,Davis
56 | **Texas** | EXP MLB DEBUT: 2024 | H/W: 5-10 206 | FUT: Utility player | **7E**

Bats R Age 26	Year	Lev	Team	AB	R	H	HR	RBI	Avg	OB	Slg	OPS	bb%	ct%	Eye	SB	CS	x/h%	Iso	RC/G
2019 (1) Baylor	2021	AA	Frisco	159	23	38	6	23	239	328	390	718	12	73	0.49	1	2	32	151	4.44
Pwr +++	2021	AAA	Round Rock	28	5	6	1	2	214	267	464	731	7	71	0.25	0	0	83	250	4.66
BAvg ++	2022	Rk	ACL Rangers	19	1	2	0	1	105	190	211	401	10	63	0.29	0	0	100	105	-0.01
Spd +	2022	AAA	Round Rock	314	43	65	17	51	207	291	398	689	11	70	0.39	2	1	40	191	3.92
Def +++	2023	AAA	Round Rock	453	84	107	30	74	236	347	477	824	15	72	0.60	3	3	46	241	5.93

AAA repeat saw conditioning gains reap massive power explosion with EVs to support it. Still above-average defensively on left side of dirt, has some sneaky 2nd-division starter upside but absent a catastrophe will need to be in different org. RHP splits says he's more utility but late-game power/on-dirt defense locks in MLB floor.

Werner,Trevor
5 | **Kansas City** | EXP MLB DEBUT: 2026 | H/W: 6-3 225 | FUT: Reserve 3B | **6A**

Bats R Age 23	Year	Lev	Team	AB	R	H	HR	RBI	Avg	OB	Slg	OPS	bb%	ct%	Eye	SB	CS	x/h%	Iso	RC/G
2023 (7) Texas A&M																				
Pwr +++																				
BAvg ++	2023	NCAA	Texas A&M	218	43	55	14	52	252	356	514	869	14	69	0.51	12	3	51	261	6.73
Spd ++	2023	Rk	ACL Royals B	15	4	5	1	4	333	375	733	1108	6	60	0.17	2	0	60	400	11.41
Def +++	2023	A	Columbia	113	32	40	8	36	354	455	699	1154	16	73	0.68	8	4	53	345	10.75

The Royals 2023 seventh rounder made himself a name to monitor by 214 wRC+ through 31 games in Single-A. He likes to use his physical swing to pull the ball. The college bat might've just been too advanced for the level, or just on a hot streak, but his performance makes him a name to monitor heading into next year.

Whitcomb,Shay
456 | **Houston** | EXP MLB DEBUT: 2024 | H/W: 6-1 202 | FUT: Reserve IF | **6D**

Bats R Age 25	Year	Lev	Team	AB	R	H	HR	RBI	Avg	OB	Slg	OPS	bb%	ct%	Eye	SB	CS	x/h%	Iso	RC/G
2020 (5) UC San Diego	2021	A	Fayetteville	163	32	46	7	22	282	361	429	790	11	67	0.38	14	2	22	147	5.52
Pwr ++++	2021	A+	Asheville	233	49	70	16	56	300	353	601	954	8	65	0.23	16	3	54	300	8.03
BAvg +	2022	AA	Corpus Christi	461	67	101	19	60	219	276	399	675	7	64	0.22	20	2	43	180	3.88
Spd ++	2023	AA	Corpus Christi	176	35	48	12	36	273	340	545	886	9	68	0.32	8	2	50	273	6.80
Def ++	2023	AAA	Sugar Land	362	44	81	23	66	224	272	434	706	6	66	0.20	12	5	37	210	4.05

Older middle infielder reached Triple-A for first time. Has huge raw power, some SB upside, poor hit tool. Ultra pull-heavy approach designed to lift balls up and out of park. Susceptible to chasing outside pitches, contact% suffers. Limited defensively, likely corner role long-term. Has raw power to be impact player, if hit tool abides.

White,Lonnie

8 | Pittsburgh | EXP MLB DEBUT: 2026 | H/W: 6-3 212 | FUT: Starting OF | 8D

Bats R Age 21 — 2021 (2) HS (PA)

Skill	Rating	Year	Lev	Team	AB	R	H	HR	RBI	Avg	OB	Slg	OPS	bb%	ct%	Eye	SB	CS	x/h%	Iso	RC/G
Pwr	+++	2021	Rk	FCL Pirates B	31	6	8	2	5	258	303	516	819	6	55	0.14	0	0	50	258	6.95
BAvg	++	2022	Rk	FCL Pirates B	7	1	2	1	3	286	286	857	1143	0	57	0.00	0	0	100	571	11.87
Spd	++++	2023	Rk	FCL Pirates B	63	13	20	1	10	317	419	444	863	15	70	0.58	6	2	30	127	6.94
Def	++++	2023	A	Bradenton	162	36	42	8	30	259	381	488	869	16	65	0.57	12	1	48	228	7.12

Exceptional athlete who returned from injury in early June and fared well. Blistering speed serves as best tool with ability to steal bases and exhibit plus CF range. Has fairly short swing but expands zone against breaking balls. Possesses high ceiling and will need time to develop hit tool and power. Has been injury prone.

White,TJ

3 | Washington | EXP MLB DEBUT: 2026 | H/W: 6-2 210 | FUT: Reserve 1B | 7D

Bats B Age 20 — 2021 (5) HS (SC)

Skill	Rating	Year	Lev	Team	AB	R	H	HR	RBI	Avg	OB	Slg	OPS	bb%	ct%	Eye	SB	CS	x/h%	Iso	RC/G
Pwr	+++																				
BAvg	++	2021	Rk	FCL Nationals	53	11	15	4	12	283	345	547	892	9	74	0.36	1	0	40	264	6.48
Spd	+	2022	A	Fredericksburg	329	55	85	11	52	258	346	432	777	12	68	0.42	8	1	39	173	5.49
Def	+	2023	A+	Wilmington	247	23	42	6	25	170	273	279	552	12	58	0.34	0	2	31	109	2.21

Rough year at High-A, where strikeouts continued to pile up and everything looked out of sync. A power/speed CF prospect just a few years ago, he now has moved to 1B exclusively, his pop is only middle-of-the-road, and his speed has evaporated. That won't cut it as a starter at that position. Young enough to rebound, but the mountain looks steep.

Wilken,Brock

5 | Milwaukee | EXP MLB DEBUT: 2025 | H/W: 6-4 225 | FUT: Starting 3B | 8C

Bats R Age 21 — 2023 (1) Wake Forest

Skill	Rating	Year	Lev	Team	AB	R	H	HR	RBI	Avg	OB	Slg	OPS	bb%	ct%	Eye	SB	CS	x/h%	Iso	RC/G
Pwr	++++	2023	NCAA	Wake Forest	238	90	82	31	82	345	492	807	1299	22	76	1.19	1	0	57	462	12.44
BAvg	++	2023	Rk	ACL Brewers G	21	3	7	1	6	333	440	571	1011	16	71	0.67	1	0	29	238	8.89
Spd	+	2023	A+	Wisconsin	121	21	35	2	15	289	419	438	857	18	74	0.84	3	0	31	149	6.89
Def	++	2023	AA	Biloxi	23	3	5	2	8	217	280	565	845	8	61	0.22	0	0	80	348	6.66

Power-hitting 3B who reached AA shortly after draft. Combines power and patience to provide nice upside with stick. Will swing and miss but should be acceptable trade-off for plus pop. Has improved against breaking balls. Plays acceptable defense at 3B but may move across diamond as range and hands are a tad short.

Willems,Creed

23 | Baltimore | EXP MLB DEBUT: 2026 | H/W: 6-0 225 | FUT: Reserve 1B | 6D

Bats L Age 20 — 2021 (8) HS (TX)

Skill	Rating	Year	Lev	Team	AB	R	H	HR	RBI	Avg	OB	Slg	OPS	bb%	ct%	Eye	SB	CS	x/h%	Iso	RC/G
		2021	Rk	FCL Orioles B	2	1	0	0	0	0	0	0	0	0	100		0	0		0	-2.66
Pwr	+++	2021	Rk	FCL Orioles O	22	3	4	0	1	182	250	227	477	8	68	0.29	0	1	25	45	1.09
BAvg	++	2022	A	Delmarva	221	21	42	4	23	190	238	321	560	6	69	0.21	0	0	40	131	2.20
Spd	++	2023	A	Delmarva	96	20	29	8	28	302	422	615	1037	17	70	0.69	2	0	48	313	9.17
Def	++	2023	A+	Aberdeen	276	22	53	9	47	192	262	319	580	9	69	0.30	0	1	32	127	2.41

Has some power and some control of the zone. His hit tool and defense, however, will need improvement for him to become fantasy relevant. In a crowded catching situation already budding in Baltimore, a move elsewhere is likely.

Williams,Carson

6 | Tampa Bay | EXP MLB DEBUT: 2025 | H/W: 6-1 180 | FUT: Starting SS | 8C

Bats R Age 20 — 2021 (1) HS (CA)

Skill	Rating	Year	Lev	Team	AB	R	H	HR	RBI	Avg	OB	Slg	OPS	bb%	ct%	Eye	SB	CS	x/h%	Iso	RC/G
		2021	Rk	FCL Rays	39	8	11	0	8	282	378	436	814	13	67	0.46	2	2	45	154	6.51
Pwr	++++	2022	A	Charleston	452	81	114	19	70	252	336	471	807	11	63	0.34	28	10	45	219	6.22
BAvg	++	2023	A+	Bowling Green	401	69	102	23	77	254	341	506	848	12	63	0.36	17	9	47	252	6.73
Spd	+++	2023	AA	Montgomery	21	4	9	0	4	429	520	524	1044	16	76	0.80	3	1	22	95	9.34
Def	++++	2023	AAA	Durham	13	3	1	0	0	77	200	154	354	13	54	0.33	0	0	100	77	-1.14

Defensively skilled SS with fantasy power had a brief stint late in upper minors. Athletic frame with room still to grow. Upright, open stance. Top hand heavy swinger, contributes to high zone miss rate, dampening hit tool projection. Works counts, doesn't chase often. Plus power in frame and swing. High EV rates. Potential Gold Glove SS.

Williams,Jett

68 | New York (N) | EXP MLB DEBUT: 2025 | H/W: 5-6 175 | FUT: Starting CF | 9C

Bats R Age 20 — 2022 (1) HS (TX)

Skill	Rating	Year	Lev	Team	AB	R	H	HR	RBI	Avg	OB	Slg	OPS	bb%	ct%	Eye	SB	CS	x/h%	Iso	RC/G
Pwr	+++	2022	Rk	FCL Mets	32	7	8	1	6	250	333	438	771	11	81	0.67	6	0	38	188	5.22
BAvg	++++	2023	A	St. Lucie	261	51	65	6	35	249	406	410	816	21	71	0.91	32	6	37	161	6.42
Spd	++++	2023	A+	Brooklyn	127	25	38	7	18	299	444	567	1011	21	75	1.03	12	1	47	268	8.89
Def	+++	2023	AA	Binghamton	22	5	5	0	2	227	292	273	564	8	55	0.20	1	0	20	45	2.71

Athletic, short-statured prospect enjoyed big first full season as professional. Plus athlete with strength despite limited size. Spray hitter with compact, line drive oriented swing. Will work counts, pester pitchers. Attacks middle-in pitches with power to pull field. Could get to 20-25 HR at maturity. Plus runner with 85% SB%. Fits best in CF.

Williamson,Ben

5 | Seattle | EXP MLB DEBUT: 2026 | H/W: 6-0 190 | FUT: Starting 3B | 7D

Bats R Age 23 — 2023 (2) William & Mary

Skill	Rating	Year	Lev	Team	AB	R	H	HR	RBI	Avg	OB	Slg	OPS	bb%	ct%	Eye	SB	CS	x/h%	Iso	RC/G
Pwr	+																				
BAvg	+++	2023	NCAA	William & Mary	210	57	82	12	49	390	488	662	1150	16	90	1.82	14	1	34	271	9.87
Spd	+++	2023	Rk	ACL Mariners	6	1	3	0	0	500	500	833	1333	0	67	0.00	0	0	33	333	13.81
Def	+++	2023	A	Modesto	35	3	8	0	6	229	270	343	613	5	71	0.20	1	0	38	114	3.07

Sleeper prospect with advanced batting approach and makes easy contact with short, quick stroke. Rarely chases balls out of zone and can recognize spin. Not much power in tank but can drive ball hard to gaps. Runs bases with aplomb with average speed and has solid defensive actions at 3B. Brings good range and arm to table.

Wilson,Ethan

79 | Philadelphia | EXP MLB DEBUT: 2025 | H/W: 6-0 210 | FUT: Reserve OF | 7E

Bats L Age 24 — 2021 (2) South Alabama

Skill	Rating	Year	Lev	Team	AB	R	H	HR	RBI	Avg	OB	Slg	OPS	bb%	ct%	Eye	SB	CS	x/h%	Iso	RC/G
		2021	NCAA	South Alabama	209	38	66	8	34	316	409	531	940	14	90	1.57	9	4	38	215	7.38
Pwr	++	2021	A	Clearwater	107	15	23	3	17	215	282	374	656	9	77	0.40	2	2	39	159	3.59
BAvg	+++	2022	A+	Jersey Shore	424	39	101	7	45	238	285	344	630	6	78	0.30	25	7	29	106	3.16
Spd	+	2022	AA	Reading	70	7	15	1	3	214	267	286	552	7	70	0.24	1	2	20	71	2.03
Def	++	2023	AA	Reading	420	52	105	17	61	250	302	443	744	7	74	0.28	12	7	42	193	4.63

Has been a disappointment after a power binge in college pushed him up draft boards. Good frame, but has no real standout tool - power has been only average - and seems to have plateaued in Double-A. Does have some speed that could get double-digit SB in the majors, but as a left fielder he may not have the hit or pop to hold down a regular role.

Wilson,Jacob

6 | Oakland | EXP MLB DEBUT: 2025 | H/W: 6-3 190 | FUT: Starting SS | 7A

Bats R Age 22 — 2023 (1) Grand Canyon

Skill	Rating	Year	Lev	Team	AB	R	H	HR	RBI	Avg	OB	Slg	OPS	bb%	ct%	Eye	SB	CS	x/h%	Iso	RC/G
Pwr	++																				
BAvg	++++	2023	NCAA	Grand Canyon	192	41	79	6	61	411	464	635	1100	9	97	3.80	8	1	34	224	8.80
Spd	+++	2023	Rk	ACL Athletics	11	4	5	0	5	455	455	636	1091	0	91	0.00	0	0	40	182	8.16
Def	+++	2023	A+	Lansing	88	13	28	1	8	318	362	455	816	6	89	0.60	4	1	36	136	5.57

Lean, contact-oriented SS with plus instincts and pure hitting ability. Doesn't swing and miss much as he owns short stroke and elite pitch recognition. Rarely chases and can read spin. Not much focus on power, though could get to double-digit HR with more reps. Doesn't have great quickness but should stick at SS with strong arm and enough range.

Wilson,Peyton

4 | Kansas City | EXP MLB DEBUT: 2025 | H/W: 5-8 180 | FUT: Reserve OF | 6B

Bats B Age 24 — 2021 (2) Alabama

Skill	Rating	Year	Lev	Team	AB	R	H	HR	RBI	Avg	OB	Slg	OPS	bb%	ct%	Eye	SB	CS	x/h%	Iso	RC/G
		2021	Rk	ACL Royals B	3	0	0	0	0	0	250	0	250	25	67	1.00	0	0		0	-2.42
Pwr	++	2021	Rk	ACL Royals G	32	7	7	1	7	219	324	469	793	14	69	0.50	2	2	71	250	5.93
BAvg	++	2021	A	Columbia	39	6	9	0	1	231	302	359	661	9	74	0.40	5	0	44	128	3.91
Spd	+++	2022	A+	Quad Cities	340	60	91	14	44	268	346	456	802	11	71	0.42	23	2	36	188	5.64
Def	+++	2023	AA	NW Arkansas	489	70	140	6	65	286	358	411	769	10	79	0.54	19	7	31	125	5.21

He's athletic with some speed. His bat is coming around more and more. He rocks his weight back with his load then explodes forward. When he gets into a ball, he can hit it hard. He just needs to do it more often.

Winn,Masyn

6 | St. Louis | EXP MLB DEBUT: 2023 | H/W: 5-11 180 | FUT: Starting SS | 8B

Bats R Age 22 — 2020 (2) HS (TX)

Skill	Rating	Year	Lev	Team	AB	R	H	HR	RBI	Avg	OB	Slg	OPS	bb%	ct%	Eye	SB	CS	x/h%	Iso	RC/G
		2021	A+	Peoria	148	26	31	2	10	209	240	304	544	4	73	0.15	16	3	26	95	1.90
Pwr	++	2022	A+	Peoria	129	22	45	1	15	349	408	566	974	9	78	0.45	15	0	42	217	8.02
BAvg	+++	2022	AA	Springfield	345	69	89	11	48	258	352	432	784	13	75	0.58	28	5	42	174	5.46
Spd	++++	2023	AAA	Memphis	445	99	128	18	61	288	352	474	826	9	81	0.53	17	2	31	187	5.68
Def	+++++	2023	MLB	St. Louis	122	8	21	2	12	172	235	238	473	8	79	0.38	2	1	19	66	1.19

Elite athleticism still needs to translate into in-game production and was clearly over-matched in MLB debut. Plus bat speed and average raw power, but struggles against elite in-zone velocity and can be induced to chase as well. Will need to make better swing decisions to reach offensive potential. Plus defender with an 80-grade arm to stick at SS.

Winokur,Brandon | 68 | **Minnesota** | EXP MLB DEBUT: 2027 | H/W: 6-5 210 | FUT: Starting CF | **8E**

Bats R Age 19	Year	Lev	Team	AB	R	H	HR	RBI	Avg	OB	Slg	OPS	bb%	ct%	Eye	SB	CS	x/h%	Iso	RC/G
2023 (3) HS (CA)																				
Pwr +++																				
BAvg ++																				
Spd +++																				
Def +++	2023	Rk	FCL Twins	66	14	19	4	17	288	329	545	874	6	65	0.17	0	1	47	258	6.75

Large-framed RHH with 5 tool capability. Long arms have led to long swing and Ks. Struggles with velocity up in zone. Significant raw power to all fields but can be pull conscious. Should benefit from pro coaching, particularly with finding consistent swing. Plays SS and CF despite XL frame and has above average speed and arm.

Wolkow,George | 89 | **Chicago (A)** | EXP MLB DEBUT: 2027 | H/W: 6-7 239 | FUT: Starting OF | **8E**

Bats L Age 18	Year	Lev	Team	AB	R	H	HR	RBI	Avg	OB	Slg	OPS	bb%	ct%	Eye	SB	CS	x/h%	Iso	RC/G
2023 (7) HS (IL)																				
Pwr ++++																				
BAvg ++																				
Spd +++																				
Def +++	2023	Rk	ACL White Sox	40	6	9	1	3	225	367	325	692	18	58	0.53	2	0	22	100	4.73

Long-limbed, power hitting COF prospect struggled with contact in pro debut. Long frame with room to grow into more mass. Could have double-plus power at projection. Open stance with a slight hitch in load. Uppercut swing trajectory sells out to lofted contact. Aggressive approach will chase. 35+ HR potential if contact allows for it.

Wood,James | 89 | **Washington** | EXP MLB DEBUT: 2024 | H/W: 6-6 240 | FUT: Starting OF | **9D**

Bats L Age 21	Year	Lev	Team	AB	R	H	HR	RBI	Avg	OB	Slg	OPS	bb%	ct%	Eye	SB	CS	x/h%	Iso	RC/G
2021 (2) HS (FL)	2022	Rk	ACL Padres	16	1	2	0	0	125	263	125	388	16	56	0.43	1	0	0	0	-0.65
Pwr ++++	2022	A	Fredericksburg	82	14	24	2	17	293	370	463	833	11	68	0.38	4	0	42	171	6.37
BAvg +++	2022	A	Lake Elsinore	193	55	65	10	45	337	443	601	1045	16	78	0.88	15	5	46	264	8.98
4.12 Spd +++	2023	A+	Wilmington	150	32	44	8	36	293	398	580	978	15	67	0.53	8	1	50	287	8.65
Def +++	2023	AA	Harrisburg	323	48	80	18	55	248	329	492	821	11	62	0.31	10	2	50	245	6.41

Has the kind of build where immense and easy natural strength comes out of his long levers, which result in high exit velocities and monster HR shots, along with big K rates. But hit tool is surprisingly good; he manipulates the barrel well and has learned to use the opposite field. His current speed shows up on both the bases and in the field.

Wood,Matthew | 2 | **Milwaukee** | EXP MLB DEBUT: 2025 | H/W: 5-10 190 | FUT: Reserve C | **6B**

Bats L Age 23	Year	Lev	Team	AB	R	H	HR	RBI	Avg	OB	Slg	OPS	bb%	ct%	Eye	SB	CS	x/h%	Iso	RC/G
2022 (4) Penn State																				
Pwr ++	2022	NCAA	Penn St.	198	55	75	12	53	379	474	667	1141	15	87	1.38	5	3	40	288	9.78
BAvg +++	2022	Rk	ACL Brewers B	5	0	1	0	1	200	200	200	400	0	100		0	0	0	0	1.14
Spd ++	2023	A	Carolina	82	13	24	3	20	293	463	488	951	24	82	1.73	1	0	42	195	8.18
Def ++	2023	A+	Wisconsin	306	28	74	1	43	242	343	284	627	13	83	0.89	2	1	14	42	3.62

Patient, contact-oriented C who enjoyed first full season as pro. Struggled in High-A at end of year. Brings disciplined eye to plate and puts ball in play. However, has very little power and lacks projection. Not much bat speed and doesn't run well either. Has ample agility and strong enough arm with quick release. Limited upside with bat.

Yorke,Nick | 4 | **Boston** | EXP MLB DEBUT: 2025 | H/W: 5-11 200 | FUT: Starting 2B | **7B**

Bats R Age 22	Year	Lev	Team	AB	R	H	HR	RBI	Avg	OB	Slg	OPS	bb%	ct%	Eye	SB	CS	x/h%	Iso	RC/G
2020 (1) HS (CA)																				
Pwr +++	2021	A	Salem	294	59	95	10	47	323	406	500	906	12	84	0.87	11	8	29	177	6.88
BAvg +++	2021	A+	Greenville	84	17	28	4	15	333	411	571	982	12	74	0.50	2	1	39	238	8.09
Spd ++	2022	A+	Greenville	337	48	78	11	45	231	300	365	665	9	72	0.35	8	4	28	134	3.62
Def ++	2023	AA	Portland	444	74	119	13	61	268	343	435	778	10	73	0.42	18	5	36	167	5.34

Offensive-minded 2B with solid offensive tools and approach. Works counts with discerning eye and can recognize pitches. Can shorten swing when behind in count. Power could get to above average with swing change. Set career high in SB more on instincts and smarts. Lacks quickness and arm strength and will need to improve with glove.

Young,Cole | 6 | **Seattle** | EXP MLB DEBUT: 2025 | H/W: 6-0 180 | FUT: Starting SS | **8B**

Bats L Age 20	Year	Lev	Team	AB	R	H	HR	RBI	Avg	OB	Slg	OPS	bb%	ct%	Eye	SB	CS	x/h%	Iso	RC/G
2022 (1) HS (PA)																				
Pwr ++	2022	Rk	ACL Mariners	21	6	7	0	5	333	440	476	916	16	81	1.00	3	0	29	143	7.56
BAvg ++++	2022	A	Modesto	39	11	15	2	9	385	442	538	980	9	90	1.00	1	2	13	154	7.31
Spd +++	2023	A	Modesto	303	60	81	5	39	267	378	429	807	15	83	1.04	17	5	40	162	6.00
Def +++	2023	A+	Everett	192	32	56	6	23	292	398	479	877	15	80	0.89	5	5	39	188	6.78

Quick-rising SS who fared better in High-A upon promotion. Finished 2nd in org in doubles and walks. Tough out with keen batting eye and easy contact. Has added strength but power still a little short. Swing mechanics are smooth and sound and rarely beats himself by chasing. Has range and arm to be above average SS.

Young,Jacob | 8 | **Washington** | EXP MLB DEBUT: 2023 | H/W: 5-11 180 | FUT: Starting OF | **7D**

Bats R Age 22	Year	Lev	Team	AB	R	H	HR	RBI	Avg	OB	Slg	OPS	bb%	ct%	Eye	SB	CS	x/h%	Iso	RC/G
2021 (7) Florida	2022	A	Fredericksburg	465	118	122	2	46	262	345	331	677	11	82	0.72	52	7	16	69	4.13
Pwr ++	2023	A+	Wilmington	212	28	65	2	28	307	380	401	781	11	85	0.81	22	4	22	94	5.37
BAvg +++	2023	AA	Harrisburg	204	30	62	3	28	304	357	431	789	8	82	0.46	17	3	27	127	5.28
Spd ++++	2023	AAA	Rochester	17	2	5	1	2	294	294	471	765	0	88	0.00	0	0	20	176	4.22
Def +++	2023	MLB	Washington	107	9	27	0	12	252	316	336	653	9	79	0.45	13	0	30	84	3.71

Unheralded, moved up quickly; forced his way onto WAS roster in September. Slasher that makes solid contact that rarely goes over the fence. But he peppers balls into gaps with strong bat-to-ball skills and once on base (career .359 OBP), he takes off often. Scant power and just an adequate defender that likely ends up in a corner.

Zamora,Freddy | 6 | **Milwaukee** | EXP MLB DEBUT: 2025 | H/W: 5-10 190 | FUT: Starting SS | **7D**

Bats R Age 25	Year	Lev	Team	AB	R	H	HR	RBI	Avg	OB	Slg	OPS	bb%	ct%	Eye	SB	CS	x/h%	Iso	RC/G
2020 (2) Miami																				
Pwr ++	2021	A	Carolina	268	58	77	5	40	287	390	399	789	14	79	0.79	9	5	25	112	5.63
BAvg ++	2021	A+	Wisconsin	79	12	27	1	9	342	429	494	922	13	76	0.63	1	0	37	152	7.49
Spd +++	2022	AA	Biloxi	91	10	19	1	5	209	250	286	536	5	76	0.23	4	0	26	77	1.87
Def ++++	2023	AA	Biloxi	377	64	96	7	51	255	347	361	707	12	76	0.60	17	3	26	106	4.44

Solid defensive SS who has been maligned by variety of injuries. Spent all of 2023 in AA and has room to grow offensively. Uses short swing to put bat to ball but has limited power upside without swing adjustments. Has above average speed and quickness to enhance SS package. Makes nifty plays but can be careless at times too.

Zanetello,Nazzan | 6 | **Boston** | EXP MLB DEBUT: 2027 | H/W: 6-2 180 | FUT: Starting SS | **8D**

Bats R Age 18	Year	Lev	Team	AB	R	H	HR	RBI	Avg	OB	Slg	OPS	bb%	ct%	Eye	SB	CS	x/h%	Iso	RC/G
2023 (2) HS (MO)																				
Pwr ++																				
BAvg ++																				
Spd +++	2023	Rk	FCL Red Sox	36	6	5	0	1	139	311	222	533	20	58	0.60	5	1	60	83	2.12
Def +++	2023	A	Salem	2	0	1	0	1	500	500	500	1000	0	100		0	0	0	0	6.83

Tall, lean SS with plenty of athleticism and projection. Offers hint of all five tools and will need plenty of seasoning to reach potential. Swing can get long and handsy, though has natural strength and quick stroke. Has advanced knowledge of strike zone. Could outgrow SS and has the arm and feet to play 3B or OF.

Zavala,Aaron | 789 | **Texas** | EXP MLB DEBUT: 2025 | H/W: 6-0 193 | FUT: Reserve OF | **7D**

Bats L Age 23	Year	Lev	Team	AB	R	H	HR	RBI	Avg	OB	Slg	OPS	bb%	ct%	Eye	SB	CS	x/h%	Iso	RC/G
2021 (2) Oregon	2021	Rk	ACL Rangers	22	5	6	0	2	273	360	318	678	12	68	0.43	2	0	17	45	4.17
Pwr ++	2021	A	Down East	53	13	16	1	7	302	413	434	847	16	75	0.77	7	0	31	132	6.54
BAvg +++	2022	A+	Hickory	299	61	83	11	41	278	411	441	853	19	74	0.86	10	5	29	164	6.66
Spd +++	2022	AA	Frisco	112	28	31	5	21	277	391	482	873	16	74	0.72	4	1	42	205	6.78
Def ++	2023	AA	Frisco	341	47	66	5	40	194	334	284	619	17	53	0.45	7	3	32	91	3.70

Whether or not 2023 BA plummet was due to regression or lingering AFL elbow injury remains unknown but a results were scary. Power likely only fringe, speed may slip there, too, and D also below average, so he has to hit and he's not on a repeat of AA. Lefty splits also awful. Stock is down big without other tool support.

Zavala,Samuel | 8 | **San Diego** | EXP MLB DEBUT: 2026 | H/W: 6-1 175 | FUT: Starting OF | **8D**

Bats L Age 19	Year	Lev	Team	AB	R	H	HR	RBI	Avg	OB	Slg	OPS	bb%	ct%	Eye	SB	CS	x/h%	Iso	RC/G
2021 FA (VZ)	2021	Rk	DSL Padres	195	44	58	3	40	297	396	487	884	14	82	0.89	11	7	43	190	6.94
Pwr +++	2022	Rk	ACL Padres	29	6	10	1	6	345	424	621	1045	12	62	0.36	0	0	50	276	10.38
BAvg +++	2022	A	Lake Elsinore	122	24	31	7	26	254	355	508	863	13	70	0.51	5	3	48	254	6.64
Spd +++	2023	A	Lake Elsinore	348	83	93	14	71	267	416	451	868	20	65	0.74	20	6	39	184	7.27
Def +++	2023	A+	Fort Wayne	51	4	4	0	6	78	161	98	259	9	63	0.26	1	1	25	20	-2.48

Advanced young OF who finished 2nd in org in BB, though also most K. Struggled in brief taste of High-A. Does many things very well, but no plus tools. Has ability to get to average power with patient approach. Hits well from left side with whippy swing. Puts ball in air consistently with sound bat control. Could evolve into terrific defensive CF.

Pitchers are classified as Starters (SP) or Relievers (RP).

THROWS: Handedness — right (RH) or left (LH).

AGE: Pitcher's age, as of April 1, 2024.

DRAFTED: The year, round, and school that the pitcher performed at as an amateur if drafted, or the year and country where the player was signed from, if a free agent.

EXP MLB DEBUT: The year a player is expected to debut in the major leagues.

H/W: The player's height and weight.

FUT: The role that the pitcher is expected to have for the majority of his major league career, not necessarily his greatest upside.

PITCHES: Each pitch that a pitcher throws is graded and designated with a "+", indicating the quality of the pitch, taking into context the pitcher's age and level pitched. Pitches are graded for their velocity, movement, and command. An average pitch will receive three "+" marks. If known, a pitcher's velocity for each pitch is indicated.

FB	fastball
CB	curveball
SP	split-fingered fastball
SL	slider
CU	change-up
CT	cut-fastball
KC	knuckle-curve
KB	knuckle-ball
SC	screwball
SU	slurve

PLAYER STAT LINES: Pitcher's statistics for the last five teams that he played for (if applicable), including college and the major leagues.

TEAM DESIGNATIONS: Each team that the pitcher performed for during a given year is included.

LEVEL DESIGNATIONS: The level for each team a player performed is included. "AAA" means Triple-A, "AA" means Double-A, "A+" means high Class-A, "A" means full-season low Class-A, and "Rk" means rookie level. Prior to 2020, an "A-" referred to short-season Class-A, a level between rookie level and full-season low-A. Starting in 2021, that level no longer exists.

SABERMETRIC CATEGORIES: Descriptions of all the sabermetric categories appear in the glossary.

CAPSULE COMMENTARIES: For each pitcher, a brief analysis of their skills/statistics, and their future potential is provided.

ELIGIBILITY: Eligibility for inclusion is the standard for which Major League Baseball adheres to; less than 50 innings pitched and less than 45 days in the 26-man roster.

POTENTIAL RATINGS: The Potential Ratings are a two-part system in which a player is assigned a number rating based on his upside potential (1-10) and a letter rating based on the probability of reaching that potential (A-E).

Potential

10:	Hall of Famer	5:	MLB reserve
9:	Elite player	4:	Top minor leaguer
8:	Solid regular	3:	Average minor leaguer
7:	Average regular	2:	Minor league reserve
6:	Platoon player	1:	Minor league roster filler

Probability Rating

A:	90% probability of reaching potential
B:	70% probability of reaching potential
C:	50% probability of reaching potential
D:	30% probability of reaching potential
E:	10% probability of reaching potential

FASTBALL: Scouts grade a fastball in terms of both velocity and movement. Movement of a pitch is purely subjective, but one can always watch the hitter to see how he reacts to a pitch or if he swings and misses. Pitchers throw four types of fastballs with varying movement. A two-seam fastball is often referred to as a sinker. A four-seam fastball appears to maintain its plane at high velocities. A cutter can move in different directions and is caused by the pitcher both cutting-off his extension out front and by varying the grip. A split-fingered fastball (forkball) is thrown with the fingers spread apart against the seams and demonstrates violent downward movement. Velocity is often graded on the 20-80 scale and is indicated by the chart below.

Scout Grade	Velocity (mph)
80	96+
70	94-95
60	92-93
50 (avg)	89-91
40	87-88
30	85-86
20	82-84

PITCHER RELEASE TIMES: The speed (in seconds) that a pitcher releases a pitch from the stretch is extremely important in terms of halting the running game and establishing good pitching mechanics. Pitchers are timed from the movement of the front leg until the baseball reaches the catcher's mitt. The phrases "slow to the plate" or "quick to the plate" may appear in the capsule commentary box.

1.0-1.2	+
1.3-1.4	MLB average
1.5+	–

Abel,Mick

SP | **Philadelphia** | EXP MLB DEBUT: 2024 | H/W: 6-5 190 | FUT: #3 starter | **8C**

Thrws R Age 22	Year	Lev	Team	W	L	Sv	IP	K	ERA	WHIP	BF/G	OBA	H%	S%	xERA	Ctl	Dom	Cmd	hr/9	BPV
2020 (1) HS (OR)	2021	A	Clearwater	1	3	0	44	66	4.48	1.22	12.8	178	27	65	2.75	5.5	13.4	2.4	1.0	111
94-97 FB ++++	2022	A+	Jersey Shore	7	8	0	85	103	4.02	1.33	19.6	238	33	70	3.40	4.0	10.9	2.7	0.6	106
80-84 CB +++	2022	AA	Reading	1	3	0	23	27	3.52	1.35	19.2	227	27	85	4.55	4.7	10.6	2.3	2.0	81
84-86 SL +++	2023	AA	Reading	5	5	0	108	126	4.16	1.25	20.0	193	24	71	3.23	5.2	10.5	2.0	1.2	67
87-90 CU +++	2023	AAA	Lehigh Valley	0	1	0	4	6	4.29	1.90	19.8	297	46	75	5.06	6.4	12.9	2.0	0.0	76

Tall, lean starter whose stuff and overall arsenal has ticked up, but command has not progressed. Mid-90s FB gets whiffs and low-80s CB has replaced SL as his best breaking pitch. Change-up can get firm, but has improved. Tends to nibble and walks have been a problem at higher levels. Poised and athletic; a mid-rotation outcome.

Acker,Dane

SP | **Texas** | EXP MLB DEBUT: 2024 | H/W: 6-2 189 | FUT: #5 SP/swingman | **6C**

Thrws R Age 25	Year	Lev	Team	W	L	Sv	IP	K	ERA	WHIP	BF/G	OBA	H%	S%	xERA	Ctl	Dom	Cmd	hr/9	BPV
2020 (4) Oklahoma	2021	A	Down East	0	1	0	6	11	2.95	0.82	11.1	189	39	60	0.87	1.5	16.2	11.0	0.0	270
87-95 FB +++	2022	Rk	ACL Rangers	0	0	0	13	14	2.08	0.92	9.7	160	21	82	1.54	3.5	9.7	2.8	0.7	99
78-81 CB +++	2022	A+	Hickory	0	3	0	12	17	11.07	2.13	15.1	317	43	48	8.04	7.4	12.5	1.7	2.2	45
85-88 CU +++	2023	A+	Hickory	0	0	0	21	25	2.13	1.00	13.4	156	21	84	1.82	4.3	10.7	2.5	0.9	95
	2023	AA	Frisco	1	1	0	46	51	2.74	1.28	15.7	203	27	82	3.00	5.1	10.0	2.0	0.8	60

It's impressive that despite missing nearly 2 years with Tommy John, he found a few ticks on his FB. Now it's staying healthy. Both his CB and CU look above-average and he's stayed on a starter's workload. But 67 IP max load and health questions push him towards bullpen/swingman outcome.

Acuna,Jose

SP | **Cincinnati** | EXP MLB DEBUT: 2025 | H/W: 6-2 175 | FUT: #5 SP/swingman | **6C**

Thrws R Age 21	Year	Lev	Team	W	L	Sv	IP	K	ERA	WHIP	BF/G	OBA	H%	S%	xERA	Ctl	Dom	Cmd	hr/9	BPV
2019 FA (VZ)	2021	Rk	FCL Mets	1	0	0	7		3.86	0.86	6.4	132	7	75	2.86	3.9	9.0	2.3	2.6	76
91-94 FB +++	2022	Rk	FCL Mets	3	0	0	25	36	3.21	0.99	16.0	202	31	70	2.17	2.5	12.9	5.1	0.7	182
81-83 SL +++	2022	A	Daytona	0	1	0	31	35	3.18	0.87	16.4	162	23	62	1.04	2.9	10.1	3.5	0.3	122
83-85 CU +++	2022	A	St. Lucie	0	0	0	8	12	1.13	1.13	15.8	151	27	89	1.26	5.6	13.5	2.4	0.0	109
	2023	A+	Dayton	7	3	0	100	100	3.95	1.24	18.5	221	27	73	3.56	4.0	9.0	2.3	1.3	73

Crafty 3/4s RHP enjoyed solid season at High-A. Athletic delivery with some deceptive timing. Shoulder tends to fly open when missing zone. Average stuff across the board. Ride/run profile of 4-seam FB contributed to high 30% whiff rate, likely to drop as competition improves. Sells late fading CU well. Struggles landing SL for strikes.

Adcock,Ty

RP | **Seattle** | EXP MLB DEBUT: 2023 | H/W: 6-0 213 | FUT: Setup reliever | **7D**

Thrws R Age 27	Year	Lev	Team	W	L	Sv	IP	K	ERA	WHIP	BF/G	OBA	H%	S%	xERA	Ctl	Dom	Cmd	hr/9	BPV
2019 (8) Elon	2022	Rk	ACL Mariners	0	0	0	2	5	4.50	1.50	4.3	151	61	67	2.11	9.0	22.5	2.5	0.0	180
94-97 FB ++++	2022	A	Modesto	0	1	0	6	6	9.00	1.67	4.5	321	42	40	4.88	3.0	9.0	3.0	0.0	99
87-89 SL +++	2023	A+	Everett	1	0	1	7	9	0.00	0.43	3.8	48	9	100		2.6	11.6	4.5	0.0	157
	2023	AA	Arkansas	0	0	2	13	13	2.73	0.83	3.7	177	22	70	1.49	2.0	8.9	4.3	0.7	122
	2023	MLB	Seattle	0	0	0	15	11	3.55	0.72	4.5	204	18	71	3.14	0.0	6.5		2.4	135

Injury-riddled RP who made it to SEA despite only 28 innings in pro career. Beset by shoulder and elbow problems previously. Aggressive pitcher who operates with dynamic FB/SL combination. Throws strikes with pure arm strength and may need to upgrade FB command in order to hit spots on edges. SL can be nasty with plus break.

Adler,Eric

RP | **Chicago (A)** | EXP MLB DEBUT: 2025 | H/W: 6-2 190 | FUT: Setup reliever | **7E**

Thrws R Age 23	Year	Lev	Team	W	L	Sv	IP	K	ERA	WHIP	BF/G	OBA	H%	S%	xERA	Ctl	Dom	Cmd	hr/9	BPV
2022 (6) Wake Forest	2022	NCAA	Wake Forest	0	1	4	21	37	8.96	1.80	4.4	179	33	47	4.05	10.7	15.8	1.5	0.9	14
93-95 FB ++++	2022	Rk	ACL White Sox	0	0	0	1	3	8.18	1.82	2.6	0	0	50	1.57	16.4	24.5	1.5	0.0	18
86-88 SL ++++	2022	A	Kannapolis	0	0	0	3	5	5.81	3.87	5.2	364	57	83	11.12	20.3	14.5	0.7	0.0	-269
80-82 CB ++	2023	A	Kannapolis	0	0	2	11	19	3.24	1.17	3.7	161	29	75	2.22	5.7	15.4	2.7	0.8	142
	2023	A+	Winston Salem	2	0	3	20	23	2.70	1.40	5.3	232	34	79	2.91	5.0	10.4	2.1	0.0	71

Hard-tossing, low 3/4s RHP improved strike throwing ability on way to solid season. Jerky RP delivery with below average extension. Primarily two-pitch pitcher. 4-seam FB has flat approach angle with above-average ride out of lower slot. SL is a tight spinning gyro shaped pitch with plus potential. Also throws 11-to-5 CB.

Aguiar,Julian

SP | **Cincinnati** | EXP MLB DEBUT: 2024 | H/W: 6-3 180 | FUT: #4 starter | **7C**

Thrws R Age 22	Year	Lev	Team	W	L	Sv	IP	K	ERA	WHIP	BF/G	OBA	H%	S%	xERA	Ctl	Dom	Cmd	hr/9	BPV
2021 (12) Cypress JC	2021	Rk	ACL Reds	3	0	1	8	14	3.29	1.10	6.4	280	47	75	3.79	0.0	15.4		1.1	295
94-96 FB +++	2022	A	Daytona	7	7	0	88	103	3.17	1.18	15.3	248	32	79	3.72	2.2	10.5	4.7	1.2	147
80-82 SL ++++	2022	A+	Dayton	0	1	0	8	10	6.75	1.63	17.8	262	36	58	4.93	5.6	11.3	2.0	1.1	69
85-88 CU +++	2023	A+	Dayton	4	1	0	70	77	1.93	0.97	19.0	182	26	80	1.48	3.1	9.9	3.2	0.3	113
80-82 CB +++	2023	AA	Chattanooga	4	4	0	54	61	4.32	1.29	20.3	272	36	69	4.11	2.2	10.1	4.7	1.0	142

Athletic, low 3/4s RHP enjoyed breakout season as stuff ticked up. Repeatable delivery, stays on-time with release point. Mixes 4-seam and 2-seam FBs. Commands heavy, arm-side running 2-seamer well. Best pitch is SL with two-plane break, including late sweep and plus command. 11-to-5 CB is also effective weapon. Fringe CU completes the arsenal.

Albright,Luke

SP | **Arizona** | EXP MLB DEBUT: 2024 | H/W: 6-4 215 | FUT: #5 SP/swingman | **6B**

Thrws R Age 24	Year	Lev	Team	W	L	Sv	IP	K	ERA	WHIP	BF/G	OBA	H%	S%	xERA	Ctl	Dom	Cmd	hr/9	BPV
2021 (6) Kent State	2020	NCAA	Kent St.	2	2	0	23	22	1.94	1.21	23.4	234	32	82	2.47	3.1	8.5	2.8	0.0	88
92-94 FB ++	2021	NCAA	Kent St.	6	4	0	82	102	3.40	1.28	22.4	219	30	78	3.48	4.4	11.2	2.6	1.1	101
86-89 SL +++	2021	A	Visalia	2	0	0	23	22	3.51	1.39	16.2	244	29	79	4.15	4.3	8.6	2.0	1.2	57
77-82 CB ++	2022	A+	Hillsboro	6	10	0	123	130	5.49	1.47	20.3	265	33	65	4.71	4.1	9.5	2.3	1.2	79
90-91 CU ++	2023	AA	Amarillo	8	5	0	112	136	5.46	1.67	20.1	272	37	68	4.96	5.5	10.9	2.0	0.9	65

RHP with starter's build attacks batters with FB/SL-dominant mix. Best pitch is tight SL, pairs well with mid-90s FB. Opposing batters see CB out of hand well, are comfortable laying off it. Has mixed in CT but does not feature it frequently. Repertoire, command may necessitate move to bullpen where FB/SL combo can play up.

Albright,Mason

SP | **Colorado** | EXP MLB DEBUT: 2025 | H/W: 6-0 190 | FUT: #5 SP/swingman | **6C**

Thrws L Age 21	Year	Lev	Team	W	L	Sv	IP	K	ERA	WHIP	BF/G	OBA	H%	S%	xERA	Ctl	Dom	Cmd	hr/9	BPV
2021 (12) HS (FL)	2022	A	Inland Empire	0	4	0	48	53	9.00	1.98	19.2	347	42	57	8.22	4.3	9.9	2.3	2.3	80
91-93 FB ++	2022	A+	Tri-City	0	0	0	4	4	9.00	2.50	7.1	307	41	60	6.76	11.3	9.0	0.8	0.0	-124
74-76 CB ++	2023	A	Fresno	1	0	0	5	9	0.00	0.80	18.1	124	28	100	0.15	3.6	16.2	4.5	0.0	212
81-83 CU ++	2023	A	Inland Empire	9	4	0	79	86	3.64	1.24	21.4	259	33	75	3.93	2.3	9.8	4.3	1.1	133
CT ++	2023	A+	Spokane	2	0	0	25	24	2.88	1.44	21.3	254	30	88	4.67	4.3	8.6	2.0	1.4	57

Acquired from the Angels in the Grichuk trade. Short lefty lacks projection but has a sturdy frame, a four-pitch mix, and had a breakout campaign. Long arm action with a low ¾ arm slot and FB that sits in the low-90s, topping at 95. Plus CB is best offering, but can get slurvy at times and needs consistency. Development of fringe CU will be key.

Aquino,Patricio

SP | **Milwaukee** | EXP MLB DEBUT: 2026 | H/W: 6-0 175 | FUT: #4 starter | **7D**

Thrws R Age 20	Year	Lev	Team	W	L	Sv	IP	K	ERA	WHIP	BF/G	OBA	H%	S%	xERA	Ctl	Dom	Cmd	hr/9	BPV
2021 FA (DR)																				
90-93 FB +++																				
80-84 SL ++	2021	Rk	DSL Brewers 1	1	2	0	44	54	2.66	1.41	16.9	220	33	79	2.78	5.5	11.0	2.0	0.0	68
83-86 CU ++	2022	Rk	ACL Brewers G	2	1	0	34	49	4.75	1.35	17.8	238	36	65	3.58	4.2	12.9	3.1	0.8	137
	2023	A	Carolina	5	3	0	88	86	2.76	1.26	17.1	244	31	80	3.30	3.2	8.8	2.8	0.6	91

Short SP who had excellent start in 1st year in full season ball. Faded down stretch as stamina was tested. Induces GB with variety of pitches with quality movement. Uses low ¾ slot to command FB low in zone. SL has potential but could use a few more ticks of velo. Has to upgrade CU to battle LHH. K rate dropped but control improved.

Arias,Michael

SP | **Chicago (N)** | EXP MLB DEBUT: 2025 | H/W: 6-0 155 | FUT: Setup reliever | **7D**

Thrws R Age 22	Year	Lev	Team	W	L	Sv	IP	K	ERA	WHIP	BF/G	OBA	H%	S%	xERA	Ctl	Dom	Cmd	hr/9	BPV
2018 FA (DR)	2021	Rk	DSL Cubs Blue	4	1	3	23	22	3.12	1.30	5.9	197	25	79	2.99	5.5	8.6	1.6	0.8	25
94-97 FB ++++	2022	Rk	ACL Cubs	0	3	0	13	18	4.85	1.62	7.2	120	14	74	3.50	11.1	12.5	1.1	1.4	-57
83-85 SL +++	2022	A	Myrtle Beach	0	1	0	4	5	4.50	2.50	10.6	262	39	80	6.07	13.5	11.3	0.8	0.0	-144
86-88 CU +++	2023	A	Myrtle Beach	1	4	0	42	64	2.57	1.16	15.2	168	30	77	1.74	5.3	13.7	2.6	0.2	120
	2023	A+	South Bend	0	6	0	39	46	5.77	1.74	16.2	276	38	65	4.81	6.0	10.6	1.8	0.5	47

Converted SS is a short, athletic hurler from the D.R. Works from a low 3/4 almost sidearm slot. Plus mid-90s FB gets on hitters quickly and is an uncomfortable AB for RHB - .128 BAA at A-ball. Struggled to adjust when moved up. CU and SL both flash plus but need to be more consistent. Still raw and likely ticketed for relief role where he could thrive.

Armbruester,Justin

SP | **Baltimore** | EXP MLB DEBUT: 2024 | H/W: 6-4 235 | FUT: #4 starter | **7C**

Thrws R Age 25	Year	Lev	Team	W	L	Sv	IP	K	ERA	WHIP	BF/G	OBA	H%	S%	xERA	Ctl	Dom	Cmd	hr/9	BPV
2021 (12) New Mexico	2021	A	Delmarva	0	0	0	7	13	2.54	0.99	3.9	130	22	83	1.86	5.1	16.5	3.3	1.3	178
91-94 FB ++++	2022	A+	Aberdeen	2	1	0	53	63	4.06	1.13	17.5	219	28	69	3.33	3.0	10.7	3.5	1.4	128
81-87 SL +++	2022	AA	Bowie	4	1	2	63	63	3.71	1.03	17.4	216	24	75	3.54	2.3	9.0	3.9	1.9	118
77-80 CB +++	2023	AA	Bowie	3	2	0	62	43	2.47	1.15	20.5	229	26	82	2.96	2.8	6.2	2.3	0.7	56
87-90 CT ++	2023	AAA	Norfolk Tides	3	4	0	59	66	4.72	1.47	18.1	248	31	72	4.60	4.9	10.1	2.1	1.4	67

High 3/4s RHP struggled after Triple-A promotion. Long arm path delivery plus head whack = command concerns. FB jumps out of hand and can get on the hitter quickly. It plays well up in the zone, especially off sweeping SL. Doesn't generate as many whiffs as profile should based on arsenal. Susceptible to hard contact due to command struggles.

Arrighetti,Spencer | SP | Houston | EXP MLB DEBUT: 2024 | H/W: 6-2 186 | FUT: #4 starter | 7C

Thrws R Age 24	Year	Lev	Team	W	L	Sv	IP	K	ERA	WHIP	BF/G	OBA	H%	S%	xERA	Ctl	Dom	Cmd	hr/9	BPV
2021 (6) La-Lafayette	2021	A	Fayetteville	2	1	0	9	16	2.93	0.54	7.7	104	17	50	0.23	2.0	15.7	8.0	1.0	247
93-94 FB + +	2022	A+	Asheville	6	5	2	85	124	5.07	1.57	17.0	268	41	67	4.40	4.9	13.1	2.7	0.6	123
80-86 SL + + +	2022	AA	Corpus Christi	1	1	0	21	28	3.43	1.05	16.2	180	24	74	2.60	3.9	12.0	3.1	1.3	130
86-89 CU + +	2023	AA	Corpus Christi	7	2	0	60	79	4.19	1.18	18.5	220	33	64	2.76	3.4	11.8	3.4	0.6	138
77-79 CB +	2023	AAA	Sugar Land	2	5	0	64	62	4.64	1.33	17.7	214	26	67	3.45	5.1	8.7	1.7	1.0	38

RHP continued climb through minors, spent second half at AAA. Gets good results with FB/SL-heavy approach. Short-statured, but gets down mound with long stride. Clean delivery, throws from high arm slot. Best pitch is high-spin SL with real bat-missing ability. However, batters see it well, like to sit FB. Command, stuff fell off at AAA.

Ashcraft,Braxton | SP | Pittsburgh | EXP MLB DEBUT: 2024 | H/W: 6-5 195 | FUT: #3 starter | 8C

Thrws R Age 24	Year	Lev	Team	W	L	Sv	IP	K	ERA	WHIP	BF/G	OBA	H%	S%	xERA	Ctl	Dom	Cmd	hr/9	BPV
2018 (2) HS (TX)	2019	A-	West Virginia	1	9	0	53	39	5.77	1.34	20.0	247	29	55	3.63	3.7	6.6	1.8	0.7	36
93-97 FB + + + +	2021	A+	Greensboro	1	1	0	38	41	5.42	1.23	15.5	245	29	62	4.44	2.8	9.7	3.4	1.9	116
80-82 CB + + +	2023	A	Bradenton	0	0	0	6	11	0.00	0.66	10.6	149	33	100	0.03	1.5	16.2	11.0	0.0	270
85-88 SL + + +	2023	A+	Greensboro	0	2	0	26	29	3.79	1.30	12.0	283	36	77	4.66	1.7	10.0	5.8	1.4	151
85-87 CU + +	2023	AA	Altoona	0	1	0	20	23	1.35	0.95	9.4	199	30	84	1.38	2.3	10.4	4.6	0.0	144

Tall, lean SP who returned from Tommy John surgery and had best season of career. Mostly short outings and ended season in early August. Led org in ERA and lowest BB/9. Lively FB is best pitch and has grown to plus status. Uses both SL and CB, both with big breaking action. Has added few ticks to all pitches, though CU can be too firm.

Askew,Keyshawn | RP | Tampa Bay | EXP MLB DEBUT: 2025 | H/W: 6-4 190 | FUT: Middle reliever | 6C

Thrws L Age 24	Year	Lev	Team	W	L	Sv	IP	K	ERA	WHIP	BF/G	OBA	H%	S%	xERA	Ctl	Dom	Cmd	hr/9	BPV
2021 (10) Clemson	2021	Rk	FCL Mets	2	0	0	9		1.00	0.78	8.1	106	15	100	0.88	4.0	14.0	3.5	1.0	162
90-92 FB + + +	2022	A	St. Lucie	4	0	1	46	64	1.95	1.02	13.6	177	27	84	1.83	3.7	12.5	3.4	0.6	142
73-78 SL + + +	2022	A+	Brooklyn	1	0	0	19	28	3.75	1.25	15.6	217	36	67	2.32	4.2	13.1	3.1	0.0	140
81-84 CU + + +	2023	A+	Bowling Green	8	6	2	75	104	3.72	1.20	12.6	215	33	70	2.85	3.8	12.5	3.3	0.7	139
	2023	AA	Montgomery	1	0	3	21	26	5.09	1.37	8.1	201	29	61	2.84	5.9	11.0	1.9	0.4	56

Sidearm LHP with funk continued march to big leagues with solid 2023 campaign. Started working as RP, which is long term role. Deceptive, crossfire delivery with deception from low release height. Primarily 2-seam FB/sweeping SL pitcher. Changes speed with SL without tell. Will mix in average CU to stay honest against RHH.

Barco,Hunter | SP | Pittsburgh | EXP MLB DEBUT: 2025 | H/W: 6-4 210 | FUT: #4 starter | 7C

Thrws L Age 23	Year	Lev	Team	W	L	Sv	IP	K	ERA	WHIP	BF/G	OBA	H%	S%	xERA	Ctl	Dom	Cmd	hr/9	BPV
2022 (2) Florida																				
90-93 FB + + +																				
80-83 SL + + +																				
85-88 CU + + +	2023	Rk	FCL Pirates B	0	0	0	7	9	1.25	0.83	8.8	165	26	83	0.69	2.5	11.3	4.5	0.0	153
	2023	A	Bradenton	0	2	0	10	19	5.29	1.67	7.6	311	57	65	4.65	3.5	16.8	4.8	0.0	224

Returned from Tommy John surgery in July and enjoyed first pro experience. Will need time to improve FB command and may eventually move to pen without more stamina and durability. Offers three quality offerings thrown from crossfire delivery. Good velo on FB complemented by slower SL and average CU. When SL on, can be dominant.

Barnett,Mason | SP | Kansas City | EXP MLB DEBUT: 2025 | H/W: 6-0 218 | FUT: #3 starter | 8C

Thrws R Age 23	Year	Lev	Team	W	L	Sv	IP	K	ERA	WHIP	BF/G	OBA	H%	S%	xERA	Ctl	Dom	Cmd	hr/9	BPV
2022 (3) Auburn	2022	NCAA	Auburn	3	3	0	63	83	4.41	1.50	14.4	261	38	71	4.22	4.6	11.8	2.6	0.7	108
93-96 FB + + + +	2022	Rk	ACL Royals B	0	0	0	1	1	0.00	0.00	2.8	0				0.0	9.0		0.0	180
78-81 CB + + +	2022	A	Columbia	1	0	0	7	11	0.00	0.14	6.9	0	0	100		1.3	14.1	11.0	0.0	238
85-88 SL + + +	2023	A+	Quad Cities	4	6	0	82	94	3.18	1.18	20.5	203	29	72	2.33	4.2	10.3	2.5	0.3	91
83-86 CU + +	2023	AA	NW Arkansas	2	1	0	32	43	3.63	1.21	18.5	229	34	70	2.91	3.4	12.0	3.6	0.6	144

Former 1st round pick saw stock explode after big 2nd half in Double-A. Over-the-top slot with long arm path to release point, struggles with secondary command. Flat-angled FB became big weapon during 2nd half emergence. Feautres three secondary offerings. The CB is ahead of the SL at this point. The CU is coming along too.

Barriera,Brandon | SP | Toronto | EXP MLB DEBUT: 2025 | H/W: 6-2 180 | FUT: #3 starter | 8C

Thrws L Age 20	Year	Lev	Team	W	L	Sv	IP	K	ERA	WHIP	BF/G	OBA	H%	S%	xERA	Ctl	Dom	Cmd	hr/9	BPV
2022 (1) HS (FL)																				
91-94 FB + + +																				
82-84 SL + + +																				
80-81 CB + +	2023	Rk	FCL Blue Jays	0	0	0	2	2	0.00	0.50	6.6	0	0	100		4.5	9.0	2.0	0.0	59
85-88 CU + +	2023	A	Dunedin	0	2	0	18	23	4.48	0.99	11.5	164	26	50	1.09	4.0	11.4	2.9	0.0	116

Strong, aggressive LHP who was saddled with injuries throughout 2023 and ended season in July. Works with quick delivery to produce good FB with cutting action. Hitters have difficulty squaring up ball due to movement. SL shows flashes of plus while CB and CU could get to average. Has to improve durability and FB command.

Bastardo,Angel | SP | Boston | EXP MLB DEBUT: 2025 | H/W: 6-1 175 | FUT: #3 starter | 8E

Thrws R Age 21	Year	Lev	Team	W	L	Sv	IP	K	ERA	WHIP	BF/G	OBA	H%	S%	xERA	Ctl	Dom	Cmd	hr/9	BPV
2018 FA (VZ)																				
93-95 FB + + +	2021	Rk	FCL Red Sox	1	3	0	29	33	6.78	1.95	13.9	353	47	63	6.43	3.7	10.2	2.8	0.3	101
82-85 CB + + +	2022	A	Salem	3	4	0	82	85	4.50	1.55	16.3	262	35	70	4.11	4.9	9.3	1.9	0.4	53
86-88 SL + +	2023	A+	Greenville	2	7	0	103	139	4.63	1.28	20.1	228	33	65	3.45	4.0	12.1	3.0	1.0	128
84-87 CU + + +	2023	AA	Portland	0	1	0	16	10	5.06	1.31	22.0	210	20	67	4.06	5.1	5.6	1.1	1.7	-17

Projectable RHP who led SAL in K before promotion to AA. Lacks consistency in delivery, arm action and performance. Throws multiple pitches and shows some feel for changing speeds. CU works well off of sinking FB and features late fade. Mixes two breaking balls with slower CB ahead of SL. Will work to add strength and velocity.

Baumann,Garrett | SP | Atlanta | EXP MLB DEBUT: 2026 | H/W: 6-8 245 | FUT: #4 starter | 7E

Thrws R Age 19	Year	Lev	Team	W	L	Sv	IP	K	ERA	WHIP	BF/G	OBA	H%	S%	xERA	Ctl	Dom	Cmd	hr/9	BPV
2023 (4) HS (FL)																				
90-93 FB + + + +																				
80-82 SL + +																				
81-83 CU + + +																				
	2023	A	Augusta	0	0	0	2	1	4.50	1.50	8.6	151	18	67	2.29	9.0	4.5	0.5	0.0	-144

Tall, projectable prep arm was selected by ATL in 4th round. Cuts short high 3/4s slot delivery, doesn't make the most out of his size. 3-pitch pitcher. Throws strikes with both FB variations. 2-seam is ahead of 4-seam in development. However, flat-angled approach of 4-seam FB likely to take lead in coming years. Struggles with secondary offerings.

Baumeister,Jackson | SP | Baltimore | EXP MLB DEBUT: 2025 | H/W: 6-4 224 | FUT: #4 starter | 7C

Thrws R Age 21	Year	Lev	Team	W	L	Sv	IP	K	ERA	WHIP	BF/G	OBA	H%	S%	xERA	Ctl	Dom	Cmd	hr/9	BPV
2023 (2) Florida State																				
91-95 FB + + +																				
75-76 CB + + +																				
84-86 CU + +																				
80-82 SL +																				

Low 3/4s RHP taken in 2nd round of 2023 draft did not make pro debut later in summer. Jerky delivery with some effort to get to top end velocity. Touches upper-90s with 4-seam FB, living mostly in the lower 90s range.12-to-6 CB is best secondary. Needs to redine CU. Starter's build with pitch mix to stay to stay in the rotation.

Baumler,Carter | SP | Baltimore | EXP MLB DEBUT: 2027 | H/W: 6-2 195 | FUT: #5 SP/swingman | 7E

Thrws R Age 22	Year	Lev	Team	W	L	Sv	IP	K	ERA	WHIP	BF/G	OBA	H%	S%	xERA	Ctl	Dom	Cmd	hr/9	BPV
2020 (5) HS (IA)																				
90-92 FB + + +																				
77-80 CB + + +	2022	A	Delmarva	0	0	0	11	20	1.61	1.25	11.4	181	38	86	1.88	5.6	16.1	2.9	0.0	155
81-83 CU + +	2023	Rk	FCL Orioles B	0	0	0	8	11	1.13	0.88	7.4	151	26	86	0.64	3.4	12.4	3.7	0.0	150
83-86 SL + +	2023	A	Delmarva	1	0	0	9	10	5.00	1.33	12.5	191	28	58	2.26	6.0	10.0	1.7	0.0	36

Injury prone RHP has dealt with Tommy John surgery and shoulder issues throughout pro career. Has tossed 29.2 innings since 2020 draft. 3/4 slot delivery with repeatable mechanics and solid extension. 4-seam FB is best offering with flat-angle approach and plus riding action. The secondaries are a mixed bag with the CB ahead of the SL and CU.

Beck,Brendan | SP | New York (A) | EXP MLB DEBUT: 2025 | H/W: 6-2 205 | FUT: #4 starter | 7D

Thrws R Age 25	Year	Lev	Team	W	L	Sv	IP	K	ERA	WHIP	BF/G	OBA	H%	S%	xERA	Ctl	Dom	Cmd	hr/9	BPV
2021 (2) Stanford																				
90-92 FB + + +																				
82-84 SL + + +	2021	--	Did Not Play																	
83-85 CU + + +	2023	Rk	FCL Yankees	0	0	0	3	5	0.00	0.00	8.5	0	0			0.0	15.0		0.0	288
76-78 CB + + +	2023	A+	Hudson Valley	0	1	0	31	35	1.74	1.00	13.2	215	30	86	2.25	2.0	10.2	5.0	0.6	146

Athletic, over-the-top RHP enjoyed splendid return from Tommy John surgery. Former 2-way player at Stanford. Repeats delivery well with solid extension. Average-to-above stuff across the board. 4-seam FB has plus riding action and flat angled at lower velocity band. SL has gyro characteristics while CB is 12-6 variety. Has feel for CU.

Bedell,Ian | SP | St. Louis

EXP MLB DEBUT: 2024 | H/W: 6-2 214 | FUT: #4 starter | 7D

Thrws R Age 24			Year	Lev	Team	W	L	Sv	IP	K	ERA	WHIP	BF/G	OBA	H%	S%	xERA	Ctl	Dom	Cmd	hr/9	BPV
2020 (4) Missouri			2020	NCAA	Missouri	2	2	0	24	35	3.73	1.00	23.0	227	31	74	3.57	1.5	13.1	8.8	1.9	213
90-93	FB	+++	2021	A+	Peoria	0	1	0	2	4	12.27	4.09	7.6	530	76	67	15.82	8.2	16.4	2.0	0.0	92
77-79	CB	++	2022	Rk	FCL Cardinals	0	0	0	3	6	0.00	1.67	4.5	262	55	100	3.91	6.0	18.0	3.0	0.0	180
80-83	SL	++	2022	A	Palm Beach	0	0	0	2	4	8.18	3.18	4.4	492	73	71	12.33	4.1	16.4	4.0	0.0	202
83-85	CU	+++	2023	A+	Peoria	4	2	0	96	106	2.44	1.15	14.1	219	30	82	2.74	3.2	9.9	3.1	0.7	111

Comes at hitters with quick and efficient delivery and short arm action that allows low-90s FB to play up. FB has arm side run and carry up in the zone generating plenty of swing and miss, but might not play as well at higher levels. Upper-70s CB has potential, but lacks consistency. CU plays average with fade and sink. Improved command bodes well.

Bednar,Will | SP | San Francisco

EXP MLB DEBUT: 2025 | H/W: 6-2 230 | FUT: #4 starter | 8E

Thrws R Age 23			Year	Lev	Team	W	L	Sv	IP	K	ERA	WHIP	BF/G	OBA	H%	S%	xERA	Ctl	Dom	Cmd	hr/9	BPV
2021 (1) Mississippi State			2021	NCAA	Mississippi St	9	1	0	92	139	3.13	1.06	18.8	217	33	77	2.95	2.5	13.6	5.3	1.2	194
90-95	FB	+++	2021	Rk	ACL Giants O	0	0	0	2	3	0.00	0.50	3.3	0	0	100		4.5	13.5	3.0	0.0	140
80-84	SL	+++	2021	A	San Jose	0	0	0	5	3	1.80	1.20	10.1	299	35	83	3.39	0.0	5.4		0.0	115
81-83	CU	++	2022	A	San Jose	1	3	0	43	51	4.19	1.09	14.0	171	20	68	2.80	4.6	10.7	2.3	1.5	86
			2023	Rk	ACL Giants O	1	2	0	10	15	4.41	1.57	11.2	238	40	69	3.39	6.2	13.2	2.1	0.0	89

14th overall pick in 2021 continues to be sidetracked by injuries. Back issues limited time in 23, including stint in AFL cut short. Only 60 pro IP since signing. Struggles to throw strikes but has impressive pitch mix when on mound. FB features plus, heavy life though velocity backed up. Good break on SL and fading CU has its moments.

Beers,Blake | SP | Oakland

EXP MLB DEBUT: 2024 | H/W: 6-4 215 | FUT: #4 starter | 7D

Thrws R Age 25			Year	Lev	Team	W	L	Sv	IP	K	ERA	WHIP	BF/G	OBA	H%	S%	xERA	Ctl	Dom	Cmd	hr/9	BPV
2021 (19) Michigan			2021	Rk	ACL Athletics	0	0	0	1		9.00	2.00	4.8	415	35	100	15.95	0.0	9.0		9.0	180
93-95	FB	+++	2022	A	Stockton	2	2	0	39	51	4.13	1.15	22.2	256	34	71	4.09	1.6	11.7	7.3	1.6	185
81-84	SL	++++	2022	A+	Lansing	0	4	0	53	49	4.08	1.40	22.3	251	31	71	3.81	4.1	8.3	2.0	0.7	58
83-86	CU	++	2023	A+	Lansing	4	1	0	34	35	2.91	1.21	19.6	226	30	77	2.86	3.4	9.3	2.7	0.5	92
			2023	AA	Midland	3	10	0	80	74	7.86	1.65	19.9	302	35	53	6.23	3.8	8.3	2.2	1.8	64

Had disastrous last two months of season and struggled in AA upon promotion. Stuff appears better than numbers indicate, led by solid FB/SL combo. FB can be flat and lack movement, leading to hard hit balls. CU hasn't improved much since signing and only shows average potential. When on, SL features plus break and is tough to elevate.

Beeter,Clayton | SP | New York (A)

EXP MLB DEBUT: 2024 | H/W: 6-2 220 | FUT: Setup reliever | 7C

Thrws R Age 25			Year	Lev	Team	W	L	Sv	IP	K	ERA	WHIP	BF/G	OBA	H%	S%	xERA	Ctl	Dom	Cmd	hr/9	BPV
2020 (2) Texas Tech			2021	AA	Tulsa	0	2	0	15	23	4.20	1.13	11.9	191	29	67	2.85	4.2	13.8	3.3	1.2	153
92-94	FB	+++	2022	AA	Somerset	0	0	0	25	41	2.15	1.08	14.0	184	33	81	1.82	3.9	14.7	3.7	0.4	176
83-85	SL	++++	2022	AA	Tulsa	0	3	0	51	88	5.80	1.62	12.6	250	40	68	5.30	6.2	15.5	2.5	1.8	130
80-82	CB	++	2023	AA	Somerset	6	2	0	60	76	2.09	1.25	20.4	206	30	85	2.62	4.6	11.4	2.5	0.4	97
86-88	CU	+	2023	AAA	Scranton/WB	3	5	0	71	89	4.94	1.48	20.3	234	29	73	4.91	5.6	11.3	2.0	1.9	70

Over-the-top RHP enjoyed big 1st half in Double-A before struggling with strikes in Triple-A. Long arm circle contributes to losing release point, dampening control/command upside. Primarily FB/SL pitcher. 4-seam FB is best up in the zone with it's vertical rise profile. Gyro spinning SL is one of the best breakers in MiLB. Also throws CB and CU.

Bellozo,Valente | RP | Houston

EXP MLB DEBUT: 2025 | H/W: 5-10 170 | FUT: Middle reliever | 6B

Thrws R Age 24			Year	Lev	Team	W	L	Sv	IP	K	ERA	WHIP	BF/G	OBA	H%	S%	xERA	Ctl	Dom	Cmd	hr/9	BPV
2017 FA (MX)			2022	Rk	FCL Astros	0	1	0	1	2	18.00	4.00	6.8	587	83	50	17.75	0.0	18.0		0.0	342
91-93	FB	++	2022	Rk	FCL Astros O	0	1	0	6	9	6.00	1.33	6.2	293	47	50	3.55	1.5	13.5	9.0	0.0	221
81-82	SL	++	2022	A	Fayetteville	3	2	0	41	43	1.75	1.09	16.1	194	27	84	1.90	3.7	9.4	2.5	0.2	87
83-85	CU	+++	2023	A+	Asheville	3	3	3	94	94	6.21	1.40	18.1	285	33	60	5.54	2.5	9.0	3.6	2.0	113
76-78	CB	+	2023	AA	Corpus Christi	0	1	1	15	12	1.78	0.99	14.5	174	18	92	2.33	3.6	7.1	2.0	1.2	50

Diminutive pitcher shelled in hitter-friendly High-A Asheville despite good command, ability to miss bats. Mostly three-pitch mix composed of FB, SL, CU. Lands low-90s FB, SL for plenty of strikes. CU effective chase pitch. Potentially better suited for long relief role as arsenal could play up better in shorter stints.

Bennett,Jake | SP | Washington

EXP MLB DEBUT: 2027 | H/W: 6-6 234 | FUT: #3 starter | 8E

Thrws L Age 23			Year	Lev	Team	W	L	Sv	IP	K	ERA	WHIP	BF/G	OBA	H%	S%	xERA	Ctl	Dom	Cmd	hr/9	BPV
2022 (2) Oklahoma																						
89-92	FB	+++																				
79-81	SL	++																				
81-83	CU	++++	2023	A	Fredericksburg	1	3	0	42	54	1.93	1.00	17.8	223	33	83	2.19	1.7	11.6	6.8	0.4	180
74-77	CB	++	2023	A+	Wilmington	0	3	0	21	19	5.57	1.62	15.5	305	37	66	5.32	3.4	8.1	2.4	0.9	72

Tall lefty with elite extension helps pitches to play up; especially a low-90s two-seamer with good whiff and chase rates that he commands well. Slider is best secondary, and throws for both strikes and chases. Unfortunately mid-season elbow pain led to August Tommy John surgery and he'll miss all of 2024. Promise, but it's a long road.

Bergert,Ryan | SP | San Diego

EXP MLB DEBUT: 2025 | H/W: 6-1 210 | FUT: #4 starter | 7C

Thrws R Age 24			Year	Lev	Team	W	L	Sv	IP	K	ERA	WHIP	BF/G	OBA	H%	S%	xERA	Ctl	Dom	Cmd	hr/9	BPV
2021 (6) West Virginia			2020	NCAA	West Virginia	2	1	0	24	30	2.98	1.03	23.3	170	25	71	1.61	4.1	11.2	2.7	0.4	108
91-94	FB	+++	2021	Rk	ACL Padres	1	0	1	11	14	0.00	0.27	4.9	88	15	100		0.0	11.5		0.0	224
77-80	CB	+++	2022	A+	Fort Wayne	4	10	0	103	129	5.85	1.61	19.0	299	40	67	5.85	3.7	11.3	3.1	1.6	122
82-85	SL	+++	2023	A+	Fort Wayne	5	2	0	61	75	2.65	1.19	17.5	207	30	79	2.49	4.1	11.0	2.7	0.4	105
82-84	CU	++	2023	AA	San Antonio	1	2	0	44	51	2.86	1.14	19.3	205	30	73	2.11	3.7	10.4	2.8	0.2	106

Returned to High-A to begin year before ascension to AA in mid-July. Showed improvement with all facets of pitching and was much tougher to hit than previously. Improved both breaking balls that feature varying shapes and velocities. Establishes plate with good FB with tailing action. May not have true out pitch and needs better CU.

Berroa,Prelander | RP | Seattle

EXP MLB DEBUT: 2023 | H/W: 5-11 170 | FUT: Setup reliever | 7C

Thrws R Age 23			Year	Lev	Team	W	L	Sv	IP	K	ERA	WHIP	BF/G	OBA	H%	S%	xERA	Ctl	Dom	Cmd	hr/9	BPV
2016 FA (DR)			2022	A+	Eugene	0	0	0	13	16	0.69	0.84	12.0	119	19	91	0.25	4.1	11.0	2.7	0.0	105
95-98	FB	++++	2022	A+	Everett	2	2	0	52	81	2.42	1.17	16.0	165	29	80	1.84	5.5	14.0	2.5	0.3	121
82-85	SL	+++	2022	AA	Arkansas	2	1	0	35	53	4.37	1.29	16.0	168	27	67	2.58	6.4	13.6	2.1	0.8	90
89-92	CU	++	2023	AA	Arkansas	5	1	6	65	101	2.90	1.29	6.2	197	34	77	2.44	5.4	14.0	2.6	0.3	124
			2023	MLB	Seattle	0	0	0	1	3	0.00	2.50	3.2	0	0	100	3.31	22.5	22.5	1.0	0.0	-185

Short, athletic RHP who pitched mostly out of pen, including in 2 games with SEA. Has swing and miss stuff and posts very high K rate and rarely allows HR. Throws on flat plane to get Ks and induce GB. SL with cutting action exhibits plus break while FB reaches 100. Command and control limit upside. Tough to square up riding FB.

Birdsong,Hayden | SP | San Francisco

EXP MLB DEBUT: 2025 | H/W: 6-4 215 | FUT: #3 starter | 8D

Thrws R Age 22			Year	Lev	Team	W	L	Sv	IP	K	ERA	WHIP	BF/G	OBA	H%	S%	xERA	Ctl	Dom	Cmd	hr/9	BPV
2022 (6) Eastern Illinois			2022	Rk	ACL Giants O	0	0	0	5	12	1.73	0.38	4.2	120	43	50		0.0	20.8		0.0	392
92-96	FB	++++	2022	A	San Jose	1	0	0	6	11	4.50	1.83	9.3	321	57	73	5.23	4.5	16.5	3.7	0.0	194
77-79	CB	+++	2023	A	San Jose	0	0	0	41	70	2.18	1.36	14.3	226	42	82	2.69	4.8	15.3	3.2	0.0	163
80-83	SL	+++	2023	A+	Eugene	2	2	0	36	46	3.25	0.92	16.8	191	26	69	2.14	2.3	11.5	5.1	1.0	164
81-84	CU	++	2023	AA	Richmond	0	3	0	23	33	5.48	1.48	12.4	245	37	63	3.99	5.1	12.9	2.5	0.8	113

Tall, strong-framed SP who pitched on three levels and faded down stretch. Posted 3rd most Ks in org and gets mileage out of pitch movement and spin rates. Owns deep mix of pitches highlighted by plus FB with riding life. Two breaking balls at disposal and both have good movement. LHH have given him issues and fading CU needs to improve.

Black,Mason | SP | San Francisco

EXP MLB DEBUT: 2024 | H/W: 6-3 230 | FUT: #3 starter | 8D

Thrws R Age 24			Year	Lev	Team	W	L	Sv	IP	K	ERA	WHIP	BF/G	OBA	H%	S%	xERA	Ctl	Dom	Cmd	hr/9	BPV
2021 (3) Lehigh																						
93-96	FB	++++	2022	A	San Jose	1	1	0	34	44	1.58	0.97	16.1	206	32	84	1.75	2.1	11.6	5.5	0.3	170
81-85	SL	++++	2022	A+	Eugene	5	3	0	77	92	3.96	1.27	19.7	243	32	74	3.93	3.3	10.7	3.3	1.3	123
80-82	CU	++	2023	AA	Richmond	1	5	0	63	83	3.57	1.05	15.2	202	29	69	2.59	3.0	11.9	4.0	1.0	150
			2023	AAA	Sacramento	3	4	0	60	72	3.89	1.40	19.5	238	31	77	4.24	4.6	10.8	2.3	1.3	87

Strong, durable RHP who is advancing quickly and was effective at both AA and AAA. Continues to post high K rates with plus FB and SL. Both thrown with fast arm speed and feature plenty of late movement. Deceptive delivery adds to mix, particularly with flat angle to plate. Gets lot of extension. May be ideal for short stints in bullpen.

Blalock,Bradley | SP | Milwaukee

EXP MLB DEBUT: 2025 | H/W: 6-2 200 | FUT: #4 starter | 7C

Thrws R Age 23			Year	Lev	Team	W	L	Sv	IP	K	ERA	WHIP	BF/G	OBA	H%	S%	xERA	Ctl	Dom	Cmd	hr/9	BPV
2019 (32) HS (GA)																						
91-95	FB	+++	2021	A	Salem	3	6	0	86	85	4.29	1.53	16.3	283	37	72	4.46	3.8	8.9	2.4	0.5	76
76-79	CB	+++	2023	A	Salem	1	0	0	18	22	1.50	0.78	16.2	165	24	85	1.03	2.0	11.0	5.5	0.5	162
82-85	SL	++	2023	A+	Greenville	5	1	0	35	36	2.56	1.14	19.9	238	31	81	3.08	2.3	9.2	4.0	0.8	122
86-88	SP	++	2023	A+	Wisconsin	0	0	0	14	17	5.18	1.44	14.8	249	31	71	5.05	4.5	11.0	2.4	1.9	94

Acquired from BOS at deadline. Returned from TJ surgery after missing all of 22. Profiles as back-end starter as he lacks true put-away pitch. K rate rose while improving control. Effectively battles LHH with variety of secondary offerings. Throws consistent strikes with all pitches and learning to mix better. Not much projection remaining.

Blubaugh, A.J. — SP — Houston

EXP MLB DEBUT: 2025 | H/W: 6-2 190 | FUT: #5 SP/swingman | 7E

Thrws R | Age 23
2022 (7) Milwaukee

			Year	Lev	Team	W	L	Sv	IP	K	ERA	WHIP	BF/G	OBA	H%	S%	xERA	Ctl	Dom	Cmd	hr/9	BPV
			2022	NCAA	Milwaukee	3	3	6	52	51	3.28	1.07	12.7	214	27	71	2.53	2.8	8.8	3.2	0.7	102
92-94	FB	++	2022	Rk	FCL Astros	0	0	0	5	4	3.46	1.15	6.9	170	22	67	1.60	5.2	6.9	1.3	0.0	2
80-82	SL	++	2022	A	Fayetteville	2	1	0	13	20	4.85	1.08	16.9	231	40	50	2.05	2.1	13.8	6.7	0.0	211
82-83	CU	+++	2023	A+	Asheville	6	3	1	85	93	4.96	1.43	16.5	261	34	67	4.38	3.9	9.8	2.5	1.1	89
77-79	CB	++	2023	AA	Corpus Christi	0	0	0	14	19	1.28	0.85	12.9	91	13	91	0.61	5.1	12.1	2.4	0.6	98

RHP performed well in first full pro season. Throws from high arm slot, tends to fall off toward 1B side at end of delivery. FB-heavy approach, lands it for strikes. Has good command of SL but needs to miss more bats to be reliable out pitch. CU is best pitch, effective against LHB. Projects as starter, but lacks significant upside.

Bolton, Cody — RP — Seattle

EXP MLB DEBUT: 2023 | H/W: 6-2 210 | FUT: Middle reliever | 7D

Thrws R | Age 25
2017 (6) HS (CA)

			Year	Lev	Team	W	L	Sv	IP	K	ERA	WHIP	BF/G	OBA	H%	S%	xERA	Ctl	Dom	Cmd	hr/9	BPV
			2019	A+	Bradenton	6	3	0	61	69	1.62	0.97	18.8	184	27	81	1.14	2.1	10.1	4.9	0.1	145
92-96	FB	+++	2019	AA	Altoona	2	3	0	40	33	5.85	1.33	18.4	247	28	57	4.22	3.6	7.4	2.1	1.4	54
81-85	SL	+++	2022	AAA	Indianapolis	4	2	0	75	82	3.11	1.29	10.3	212	29	76	2.84	4.8	9.8	2.1	0.5	65
89-91	CU	+++	2023	AAA	Indianapolis	3	4	1	46	47	3.90	1.23	5.5	230	31	67	2.86	3.5	9.2	2.6	0.4	88
			2023	MLB	Pittsburgh	1	0	0	21	22	6.40	2.13	6.5	335	42	71	7.49	6.4	9.4	1.5	1.3	14

Acquired from PIT in November, was converted to RP in 2022. Repeated AAA with limited success in majors. Long arm action hinders command but has three good pitches at disposal. Likes to use FB to get ahead and leverage sweeping action on SL to get hitters to chase. Durability in question and likely to stick as RP.

Bowen, Darren — SP — Seattle

EXP MLB DEBUT: 2025 | H/W: 6-3 180 | FUT: #4 starter | 7D

Thrws R | Age 23
2022 (13) UNC-Pembroke

			Year	Lev	Team	W	L	Sv	IP	K	ERA	WHIP	BF/G	OBA	H%	S%	xERA	Ctl	Dom	Cmd	hr/9	BPV
93-96	FB	+++																				
83-85	SL	+++																				
79-80	CB	++																				
85-87	CU	+	2023	A	Modesto	4	2	0	55	59	3.91	1.11	11.4	188	26	63	1.96	4.1	9.6	2.4	0.3	81

Intriguing SP with breakout potential. Began first pro season showcased lively, hard FB and two breaking balls that can be average or better. Very tough on RHH though will need better CU to combat LHH. Has long arm action but repeats mechanics and slot. Tough to make hard contact against. Does not have plus offering.

Boyle, Joe — SP — Oakland

EXP MLB DEBUT: 2023 | H/W: 6-7 240 | FUT: #3 starter | 8E

Thrws R | Age 24
2020 (5) Notre Dame

			Year	Lev	Team	W	L	Sv	IP	K	ERA	WHIP	BF/G	OBA	H%	S%	xERA	Ctl	Dom	Cmd	hr/9	BPV
			2022	AA	Chattanooga	0	2	0	26	31	4.85	1.77	19.9	223	30	74	4.70	8.7	10.7	1.2	1.0	-23
96-100	FB	+++++	2023	AA	Chattanooga	6	5	0	84	122	4.50	1.64	19.7	210	33	73	3.83	8.0	13.1	1.6	0.6	36
85-88	SL	+++	2023	AA	Midland	2	1	0	17	28	2.11	1.11	22.4	199	37	79	1.75	3.7	14.7	4.0	0.0	184
81-85	CB	+++	2023	AAA	Las Vegas	0	2	0	16	18	2.25	1.19	21.4	151	21	83	1.98	6.2	10.1	1.6	0.6	33
88-89	CU	+	2023	MLB	Oakland	2	0	0	16	16	1.69	0.81	19.4	151	19	83	1.05	2.8	8.4	3.0	0.6	94

Improving, tall SP with lethal FB that allowed him to finish 5th in minors in K and 7th in oppBA. Atrocious control got better over last 2 months, including in majors. Misses ton of bats with triple-digit FB and knockout SL. Flashes decent CB as well. Has little ability to change speeds as CU too firm. May be best served in pen.

Bratt, Mitch — SP — Texas

EXP MLB DEBUT: 2025 | H/W: 6-1 190 | FUT: #4 starter | 7C

Thrws L | Age 20
2021 (5) HS (GA)

			Year	Lev	Team	W	L	Sv	IP	K	ERA	WHIP	BF/G	OBA	H%	S%	xERA	Ctl	Dom	Cmd	hr/9	BPV
89-92	FB	+++																				
84-86	CU	++	2021	Rk	ACL Rangers	0	0	0	6	13	0.00	0.67	5.2	191	51	100	0.49	0.0	19.5		0.0	369
77-80	SL	++	2022	A	Down East	5	5	0	80	99	2.47	1.17	16.9	226	33	80	2.68	3.1	11.1	3.5	0.4	133
75-79	CB	++	2023	A+	Hickory	2	3	0	61	73	3.54	1.26	15.6	259	35	75	3.75	2.5	10.8	4.3	0.9	144

Always a long-term play, Bratt remained solid-not-spectacular in third year but failed to up his IP count. Lat injury erased Aug and fastball velo ticked down in 2023 sitting just 90 but played above it. Average change and slider were more used, but curve best SwK in arsenal. Command remained promising though RHB got to him.

Bright, Trace — SP — Baltimore

EXP MLB DEBUT: 2025 | H/W: 6-4 199 | FUT: Middle reliever | 6A

Thrws R | Age 23
2022 (5) Auburn

			Year	Lev	Team	W	L	Sv	IP	K	ERA	WHIP	BF/G	OBA	H%	S%	xERA	Ctl	Dom	Cmd	hr/9	BPV
			2022	NCAA	Auburn	5	4	0	80	94	5.16	1.45	19.0	256	35	65	4.20	4.3	10.5	2.5	0.9	93
91-95	FB	+++	2022	Rk	FCL Orioles B	0	0	0	2	4	0.00	0.00	5.6	0	0			0.0	18.0		0.0	342
83-86	SL	++	2022	A	Delmarva	0	0	1	7	5	2.50	0.83	8.9	90	12	67	0.01	5.0	6.3	1.3	0.0	-5
76-79	CB	+++	2023	A+	Aberdeen	2	6	0	82	127	4.38	1.34	15.5	211	34	69	3.29	5.3	13.9	2.6	0.9	126
84-87	CU	++	2023	AA	Bowie	1	0	0	17	20	2.12	1.24	17.2	213	30	85	2.77	4.2	10.6	2.5	0.5	94

Tall, thin RHP pitched well at times in first full season. Over-the-top slot delivery with plus extension. 4-seam FB gets on hitters quickly and plays up to plus due to late riding action. Varies between a CB and SL as main secondary. Slower CB is ahead in development and effectiveness. Doesn't have much of a feel for CU.

Brnovich, Kyle — SP — Baltimore

EXP MLB DEBUT: 2025 | H/W: 6-2 190 | FUT: #5 SP/swingman | 6A

Thrws R | Age 26
2019 (8) Elon

			Year	Lev	Team	W	L	Sv	IP	K	ERA	WHIP	BF/G	OBA	H%	S%	xERA	Ctl	Dom	Cmd	hr/9	BPV
			2022	AAA	Norfolk Tides	0	0	0	8	4	5.63	1.50	17.3	181	18	64	3.68	7.9	4.5	0.6	1.1	-114
91-93	FB	++	2023	Rk	FCL Orioles B	0	0	0	2	2	0.00	0.00	5.6	0	0			0.0	9.0		0.0	180
82-84	CB	++++	2023	A	Delmarva	0	0	0	3	2	0.00	0.00	11.5	106	13	100	0.58	6.0	6.0	1.0	0.0	-36
84-86	SL	+++	2023	A+	Aberdeen	0	0	0	7	11	1.29	0.86	12.9	233	41	83	1.52	0.0	14.1		0.0	273
84-86	CU	+++	2023	AA	Bowie	0	2	0	14	19	7.71	1.36	14.6	262	31	50	6.20	3.2	12.2	3.8	3.2	151

Older prospect returned from Tommy John surgery but struggled with in-zone command at Double-A. Side-thrower with jerky delivery. Stuff plays up due to plus extension. Both secondaries are good offerings with the CB ahead of the SL. 4-Seam FB struggles with in-zone whiffs, resulting mostly in harder contact due to living in the fat part of the plate.

Brown, Ben — SP — Chicago (N)

EXP MLB DEBUT: 2024 | H/W: 6-6 210 | FUT: #3 starter | 8D

Thrws R | Age 24
2017 (33) HS (NY)

			Year	Lev	Team	W	L	Sv	IP	K	ERA	WHIP	BF/G	OBA	H%	S%	xERA	Ctl	Dom	Cmd	hr/9	BPV
			2021	A+	Jersey Shore	0	0	0	12	14	7.50	1.58	13.2	262	34	53	5.18	5.3	10.5	2.0	1.5	65
94-96	FB	++++	2022	A+	Jersey Shore	3	5	0	73	105	3.08	1.04	17.6	205	31	74	2.46	2.8	12.9	4.6	0.9	174
83-86	CB	++++	2022	AA	Tennessee	3	0	0	31	44	4.06	1.48	19.1	274	41	74	4.49	3.8	12.8	3.4	0.9	146
88-89	SL	++++	2023	AA	Tennessee	2	0	0	20	30	0.45	0.95	18.9	187	31	100	1.64	2.7	13.5	5.0	0.5	188
82-84	CU		2023	AAA	Iowa	6	8	0	72	100	5.36	1.54	14.3	228	33	67	4.24	6.4	12.5	2.0	1.1	71

Large framed RHP comes after hitters from a high ¾ slot with a potentially plus 3-pitch mix. Crossfire delivery with good extension and FB sits at 94-96 with good arm side run, topping at 98. Mid-80s, 12-to-6 CB gets plenty of swing-and-miss and upper-80s SL has sharp late break with cutter action. High upside but raw and needs to improve command.

Brown, Cam — SP — Philadelphia

EXP MLB DEBUT: 2026 | H/W: 6-3 225 | FUT: #4 starter | 7D

Thrws R | Age 22
2023 (10) TCU

			Year	Lev	Team	W	L	Sv	IP	K	ERA	WHIP	BF/G	OBA	H%	S%	xERA	Ctl	Dom	Cmd	hr/9	BPV
92-95	FB	++																				
83-85	SL	+++	2023	NCAA	TCU	3	2	0	55	62	5.23	1.45	14.7	205	27	64	3.48	6.5	10.1	1.6	0.8	24
84-86	CU	+	2023	Rk	FCL Phillies	0	0	0	0	0		40.00	4.3	780	78	50	#####		0.0	0.0	0.0	-7272
			2023	A	Clearwater	0	1	0	1	1	24.55	7.27	5.6	492	59	63	22.72	40.9	8.2	0.2	0.0	-939

Well built and physical, but not a lot of sizzle. Two-plane slider is his best pitch and got whiffs with it in college. Fastball comes in at low-to-mid 90s; command issues with both. Lacks feel for upper-80s CU, and only received a couple cameo appearances post-draft. Significant reliever risk, especially with his walk rate struggles.

Bruns, Maddux — SP — Los Angeles (N)

EXP MLB DEBUT: 2025 | H/W: 6-2 205 | FUT: #3 starter | 8E

Thrws L | Age 21
2021 (1) HS (AL)

			Year	Lev	Team	W	L	Sv	IP	K	ERA	WHIP	BF/G	OBA	H%	S%	xERA	Ctl	Dom	Cmd	hr/9	BPV
93-96	FB	++++	2021	Rk	ACL Dodgers	0	2	0	5	5	16.20	3.00	7.3	362	40	46	12.33	12.6	9.0	0.7	3.6	-160
80-83	CB	++++	2022	A	Rancho Cuca	0	3	0	44	67	5.71	1.84	9.8	224	38	66	4.08	9.2	13.7	1.5	0.2	16
73-75	SL	++++	2023	A	Rancho Cuca	0	0	0	21	33	1.29	1.14	13.9	157	30	88	1.36	5.6	14.1	2.5	0.0	122
			2023	A+	Great Lakes	0	7	0	76	93	4.74	1.45	16.2	207	29	68	3.50	6.4	11.0	1.7	0.8	44

Has some of the best raw stuff in the system, featuring three above-average to plus offerings, but struggles with command and owns a career 7.3/9 walk rate. FB sits at 93-96 topping out at 99 from a high ¾ arm slot with arm side run and late life. Mixes in 12-to-6 CB with late break and power SL that generates swing and miss. Lots of upside.

Burke, Sean — SP — Chicago (A)

EXP MLB DEBUT: 2024 | H/W: 6-6 230 | FUT: #5 SP/swingman | 6C

Thrws R | Age 24
2021 (3) Maryland

			Year	Lev	Team	W	L	Sv	IP	K	ERA	WHIP	BF/G	OBA	H%	S%	xERA	Ctl	Dom	Cmd	hr/9	BPV
91-94	FB	+++	2021	A	Kannapolis	0	1	0	14	20	3.21	1.36	11.7	186	32	74	2.23	6.4	12.9	2.0	0.0	76
82-84	SL	++	2022	A+	Winston-Salem	2	1	0	28	31	2.89	1.29	19.2	233	30	82	3.55	3.9	10.0	2.6	1.0	93
76-78	CB	++	2022	AA	Birmingham	2	7	0	73	99	4.81	1.44	16.4	259	36	70	4.63	4.1	12.2	3.0	1.4	128
83-85	CU	+++	2022	AAA	Charlotte	0	2	0	7	7	11.57	2.14	17.4	378	46	43	8.30	3.9	9.0	2.3	1.3	76
			2023	AAA	Charlotte	1	4	0	34	34	7.71	1.74	18.3	261	28	59	6.27	6.7	8.5	1.3	2.2	-11

Tall RHP was mostly ineffective or dealing with shoulder issues during lost 2023. Command/control RHP prior to billing. Over-the-top delivery with plus extension but struggles creating deception with release. 4-seam FB has plus riding action but below-average command and shape. Cannot command spin, thus lacking out pitch.

Burkhalter,Blake | RP | Atlanta | EXP MLB DEBUT: 2025 | H/W: 6-0 204 | FUT: Setup reliever | 7D

Thrws R Age 23	Year	Lev	Team	W	L	Sv	IP	K	ERA	WHIP	BF/G	OBA	H%	S%	xERA	Ctl	Dom	Cmd	hr/9	BPV
2022 (2) Auburn																				
92-95 FB ++++	2022	NCAA	Auburn	4	2	16	46	71	3.71	0.91	5.7	212	31	70	3.05	1.4	13.9	10.1	1.8	231
88-90 CT +++	2022	Rk	FCL Braves	0	0	0	0	0		40.00	4.3	914	91	50	#####	90.0	0.0	0.0	0.0	-2412
82-85 CU ++	2022	A	Augusta	1	0	0	4	7	0.00	0.24	6.3	80	18	100		0.0	15.4		0.0	295
	2023	--	Did Not Play																	

Missed all of 2023 after spring Tommy John surgery. Over-the-top college RP is shorter in stature and at physical projection. Quick RP delivery with below-average extension. 3-pitch pitcher. Flat-angled FB with plus riding action. Plays up due to low release height. CT has short, late break profile. Works in CU.

Burns,Tanner | RP | Cleveland | EXP MLB DEBUT: 2024 | H/W: 6-0 210 | FUT: Middle reliever | 7D

Thrws R Age 25	Year	Lev	Team	W	L	Sv	IP	K	ERA	WHIP	BF/G	OBA	H%	S%	xERA	Ctl	Dom	Cmd	hr/9	BPV
2020 (1) Auburn																				
90-95 FB +++	2020	NCAA	Auburn	3	1	0	22	32	2.44	1.00	21.1	194	30	80	2.18	2.9	13.0	4.6	0.8	176
77-79 CB +++	2021	A+	Lake County	2	5	0	75	91	3.59	1.24	16.9	232	31	76	3.62	3.5	10.9	3.1	1.2	120
82-85 SL +++	2022	AA	Akron	3	7	0	88	92	3.57	1.36	17.6	232	28	80	4.17	4.6	9.4	2.0	1.4	63
81-83 CU +++	2023	AA	Akron	5	3	1	86	86	3.03	1.26	12.1	219	27	82	3.50	4.3	9.0	2.1	1.1	64

Versatile arm who repeated AA and worked as both SP and RP. Mostly shorter outings as SP, though didn't see velo increase as hoped. Gets good armside run on FB and generally commands it well. Secondary offerings show promise, highlighted by hard SL and sinking CU. Durability in question and control is erratic.

Burrows,Michael | SP | Pittsburgh | EXP MLB DEBUT: 2025 | H/W: 6-1 190 | FUT: #4 starter | 7C

Thrws R Age 24	Year	Lev	Team	W	L	Sv	IP	K	ERA	WHIP	BF/G	OBA	H%	S%	xERA	Ctl	Dom	Cmd	hr/9	BPV
2018 (11) HS (CT)	2019	A-	West Virginia	2	3	0	43		4.38	1.48	16.9	265	35	69	3.97	4.2	9.0	2.2	0.4	67
92-96 FB +++	2021	A+	Greensboro	2	2	0	49	66	2.20	0.90	14.0	148	23	78	1.19	3.7	12.1	3.3	0.6	137
78-82 CB +++	2022	AA	Altoona	4	2	0	52	69	2.94	1.10	17.0	206	31	74	2.30	3.3	11.9	3.6	0.5	144
85-87 SL ++	2022	AAA	Indianapolis	1	4	0	42	42	5.34	1.35	14.6	275	34	62	4.39	2.6	9.0	3.5	1.1	110
86-88 CU +++	2023	AAA	Indianapolis	0	0	0	6	3	2.90	0.97	11.7	186	12	100	4.07	2.9	4.4	1.5	2.9	18

Promising RHP who underwent Tommy John surgery in April 2023. Advanced pitchability and solid velocity have led to minors success. Limited IP as pro yet has made it to AAA and on verge of majors. Operates with four pitches in average to above average arsenal. Locates all pitches well and uses high spin CB as K pitch. CU has made big strides.

Bush,Ky | SP | Chicago (A) | EXP MLB DEBUT: 2024 | H/W: 6-6 240 | FUT: #5 SP/swingman | 6D

Thrws L Age 24	Year	Lev	Team	W	L	Sv	IP	K	ERA	WHIP	BF/G	OBA	H%	S%	xERA	Ctl	Dom	Cmd	hr/9	BPV
2021 (2) St. Mary's (CA)	2021	A+	Tri-City	0	2	0	12	20	4.50	1.58	10.6	293	50	68	4.17	3.8	15.0	4.0	0.0	187
91-93 FB ++	2022	AA	Rocket City	7	4	0	103	101	3.67	1.18	19.6	243	29	74	3.67	2.5	8.8	3.5	1.2	108
82-84 SL +++	2023	Rk	ACL Angels	0	1	0	4	9	15.75	2.75	11.1	470	81	36	10.60	2.3	20.3	9.0	0.0	322
76-78 CB ++	2023	AA	Birmingham	3	4	0	41	36	6.77	1.70	20.7	292	32	65	6.58	4.8	7.9	1.6	2.2	30
84-86 CU ++	2023	AA	Rocket City	1	3	0	26	33	5.88	1.42	18.4	239	30	65	5.00	4.8	11.4	2.4	2.1	93

Command/control LHP lost ability to command and control pitches, was abused by upper minors pitching in 2023. Over-the-top delivery. Has lost previous feel for release point. FB has always been below-average but regressed. SL is an above-average pitch with a solid, tight movement profile. CB and CU have each backed up.

Cabrera,Jean | SP | Philadelphia | EXP MLB DEBUT: 2026 | H/W: 6-0 145 | FUT: #4 starter | 7C

Thrws R Age 22	Year	Lev	Team	W	L	Sv	IP	K	ERA	WHIP	BF/G	OBA	H%	S%	xERA	Ctl	Dom	Cmd	hr/9	BPV
2019 FA (VZ)																				
92-95 FB +++																				
82-85 SL ++++	2021	Rk	DSL Phillies White	3	2	0	52	61	1.55	0.84	14.7	188	28	81	1.14	1.7	10.5	6.1	0.2	161
85-88 CU +++	2022	A	Clearwater	2	4	0	46	51	5.27	1.78	17.7	293	37	74	6.19	5.5	10.0	1.8	1.6	50
	2023	A	Clearwater	5	7	1	81	86	4.33	1.60	18.9	321	42	72	5.02	2.4	9.5	3.9	0.3	124

Intriguing under-the-radar arm. Throws both 4S and 2S fastballs and commands both in the zone. Focused on SL instead of CB as primary breaker, and has developed into a good chase and a good whiff pitch. Change-up has also improved; lots of fade. Could add some strength, but strike-throwing skill points to an eventual rotation piece.

Caceres,Kelvin | RP | Los Angeles (A) | EXP MLB DEBUT: 2023 | H/W: 6-1 205 | FUT: Setup reliever | 7C

Thrws R Age 24	Year	Lev	Team	W	L	Sv	IP	K	ERA	WHIP	BF/G	OBA	H%	S%	xERA	Ctl	Dom	Cmd	hr/9	BPV
2018 FA (DR)	2022	A	Inland Empire	3	2	4	77	117	3.85	1.30	8.8	175	29	71	2.49	6.3	13.7	2.2	0.6	94
94-97 FB ++++	2023	A+	Tri City	0	0	5	11	21	2.45	1.18	4.0	205	44	77	1.97	4.1	17.2	4.2	0.0	217
83-85 SL +++	2023	AA	Rocket City	5	1	2	33	53	5.69	1.57	4.3	243	40	63	4.20	6.0	14.4	2.4	0.8	116
82-84 CB +++	2023	AAA	Salt Lake	1	0	1	10	11	0.90	1.00	5.5	151	23	90	0.98	4.5	9.9	2.2	0.0	75
88-90 CU +++	2023	MLB	LA Angels	0	0	0	1	1	8.18	3.64	3.6	392	49	75	11.14	16.4	8.2	0.5	0.0	-277

Strong-bodied, flame throwing sinkerball pitcher eclipsed 3 levels on way to making MLB debut in 2023. Low 3/4s delivery effort and below-average extension. Must live in lower half with mid-90s sinker, which produces heavy groundball rate. Struggles throwing strikes with pitch. Throws 3 secondaries in the average-to-above-average range.

Cameron,Noah | SP | Kansas City | EXP MLB DEBUT: 2025 | H/W: 6-3 220 | FUT: #5 SP/swingman | 7C

Thrws L Age 24	Year	Lev	Team	W	L	Sv	IP	K	ERA	WHIP	BF/G	OBA	H%	S%	xERA	Ctl	Dom	Cmd	hr/9	BPV
2021 (7) Central Arkansas	2022	Rk	ACL Royals B	0	1	0	5	7	3.46	1.73	7.9	380	51	88	7.69	0.0	12.1		1.7	236
90-93 FB ++	2022	A	Columbia	0	1	0	29	39	3.72	1.07	16.1	212	31	68	2.69	2.8	12.1	4.3	0.9	160
80-82 CU +++	2022	A+	Quad Cities	2	1	0	31	53	3.48	1.10	13.5	236	42	69	2.70	2.0	15.4	7.6	0.6	240
78-80 CB +++	2023	A+	Quad Cities	2	2	0	35	58	3.60	1.06	19.4	221	36	72	3.08	2.3	14.9	6.4	1.3	224
	2023	AA	NW Arkansas	3	10	0	72	74	6.12	1.57	18.6	300	36	65	5.93	3.2	9.2	2.8	1.7	97

Command-oriented LHP that can fill up the zone with strikes. Contolled, high 3/4s slot delivery with below-average extension. Deceptive CU with lots of fade is best pitch, generates whiffs. Also features a solid CB. Struggles commanding 4-seam FB. Lack of velocity and poor in-zone command makes FB ineffective.

Campbell,Justin | SP | Cleveland | EXP MLB DEBUT: 2025 | H/W: 6-7 219 | FUT: #4 starter | 7C

Thrws R Age 23	Year	Lev	Team	W	L	Sv	IP	K	ERA	WHIP	BF/G	OBA	H%	S%	xERA	Ctl	Dom	Cmd	hr/9	BPV
2022 (1) Oklahoma State																				
91-94 FB +++																				
75-78 CB +++																				
81-84 SL ++																				
81-85 CU +++																				

Hasn't yet pitched as pro due to elbow surgery in May 2022. Tall, strong-framed RHP with clean delivery and potential to add velocity to average FB. Repeats delivery and slot well for size. Best pitch is CU with lively action and deceptive arm speed. Fits more of a back-end profile without knockout breaking pitch. Soft SL lacks spin.

Cannon,Jonathan | SP | Chicago (A) | EXP MLB DEBUT: 2024 | H/W: 6-6 213 | FUT: #4 starter | 7D

Thrws R Age 23	Year	Lev	Team	W	L	Sv	IP	K	ERA	WHIP	BF/G	OBA	H%	S%	xERA	Ctl	Dom	Cmd	hr/9	BPV
2022 (3) Georgia	2022	NCAA	Georgia	9	4	0	78	68	4.03	1.01	23.0	233	27	64	3.06	1.4	7.8	5.7	1.2	122
93-95 FB +++	2022	Rk	ACL White Sox	0	0	1	1	1	0.00	1.00	3.8	0	0	100		9.0	9.0	1.0	0.0	-63
83-86 SL +++	2022	A	Kannapolis	0	0	0	6	3	1.48	0.98	7.7	189	22	83	1.41	3.0	4.4	1.5	0.0	18
79-81 CB +++	2023	A+	Winston Salem	5	2	0	72	67	3.61	1.23	20.9	242	30	73	3.46	3.0	8.4	2.8	0.9	88
90-92 CT +++	2023	AA	Birmingham	1	4	0	48	39	5.80	1.58	19.2	310	35	66	5.91	2.8	7.3	2.6	1.5	74

Big-bodied, pitchability RHP struggled during stint in Double-A after solid season in High-A. Strike-thrower. 3/4s delivery but doesn't use massive height well to extend out. Throws kitchen sink at hitters. Everything average-to-above-average offerings. Lacking true swing and miss pitch with less than 25% whiff rate last season.

Canterino,Matt | SP | Minnesota | EXP MLB DEBUT: 2024 | H/W: 6-2 222 | FUT: Setup reliever | 8E

Thrws R Age 26	Year	Lev	Team	W	L	Sv	IP	K	ERA	WHIP	BF/G	OBA	H%	S%	xERA	Ctl	Dom	Cmd	hr/9	BPV
2019 (2) Rice	2021	A	Fort Myers	0	0	0	2	2	0.00	0.00	5.6	0	0			0.0	9.0		0.0	180
93-97 FB +++	2021	A+	Cedar Rapids	1	0	0	21	43	0.86	0.67	14.6	144	36	92	0.39	1.7	18.4	10.8	0.4	303
84-87 SL +++	2022	Rk	FCL Twins	0	0	0	2	4	4.09	1.82	5.1	326	48	100	9.11	4.1	16.4	4.0	4.1	202
80-83 CB +++	2022	AA	Wichita	0	1	0	34	50	1.85	1.14	12.3	150	26	84	1.55	5.8	13.2	2.3	0.3	99
80-82 CU +++	2023	--	Did Not Play																	

DNP in 2023 due to recovery from Tommy John surgery in August 2022. Cannot stay healthy. Only 85 IP in career since 2019 draft. May have best pure stuff in org. Uses four pitches and all grade as average to plus. Electric FB can dominate hitters and mixes in hard and slower breaking balls and tumbling CU. Could be moved to pen to preserve arm.

Cantillo,Joey | SP | Cleveland | EXP MLB DEBUT: 2024 | H/W: 6-4 225 | FUT: #4 starter | 7C

Thrws L Age 24	Year	Lev	Team	W	L	Sv	IP	K	ERA	WHIP	BF/G	OBA	H%	S%	xERA	Ctl	Dom	Cmd	hr/9	BPV
2017 (16) HS (HI)	2021	Rk	ACL Indians	0	0	0	5	7	0.00	0.60	8.6	124	22	100		1.8	12.6	7.0	0.0	196
92-96 FB +++	2021	AA	Akron	0	2	0	8	12	4.50	2.25	8.1	262	43	78	5.42	11.3	13.5	1.2	0.0	-43
75-77 CB ++	2022	AA	Akron	4	3	0	60	87	1.94	1.10	16.8	183	30	83	1.82	4.2	13.0	3.1	0.3	139
81-84 SL ++	2023	AA	Akron	1	0	0	24	35	1.87	1.16	16.0	171	27	88	2.27	5.2	13.1	2.5	0.7	112
79-82 CU ++++	2023	AAA	Columbus	6	4	0	95	111	4.64	1.52	20.6	249	32	74	4.86	5.2	10.5	2.0	1.5	67

Consistent LHP who dominated AA before promotion to AAA. Only struggles as pro was in AAA. Led org in K despite lacking plus FB or breaking ball. CU is best pitch and falls off table with dramatic late tumbling action. Both SL and CB lack consistency though can play off one another. Adds deception to delivery and hides ball well.

Carela,Juan — SP — Chicago (A)

EXP MLB DEBUT: 2025 | H/W: 6-3 186 | FUT: Setup reliever | 7D

Thrws R Age 22

Pitches	Year	Lev	Team	W	L	Sv	IP	K	ERA	WHIP	BF/G	OBA	H%	S%	xERA	Ctl	Dom	Cmd	hr/9	BPV
2018 FA (DR)	2021	A	Tampa	0	2	0	20	22	11.64	2.49	17.8	361	46	51	8.89	8.1	9.9	1.2	1.3	-22
81-84 SL ++++	2022	A	Tampa	7	2	0	79	110	2.96	1.06	19.2	180	28	73	1.97	4.0	12.5	3.1	0.6	136
90-93 FB +++	2022	A+	Hudson Valley	1	4	0	28	21	7.71	1.50	17.3	240	27	47	4.52	5.5	6.8	1.2	1.3	-8
83-86 CU +++	2023	A+	Hudson Valley	2	4	0	83	109	3.68	1.17	19.5	217	32	70	2.84	3.5	11.8	3.4	0.8	137
77-79 CB ++	2023	A+	Winston Salem	1	3	0	32	27	3.36	1.28	21.9	249	28	81	4.17	3.1	7.6	2.5	1.4	71

Crafty 3/4 RHP, acquired mid-season from NYY, rode a 62% SL usage throughout 2023 season. Repeatable delivery despite occasionally altering slot. Can throw SL in and out of zone with plus command. It's a two-plane mover with late downward bite. CU is also an effective weapon but plays down due to struggles with FB. Also flashes 11-to-5 CB.

Carr,Kyle — SP — New York (A)

EXP MLB DEBUT: 2026 | H/W: 6-1 175 | FUT: #3 starter | 8E

Thrws L Age 21

Pitches	Year	Lev	Team	W	L	Sv	IP	K	ERA	WHIP	BF/G	OBA	H%	S%	xERA	Ctl	Dom	Cmd	hr/9	BPV
2023 (3) Palomar JC																				
90-94 FB ++++																				
80-83 SL +++																				
85-87 CU +++																				
	2023	--	Did Not Play																	

Athletic, developing LHP was best prospect in draft from JuCo circuit. Repeats 3/4s delivery well. Frame has room to grow into muscle, which could add future velocity. FB has makings of plus pitch, especially when kept up in zone where the ride comes out and plays. SL variates in shape but best as sweeper. Has feel for average CU.

Cavalli,Cade — SP — Washington

EXP MLB DEBUT: 2022 | H/W: 6-4 232 | FUT: #2 starter | 9D

Thrws R Age 25

Pitches	Year	Lev	Team	W	L	Sv	IP	K	ERA	WHIP	BF/G	OBA	H%	S%	xERA	Ctl	Dom	Cmd	hr/9	BPV
2020 (1) Oklahoma	2021	AA	Harrisburg	3	3	0	58		2.79	1.28	21.6	193	31	78	2.40	5.4	12.4	2.3	0.3	95
94-98 FB +++++	2021	AAA	Rochester	1	5	0	24	24	7.44	1.90	19.0	326	41	59	6.25	4.8	8.9	1.8	0.7	48
84-87 CB ++++	2022	AAA	Rochester	6	4	0	97	104	3.71	1.18	19.4	215	30	67	2.41	3.6	9.6	2.7	0.3	94
87-90 SL +++	2022	MLB	Washington	0	1	0	4	6	15.37	1.95	19.6	342	52	13	5.90	4.4	13.2	3.0	0.0	137
86-89 CU +++	2023	--	Did Not Play																	

Missed all of 2023 due to March Tommy John surgery after competing for #5 rotation spot. Has the tools to succeed: top-shelf FB, CB with huge bite, and SL and CU that grade out as average but keep hitters honest. Control and command hold the key to how successful he becomes ... after he gets back on the MLB mound, likely in mid-season 2024.

Cecconi,Slade — SP — Arizona

EXP MLB DEBUT: 2023 | H/W: 6-4 219 | FUT: #5 SP/swingman | 7E

Thrws R Age 24

Pitches	Year	Lev	Team	W	L	Sv	IP	K	ERA	WHIP	BF/G	OBA	H%	S%	xERA	Ctl	Dom	Cmd	hr/9	BPV
2020 (1) Miami	2020	NCAA	Miami	2	1	0	21	30	3.84	1.04	20.4	201	31	65	2.42	3.0	12.8	4.3	0.9	168
94-96 FB ++	2021	A+	Hillsboro	4	2	0	59	63	4.12	1.24	19.9	242	32	68	3.35	3.1	9.6	3.2	0.8	109
82-85 SL ++++	2022	AA	Amarillo	7	6	0	129	127	4.39	1.32	20.6	276	33	72	4.77	2.2	8.8	4.0	1.5	117
73-77 CB +++	2023	AAA	Reno	5	9	0	116	118	6.12	1.38	21.2	275	32	60	5.20	2.8	9.1	3.3	1.9	107
83-85 CU +	2023	MLB	Arizona	0	1	0	27	20	4.33	1.15	15.3	262	29	67	3.97	1.3	6.7	5.0	1.3	102

Tall, muscular RHP gets by with pitch-to-contact approach. Finds zone early, often despite spotty control. FB gets tons of swings, contact. Best pitch is SL with lots of whiffs. Does not fool batters with CB, CU. Lack of whiffs overall caps K upside, amount of contact given up limits run prevention efficiency.

Champlain,Chandler — SP — Kansas City

EXP MLB DEBUT: 2024 | H/W: 6-5 220 | FUT: #5 SP/swingman | 7A

Thrws R Age 24

Pitches	Year	Lev	Team	W	L	Sv	IP	K	ERA	WHIP	BF/G	OBA	H%	S%	xERA	Ctl	Dom	Cmd	hr/9	BPV
2021 (9) USC																				
93-96 FB +++	2022	A	Tampa	2	5	0	73	94	4.31	1.24	18.6	259	35	70	4.14	2.3	11.6	4.9	1.4	163
79-82 CB +++	2022	A+	Quad Cities	1	3	0	32	22	9.84	2.16	19.9	391	45	52	8.21	3.1	6.2	2.0	0.8	46
83-88 SL +++	2023	A+	Quad Cities	6	3	0	62	61	2.75	1.06	21.9	215	27	77	2.55	2.6	8.8	3.4	0.7	107
83-86 CU ++	2023	AA	NW Arkansas	5	5	0	73	64	3.82	1.22	21.1	237	27	74	3.83	3.1	7.9	2.6	1.4	77

Big RHP has continued to mature into future backend rotation arm. Features three usable pitches with FB and both breaking balls. 4-seam FB best pitch with solid riding action and plus command. Shows more confidence in CB than SL. Will need to improve strike% of breakers to remain in rotation.

Chandler,Bubba — SP — Pittsburgh

EXP MLB DEBUT: 2024 | H/W: 6-2 200 | FUT: #3 starter | 8C

Thrws R Age 21

Pitches	Year	Lev	Team	W	L	Sv	IP	K	ERA	WHIP	BF/G	OBA	H%	S%	xERA	Ctl	Dom	Cmd	hr/9	BPV
2021 (3) HS (GA)	2021	--	Did Not Play																	
93-96 FB ++++	2022	Rk	FCL Pirates B	0	0	0	15	27	0.00	0.86	9.3	66	16	100		6.0	16.1	2.7	0.0	147
84-87 SL +++	2022	A	Bradenton	1	1	0	26	33	4.15	1.46	13.9	214	30	74	3.82	6.2	11.4	1.8	1.0	55
79-82 CB +++	2023	A+	Greensboro	9	4	0	106	120	4.75	1.50	19.1	265	34	72	4.81	4.3	10.2	2.4	1.3	84
86-88 CU ++	2023	AA	Altoona	1	0	0	5	8	0.00	0.20	15.1	66	14	100		0.0	14.4		0.0	277

Strong, athletic RHP who showed considerable improvement in art of pitching. Induces ton of GB with sinking, hard FB. Continues to miss bats with variety of offerings. High spin CB is plus already and can dominate up in zone. SL and CB have varying velocities and shapes. Doesn't use CU enough. Still room to improve FB command.

Chen,Po Yu — SP — Pittsburgh

EXP MLB DEBUT: 2025 | H/W: 6-2 187 | FUT: #4 starter | 7D

Thrws R Age 22

Pitches	Year	Lev	Team	W	L	Sv	IP	K	ERA	WHIP	BF/G	OBA	H%	S%	xERA	Ctl	Dom	Cmd	hr/9	BPV
2020 FA (TW)																				
90-94 FB +++	2021	Rk	FCL Pirates B	2	0	0	26	29	0.69	0.69	15.2	197	29	89	0.71	0.0	10.0		0.0	199
79-82 CB +++	2021	A	Bradenton	1	1	0	16	15	5.63	1.69	18.0	250	30	68	4.94	6.8	8.4	1.3	1.1	-12
83-85 SL +++	2022	A	Bradenton	4	8	0	98	103	4.59	1.26	18.2	241	32	64	3.39	3.3	9.4	2.9	0.7	99
84-85 CU +++	2023	A+	Greensboro	5	8	0	119	124	4.45	1.38	20.0	266	32	74	4.83	3.2	9.4	2.9	1.6	99

Underrated SP who finished 5th in SAL in K, however, allowed most HR in org. Uses deep pitch mix to attack hitters to both sides of plate. Able to hold velocity deep into games and has been relatively unscathed from arm issues. Spins ball well and able to thrive with multiple breaking balls. FB has chance to add velocity.

Church,Marc — RP — Texas

EXP MLB DEBUT: 2024 | H/W: 6-3 189 | FUT: Setup reliever | 7D

Thrws R Age 23

Pitches	Year	Lev	Team	W	L	Sv	IP	K	ERA	WHIP	BF/G	OBA	H%	S%	xERA	Ctl	Dom	Cmd	hr/9	BPV
2019 (18) HS (GA)	2021	A	Down East	3	1	3	27	49	4.32	1.11	5.6	224	40	65	3.26	2.7	16.3	6.1	1.3	239
94-97 FB +++	2022	A+	Hickory	2	2	4	34	57	2.91	1.03	5.7	226	35	86	3.60	1.9	15.1	8.1	1.9	240
84-89 CT +++	2022	AA	Frisco	1	3	1	15	21	7.20	1.67	4.8	299	40	62	6.75	4.2	12.6	3.0	2.4	131
	2023	AA	Frisco	2	3	0	18	31	4.00	1.33	5.8	216	38	73	3.44	5.0	15.5	3.1	1.0	162
	2023	AAA	Round Rock	7	1	2	44	48	3.48	1.55	6.4	244	32	81	4.40	5.7	9.8	1.7	1.0	40

Things looked good coming into 2023 but FB command backed up, playing pitch below 97-mph velo. CT/SL remains plus-plus in projection also playing below grade. But maintains MLB floor due to whiffs he gets. If he finds consistent release point there's closer upside; until then it's setup.

Clemmey,Alex — SP — Cleveland

EXP MLB DEBUT: 2027 | H/W: 6-6 205 | FUT: #3 starter | 8D

Thrws L Age 18

Pitches	Year	Lev	Team	W	L	Sv	IP	K	ERA	WHIP	BF/G	OBA	H%	S%	xERA	Ctl	Dom	Cmd	hr/9	BPV
2023 (2) HS (RI)																				
91-96 FB ++++																				
77-81 CB +++																				
82-86 CU +																				

Tall, projectable LHP with lot of development time ahead. Commands FB well for age and uses height effectively with release. Lot of riding life to FB. Uses CB that flashes plus and may add SL to mix. Slows arm on CU and struggles to repeat mechanics and release point. Has requisite pitches and body to offer nice upside.

Coffey,Isaac — SP — Boston

EXP MLB DEBUT: 2025 | H/W: 6-1 205 | FUT: #4 starter | 7D

Thrws R Age 23

Pitches	Year	Lev	Team	W	L	Sv	IP	K	ERA	WHIP	BF/G	OBA	H%	S%	xERA	Ctl	Dom	Cmd	hr/9	BPV
2022 (10) Oral Roberts																				
88-91 FB +++																				
76-80 SL ++	2022	Rk	FCL Red Sox	0	0	0	1	0	15.00	3.33	3.7	371	37	50	10.06	15.0	0.0	0.0	0.0	-387
81-84 CU ++	2023	A+	Greenville	4	2	0	60	83	2.85	1.01	21.0	231	32	84	3.46	1.5	12.4	8.3	1.6	201
	2023	AA	Portland	7	4	0	57	72	3.94	1.21	19.2	222	28	76	3.93	3.6	11.3	3.1	1.7	124

Athletic, strong RHP who was 2nd in org in Ks in first full season. Uses short arm action to command FB to all quadrants of strike zone. Repeats delivery from sidearm slot and provides deception. Velocity a tad short and lacks plus secondary pitch. Sequences well and is able to locate sweeping SL and fading CU. HR prone as flyballer.

Cooke,Connor — RP — Toronto

EXP MLB DEBUT: 2024 | H/W: 6-1 203 | FUT: Setup reliever | 7C

Thrws R Age 24

Pitches	Year	Lev	Team	W	L	Sv	IP	K	ERA	WHIP	BF/G	OBA	H%	S%	xERA	Ctl	Dom	Cmd	hr/9	BPV
2021 (10) La-Lafayette	2022	A	Dunedin	2	5	1	46	63	4.88	1.26	13.4	253	38	60	3.36	2.7	12.3	4.5	0.6	166
93-96 FB +++	2022	A+	Vancouver	0	2	8	10	12	7.06	1.18	3.7	238	29	40	4.09	2.6	10.6	4.0	1.8	137
83-86 SL +++	2023	A+	Vancouver	0	0	1	9	19	2.97	1.10	4.0	214	47	78	2.78	3.0	18.8	6.3	1.0	276
87-88 CU +	2023	AA	New Hampshire	1	2	3	24	46	4.46	1.49	5.2	298	54	73	5.04	2.6	17.1	6.6	1.1	256
	2023	AAA	Buffalo	2	0	0	10	15	4.46	1.49	4.8	174	27	71	3.25	8.0	13.4	1.7	0.9	42

Athletic RP who pitched on 3 levels and demonstrated amazing K rate. Spent most of career in pen and has the aggressive nature to be potent. All pitches exhibit plus spin and late action while missing bats. Sequences well for RP. Not much need for CU but he adds that to mix. Due to pitch movement, can have trouble throwing strikes.

Corniell,Jose — SP — Texas

EXP MLB DEBUT: 2025 | H/W: 6-3 165 | FUT: #4 starter | 7C

Thrws R Age 20
2019 FA (DR)

Velo	Pitch	Grade
93-96	FB	++++
82-89	SL	+++
85-88	CU	+
78-81	CB	+++

Year	Lev	Team	W	L	Sv	IP	K	ERA	WHIP	BF/G	OBA	H%	S%	xERA	Ctl	Dom	Cmd	hr/9	BPV
2021	Rk	ACL Rangers	1	3	0	38	44	7.07	1.52	12.7	290	37	55	5.56	3.3	10.4	3.1	1.6	116
2022	A	Down East	3	5	3	66	71	5.45	1.39	12.6	238	30	63	4.13	4.6	9.7	2.1	1.2	67
2023	A	Down East	4	1	1	43	56	2.71	0.93	16.2	176	25	75	1.84	2.9	11.7	4.0	0.8	150
2023	A+	Hickory	4	2	1	58	63	3.10	1.05	17.3	212	27	76	2.81	2.6	9.8	3.7	1.1	123

Finally enjoyed breakout 2023 across two levels and eclipsed 100 IP for first time. Everything but the change is above average, with both a 4S and 2S fastball and a cutter, alongside mean slider. All secondaries featuring 36%+ whiff rates. Change still lags and isn't effective against LHB who hit much better than RHB.

Coupet,Isaiah — SP — Colorado

EXP MLB DEBUT: 2026 | H/W: 6-1 190 | FUT: #5 SP/swingman | 6B

Thrws L Age 21
2023 (4) Ohio State

Velo	Pitch	Grade
89-91	FB	+
78-82	SL	++++
73-75	CB	++++
84-86	CU	++

Year	Lev	Team	W	L	Sv	IP	K	ERA	WHIP	BF/G	OBA	H%	S%	xERA	Ctl	Dom	Cmd	hr/9	BPV
2023	NCAA	Ohio St	4	3	0	50	72	3.59	1.14	18.1	225	34	71	2.97	2.9	12.9	4.5	0.9	173
2023	Rk	ACL Rockies	0	0	0	2	3	0.00	0.50	3.3	0	0	100		4.5	13.5	3.0	0.0	140
2023	A	Fresno	0	0	0	2	3	0.00	0.48	2.3	144	25	100		0.0	12.9		0.0	249

Short, athletic lefty had some of the best feel for spin in draft class. FB sits at 89-91 and lacks deception or movement. More than makes up for it with a pair of breaking balls. High spin SL and CB are both plus, swing-and-miss offerings and CU has the potential to be average. Improved command, and will make full-season debut in 2024.

Cox,Jackson — SP — Colorado

EXP MLB DEBUT: 2027 | H/W: 6-2 200 | FUT: #4 starter | 7D

Thrws R Age 20
2022 (2) HS (WA)

Velo	Pitch	Grade
91-94	FB	+++
80-83	CB	++++
83-86	CU	++

Year	Lev	Team	W	L	Sv	IP	K	ERA	WHIP	BF/G	OBA	H%	S%	xERA	Ctl	Dom	Cmd	hr/9	BPV
2023	A	Fresno	1	0	0	31	32	7.26	1.90	14.6	308	40	60	5.82	5.8	9.3	1.6	0.6	28

2nd rounder made just 9 starts before Tommy John surgery; will miss most of 2024. Quick, compact delivery with short stride and reliance on strong shoulder rotation. When healthy, features a low-90s heater with arm side run and late life, but below average command. Best secondary is plus high-spin 1-to-7 CB that dives out of the zone. Some feel for CU.

Crawford,Reggie — SP — San Francisco

EXP MLB DEBUT: 2025 | H/W: 6-4 235 | FUT: #3 starter | 8C

Thrws L Age 23
2022 (1) Connecticut

Velo	Pitch	Grade
94-96	FB	++++
83-86	SL	++++
83-85	CU	+

Year	Lev	Team	W	L	Sv	IP	K	ERA	WHIP	BF/G	OBA	H%	S%	xERA	Ctl	Dom	Cmd	hr/9	BPV
2023	A	San Jose	0	0	0	11	18	4.09	1.18	6.3	225	32	80	4.54	3.3	14.7	4.5	2.5	195
2023	A+	Eugene	0	0	0	8	14	1.13	1.50	5.8	210	41	92	2.84	6.8	15.8	2.3	0.0	119

Made pro debut with very short starts and features high-octane FB that could get to double-plus level. All about power with FB/SL combo. Velocity has returned from Tommy John surgery and will need to improve CU to stick as SP. SL also a plus offering and features power and break. Control and command should return to pre-surgery levels.

Crow,Coleman — SP — Milwaukee

EXP MLB DEBUT: 2025 | H/W: 6-0 175 | FUT: #4 starter | 7D

Thrws R Age 23
2019 (28) HS (GA)

Velo	Pitch	Grade
90-92	FB	+++
75-77	CB	+++
84-86	SL	+++
85-86	CU	++

Year	Lev	Team	W	L	Sv	IP	K	ERA	WHIP	BF/G	OBA	H%	S%	xERA	Ctl	Dom	Cmd	hr/9	BPV
2021	A	Inland Empire	4	3	0	62	62	4.20	1.56	20.9	280	35	76	4.94	4.2	9.0	2.1	1.0	66
2022	AA	Rocket City	9	3	0	128	128	4.85	1.31	22.0	269	33	67	4.53	2.5	9.0	3.7	1.4	114
2023	AA	Rocket City	2	0	0	24	31	1.88	0.63	20.7	117	14	83	0.74	2.3	11.6	5.2	1.1	167

Pitchability RHP saw stuff play up prior to an elbow injury, resulting in Tommy John surgery. Repeatable low 3/4s delivery with high overall strike rate. Stuff tick up might be result of pre-tack experimental ball. 4-seam FB produced flatter angled approach and exceptional ride. Achieved incredible break with CB. SL and CU are 3rd and 4th pitches.

Cruz,Deivy — SP — Baltimore

EXP MLB DEBUT: 2027 | H/W: 5-11 154 | FUT: #5 SP/swingman | 7D

Thrws L Age 20
2021 FA (DR)

Velo	Pitch	Grade
90-92	FB	++
79-81	SL	+++
78-80	CU	+++
84-87	CB	++

Year	Lev	Team	W	L	Sv	IP	K	ERA	WHIP	BF/G	OBA	H%	S%	xERA	Ctl	Dom	Cmd	hr/9	BPV
2021	Rk	DSL Orioles	2	5	0	45	63	5.20	1.51	15.0	257	40	64	3.88	4.8	12.6	2.6	0.4	115
2022	Rk	FCL Orioles B	0	2	0	13	17	2.77	1.23	17.6	179	26	80	2.50	5.5	11.8	2.1	0.7	80
2022	A	Delmarva	1	1	0	53	52	4.06	1.54	17.8	231	30	73	3.75	6.3	8.8	1.4	0.5	7
2023	A	Delmarva	8	4	0	97	103	3.62	1.28	15.9	213	28	73	2.99	4.6	9.6	2.1	0.6	65

Short-statured LHP with low arm slot relies heavily on deception, keeping hitter off balance. Struggles repeating release point, contributing to below-average command. SL is solid offering with horizontal break profile. The sum of all parts equals potential big league SP. Likely low strikeout profile if the stuff survives at upper levels.

Culpepper,C.J. — SP — Minnesota

EXP MLB DEBUT: 2025 | H/W: 6-3 193 | FUT: #4 starter | 7C

Thrws R Age 22
2022 (13) California Baptist

Velo	Pitch	Grade
93-97	FB	+++
82-84	SL	+++
80-82	CB	++
85-89	CU	++

Year	Lev	Team	W	L	Sv	IP	K	ERA	WHIP	BF/G	OBA	H%	S%	xERA	Ctl	Dom	Cmd	hr/9	BPV
2022	NCAA	Cal Baptist	5	3	1	69	76	3.26	1.14	17.1	220	30	72	2.62	3.1	9.9	3.2	0.5	112
2022	Rk	FCL Twins	0	0	0	1	1	0.00	1.00	3.8	0	0	100		9.0	9.0	1.0	0.0	-63
2023	A	Fort Myers	4	3	0	46	53	2.34	1.02	16.1	198	28	78	1.91	2.9	10.3	3.5	0.4	125
2023	A+	Cedar Rapids	2	2	0	39	36	5.05	1.43	16.7	266	34	63	3.89	3.7	8.3	2.3	0.5	68

Long, lean SP who got off to hot start in Low-A before promotion to High-A. Faded down stretch and will work towards adding strength for deeper outings. Heavy GB guy with solid sinker. Can pitch up in zone with good spin and counters with slower CB and sweeping SL. Focus will be on FB command and upgrading CU. Big time sleeper.

Curet,Yoniel — SP — Tampa Bay

EXP MLB DEBUT: 2025 | H/W: 6-2 190 | FUT: Closer | 8E

Thrws R Age 21
2019 FA (DR)

Velo	Pitch	Grade
96-98	FB	++++
85-87	SL	++++
88-90	CT	+++

Year	Lev	Team	W	L	Sv	IP	K	ERA	WHIP	BF/G	OBA	H%	S%	xERA	Ctl	Dom	Cmd	hr/9	BPV
2021	Rk	DSL Rays 2	2	4	0	51	63	3.71	1.25	14.8	205	31	67	2.21	4.8	11.1	2.3	0.0	89
2022	Rk	FCL Rays	2	1	0	36	48	1.75	1.11	10.9	158	23	89	2.02	5.3	12.0	2.3	0.8	92
2022	A	Charleston	0	0	0	6	10	4.50	2.17	15.0	262	46	77	5.20	10.5	15.0	1.4	0.0	5
2023	A	Charleston	6	1	0	80	111	2.47	1.10	15.7	131	22	76	1.11	6.1	12.5	2.1	0.1	79
2023	A+	Bowling Green	2	0	0	23	33	4.66	1.55	16.9	206	33	69	3.32	7.4	12.8	1.7	0.4	49

Hard-throwing low 3/4s RHP dazzled lower minor competition with high spin rate 4-seam FB. Strong frame, at physical projection with tree trunks for legs. Struggles with repeating release point in delivery. Double-plus 4-seam FB combines plus ride with late running action. Varies between SL and CT with SL being better offering. Likely RP.

Curry,Aidan — SP — Texas

EXP MLB DEBUT: 2025 | H/W: 6-5 205 | FUT: #4 starter | 7B

Thrws R Age 21
2020 FA (NY)

Velo	Pitch	Grade
90-94	FB	+++
81-86	SL	+++
85-87	CU	++
79-82	CB	++

Year	Lev	Team	W	L	Sv	IP	K	ERA	WHIP	BF/G	OBA	H%	S%	xERA	Ctl	Dom	Cmd	hr/9	BPV
2021	Rk	ACL Rangers	0	1	0	15	23	14.21	2.43	7.3	349	53	36	7.80	8.3	13.6	1.6	0.6	39
2022	Rk	ACL Rangers	1	1	0	35	50	4.63	1.54	13.9	273	40	72	4.76	4.4	12.9	2.9	1.0	131
2022	A	Down East	0	0	0	3	6	0.00	1.94	14.7	103	27	100	2.79	14.5	17.4	1.2	0.0	-60
2023	A	Down East	6	3	0	82	99	2.30	0.93	16.2	169	25	76	1.39	3.2	10.9	3.4	0.4	128
2023	A+	Hickory	0	0	0	6	5	8.85	3.11	18.1	343	33	81	13.08	14.8	7.4	0.5	4.4	-248

Projectable frame met burgeoning stuff for a breakout 2023 performance. Big extension down mound with solid three-pitch mix though nothing plus yet. Has feel for fastball, slider, and change, though poor LHB splits say change has more distance to travel and looked gassed in Aug and Sept. Nice mid-rotation upside.

Cusick,Ryan — SP — Oakland

EXP MLB DEBUT: 2024 | H/W: 6-6 235 | FUT: #4 starter | 7C

Thrws R Age 24
2021 (1) Wake Forest

Velo	Pitch	Grade
93-95	FB	++++
82-84	SL	+++
80-81	CB	++
84-85	CU	++

Year	Lev	Team	W	L	Sv	IP	K	ERA	WHIP	BF/G	OBA	H%	S%	xERA	Ctl	Dom	Cmd	hr/9	BPV
2022	Rk	ACL Athletics	0	0	0	2	3	9.00	1.50	8.6	347	53	33	4.86	0.0	13.5		0.0	261
2022	AA	Midland	1	6	0	41	43	7.02	2.02	16.6	314	40	65	6.49	6.6	9.4	1.4	0.9	10
2023	Rk	ACL Athletics	0	0	0	3	5	0.00	1.00	11.5	106	22	100	0.49	6.0	15.0	2.5	0.0	126
2023	AA	Midland	5	7	0	94	84	4.78	1.49	18.4	238	27	73	4.77	5.5	8.0	1.5	1.6	15
2023	AAA	Las Vegas	0	1	0	2	2	20.45	4.55	16.2	326	42	50	12.22	28.6	8.2	0.3	0.0	-608

Tall-framed SP who repeated AA with slightly better results. Most walks in org as he struggled to command FB and repeat delivery. When on, can be very tough to barrel, but hasn't happened often enough. Plus FB can be elevated in zone and has good carry. K rate has fallen and will need to find consistent CB and CU.

Dallas,Chad — SP — Toronto

EXP MLB DEBUT: 2025 | H/W: 5-11 206 | FUT: #4 starter | 7D

Thrws R Age 23
2021 (4) Tennessee

Velo	Pitch	Grade
91-95	FB	+++
81-82	CB	++
83-85	SL	+++
83-86	CU	++

Year	Lev	Team	W	L	Sv	IP	K	ERA	WHIP	BF/G	OBA	H%	S%	xERA	Ctl	Dom	Cmd	hr/9	BPV
2022	A+	Vancouver	1	7	0	88	86	4.60	1.55	18.3	255	31	74	4.85	5.2	8.8	1.7	1.3	35
2023	A+	Vancouver	2	0	0	26	37	2.06	0.95	19.8	150	25	79	1.15	4.1	12.7	3.1	0.3	135
2023	AA	New Hampshire	7	3	0	96	107	4.12	1.27	21.8	239	30	73	3.99	3.5	10.0	2.9	1.4	105

Short, durable SP who led org in Ks. Shows advanced mixing ability with intriguing offerings. Despite K rate falling in AA, has sweeping SL with plus spin that is effective against RHH and LHH. Holds velocity deep into games. Needs to enhance CU to keep LHH off-guard with change-of-pace. May end up in bullpen long-term.

Dana,Caden

SP | **Los Angeles (A)** | EXP MLB DEBUT: 2025 | H/W: 6-4 215 | FUT: #2 starter | **9D**

Thrws R Age 20			Year	Lev	Team	W	L	Sv	IP	K	ERA	WHIP	BF/G	OBA	H%	S%	xERA	Ctl	Dom	Cmd	hr/9	BPV
2022 (11) HS (NJ)																						
91-96	FB	++++	2022	Rk	ACL Angels	0	0	0	6	6	1.45	0.97	7.8	255	34	83	2.15	0.0	8.7		0.0	175
82-84	SL	++++	2022	A	Inland Empire	0	0	0	1	2	37.50	5.83	10.4	639	81	29	25.06	7.5	15.0	2.0	0.0	86
79-81	CB	+++	2023	A	Inland Empire	1	1	0	15	18	1.20	0.80	18.1	124	17	91	0.76	3.6	10.8	3.0	0.6	115
83-85	CU	++	2023	A+	Tri City	2	4	0	53	71	4.24	1.30	19.9	231	35	67	3.11	4.1	12.0	3.0	0.5	125

Hard-throwing hurler had periods of domination against older competition. Repeats balanced, high 3/4s delivery with below average extension. Throws strikes with primary arsenal. Double-plus 4-seam FB has tremendous ride profile mixed in with plus arm-side action. Gyro SL has emerged as plus offering. Mixes in solid CB and occasional CU.

Daniel,Davis

SP | **Los Angeles (A)** | EXP MLB DEBUT: 2023 | H/W: 6-1 190 | FUT: #4 starter | **7C**

Thrws R Age 26			Year	Lev	Team	W	L	Sv	IP	K	ERA	WHIP	BF/G	OBA	H%	S%	xERA	Ctl	Dom	Cmd	hr/9	BPV
2019 (7) Auburn			2022	AAA	Salt Lake	6	7	0	102	83	4.50	1.21	19.6	242	28	66	3.77	2.8	7.3	2.6	1.2	74
91-93	FB	+++	2023	Rk	ACL Angels	0	0	0	5	9	1.80	0.80	9.1	221	44	75	1.21	0.0	16.2		0.0	310
80-82	SL	+++	2023	A	Inland Empire	1	1	0	20	28	1.79	1.00	19.2	209	34	80	1.59	2.2	12.5	5.6	0.0	183
73-76	CB	+++	2023	AAA	Salt Lake	0	1	0	4	5	4.50	2.25	20.3	151	24	78	4.12	15.8	11.3	0.7	0.0	-205
83-86	CU	+++	2023	MLB	LA Angels	1	1	0	12	9	2.23	1.32	16.7	170	19	87	2.73	6.7	6.7	1.0	0.7	-42

Over-the-top SP made MLB debut as RP after shoulder injury derailed most of 2023 season. Athletic frame is near projection. Repeats delivery well with solid extension. 4-seam FB sits low 90s with flat approach, solid ride and late arm-side run. Sweeping SL plays up due to tremendous command. Struggles to throw CB for strikes. CU is a solid pitch.

Danner,Hagen

RP | **Toronto** | EXP MLB DEBUT: 2023 | H/W: 6-1 215 | FUT: Closer | **7D**

Thrws R Age 25			Year	Lev	Team	W	L	Sv	IP	K	ERA	WHIP	BF/G	OBA	H%	S%	xERA	Ctl	Dom	Cmd	hr/9	BPV
2017 (2) HS (CA)			2022	AA	New Hampshire	0	0	2	3		5.63	2.50	4.3	357	38	75	7.65	8.4	2.8	0.3	0.0	-159
95-98	FB	++++	2023	A	Dunedin	0	0	0	2	5	4.50	1.50	4.3	151	61	67	2.11	9.0	22.5	2.5	0.0	180
77-79	CB	+++	2023	AA	New Hampshire	1	1	0	9	16	3.00	1.22	4.5	262	49	73	2.81	2.0	16.0	8.0	0.0	252
86-88	SL	+++	2023	AAA	Buffalo	0	1	1	28	35	3.84	0.96	4.6	202	21	79	3.84	2.2	11.2	5.0	2.6	159
			2023	MLB	Toronto	0	0	0	0	0	0.00	0.00	0.3	0	0			0.0	0.0		0.0	18

Overpowering RP who reached TOR, pitched 1 game and was done for year with oblique strain. Explosive FB is blown by hitters up in zone. Lot of armside run and CT to heater. SL features cutting action and tough to elevate. Delivery has lot of moving parts and difficult to repeat. Has been beset by injuries in career.

De Avila,Luis

SP | **Atlanta** | EXP MLB DEBUT: 2024 | H/W: 5-9 215 | FUT: #5 SP/swingman | **6C**

Thrws L Age 22			Year	Lev	Team	W	L	Sv	IP	K	ERA	WHIP	BF/G	OBA	H%	S%	xERA	Ctl	Dom	Cmd	hr/9	BPV
2017 FA (CB)			2021	Rk	ACL Royals G	0	0	0	5	5	3.53	1.76	7.8	218	30	78	3.67	8.8	8.8	1.0	0.0	-61
90-94	FB	+++	2021	A	Columbia	5	4	0	52	59	5.18	1.69	9.8	320	43	69	5.55	3.3	10.2	3.1	0.7	113
86-88	CU	++++	2022	A+	Rome	6	8	0	126	129	3.50	1.27	21.5	244	31	74	3.49	3.2	9.2	2.9	0.8	97
82-84	SL	+++	2023	AA	Mississippi	6	10	0	123	125	3.29	1.30	20.3	222	29	76	3.10	4.5	9.1	2.0	0.6	62
79-81	CB	++	2023	AAA	Gwinnett	0	0	0	3	3	2.81	2.50	17.0	307	40	88	6.76	11.3	8.4	0.8	0.0	-134

Short-statured, low 3/4s LHP had successful upper minors run despite low strike rate. Two FB varieties: 2-seam FB gas solid sink with above-average arm-side run; 4-seam FB isn't effective. Best pitch is a late fading CU with solid strike rate and lots of chase potential. SL is slightly below-average offering. Struggles with CB consistency.

De La Cruz,Juan

SP | **Miami** | EXP MLB DEBUT: 2026 | H/W: 6-3 180 | FUT: #4 starter | **7E**

Thrws R Age 19			Year	Lev	Team	W	L	Sv	IP	K	ERA	WHIP	BF/G	OBA	H%	S%	xERA	Ctl	Dom	Cmd	hr/9	BPV
2022 FA (DR)																						
90-92	FB	+++																				
72-75	CB	+++	2022	Rk	DSL Marlins	3	2	0	41	28	4.17	1.37	15.6	247	29	70	3.69	4.0	6.1	1.6	0.7	22
84-87	CU	++	2023	Rk	FCL Marlins	1	1	0	9	8	2.00	1.11	17.7	136	19	80	1.13	6.0	8.0	1.3	0.0	0
			2023	A	Jupiter	1	4	0	43	42	4.59	1.86	16.8	283	36	75	5.37	6.7	8.8	1.3	0.6	-5

High waisted, projectable RHP made US debut in 2nd half of 2023 season. Plus frame to grow in muscle, should be hard-thrower at projection. 3/4s delivery needs refinement. 4-seam FB has makings of solid offering, potentially plus with velocity. Has feel for spin with sweeping CB. Also throws CU, which is mostly ineffective.

De Leon,Luis

SP | **Baltimore** | EXP MLB DEBUT: 2026 | H/W: 6-3 168 | FUT: #4 starter | **8E**

Thrws L Age 20			Year	Lev	Team	W	L	Sv	IP	K	ERA	WHIP	BF/G	OBA	H%	S%	xERA	Ctl	Dom	Cmd	hr/9	BPV
2021 FA (DR)																						
93-96	FB	+++	2022	Rk	DSL Orioles 2	3	4	0	24	37	6.00	1.17	10.6	181	33	43	1.69	4.9	13.9	2.8	0.0	136
85-87	CU	+++	2022	Rk	DSL Orioles	1	0	0	4	8	0.00	0.25	12.3	81	23	100		0.0	18.0		0.0	342
83-85	SL	++	2023	Rk	FCL Orioles B	2	0	0	27	36	1.66	1.37	18.9	231	36	86	2.80	4.6	12.0	2.6	0.0	108
			2023	A	Delmarva	3	1	0	26	31	2.41	1.26	11.8	188	29	79	2.04	5.5	10.7	1.9	0.0	61

Low 3/4s LHP with whippy arm enjoyed exceptional US debut. Dreams need apply with this profile. Solid size with room to grow into, could hit triple digits someday on radar gun. Possesses FB velocity mixed with two decent and improving offspeed pitches, making for interesting profile. Could make huge leap in development with improved FB shape.

Del Rosario,Joelvis

SP | **Oakland** | EXP MLB DEBUT: 2025 | H/W: 5-11 170 | FUT: #4 starter | **7E**

Thrws R Age 22			Year	Lev	Team	W	L	Sv	IP	K	ERA	WHIP	BF/G	OBA	H%	S%	xERA	Ctl	Dom	Cmd	hr/9	BPV
2018 FA (DR)																						
92-95	FB	+++	2021	Rk	FCL Pirates G	4	2	1	38	52	3.30	1.10	12.5	229	34	72	2.77	2.4	12.3	5.2	0.7	175
81-84	SL	++	2022	A	Bradenton	7	4	0	93	76	3.68	1.29	19.1	266	31	76	4.21	2.4	7.4	3.0	1.2	85
83-85	CU	+++	2023	A+	Lansing	3	9	0	80	69	4.83	1.37	17.7	259	31	66	4.18	3.5	7.8	2.2	1.0	64
			2023	AA	Midland	2	1	0	23	16	7.37	1.72	21.1	342	36	62	7.59	2.3	6.2	2.7	2.3	67

Short power pitcher who increased velocity but still struggled to miss bats. Could be ideal RP due to lack of size and consistent 2nd pitch. Firm CU can fit bill and needs to find consistency with it for LHH. Repeats smooth delivery well and exhibits above average control. Needs to upgrade SL to remain SP.

Denoyer,Noah

RP | **Baltimore** | EXP MLB DEBUT: 2025 | H/W: 6-5 250 | FUT: Middle reliever | **6B**

Thrws R Age 26			Year	Lev	Team	W	L	Sv	IP	K	ERA	WHIP	BF/G	OBA	H%	S%	xERA	Ctl	Dom	Cmd	hr/9	BPV
2019 FA (CA)			2021	A+	Aberdeen	0	0	1	12	10	2.25	1.25	9.8	228	27	86	3.22	3.8	7.5	2.0	0.8	52
91-94	FB	++	2022	Rk	FCL Orioles B	0	0	0	2	3	0.00	0.50	6.6	151	27	100		0.0	13.5		0.0	261
86-89	CT	+++	2022	A+	Aberdeen	4	0	0	18	27	4.00	1.39	12.6	272	44	68	3.40	3.0	13.5	4.5	0.0	180
80-82	CB	+++	2022	AA	Bowie	1	2	2	51	69	2.64	0.80	13.2	172	23	79	2.00	1.9	12.1	6.3	1.4	184
81-84	SL	++	2023	AAA	Norfolk Tides	3	0	1	51	63	5.64	1.72	9.3	258	34	71	5.55	6.7	11.1	1.7	1.6	37

Over-achiveing former UDFA struggled in Triple-A during 2023 season. Underwent Tommy John in September and will miss entire 2024 season. Relies heavily on CT with solid attributes. Struggled commanding FB that doesn't miss bats. CB is a solid secondary, which plays down due to FB struggles. Also throws SL.

Denton,Cade

SP | **Colorado** | EXP MLB DEBUT: 2025 | H/W: 6-3 180 | FUT: Setup reliever | **7C**

Thrws R Age 22			Year	Lev	Team	W	L	Sv	IP	K	ERA	WHIP	BF/G	OBA	H%	S%	xERA	Ctl	Dom	Cmd	hr/9	BPV
2023 (6) Oral Roberts																						
93-95	FB	+++																				
80-83	SL	+++	2023	NCAA	Oral Roberts	3	1	15	64	86	1.83	0.98	7.0	210	33	82	1.85	2.1	12.1	5.7	0.3	179
86-88	CU	+	2023	Rk	ACL Rockies	0	0	1	5	7	3.60	1.20	5.0	262	41	67	2.78	1.8	12.6	7.0	0.0	196
			2023	A	Fresno	0	0	0	5	5	18.00	2.20	6.3	390	47	10	9.16	3.6	9.0	2.5	1.8	83

Righty reliever helped lead Oral Roberts to College World Series. Attacks hitters from a low ¾ slot and features an above-average mid-90s FB that has carry and arm side run. Backs up the heater with a plus sweeper that is nails vs RHB. The lack of a usable CU will keep him in a relief role, but given his experience and stuff he could move up quickly.

Dettmer,Nathan

SP | **Oakland** | EXP MLB DEBUT: 2025 | H/W: 6-4 230 | FUT: #4 starter | **7D**

Thrws R Age 21			Year	Lev	Team	W	L	Sv	IP	K	ERA	WHIP	BF/G	OBA	H%	S%	xERA	Ctl	Dom	Cmd	hr/9	BPV
2023 (5) Texas A&M																						
92-94	FB	+++																				
79-85	SL	+++																				
84-85	CU	+	2023	NCAA	Texas A&M	1	4	0	72	65	6.36	1.66	19.0	277	33	63	5.38	5.2	8.1	1.5	1.2	22
			2023	Rk	ACL Athletics	0	0	0	3	3	0.00	1.00	5.7	191	27	100	1.43	3.0	9.0	3.0	0.0	99

Physical SP who pitches aggressively to all quadrants of strike zone. Sinking FB remains best pitch and induces high number of GB. Needs to keep FB down in zone. Complements FB with average SL that operates as bat misser. Lacks touch and feel for changing speeds and hope is pro instruction will help. Could be innings eater.

Diaz,Joel

SP | **New York (N)** | EXP MLB DEBUT: 2026 | H/W: 6-2 208 | FUT: #4 starter | **7D**

Thrws R Age 20			Year	Lev	Team	W	L	Sv	IP	K	ERA	WHIP	BF/G	OBA	H%	S%	xERA	Ctl	Dom	Cmd	hr/9	BPV
2021 FA (DR)																						
92-95	FB	+++	2021	Rk	DSL Mets 2	0	2	0	49	62	0.55	0.77	12.6	173	27	92	0.63	1.6	11.4	6.9	0.0	178
76-78	CB	+++	2021	Rk	DSL Mets	0	0	0	1	1	0.00	0.00	2.8	0	0			0.0	9.0		0.0	180
84-87	CU	+++	2022	A	St. Lucie	3	2	0	55	51	5.88	1.58	15.1	285	35	64	5.19	4.1	8.3	2.0	1.1	58
			2023	--	Did Not Play																	

Projectable RHP with solid command/control tendencies missed all of 2023 after March Tommy John surgery. Athletic build with room to grow into frame. Stays online throughout 3/4s delivery with solid extension. Flat-angled FB has solid ride profile. Must live up to survive. 11-to-5 CB struggles with shape. Has a feel for late-fading CU.

Dodd,Dylan — SP — Atlanta — EXP MLB DEBUT: 2023 — H/W: 6-2 210 — FUT: #5 SP/swingman — 6C

Thrws L Age 25	Year	Lev	Team	W	L	Sv	IP	K	ERA	WHIP	BF/G	OBA	H%	S%	xERA	Ctl	Dom	Cmd	hr/9	BPV
2021 (3) SE Missouri St	2022	AA	Mississippi	2	4	0	46	55	3.12	1.28	21.0	261	36	77	3.55	2.5	10.7	4.2	0.6	143
91-93 FB +++	2022	AAA	Gwinnett	1	0	0	6	7	4.35	0.97	23.5	222	28	60	3.07	1.5	10.2	7.0	1.5	162
80-83 SL +++	2023	Rk	FCL Braves	0	0	0	3	4	0.00	0.00	8.7	0	0			0.0	11.6		0.0	227
81-83 CU +++	2023	AAA	Gwinnett	4	6	0	74	67	5.94	1.56	20.3	291	34	66	5.76	3.6	8.1	2.2	1.7	66
86-88 CT +++	2023	MLB	Atlanta	2	2	0	34	15	7.65	1.91	23.0	355	35	64	8.35	3.2	4.0	1.3	2.4	4

High 3/4s LHP shuttled between Triple-A and MLB with wayward results. Repeats jerky delivery well with some deception. 4-pitch arsenal but lacks out pitch. 4-seam FB has average characteristics across the board, struggles with in zone command. SL flashes plus but lacks break consistency. CU has solid fade profile but not enough strikes. Throws CT.

Dollander,Chase — SP — Colorado — EXP MLB DEBUT: 2026 — H/W: 6-2 200 — FUT: #2 starter — 9D

Thrws R Age 22	Year	Lev	Team	W	L	Sv	IP	K	ERA	WHIP	BF/G	OBA	H%	S%	xERA	Ctl	Dom	Cmd	hr/9	BPV
2023 (1) Tennessee																				
94-97 FB +++++																				
74-76 CB ++++																				
84-86 SL ++																				
83-85 CU +++																				

Entered the year as the top collegiate arm in the class, but with surprisingly hittable stuff. Attacks from a low 3/4 arm slot that allows his plus upper-90s FB to carry up in the zone. Works off the FB but backs it up with a high spin SL gives that is potentially a second plus offering. CU has swing-and-miss fade and sink and rarely used CB vs LHB

Dollard,Taylor — SP — Seattle — EXP MLB DEBUT: 2025 — H/W: 6-3 195 — FUT: #4 starter — 7C

Thrws R Age 25	Year	Lev	Team	W	L	Sv	IP	K	ERA	WHIP	BF/G	OBA	H%	S%	xERA	Ctl	Dom	Cmd	hr/9	BPV
2020 (5) Cal Poly	2020	NCAA	Cal Poly	1	0	0	27		1.67	0.89	25.0	208	33	79	1.32	1.3	12.0	9.0	0.0	198
90-94 FB +++	2021	A	Modesto	3	2	0	37	59	3.39	1.34	22.1	276	45	75	3.78	2.4	14.3	5.9	0.5	210
78-82 SL +++	2021	A+	Everett	6	2	0	67	74	6.17	1.37	23.4	292	36	58	5.19	1.9	9.9	5.3	1.6	146
70-74 CB ++	2022	AA	Arkansas	16	2	0	144	131	2.25	0.95	20.1	207	26	79	2.03	1.9	8.2	4.2	0.6	113
80-83 CU +++	2023	AAA	Tacoma	0	2	0	8	8	7.78	1.48	11.6	283	25	63	8.00	3.3	8.9	2.7	4.4	88

Command and control RHP who ended season in mid-April after labrum surgery. Not a dominator as K rate has fallen in upper minors. Lacks velocity and wipeout offering. Hits spots with precision and gets good extension in easy delivery. Sequences well and uses split CU to keep hitters off guard. Low ceiling, but high floor guy.

Dombroski,Trey — SP — Houston — EXP MLB DEBUT: 2026 — H/W: 6-5 235 — FUT: #4 starter — 7E

Thrws L Age 23	Year	Lev	Team	W	L	Sv	IP	K	ERA	WHIP	BF/G	OBA	H%	S%	xERA	Ctl	Dom	Cmd	hr/9	BPV
2022 (4) Monmouth																				
90-91 FB ++																				
78-80 CB +++																				
84-85 CU +++																				
79-80 SL ++	2023	A	Fayetteville	7	9	1	119	148	3.71	1.12	18.0	224	30	71	3.17	2.7	11.2	4.1	1.1	146

Southpaw showed impressive bat-missing stuff in Low-A pro debut. Arsenal headlined by tablesetting FB/CB combo, CU/SL are effective out pitches. Size results in good extension, helping velo play up. Needs to prove stuff can hold up against advanced batters. Could be quick riser if it does.

Drohan,Shane — SP — Chicago (A) — EXP MLB DEBUT: 2024 — H/W: 6-3 195 — FUT: #4 starter — 7C

Thrws L Age 25	Year	Lev	Team	W	L	Sv	IP	K	ERA	WHIP	BF/G	OBA	H%	S%	xERA	Ctl	Dom	Cmd	hr/9	BPV
2020 (5) Florida State	2021	A	Salem	7	4	0	88	86	3.98	1.43	16.3	246	32	71	3.47	4.6	8.8	1.9	0.3	52
91-94 FB ++	2022	A+	Greenville	6	7	0	105	136	4.02	1.25	19.4	235	32	72	3.75	3.4	11.6	3.4	1.3	135
74-77 CB +++	2022	AA	Portland	1	1	0	24	21	3.38	1.33	19.9	237	26	85	4.60	4.1	7.9	1.9	1.9	48
83-86 SL +++	2023	AA	Portland	5	0	0	34	36	1.32	0.82	20.6	165	23	85	0.94	2.4	9.5	4.0	0.3	125
81-85 CU ++++	2023	AAA	Worcester	5	7	0	89	93	6.47	1.87	19.9	291	35	69	6.71	6.4	9.4	1.5	1.9	15

Tale of two seasons for deceptive LHP. Excellent in AA, though struggled mightily in AAA upon promotion. Gets lively action on sub-par FB while hard SL features cutting action and big-bending CB misses bats. Needs to be more consistent within zone, particularly due to lack of velocity. CU ranks among best in org.

Echavarria,Steven — SP — Oakland — EXP MLB DEBUT: 2027 — H/W: 6-1 180 — FUT: #3 starter — 8E

Thrws R Age 18	Year	Lev	Team	W	L	Sv	IP	K	ERA	WHIP	BF/G	OBA	H%	S%	xERA	Ctl	Dom	Cmd	hr/9	BPV
2023 (3) HS (NJ)																				
92-95 FB +++																				
83-85 SL +++																				
79-82 CB ++																				
80-82 CU ++																				

Gifted SP with intriguing combo of pitchability and projection. Operates with four pitches and repeats simple delivery and arm slot. Has plenty of room to add muscle to increase stamina. Can throw solid average FB up in zone and get hitters to chase high-spin SL. Advanced CU with late drop. May need to shelve CB.

Eder,Jake — SP — Chicago (A) — EXP MLB DEBUT: 2025 — H/W: 6-4 215 — FUT: #4 starter — 7C

Thrws L Age 25	Year	Lev	Team	W	L	Sv	IP	K	ERA	WHIP	BF/G	OBA	H%	S%	xERA	Ctl	Dom	Cmd	hr/9	BPV
2020 (4) Vanderbilt	2020	NCAA	Vanderbilt	1	1	0	20	27	3.60	1.45	21.4	262	39	75	3.84	4.1	12.2	3.0	0.5	127
91-93 FB +++	2021	AA	Pensacola	3	5	0	71	99	1.77	0.98	18.0	177	28	84	1.55	3.4	12.5	3.7	0.4	151
78-80 SL ++++	2023	A+	Jupiter	0	2	0	9	10	4.89	1.63	13.6	278	39	67	4.13	4.9	9.8	2.0	0.0	62
82-84 CU +++	2023	AA	Birmingham	0	3	0	18	22	11.12	2.36	18.4	350	46	51	8.52	7.6	11.1	1.5	1.5	13
77-79 CB	2023	AA	Pensacola	2	1	0	29	38	4.01	1.30	20.1	211	29	74	3.55	4.9	11.7	2.4	1.2	96

Projectable LHP struggled with command in return from Tommy John surgery. Traded mid-season from MIA. 3/4s delivery with above-average extension. Doesn't consistently stay balanced. Best pitch is slurvy SL with sudden downward break late in the pitch progression. Struggled with FB consistency throughout. Has feel for above-average CU.

Elbis,Joe — SP — Arizona — EXP MLB DEBUT: 2026 — H/W: 6-1 150 — FUT: #4 starter — 7C

Thrws R Age 21	Year	Lev	Team	W	L	Sv	IP	K	ERA	WHIP	BF/G	OBA	H%	S%	xERA	Ctl	Dom	Cmd	hr/9	BPV
2019 FA (VZ)	2021	Rk	ACL Dbacks	3	2	0	39	46	3.44	1.10	17.1	261	35	72	3.39	0.9	10.6	11.5	0.9	183
90-93 FB ++	2021	A	Visalia	0	1	0	14	13	3.86	1.14	18.5	248	33	63	2.49	1.9	8.4	4.3	0.0	116
76-79 CB +++	2022	A	Visalia	0	2	0	10	14	9.00	1.70	15.1	316	48	41	4.84	3.6	12.6	3.5	0.0	148
82-85 SL +++	2023	A	Visalia	3	2	0	41	37	1.76	1.17	16.4	227	30	85	2.51	3.1	8.1	2.6	0.2	81
84-86 CU ++	2023	A+	Hillsboro	1	7	0	74	60	4.86	1.43	22.5	248	29	68	4.26	4.5	7.3	1.6	1.1	28

Lanky RHP with some physical projection left features solid repertoire. Attacks zone with FB-heavy approach. Can land CB/SL for strikes, keeping batters honest despite so-so movement. Some effort in delivery, inconsistent command. Stuff doesn't jump off page, but shows starter attributes and could grow into more velo with added muscle.

Eldridge P,Bryce — SP — San Francisco — EXP MLB DEBUT: 2026 — H/W: 6-7 223 — FUT: #3 starter — 8D

Thrws R Age 19	Year	Lev	Team	W	L	Sv	IP	K	ERA	WHIP	BF/G	OBA	H%	S%	xERA	Ctl	Dom	Cmd	hr/9	BPV
2023 (1) HS (VA)																				
91-94 FB +++																				
81-84 SL +++																				
79-81 CB ++																				
82-84 CU ++																				

Two-way player with tall frame and arm strength that could lead to high-90s FB eventually. Very athletic with ability to repeat delivery despite age. Downhill plane to plane adds deception to mix, particularly with FB thrown from ¾ slot. Mixes two distinct breaking balls and is able to change speeds. Needs time to develop but has high upside.

Enlow,Blayne — SP — San Francisco — EXP MLB DEBUT: 2024 — H/W: 6-3 170 — FUT: #5 SP/swingman — 6B

Thrws R Age 25	Year	Lev	Team	W	L	Sv	IP	K	ERA	WHIP	BF/G	OBA	H%	S%	xERA	Ctl	Dom	Cmd	hr/9	BPV
2017 (3) HS (LA)	2021	A+	Cedar Rapids	1	1	0	14	23	1.90	1.34	19.7	245	41	89	3.48	3.8	14.6	3.8	0.6	178
90-93 FB +++	2022	A+	Cedar Rapids	0	0	0	1	1	22.50	5.00	9.4	596	63	60	27.87	7.5	7.5	1.0	7.5	-50
87-89 CT +++	2022	AA	Wichita	1	3	3	57	64	4.41	1.58	10.5	271	37	72	4.48	4.7	10.1	2.1	0.6	72
78-81 CB ++	2023	AA	Wichita	3	1	0	54	65	3.17	1.13	19.4	240	32	76	3.27	2.2	10.8	5.0	1.0	155
86-89 CU ++	2023	AAA	St. Paul	2	5	0	45	44	7.98	1.60	13.3	294	34	52	6.16	3.8	8.8	2.3	2.0	74

Tall RHP who has seen stuff regress but still has enough to challenge for big league spot. Control was vastly improved in 23 and learned to locate FB to both sides of plate. Solid-average CT is best pitch and gets RHH to make weak contact. Durability has been issue and could be bullpen candidate. Hope would be to add velocity in short stints.

Ercolani,Alesandro — SP — Pittsburgh — EXP MLB DEBUT: 2026 — H/W: 6-2 185 — FUT: #4 starter — 7D

Thrws R Age 19	Year	Lev	Team	W	L	Sv	IP	K	ERA	WHIP	BF/G	OBA	H%	S%	xERA	Ctl	Dom	Cmd	hr/9	BPV
2021 FA (Italy)																				
92-95 FB +++																				
77-79 SL +++	2021	Rk	FCL Pirates G	2	3	0	18	20	5.47	1.55	7.9	282	38	63	4.43	4.0	9.9	2.5	0.5	90
80-83 CB ++	2022	Rk	FCL Pirates B	1	0	1	30	39	1.20	1.30	12.4	183	29	90	2.05	6.0	11.7	2.0	0.0	66
84-86 CU +	2023	A	Bradenton	4	5	0	65	66	4.43	1.43	16.3	253	32	72	4.32	4.3	9.1	2.1	1.1	67

Improving RHP who found success in first full season as pro, though ended season in July. Pitched in AFL after campaign. Added more electricity to average FB and can now attack up in zone. CU also has improved and thrown with same arm speed. Occasional CT gives different look. LHH have been challenging and can be hittable.

Espino,Daniel | SP | Cleveland

EXP MLB DEBUT: 2025 | H/W: 6-2 225 | FUT: #1 starter | 9E

Thrws R Age 23
2019 (1) HS (GA)

95-99	FB	+++++
80-83	CB	+++
84-88	SL	++++
83-86	CU	++

Year	Lev	Team	W	L	Sv	IP	K	ERA	WHIP	BF/G	OBA	H%	S%	xERA	Ctl	Dom	Cmd	hr/9	BPV
2019	A-	MahoningVal	0	2	0	10	18	6.30	1.40	14.1	242	44	54	3.83	4.5	16.2	3.6	0.9	188
2021	A	Lynchburg	1	2	0	42	64	3.41	1.35	17.6	222	37	75	3.04	4.9	13.6	2.8	0.4	131
2021	A+	Lake County	2	6	0	49	88	4.04	0.94	18.4	178	31	62	2.27	2.9	16.2	5.5	1.3	230
2022	AA	Akron	1	0	0	18	35	2.49	0.72	16.0	150	24	89	2.06	2.0	17.4	8.8	2.0	278
2023	--	Did Not Play																	

Hasn't pitched in game action since April 2022. Surgery in May 23 to repair shoulder and could return in mid-24. Few can compare with electric stuff, led by elite FB and incredible SL. Lots of movement with pitches and uses downhill plane effectively. Very athletic delivery with minimal effort though arm action is long. Misses ton of bats.

Estes,Joey | SP | Oakland

EXP MLB DEBUT: 2023 | H/W: 6-2 190 | FUT: #4 starter | 7B

Thrws R Age 22
2019 (16) HS (CA)

92-96	FB	+++
80-84	SL	+++
79-82	CB	++
85-87	CU	++

Year	Lev	Team	W	L	Sv	IP	K	ERA	WHIP	BF/G	OBA	H%	S%	xERA	Ctl	Dom	Cmd	hr/9	BPV
2021	A	Augusta	3	6	0	99	127	2.91	0.96	18.7	191	28	72	1.90	2.6	11.5	4.4	0.6	155
2022	A+	Lansing	3	7	0	91	92	4.55	1.27	18.6	251	30	71	4.44	3.0	9.1	3.1	1.7	102
2023	AA	Midland	6	6	0	104	100	3.29	1.10	20.4	222	27	76	3.21	2.7	8.6	3.2	1.2	101
2023	AAA	Las Vegas	3	0	0	32	31	5.31	1.37	19.3	261	27	74	5.85	3.4	8.7	2.6	2.8	83
2023	MLB	Oakland	0	1	0	10	7	7.20	1.40	21.1	299	27	60	7.27	1.8	6.3	3.5	3.6	83

Athletic, fast-armed RHP who led org in wins and 2nd in Ks. Ascended to majors on heels of consistent campaign in AA. Operates with two effective offerings in FB and sneaky good SL and aggressively pitches inside. FB features good carry up in zone but allows lot of HR. Owns pitch mix to stick as SP but needs polish.

Ferris,Jackson | SP | Los Angeles (N)

EXP MLB DEBUT: 2026 | H/W: 6-4 195 | FUT: #3 starter | 8D

Thrws L Age 20
2022 (2) HS (FL)

92-95	FB	++++
75-77	CB	++++
78-81	SL	+++
84-86	CU	++

Year	Lev	Team	W	L	Sv	IP	K	ERA	WHIP	BF/G	OBA	H%	S%	xERA	Ctl	Dom	Cmd	hr/9	BPV
2023	A	Myrtle Beach	2	3	0	56	77	3.38	1.21	12.6	181	30	70	1.98	5.3	12.4	2.3	0.2	98

Inked an above slot $3 million deal and features a potentially plus 4-pitch mix. Athletic frame with high ¾ arm slot and good front side mechanics, but varies release point. FB sits at 92-95, topping at 97 with good arm side run and CB, CU, and SL all flash above-average. Refining mechanics and improving command will be key to long-term success.

Festa,David | SP | Minnesota

EXP MLB DEBUT: 2024 | H/W: 6-6 185 | FUT: #4 starter | 7B

Thrws R Age 24
2021 (13) Seton Hall

92-96	FB	++++
85-88	SL	+++
78-82	CB	++
83-86	CU	+++

Year	Lev	Team	W	L	Sv	IP	K	ERA	WHIP	BF/G	OBA	H%	S%	xERA	Ctl	Dom	Cmd	hr/9	BPV
2021	A	Fort Myers	0	0	0	3	4	11.61	1.94	7.4	186	30	33	3.70	11.6	11.6	1.0	0.0	-87
2022	A	Fort Myers	2	1	0	24	33	1.50	0.75	17.1	151	24	82	0.68	2.3	12.4	5.5	0.4	180
2022	A+	Cedar Rapids	7	3	0	79	75	2.73	1.20	19.9	231	29	79	2.95	3.2	8.5	2.7	0.6	86
2023	AA	Wichita	3	3	0	80	104	4.39	1.36	15.9	252	36	69	3.91	3.7	11.7	3.2	0.9	128
2023	AAA	St. Paul	1	1	0	12	15	2.98	1.57	17.7	227	32	83	3.97	6.7	11.2	1.7	0.7	38

Tall, lean SP who led org in K and even increased K rate. Hits mid-90s with present FB and may have more in tank as he adds muscle. Control took step back. Does decent job of locating FB but SL and CB can be erratic. Lot of spin on SL and hitters often chase. CU getting better, though needs more separation from FB. Induces groundballs.

Fitts,Richard | SP | Boston

EXP MLB DEBUT: 2024 | H/W: 6-3 230 | FUT: #4 starter | 7C

Thrws R Age 24
2021 (6) Auburn

92-94	FB	++++
83-85	SL	++++
86-88	CU	+++
86-88	CT	++

Year	Lev	Team	W	L	Sv	IP	K	ERA	WHIP	BF/G	OBA	H%	S%	xERA	Ctl	Dom	Cmd	hr/9	BPV
2022	A	Tampa	3	8	0	79	93	5.01	1.14	18.4	247	32	60	3.84	1.9	10.6	5.5	1.5	156
2022	A+	Hudson Valley	4	0	0	33	38	0.55	0.61	22.6	154	23	95	0.28	0.8	10.4	12.7	0.3	182
2023	AA	Somerset	11	5	0	152	163	3.49	1.14	22.3	234	29	76	3.52	2.5	9.6	3.8	1.3	123

Over-the-top, big-bodied RHP took step closer to MLB in 2023. Frame bordering on XXL. Stiff delivery with jerky leg lift and average extension. Mostly FB/SL pitcher. Flat-angled 4-seam FB has plus ride but limited run. SL is best pitch with varying plus two-plane movement. CU is an average offering. Also throws CT. Backend SP upside, RP floor.

Flores,Wilmer | SP | Detroit

EXP MLB DEBUT: 2024 | H/W: 6-4 225 | FUT: #4 starter | 8D

Thrws R Age 23
2020 FA (Arizona Western JC)

92-96	FB	++++
76-79	CB	++++
85-87	CU	++
82-84	CT	+++

Year	Lev	Team	W	L	Sv	IP	K	ERA	WHIP	BF/G	OBA	H%	S%	xERA	Ctl	Dom	Cmd	hr/9	BPV
2021	A	Lakeland	4	3	0	53	72	3.40	1.30	19.9	239	37	72	2.90	3.7	12.2	3.3	0.2	137
2022	A+	West Michigan	1	0	0	19	35	1.88	0.83	11.7	205	39	86	1.98	0.9	16.4	17.5	0.9	288
2022	AA	Erie	6	4	0	83	95	3.03	1.06	17.0	222	30	75	2.74	2.3	10.3	4.5	0.9	142
2023	A+	West Michigan	0	1	0	8	8	12.22	1.60	11.9	344	45	15	5.12	1.1	8.9	8.0	0.0	148
2023	AA	Erie	5	3	0	80	82	3.93	1.30	18.3	241	32	70	3.32	3.6	9.2	2.6	0.6	87

Took a step back in 2023. Mid-90s FB has arm side run and late life, but lack of athleticism and difficulty repeating mechanics limits upside. Velocity down a tick or two and tends to miss up and away with FB. Power CB is best secondary with below-average CU and CT rounding out the mix. Will need to improve control and command to remain a starter.

Floyd,Ty | SP | Cincinnati

EXP MLB DEBUT: 2025 | H/W: 6-2 200 | FUT: Setup reliever | 7C

Thrws R Age 22
2023 (2) Louisiana State

93-95	FB	++++
81-83	SL	++
83-85	CU	+++
77-79	CB	++

Year	Lev	Team	W	L	Sv	IP	K	ERA	WHIP	BF/G	OBA	H%	S%	xERA	Ctl	Dom	Cmd	hr/9	BPV

Athletic RHP with plus-plus arm speed was drafted 38th overall after solid Junior season at LSU. Repeatable, 3/4s delivery with solid extension. Near physical projection with frame. Relies heavily on FB with natural arm-side ride and late run. Struggles with feel for spin. Both breakers below average. Has a solid feel for a late-fading CU.

Fluharty,Mason | RP | Toronto

EXP MLB DEBUT: 2024 | H/W: 6-2 215 | FUT: Setup reliever | 6B

Thrws L Age 22
2022 (5) Liberty

90-92	FB	++
83-85	SL	+++
87-89	CT	+++

Year	Lev	Team	W	L	Sv	IP	K	ERA	WHIP	BF/G	OBA	H%	S%	xERA	Ctl	Dom	Cmd	hr/9	BPV
2022	NCAA	Liberty	6	3	2	50	83	2.87	1.12	7.6	245	43	74	2.66	1.8	14.9	8.3	0.4	237
2022	A+	Vancouver	1	1	0	15	21	3.58	1.46	6.5	260	38	80	4.53	4.2	12.5	3.0	1.2	131
2023	A+	Vancouver	1	0	1	15	21	0.60	0.79	4.5	141	22	100	0.90	3.0	12.5	4.2	0.6	163
2023	AA	New Hampshire	2	5	4	42	54	4.28	1.59	5.2	292	40	77	5.42	3.8	11.5	3.0	1.3	122

Deceptive RP who could be lethal lefty specialist. Throws from low slot and slings ball to plate. May not have much velo but can spot lively pitches up and down in zone. Commands SL well and mixes in quick CT to keep RHH off guard. K rate more about deception than stuff. Rare pitcher who doesn't use FB that frequently.

Ford,Walter | SP | Seattle

EXP MLB DEBUT: 2026 | H/W: 6-3 198 | FUT: #3 starter | 8E

Thrws R Age 19
2022 (2) HS (FL)

92-95	FB	+++
81-83	SL	++
80-83	CB	++
81-83	CU	++

Year	Lev	Team	W	L	Sv	IP	K	ERA	WHIP	BF/G	OBA	H%	S%	xERA	Ctl	Dom	Cmd	hr/9	BPV
2023	Rk	ACL Mariners	0	0	0	22	23	3.65	1.58	10.8	285	38	76	4.48	4.1	9.3	2.3	0.4	76

Young, projectable RHP who has limited pitching experience and being treated with kid gloves. Has chance to be dominant type with knockout pitches aplenty. Mechanics are crude and often overthrows with long arm action. Inconsistent velocity as well. Has pure arm strength and feel for spin. Could have 3 plus pitches down the road.

Franklin,Kohl | SP | Chicago (N)

EXP MLB DEBUT: 2024 | H/W: 6-4 195 | FUT: #5 SP/swingman | 7D

Thrws R Age 24
2018 (6) HS (OK)

94-96	FB	+++
78-82	CB	++
80-82	SL	++
83-85	CU	+++

Year	Lev	Team	W	L	Sv	IP	K	ERA	WHIP	BF/G	OBA	H%	S%	xERA	Ctl	Dom	Cmd	hr/9	BPV
2019	A-	Eugene	1	3	0	39	49	2.31	1.15	15.5	220	32	81	2.57	3.2	11.3	3.5	0.5	134
2019	A+	South Bend	0	0	0	3	3	3.00	1.67	13.5	0	0	80	1.34	15.0	9.0	0.6	0.0	-225
2022	A+	South Bend	3	7	0	69	75	6.90	1.64	13.4	270	35	57	5.00	5.3	9.8	1.8	1.0	50
2023	A+	South Bend	0	2	0	19	30	2.83	1.31	15.8	194	32	83	3.08	5.7	14.1	2.5	0.9	120
2023	AA	Tennessee	4	10	0	85	86	6.02	1.50	17.5	273	32	65	5.62	4.0	9.1	2.3	2.0	73

Features four average to above offerings, but has yet to have sustained success as a professional and was left off the Cubs 40-man. FB sits 94-96 up to 99 with heavy fade CU, knee-bending knuckle CB, and sweeping SL. Below-average control and command will need to be addressed to remain in a starting role, but FB/CU mix could play well in relief.

Frasso,Nick | SP | Los Angeles (N)

EXP MLB DEBUT: 2024 | H/W: 6-5 200 | FUT: #2 SP/closer | 9E

Thrws R Age 25
2020 (4) Loyola Marymount

94-97	FB	+++++
86-89	SL	+++
84-86	CU	++

Year	Lev	Team	W	L	Sv	IP	K	ERA	WHIP	BF/G	OBA	H%	S%	xERA	Ctl	Dom	Cmd	hr/9	BPV
2022	A+	Great Lakes	0	0	0	5	9	1.73	0.96	9.8	254	47	80	2.05	0.0	15.6		0.0	298
2022	A+	Vancouver	0	0	0	11	15	0.82	0.45	12.0	88	11	100		1.6	12.3	7.5	0.8	195
2022	AA	Tulsa	0	0	0	11	10	5.63	1.70	12.6	275	34	67	5.02	5.6	8.0	1.4	0.8	11
2023	AA	Tulsa	3	4	0	73	94	3.93	1.26	14.2	248	36	68	3.21	3.0	11.6	3.9	0.5	146
2023	AAA	Oklahoma City	1	2	0	19	13	3.30	1.36	20.0	261	32	73	3.24	3.3	6.1	1.9	0.0	39

2022 breakout and early success at AA raised profile, but suffered elbow-brace surgery to repair partial UCL tear and has yet to prove he can go deep into games. Plus upper-90s FB with carry up gets plenty of swings and misses. SL shows potential but remains inconsistent. A fringe CU makes move to relief likely.

Fuentes,Didier — SP — Atlanta — EXP MLB DEBUT: 2026 — H/W: 6-0 170 — FUT: #4 starter — 7E

Thrws R Age 18 — 2022 FA (CB)

Velo	Pitch	Grade
91-94	FB	+++
80-83	SL	+++
86-88	CU	++
76-79	CB	+++

Year	Lev	Team	W	L	Sv	IP	K	ERA	WHIP	BF/G	OBA	H%	S%	xERA	Ctl	Dom	Cmd	hr/9	BPV
2022	Rk	DSL Braves	1	1	0	44	50	2.25	1.02	15.4	220	31	79	2.20	2.0	10.2	5.0	0.4	147
2023	A	Augusta	0	4	0	26	27	7.27	1.69	11.7	304	36	61	6.62	4.2	9.3	2.3	2.1	74

Low 3/4s RHP struggled in aggressive full-season assignment as 17-year-old. Effort in delivery, achieves above-average extension. 4-pitch arsenal. Low-90s FB has flat-angled, arm-side running profile. Throws a hybrid SL with solid horizontal break. Also throws occasional CB & CU. Needs to improve consistency with delivery and strikes.

Fulton,Dax — SP — Miami — EXP MLB DEBUT: 2024 — H/W: 6-7 235 — FUT: #4 starter — 7C

Thrws L Age 22 — 2020 (2) HS (OK)

Velo	Pitch	Grade
92-95	FB	+++
81-84	SL	+++
87-88	CU	+++

Year	Lev	Team	W	L	Sv	IP	K	ERA	WHIP	BF/G	OBA	H%	S%	xERA	Ctl	Dom	Cmd	hr/9	BPV
2021	A	Jupiter	2	4	0	58	66	4.33	1.37	16.3	234	32	68	3.31	4.6	10.2	2.2	0.5	76
2021	A+	Beloit	0	1	0	19	18	5.63	1.51	16.6	279	33	65	5.18	3.8	8.4	2.3	1.4	69
2022	A+	Beloit	5	6	0	97	120	4.08	1.43	20.6	275	39	71	4.09	3.2	11.1	3.4	0.6	131
2022	AA	Pensacola	1	1	0	21	30	2.57	0.76	18.8	132	19	71	0.97	3.0	12.9	4.3	0.9	168
2023	AA	Pensacola	2	4	0	33	39	5.18	1.55	20.6	256	34	68	4.62	5.2	10.6	2.1	1.1	70

High 3/4s LHP made return from Tommy John surgery in 2023. Stuff has returned but command was lacking. Repeatable, crossfire delivery creates deceptive look. 3-pitch pitcher. 4-seam FB has ride up in the zone with high whiff rate. Sweeping SL is best secondary. Both pitches rate as above-average offerings. Arm-side fading CU is viable 3rd pitch.

Gasser,Robert — SP — Milwaukee — EXP MLB DEBUT: 2024 — H/W: 6-0 192 — FUT: #4 starter — 7B

Thrws L Age 24 — 2021 (2) Houston

Velo	Pitch	Grade
91-94	FB	+++
79-80	SL	++++
85-87	CB	+++
85-89	CU	+++

Year	Lev	Team	W	L	Sv	IP	K	ERA	WHIP	BF/G	OBA	H%	S%	xERA	Ctl	Dom	Cmd	hr/9	BPV
2021	A	Lake Elsinore	0	0	0	14		1.29	0.93	10.5	218	27	92	2.18	1.3	8.4	6.5	0.6	134
2022	A+	Fort Wayne	4	9	0	90	115	4.20	1.27	20.4	253	36	68	3.59	2.8	11.5	4.1	0.8	149
2022	AA	Biloxi	1	1	0	20	26	2.24	1.09	19.7	198	28	85	2.56	3.6	11.6	3.3	0.9	131
2022	AAA	Nashville	2	2	0	26	31	4.48	1.61	23.1	261	37	71	4.15	5.5	10.7	1.9	0.3	61
2023	AAA	Nashville	9	1	0	135	166	3.80	1.28	21.3	244	34	72	3.52	3.3	11.1	3.3	0.8	127

Consistent LHP who led IL in K. Continues to impress with deep repertoire and one of nastiest SL in org. Uses SL against both RHH and LHH and features great horizontal sweep. Mixes in big-bending CB and average CU. Not a flamethrower but knows how to sequence. Lacks ideal size and command often comes and goes.

Gil,Luis — SP — New York (A) — EXP MLB DEBUT: 2021 — H/W: 6-2 185 — FUT: #4 starter — 8E

Thrws R Age 25 — 2015 FA (DR)

Velo	Pitch	Grade
94-97	FB	++++
85-87	SL	++++
88-90	CU	+++

Year	Lev	Team	W	L	Sv	IP	K	ERA	WHIP	BF/G	OBA	H%	S%	xERA	Ctl	Dom	Cmd	hr/9	BPV
2021	AAA	Scranton/WB	4	0	1	48	67	4.85	1.39	15.6	205	29	68	3.76	6.0	12.5	2.1	1.3	82
2021	MLB	New York	1	1	0	29	38	3.09	1.34	20.2	196	27	83	3.48	5.9	11.8	2.0	1.2	71
2022	AAA	Scranton/WB	0	3	0	21	31	8.07	1.70	16.0	260	34	57	6.40	6.4	13.2	2.1	2.5	83
2022	MLB	New York (A)	0	0	0	4	5	9.00	1.75	18.3	307	44	43	4.85	4.5	11.3	2.5	0.0	99
2023	A	Tampa	0	0	0	4	6	11.25	2.25	10.1	347	53	44	6.75	6.8	13.5	2.0	0.0	79

Hard-throwing RHP, made MLB debut in 2021, has struggled in his recovering from Tommy John surgery. Tall, lanky frame creates deception in 3/4s slot delivery. Stuff was back during rehab assignment but command and control were no where to be found. At his best, flat-angled 4-seam FB with ride and vertical breaking SL carry profile.

Ginn,J.T. — SP — Oakland — EXP MLB DEBUT: 2024 — H/W: 6-2 200 — FUT: #4 starter — 7D

Thrws R Age 24 — 2020 (2) Mississippi State

Velo	Pitch	Grade
91-94	FB	+++
81-84	SL	+++
83-85	CU	++

Year	Lev	Team	W	L	Sv	IP	K	ERA	WHIP	BF/G	OBA	H%	S%	xERA	Ctl	Dom	Cmd	hr/9	BPV
2021	A+	Brooklyn	3	4	0	53	46	3.39	1.15	21.1	247	32	67	2.50	2.0	7.8	3.8	0.0	103
2022	Rk	ACL Athletics	0	0	0	7	5	0.00	0.57	11.9	168	21	100	0.12	0.0	6.4		0.0	134
2022	AA	Midland	1	4	0	35	41	6.15	1.48	15.1	277	38	57	4.46	3.6	10.5	2.9	0.8	110
2023	Rk	ACL Athletics	0	1	0	4	6	4.39	1.95	9.8	302	47	75	5.25	6.6	13.2	2.0	0.0	77
2023	AA	Midland	1	2	0	22	11	8.14	1.81	17.1	302	33	53	5.76	5.3	4.5	0.8	0.8	-44

Missed most of season with biceps tendinitis and not able to gain traction. Throws consistent strikes with power sink and hard SL combination. True GB pitcher who doesn't allow many HR. Doesn't have the riding life on FB to pitch up in zone but thrives with control and command. Injury history a concern and will need CU to last as SP.

Gipson Long,Sawyer — SP — Detroit — EXP MLB DEBUT: 2023 — H/W: 6-4 225 — FUT: #5 SP/swingman — 6A

Thrws R Age 26 — 2019 (6) Mercer

Velo	Pitch	Grade
91-94	FB	+
81-84	SL	+++
84-86	CU	+++
86-88	CT	++

Year	Lev	Team	W	L	Sv	IP	K	ERA	WHIP	BF/G	OBA	H%	S%	xERA	Ctl	Dom	Cmd	hr/9	BPV
2022	AA	Erie	2	2	0	35	35	4.60	1.31	20.8	272	32	72	4.91	2.3	8.9	3.9	1.8	117
2022	AA	Wichita	3	4	0	37	35	7.26	1.40	19.6	305	37	47	5.09	1.5	8.5	5.8	1.2	131
2023	AA	Erie	6	5	0	65	76	3.74	1.02	17.8	218	27	72	3.33	2.1	10.5	5.1	1.7	151
2023	AAA	Toledo	2	3	0	34	50	5.53	1.37	17.9	255	35	67	5.10	3.7	13.2	3.6	2.1	155
2023	MLB	Detroit	1	0	0	20	26	2.70	1.10	19.6	199	28	80	2.59	3.6	11.7	3.3	0.9	131

Four-pitch mix and above-average command compensate for pedestrian 90-93 mph FB. SL and CU are both above-average offerings with plenty of swing and miss (41% and 50% whiff rates). Simple, repeatable mechanics with good tunneling and E/W action keeps hitters off-balance. Fly ball tendencies and lack of velo limit upside, but the floor is solid.

Gomez,Raimon — RP — New York (N) — EXP MLB DEBUT: 2025 — H/W: 6-2 175 — FUT: Setup reliever — 7E

Thrws R Age 22 — 2021 FA (VZ)

Velo	Pitch	Grade
97-99	FB	++++
85-88	SL	+++
89-91	CT	++
87-89	CU	+

Year	Lev	Team	W	L	Sv	IP	K	ERA	WHIP	BF/G	OBA	H%	S%	xERA	Ctl	Dom	Cmd	hr/9	BPV
2021	Rk	DSL Mets	1	1	0	12	14	2.23	1.32	5.6	227	31	87	3.35	4.5	10.4	2.3	0.7	85
2022	A	St. Lucie	4	5	3	47	54	3.81	1.33	8.2	244	35	69	3.09	3.8	10.3	2.7	0.2	100
2023	A+	Brooklyn	0	0	0	7	12	6.43	1.86	10.9	168	28	67	4.48	11.6	15.4	1.3	1.3	-17

Hard-throwing RHP with helium coming out of Spring Training, needed Tommy John Surgery after 3rd start of season. Strong frame, near physical projection. 3/4s delivery with longer arm path and plus extension. Double-plus arm-speed propels high velocity 4-seam FB. SL is short breaker with inconsistent spin profile. Toys with CT and CU.

Gomez,Yoendrys — SP — New York (A) — EXP MLB DEBUT: 2023 — H/W: 6-3 212 — FUT: Setup reliever — 7D

Thrws R Age 24 — 2016 FA (VZ)

Velo	Pitch	Grade
92-94	FB	++++
83-85	SL	++
87-89	CT	+++
79-81	CB	+++

Year	Lev	Team	W	L	Sv	IP	K	ERA	WHIP	BF/G	OBA	H%	S%	xERA	Ctl	Dom	Cmd	hr/9	BPV
2022	Rk	FCL Yankees	0	0	0	2	3	0.00	1.36	9.2	326	48	100	4.16	0.0	12.3		0.0	239
2022	A+	Hudson Valley	0	0	0	28	27	1.93	1.14	11.1	202	28	81	1.92	3.9	8.7	2.3	0.0	70
2022	AA	Somerset	1	0	0	16	19	3.91	1.24	16.4	236	33	68	3.09	3.4	10.6	3.2	0.6	119
2023	AA	Somerset	0	3	0	65	78	3.59	1.29	14.1	204	28	74	3.07	5.1	10.8	2.1	0.8	74
2023	MLB	New York (A)	0	0	0	2	4	0.00	0.50	6.6	151	38	100		0.0	18.0		0.0	342

SP had solid MiLB season, earning late-season callup, working 2 innings of dominant relief. High 3/4s delivery with effort. Struggles with release point consistently. Arsenal, especially FB, played up as RP. Flat-angled 4-seam FB has solid ride and late run profile. Secondaries are average-or-less. CB has best shot developing of bunch.

Gonzalez,Wikelman — SP — Boston — EXP MLB DEBUT: 2024 — H/W: 6-0 167 — FUT: #3 starter — 8C

Thrws R Age 22 — 2018 FA (VZ)

Velo	Pitch	Grade
93-97	FB	+++
77-80	CB	+++
84-88	SL	++
83-87	CU	+++

Year	Lev	Team	W	L	Sv	IP	K	ERA	WHIP	BF/G	OBA	H%	S%	xERA	Ctl	Dom	Cmd	hr/9	BPV
2021	A	Salem	0	0	0	17	20	1.57	1.22	17.4	211	30	90	2.70	4.2	10.5	2.5	0.5	93
2022	A	Salem	4	3	0	81	98	4.55	1.37	16.2	216	32	64	2.84	5.3	10.9	2.0	0.2	70
2022	A+	Greenville	0	0	0	17	23	2.65	1.12	16.7	213	34	74	1.96	3.2	12.2	3.8	0.0	151
2023	A+	Greenville	6	3	0	63	105	5.14	1.44	17.9	216	38	64	3.46	6.0	15.0	2.5	0.7	126
2023	AA	Portland	3	1	0	48	63	2.43	1.14	19.1	166	26	79	1.84	5.2	11.8	2.3	0.4	89

Live-armed SP who had highest K% in org in breakout season. Performed better in AA as he was tough to hit with variety of solid offerings. May not have plus pitch yet but all work in tandem well. Dynamic FB thrown from flat angle and CU thrown with similar arm speed. Has some effort in delivery, though adds hint of deception

Gordon,Colton — SP — Houston — EXP MLB DEBUT: 2024 — H/W: 6-4 225 — FUT: #4 starter — 7E

Thrws L Age 25 — 2021 (8) Central Florida

Velo	Pitch	Grade
91-92	FB	+++
79-84	SL	++
74-77	CB	+++
86-89	CU	++

Year	Lev	Team	W	L	Sv	IP	K	ERA	WHIP	BF/G	OBA	H%	S%	xERA	Ctl	Dom	Cmd	hr/9	BPV
2022	Rk	FCL Astros	0	1	0	7	11	0.00	0.57	5.9	132	26	100		1.3	14.1	11.0	0.0	238
2022	A	Fayetteville	0	0	0	20	27	2.24	0.80	14.5	187	29	73	1.25	1.3	12.1	9.0	0.4	199
2022	A+	Asheville	2	0	1	20	29	2.69	0.80	18.2	187	28	71	1.67	1.3	13.0	9.7	0.9	215
2023	AA	Corpus Christi	4	5	1	93	121	3.96	1.19	18.7	222	32	69	3.07	3.5	11.7	3.4	0.9	135
2023	AAA	Sugar Land	3	2	0	35	30	4.63	1.74	17.7	283	31	81	6.44	5.7	7.7	1.4	2.1	4

LHP takes unique kitchen-sink approach. Tall frame, throws from low arm slot with long stride. Pitch mix headlined by low-90s sinker. High-spin SL has good shape but doesn't miss many bats. Changed pitch mix at AAA to feature offspeed stuff, avoid heart of zone. Lost command, Ks as a result. Lacks high-end velocity, needs to work on sequencing.

Graceffo,Gordon — SP — St. Louis — EXP MLB DEBUT: 2024 — H/W: 6-4 210 — FUT: #4 starter — 8D

Thrws R Age 24 — 2021 (5) Villanova

Velo	Pitch	Grade
93-95	FB	+++
84-86	SL	++++
77-79	CB	++
80-83	CU	++

Year	Lev	Team	W	L	Sv	IP	K	ERA	WHIP	BF/G	OBA	H%	S%	xERA	Ctl	Dom	Cmd	hr/9	BPV
2021	NCAA	Villanova	7	2	0	82	86	1.54	0.96	28.2	222	31	82	1.70	1.4	9.4	6.6	0.0	149
2021	A	Palm Beach	1	0	1	26	37	1.73	1.42	10.0	276	43	89	3.87	3.1	12.8	4.1	0.3	164
2022	A+	Peoria	3	2	0	45	56	1.00	0.69	19.8	175	27	87	0.62	0.8	11.2	14.0	0.2	197
2022	AA	Springfield	7	4	0	93	83	3.96	1.07	20.2	224	25	70	3.47	2.3	8.0	3.5	1.5	100
2023	AAA	Memphis	4	3	0	86	81	4.92	1.53	17.8	264	33	69	4.58	4.7	8.5	1.8	0.9	43

Coils well and uses thick lower half to drive towards home. Missed two months with shoulder inflammation and struggled down the stretch. Simple, repeatable mechanics and attacks with a plus 4-pitch mix. FB has been up to 100, but sits in the mid-90s Best offering is a plus 1-to-7 SL that dives out of zone with fringe CU and overhand CB lacks depth.

Granillo,Andre

RP | **St. Louis** | EXP MLB DEBUT: 2024 | H/W: 6-4 245 | FUT: Middle reliever | **6B**

Thrws R Age 23 — 2021 (14) UC Riverside

Velo	Pitch	Grade
94-96	FB	+++
77-80	SL	++++
73-75	CB	+

Year	Lev	Team	W	L	Sv	IP	K	ERA	WHIP	BF/G	OBA	H%	S%	xERA	Ctl	Dom	Cmd	hr/9	BPV
2022	A	Palm Beach	3	1	2	15	26	2.96	1.25	6.2	189	32	82	3.09	5.3	15.4	2.9	1.2	151
2022	A+	Peoria	1	4	5	34	51	3.68	1.35	5.5	219	35	74	3.32	5.0	13.4	2.7	0.8	125
2022	AA	Springfield	0	1	1	2	5	22.50	4.50	4.9	554	92	44	17.64	9.0	22.5	2.5	0.0	180
2023	AA	Springfield	3	4	14	55	72	4.42	1.22	5.0	213	30	66	3.13	4.1	11.8	2.9	1.0	120
2023	AAA	Memphis	0	0	0	13	17	6.18	1.76	6.7	213	29	67	4.86	8.9	11.7	1.3	1.4	-13

Tall, thick framed reliever works with a quick tempo and short arm action. Falls off towards 1B with poor front-side mechanics that below-average control. Mid-90s FB has good late life and when paired with plus SL generates plenty of swing-and-miss (11.7 K/9). Below-average 12-to-6 CB has largely been shelved. Profiles as a middle reliever.

Gray,Drew

SP | **Chicago (N)** | EXP MLB DEBUT: 2026 | H/W: 6-3 190 | FUT: #4 starter | **7D**

Thrws L Age 20 — 2021 (3) HS (FL)

Velo	Pitch	Grade
91-94	FB	+++
74-76	CB	++++
80-83	SL	++
	CU	+

Year	Lev	Team	W	L	Sv	IP	K	ERA	WHIP	BF/G	OBA	H%	S%	xERA	Ctl	Dom	Cmd	hr/9	BPV
2021	Rk	ACL Cubs	0	1	0	4	9	0.00	1.00	7.6	210	57	100	1.54	2.3	20.3	9.0	0.0	322
2023	Rk	ACL Cubs	0	0	0	6	11	5.90	1.48	8.7	149	33	56	2.09	8.9	16.2	1.8	0.0	71
2023	A	Myrtle Beach	0	3	0	27	45	4.30	1.54	10.8	199	37	69	2.83	7.6	14.9	2.0	0.0	81

Lefty out of IMG showed glimpses in pro debut following Tommy John surgery. Attacks from 1B side with slow tempo before exploding towards the plate. Low-90s FB has spin and carry at the top of zone. Best secondary is above-average power CB while SL and CU are fringe. Struggles with control and command, but there is some upside here.

Grice,Caden

SP | **Arizona** | EXP MLB DEBUT: 2026 | H/W: 6-6 250 | FUT: #4 starter | **7E**

Thrws L Age 21 — 2023 (2) Clemson

Velo	Pitch	Grade
90-93	FB	++
83-86	CU	+++
78-80	CB	+++

Year	Lev	Team	W	L	Sv	IP	K	ERA	WHIP	BF/G	OBA	H%	S%	xERA	Ctl	Dom	Cmd	hr/9	BPV

Hulking two-way prospect generates debate surrounding future role. Huge raw power with bat, but contact issues at plate suggest pitching is best path. Low-90s FB keeps batters honest, CU plays off it well. CB also gets lots of whiffs, GBs. General delivery maintenance (cleaner arm action, sequencing) could lead to improvements with experience.

Groome,Jay

SP | **San Diego** | EXP MLB DEBUT: 2024 | H/W: 6-6 262 | FUT: #4 starter | **7E**

Thrws L Age 25 — 2016 (1) HS (NJ)

Velo	Pitch	Grade
91-93	FB	+++
77-81	CB	+++
84-87	SL	++
80-82	CU	+++

Year	Lev	Team	W	L	Sv	IP	K	ERA	WHIP	BF/G	OBA	H%	S%	xERA	Ctl	Dom	Cmd	hr/9	BPV
2021	AA	Portland	2	0	0	15	26	2.37	1.05	19.6	219	42	75	1.82	2.4	15.4	6.5	0.0	231
2022	AA	Portland	3	4	0	76	81	3.54	1.26	19.4	213	26	78	3.55	4.5	9.6	2.1	1.3	69
2022	AAA	El Paso	3	2	0	51	44	3.17	1.39	21.5	265	32	79	4.02	3.3	7.7	2.3	0.7	67
2022	AAA	Worcester	1	1	0	16	15	3.94	1.50	23.0	274	33	77	4.80	3.9	8.4	2.1	1.1	64
2023	AAA	El Paso	4	10	0	134	137	8.58	2.11	22.0	311	38	60	7.41	7.5	9.2	1.2	1.7	-19

Huge-framed SP who had awful season after leading PCL in BB and HR allowed while also finishing 2nd in K. Massive problem with control: walk rate elevated as he couldn't command FB or CB. Velocity has declined in last 2 years. Still hope that he can tame delivery and find consistent breaking ball and return FB to plus status.

Guerrero,Luis

RP | **Boston** | EXP MLB DEBUT: 2024 | H/W: 6-0 215 | FUT: Setup reliever | **7D**

Thrws R Age 23 — 2021 (17) Chipola JC

Velo	Pitch	Grade
95-98	FB	+++
85-88	SL	+++
84-86	CU	+++

Year	Lev	Team	W	L	Sv	IP	K	ERA	WHIP	BF/G	OBA	H%	S%	xERA	Ctl	Dom	Cmd	hr/9	BPV
2022	Rk	FCL Red Sox	0	0	2	2	3	0.00	0.00	3.0	0	0			0.0	12.9		0.0	249
2022	A	Salem	4	3	6	23	37	4.27	1.25	5.2	187	33	64	2.32	5.4	14.4	2.6	0.4	130
2022	A+	Greenville	0	2	1	13	19	2.08	1.08	7.2	231	38	79	2.06	2.1	13.2	6.3	0.0	199
2023	AA	Portland	3	2	18	49	59	1.83	1.14	4.5	158	23	85	1.74	5.5	10.8	2.0	0.4	64
2023	AAA	Worcester	0	1	1	4	9	8.57	2.62	3.8	252	51	70	8.18	15.0	19.3	1.3	2.1	-40

Career RP who is on fast track and led EL in saves. Posted lowest oppBA in org and was tough to square up with solid-average FB and potential plus SL. Flies under radar despite success. Can be victimized by walks and poor FB command. Uses unusual delivery to fire FB and hard SL to plate. Has split CU that also shows flashes.

Guerrero,Tyson

SP | **Kansas City** | EXP MLB DEBUT: 2025 | H/W: 6-1 188 | FUT: Middle reliever | **6C**

Thrws L Age 25 — 2021 (12) Washington

Velo	Pitch	Grade
91-94	FB	+++
80-83	SL	++++
75-77	CB	++
84-86	CU	++

Year	Lev	Team	W	L	Sv	IP	K	ERA	WHIP	BF/G	OBA	H%	S%	xERA	Ctl	Dom	Cmd	hr/9	BPV
2021	Rk	ACL Royals B	0	0	0	8	12	2.25	1.25	6.5	210	36	80	2.24	4.5	13.5	3.0	0.0	140
2021	A	Columbia	0	1	0	7	6	9.00	2.00	11.2	336	37	58	8.40	5.1	7.7	1.5	2.6	18
2022	A+	Quad Cities	0	3	0	23	22	6.23	1.47	16.5	269	31	62	5.44	3.9	8.6	2.2	1.9	67
2023	A+	Quad Cities	2	4	0	84	106	3.64	1.12	18.4	215	30	71	2.99	3.1	11.3	3.7	1.1	138
2023	AA	NW Arkansas	1	2	0	11	15	6.55	1.36	15.3	244	33	54	4.50	4.1	12.3	3.0	1.6	128

Over-achieving, college LHP that had fantastic season in High-A prior to Double-A callup. Pitch arsenal led by wipeout SL with tons of movement, generating lots of swing and miss. Posted high strikeout rates using mostly a FB/SL combination. A high effort delivery and lacking FB command likely means RP future.

Hackenberg,Drue

SP | **Atlanta** | EXP MLB DEBUT: 2025 | H/W: 6-2 220 | FUT: #4 starter | **7C**

Thrws R Age 22 — 2023 (2) Virginia Tech

Velo	Pitch	Grade
91-94	FB	+++
83-86	SU	+++
85-87	CU	++

Year	Lev	Team	W	L	Sv	IP	K	ERA	WHIP	BF/G	OBA	H%	S%	xERA	Ctl	Dom	Cmd	hr/9	BPV
2023	NCAA	Virginia Tech	5	8	0	85	99	5.71	1.63	25.3	320	43	65	5.56	2.7	10.5	3.8	0.8	132
2023	A	Augusta	0	0	0	5	12	0.00	0.96	9.8	170	53	100	0.98	3.5	20.8	6.0	0.0	298

Command/control groundball machine was 2nd round pick after stellar college career. Made it to Double-A during debut. Repeats 3/4 delivery with below-average extension. Primarily sinker heavy diet of FBs. Will mix in average 4-seam FB. Throws slurve, which likely becomes a true SL in ATL organization. CU is firm and usable.

Hall,DL

SP | **Baltimore** | EXP MLB DEBUT: 2022 | H/W: 6-2 210 | FUT: #2 SP/closer | **9D**

Thrws L Age 25 — 2017 (1) HS (GA)

Velo	Pitch	Grade
92-96	FB	++++
84-87	SL	++++
78-81	CB	++
83-86	CU	++

Year	Lev	Team	W	L	Sv	IP	K	ERA	WHIP	BF/G	OBA	H%	S%	xERA	Ctl	Dom	Cmd	hr/9	BPV
2022	AAA	Norfolk Tides	3	7	0	76	125	4.72	1.46	14.8	224	37	70	4.02	5.8	14.8	2.6	1.2	127
2022	MLB	Baltimore	1	1	1	13	19	6.14	1.74	5.5	314	48	61	4.91	4.1	13.0	3.2	0.0	141
2023	Rk	FCL Orioles B	1	0	0	3	8	0.00	1.00	5.7	106	68	100	0.40	6.0	24.0	4.0	0.0	288
2023	AAA	Norfolk Tides	1	2	1	49	70	4.22	1.39	12.1	216	31	74	3.87	5.5	12.9	2.3	1.3	101
2023	MLB	Baltimore	3	0	0	19	23	3.30	1.20	4.3	250	34	76	3.54	2.4	10.8	4.6	0.9	149

Athletic LHP made MLB debut, working successfully as RP. Not much has changed: has the stuff to be a frontline SP or high-leverage RP, but struggles throwing strikes with consistency. With his nasty offerings, even minor strides in command would go a long way. FB and SL both plus pitches. Only threw 60% strikes in minors with arsenal.

Hall,Tanner

SP | **Minnesota** | EXP MLB DEBUT: 2025 | H/W: 6-1 186 | FUT: #4 starter | **7C**

Thrws R Age 22 — 2023 (4) Southern Miss

Velo	Pitch	Grade
88-92	FB	+++
81-84	SL	++
81-83	CU	+++

Year	Lev	Team	W	L	Sv	IP	K	ERA	WHIP	BF/G	OBA	H%	S%	xERA	Ctl	Dom	Cmd	hr/9	BPV

Consistent, control-oriented SP with high floor and average pitch mix. Has outstanding ability to command FB to all quadrants of strike zone. More about pitch location than velocity or movement. Hits spots and induces weak contact. Likes to mix and match FB and CU while getting hitters to chase SL.

Hamel,Dominic

SP | **New York (N)** | EXP MLB DEBUT: 2024 | H/W: 6-2 206 | FUT: #4 starter | **7C**

Thrws R Age 25 — 2021 (3) Dallas Baptist

Velo	Pitch	Grade
92-94	FB	++++
81-83	SL	+++
76-78	CB	+++
84-86	CU	+++

Year	Lev	Team	W	L	Sv	IP	K	ERA	WHIP	BF/G	OBA	H%	S%	xERA	Ctl	Dom	Cmd	hr/9	BPV
2021	NCAA	Dallas Baptist	13	2	1	91	136	4.24	1.12	20.0	209	30	69	3.38	3.4	13.4	4.0	1.6	169
2021	Rk	FCL Mets	0	0	0	3	7	0.00	0.00	4.2	0	0			0.0	21.0		0.0	396
2022	A	St. Lucie	5	2	0	63	71	3.85	1.22	18.2	212	29	69	2.89	4.1	10.1	2.4	0.7	89
2022	A+	Brooklyn	5	1	0	55	74	2.61	1.09	19.6	184	30	73	1.53	4.1	12.1	3.0	0.0	125
2023	AA	Binghamton	8	6	0	124	160	3.85	1.27	19.5	236	34	72	3.44	3.6	11.6	3.3	0.9	131

Over-the-top RHP enjoyed solid development year at Double-A. Not the most fluid delivery but repeats well and throws strikes. Best pitch is 4-seam FB with plus vertical break. Complements FB with 3 secondaries. Horizontal SL is the best of the bunch with above-average upside. CU and CB are future average or fringe offerings.

Hampton,Chase

SP | **New York (A)** | EXP MLB DEBUT: 2024 | H/W: 6-2 220 | FUT: #3 starter | **8C**

Thrws R Age 22 — 2022 (6) Texas Tech

Velo	Pitch	Grade
92-94	FB	++++
84-86	SL	+++
88-90	CT	+++
78-81	CB	+++

Year	Lev	Team	W	L	Sv	IP	K	ERA	WHIP	BF/G	OBA	H%	S%	xERA	Ctl	Dom	Cmd	hr/9	BPV
2023	A+	Hudson Valley	2	1	0	47	77	2.68	1.00	19.9	190	32	79	2.25	3.1	14.7	4.8	1.0	201
2023	AA	Somerset	2	2	0	59	68	4.41	1.27	22.0	244	32	69	3.88	3.2	10.3	3.2	1.2	118

High 3/4s RHP enjoyed dynamic season in pro debut. Repeatable delivery despite longer arm action. 4-pitch pitcher. 4-seam FB combines flat-approach angle with plus ride and above-average run to pile up Ks. Secondaries are all in average-to-above bucket. SL is best pitch with plus sweep and command. CT is unique wrinkle for FB/SL combo.

Hancock,Emerson — SP — Seattle

EXP MLB DEBUT: 2023 | H/W: 6-4 213 | FUT: #3 starter | 8C

Thrws R Age 24
2020 (1) Georgia

Velo	Pitch	Grade
92-95	FB	+++
80-83	CB	+++
82-85	SL	+++
84-86	CU	+++

Year	Lev	Team	W	L	Sv	IP	K	ERA	WHIP	BF/G	OBA	H%	S%	xERA	Ctl	Dom	Cmd	hr/9	BPV
2021	A+	Everett	2	0	0	31	30	2.32	1.03	13.3	179	24	77	1.64	3.8	8.7	2.3	0.3	73
2021	AA	Arkansas	1	1	0	13	13	3.41	1.06	17.1	212	29	64	1.83	2.7	8.9	3.3	0.0	104
2022	AA	Arkansas	7	4	0	98	92	3.76	1.20	18.8	224	26	75	3.72	3.5	8.4	2.4	1.5	76
2023	AA	Arkansas	11	5	0	98	107	4.32	1.23	19.9	231	30	66	3.27	3.5	9.8	2.8	0.8	101
2023	MLB	Seattle	0	0	0	12	6	4.50	1.33	16.6	278	30	67	4.13	2.3	4.5	2.0	0.8	38

Tall, strong-armed SP who repeated AA and started 3 games in majors. Ended season early due to shoulder strain. Posted higher K rate thanks in part to better command and improved, sharp SL. CU has evolved into above average offering, though velocity backed up on FB. Has stuff, size and control to be solid mid-rotation option.

Hansen,Pete — SP — St. Louis

EXP MLB DEBUT: 2025 | H/W: 6-2 205 | FUT: #4 starter | 7D

Thrws L Age 23
2022 (3) Texas

Velo	Pitch	Grade
89-92	FB	+
80-83	SL	++++
72-75	CB	++
80-83	CU	++

Year	Lev	Team	W	L	Sv	IP	K	ERA	WHIP	BF/G	OBA	H%	S%	xERA	Ctl	Dom	Cmd	hr/9	BPV
2023	A	Palm Beach	11	3	0	112	126	3.13	1.17	19.5	225	30	76	3.00	3.1	10.1	3.2	0.8	115
2023	AAA	Memphis	0	0	0	1	0	0.00	0.00	2.8	0	0			0.0	0.0		0.0	18

Soft tossing lefty out of Texas thrives due to 4-pitch mix and ability to pound the strike zone. Works off low-90s FB that is well located but lacks movement and spin. Best offering is SL that is nasty vs LHB. CB and CU show potential but are underdeveloped right now. Solid pro debut bodes well.

Harrington,Thomas — SP — Pittsburgh

EXP MLB DEBUT: 2024 | H/W: 6-2 185 | FUT: #3 starter | 8C

Thrws R Age 22
2022 (1) Campbell

Velo	Pitch	Grade
92-95	FB	+++
78-82	CB	+++
81-84	SL	+++
86-88	CU	+++

Year	Lev	Team	W	L	Sv	IP	K	ERA	WHIP	BF/G	OBA	H%	S%	xERA	Ctl	Dom	Cmd	hr/9	BPV
2023	A	Bradenton	4	1	0	39	40	2.77	1.10	19.1	220	29	78	2.68	2.8	9.2	3.3	0.7	109
2023	A+	Greensboro	3	5	0	88	106	3.88	1.31	20.2	257	34	74	4.06	3.0	10.8	3.7	1.1	133

Athletic, durable SP with strong velocity and feel for pitching. Tends to allow inordinate number of flyballs but also is K artist. Sequences well and can find success with establishing control with CU. High spin rate on FB while sweeping SL can be used as chaser. Low ¾ delivery adds some deception and can be tough to make hard contact against.

Harrison,Kyle — SP — San Francisco

EXP MLB DEBUT: 2023 | H/W: 6-2 200 | FUT: #2 starter | 8A

Thrws L Age 22
2020 (3) HS (CA)

Velo	Pitch	Grade
93-96	FB	++++
84-86	SL	++++
85-88	CU	+++

Year	Lev	Team	W	L	Sv	IP	K	ERA	WHIP	BF/G	OBA	H%	S%	xERA	Ctl	Dom	Cmd	hr/9	BPV
2022	A+	Eugene	0	1	0	29	59	1.55	1.00	15.8	189	43	89	1.89	3.1	18.3	5.9	0.6	264
2022	AA	Richmond	4	2	0	84	127	3.11	1.18	18.7	202	31	80	3.07	4.2	13.6	3.3	1.2	150
2023	Rk	ACL Giants B	0	0	0	2	4	0.00	0.00	5.6	0	0			0.0	18.0		0.0	342
2023	AAA	Sacramento	1	3	0	65	105	4.69	1.53	14.2	220	35	73	4.37	6.6	14.5	2.2	1.4	100
2023	MLB	San Francisco	1	1	0	34	35	4.21	1.17	19.5	231	25	75	4.32	2.9	9.2	3.2	2.1	106

High-upside arm who reached majors and continues to show promise. Treated cautiously in minors but exhibits high-quality pitch mix with bat-missing ability. Lethal to LHH and enhances pitchability with lower arm slot and angle to plate. Allows high number of flyballs, but improved control and high K rate could lead to fronting rotation.

Harrison,Trevor — SP — Tampa Bay

EXP MLB DEBUT: 2027 | H/W: 6-4 225 | FUT: #4 starter | 7D

Thrws R Age 18
2023 (5) HS (FL)

Velo	Pitch	Grade
90-93	FB	+++
78-82	SL	+++
80-82	CU	+++

Year	Lev	Team	W	L	Sv	IP	K	ERA	WHIP	BF/G	OBA	H%	S%	xERA	Ctl	Dom	Cmd	hr/9	BPV

Physical RHP was drafted and signed out of commitment to Florida State. Frame is strong, close to projection. Utilizes low 3/4s slot in delivery with longer arm path. TAM will refine delivery. 3-pitch pitcher. FB has above-average running profile. CB has a chance at an above-average outcome with better shape. Throws fading CU with conviction.

Harvey,Ryan — SP — New York (A)

EXP MLB DEBUT: 2026 | H/W: 6-3 195 | FUT: Middle reliever | 6C

Thrws R Age 23
2022 (11) UC Santa Barbara

Velo	Pitch	Grade
90-92	FB	+++
81-83	SL	+++
82-84	CU	++
75-79	CB	++

Year	Lev	Team	W	L	Sv	IP	K	ERA	WHIP	BF/G	OBA	H%	S%	xERA	Ctl	Dom	Cmd	hr/9	BPV
2023	Rk	FCL Yankees	0	1	0	19	29	3.77	1.52	13.8	290	45	78	4.86	3.3	13.7	4.1	0.9	175
2023	A	Tampa	1	2	0	26	19	4.14	1.38	15.7	222	24	75	4.07	5.2	6.6	1.3	1.4	-4

Former college RP transitioned to pro SP role in 2023. Repeatable 3/4s delivery. Lives up in zone with flat-angled 4-seam FB with solid vertical riding action. Complements FB well with 2-plane slider and occasionally throws sweeping CB. SL projects to be average offering with CB less than that. Struggles throwing CU for strikes.

Hawkins,Garrett — SP — San Diego

EXP MLB DEBUT: 2025 | H/W: 6-5 230 | FUT: #3 starter | 8E

Thrws R Age 24
2021 (9) British Columbia

Velo	Pitch	Grade
92-95	FB	++++
81-85	SL	++
84-86	CU	+++

Year	Lev	Team	W	L	Sv	IP	K	ERA	WHIP	BF/G	OBA	H%	S%	xERA	Ctl	Dom	Cmd	hr/9	BPV
2020	NAIA	British Columbia	3	1	0	32	46	3.66	1.25	21.7	274	40	75	4.13	1.7	12.9	7.7	1.1	205
2021	Rk	ACL Padres	3	1	0	15	27	2.38	1.13	8.5	260	47	81	3.10	1.2	16.1	13.5	0.6	275
2022	A	Lake Elsinore	5	5	0	77	108	3.96	1.20	18.3	251	37	70	3.64	2.3	12.6	5.4	1.0	182
2022	A+	Fort Wayne	0	3	0	15	12	8.94	2.12	18.6	341	34	65	9.73	6.0	7.2	1.2	3.6	-14
2023	A+	Fort Wayne	0	2	0	15	15	3.60	1.53	16.3	287	35	81	5.14	3.6	9.0	2.5	1.2	83

Large-framed RHP who ended season in May due to lat strain. Has reliever risk due to lack of dependable secondary offerings. Explosive FB is best pitch and is enhanced by great extension in delivery. Tough on LHH with CU but struggles to repeat arm speed at times. SL comes and goes but has potential.

Haynes,Jagger — SP — San Diego

EXP MLB DEBUT: 2026 | H/W: 6-3 170 | FUT: #3 starter | 8E

Thrws L Age 21
2020 (5) HS (NC)

Velo	Pitch	Grade
91-94	FB	+++
81-83	SL	+++
81-85	CU	+++

Year	Lev	Team	W	L	Sv	IP	K	ERA	WHIP	BF/G	OBA	H%	S%	xERA	Ctl	Dom	Cmd	hr/9	BPV
2021	--	Did Not Play																	
2022	--	Did Not Play																	
2023	A	Lake Elsinore	0	3	0	25	29	3.94	1.35	9.5	237	32	72	3.54	4.3	10.4	2.4	0.7	89

Injury-prone but talented LHP who had 1st pro experience since 2020 draft. Ended season in late July, however, due to blister issues. Lottery ticket type with plus athleticism, size and projection. FB has plus potential along with SL. Has nice delivery and deceptive arm slot that can baffle hitters. Has to prove health to rise up prospect lists.

Hence,Tink — SP — St. Louis

EXP MLB DEBUT: 2024 | H/W: 6-1 185 | FUT: #2 starter | 9D

Thrws R Age 21
2020 (2) HS (AR)

Velo	Pitch	Grade
94-96	FB	+++++
77-79	CB	++++
82-85	SL	+++
82-84	CU	+++

Year	Lev	Team	W	L	Sv	IP	K	ERA	WHIP	BF/G	OBA	H%	S%	xERA	Ctl	Dom	Cmd	hr/9	BPV
2021	Rk	FCL Cardinals	0	1	1	8	14	9.00	1.75	4.6	328	54	46	6.19	3.4	15.8	4.7	1.1	210
2022	A	Palm Beach	0	1	0	52	81	1.38	0.88	12.1	174	31	84	1.06	2.6	14.0	5.4	0.2	200
2023	A+	Peoria	2	1	0	41	46	2.84	1.12	14.7	226	30	79	2.96	2.6	10.0	3.8	0.9	128
2023	AA	Springfield	2	5	0	54	53	5.49	1.52	19.5	282	34	66	5.16	3.7	8.8	2.4	1.3	78

Works primarily off a mid-90s FB that has plenty of late life. Backs up the heater with a plus upper-70s CB with good spin and late action and an improved low-80s CU. Concerns about his durability as a starter, but stuff can be electric. While there is work to be done here, the Cardinals don't have many arms like this and should be up in 2024.

Henderson,Logan — SP — Milwaukee

EXP MLB DEBUT: 2025 | H/W: 5-11 194 | FUT: #4 starter | 7C

Thrws R Age 22
2021 (4) McLennan CC

Velo	Pitch	Grade
91-94	FB	+++
79-83	SL	++
78-81	CU	++++

Year	Lev	Team	W	L	Sv	IP	K	ERA	WHIP	BF/G	OBA	H%	S%	xERA	Ctl	Dom	Cmd	hr/9	BPV
2022	Rk	ACL Brewers B	0	0	0	2	5	0.00	0.50	3.3	151	61	100		0.0	22.5		0.0	423
2022	A	Carolina	0	1	0	11	18	4.82	1.79	10.3	307	51	70	4.90	4.8	14.5	3.0	0.0	148
2023	A	Carolina	4	3	0	78	106	2.76	0.97	16.5	185	27	76	2.12	3.0	12.2	4.1	0.9	157

Short, live-armed SP who was terrific over last 3 months of season. Posted 2nd highest K% in org. Flat arm angle generates lively FB and plus CU features late tumble and drop. Doesn't have dependable breaking ball and stamina is in question due to injury history and shorter outings. Could be potent high leverage RP if desired.

Henry,Cole — SP — Washington

EXP MLB DEBUT: 2025 | H/W: 6-4 215 | FUT: Middle reliever | 7D

Thrws R Age 24
2020 (2) LSU

Velo	Pitch	Grade
91-94	FB	+++
81-83	SL	++
83-86	CU	+++

Year	Lev	Team	W	L	Sv	IP	K	ERA	WHIP	BF/G	OBA	H%	S%	xERA	Ctl	Dom	Cmd	hr/9	BPV
2022	AA	Harrisburg	0	0	0	23	28	0.78	0.60	11.3	71	10	92		3.5	10.9	3.1	0.4	119
2022	AAA	Rochester	1	0	0	8	6	4.50	1.38	16.8	285	33	70	4.67	2.3	6.8	3.0	1.1	79
2023	A	Fredericksburg	0	0	0	7	11	0.00	0.57	11.9	168	31	100	0.05	0.0	14.1		0.0	273
2023	A+	Wilmington	0	1	0	8	5	2.25	1.13	15.8	210	22	88	3.06	3.4	5.6	1.7	1.1	28
2023	AA	Harrisburg	0	2	0	18	21	10.44	1.99	8.7	311	37	48	7.85	6.5	10.4	1.6	2.5	31

Worked all the way back from 2022's thoracic outlet syndrome surgery; got feet wet and ended season in Double-A. Went from curveball to a harder slider; change-up had improved before surgery, when good control and a strong strikeout rate held some promise. All depends on holding up over a full season; some more reliever risk now.

Hernandez,Daysbel — RP — Atlanta

EXP MLB DEBUT: 2023 | H/W: 5-10 220 | FUT: Middle reliever | 6C

Thrws R Age 27
2017 FA (CU)

- 95-97 FB + + +
- 86-88 SL + + + +
- 88-90 CT + +

Year	Lev	Team	W	L	Sv	IP	K	ERA	WHIP	BF/G	OBA	H%	S%	xERA	Ctl	Dom	Cmd	hr/9	BPV
2021	AAA	Gwinnett	0	1	0	9	12	7.83	1.63	4.1	236	33	50	4.45	6.8	11.7	1.7	1.0	44
2023	A+	Rome	2	0	0	5	6	8.82	1.96	4.1	258	32	56	6.33	8.8	10.6	1.2	1.8	-30
2023	AA	Mississippi	1	0	2	14	19	0.00	0.64	4.0	92	16	100		3.2	12.2	3.8	0.0	151
2023	AAA	Gwinnett	0	0	0	5	11	1.76	0.98	3.9	122	37	80	0.55	5.3	19.4	3.7	0.0	224
2023	MLB	Atlanta	1	0	0	3	6	8.44	2.81	4.5	399	62	75	11.77	8.4	16.9	2.0	2.8	94

Hard-throwing RP made return from Tommy John surgery. Dominated upper levels, earning MLB callup. High 3/4s delivery with long arm path. Struggles maintaining slot. Two-plane SL best pitch with MiLB whiff rate of near 50%. Riding 4-seam FB has flat-angled approach. Tends to overthrow. Also mixes in CT to round our arsenal.

Herz,DJ — SP — Washington

EXP MLB DEBUT: 2024 | H/W: 6-2 175 | FUT: #4 starter | 7D

Thrws L Age 23
2019 (8) HS (NC)

- 90-94 FB + + +
- 82-85 SL + +
- 78-82 CU + + + +
- 78-81 CB +

Year	Lev	Team	W	L	Sv	IP	K	ERA	WHIP	BF/G	OBA	H%	S%	xERA	Ctl	Dom	Cmd	hr/9	BPV
2021	A+	South Bend	1	0	0	16	26	2.81	1.00	20.4	181	32	73	1.79	3.4	14.6	4.3	0.6	190
2022	A+	South Bend	2	2	0	63	99	2.28	1.11	14.6	156	27	81	1.67	5.3	14.1	2.7	0.4	130
2022	AA	Tennessee	1	4	0	31	42	8.37	1.83	16.1	214	29	54	5.11	9.5	12.1	1.3	1.4	-21
2023	AA	Harrisburg	2	2	0	35	53	2.56	1.14	17.4	168	29	77	1.72	5.1	13.6	2.7	0.3	124
2023	AA	Tennessee	1	1	0	59	80	3.97	1.42	17.9	220	33	73	3.38	5.6	12.2	2.2	0.6	85

Part of the return for Candelario in 2023, the athletic southpaw gets more Ks than expected due to elite deception via crossfire delivery and a masterful change-up. Unique arm angle and good extension makes his FB play up and sets up CU. SL the better of his two breakers; needs to command all pitches better to cut down on walks.

Heubeck,Peter — SP — Los Angeles (N)

EXP MLB DEBUT: 2025 | H/W: 6-3 170 | FUT: Setup reliever | 8E

Thrws R Age 21
2021 (3) HS (MD)

- 92-95 FB + + +
- 78-81 CB + + + +
- 83-85 CU + +

Year	Lev	Team	W	L	Sv	IP	K	ERA	WHIP	BF/G	OBA	H%	S%	xERA	Ctl	Dom	Cmd	hr/9	BPV
2021	Rk	ACL Dodgers	0	0	0	4	9	0.00	0.75	7.1	81	30	100		4.5	20.3	4.5	0.0	261
2022	A	Rancho Cuca	0	1	0	31	42	7.50	1.51	9.0	200	25	53	4.68	7.2	12.1	1.7	2.0	41
2023	A	Rancho Cuca	3	5	0	68	91	5.15	1.30	14.8	222	32	61	3.41	4.5	12.0	2.7	0.9	113
2023	A+	Great Lakes	2	2	0	17	16	8.47	1.76	13.0	305	35	54	6.86	4.8	8.5	1.8	2.1	42

Athletic, projectable frame. Comes at hitters from 3/4 arm slot with a short stride. Plus 12-to-6 CB is best offering with late break leading to swing-and-miss. FB sits at 92-95 with arm side run and carry. CU is below-average and needs to improve to remain a starter. Struggles with control and now owns a career 5.2 BB/9 making a move to relief likely.

Hill,Jaden — SP — Colorado

EXP MLB DEBUT: 2025 | H/W: 6-4 234 | FUT: Setup reliever | 8E

Thrws R Age 25
2021 (2) LSU

- 94-96 FB + + + +
- 86-88 SL + + +
- 80-83 CU + + +

Year	Lev	Team	W	L	Sv	IP	K	ERA	WHIP	BF/G	OBA	H%	S%	xERA	Ctl	Dom	Cmd	hr/9	BPV
2021		Did Not Play																	
2022	Rk	ACL Rockies	0	0	0	10	11	3.56	1.49	6.2	279	39	73	3.77	3.6	9.8	2.8	0.0	98
2022	A	Fresno	0	0	0	7	14	2.54	1.27	9.7	259	54	78	2.86	2.5	17.7	7.0	0.0	269
2023	A+	Spokane	0	9	0	43	57	9.58	1.83	12.6	307	40	49	7.19	5.2	11.9	2.3	2.3	91

Talented 2nd rounder can't stay healthy and took a huge step back. Had Tommy John surgery in 2021 and while velo is back in mid-90s, touching 99 with spin/carry up in the zone, command is well below average. SL flashes plus while CU has good late fade and sink. Inability to throw strikes clouds his future, which most likely will be in relief.

Hitt,Grayson — SP — Arizona

EXP MLB DEBUT: 2026 | H/W: 6-3 210 | FUT: #3 starter | 8E

Thrws L Age 22
2023 (4) Alabama

- 92-96 FB + + +
- 87-90 CT + + + +
- 73-76 CB + +
- 84-86 SL +

Year	Lev	Team	W	L	Sv	IP	K	ERA	WHIP	BF/G	OBA	H%	S%	xERA	Ctl	Dom	Cmd	hr/9	BPV

Lefty with big stuff projected as 1st round pick, went in 4th due to Tommy John surgery. FB gained velo before shutdown, CT served as true out pitch. Misses bats, but overall lack of command could force move to bullpen.

Hjerpe,Cooper — SP — St. Louis

EXP MLB DEBUT: 2025 | H/W: 6-3 200 | FUT: #3 starter | 8D

Thrws L Age 23
2022 (1) Oregon State

- 89-93 FB + + +
- 76-79 SL + + + +
- 74-76 CB + + +
- 79-82 CU + + +

Year	Lev	Team	W	L	Sv	IP	K	ERA	WHIP	BF/G	OBA	H%	S%	xERA	Ctl	Dom	Cmd	hr/9	BPV
2023	A+	Peoria	2	3	0	41	51	3.51	1.24	16.7	184	22	81	3.59	5.5	11.2	2.0	1.8	71

Showcased electric stuff in debut, but struggles with control and an elbow injury are red flags. Minor surgery cleaned out elbow and was back in action in the AFL. Slings it from a low 3/4 slot with crossfire action creating deception and allowing low-90s FB to play up. Best offering is a plus SL and shows feel for CU that tunnels well off the FB.

Hodge,Porter — SP — Chicago (N)

EXP MLB DEBUT: 2024 | H/W: 6-4 230 | FUT: #4 starter | 7C

Thrws R Age 23
2019 (13) HS (UT)

- 92-96 FB + + + +
- 82-85 SL + + + +
- 77-79 CB + +
- 86-88 CU +

Year	Lev	Team	W	L	Sv	IP	K	ERA	WHIP	BF/G	OBA	H%	S%	xERA	Ctl	Dom	Cmd	hr/9	BPV
2021	Rk	ACL Cubs	1	2	0	29	35	7.45	1.55	18.1	306	40	53	5.79	2.8	10.9	3.9	1.6	138
2021	A	Myrtle Beach	1	1	0	21	29	3.82	1.27	12.4	241	38	67	2.70	3.4	12.3	3.6	0.0	148
2022	A	Myrtle Beach	4	2	0	69	90	3.00	1.35	16.9	217	34	76	2.71	5.1	11.7	2.3	0.1	92
2022	A+	South Bend	3	3	0	40	51	2.02	1.05	19.4	187	27	85	2.11	3.6	11.4	3.2	0.7	127
2023	AA	Tennessee	6	7	0	80	103	5.16	1.41	9.7	221	33	61	3.10	5.5	11.6	2.1	0.3	78

Big, strong framed RHP took a step back after 2022 breakout. Drop and drive delivery with long arm action and a bit of crossfire that gives mid-90s heater late life up in the zone. Also cuts FB away from RHB. Plus sweeper gets plenty of swing-and-miss, but struggles to keep it in the zone. CB and CU flash above-average but need consistency.

Hoglund,Gunnar — SP — Oakland

EXP MLB DEBUT: 2024 | H/W: 6-4 220 | FUT: #3 starter | 8E

Thrws R Age 24
2021 (1) Mississippi

- 90-95 FB + + +
- 80-82 CB + + +
- 81-84 SL + + +
- 82-85 CU + +

Year	Lev	Team	W	L	Sv	IP	K	ERA	WHIP	BF/G	OBA	H%	S%	xERA	Ctl	Dom	Cmd	hr/9	BPV
2022	Rk	ACL Athletics	0	1	0	5	7	0.00	0.80	9.1	221	36	100	1.24	0.0	12.6		0.0	245
2022	A	Stockton	0	0	0	3	1	0.00	1.33	12.5	262	29	100	3.22	3.0	3.0	1.0	0.0	-9
2023	A	Stockton	1	5	0	43	27	7.52	1.53	15.6	315	33	53	6.25	2.1	5.6	2.7	1.9	63
2023	A+	Lansing	1	0	0	12	14	1.48	0.57	13.8	127	20	71		1.5	10.3	7.0	0.0	164
2023	AA	Midland	0	0	0	5	5	5.40	1.20	20.1	299	40	50	3.35	0.0	9.0		0.0	180

Injury-riddled RHP who pitched on 3 levels in first full season. Possesses well above average control but K rate has been disappointing. Should continue to improve as velocity returns and SL regains bite. CU could end up being best pitch but needs more innings to master. Got better as season evolved and one to keep an eye on.

Hollan,Hunter — SP — Cincinnati

EXP MLB DEBUT: 2026 | H/W: 6-5 200 | FUT: #4 starter | 7E

Thrws L Age 22
2023 (3) Arkansas

- 89-91 FB + + +
- 78-81 SL + + + +
- 72-74 CB + + +
- 84-86 CU + + +

Year	Lev	Team	W	L	Sv	IP	K	ERA	WHIP	BF/G	OBA	H%	S%	xERA	Ctl	Dom	Cmd	hr/9	BPV

Projectable, 3/4s LHP struggled maintaining velocity during college season. Thin frame, scouts hope he adds strength, playing up arsenal. Repeats crossfire delivery well. 4-pitch pitcher. 4-seam FB isn't flashy but commands well enough. Potentially plus sweeping SL and vertical breaking CB are best offerings. Has feel for CU.

Horton,Cade — SP — Chicago (N)

EXP MLB DEBUT: 2024 | H/W: 6-1 211 | FUT: #2 starter | 9C

Thrws R Age 22
2022 (1) Oklahoma

- 94-96 FB + + + +
- 84-86 SL + + + + +
- 80-83 CB + + +
- 83-85 CU +

Year	Lev	Team	W	L	Sv	IP	K	ERA	WHIP	BF/G	OBA	H%	S%	xERA	Ctl	Dom	Cmd	hr/9	BPV
2023	A	Myrtle Beach	0	0	0	14	21	1.28	0.85	12.9	167	27	91	1.35	2.6	13.4	5.3	0.6	190
2023	A+	South Bend	3	3	0	47	65	3.83	1.00	16.3	209	30	66	2.68	2.3	12.4	5.4	1.1	180
2023	AA	Tennessee	1	1	0	27	31	1.33	1.07	17.5	191	29	86	1.60	3.7	10.3	2.8	0.0	105

Strong, athletic hurler had impressive pro debut. Simple, repeatable mechanics with high ¾ arm slot and slight hesitation in delivery. Plus FB sits at 94-96 with arm side run and carry. Best secondary is a plus-plus SL that generates tons of swing-and-miss. CB and CU lag behind but show potential and should be in Chicago sooner than anticipated.

Hughes,Gabriel — SP — Colorado

EXP MLB DEBUT: 2025 | H/W: 6-4 220 | FUT: #5 SP/swingman | 7D

Thrws R Age 22
2022 (1) Gonzaga

- 93-95 FB + + + +
- 83-85 SL + + +
- 80-83 CU + +

Year	Lev	Team	W	L	Sv	IP	K	ERA	WHIP	BF/G	OBA	H%	S%	xERA	Ctl	Dom	Cmd	hr/9	BPV
2022	NCAA	Gonzaga	8	3	0	98	138	3.21	1.14	25.9	213	34	72	2.45	3.4	12.7	3.7	0.5	154
2022	A	Fresno	0	0	0	3	1	0.00	0.67	10.5	106	12	100		3.0	3.0	1.0	0.0	-9
2023	A+	Spokane	4	3	0	37	54	5.56	1.21	18.7	222	33	55	3.43	3.6	13.1	3.6	1.2	155
2023	AA	Hartford	2	2	0	29	29	7.14	1.55	21.1	294	34	58	6.21	3.4	9.0	2.6	2.2	88

10th pick in '22 had rough full-season debut, giving up 12 HR in 66.2 IP before Tommy John surgery in July. Prior to the injury featured a 94-96 mph FB with good cutting and sinking action. Backs up FB with an above-average slider and fringy CU. Given the injury and lack of a quality third offering, a move to relief would not be a huge surprise.

Humphries,Jackson — SP — Cleveland

EXP MLB DEBUT: 2026 | H/W: 6-1 200 | FUT: #4 starter | 7D

Thrws L Age 19
2022 (8) HS (NC)

Velo	Pitch	Grade
90-95	FB	+ + +
77-80	CB	+ + +
80-82	SL	+ + +
81-83	CU	+ +

Year	Lev	Team	W	L	Sv	IP	K	ERA	WHIP	BF/G	OBA	H%	S%	xERA	Ctl	Dom	Cmd	hr/9	BPV
2023	Rk	ACL Indians	0	6	0	33	48	5.69	1.54	16.1	243	38	61	3.88	5.7	13.0	2.3	0.5	99
2023	A	Lynchburg	0	1	0	23	24	5.43	1.21	15.6	234	29	56	3.56	3.1	9.3	3.0	1.2	102

Durable SP who fits CLE mold with good analytics. Lot of spin on all pitches, particularly FB, CB and SL. None are plus but all feature lots of movement. Has experienced difficulty with command, though should improve with more IP. Changes speeds and has advanced sequencing for age. Not much projection or hope for velo uptick.

Hurt,Kyle — SP — Los Angeles (N)

EXP MLB DEBUT: 2023 | H/W: 6-3 240 | FUT: #3 starter | 8D

Thrws R Age 25
2020 (5) USC

Velo	Pitch	Grade
94-96	FB	+ + + +
86-89	SL	+ + +
77-80	CB	+ + +
87-88	CU	+ + + +

Year	Lev	Team	W	L	Sv	IP	K	ERA	WHIP	BF/G	OBA	H%	S%	xERA	Ctl	Dom	Cmd	hr/9	BPV
2022	A+	Great Lakes	4	2	0	40	64	2.24	1.07	12.0	156	29	79	1.38	4.9	14.3	2.9	0.2	143
2022	AA	Tulsa	1	5	0	31	45	9.29	2.32	13.3	286	43	58	6.77	10.7	13.1	1.2	0.9	-37
2023	AA	Tulsa	2	3	0	65	110	4.15	1.28	14.0	214	37	70	3.25	4.6	15.2	3.3	1.0	169
2023	AAA	Oklahoma City	2	1	0	27	42	3.33	1.11	15.2	200	32	74	2.70	3.7	14.0	3.8	1.0	171
2023	MLB	Los Angeles	0	0	0	2	3	0.00	0.00	5.6	0	0			0.0	13.5		0.0	261

Strong, stocky frame with max-effort delivery. Flies open on release, resulting in command issues, but plus mid-90s FB has good carry and arm-side run. Change-up is best secondary with swing-and-miss action, while CB and SL are above average. FB/CU profile well in relief, but will remain a starter for now.

Hurter,Brant — SP — Detroit

EXP MLB DEBUT: 2024 | H/W: 6-6 250 | FUT: #5 SP/swingman | 7D

Thrws L Age 25
2021 (7) Georgia Tech

Velo	Pitch	Grade
92-94	FB	+ + +
81-83	SL	+ + +
82-85	CU	+

Year	Lev	Team	W	L	Sv	IP	K	ERA	WHIP	BF/G	OBA	H%	S%	xERA	Ctl	Dom	Cmd	hr/9	BPV
2022	A	Lakeland	3	3	0	42	57	2.99	0.95	15.9	223	33	72	2.45	1.3	12.2	9.5	0.9	203
2022	A+	West Michigan	4	1	0	50	62	3.23	1.10	17.9	237	35	70	2.54	2.0	11.1	5.6	0.4	165
2022	AA	Erie	0	2	0	13	17	8.18	1.89	15.6	361	50	54	6.75	2.7	11.6	4.3	0.7	153
2023	AA	Erie	6	7	0	118	133	3.28	1.19	18.2	245	34	73	3.07	2.5	10.1	4.0	0.5	133

LHP comes after hitters from a low 3/4 arm slot. Hides the ball well with a short arm action, but lacks extension and fluidity. Attacks with a sinker/sweeper mix with horizontal action. Two seamer sits at 92-94 and 4 seamer at 95-96, but lacks elite spin or carry. Mid-80s sweeper is best offering and below-average CU will need to improve to remain a SP.

Ingram,Kolton — RP — Los Angeles (A)

EXP MLB DEBUT: 2023 | H/W: 5-9 170 | FUT: Middle reliever | 6B

Thrws L Age 27
2019 (37) Columbus State

Velo	Pitch	Grade
91-94	FB	+ + +
80-83	SL	+ + +
85-87	CT	+ + +

Year	Lev	Team	W	L	Sv	IP	K	ERA	WHIP	BF/G	OBA	H%	S%	xERA	Ctl	Dom	Cmd	hr/9	BPV
2021	AA	Rocket City	0	0	4	14	17	1.28	1.06	4.6	185	28	87	1.50	3.8	10.9	2.8	0.0	110
2022	AA	Rocket City	6	2	10	60	73	2.69	0.93	4.5	187	25	76	2.03	2.5	10.9	4.3	0.9	146
2023	AA	Rocket City	1	1	2	27	38	2.66	1.33	4.9	182	29	80	2.43	6.3	12.6	2.0	0.3	75
2023	AAA	Salt Lake	2	3	2	33	39	3.25	1.17	6.0	204	29	73	2.51	4.1	10.6	2.6	0.5	99
2023	MLB	LA Angels	0	0	0	5	7	8.82	2.55	5.5	357	45	73	11.01	8.8	12.4	1.4	3.5	2

3/4s relief-only prospect made MLB debut after solid minor league season. 3/4s LHP with longer arm cirle, creates deception with cross-fire delivery and plus extension. 3-pitch arsenal. High spin 4-seam FB keeps hitters off balance. Sweeping SL is best pitch with plus horizontal break profile. Mixes CT in to stay honest against RHH.

Iriarte,Jairo — SP — San Diego

EXP MLB DEBUT: 2024 | H/W: 6-2 160 | FUT: #3 starter | 8D

Thrws R Age 22
2018 FA (VZ)

Velo	Pitch	Grade
92-96	FB	+ + + +
84-86	SL	+ +
83-87	CU	+ + +

Year	Lev	Team	W	L	Sv	IP	K	ERA	WHIP	BF/G	OBA	H%	S%	xERA	Ctl	Dom	Cmd	hr/9	BPV
2021	Rk	ACL Padres	0	1	0	21	25	4.71	1.19	10.5	233	33	58	2.80	3.0	10.7	3.6	0.4	130
2021	A	Lake Elsinore	0	4	0	9	9	27.00	3.44	14.1	496	55	15	17.90	6.0	9.0	1.5	5.0	18
2022	A	Lake Elsinore	4	7	0	91	109	5.14	1.37	18.2	244	32	65	4.21	4.1	10.8	2.6	1.3	100
2023	A+	Fort Wayne	3	3	0	61	77	3.10	1.28	17.9	225	34	75	2.79	4.1	11.4	2.8	0.3	111
2023	AA	San Antonio	0	1	0	29	51	4.33	1.31	9.2	204	38	67	2.86	5.3	15.8	3.0	0.6	160

Unheralded RHP who posted highest K% in org and reached AA in July. Increased velocity with added strength gains and has excellent extension in delivery. Pitches aggressively with FB yet has deceptive CU that drops dramatically late. Misses bats with all pitches and could use better command within zone. Will need to enhance SL to last as SP.

Izzi,Ashton — SP — Seattle

EXP MLB DEBUT: 2026 | H/W: 6-3 165 | FUT: #3 starter | 8E

Thrws R Age 20
2022 (4) HS (IL)

Velo	Pitch	Grade
91-95	FB	+ + +
81-84	SL	+ +
83-85	CU	+ +

Year	Lev	Team	W	L	Sv	IP	K	ERA	WHIP	BF/G	OBA	H%	S%	xERA	Ctl	Dom	Cmd	hr/9	BPV
2023	Rk	ACL Mariners	0	2	0	18	13	8.45	2.10	9.9	370	42	60	8.26	4.0	6.5	1.6	1.5	27

Tall, lean, projectable SP who has been treated cautiously since drafted. All about cleaning up delivery and adding velocity. More of a thrower than pitcher at present and has potential for plus FB and SL if he continues to improve. Command is well short of the mark and needs to find consistency with CU. Can vary arm speed.

Jacob,Alek — RP — San Diego

EXP MLB DEBUT: 2023 | H/W: 6-3 190 | FUT: Middle reliever | 6A

Thrws R Age 25
2021 (16) Gonzaga

Velo	Pitch	Grade
86-88	FB	+ +
71-75	SL	+ + +
71-76	CU	+ + + +

Year	Lev	Team	W	L	Sv	IP	K	ERA	WHIP	BF/G	OBA	H%	S%	xERA	Ctl	Dom	Cmd	hr/9	BPV
2022	A+	Fort Wayne	3	0	0	9	16	0.00	0.44	7.3	136	30	100		0.0	16.0		0.0	306
2022	AA	San Antonio	1	0	2	34	43	1.85	1.09	5.8	219	33	83	2.20	2.6	11.3	4.3	0.3	151
2022	AAA	El Paso	1	1	2	13	18	6.82	1.74	3.8	326	42	68	7.68	3.4	12.3	3.6	2.7	147
2023	AA	San Antonio	1	0	5	27	32	1.33	1.00	5.7	199	29	88	1.81	2.7	10.6	4.0	0.3	138
2023	MLB	San Diego	0	0	0	3	5	0.00	0.33	3.2	0	0	100		3.0	15.0	5.0	0.0	207

Funky sidearmer who reached majors despite return to AA to begin 2023. Ended year in late July due to elbow sprain. Works off FB featuring very heavy sink and armside run. Tough to elevate FB when in lower half. CU is plus offering and thrown with same arm speed while hiding ball in release. Sweepy SL is third pitch and just average.

Jang,Hyun Seok — SP — Los Angeles (N)

EXP MLB DEBUT: 2027 | H/W: 6-4 200 | FUT: #3 starter | 8D

Thrws R Age 20
2023 FA (KR)

Velo	Pitch	Grade
92-95	FB	+ + + +
77-80	CB	+ + +
84-87	SL	+ + +
82-85	CU	+ +

Year	Lev	Team	W	L	Sv	IP	K	ERA	WHIP	BF/G	OBA	H%	S%	xERA	Ctl	Dom	Cmd	hr/9	BPV

Korean hurler opted not to play in the KBO and sign with the Dodgers for $900,000. after winning gold in Asian Games earning an exemption from military service. FB sits in the low-to-mid 90s topping at 97. Backs up the FB with SL and CB, both of which project to be above-average to plus and a CU that needs work. Will make state-side debut in 2024.

Jarvis,Bryce — SP — Arizona

EXP MLB DEBUT: 2023 | H/W: 6-2 195 | FUT: #5 SP/swingman | 6C

Thrws R Age 26
2020 (1) Duke

Velo	Pitch	Grade
95-96	FB	+
84-85	SL	+ + +
84-86	CU	+ +
	CB	+

Year	Lev	Team	W	L	Sv	IP	K	ERA	WHIP	BF/G	OBA	H%	S%	xERA	Ctl	Dom	Cmd	hr/9	BPV
2021	AA	Amarillo	1	2	0	35	40	5.66	1.40	18.5	245	29	66	5.02	4.4	10.3	2.4	2.1	85
2022	AA	Amarillo	3	6	0	106	110	8.31	1.89	20.0	320	38	59	7.58	5.1	9.3	1.8	2.3	49
2023	AA	Amarillo	2	1	0	14	17	3.86	1.07	18.2	168	26	60	1.34	4.5	10.9	2.4	0.0	93
2023	AAA	Reno	7	5	0	92	96	5.28	1.50	16.6	262	33	66	4.48	4.5	9.4	2.1	1.0	65
2023	MLB	Arizona	2	1	0	23	12	3.10	0.99	8.0	176	17	75	2.38	3.5	4.7	1.3	1.2	8

Former 1st rounder reached MLB with solid AAA performance, but struggles with control despite easy delivery. Straight FB reaches solid mid-90s velo but is hittable, lacks deception. Uses SL to get batters to chase and whiff, but gives up plenty of contact on other pitches. Backend option or long reliever most likely.

Jarvis,Justin — SP — New York (N)

EXP MLB DEBUT: 2024 | H/W: 6-2 183 | FUT: #4 starter | 7D

Thrws R Age 24
2018 (5) HS (NC)

Velo	Pitch	Grade
93-95	FB	+ + +
80-82	SL	+ + +
74-76	CB	+ +
82-85	SP	+ + +

Year	Lev	Team	W	L	Sv	IP	K	ERA	WHIP	BF/G	OBA	H%	S%	xERA	Ctl	Dom	Cmd	hr/9	BPV
2022	A+	Wisconsin	9	8	0	121	134	4.02	1.29	20.7	235	29	74	4.01	3.8	10.0	2.6	1.4	95
2022	AA	Biloxi	2	1	0	20	16	2.70	1.50	21.6	210	26	83	3.35	6.8	7.2	1.1	0.5	-35
2023	AA	Biloxi	6	4	0	75	91	3.35	1.26	21.9	245	33	79	3.87	3.1	10.9	3.5	1.2	130
2023	AAA	Nashville	0	2	0	11	11	11.25	2.59	20.2	350	42	56	9.21	9.6	8.8	0.9	1.6	-83
2023	AAA	Syracuse	0	5	0	32	36	7.92	2.04	17.2	324	39	65	8.00	6.2	10.2	1.6	2.3	33

Over-the-top RHP acquired from MIL in mid-season trade struggled in Triple-A. Uphill delivery with long arm path and above-average extension. Lost release point in 2nd half. 4-pitch mix. Struggled with flat-angled 4-seam FB becoming too hittable. Lacks consistent swing-and-miss secondary since CU strike% is poor. Also throws CB and SL.

Jobe,Jackson — SP — Detroit

EXP MLB DEBUT: 2025 | H/W: 6-2 190 | FUT: #1 starter | 9D

Thrws R Age 21
2021 (1) HS (OK)

Velo	Pitch	Grade
93-96	FB	+ + + + +
80-83	SL	+ + + +
83-85	CU	+ + + +
	CT	+ + +

Year	Lev	Team	W	L	Sv	IP	K	ERA	WHIP	BF/G	OBA	H%	S%	xERA	Ctl	Dom	Cmd	hr/9	BPV
2022	A+	West Michigan	2	0	0	15	10	1.18	0.99	19.3	189	20	100	2.52	3.0	5.9	2.0	1.2	45
2023	Rk	FCL Tigers East	0	0	0	2	4	0.00	0.00	5.6	0	0			0.0	18.0		0.0	342
2023	A	Lakeland	0	1	0	16	20	2.25	1.06	10.4	237	32	87	3.18	1.7	11.3	6.7	1.1	175
2023	A+	West Michigan	2	3	0	40	54	3.60	1.05	19.4	257	35	74	3.82	0.7	12.2	18.0	1.6	218
2023	AA	Erie	0	0	0	6	6	0.00	0.67	20.9	191	27	100	0.59	0.0	9.0		0.0	180

When drafted featured a mid-90s heater and 3000 rpm breaking ball, but health and inconsistency clouded his future. After a delayed start in 2023 was one of the best pitchers in the minors. Vastly improved CU is now a plus offering and FB command is near elite. Also added a CT this year. Frontline starter potential if he can stay healthy.

Johnson,Marcus — SP — Tampa Bay

EXP MLB DEBUT: 2025 | H/W: 6-6 200 | FUT: #4 starter | 7C

Thrws R Age 23 — 2022 (4) Duke

Velo	Pitch	Grade
91-93	FB	+++
80-83	SL	+++
76-79	CB	+++
84-86	CU	+++

Year	Lev	Team	W	L	Sv	IP	K	ERA	WHIP	BF/G	OBA	H%	S%	xERA	Ctl	Dom	Cmd	hr/9	BPV
2022	NCAA	Duke	1	8	0	69	76	5.61	1.52	23.0	291	35	70	6.01	3.3	9.9	3.0	2.1	108
2022	Rk	FCL Marlins	0	1	0	4	5	8.78	2.20	10.3	302	43	56	5.89	8.8	11.0	1.3	0.0	-22
2022	A	Jupiter	1	2	0	12	24	5.21	1.16	16.0	170	33	58	2.90	5.2	17.9	3.4	1.5	199
2023	A	Charleston	5	6	0	130	114	3.74	1.16	19.9	262	32	70	3.51	1.5	7.9	5.4	0.8	121

Tall, high 3/4s RHP put up solid numbers in Low-A after being acquired in off-season trade. Former RP in college, improved command and delivery in spring. All four pitches project as average-to-above offerings. Features plus control of 4-seam FB with solid ride profile. Also command SL at high rate. Needs to find more whiffs in arsenal.

Johnson,Seth — SP — Baltimore

EXP MLB DEBUT: 2025 | H/W: 6-1 205 | FUT: #4 starter | 7C

Thrws R Age 25 — 2019 (1) Campbell

Velo	Pitch	Grade
94-97	FB	++++
75-78	CB	+++
84-87	SL	+++
82-85	CU	++

Year	Lev	Team	W	L	Sv	IP	K	ERA	WHIP	BF/G	OBA	H%	S%	xERA	Ctl	Dom	Cmd	hr/9	BPV
2022	A+	Bowling Green	1	1	0	27	41	3.00	1.26	15.7	232	35	83	3.78	3.7	13.7	3.7	1.3	165
2023	Rk	FCL Orioles B	0	0	0	1	2	0.00	1.00	3.8	262	55	100	2.23	0.0	18.0		0.0	342
2023	A	Delmarva	0	0	0	2	1	0.00	0.50	6.6	151	18	100		0.0	4.5		0.0	99
2023	A+	Aberdeen	0	1	0	4	7	8.78	1.71	9.3	257	47	43	3.97	6.6	15.4	2.3	0.0	117
2023	AA	Bowie	0	0	0	3	4	3.00	1.67	13.5	262	31	100	6.79	6.0	12.0	2.0	3.0	72

Former first round pick struggled during late season return from Tommy John surgery. When healthy, possesses plus FB that touches upper-90s and a SL that is a near-plus offering too. A low-effort, over-the-top delivery where his arm stays on time gives good shot to stick as RP if health returns to pre surgery levels.

Jones,Jared — SP — Pittsburgh

EXP MLB DEBUT: 2024 | H/W: 6-1 190 | FUT: #2 starter | 8B

Thrws R Age 22 — 2020 (2) HS (CA)

Velo	Pitch	Grade
94-98	FB	++++
80-82	CB	+++
89-90	SL	+++
88-89	CU	++

Year	Lev	Team	W	L	Sv	IP	K	ERA	WHIP	BF/G	OBA	H%	S%	xERA	Ctl	Dom	Cmd	hr/9	BPV
2021	A	Bradenton	3	6	0	66	103	4.64	1.47	15.7	253	41	69	4.10	4.6	14.0	3.0	0.8	146
2022	A+	Greensboro	5	7	0	122	142	4.64	1.36	19.6	250	32	70	4.36	3.8	10.5	2.8	1.4	105
2023	AA	Altoona	1	4	0	44	47	2.24	1.09	17.2	205	27	82	2.38	3.3	9.6	2.9	0.6	102
2023	AAA	Indianapolis	4	5	0	82	99	4.72	1.32	21.2	242	33	66	3.76	3.7	10.9	2.9	1.0	113

Tied for most K in org and had higher K rate in AAA than AA where he had better ERA. Brings solid pitch mix to mound highlighted by exceptional FB. Mixes two breaking balls, and hard SL could evolve to plus status. Repeats arm speed and slot on CU but can overthrow. Improving command overall but still work to be done.

Joyce,Ben — RP — Los Angeles (A)

EXP MLB DEBUT: 2023 | H/W: 6-5 225 | FUT: Closer | 8E

Thrws R Age 23 — 2022 (3) Tennessee

Velo	Pitch	Grade
98-102	FB	+++++
87-91	SL	++++
88-91	CT	+++

Year	Lev	Team	W	L	Sv	IP	K	ERA	WHIP	BF/G	OBA	H%	S%	xERA	Ctl	Dom	Cmd	hr/9	BPV
2022	NCAA	Tennessee	2	1	0	32	53	2.24	1.00	4.5	166	26	89	2.40	3.9	14.9	3.8	1.4	179
2022	AA	Rocket City	1	0	1	13	20	2.08	1.15	4.0	231	40	80	2.25	2.8	13.8	5.0	0.0	192
2023	A	Inland Empire	0	0	0	2	2	0.00	1.00	3.8	151	22	100	0.99	4.5	9.0	2.0	0.0	59
2023	AA	Rocket City	0	1	4	15	24	4.74	1.32	4.5	140	24	63	2.18	7.7	14.2	1.8	0.6	66
2023	MLB	LA Angels	1	1	0	10	10	5.40	1.80	3.9	242	31	71	4.91	8.1	9.0	1.1	0.9	-39

Flame-throwing RP who averages 100 MPH on FB struggled to throw strikes in 2023. Relies heavily on 2-seam FB with plus arm-side run but poor command. Strike rate on pitch was under 55% in minors. Varies between sweeping SL and CT in the same velocity band. SL is plus pitch but plays down due to FB command.

Joyce,Jimmy — SP — Seattle

EXP MLB DEBUT: 2024 | H/W: 6-2 210 | FUT: #4 starter | 7D

Thrws R Age 25 — 2021 (16) Hofstra

Velo	Pitch	Grade
92-94	FB	+++
82-84	CB	++
82-84	CU	+++

Year	Lev	Team	W	L	Sv	IP	K	ERA	WHIP	BF/G	OBA	H%	S%	xERA	Ctl	Dom	Cmd	hr/9	BPV
2021	A+	Everett	0	0	0	17	25	3.68	1.35	17.8	261	39	76	4.12	3.2	13.2	4.2	1.1	170
2022	A	Modesto	0	1	0	8	7	3.33	1.60	17.9	208	27	77	3.16	7.8	7.8	1.0	0.0	-52
2022	A+	Everett	7	11	0	112	133	5.78	1.36	20.4	251	33	58	4.12	3.8	10.7	2.8	1.1	108
2023	A+	Everett	2	0	0	39	54	1.61	0.97	16.5	203	30	91	2.32	2.3	12.4	5.4	0.9	180
2023	AA	Arkansas	0	3	0	30	29	3.87	1.29	17.7	254	33	68	3.23	3.0	8.6	2.9	0.3	93

Returned to High-A to begin season and made huge improvement before earning promotion to AA midseason. Average stuff plays up due to unusual delivery. Lot of pitch movement and nothing comes out of hand straight. CU has excellent fading action and tough to square up for RHH. No single pitch grades as plus.

Juarez,Victor — SP — Colorado

EXP MLB DEBUT: 2026 | H/W: 6-0 173 | FUT: #4 starter | 7D

Thrws R Age 20 — 2019 FA (MX)

Velo	Pitch	Grade
91-93	FB	++
75-78	CB	+++
83-86	CU	+++

Year	Lev	Team	W	L	Sv	IP	K	ERA	WHIP	BF/G	OBA	H%	S%	xERA	Ctl	Dom	Cmd	hr/9	BPV
2021	Rk	ACL Rockies	0	1	0	10	13	6.30	1.40	14.1	316	42	58	5.78	0.9	11.7	13.0	1.8	204
2021	Rk	DSL Colorado	2	0	0	26	34	0.69	0.65	13.0	130	22	88		2.1	11.7	5.7	0.0	173
2022	A	Fresno	6	5	0	103	100	4.98	1.31	20.3	260	31	65	4.31	2.9	8.7	3.0	1.3	97
2023	A+	Spokane	6	6	0	91	94	6.41	1.66	20.4	311	38	64	6.17	3.5	9.3	2.7	1.6	92

Polished hurler works from a high ¾ arm slot and gets arm side ride and run on low-90s FB. Repeats delivery well with a short stride and close to max effort, but does have some less than ideal head movement. Potentially plus CU and sharp, late breaking CB give him two solid secondaries. Gave up 16 HR in 91 IP and will need to show better control.

Juenger,Hayden — RP — Toronto

EXP MLB DEBUT: 2024 | H/W: 6-0 180 | FUT: Setup reliever | 7D

Thrws R Age 23 — 2021 (6) Missouri State

Velo	Pitch	Grade
93-96	FB	+++
86-88	SL	+++
85-87	CU	++

Year	Lev	Team	W	L	Sv	IP	K	ERA	WHIP	BF/G	OBA	H%	S%	xERA	Ctl	Dom	Cmd	hr/9	BPV
2021	NCAA	Missouri St	2	2	6	21	31	3.86	1.24	5.3	252	38	74	3.95	2.6	13.3	5.2	1.3	188
2021	A+	Vancouver	2	0	0	20	34	2.70	0.75	6.5	163	33	60	0.43	1.8	15.3	8.5	0.0	245
2022	AA	New Hampshire	0	5	0	56	67	4.02	1.09	10.9	202	24	73	3.58	3.4	10.8	3.2	1.9	121
2022	AAA	Buffalo	3	2	2	32	33	3.35	1.21	7.2	202	23	82	3.66	4.5	9.2	2.1	1.7	63
2023	AAA	Buffalo	5	2	2	75	92	6.35	1.66	6.2	289	39	63	5.59	4.7	11.0	2.4	1.3	90

Short RHP who was converted to RP in AAA. Had disastrous season as FB became flat and couldn't find consistency with SL. Hitters able to square up pitches while walk rate regressed. Still has pitch mix to be lethal, particularly to RHH. Firm CU has chance to become solid offering. Has demonstrated durability with multiple innings.

Keener,Seth — SP — Chicago (A)

EXP MLB DEBUT: 2026 | H/W: 6-2 195 | FUT: #4 starter | 7D

Thrws R Age 22 — 2023 (3) Wake Forest

Velo	Pitch	Grade
91-95	FB	+++
82-85	SL	+++
83-87	CU	+++

Year	Lev	Team	W	L	Sv	IP	K	ERA	WHIP	BF/G	OBA	H%	S%	xERA	Ctl	Dom	Cmd	hr/9	BPV
2023	NCAA	Wake Forest	8	2	1	70	94	2.70	0.87	11.2	172	26	70	1.34	2.6	12.1	4.7	0.5	166
2023	Rk	ACL White Sox	1	0	0	6	7	1.50	0.67	5.2	106	17	75		3.0	10.5	3.5	0.0	126
2023	A	Kannapolis	0	1	0	6	7	7.38	1.80	9.4	343	44	60	6.98	3.0	10.3	3.5	1.5	124

Low 3/4s RHP with advanced feel for spin made solid pro debut after draft. Repeatable delivery despite longer arm circle. Stays on time through release. Heavy SL usage in college continued into pros. SL is an above-average offering with solid gyro movement profile. Struggles to command flat-angled FB. Has feel for late fading CU.

Keller,Seth — SP — Atlanta

EXP MLB DEBUT: 2026 | H/W: 5-10 180 | FUT: #4 starter | 7E

Thrws R Age 19 — 2022 (6) HS (VA)

Velo	Pitch	Grade
88-92	FB	+++
83-85	CU	+++
78-80	CB	++
81-83	SL	++

Year	Lev	Team	W	L	Sv	IP	K	ERA	WHIP	BF/G	OBA	H%	S%	xERA	Ctl	Dom	Cmd	hr/9	BPV
2022	Rk	FCL Braves	0	0	0	2	1	18.00	2.50	5.3	0	0	20	3.49	22.5	4.5	0.2	0.0	-509
2023	A	Augusta	2	4	0	46	32	6.26	1.54	12.5	253	31	56	3.78	5.3	6.3	1.2	0.2	-12

Raw, athletic hurler struggled mightily in full-season debut. Low 3/4s delivery with below average extension, lacking deception and refinement. 2-seam FB has solid arm-side run profile but struggles throwing for strikes. Is challenged to spin breaking pitches. SL more likely to develop than CB. Has a feel for CU but pitch is extremely raw.

Kelley,Jared — RP — Chicago (A)

EXP MLB DEBUT: 2025 | H/W: 6-3 230 | FUT: Middle reliever | 6C

Thrws R Age 22 — 2020 (2) HS (TX)

Velo	Pitch	Grade
93-95	FB	+++
83-85	SL	+++
79-82	CU	+++

Year	Lev	Team	W	L	Sv	IP	K	ERA	WHIP	BF/G	OBA	H%	S%	xERA	Ctl	Dom	Cmd	hr/9	BPV
2021	A	Kannapolis	0	5	0	21	25	6.86	2.05	10.2	262	37	64	5.34	9.4	10.7	1.1	0.4	-44
2022	A	Kannapolis	1	4	0	64	59	3.36	1.43	15.2	223	27	79	3.70	5.6	8.3	1.5	0.8	15
2022	AA	Birmingham	0	2	0	12	12	4.50	1.67	17.9	278	33	78	5.63	5.3	9.0	1.7	1.5	38
2023	A+	Winston Salem	2	4	0	42	47	5.14	1.45	15.0	233	32	63	3.47	5.4	10.1	1.9	0.4	55
2023	AA	Birmingham	0	3	0	23	28	11.74	2.74	8.0	344	46	55	9.05	11.3	11.0	1.0	1.2	-91

XXL frame, former 2nd round pick, moved to pen fulltime in 2023. Continues to be averse to throwing strikes. Struggles repeating high 3/4s delivery, which is a lot of the issues. However, throws hard with poor 2-seam and 4-seam FB shape. Best present offering is CU but better hitters lay off late fading movement. Also throws solid SL.

Kelly,Antoine — RP — Texas

EXP MLB DEBUT: 2024 | H/W: 6-5 205 | FUT: Setup reliever | 7D

Thrws L Age 24 — 2019 (2) Wabash Valley CC

Velo	Pitch	Grade
96-99	FB	++++
84-87	SL	+++

Year	Lev	Team	W	L	Sv	IP	K	ERA	WHIP	BF/G	OBA	H%	S%	xERA	Ctl	Dom	Cmd	hr/9	BPV
2021	A+	Wisconsin	0	1	0	1	3	65.45	5.45	9.1	492	97		17.97	24.5	24.5	1.0	0.0	-203
2022	A+	Wisconsin	2	4	0	91	119	3.86	1.23	19.4	190	28	69	2.52	5.1	11.8	2.3	0.6	91
2022	AA	Frisco	0	0	0	18	24	7.42	1.70	11.8	190	31	52	3.15	9.4	11.9	1.3	0.0	-22
2023	AA	Frisco	3	1	11	50	69	1.97	1.18	4.7	207	31	87	2.70	3.9	12.4	3.1	0.7	134
2023	AAA	Round Rock	0	0	0	6	10	2.90	1.45	4.4	314	52	78	4.17	1.5	14.5	10.0	0.0	240

Profile has remained "if only he had command" but seemingly found it in 2023. Plus 97-mph FB and SL have screamed impact reliever, but poor command held everything back. Improved strike-throwing as the season went on. If command gains hold, he's a setup option in 2024 and beyond.

Kempner,William | RP | San Francisco | EXP MLB DEBUT: 2024 | H/W: 6-0 222 | FUT: Setup reliever | 7D

Thrws R Age 22
2022 (3) Gonzaga

Velo	Pitch	Grade
93-96	FB	++++
84-88	SL	+++
85-87	CU	+

Year	Lev	Team	W	L	Sv	IP	K	ERA	WHIP	BF/G	OBA	H%	S%	xERA	Ctl	Dom	Cmd	hr/9	BPV
2022	Rk	ACL Giants B	1	0	0	3	5	2.90	1.94	7.4	314	52	83	5.39	5.8	14.5	2.5	0.0	123
2022	A	San Jose	0	0	0	5	6	6.92	1.92	8.2	290	37	67	6.66	6.9	10.4	1.5	1.7	18
2023	A	San Jose	1	3	1	27	29	4.67	1.33	8.0	216	31	61	2.56	5.0	9.7	1.9	0.0	57
2023	A+	Eugene	3	2	0	34	47	2.91	1.21	6.0	226	32	83	3.58	3.4	12.4	3.6	1.3	149
2023	AA	Richmond	0	0	0	1	2	7.50	4.17	8.4	470	68	80	14.22	15.0	15.0	1.0	0.0	-117

Short, strong RP who pitched mostly out of pen. Uses unusual delivery and sidearm slot to deceive hitters. May have one of best FB in org with high spin and lethal movement. Sweeping SL can miss bats, though command and control are sub-par. Lot of effort in delivery and likely to stick in bullpen full time.

Kennedy,Michael | SP | Pittsburgh | EXP MLB DEBUT: 2027 | H/W: 6-1 205 | FUT: #4 starter | 7C

Thrws L Age 19
2022 (4) HS (NY)

Velo	Pitch	Grade
88-92	FB	+++
79-82	SL	+++
80-82	CU	+++

Year	Lev	Team	W	L	Sv	IP	K	ERA	WHIP	BF/G	OBA	H%	S%	xERA	Ctl	Dom	Cmd	hr/9	BPV
2023	Rk	FCL Pirates B	2	1	0	42	55	2.14	1.05	14.8	174	27	79	1.52	4.1	11.8	2.9	0.2	120
2023	A	Bradenton	0	0	0	4	8	2.20	1.95	9.8	147	36	88	3.27	13.2	17.6	1.3	0.0	-22

Savvy, advanced LHP who pitches above age. May not have high ceiling but combats hitters with varying velocities and angles. Has short arm action which generates sneaky FB with riding life up in zone. SL can be good but not consistent. Repeats delivery which bodes well for CU. Mixes offerings to keep hitters off-guard.

Kent,Barrett | SP | Los Angeles (A) | EXP MLB DEBUT: 2026 | H/W: 6-4 215 | FUT: #4 starter | 7E

Thrws R Age 19
2023 (8) HS (TX)

Velo	Pitch	Grade
90-93	FB	+++
82-84	SL	+++
81-83	CU	+++

Year	Lev	Team	W	L	Sv	IP	K	ERA	WHIP	BF/G	OBA	H%	S%	xERA	Ctl	Dom	Cmd	hr/9	BPV
2023	Rk	ACL Angels	1	0	0	4	5	0.00	1.19	8.4	144	23	100	1.39	6.4	10.7	1.7	0.0	37
2023	A	Inland Empire	0	0	0	4	5	0.00	0.75	14.3	151	24	100	0.34	2.3	11.3	5.0	0.0	160

Tall, projectable RHP rode big prep season into nearly $1 million signing bonus. 3/4s delivery with solid athleticism and room to grow into frame. 3-pitch pitcher in pro debut, all projecting to be average-or-better offerings. Varies between 2 FBs, both fairly raw offerings. CU is the best present offering with late-fading action.

Kent,Zak | SP | Texas | EXP MLB DEBUT: 2024 | H/W: 6-3 208 | FUT: #5 SP/swingman | 6B

Thrws R Age 26
2019 (9) Va Military Inst.

Velo	Pitch	Grade
90-93	FB	++
83-87	SL	+++
86-91	CT	++
79-83	CB	++

Year	Lev	Team	W	L	Sv	IP	K	ERA	WHIP	BF/G	OBA	H%	S%	xERA	Ctl	Dom	Cmd	hr/9	BPV
2021	AA	Frisco	0	4	0	28	39	5.43	1.52	20.4	299	38	76	6.85	2.9	12.4	4.3	2.9	164
2022	AA	Frisco	2	3	0	82	87	4.71	1.37	18.1	264	33	69	4.41	3.3	9.5	2.9	1.2	101
2022	AAA	Round Rock	1	1	0	27	23	1.67	1.11	21.2	183	22	89	2.25	4.3	7.7	1.8	0.7	39
2023	Rk	ACL Rangers	0	0	0	6	9	10.16	1.77	9.5	314	37	50	9.09	4.4	13.1	3.0	4.4	136
2023	AAA	Round Rock	0	1	0	34	34	3.97	1.06	13.2	213	26	66	2.83	2.6	9.0	3.4	1.1	109

Despite still starting, he is assuredly a bullpen piece. Four-seamer plays a bit down to more average in rotation, with new two-seamer to get weak contact. The secondaries have lots of spin, led by his plus 85-mph SL with lesser used CB & CH also. Multiple injuries have stunted development and FB would play up in bullpen, only needing SL for leverage.

Kerkering,Orion | RP | Philadelphia | EXP MLB DEBUT: 2023 | H/W: 6-2 204 | FUT: Closer | 9C

Thrws R Age 23
2022 (5) South Florida

Velo	Pitch	Grade
96-99	FB	++++
85-88	SL	+++++

Year	Lev	Team	W	L	Sv	IP	K	ERA	WHIP	BF/G	OBA	H%	S%	xERA	Ctl	Dom	Cmd	hr/9	BPV
2023	A	Clearwater	1	0	4	10	18	0.00	0.30	3.5	66	16	100		0.9	16.0	18.0	0.0	283
2023	A+	Jersey Shore	2	0	3	20	27	1.79	0.95	4.2	187	27	88	2.05	2.7	12.1	4.5	0.9	163
2023	AA	Reading	0	1	7	22	33	2.05	1.09	4.1	234	37	86	2.91	2.0	13.5	6.6	0.8	206
2023	AAA	Lehigh Valley	1	0	0	1	1	0.00	2.00	4.8	415	52	100	7.49	0.0	9.0		0.0	180
2023	MLB	Philadelphia	1	0	0	3	6	0.00	1.33	4.2	191	45	100	2.18	6.0	18.0	3.0	0.0	180

Definition of "meteoric rise." Pitched in all four MiLB full-season levels, and finished in MLB bullpen. High-80s slider is elite breaking pitch with top-level chase and whiff rates. Plus fastball is consistently high 90s (tops at 99) with ride and swing-and-miss characteristics. Around the strike zone with everything. Impact reliever.

Kilian,Caleb | SP | Chicago (N) | EXP MLB DEBUT: 2022 | H/W: 6-4 180 | FUT: #5 SP/swingman | 6C

Thrws R Age 26
2019 (8) Texas Tech

Velo	Pitch	Grade
93-95	FB	+++
75-77	CB	+++
87-89	CT	++
83-86	CU	+

Year	Lev	Team	W	L	Sv	IP	K	ERA	WHIP	BF/G	OBA	H%	S%	xERA	Ctl	Dom	Cmd	hr/9	BPV
2021	AA	Richmond	3	2	0	63	64	2.43	0.94	21.5	223	30	74	1.92	1.1	9.1	8.0	0.3	152
2022	AAA	Iowa	5	4	0	106	125	4.24	1.57	17.9	265	37	73	4.34	5.0	10.6	2.1	0.6	74
2022	MLB	Chicago (N)	0	2	0	11	9	10.54	2.07	18.1	260	33	43	5.01	9.7	7.3	0.8	0.0	-113
2023	AAA	Iowa	8	3	0	120	95	4.57	1.32	19.9	266	30	69	4.41	2.7	7.1	2.6	1.3	73
2023	MLB	Chicago (N)	0	1	0	5	5	17.65	2.94	9.8	475	58	33	11.32	3.5	8.8	2.5	0.0	82

Struggled in 2nd stint in MLB. Continues to work primarily off a mid-90s FB, but overall his stuff continues to trend in the wrong direction and gave up a career worst 17 HR in 24 starts. FB sits at 93-95 with good sink and tops at 98. Mixes in above-average CB, CT, and below-average CU. Most likely destined to a relief role in 2024.

Klassen ,George | SP | Philadelphia | EXP MLB DEBUT: 2025 | H/W: 6-2 170 | FUT: Middle reliever | 8E

Thrws R Age 22
2023 (6) Minnesota

Velo	Pitch	Grade
96-98	FB	++++
83-88	SL	++
82-86	CB	++

Year	Lev	Team	W	L	Sv	IP	K	ERA	WHIP	BF/G	OBA	H%	S%	xERA	Ctl	Dom	Cmd	hr/9	BPV

Pumps gas but too often misses the tank. High-90s FB that touches triple digits is the appeal here, but lacks ideal shape at present and it plays below its velo. Also has two below-average secondaries in SL/CB that also miss their mark often. A player development challenge for sure, to turn pure arm strength into a usable pitcher.

Kloffenstein,Adam | SP | St. Louis | EXP MLB DEBUT: 2024 | H/W: 6-5 243 | FUT: #5 SP/swingman | 7D

Thrws R Age 23
2018 (3) HS (TX)

Velo	Pitch	Grade
90-93	FB	+++
80-83	SL	+++
	CB	+
83-85	CU	++

Year	Lev	Team	W	L	Sv	IP	K	ERA	WHIP	BF/G	OBA	H%	S%	xERA	Ctl	Dom	Cmd	hr/9	BPV
2021	A+	Vancouver	7	7	0	101	107	6.23	1.55	19.2	252	33	59	4.41	5.4	9.5	1.8	0.9	43
2022	A+	Vancouver	0	2	0	26	30	3.81	1.46	18.6	276	36	79	4.97	3.5	10.4	3.0	1.4	111
2022	AA	New Hampshire	2	5	0	86	88	6.07	1.66	20.3	288	36	65	5.53	4.7	9.2	2.0	1.3	57
2023	AA	New Hampshire	5	5	0	89	105	3.24	1.27	21.4	239	33	77	3.44	3.4	10.6	3.1	0.8	116
2023	AAA	Memphis	2	1	0	39	35	3.00	1.28	17.8	209	23	84	3.66	4.8	8.1	1.7	1.4	33

Big bodied hurler acquired as part of J. Hicks deal. Solid 4-pitch mix, but none are plus. Bumpy mechanics with close to max effort release results in below-average command - 4.3 BB/9. Low-90s sinking FB bores in on RHB. SL/Sweeper is offering while CT and CU are average at best. FB/SL mix does get swing-and-miss and now owns a career 9.6 K/9.

Knack,Landon | SP | Los Angeles (N) | EXP MLB DEBUT: 2024 | H/W: 6-2 220 | FUT: #4 starter | 8D

Thrws R Age 26
2020 (2) East Tenn State

Velo	Pitch	Grade
92-95	FB	+++
83-85	CB	+
76-78	SL	+++
80-83	CU	+++

Year	Lev	Team	W	L	Sv	IP	K	ERA	WHIP	BF/G	OBA	H%	S%	xERA	Ctl	Dom	Cmd	hr/9	BPV
2021	A+	Great Lakes	5	0	0	39	55	2.53	0.92	14.7	219	34	74	1.95	1.1	12.6	11.0	0.5	214
2021	AA	Tulsa	2	1	0	22	27	4.46	0.99	14.1	233	27	69	4.18	1.2	10.9	9.0	2.4	182
2022	AA	Tulsa	2	10	0	64	80	5.05	1.42	16.0	261	36	66	4.39	3.8	11.2	3.0	1.1	118
2023	AA	Tulsa	2	0	0	57	61	2.21	0.95	17.9	207	28	78	1.91	1.9	9.6	5.1	0.5	140
2023	AAA	Oklahoma City	3	1	0	43	38	2.93	1.44	18.3	266	31	86	4.68	3.8	8.0	2.1	1.3	59

Thick-bodied hurler rocks back with a high leg kick but not much extension from high 3/4 arm slot and has some effort to delivery. Mid-90s FB is best offering with arm-side run and horizontal carry. Sink on CU gives it potential, but seeks consistency. CB and above-average SL round out the arsenal. Stint at AAA looks better than it was.

Knorr,Michael | SP | Houston | EXP MLB DEBUT: 2025 | H/W: 6-5 245 | FUT: #4 starter | 7E

Thrws R Age 23
2022 (3) Coastal Carolina

Velo	Pitch	Grade
94-96	FB	++
85-87	SL	+++
76-78	CB	+++
85-87	CU	++

Year	Lev	Team	W	L	Sv	IP	K	ERA	WHIP	BF/G	OBA	H%	S%	xERA	Ctl	Dom	Cmd	hr/9	BPV
2023	A	Fayetteville	2	0	0	17	24	2.63	1.17	17.1	212	35	75	2.07	3.7	12.6	3.4	0.0	146
2023	A+	Asheville	1	5	0	41	54	4.61	1.37	15.6	252	33	73	4.73	3.7	11.9	3.2	1.8	131

Imposing righty showed impressive stuff before July injury cut season short. Repeatable delivery with quick arm action. Mid-90s FB shows decent movement. SL and CB are his bread and butter, getting plenty of chases and whiffs. Short pro track record, but could open 2024 in Double-A given in-game success. One to watch.

Knoth,Josh | SP | Milwaukee | EXP MLB DEBUT: 2028 | H/W: 6-1 190 | FUT: #2 starter | 8D

Thrws R Age 18
2023 (1) HS (NY)

Velo	Pitch	Grade
92-96	FB	+++
79-81	CB	+++
81-84	SL	++++
85-87	CU	+

Year	Lev	Team	W	L	Sv	IP	K	ERA	WHIP	BF/G	OBA	H%	S%	xERA	Ctl	Dom	Cmd	hr/9	BPV

Young, athletic SP with high upside but plenty of development time ahead. Works with clean mechanics but has some tweaks to add velocity to average FB. Velocity generated from quick arm though FB lacks spin. Uses power CB but SL is better of two. Hasn't used CU much and will need as pro. Some reliever risk in profile.

Kochanowicz,Jack — SP — Los Angeles (A)

EXP MLB DEBUT: 2024 | H/W: 6-7 228 | FUT: #4 starter | 7C

Thrws R Age 23	Year	Lev	Team	W	L	Sv	IP	K	ERA	WHIP	BF/G	OBA	H%	S%	xERA	Ctl	Dom	Cmd	hr/9	BPV
2019 (3) HS (PA)																				
94-97 FB ++++	2021	A	Inland Empire	4	2	0	83	73	6.93	1.65	18.6	303	36	58	5.79	3.8	7.9	2.1	1.3	58
79-81 CB ++	2022	A	Inland Empire	4	4	0	57	53	5.03	1.31	13.9	261	32	62	3.98	2.8	8.3	2.9	0.9	92
86-88 CU +++	2023	A+	Tri City	1	0	0	23	14	1.55	1.08	18.1	252	30	84	2.41	1.2	5.4	4.7	0.0	84
85-86 SL ++	2023	AA	Rocket City	4	5	0	70	55	6.55	1.47	18.8	291	32	59	5.74	2.8	7.1	2.5	1.9	69

Strike-throwing, sinkerball-heavy RHP finally made it to Double-A, where he struggled. Low 3/4s delivery, repeats well with solid extension. At his best, works to the arm side, and cashes in on FB's sink and run profile. Average CU is nice compliment to sinker. Struggles with breaking pitch consistently; SL over CB at present.

Kopp,Ronan — SP — Los Angeles (N)

EXP MLB DEBUT: 2025 | H/W: 6-7 250 | FUT: Setup reliever | 7D

Thrws L Age 21	Year	Lev	Team	W	L	Sv	IP	K	ERA	WHIP	BF/G	OBA	H%	S%	xERA	Ctl	Dom	Cmd	hr/9	BPV
2021 (12) South Mountain CC																				
95-97 FB ++++	2021	Rk	ACL Dodgers	0	0	0	2	5	0.00	1.50	2.9	262	76	100	3.44	4.5	22.5	5.0	0.0	302
84-86 SL +++	2022	A	Rancho Cuca	5	2	1	57	102	2.83	1.28	9.8	182	36	79	2.40	5.8	16.0	2.8	0.5	150
CU +	2022	A+	Great Lakes	0	1	0	4	6	2.14	2.14	6.9	202	34	89	4.40	12.9	12.9	1.0	0.0	-98
	2023	A+	Great Lakes	0	4	1	72	107	3.00	1.32	9.9	181	29	80	2.78	6.2	13.4	2.1	0.7	90

Huge lefty features two plus offerings, highlighted by a 95-97 FB that tops at 99 with late life and a power SL with downhill tilt. Closed stance and hides the ball well as he comes at hitters from a high ¾ slot, working mostly top to bottom. Command is a work in progress and will determine if he can remain a starter, but FB/SL mix works well in relief.

Kouba,Rhett — SP — Houston

EXP MLB DEBUT: 2025 | H/W: 6-0 180 | FUT: #5 SP/swingman | 7E

Thrws R Age 24	Year	Lev	Team	W	L	Sv	IP	K	ERA	WHIP	BF/G	OBA	H%	S%	xERA	Ctl	Dom	Cmd	hr/9	BPV
2021 (12) Dallas Baptist	2021	A	Fayetteville	0	0	0	13		1.37	0.92	12.2	229	29	91	2.32	0.7	8.9	13.0	0.7	160
92-93 FB ++	2022	A	Fayetteville	1	0	0	15	20	2.40	1.07	14.6	206	31	80	2.31	3.0	12.0	4.0	0.6	153
84-87 CU +++	2022	A+	Asheville	5	3	0	55	65	4.57	1.39	16.6	261	34	71	4.51	3.6	10.6	3.0	1.3	112
81-83 SL ++	2023	AA	Corpus Christi	7	5	0	110	118	3.27	1.07	18.6	234	30	74	3.05	1.9	9.7	5.1	1.0	141
79-80 CB ++	2023	AAA	Sugar Land	1	2	0	18	18	4.50	1.94	17.2	293	37	79	6.08	7.0	9.0	1.3	1.0	-9

Former 12th-rounder reached Triple-A in third pro season. Not particularly tall but gets good extension down mound. Pounds zone with low-90s FB, gets lots of swings but struggles to miss bats. Best pitch is mid-80s change-up which plays well off FB to LHB. Strike-thrower lacks overpowering stuff, likely innings-eater at next level.

Krob,Austin — SP — San Diego

EXP MLB DEBUT: 2024 | H/W: 6-3 205 | FUT: #4 starter | 7D

Thrws L Age 24	Year	Lev	Team	W	L	Sv	IP	K	ERA	WHIP	BF/G	OBA	H%	S%	xERA	Ctl	Dom	Cmd	hr/9	BPV
2022 (12) TCU	2022	NCAA	TCU	2	0	0	31	45	5.19	1.47	10.3	261	40	64	4.00	4.3	13.0	3.0	0.6	135
90-93 FB ++	2022	Rk	ACL Padres	0	0	0	1	0	0.00	0.00	2.8	0	0			0.0	0.0		0.0	18
76-79 CB ++	2022	A	Lake Elsinore	0	0	0	3	4	14.52	2.58	8.4	407	51	43	11.48	5.8	11.6	2.0	2.9	70
82-84 SL +++	2023	A	Lake Elsinore	0	1	0	50	59	2.34	1.36	19.0	246	35	82	3.16	4.0	10.6	2.7	0.2	102
83-85 CU +++	2023	A+	Fort Wayne	5	3	0	59	65	3.05	1.32	22.2	255	34	78	3.59	3.2	9.9	3.1	0.6	110

Durable SP who split season between Low-A and High-A and was successful at both levels. Finished 6th in minors in ERA and missed more bats than stuff suggests. Keeps ball low in zone to induce GB and gets hitters to chase solid SL. Not much velocity in tank but he locates FB well. CB could be shelved while CU has good upside.

Kudrna,Ben — SP — Kansas City

EXP MLB DEBUT: 2026 | H/W: 6-3 175 | FUT: #5 SP/swingman | 7D

Thrws R Age 21	Year	Lev	Team	W	L	Sv	IP	K	ERA	WHIP	BF/G	OBA	H%	S%	xERA	Ctl	Dom	Cmd	hr/9	BPV
2021 (2) HS (KS)																				
92-95 FB +++																				
83-86 SL ++++	2022	A	Columbia	2	5	0	72	61	3.50	1.36	17.7	245	30	74	3.48	4.0	7.6	1.9	0.5	47
84-88 CU +++	2023	A	Columbia	4	3	0	68	70	3.57	1.42	20.6	259	33	78	4.21	4.0	9.3	2.3	0.9	77
	2023	A+	Quad Cities	1	4	0	40	34	5.39	1.67	22.5	315	36	72	6.28	3.4	7.6	2.3	1.6	64

Former 2nd rounder struggled with strikes and inducing whiffs during so-so 2024. Throws hard but lacks solid FB shape. It plays very below average. Both secondaries are above-average or better. The SL has a gyro spin profile and can pile up whiffs while also stealing strikes. CU has solid fading profile with occasional late drop.

Kuehler,Cade — SP — Atlanta

EXP MLB DEBUT: 2025 | H/W: 6-0 215 | FUT: #4 starter | 7D

Thrws R Age 21	Year	Lev	Team	W	L	Sv	IP	K	ERA	WHIP	BF/G	OBA	H%	S%	xERA	Ctl	Dom	Cmd	hr/9	BPV
2023 (2) Campbell																				
92-95 FB ++++																				
83-85 SL +++																				
80-83 CU +++	2023	NCAA	Campbell	8	1	0	73	91	2.71	1.10	22.0	208	31	75	2.19	3.2	11.2	3.5	0.4	133
	2023	A	Augusta	0	0	0	7	8	0.00	0.71	12.4	48	8	100		5.1	10.3	2.0	0.0	64

3/4s RHP with history of success in college made pro debut. Near physical projection. Short-armed 3/4s delivery with some jerkiness. 4-seam FB has significant riding profile and heavy whiff/strike rate. Ditched CB in pro debut, refining gyro SL, with above-average upside. Throws split-CU with fringe-average characteristics.

Lagrange,Carlos — SP — New York (A)

EXP MLB DEBUT: 2026 | H/W: 6-7 195 | FUT: #3 starter | 8E

Thrws R Age 20	Year	Lev	Team	W	L	Sv	IP	K	ERA	WHIP	BF/G	OBA	H%	S%	xERA	Ctl	Dom	Cmd	hr/9	BPV
2022 FA (DR)																				
96-98 FB ++++																				
81-84 SL ++++																				
86-87 CU +++	2022	Rk	DSL Yankees 2	0	1	0	33	43	3.00	0.88	11.1	97	15	64	0.39	5.2	11.7	2.3	0.3	89
	2023	Rk	FCL Yankees	0	0	0	41	63	5.02	1.41	14.5	226	36	65	3.65	5.2	13.8	2.6	0.9	124

Tall, projectable RHP flashed two plus pitches in US debut. Struggles staying balanced with 3/4s delivery. Has room to grow into frame but already possesses strong frame. Varies between heavy 2-seam and riding 4-seam FB. Both potential plus offerings, with 4-seam FB potentially double-plus. SL with sharp break potentially plus too.

Lalane,Henry — SP — New York (A)

EXP MLB DEBUT: 2026 | H/W: 6-7 211 | FUT: #1 starter | 9E

Thrws L Age 19	Year	Lev	Team	W	L	Sv	IP	K	ERA	WHIP	BF/G	OBA	H%	S%	xERA	Ctl	Dom	Cmd	hr/9	BPV
2021 FA (NY)																				
93-95 FB ++++																				
77-79 SL ++++	2021	Rk	DSL Yankees 2	1	3	0	41	39	3.72	1.63	15.2	266	34	77	4.38	5.5	8.5	1.6	0.4	24
83-85 CU +++	2022	Rk	DSL Yankees 2	3	3	0	48	52	2.99	1.02	16.8	205	30	67	1.63	2.6	9.7	3.7	0.0	122
	2023	Rk	FCL Yankees	1	0	0	21	34	4.67	0.99	10.1	221	35	56	2.91	1.7	14.4	8.5	1.3	232

Tall, projectable low 3/4s LHP wowed complex scouts with combination of stuff and advanced strike throwing skills. Repeatable delivery with plus extension. FBs has significant riding action, played up by arm slot. Sweeping SL has significant horizontal movement profile with a chance to be plus. CU also flashes plus but less refined.

Lara,Andry — SP — Washington

EXP MLB DEBUT: 2026 | H/W: 6-4 180 | FUT: #3 starter | 7C

Thrws R Age 21	Year	Lev	Team	W	L	Sv	IP	K	ERA	WHIP	BF/G	OBA	H%	S%	xERA	Ctl	Dom	Cmd	hr/9	BPV
2019 FA (VZ)																				
91-93 FB +++	2021	Rk	FCL Nationals	3	2	0	39	47	4.59	1.22	17.6	240	32	65	3.66	3.0	10.8	3.6	1.1	132
82-85 SL ++++	2021	A	Fredericksburg	0	1	0	8	5	5.49	1.71	18.6	206	18	75	5.48	8.8	5.5	0.6	2.2	-120
84-87 CU +++	2022	A	Fredericksburg	3	8	0	101	105	5.52	1.45	18.8	265	34	62	4.34	3.9	9.3	2.4	0.9	80
	2023	A+	Wilmington	6	8	0	98	66	4.59	1.26	17.4	245	27	65	3.74	3.1	6.1	1.9	1.0	43

Athletic, young and still projectable, the right-hander has not had the breakout season many expected when WAS signed him for $1.25M in 2019. Sinker is only average, slider and change are both a tick above, but did not get the strikeouts in High-A and was hittable. Control only passable the past two seasons. Needs to take another step.

Lara,Jhancarlos — SP — Atlanta

EXP MLB DEBUT: 2025 | H/W: 6-3 190 | FUT: #3 starter | 8E

Thrws R Age 21	Year	Lev	Team	W	L	Sv	IP	K	ERA	WHIP	BF/G	OBA	H%	S%	xERA	Ctl	Dom	Cmd	hr/9	BPV
2021 FA (DR)																				
94-97 FB +++																				
86-88 SL ++++	2022	Rk	DSL Braves	1	1	0	30	38	1.79	1.53	13.1	191	30	87	2.73	7.8	11.4	1.5	0.0	13
89-90 CT +++	2023	A	Augusta	4	7	0	72	96	4.00	1.29	16.4	213	32	69	2.86	4.8	12.0	2.5	0.5	106
	2023	A+	Rome	0	1	0	9	18	4.95	0.99	17.3	163	28	57	2.86	4.0	17.8	4.5	2.0	232

Pop-up athletic RHP made strides during challenging full-season debut. Slim build with room to grow onto frame. 3/4s cross-fire delivery, achieving solid extension. 3-pitch pitcher. Sits mid-90s with 4-seam FB with below-average shape characteristics and performance. Gyro SL has devastating vertical break action. CT projects to be above-average.

Leasure,Jordan — RP — Chicago (A)

EXP MLB DEBUT: 2024 | H/W: 6-3 215 | FUT: Closer | 8E

Thrws R Age 25	Year	Lev	Team	W	L	Sv	IP	K	ERA	WHIP	BF/G	OBA	H%	S%	xERA	Ctl	Dom	Cmd	hr/9	BPV
2021 (14) Tampa	2021	A	Rancho Cuca	1	0	0	5	6	5.19	1.54	5.7	254	26	83	6.81	5.2	10.4	2.0	3.5	65
96-98 FB ++++	2022	A+	Great Lakes	0	0	2	9	21	1.98	0.99	6.9	135	46	78	0.68	4.9	20.8	4.2	0.0	258
86-89 SL +++	2022	AA	Tulsa	2	2	5	49	63	3.67	1.16	4.4	215	28	76	3.47	3.5	11.5	3.3	1.5	132
	2023	AA	Tulsa	2	2	9	35	56	3.09	1.06	4.7	175	26	81	2.79	4.1	14.4	3.5	1.5	166
	2023	AAA	Charlotte	0	2	2	13	23	6.18	1.83	4.1	302	48	71	6.87	5.5	15.8	2.9	2.1	154

Hard-throwing RP, acquired from LAD mid-season, looks to be future high-leverage RP. Over-the-top delivery with plus extension causes high 90s FB to look harder. Uses flat-angled approach with FB, playing up plus vertical breaking profile. Tight SL has chance to be plus with a deeper break profile. Arm isn't ready to close but could be option.

Leiter,Jack — SP — Texas

EXP MLB DEBUT: 2024 | H/W: 6-1 205 | FUT: #3 starter | 8D

Thrws R Age 23 — 2021 (1) Vanderbilt

Velo	Pitch	Grade
94-97	FB	+++
85-88	SL	++++
78-83	CB	++
86-89	CT	+

Year	Lev	Team	W	L	Sv	IP	K	ERA	WHIP	BF/G	OBA	H%	S%	xERA	Ctl	Dom	Cmd	hr/9	BPV
2021	--	Did Not Play																	
2022	AA	Frisco	3	10	0	92	109	5.56	1.56	17.6	253	34	65	4.60	5.5	10.6	1.9	1.1	62
2023	AA	Frisco	2	6	0	81	110	5.10	1.40	18.1	226	31	68	4.30	5.2	12.2	2.3	1.6	97
2023	AAA	Round Rock	0	0	0	3	4	8.71	3.23	18.7	478	56	88	17.55	5.8	11.6	2.0	5.8	70

While 2023 results were better than 2022, still not befitting a #2 overall selection. Fastball location still rough though it still is nearly unhittable at letters. SL also remains plus but command poor here as well. Still lacking dependable 3rd pitch as change-up remains stagnant; profile is thus unable to silence bullpen whispers.

Lesko,Dylan — SP — San Diego

EXP MLB DEBUT: 2026 | H/W: 6-2 195 | FUT: #2 starter | 9D

Thrws R Age 20 — 2022 (1) HS (GA)

Velo	Pitch	Grade
91-96	FB	++++
77-80	CB	+++
80-84	CU	++++

Year	Lev	Team	W	L	Sv	IP	K	ERA	WHIP	BF/G	OBA	H%	S%	xERA	Ctl	Dom	Cmd	hr/9	BPV
2023	Rk	ACL Padres	0	1	0	5	9	10.80	2.20	6.3	362	58	50	8.55	5.4	16.2	3.0	1.8	164
2023	A	Lake Elsinore	0	3	0	16	23	4.50	1.31	13.2	224	35	65	3.09	4.5	12.9	2.9	0.6	129
2023	A+	Fort Wayne	1	1	0	12	20	4.50	1.58	17.6	191	34	72	3.55	8.3	15.0	1.8	0.8	65

Returned from Tommy John surgery and pitched well, mostly in short stints. Flashes dominance with advanced pitch sequencing and three potential plus offerings. Diving CU may be best in org while FB features carry up in zone. Could add more velocity with more strength. Durability is the main question but could be stud.

Lewis,Cory — SP — Minnesota

EXP MLB DEBUT: 2025 | H/W: 6-5 220 | FUT: #4 starter | 7D

Thrws R Age 23 — 2022 (9) UC Santa Barbara

Velo	Pitch	Grade
91-94	FB	+++
80-83	SL	+++
83-86	KC	+++
81-82	CU	++

Year	Lev	Team	W	L	Sv	IP	K	ERA	WHIP	BF/G	OBA	H%	S%	xERA	Ctl	Dom	Cmd	hr/9	BPV
2023	A	Fort Myers	4	3	0	39	55	2.76	1.05	16.8	191	29	76	2.16	3.5	12.7	3.7	0.7	153
2023	A+	Cedar Rapids	5	1	0	62	63	2.32	1.06	18.5	215	29	79	2.29	2.6	9.1	3.5	0.4	112

Consistent, steady SP who finished 2nd in org in K while holding hitters to a .198 oppBA. K rate was a bit of a surprise as he doesn't have plus velocity or wipeout breaking ball. Gets excellent extension on FB while exhibiting high spin rates. Slow CB serves as out pitch. MIN would like to see more velocity and better sequencing.

Lin,Yu Min — SP — Arizona

EXP MLB DEBUT: 2024 | H/W: 5-11 160 | FUT: #3 starter | 8E

Thrws L Age 20 — 2021 FA (TW)

Velo	Pitch	Grade
90-92	FB	+++
80-86	CU	++++
78-80	CB	++
83-86	SL	++

Year	Lev	Team	W	L	Sv	IP	K	ERA	WHIP	BF/G	OBA	H%	S%	xERA	Ctl	Dom	Cmd	hr/9	BPV
2022	Rk	ACL DBacks Reds	0	2	0	23	41	2.35	0.65	11.4	122	27	60		2.3	16.0	6.8	0.0	243
2022	A	Visalia	2	0	0	33	50	2.99	1.42	20.0	249	40	80	3.67	4.4	13.6	3.1	0.5	145
2023	A+	Hillsboro	1	3	0	60	76	3.44	1.15	18.3	217	32	70	2.51	3.3	11.4	3.5	0.4	134
2023	AA	Amarillo	5	2	0	61	64	4.28	1.23	22.5	222	28	68	3.34	3.8	9.4	2.5	1.0	84

Prototypical crafty lefty makes up for lack of physicality, velocity with pitchability and deception. Deep pitch mix headlined by low-90s two-seamer, pairs with excellent CU. CB/SL are usable but don't particularly wow. Lacks physical projection to bank on more velo, so secondary development is crucial to continued success as starter.

Lindsey,Andrew — SP — Tampa Bay

EXP MLB DEBUT: 2026 | H/W: 6-3 216 | FUT: #4 starter | 7D

Thrws R Age 24 — 2023 (5) Tennessee

Velo	Pitch	Grade
92-95	FB	+++
86-88	SL	+++
77-79	CB	++
84-86	CU	++

Year	Lev	Team	W	L	Sv	IP	K	ERA	WHIP	BF/G	OBA	H%	S%	xERA	Ctl	Dom	Cmd	hr/9	BPV
2023	NCAA	Tennessee	3	4	0	71	73	2.91	1.11	13.3	230	29	80	3.25	2.4	9.2	3.8	1.1	119
2023	Rk	FCL Marlins	0	1	0	4	2	8.78	1.71	9.3	342	39	43	5.37	2.2	4.4	2.0	0.0	38

Groundball-inducing RHP was drafted by MIA in 5th round ub July, traded to TAM in the fall. Repeatable delivery despite longer arm path out of low 3/4s slot. Thrives on heavy 2-seam FB usage; gets plus sink but struggles with command in zone. Two-plane SL is best secondary with above-average potential. Other pitches need refinement.

Little,Luke — RP — Chicago (N)

EXP MLB DEBUT: 2023 | H/W: 6-8 220 | FUT: Setup reliever | 6B

Thrws L Age 23 — 2020 (4) San Jacinto JC

Velo	Pitch	Grade
94-98	FB	++++
80-83	SL	++++
	CU	+

Year	Lev	Team	W	L	Sv	IP	K	ERA	WHIP	BF/G	OBA	H%	S%	xERA	Ctl	Dom	Cmd	hr/9	BPV
2022	A+	South Bend	0	1	0	13	17	0.69	0.92	12.2	141	23	92	0.66	4.2	11.8	2.8	0.0	118
2023	A+	South Bend	0	0	0	17	21	0.53	1.11	13.4	199	31	95	1.78	3.7	11.1	3.0	0.0	117
2023	AA	Tennessee	3	2	0	34	63	3.16	1.40	6.3	172	36	77	2.40	7.4	16.6	2.3	0.3	117
2023	AAA	Iowa	2	0	1	11	21	1.61	1.34	5.8	202	43	87	2.33	5.6	16.9	3.0	0.0	170
2023	MLB	Chicago (N)	0	0	0	6	12	0.00	1.45	3.8	222	48	100	2.86	5.8	17.4	3.0	0.0	175

Huge LHP has uses plus FB to blow hitters away and made his MLB debut. FB sits in the upper-90s, topping at 102 with late and plus SL has late two-plane break. Starts on 1B side of the mound and attacks with crossfire action. Moved to relief role and now owns a career 14.4 K/9, but struggles with command continue to be an issue (5.5 BB/9).

Lizarraga,Victor — SP — San Diego

EXP MLB DEBUT: 2025 | H/W: 6-3 180 | FUT: #4 starter | 7D

Thrws R Age 20 — 2020 FA (MX)

Velo	Pitch	Grade
91-94	FB	+++
79-82	CB	++
82-84	CU	+++

Year	Lev	Team	W	L	Sv	IP	K	ERA	WHIP	BF/G	OBA	H%	S%	xERA	Ctl	Dom	Cmd	hr/9	BPV
2021	Rk	ACL Padres	0	4	0	30	35	5.10	1.33	11.3	228	29	66	4.11	4.5	10.5	2.3	1.5	86
2022	A	Lake Elsinore	8	3	0	94	95	3.44	1.29	19.3	247	32	73	3.28	3.3	9.1	2.8	0.5	94
2023	A+	Fort Wayne	4	7	0	94	78	4.11	1.26	18.3	242	30	67	3.18	3.2	7.5	2.3	0.5	64

Durable RHP with solid repertoire and some projection remaining. K rate has declined over each of last three seasons, mainly due to inability to find consistent CB. Likes to use FB early in count and can leverage up in zone. CU is best present offering and can stymie LHH. When on, induces weak contact and limits walks.

Lopez,Jacob — SP — Tampa Bay

EXP MLB DEBUT: 2023 | H/W: 6-4 220 | FUT: #5 SP/swingman | 7D

Thrws L Age 26 — 2018 (26) Col of Canyons

Velo	Pitch	Grade
90-92	FB	+++
86-88	CU	++
78-80	SL	++++

Year	Lev	Team	W	L	Sv	IP	K	ERA	WHIP	BF/G	OBA	H%	S%	xERA	Ctl	Dom	Cmd	hr/9	BPV
2021	A+	Bowling Green	3	1	2	54	88	2.32	1.05	15.0	207	34	84	2.63	2.8	14.6	5.2	1.0	205
2021	AA	Montgomery	0	0	0	5	8	3.60	0.80	18.1	175	33	50	0.69	1.8	14.4	8.0	0.0	229
2023	AA	Montgomery	0	0	0	28	45	2.57	0.82	12.7	151	26	71	1.09	2.9	14.5	5.0	0.6	200
2023	AAA	Durham	4	5	0	79	87	2.73	1.33	18.2	206	27	83	3.17	5.3	9.9	1.9	0.8	52
2023	MLB	Tampa Bay	1	0	1	12	8	4.46	1.32	12.5	291	35	63	3.57	1.5	6.0	4.0	0.0	85

Deceptive, near sidearm LHP returned from Tommy John surgery to earn late season MLB roster spot. 3-pitch pitcher. 2-seam fastball has significant running action but low strike rate brings performance down to average. Slow SL is best offering with horizontal running profile. CU is an fringe offering, playing off FB/SL usage profile to combat RHH.

Lord,Kiefer — SP — Baltimore

EXP MLB DEBUT: 2026 | H/W: 6-3 195 | FUT: #4 starter | 7A

Thrws R Age 21 — 2023 (3) Washington

Velo	Pitch	Grade
94-97	FB	+++
80-83	SL	++++
84-86	CU	++

Year	Lev	Team	W	L	Sv	IP	K	ERA	WHIP	BF/G	OBA	H%	S%	xERA	Ctl	Dom	Cmd	hr/9	BPV
2023	NCAA	Washington	6	5	0	75	78	6.22	1.37	21.0	289	35	57	5.20	2.0	9.3	4.6	1.7	131
2023	Rk	FCL Orioles B	0	0	0	2	1	0.00	0.50	6.6	0	0	100		4.5	4.5	1.0	0.0	-23

Former Division 3 SP battled inconsistencies at in Pac12 before being drafted into pro ball. Recipe for success there. Strike thrower with poor in zone command. Refinement needed with pitch shape, especially high velocity FB, which is powered by plus-plus arm speed. Two-plane SL has chance to be plus pitch. Also throws CB and CU.

Lowder,Rhett — SP — Cincinnati

EXP MLB DEBUT: 2024 | H/W: 6-2 200 | FUT: #3 starter | 8C

Thrws R Age 22 — 2023 (1) Wake Forest

Velo	Pitch	Grade
92-95	FB	+++
84-86	SL	++++
86-88	CU	++++

Year	Lev	Team	W	L	Sv	IP	K	ERA	WHIP	BF/G	OBA	H%	S%	xERA	Ctl	Dom	Cmd	hr/9	BPV

Near-ready, athletic hurler was drafted after stellar career at Wake Forest. Athletic frame, near projection. Repeatable 3/4s delivery with solid extension. Varies between FB. 4-seam FB has an above-average ride profile, playing up due to command. Each secondary is a whiff-inducing pitch. Late-fading CU is ahead of SL with late vertical action.

Lowe,Isaiah — SP — San Diego

EXP MLB DEBUT: 2026 | H/W: 6-1 220 | FUT: #3 starter | 8E

Thrws R Age 20 — 2022 (11) HS (NC)

Velo	Pitch	Grade
92-95	FB	+++
81-83	SL	+++
82-84	CU	++

Year	Lev	Team	W	L	Sv	IP	K	ERA	WHIP	BF/G	OBA	H%	S%	xERA	Ctl	Dom	Cmd	hr/9	BPV
2023	Rk	ACL Padres	0	0	0	1	1	9.00	2.00	4.8	262	35	50	4.84	9.0	9.0	1.0	0.0	-63
2023	A	Lake Elsinore	0	1	0	11	17	1.62	1.17	14.8	223	36	92	2.96	3.2	13.8	4.3	0.8	179

Promising young RHP with high upside, but rarely pitched due to shoulder issues. History of injuries and current frame give some pause. Outside of CU, has two average to above average pitches in FB and SL. Throws with good control and mixing ability despite inexperience. Could make for intriguing RP if can't demonstrate stamina.

Macko, Adam — SP — Toronto

EXP MLB DEBUT: 2025 | H/W: 6-0 170 | FUT: #4 starter | 7C

Thrws L | Age 23
2019 (7) HS (AB)

92-96	FB	+++	
81-83	CB	+++	
82-85	SL	+++	
85-86	CU	++	

Year	Lev	Team	W	L	Sv	IP	K	ERA	WHIP	BF/G	OBA	H%	S%	xERA	Ctl	Dom	Cmd	hr/9	BPV
2019	Rk	AZL Mariners	0	3	0	21	31	3.41	1.42	11.2	242	39	76	3.47	4.7	13.2	2.8	0.4	129
2019	A-	Everett	0	0	0	2	1	0.00	0.50	6.6	0	0	100		4.5	4.5	1.0	0.0	-23
2021	A	Modesto	2	2	0	33	56	4.62	1.51	15.9	237	43	67	3.47	5.7	15.2	2.7	0.3	138
2022	A+	Everett	0	2	0	38	60	4.02	1.39	20.1	235	38	73	3.78	4.7	14.2	3.0	0.9	146
2023	A+	Vancouver	5	5	0	86	106	4.81	1.35	17.9	239	34	64	3.55	4.2	11.1	2.7	0.7	105

Short-framed SP who has added strength and gotten to more consistent velocity. Has advanced one level per year and on verge of majors. Stuff is better than stats indicate. Can effectively change speeds and eye levels, particularly with FB and CB. Can pitch up in zone. Hasn't been challenged with long outings; command could be better.

Madden, Jake — SP — Colorado

EXP MLB DEBUT: 2025 | H/W: 6-6 185 | FUT: Setup reliever | 7D

Thrws R | Age 22
2022 (4) NW Florida State

94-96	FB	++++	
84-86	SL	+++	
86-88	CU	++	

Year	Lev	Team	W	L	Sv	IP	K	ERA	WHIP	BF/G	OBA	H%	S%	xERA	Ctl	Dom	Cmd	hr/9	BPV
2023	A	Fresno	0	2	0	15	14	7.80	1.80	11.6	299	33	61	7.12	5.4	8.4	1.6	2.4	23
2023	A	Inland Empire	2	6	0	64	66	5.48	1.59	20.2	258	33	66	4.68	5.5	9.3	1.7	1.0	37

Tall, projectable hurler had Tommy John surgery in 2020. Owns a plus mid-90s FB that tops at 98 with good spin. Lots of moving parts to quick-tempo delivery that creates some deception, but inconsistent arm slot and below average command. Shows some feel for CU and SL flashes plus when he's on. Improved control and command will be critical.

Madden, Ty — SP — Detroit

EXP MLB DEBUT: 2024 | H/W: 6-3 215 | FUT: #4 starter | 7B

Thrws R | Age 24
2021 (1) Texas

93-96	FB	+++	
83-85	SL	++++	
85-88	CU	++	
88-90	CT		

Year	Lev	Team	W	L	Sv	IP	K	ERA	WHIP	BF/G	OBA	H%	S%	xERA	Ctl	Dom	Cmd	hr/9	BPV
2022	A+	West Michigan	6	4	0	87	84	3.10	1.09	17.9	220	27	76	2.97	2.7	8.7	3.2	1.0	102
2022	AA	Erie	2	2	0	35	49	2.81	1.14	19.9	220	30	85	3.52	3.1	12.5	4.1	1.5	161
2023	AA	Erie	3	4	0	118	146	3.43	1.28	18.6	233	31	79	3.76	3.8	11.1	2.9	1.2	115

Lowered arm slot has led to better pitch shape and carry on mid-90s FB. Strong, durable frame and works better up in the zone. Short SL is best secondary with CT, CB, and CU rounding out the arsenal. Struggles vs LHB to the tune of a .900+ OPS. CU remains erratic, but flashes plus. CU development will determine whether or not he remains a starter.

Mahoney, Jack — SP — Colorado

EXP MLB DEBUT: 2025 | H/W: 6-3 205 | FUT: #4 starter | 7D

Thrws R | Age 22
2023 (3) South Carolina

92-95	FB	+++	
83-85	SL	+++	
82-83	CU	+++	

Year	Lev	Team	W	L	Sv	IP	K	ERA	WHIP	BF/G	OBA	H%	S%	xERA	Ctl	Dom	Cmd	hr/9	BPV
2023	Rk	ACL Rockies	0	0	0	2	3	9.00	2.00	4.8	347	43	67	10.35	4.5	13.5	3.0	4.5	140

Compact RHP pitched after having Tommy John surgery in 2022. Quick tempo, close to max-effort delivery highlighted by plus mid-90s FB that tops at 97 with carry up in the zone. Mid-80s SL is above-average secondary while CU is a also above-average. Solid command gives him a chance to develop into a solid back-end starter.

Maier, Adam — SP — Atlanta

EXP MLB DEBUT: 2025 | H/W: 6-0 203 | FUT: #4 starter | 7D

Thrws R | Age 22
2022 (7) Oregon

90-93	FB	+++	
80-83	SL	+++	
83-85	CU	++	

Missed entire 2023 season rehabbing UCL brace surgery. Repeats 3/4s delivery with above-average arm speed. 3-pitch hurler. 4-seam FB is mostly an arm-side runner with limited ride. Two-plane SL has above-average potential, especially if tightened up and thrown harder. Feel for changing speeds with CU but lacks movement consistency.

Maldonado, Anthony — RP — Miami

EXP MLB DEBUT: 2024 | H/W: 6-4 220 | FUT: Setup reliever | 7D

Thrws R | Age 26
2019 (11) Bethune-Cookman

92-94	FB	+++	
83-86	CT	++++	
81-84	SL	++++	

Year	Lev	Team	W	L	Sv	IP	K	ERA	WHIP	BF/G	OBA	H%	S%	xERA	Ctl	Dom	Cmd	hr/9	BPV
2021	AA	Pensacola	0	1	3	5	5	3.53	0.98	3.9	218	35	60	1.64	1.8	14.1	8.0	0.0	224
2022	AA	Pensacola	3	3	1	41	58	3.71	1.17	6.1	221	30	78	3.81	3.3	12.7	3.9	1.7	158
2022	AAA	Jacksonville	1	0	3	20	28	1.78	0.89	5.0	186	29	82	1.48	2.2	12.5	5.6	0.4	182
2023	A	Jupiter	0	0	0	4	7	0.00	0.25	4.1	81	19	100		0.0	15.8		0.0	302
2023	AAA	Jacksonville	7	3	9	46	71	1.76	0.96	5.1	151	23	90	1.75	4.1	13.9	3.4	1.0	157

XXL frame RP with feel for spin had excellent season, earning 40-man roster slot. Missed time due to injury late, preventing MLB debut. RP delivery with short arm action and head whack. Equal diet of 3 pitches. CT is best pitch with solid tilt/axis profile. SL is a gyro spinner with whiff potential. Intertwines 2-seam FB nicely with arsenal.

Maldonado, Gerelmi — SP — San Francisco

EXP MLB DEBUT: 2026 | H/W: 6-2 170 | FUT: #3 starter | 8D

Thrws R | Age 20
2021 FA (VZ)

93-96	FB	++++	
81-84	SL	+++	
83-86	CU	+	

Year	Lev	Team	W	L	Sv	IP	K	ERA	WHIP	BF/G	OBA	H%	S%	xERA	Ctl	Dom	Cmd	hr/9	BPV
2021	Rk	DSL Giants B	2	1	0	29	30	5.26	1.44	9.5	234	32	60	3.06	5.3	9.3	1.8	0.0	43
2022	Rk	ACL Giants O	0	2	1	39	59	2.30	1.30	11.5	224	36	85	3.19	4.4	13.5	3.1	0.7	144
2023	A	San Jose	1	1	0	65	81	4.71	1.42	14.5	221	31	67	3.46	5.5	11.2	2.0	0.7	70

Ended season in July, but impressed org with power arm and ability to miss bats. Will need to address command issues, but more reflective of age and more throwing than pitching. FB has potential to be special due to lively action and deceptive throwing motion. CU purely in infancy stage and often slows arm to aim ball.

Marcheco, Jorge — SP — Los Angeles (A)

EXP MLB DEBUT: 2025 | H/W: 6-1 185 | FUT: #4 starter | 7E

Thrws R | Age 21
2021 FA (CU)

87-90	FB	+++	
73-75	CB	++	
76-79	CU	+++	
83-86	SL	++	

Year	Lev	Team	W	L	Sv	IP	K	ERA	WHIP	BF/G	OBA	H%	S%	xERA	Ctl	Dom	Cmd	hr/9	BPV
2022	Rk	ACL Angels	5	2	0	50	76	3.23	1.08	17.8	229	37	71	2.53	2.2	13.6	6.3	0.5	205
2022	A	Inland Empire	0	1	0	11	14	4.86	0.99	14.1	204	29	50	2.29	2.4	11.4	4.7	0.8	157
2023	A	Inland Empire	7	5	0	93	91	4.06	1.08	21.3	227	28	65	3.05	2.2	8.8	4.0	1.1	116
2023	A+	Tri City	3	1	0	28	33	1.91	0.89	20.9	217	28	90	2.63	1.0	10.5	11.0	1.3	182

Command/control RHP had strong second half, especially during High-A stint. Low 3/4s delivery with limited extension. Repeats delivery well, especially release point. Best two pitches are 2-seam and 4-seam FBs. Plays up by tunneling each pitch off each other. CU is best secondary with natural fade. Both breakers below average pitches.

Maroudis, Landen — SP — Toronto

EXP MLB DEBUT: 2027 | H/W: 6-3 190 | FUT: #3 starter | 8E

Thrws R | Age 19
2023 (4) HS (FL)

89-93	FB	+++	
77-79	CB	++	
81-82	SL	++	
80-83	CU	+++	

Athletic, projectable SP with impressive, deep arsenal. Throws with fast arm speed, though has enough effort to impact command. Able to repeat arm action and slot. Average velocity with potential to add more. Development needed with both breaking balls. Should have above average FB and CU at peak.

Martin, Payton — SP — Los Angeles (N)

EXP MLB DEBUT: 2026 | H/W: 6-0 170 | FUT: #4 starter | 7D

Thrws R | Age 19
2022 (17) HS (NC)

94-96	FB	++++	
87-89	SL	++++	
74-76	CU	++	

Year	Lev	Team	W	L	Sv	IP	K	ERA	WHIP	BF/G	OBA	H%	S%	xERA	Ctl	Dom	Cmd	hr/9	BPV
2023	A	Rancho Cuca	2	1	0	39	48	2.07	1.15	11.1	213	32	82	2.26	3.4	11.0	3.2	0.2	123

Short, athletic hurler converted from SS to SP after being drafted in the 17th round. Attacks from a high 3/4 arm slot with quick arm action. Uptick in velo and FB now sits at 94-96 topping at 98 with arm side run. Power SL sits in the upper-80, touching 90 with late break. Will need to refine CU to remain a starter, but he's worth watching.

Martin, Trevor — SP — Tampa Bay

EXP MLB DEBUT: 2025 | H/W: 6-5 238 | FUT: #4 starter | 7C

Thrws R | Age 23
2022 (3) Oklahoma State

91-93	FB	++++	
83-85	SL	+++	
77-79	CB	+++	
83-85	CU	++	

Year	Lev	Team	W	L	Sv	IP	K	ERA	WHIP	BF/G	OBA	H%	S%	xERA	Ctl	Dom	Cmd	hr/9	BPV
2022	NCAA	Oklahoma St	4	3	9	47	79	4.78	1.32	6.5	231	35	73	4.63	4.2	15.1	3.6	2.1	176
2022	Rk	FCL Rays	0	0	0	1	2	0.00	2.00	4.8	262	55	100	4.75	9.0	18.0	2.0	0.0	99
2023	A	Charleston	10	5	0	110	131	3.52	1.21	17.7	229	31	74	3.24	3.4	10.7	3.2	0.9	120

Tall, big-bodied RHP rode excellent FB pitch profile to success in full season debut. 3/4s arm path with longer arm path. Uses size well within delivery. 4-pitch pitcher. 4-seam FB features plus run and command to all quadrants of zone. SL and CB are solid secondaries. Neither act as out pitches. Will need to develop fringe CU to start.

Martinez,Jeter

SP | Seattle | EXP MLB DEBUT: 2027 | H/W: 6-4 180 | FUT: #3 starter | 8E

Thrws R Age 18
2023 FA (MX)

Velo	Pitch	Grade
90-94	FB	+++
79-84	SL	++
82-84	CU	+

Year	Lev	Team	W	L	Sv	IP	K	ERA	WHIP	BF/G	OBA	H%	S%	xERA	Ctl	Dom	Cmd	hr/9	BPV
2023	Rk	DSL Mariners	2	2	0	47	55	1.72	0.79	17.0	114	17	78	0.25	3.8	10.5	2.8	0.2	104

Tall, projectable RHP who posted miniscule oppBA in DSL. RHH couldn't make hard contact against him. Uses deceptive arm angle to baffle hitters and leverages SL to miss bats. FB features sinking action and generally throws strikes. Needs plenty of polish and consistency before making move up charts. SL shows flashes and needs better CU.

Martinez,Justin

RP | Arizona | EXP MLB DEBUT: 2023 | H/W: 6-3 180 | FUT: Setup reliever | 7E

Thrws R Age 22
2018 FA (DR)

Velo	Pitch	Grade
99-101	FB	++
88-90	SL	++++
88-90	CU	+++

Year	Lev	Team	W	L	Sv	IP	K	ERA	WHIP	BF/G	OBA	H%	S%	xERA	Ctl	Dom	Cmd	hr/9	BPV
2022	A+	Hillsboro	1	2	1	27	44	2.67	1.30	8.5	216	38	79	2.73	4.7	14.7	3.1	0.3	156
2022	AA	Amarillo	1	0	0	4	8	4.39	1.95	9.8	342	63	75	5.86	4.4	17.6	4.0	0.0	216
2022	AAA	Reno	1	0	0	4	8	4.29	1.90	6.6	202	44	75	3.76	10.7	17.1	1.6	0.0	37
2023	AAA	Reno	2	1	9	49	67	4.22	1.65	4.7	192	30	74	3.57	8.8	12.3	1.4	0.5	2
2023	MLB	Arizona	0	0	1	10	14	12.60	2.40	5.2	316	44	45	8.30	9.9	12.6	1.3	1.8	-23

Young reliever made major league debut in 2023. Hardest thrower in system, regularly touching 100+ on FB. FB is hittable pitch, garnering very few whiffs. Best pitch is SL when batters chase, but batters see it well and sit FB. Has raw arm strength and secondaries to be a high-leverage reliever, but FB needs work.

Massey,J.P.

SP | Pittsburgh | EXP MLB DEBUT: 2025 | H/W: 6-5 205 | FUT: Middle reliever | 7D

Thrws R Age 24
2022 (7) Minnesota

Velo	Pitch	Grade
91-95	FB	+++
83-86	SL	++
80-83	CB	++
85-86	CU	++

Year	Lev	Team	W	L	Sv	IP	K	ERA	WHIP	BF/G	OBA	H%	S%	xERA	Ctl	Dom	Cmd	hr/9	BPV
2023	A	Bradenton	3	3	0	49	57	3.30	1.32	18.5	228	31	77	3.37	4.4	10.4	2.4	0.7	87
2023	A+	Greensboro	2	4	0	31	26	4.65	1.35	14.4	179	21	67	3.01	6.7	7.5	1.1	0.9	-26

Athletic RHP who split time between Low-A and High-A in first full season. Had difficulty locating pitches in strike zone and was hurt by walks. Pure stuff is quite good but just can't find consistency. Delivery is a tad rough and difficult to repeat. Varies arm angles and release points. Keeps ball on ground and has stuff to miss bats.

Mata,Bryan

SP | Boston | EXP MLB DEBUT: 2024 | H/W: 6-3 223 | FUT: #4 starter | 7C

Thrws R Age 24
2016 FA (VZ)

Velo	Pitch	Grade
94-97	FB	+++
76-79	CB	+
83-88	SL	+++
85-89	CU	+++

Year	Lev	Team	W	L	Sv	IP	K	ERA	WHIP	BF/G	OBA	H%	S%	xERA	Ctl	Dom	Cmd	hr/9	BPV
2022	A	Salem	0	0	0	2	2	0.00	1.00	7.6	0	0	100		9.0	9.0	1.0	0.0	-63
2022	A+	Greenville	0	1	0	9	15	4.00	1.33	12.5	191	33	73	3.15	6.0	15.0	2.5	1.0	126
2022	AA	Portland	5	2	0	48	58	1.87	1.20	19.4	205	28	89	2.78	4.3	10.8	2.5	0.7	97
2022	AAA	Worcester	2	0	0	23	30	3.51	1.47	19.8	226	35	74	3.01	5.8	11.7	2.0	0.0	71
2023	AAA	Worcester	0	3	0	27	28	6.33	2.19	15.0	276	37	69	5.81	10.0	9.3	0.9	0.3	-84

Strong-framed SP who continues to miss time with injuries. Has as good of arsenal as any prospect in system when healthy. All about power with quick, sinking FB and hard SL. Lacks touch and feel for command and walks too many. CU can be too firm but features late drop. Can be susceptible to hard contact with flat FB.

Mathews,Quinn

SP | St. Louis | EXP MLB DEBUT: 2025 | H/W: 6-5 188 | FUT: #5 SP/swingman | 7D

Thrws L Age 23
2023 (4) Stanford

Velo	Pitch	Grade
89-93	FB	++
79-83	SL	++++
78-79	CB	+
81-82	CU	+++

Year	Lev	Team	W	L	Sv	IP	K	ERA	WHIP	BF/G	OBA	H%	S%	xERA	Ctl	Dom	Cmd	hr/9	BPV

Tossed epic 156-pitch, 16 K complete game to help the Cardinal to the College World Series. Clean, easy mechanics with above-average low-90s FB with command. Does most of his damage with SL that has two-plane sweep and plus CU, both of which give lefties fits. Pounds the zone. Slender frame, but durability isn't yet an issue.

Matthews,Zebby

SP | Minnesota | EXP MLB DEBUT: 2025 | H/W: 6-5 225 | FUT: #4 starter | 7D

Thrws R Age 23
2022 (8) Western Carolina

Velo	Pitch	Grade
92-95	FB	+++
81-84	SL	++
78-80	CB	++
84-86	CU	++

Year	Lev	Team	W	L	Sv	IP	K	ERA	WHIP	BF/G	OBA	H%	S%	xERA	Ctl	Dom	Cmd	hr/9	BPV
2022	NCAA	Western Carolina	4	6	4	95	122	3.69	1.21	17.4	259	36	74	3.85	2.0	11.5	5.8	1.1	172
2022	Rk	FCL Twins	0	0	0	1	2	0.00	1.00	3.8	262	55	100	2.23	0.0	18.0		0.0	342
2022	A	Fort Myers	0	0	0	2	4	0.00	0.00	5.6	0	0			0.0	18.0		0.0	342
2023	A	Fort Myers	3	1	0	38	53	2.59	0.94	18.0	223	35	71	1.86	1.2	12.5	10.6	0.2	211
2023	A+	Cedar Rapids	4	2	0	66	59	4.62	1.13	18.7	258	29	66	4.27	1.4	8.0	5.9	1.8	126

Command/control SP with advanced ability to hit spots. Was much better in Low-A and toyed with hitters timing before promotion to High-A. Added a few ticks to average FB and sweeping SL is getting better. Changes speeds well but not just with CU. Adds and subtracts from all pitches while maintaining arm speed and slot.

Mattison,Tyler

RP | Detroit | EXP MLB DEBUT: 2024 | H/W: 6-4 235 | FUT: Setup reliever | 7C

Thrws R Age 24
2021 (4) Bryant

Velo	Pitch	Grade
95-97	FB	+++
82-84	CB	+++
83-86	SL	++
86-88	CU	+++

Year	Lev	Team	W	L	Sv	IP	K	ERA	WHIP	BF/G	OBA	H%	S%	xERA	Ctl	Dom	Cmd	hr/9	BPV
2022	Rk	FCL Tigers East	0	1	1	7	8	1.29	0.86	8.6	168	25	83	0.80	2.6	10.3	4.0	0.0	134
2022	A	Lakeland	7	0	1	32	46	5.31	1.30	5.5	216	34	58	2.98	4.8	12.9	2.7	0.6	121
2023	A+	West Michigan	3	1	2	26	45	3.45	1.15	5.5	214	34	80	3.63	3.4	15.5	4.5	1.7	204
2023	AA	Erie	2	0	4	33	46	1.63	1.15	6.0	176	30	84	1.60	4.9	12.5	2.6	0.0	111

Hard-throwing reliever had an impressive season, posting a 38% K rate. Comes at hitters from an over-the-top arm slot with a plus 95-97 heater with arm-side run that bores in on RHB. Backs up the FB with a firm 86-88 CU and a mid-80s SL with 11-to-5 action. Command has always been an issue, but limited hitters to a .190 BA.

Mautz,Brycen

SP | St. Louis | EXP MLB DEBUT: 2025 | H/W: 6-3 190 | FUT: #5 SP/swingman | 7D

Thrws L Age 22
2022 (2) San Diego

Velo	Pitch	Grade
90-93	FB	+++
78-84	SL	++++
83-85	CU	+

Year	Lev	Team	W	L	Sv	IP	K	ERA	WHIP	BF/G	OBA	H%	S%	xERA	Ctl	Dom	Cmd	hr/9	BPV
2023	A	Palm Beach	4	9	0	104	115	3.98	1.34	18.8	243	34	69	3.22	3.9	10.0	2.6	0.3	92

LHP worked both as starter and reliever in college. Comes at hitters from a low 3/4 arm slot with crossfire action. Low-90s heater has cutter like action and is tough vs LHB. Low-80s sweeper is his best offering, but he struggles to keep it in the zone. Fringe CU and command need improvement to remain a starter, but FB/SL mix works well in relief.

Maxwell,Zach

RP | Cincinnati | EXP MLB DEBUT: 2025 | H/W: 6-6 275 | FUT: Closer | 8E

Thrws R Age 23
2022 (6) Georgia Tech

Velo	Pitch	Grade
96-99	FB	++++
88-90	SL	++++

Year	Lev	Team	W	L	Sv	IP	K	ERA	WHIP	BF/G	OBA	H%	S%	xERA	Ctl	Dom	Cmd	hr/9	BPV
2022	NCAA	Georgia Tech	5	0	4	51	84	5.28	1.66	10.9	234	37	71	4.88	7.2	14.8	2.0	1.4	89
2022	Rk	ACL Reds	0	0	1	2	3	0.00	1.00	3.8	151	27	100	0.94	4.5	13.5	3.0	0.0	140
2022	A	Daytona	0	0	0	5	7	7.06	2.16	8.5	218	35	64	4.62	12.4	12.4	1.0	0.0	-93
2023	A	Daytona	3	2	1	35	55	3.84	1.51	7.3	232	40	73	3.39	5.9	14.1	2.4	0.3	112
2023	A+	Dayton	3	2	1	25	41	4.64	1.27	7.9	193	33	63	2.75	5.4	14.6	2.7	0.7	137

Hard-throwing, XXL prospect has one of the best two-pitch RP mixes in lower minors. Jerky 3/4s delivery with below-average extension. 4-seam FB with double-plus riding action overpowers hitters. In zone FB whiff rate near 40%. Sharp, two-plane SL piles up whiffs, just like FB. Control has always plagued him; could close with more strikes.

Mazur,Adam

SP | San Diego | EXP MLB DEBUT: 2024 | H/W: 6-2 180 | FUT: #4 starter | 7B

Thrws R Age 22
2022 (2) Iowa

Velo	Pitch	Grade
90-95	FB	+++
76-79	CB	+++
82-85	SL	++++
83-85	CU	+++

Year	Lev	Team	W	L	Sv	IP	K	ERA	WHIP	BF/G	OBA	H%	S%	xERA	Ctl	Dom	Cmd	hr/9	BPV
2023	A+	Fort Wayne	4	1	0	58	47	2.02	1.03	18.6	234	29	81	2.34	1.6	7.3	4.7	0.3	107
2023	AA	San Antonio	2	3	0	38	43	4.03	1.42	13.4	305	41	73	4.66	1.7	10.2	6.1	0.7	157

Wiry RHP with strong repertoire and pitchability. Promoted to AA in mid-July and had workload monitored in first pro season. Throws deep mix of pitches with SL being best of bunch. Can live in fat part of plate too much but can keep hitters off balance with sound CU. May have more velocity in tank with added strength. Exceptional control.

McCarty,D.J.

SP | Texas | EXP MLB DEBUT: 2026 | H/W: 6-2 145 | FUT: #5 SP/swingman | 6C

Thrws R Age 21
2020 FA (CA)

Velo	Pitch	Grade
91-95	FB	++
77-80	CB	+++
82-88	SL	++

Year	Lev	Team	W	L	Sv	IP	K	ERA	WHIP	BF/G	OBA	H%	S%	xERA	Ctl	Dom	Cmd	hr/9	BPV
2021	Rk	ACL Rangers	0	3	0	26	36	7.90	2.40	8.6	328	45	69	8.43	9.3	12.4	1.3	1.7	-10
2022	Rk	ACL Rangers	3	3	0	46	51	5.27	1.65	18.7	286	39	65	4.46	4.7	10.0	2.1	0.2	71
2022	A	Down East	0	1	0	1	2	15.00	4.17	8.4	470	68	60	14.22	15.0	15.0	1.0	0.0	-117
2023	A	Down East	1	3	0	73	86	3.07	1.16	12.7	219	32	71	2.27	3.3	10.6	3.2	0.1	119

Unheralded 2020 NDFA slowly but surely moving through system. Fast arm with low 3/4 delivery, lots of GB with only 1 HRA in 2023. FT now touching 95 with CB flashing plus. Solid SL rounds out repertoire. Could add some weight to frame, and improve offspeed to project beyond a bulk guy.

McCollum,Tommy — RP — Philadelphia

EXP MLB DEBUT: 2025 | H/W: 6-5 260 | FUT: Middle reliever | 8E

Thrws R Age 24 — 2021 FA (Wingate)

Year	Lev	Team	W	L	Sv	IP	K	ERA	WHIP	BF/G	OBA	H%	S%	xERA	Ctl	Dom	Cmd	hr/9	BPV
2021	NCAA	Wingate	2	2	0	19	29	6.56	1.67	5.4	156	24	60	3.56	10.3	13.6	1.3	0.9	-16
2021	A	Clearwater	0	0	1	12	15	6.64	2.05	6.6	207	29	67	4.94	11.8	11.1	0.9	0.7	-102
2022	A	Clearwater	1	0	5	31	52	1.45	0.87	5.0	112	18	92	1.03	4.6	15.1	3.3	0.9	164
2023	A+	Jersey Shore	0	0	7	35	56	2.31	1.14	4.1	147	28	78	1.26	5.9	14.4	2.4	0.0	118
2023	AA	Reading	1	0	1	9	11	3.96	1.32	3.8	105	17	67	1.32	8.9	10.9	1.2	0.0	-27

Velo	Pitch	Grade
92-95	FB	+++
85-87	SP	+++

Undrafted Division II free agent has excelled on fastball/splitter combination and ended the season in Double-A. Four-seamer has tons of ride and misses bats; both pitches though are a bit averse to the strike zone. Has breaking balls that he rarely throws, so this will be the arsenal. Control must improve to get into an MLB bullpen.

McCullough,Brody — SP — Chicago (N)

EXP MLB DEBUT: 2025 | H/W: 6-4 205 | FUT: #5 SP/swingman | 6B

Thrws R Age 23 — 2022 (10) Wingate

Year	Lev	Team	W	L	Sv	IP	K	ERA	WHIP	BF/G	OBA	H%	S%	xERA	Ctl	Dom	Cmd	hr/9	BPV
2022	NCAA	Wingate	9	1	0	63	110	2.42	1.14	20.9	212	41	76	1.96	3.4	15.7	4.6	0.0	208
2022	Rk	ACL Cubs	1	0	0	2	3	0.00	1.00	7.6	262	43	100	2.27	0.0	13.5		0.0	261
2022	A	Myrtle Beach	1	0	0	5	9	1.80	0.80	4.5	124	28	75	0.15	3.6	16.2	4.5	0.0	212
2023	A	Myrtle Beach	5	2	0	50	74	2.87	0.92	15.6	170	28	70	1.45	3.1	13.3	4.4	0.5	175
2023	A+	South Bend	0	3	0	36	34	4.25	1.28	16.4	240	30	67	3.43	3.5	8.5	2.4	0.8	77

Velo	Pitch	Grade
92-94	FB	+++
80-83	SL	+++
76-78	CB	++
82-84	CU	+

DII All-American stands tall with short arm action and funky mechanics and doesn't use the lower half well. FB sits at 92-94 but with a bit of late life and has room for more if he cleans up mechanics. Low-80s SL is best secondary but needs more consistency while CB and CU are fringe at best. Improved command on display in solid pro debut.

McDermott,Chayce — SP — Baltimore

EXP MLB DEBUT: 2024 | H/W: 6-3 197 | FUT: #4 starter | 7C

Thrws R Age 25 — 2021 (4) Ball State

Year	Lev	Team	W	L	Sv	IP	K	ERA	WHIP	BF/G	OBA	H%	S%	xERA	Ctl	Dom	Cmd	hr/9	BPV
2022	A+	Aberdeen	0	1	0	5		3.60	0.80	9.1	175	33	67	2.35	1.8	18.0	10.0	1.8	293
2022	A+	Asheville	6	1	0	72	114	5.50	1.39	15.9	219	35	62	3.75	5.4	14.3	2.7	1.1	129
2022	AA	Bowie	1	1	0	26	36	6.18	1.41	18.5	187	21	63	4.65	6.9	12.4	1.8	2.4	55
2023	AA	Bowie	5	6	1	68	88	3.57	1.26	17.4	179	26	74	2.68	5.8	11.6	2.0	0.8	70
2023	AAA	Norfolk Tides	3	2	0	50	64	2.51	1.02	19.3	160	24	77	1.61	4.3	11.5	2.7	0.5	108

Velo	Pitch	Grade
93-96	FB	+++
82-85	SL	+++
76-79	CB	+++
84-87	CU	++

Hard-throwing, high-3/4s slot RHP had breakout season in first full season with BAL. Nearly unhittable at times, struggled with strikes and staying on time in delivery. Four-seam FB is borderline pitch with flat-angled approach and plus, uncontrollable rising action. SL is also nearly plus pitch too. Also throws average CB and fringe CU.

McDonald,Trevor — SP — San Francisco

EXP MLB DEBUT: 2025 | H/W: 6-2 200 | FUT: #4 starter | 7D

Thrws R Age 23 — 2019 (11) HS (MS)

Year	Lev	Team	W	L	Sv	IP	K	ERA	WHIP	BF/G	OBA	H%	S%	xERA	Ctl	Dom	Cmd	hr/9	BPV
2022	A	San Jose	6	3	2	90	102	2.40	1.27	13.6	226	32	80	2.68	4.0	10.2	2.6	0.2	94
2022	A+	Eugene	0	0	0	11	18	1.64	1.18	22.0	262	41	100	4.25	1.6	14.7	9.0	1.6	239
2023	Rk	ACL Giants B	0	1	0	8	11	1.10	1.22	8.3	257	40	90	2.77	2.2	12.1	5.5	0.0	176
2023	Rk	ACL Giants O	0	0	0	1	1	18.00	2.00	4.8	262	35	0	4.84	9.0	9.0	1.0	0.0	-63
2023	A+	Eugene	3	1	0	37	39	0.97	0.86	15.2	186	26	90	1.24	1.9	9.4	4.9	0.2	136

Velo	Pitch	Grade
91-96	FB	+++
78-80	CB	+++
82-84	SL	++
81-83	CU	++

Versatile RHP who moved back to SP in 2023 after RP in 2-22. Has made slow climb up ladder as injuries have taken toll. Returned in July and showed much improved control and stuff that was difficult to hit. K rate has slightly declined. Operates with FB with high spin rate and SL/CT that keeps hitters honest. Needs better CU to stick as SP.

McDougal,Tanner — SP — Chicago (A)

EXP MLB DEBUT: 2025 | H/W: 6-5 185 | FUT: Setup reliever | 7D

Thrws R Age 21 — 2021 (5) HS (NV)

Year	Lev	Team	W	L	Sv	IP	K	ERA	WHIP	BF/G	OBA	H%	S%	xERA	Ctl	Dom	Cmd	hr/9	BPV
2021	Rk	ACL White Sox	1	2	0	9	17	9.78	1.63	6.8	278	47	38	5.90	4.9	16.6	3.4	2.0	185
2023	A	Kannapolis	0	3	0	69	80	4.17	1.40	13.9	217	30	71	3.35	5.6	10.4	1.9	0.7	54

Velo	Pitch	Grade
94-96	FB	++++
78-80	CB	+++
87-89	CU	++

Tall RHP, back from Tommy John surgery, made strides in first full season of pro ball. Improved mechanics of 3/4s delivery as season wore on. It's a power RP delivery despite SP role. Plus 4-seam FB is best pitch with ride/run profile. Best secondary is a horizontal SL with above-average upside. CU has too many tells in delivery to be effective.

McFarlane,Alex — SP — Philadelphia

EXP MLB DEBUT: 2026 | H/W: 6-3 215 | FUT: #4 starter | 8D

Thrws R Age 22 — 2022 (4) Miami

Year	Lev	Team	W	L	Sv	IP	K	ERA	WHIP	BF/G	OBA	H%	S%	xERA	Ctl	Dom	Cmd	hr/9	BPV
2022	NCAA	Miami	3	2	0	45	68	4.00	1.36	7.0	244	39	71	3.49	4.0	13.6	3.4	0.6	155
2022	A	Clearwater	0	3	0	8	12	9.00	1.88	12.5	347	51	50	6.86	3.4	13.5	4.0	1.1	170
2023	A	Clearwater	0	4	0	50	69	5.75	1.68	14.1	246	37	65	4.44	6.8	12.4	1.8	0.7	57

Velo	Pitch	Grade
94-98	FB	+++
83-86	SL	++++
85-88	CT	++
85-88	CU	++

College RP transitioned to a starter with a high-spin sinker and a plus-plus slider that he get chases on and lands for strikes. Mixed in cutter and change. Needs to improve control; but is a long and loose athlete. Could use more stamina work, including holding velocity deeper into games. Given his past, there's some reliever risk.

McGarry,Griff — SP — Philadelphia

EXP MLB DEBUT: 2024 | H/W: 6-2 190 | FUT: Setup reliever | 8E

Thrws R Age 24 — 2021 (5) Virginia

Year	Lev	Team	W	L	Sv	IP	K	ERA	WHIP	BF/G	OBA	H%	S%	xERA	Ctl	Dom	Cmd	hr/9	BPV
2022	AA	Reading	1	3	0	32	39	2.24	1.02	15.5	125	19	78	1.04	5.6	10.9	2.0	0.3	63
2022	AAA	Lehigh Valley	0	2	0	8	9	9.00	2.00	5.5	237	27	57	6.61	10.1	10.1	1.0	2.3	-73
2023	A	Clearwater	0	0	0	1	2	9.00	1.00	3.8	262	0		10.69	0.0	18.0		9.0	342
2023	AA	Reading	1	1	0	54	74	3.15	1.24	16.9	169	26	76	2.37	6.0	12.3	2.1	0.7	78
2023	AAA	Lehigh Valley	0	2	0	4	5	43.90	5.37	11.2	409	55	9	15.82	30.7	11.0	0.4	0.0	-614

Velo	Pitch	Grade
93-96	FB	++++
84-87	SL	++++
79-82	CB	++
87-90	CU	+

2022 glimmer of promise evaporated quickly as throwing strikes became even more infrequent. FB/SL duo formidable on their own; CB showed flashes; but all marred by ugly control and high-pitch outings. Team is working to tweak his delivery, but looking more and more like a bullpen arm. Wide range of possible outcomes.

McGowan,Christian — SP — Philadelphia

EXP MLB DEBUT: 2026 | H/W: 6-0 205 | FUT: #3 starter | 8D

Thrws R Age 24 — 2021 (7) Eastern OK ST

Year	Lev	Team	W	L	Sv	IP	K	ERA	WHIP	BF/G	OBA	H%	S%	xERA	Ctl	Dom	Cmd	hr/9	BPV
2022	A+	Jersey Shore	0	1	0	7	7	5.07	1.41	15.0	285	35	67	4.87	2.5	8.9	3.5	1.3	109
2023	Rk	FCL Phillies	0	0	0	5	6	3.60	0.40	8.1	124	20	0		0.0	10.8		0.0	212
2023	A	Clearwater	0	1	0	2	2	18.00	3.50	12.6	470	52	50	16.83	9.0	9.0	1.0	4.5	-63
2023	A+	Jersey Shore	0	0	0	16	17	2.81	1.25	13.0	250	35	75	2.77	2.8	9.6	3.4	0.0	114
2023	AAA	Lehigh Valley	0	0	0	2	3	0.00	2.27	11.2	244	38	100	5.25	12.3	12.3	1.0	0.0	-92

Velo	Pitch	Grade
93-96	FB	+++
86-88	SL	+++
86-89	CU	++

Hard sinker/slider-centric hurler eased his way back from Tommy John surgery and finished in the Fall League. Bowling-ball 2-seamer, potential plus slider evoke a lot of GB contact. Solid starter's frame and a CU with some promise are reasons he could stay in the rotation, but could easily see this playing up in the pen as well.

McGraw,Teddy — SP — Seattle

EXP MLB DEBUT: 2026 | H/W: 6-3 210 | FUT: #4 starter | 7D

Thrws R Age 22 — 2023 (3) Wake Forest

Year	Lev	Team	W	L	Sv	IP	K	ERA	WHIP	BF/G	OBA	H%	S%	xERA	Ctl	Dom	Cmd	hr/9	BPV

Velo	Pitch	Grade
92-95	FB	+++
83-85	SL	++
85-88	CU	++

Did not pitch in 2023 due to ongoing elbow issues. Should be ready to go soon. When healthy, has potential for premium FB with velocity and run. Lot of sinking action that induces GB. Sweeping SL could be the key to pro success as it features quality depth but rarely throws for strikes. Walk rate is a concern.

McGreevy,Michael — SP — St. Louis

EXP MLB DEBUT: 2024 | H/W: 6-4 215 | FUT: #4 starter | 7D

Thrws R Age 23 — 2021 (1) UC Santa Barbara

Year	Lev	Team	W	L	Sv	IP	K	ERA	WHIP	BF/G	OBA	H%	S%	xERA	Ctl	Dom	Cmd	hr/9	BPV
2021	A	Palm Beach	0	0	0	6	4	9.00	1.83	5.6	371	41	50	7.63	1.5	6.0	4.0	1.5	86
2022	A+	Peoria	3	1	0	45	41	2.59	1.00	21.5	244	32	73	2.26	0.8	8.2	10.3	0.2	144
2022	AA	Springfield	6	4	0	99	76	4.64	1.36	20.7	281	32	69	4.72	2.4	6.9	2.9	1.3	79
2023	AA	Springfield	2	0	0	18	16	1.48	0.99	23.1	249	32	83	2.12	0.5	7.9	16.0	0.0	147
2023	AAA	Memphis	11	6	0	134	107	4.50	1.47	24.0	297	35	72	5.10	2.5	7.2	2.9	1.1	80

Velo	Pitch	Grade
90-92	FB	++
84-86	SL	+++
76-78	CB	++
83-85	CU	+

Former 1st rounder pounds the zone with a 4-pitch mix. Uses a quick tempo and repeatable mechanics, but stuff is more hittable than in college - .286 BAA. Low-90s FB has good arm side run, but lacks swing-and-miss velocity. Above-average SL is best offering and along with 12-6 CB and below-average CU has the tools to be a back-end starter.

McLean,Nolan — SP — New York (N)

EXP MLB DEBUT: 2025 | H/W: 6-4 214 | FUT: Setup reliever | 7D

Thrws R Age 22 — 2023 (3) Oklahoma State

Year	Lev	Team	W	L	Sv	IP	K	ERA	WHIP	BF/G	OBA	H%	S%	xERA	Ctl	Dom	Cmd	hr/9	BPV

Velo	Pitch	Grade
93-95	FB	++++
88-90	CT	+++
84-86	SL	+++

Two-way player being developed as both was drafted out of Oklahoma State in 2023. RP/3B prospect. At the plate, there is big power potential but questions regarding hit tool will likely push profile to RP only. 3-pitch pitcher. Heavy sinker is go to pitch, producing lots of ground ball contact. CT and SL project as average-or-better pitches.

Mederos,Victor

SP | **Los Angeles (A)** | EXP MLB DEBUT: 2023 | H/W: 6-2 227 | FUT: Setup reliever | **7D**

Thrws R Age 22		Year	Lev	Team	W	L	Sv	IP	K	ERA	WHIP	BF/G	OBA	H%	S%	xERA	Ctl	Dom	Cmd	hr/9	BPV
2022 (6) Oklahoma State																					
93-96 FB	+ + + +	2022	NCAA	Oklahoma St	4	4	0	66	62	5.59	1.36	19.7	270	31	64	5.02	2.9	8.5	3.0	1.8	93
85-87 SL	+ + + +	2022	A+	Tri-City	0	1	0	16	15	5.63	1.50	11.5	250	32	61	3.94	5.1	8.4	1.7	0.6	33
81-83 CB	+ +	2023	AA	Rocket City	4	9	0	92	99	5.67	1.48	19.8	264	31	68	5.47	4.2	9.7	2.3	2.1	79
86-88 CU	+	2023	MLB	LA Angels	0	0	0	3	3	9.00	2.67	5.5	371	48	63	8.29	9.0	9.0	1.0	0.0	-63

2022 6th round pick made MLB debut despite sideways performance in Double-A. 3/4s delivery with effort. Struggles staying balanced. 5-pitch pitcher. Mid-90s sinker is groundball darling. Two-plane breaking SL is best pitch, especially dropping out of zone. Poor overall command and lackluster complementary pitches push profile to pen.

Mejia,Juan

RP | **Colorado** | EXP MLB DEBUT: 2024 | H/W: 6-3 200 | FUT: Middle reliever | **6C**

Thrws R Age 23		Year	Lev	Team	W	L	Sv	IP	K	ERA	WHIP	BF/G	OBA	H%	S%	xERA	Ctl	Dom	Cmd	hr/9	BPV
2017 FA (DR)		2021	A	Fresno	3	5	8	46	66	4.87	1.45	4.6	252	40	65	3.65	4.5	12.9	2.9	0.4	128
95-97 FB	+ + + +	2022	A	Fresno	2	2	6	34	43	3.71	1.41	4.6	232	34	74	3.44	5.0	11.4	2.3	0.5	87
86-89 SL	+ + + +	2022	A+	Spokane	1	1	0	16	17	6.75	1.50	5.3	262	33	55	4.63	4.5	9.6	2.1	1.1	69
CU	+	2023	A+	Spokane	2	2	1	43	64	4.81	1.40	5.2	234	37	65	3.49	4.8	13.4	2.8	0.6	129
		2023	AA	Hartford	1	3	1	15	22	5.92	1.58	5.1	259	40	61	4.26	5.3	13.0	2.4	0.6	109

High octane reliever floundered at two stops, but showed enough effort in the AFL to earn a spot on the Rockies 40-man roster and avoid Rule 5 draft. Uptick in FB velocity which now sits 95-97, topping at 100 and punched out 13.2 per 9 in 2023. Also owns a potentially plus SL and fringe CU Below-average CU limits upside, but the FB/SL mix can be electric.

Melendez,Jaime

SP | **Houston** | EXP MLB DEBUT: 2024 | H/W: 5-8 190 | FUT: Middle reliever | **6D**

Thrws R Age 22		Year	Lev	Team	W	L	Sv	IP	K	ERA	WHIP	BF/G	OBA	H%	S%	xERA	Ctl	Dom	Cmd	hr/9	BPV
2019 FA (MX)		2021	A	Fayetteville	2	2	0	18		0.50	0.66	10.5	121	32	100	0.21	2.5	18.9	7.6	0.5	291
94-96 FB	+ + +	2021	A+	Asheville	2	3	0	32	41	4.78	1.81	13.5	274	39	73	5.03	6.8	11.5	1.7	0.6	43
86-88 SL	+ + +	2021	AA	Corpus Christi	0	1	0	7	11	6.25	1.67	10.8	283	46	58	4.24	5.0	13.8	2.8	0.0	131
82-85 CB	+ +	2022	AA	Corpus Christi	2	8	0	73	106	5.04	1.50	13.8	222	34	67	3.84	6.3	13.0	2.1	0.9	83
88-90 CU	+ +	2023	AA	Corpus Christi	2	0	0	9	8	5.87	1.63	13.6	236	25	69	5.41	6.8	7.8	1.1	2.0	-26

21-year-old RHP pitched very little in 2023 due to April injury, returned for Arizona Fall League. Short-statured, but has good velo on FB. Throws from high arm slot with balanced delivery. Lack of command, bat-missing stuff suggests middle relief role.

Melton,Troy

SP | **Detroit** | EXP MLB DEBUT: 2025 | H/W: 6-4 210 | FUT: #5 SP/swingman | **7D**

Thrws R Age 23		Year	Lev	Team	W	L	Sv	IP	K	ERA	WHIP	BF/G	OBA	H%	S%	xERA	Ctl	Dom	Cmd	hr/9	BPV
2022 (4) San Diego State																					
94-95 FB	+ + +	2022	NCAA	San Diego St	5	2	0	65	67	2.07	1.11	23.2	237	32	81	2.51	2.1	9.3	4.5	0.3	129
83-85 SL	+ +	2022	A	Lakeland	0	0	0	5	5	0.00	0.60	8.6	175	25	100	0.25	0.0	9.0		0.0	180
90-92 CT	+ +	2023	A	Lakeland	0	0	0	26	33	3.44	1.22	15.1	260	36	76	3.80	2.1	11.3	5.5	1.0	166
86-88 CU	+ +	2023	A+	West Michigan	3	1	0	65	61	2.49	1.12	16.0	231	30	77	2.47	2.5	8.4	3.4	0.3	103

Late developing hurler worked hard to gain strength and velo, which led to breakout. Lowered arm slot to get more carry and uptick in FB velocity, which now sits at 94-95, topping at 99. Short arm action, some deception, and improved mechanics allow secondaries to play up. SL, CU, and CT all average at best and will need to improve to remain a SP.

Mena,Cristian

SP | **Chicago (A)** | EXP MLB DEBUT: 2024 | H/W: 6-2 170 | FUT: #4 starter | **7C**

Thrws R Age 21		Year	Lev	Team	W	L	Sv	IP	K	ERA	WHIP	BF/G	OBA	H%	S%	xERA	Ctl	Dom	Cmd	hr/9	BPV
2019 FA (DR)		2022	A	Kannapolis	1	2	0	53	66	2.71	1.13	19.1	231	34	76	2.52	2.5	11.2	4.4	0.3	150
90-93 FB	+ + +	2022	A+	Winston-Salem	1	3	0	40	47	4.70	1.52	17.4	256	35	70	4.37	4.9	10.5	2.1	0.9	74
83-85 SL	+ + + +	2022	AA	Birmingham	0	1	0	10	13	6.30	1.70	15.1	362	50	63	6.49	0.9	11.7	13.0	0.9	204
81-83 CB	+ + +	2023	AA	Birmingham	7	6	0	114	136	4.66	1.35	20.7	235	31	69	4.09	4.3	10.7	2.5	1.3	94
87-89 CU	+ +	2023	AAA	Charlotte	1	1	0	19	20	6.09	1.82	22.3	324	42	65	5.77	4.2	9.4	2.2	0.5	73

Over-the-top RHP with feel for spin struggled to keep hitters off his subpar 4-seam FB. Achieves solid extension in delivery but will lose release point at times. SL and CB are best offerings. Can vary movement profile of SL. It's best as gyro SL. CB has solid depth and strong movement. Need to refine FB mix. 2-seam FB should be primary FB.

Messick,Parker

SP | **Cleveland** | EXP MLB DEBUT: 2024 | H/W: 6-0 225 | FUT: #4 starter | **7C**

Thrws L Age 23		Year	Lev	Team	W	L	Sv	IP	K	ERA	WHIP	BF/G	OBA	H%	S%	xERA	Ctl	Dom	Cmd	hr/9	BPV
2022 (2) Florida State																					
90-93 FB	+ + +																				
75-77 CB	+ +																				
77-80 SL	+ +	2023	A	Lynchburg	3	2	0	56	61	3.04	1.10	17.0	232	33	70	2.33	2.2	9.8	4.4	0.2	133
81-84 CU	+ + +	2023	A+	Lake County	2	4	0	65	75	4.43	1.34	20.8	253	32	71	4.33	3.5	10.4	3.0	1.4	111

Short lefty who had positive contributions on two levels of minors. Had higher K rate in High-A, but walk rate rose too. Works with solid FB/CU combination with repetitive arm speed and slot. Hides ball well in delivery and tough on RHH thanks to tumbling CU. Breaking balls a little short. Lot of moving parts in mechanics but throws strikes.

Messinger,Zach

SP | **New York (A)** | EXP MLB DEBUT: 2025 | H/W: 6-6 225 | FUT: #5 SP/swingman | **6C**

Thrws R Age 24		Year	Lev	Team	W	L	Sv	IP	K	ERA	WHIP	BF/G	OBA	H%	S%	xERA	Ctl	Dom	Cmd	hr/9	BPV
2021 (13) Virginia																					
90-93 FB	+ + +																				
81-83 SL	+ + +	2022	A	Tampa	1	8	2	83	112	4.33	1.36	11.2	225	34	68	3.21	4.9	12.1	2.5	0.5	105
77-79 CB	+ + +	2023	A+	Hudson Valley	1	10	0	97	113	4.36	1.39	19.5	231	30	72	4.01	4.9	10.5	2.1	1.2	74
85-87 CU	+ +	2023	AA	Somerset	0	0	0	4	7	4.39	1.22	16.6	257	40	75	4.80	2.2	15.4	7.0	2.2	235

Tall RHP with feel for spin pitched better than 2023 line would indicate. Struggled flying open from 3/4s delivery at times during season. 4-seam FB is solid offering, especially up in zone. SL and CB flashed later in the season as above-average offerings, especially the SL with sweepy break. Struggles corralling fading CU.

Meyer,Max

SP | **Miami** | EXP MLB DEBUT: 2022 | H/W: 6-0 196 | FUT: #1 starter | **9D**

Thrws R Age 25		Year	Lev	Team	W	L	Sv	IP	K	ERA	WHIP	BF/G	OBA	H%	S%	xERA	Ctl	Dom	Cmd	hr/9	BPV
2020 (1) Minnesota		2021	AAA	Jacksonville	0	1	0	10	17	0.90	0.80	18.1	175	31	100	1.53	1.8	15.3	8.5	0.9	245
94-96 FB	+ + +	2022	A	Jupiter	0	0	0	3	4	3.00	0.33	9.5	106	18	0		0.0	12.0		0.0	234
88-90 SL	+ + + +	2022	AAA	Jacksonville	3	4	0	58	65	3.72	1.00	18.5	193	26	64	2.16	2.9	10.1	3.4	0.8	120
86-89 CU	+ + + +	2022	MLB	Miami	0	1	0	6	6	7.50	1.50	13.0	293	31	57	6.84	3.0	9.0	3.0	3.0	99
		2023	--	Did Not Play																	

Hard-throwing RHP missed all of 2023 recovering from Tommy John surgery. Athletic, 3/4s delivery. Achieves solid extension despite shorter frame. 4-seam FB has solid ride but he struggles to command it. Short, tight SL has nasty movement profile. Prior to injury, CU become plus offering with solid arm-side run with late drop.

Meyer,Noble

SP | **Miami** | EXP MLB DEBUT: 2026 | H/W: 6-5 185 | FUT: #1 starter | **9D**

Thrws R Age 19		Year	Lev	Team	W	L	Sv	IP	K	ERA	WHIP	BF/G	OBA	H%	S%	xERA	Ctl	Dom	Cmd	hr/9	BPV
2023 (1) HS (OR)																					
92-95 FB	+ + + +																				
77-83 CB	+ + + +																				
83-85 SL	+ + +	2023	Rk	FCL Marlins	0	1	0	4	6	4.50	1.25	8.1	151	27	60	1.57	6.8	13.5	2.0	0.0	79
CU		2023	A	Jupiter	0	0	0	7	9	3.86	1.86	10.9	313	46	77	5.21	5.1	11.6	2.3	0.0	87

Hard-throwing low 3/4s RHP was best prep pitcher in 2024 draft. High-waisted frame with room to grow. Athletic delivery with plus-plus arm speed. Two FBs: sinker has plus arm-side run and downward break; 4-seamer is developing. Sweeping SL has plus-plus potential with devastating late two-plane break. Showcased promising CU in pro debut.

Milbrandt,Karson

SP | **Miami** | EXP MLB DEBUT: 2026 | H/W: 6-2 190 | FUT: #3 starter | **8E**

Thrws R Age 19		Year	Lev	Team	W	L	Sv	IP	K	ERA	WHIP	BF/G	OBA	H%	S%	xERA	Ctl	Dom	Cmd	hr/9	BPV
2022 (3) HS (MO)																					
93-96 FB	+ + + +																				
79-82 CB	+ + + +	2022	A	Jupiter	0	0	0	2	1	9.00	1.50	8.6	262	30	33	3.62	4.5	4.5	1.0	0.0	-23
84-87 CU	+ + +	2023	A	Jupiter	3	3	0	52	52	5.36	1.46	18.6	254	33	63	4.01	4.5	9.0	2.0	0.7	58
		2023	A+	Beloit	0	3	0	43	41	4.60	1.63	17.4	275	36	70	4.28	5.0	8.6	1.7	0.2	37

Projectable low 3/4s RHP showed promise despite struggles with command and whiffs. Tall frame with room to grow. Doesn't extend well in delivery. Varies between 4-seam and sinker as primary offering. The FBs tend to bleed into each other; 4-seam shape more conducive for long term success. CB projects to be plus offering with sharp, late break.

Miller,Cole

SP | **Oakland** | EXP MLB DEBUT: 2027 | H/W: 6-6 226 | FUT: #3 starter | **8D**

Thrws R Age 18		Year	Lev	Team	W	L	Sv	IP	K	ERA	WHIP	BF/G	OBA	H%	S%	xERA	Ctl	Dom	Cmd	hr/9	BPV
2023 (4) HS (CA)																					
90-94 FB	+ + +																				
81-85 SL	+ + +																				
80-85 CU	+ +																				

Young, tall SP with interesting ingredients and high upside. Didn't pitch upon signing and may take several years to develop. Has big frame and still growing. Will need to iron out delivery and find consistent secondary offerings. Best pitch is FB with late drop and adds solid SL with good depth. Can slow arm when using CU.

Miller,Erik | RP | San Francisco | EXP MLB DEBUT: 2024 | H/W: 6-5 240 | FUT: Setup reliever | 7D

Thrws L Age 26	Year	Lev	Team	W	L	Sv	IP	K	ERA	WHIP	BF/G	OBA	H%	S%	xERA	Ctl	Dom	Cmd	hr/9	BPV
2019 (4) Stanford	2021	A+	Jersey Shore	0	0	0	3	4	0.00	1.94	14.7	255	39	100	4.56	8.7	11.6	1.3	0.0	-8
93-96 FB +++	2022	AA	Reading	1	0	0	36	44	2.24	1.16	6.5	197	30	79	1.89	4.2	11.0	2.6	0.0	101
81-85 SL +++	2022	AAA	Lehigh Valley	0	1	0	12	18	7.50	2.33	6.2	293	39	75	8.89	10.5	13.5	1.3	3.0	-23
83-87 CU +++	2023	AA	Richmond	1	0	1	10	15	0.89	0.69	5.9	95	18	86		3.6	13.4	3.8	0.0	162
	2023	AAA	Sacramento	2	1	14	52	73	2.77	1.31	4.5	155	25	79	2.10	7.1	12.6	1.8	0.3	54

Very large RP who posted most saves in SF minors. Misses bats with pure heat, dynamic sweeping SL and deceptive delivery. Has trouble repeating high effort mechanics and control has suffered as a result. Has three solid offerings in arsenal including CU with late fade. Rarely allows HR but will need to spot FB better to get ahead in counts.

Miller,Jacob | SP | Miami | EXP MLB DEBUT: 2026 | H/W: 6-2 180 | FUT: #4 starter | 7D

Thrws R Age 20	Year	Lev	Team	W	L	Sv	IP	K	ERA	WHIP	BF/G	OBA	H%	S%	xERA	Ctl	Dom	Cmd	hr/9	BPV
2022 (2) HS (OH)																				
91-93 FB +++	2022	Rk	FCL Marlins	0	1	0	3	3	8.44	1.88	5.0	307	33	60	7.83	5.6	8.4	1.5	2.8	18
80-83 CB +++	2022	A	Jupiter	0	1	0	2	3	0.00	0.50	6.6	151	27	100		0.0	13.5		0.0	261
83-85 SL +++	2023	Rk	FCL Marlins	0	0	0	4	5	0.00	0.95	7.9	144	23	100	0.79	4.3	10.7	2.5	0.0	95
85-87 CU +++	2023	A	Jupiter	2	4	0	59	50	4.72	1.20	17.0	216	27	59	2.68	3.8	7.6	2.0	0.5	52

Developing prep arm from 2022 draft showed promise with an average to above average 4-pitch arsenal. Repeatable 3/4s delivery with below-average extension. Has room to grow in average build. Must improve spin profile of 4-seam FB to get most out of pitch. Has excellent feel for spin with distinct SL and CB as well as his average CU.

Miller,Mason | SP | Oakland | EXP MLB DEBUT: 2023 | H/W: 6-5 200 | FUT: #3 starter | 8C

Thrws R Age 25	Year	Lev	Team	W	L	Sv	IP	K	ERA	WHIP	BF/G	OBA	H%	S%	xERA	Ctl	Dom	Cmd	hr/9	BPV
2021 (3) Gardner-Webb	2022	AAA	Las Vegas	0	1	0	5		5.40	1.20	10.1	262	30	75	6.17	1.8	12.6	7.0	3.6	196
96-100 FB +++++	2023	A	Stockton	0	0	0	3	4	5.63	1.56	7.0	250	28	75	6.19	5.6	11.3	2.0	2.8	69
85-88 SL ++++	2023	AA	Midland	0	0	0	3	8	5.63	0.63	11.0	181	0		5.53	0.0	22.5		5.6	423
86-88 CU ++	2023	AAA	Las Vegas	1	0	0	12	23	0.00	0.50	10.0	81	22	100		2.3	17.3	7.7	0.0	268
	2023	MLB	Oakland	0	3	0	33	38	3.81	1.21	13.3	205	28	68	2.61	4.4	10.3	2.4	0.5	87

Tall SP who reached OAK despite only 39 IP in minors. Missed time with injuries but has wipeout stuff when on mound. Hits triple digits with ease and complements FB with plus SL. Posts incredibly high K rate but has RP risk due to lack of CU and max effort. Exhibits nice control with average FB command. Needs to stay healthy.

Misiorowski,Jacob | SP | Milwaukee | EXP MLB DEBUT: 2025 | H/W: 6-7 190 | FUT: #1 starter | 9D

Thrws R Age 22	Year	Lev	Team	W	L	Sv	IP	K	ERA	WHIP	BF/G	OBA	H%	S%	xERA	Ctl	Dom	Cmd	hr/9	BPV
2022 (2) Crowder JC	2022	NJCA/	Crowder	10	0	0	76	136	2.72	1.25	20.6	189	38	78	2.30	5.3	16.1	3.0	0.4	164
94-98 FB ++++	2022	A	Carolina	0	0	0	1	3	7.50	6.67	5.7	228	72	88	16.02	52.5	22.5	0.4	0.0	-995
79-82 CB +++	2023	A	Carolina	1	1	0	26	46	3.09	0.84	10.7	119	26	59	0.20	4.1	15.8	3.8	0.0	191
83-86 SL ++++	2023	A+	Wisconsin	1	0	0	23	28	1.94	1.25	15.7	187	29	83	1.99	5.4	10.9	2.0	0.0	67
89-92 CT +++	2023	AA	Biloxi	2	1	0	21	36	5.57	1.57	18.4	223	39	65	3.99	6.9	15.4	2.3	0.9	111

Tall, high-ceiling SP with big breakout campaign and ended season in late August due to arm fatigue. Posted highest K rate and lowest oppBA in org. Has ace potential with multiple plus pitches. Can hit triple digits with FB with plus spin rate. Hard SL is dynamic with good depth. Mixes in CB and CT. Flyball pitcher and will need to repeat delivery.

Monegro,Yordanny | SP | Boston | EXP MLB DEBUT: 2026 | H/W: 6-4 180 | FUT: #3 starter | 8E

Thrws R Age 21	Year	Lev	Team	W	L	Sv	IP	K	ERA	WHIP	BF/G	OBA	H%	S%	xERA	Ctl	Dom	Cmd	hr/9	BPV
2020 FA (DR)	2021	Rk	DSL Red Sox B	0	1	0	39	41	3.67	1.51	13.0	235	33	73	3.23	5.7	9.4	1.6	0.0	32
91-96 FB +++	2022	Rk	FCL Red Sox	1	2	0	25	24	7.50	1.90	13.2	324	36	66	7.88	5.0	8.6	1.7	2.5	37
77-80 CB +++	2023	Rk	FCL Red Sox	2	0	0	15	20	1.20	0.60	17.1	106	18	78		2.4	12.0	5.0	0.0	169
85-88 SL +	2023	A	Salem	3	2	0	40	60	2.46	1.24	18.2	225	38	78	2.41	3.8	13.4	3.5	0.0	157
84-87 CU +	2023	A+	Greenville	1	1	0	10	13	1.80	1.30	20.6	221	32	92	3.36	4.5	11.7	2.6	0.9	107

Tall, lean RHP with loads of projection. Led org in ERA and posted very high K rate due to FB/CB combo. FB can be too straight at times and could add velocity with more strength. Command comes and goes but is tough to square up when FB thrown with conviction. CB has great depth while CU in infancy stage. More thrower than pitcher.

Montalvo,Joseph | SP | Texas | EXP MLB DEBUT: 2025 | H/W: 6-2 185 | FUT: #4 starter | 7D

Thrws R Age 21	Year	Lev	Team	W	L	Sv	IP	K	ERA	WHIP	BF/G	OBA	H%	S%	xERA	Ctl	Dom	Cmd	hr/9	BPV
2021 (20) HS (FL)																				
90-93 FB ++																				
80-83 SL +++																				
85-87 CU +++	2022	Rk	ACL Rangers	4	0	0	23	36	2.34	1.08	9.0	252	42	79	2.71	1.2	14.0	12.0	0.4	239
	2023	A	Down East	7	2	0	95	107	2.84	1.19	17.3	216	29	80	2.99	3.7	10.1	2.7	0.9	101

Solid full-season debut saw both secondaries flash plus - low-80s SL and mid-80s CU - while 92-mph FF played up. Repeatable, drop-and-drive delivery has average command projection so if FF ticks up he has mid-rotation upside, impressive for a 20th rounder. Now still more backend projection but stock materially up.

Montero,Keider | SP | Detroit | EXP MLB DEBUT: 2024 | H/W: 6-1 145 | FUT: #5 SP/swingman | 7D

Thrws R Age 23	Year	Lev	Team	W	L	Sv	IP	K	ERA	WHIP	BF/G	OBA	H%	S%	xERA	Ctl	Dom	Cmd	hr/9	BPV
2016 FA (VZ)	2021	A+	West Michigan	4	8	0	61	59	5.30	1.69	18.4	328	41	69	5.87	2.8	8.7	3.1	0.9	99
93-96 FB +++	2022	A+	West Michigan	7	7	0	103	101	4.53	1.33	17.1	256	32	68	4.04	3.2	8.8	2.7	1.0	89
83-85 SL ++++	2023	A+	West Michigan	0	0	0	16	22	2.81	0.88	14.8	181	28	69	1.50	2.3	12.4	5.5	0.6	180
77-80 CB +++	2023	AA	Erie	10	2	0	69	91	4.95	1.51	19.9	273	39	68	4.57	4.0	11.9	2.9	0.9	122
86-88 CU +	2023	AAA	Toledo	5	2	0	42	47	4.93	1.33	21.8	262	32	69	4.76	3.0	10.1	3.4	1.7	118

Works from the 3b side of the mound with significant cross-fire action. FB sits at 93-96, topping out at 98 mph and also features a low-90s two-seamer. Power sweeper is best offering with a high spin. Also mixes in an 11-to-5 CB and CU that he uses almost exclusively vs LHB. Pounds the strike zone and profiles better in a relief role.

Monteverde,Patrick | SP | Miami | EXP MLB DEBUT: 2024 | H/W: 6-2 200 | FUT: #5 SP/swingman | 6C

Thrws L Age 26	Year	Lev	Team	W	L	Sv	IP	K	ERA	WHIP	BF/G	OBA	H%	S%	xERA	Ctl	Dom	Cmd	hr/9	BPV
2021 (8) Texas Tech	2021	Rk	FCL Marlins	0	0	2	14	16	3.17	1.27	8.3	259	35	76	3.54	2.5	10.1	4.0	0.6	132
89-91 FB +++	2022	A+	Beloit	3	4	0	79	90	2.51	1.11	20.7	218	29	83	2.87	3.0	10.3	3.5	0.9	123
85-87 CT ++	2022	AA	Pensacola	1	0	0	30	32	5.07	1.42	21.4	303	38	68	5.38	1.8	9.5	5.3	1.5	141
76-79 CB +++	2023	AA	Pensacola	10	5	0	114	114	3.32	1.20	21.8	221	27	77	3.25	3.6	9.0	2.5	1.0	82
82-84 CU ++++	2023	AAA	Jacksonville	1	1	0	8	7	16.46	2.56	22.1	393	41	35	12.59	6.6	7.7	1.2	4.4	-22

Soft-tossing over-the-top lefty battles hitters with craftiness. Repeatable delivery with solid extension. 5-pitch arsenal. 4-seam FB has flat-angled approach, playing up ride. CU has crazy movement profile, plus pitch. Loopy CB is the least of his offerings with 12-to-6 break. Added a CT which is a below-average offerings. Also toils with SL.

Montgomery,Mason | SP | Tampa Bay | EXP MLB DEBUT: 2024 | H/W: 6-2 195 | FUT: #4 starter | 7C

Thrws L Age 23	Year	Lev	Team	W	L	Sv	IP	K	ERA	WHIP	BF/G	OBA	H%	S%	xERA	Ctl	Dom	Cmd	hr/9	BPV
2021 (6) Texas Tech	2021	Rk	FCL Rays	1	0	0	10	20	0.88	0.49	6.8	122	31	80		0.9	17.6	20.0	0.0	312
91-93 FB ++++	2022	A+	Bowling Green	3	2	0	69	118	1.82	1.10	16.9	201	36	89	2.46	3.5	15.3	4.4	0.8	199
81-83 SL +++	2022	AA	Montgomery	3	1	0	54	53	2.50	1.04	19.0	208	26	80	2.50	2.7	8.8	3.3	0.8	105
82-84 CU ++	2023	AA	Montgomery	5	4	0	107	131	4.20	1.37	18.0	245	32	75	4.42	4.1	11.0	2.7	1.5	105
	2023	AAA	Durham	2	0	0	16	13	2.78	1.11	15.9	133	13	81	2.15	6.1	7.2	1.2	1.1	-17

Over-the-top, crossfire LHP struggled avoiding the big inning last season. Inconsistencies caused by wavering release point. 4-seam FB is best pitch with double-plus riding action. Struggles commanding FB within zone and keeping flat-angled approach. Tight SL is best secondary with above-average movement. Also flashes fringe CU.

Morales,Luis | SP | Oakland | EXP MLB DEBUT: 2025 | H/W: 6-3 190 | FUT: #3 starter | 8D

Thrws R Age 21	Year	Lev	Team	W	L	Sv	IP	K	ERA	WHIP	BF/G	OBA	H%	S%	xERA	Ctl	Dom	Cmd	hr/9	BPV
2023 FA (CU)																				
93-96 FB ++++	2023	Rk	DSL Athletics	0	0	0	11	16	0.82	0.55	9.3	114	21	83		1.6	13.1	8.0	0.0	209
79-82 CB ++	2023	Rk	ACL Athletics	0	2	0	9	11	6.00	1.33	12.5	283	41	50	3.43	2.0	11.0	5.5	0.0	162
82-84 SL +++	2023	A	Stockton	0	3	0	16	18	2.24	1.30	13.3	223	32	81	2.56	4.5	10.1	2.3	0.0	78
81-85 CU ++	2023	A+	Lansing	0	0	0	7	8	3.75	1.25	14.7	228	25	86	4.84	3.8	10.0	2.7	2.5	97

High-profile internal signee who pitched on 4 levels. Has potential for elite FB with plus arm speed and plenty of projection remaining. Delivery can be erratic but should improve with more reps and strength. SL ahead of CB at present and both could be above average in time. Controls pitches well but needs better command on margins.

Morales,Michael | SP | Seattle | EXP MLB DEBUT: 2025 | H/W: 6-2 205 | FUT: #3 starter | 8D

Thrws R Age 21	Year	Lev	Team	W	L	Sv	IP	K	ERA	WHIP	BF/G	OBA	H%	S%	xERA	Ctl	Dom	Cmd	hr/9	BPV
2021 (3) HS (PA)																				
91-93 FB +++																				
79-83 CB ++	2021	Rk	ACL Mariners	0	0	0	1	1	18.00	3.00	5.8	415	52	33	10.01	9.0	9.0	1.0	0.0	-63
82-84 CU +++	2022	A	Modesto	5	7	0	120	125	5.92	1.61	20.4	297	38	64	5.33	3.7	9.4	2.5	1.0	85
	2023	A	Modesto	5	4	0	101	106	4.54	1.31	19.0	244	32	65	3.43	3.6	9.4	2.7	0.6	92

Athletic RHP who repeated Low-A but hasn't been as dominant as natural stuff suggests. Velocity hasn't grown as anticipated, though command has improved as he's found consistency in repeatable mechanics and slot. Much lower oppBA as he's learned to pitch and sequence. Hope is for FB to tick higher and may need more strength.

Morris, Kade — SP — New York (N)

EXP MLB DEBUT: 2026 | H/W: 6-3 180 | FUT: #4 starter | **7D**

Thrws R | Age 21
2023 (3) Nevada

			FB	+++
92-95				
84-86	SL	+++
86-88	CU	+++
74-77	CB	+++

Year	Lev	Team	W	L	Sv	IP	K	ERA	WHIP	BF/G	OBA	H%	S%	xERA	Ctl	Dom	Cmd	hr/9	BPV
2023	NCAA	Nevada	4	7	0	81	85	5.44	1.52	25.1	296	39	63	4.73	3.0	9.4	3.1	0.7	107
2023	Rk	FCL Mets	0	0	0	1	0	0.00	1.00	3.8	262	26	100	2.41	0.0	0.0			18
2023	A	St. Lucie	0	0	0	2	3	4.29	1.43	8.9	144	25	67	1.97	8.6	12.9	1.5	0.0	18

2023 3rd round pick made pro debut after so-so college season. Long frame with physical projection left. Repeats low 3/4 slot delivery well but doesn't achieve appropriate extension for height. Heavy 2-seam FB/SL profile. 2-seamer has solid arm-side run and sink. SL has two-plane break profile and borderline plus offering. Has solid feel for CU.

Mozzicato, Frank — SP — Kansas City

EXP MLB DEBUT: 2026 | H/W: 6-3 175 | FUT: #3 starter | **8E**

Thrws L | Age 20
2021 (1) HS (CT)

88-91	FB	+++
79-82	CB	++++
83-86	CU	++

Year	Lev	Team	W	L	Sv	IP	K	ERA	WHIP	BF/G	OBA	H%	S%	xERA	Ctl	Dom	Cmd	hr/9	BPV
2022	A	Columbia	2	6	0	69	89	4.30	1.54	15.8	220	32	73	3.84	6.7	11.6	1.7	0.8	47
2023	A	Columbia	2	5	0	56	85	3.05	1.25	19.0	185	30	78	2.70	5.5	13.6	2.5	0.8	116
2023	A+	Quad Cities	0	4	0	36	45	7.21	1.85	18.8	250	32	63	5.91	8.2	11.2	1.4	1.7	-2

Projectable, 3/4s LHP fell apart after high-A promotion mid-season. FB/CB combination led to high strikeouts. At the same time, produced high BB numbers. CB has big 12-to-6 breaking action. Flat-angled four-seam FB has plus ride profile. Also throws CU. The moments of brilliance are spectacular. The moments of struggle are forgetable.

Mueth, Zander — SP — Pittsburgh

EXP MLB DEBUT: 2027 | H/W: 6-6 205 | FUT: #3 starter | **8E**

Thrws R | Age 18
2023 (2) HS (IL)

91-95	FB	+++
80-84	SL	+++
82-85	CU	++

Year	Lev	Team	W	L	Sv	IP	K	ERA	WHIP	BF/G	OBA	H%	S%	xERA	Ctl	Dom	Cmd	hr/9	BPV

Quick-armed, tall RHP who didn't pitch after signing. Works from low 3/4 slot and gets great horizontal action on pitches. Lot of sink and run to quality FB, though can struggle to keep in zone. Induces weak gb contact with FB and complements with sweeping SL. Command needs attention and can often slow arm speed on rudimentary CU.

Murphy, Owen — SP — Atlanta

EXP MLB DEBUT: 2025 | H/W: 6-1 190 | FUT: #3 starter | **8D**

Thrws R | Age 20
2022 (1) HS (IL)

89-92	FB	++++
82-84	SL	+++
75-79	CB	+++

Year	Lev	Team	W	L	Sv	IP	K	ERA	WHIP	BF/G	OBA	H%	S%	xERA	Ctl	Dom	Cmd	hr/9	BPV
2022	Rk	FCL Braves	0	0	0	5	7	0.00	0.40	8.1	124	22	100		0.0	12.6		0.0	245
2022	A	Augusta	0	1	0	7	10	7.71	1.57	10.2	202	34	45	2.96	7.7	12.9	1.7	0.0	41
2023	A	Augusta	6	3	0	72	97	4.74	1.25	16.3	233	34	63	3.47	3.5	12.1	3.5	1.0	141
2023	A+	Rome	0	1	0	17	16	4.76	1.47	24.3	305	39	67	4.63	2.1	8.5	4.0	0.5	113

Former 1st round pick pitched across two levels in 2023. Repeats upright 3/4s delivery well with below-average extension. Solid frame with additional growth potential. 3-pitch pitcher. Flat-angled 4-seam FB has excellent ride profile making up for lower velocity. SL has gyro spin profile but struggles with command. 12-to-6 CB doesn't steal strikes.

Murphy, Ryan — SP — San Francisco

EXP MLB DEBUT: 2024 | H/W: 6-1 190 | FUT: #5 SP/swingman | **7D**

Thrws R | Age 24
2020 (5) LeMoyne

90-94	FB	+++
76-79	CB	+++
80-82	SL	+++
82-83	CU	++

Year	Lev	Team	W	L	Sv	IP	K	ERA	WHIP	BF/G	OBA	H%	S%	xERA	Ctl	Dom	Cmd	hr/9	BPV
2022	Rk	ACL Giants B	0	0	0	1	0	9.00	2.00	4.8	415	26	100	16.04	0.0	0.0		9.0	18
2022	A	San Jose	0	0	0	1	3	15.00	3.33	7.4	470	84	67	19.09	7.5	22.5	3.0	7.5	221
2022	A+	Eugene	1	0	0	31	47	2.90	1.03	17.1	186	32	71	1.68	3.5	13.6	3.9	0.3	170
2022	AA	Richmond	1	1	0	8	7	9.88	2.32	21.1	280	30	59	7.97	11.0	7.7	0.7	2.2	-140
2023	AA	Richmond	2	9	0	107	107	4.37	1.43	15.7	252	31	73	4.45	4.3	9.0	2.1	1.3	64

Profiles as back-end SP who sequences well and maximizes fairly rudimentary pitch mix. Lacks knockout pitch yet has been able eto register Ks by keeping hitters off balance. Changes speeds well and mixes and matches two breaking balls. Control can be erratic and subject to high amount of flyballs. Has been durable in career.

Nastrini, Nick — SP — Chicago (A)

EXP MLB DEBUT: 2024 | H/W: 6-3 215 | FUT: #3 starter | **8C**

Thrws R | Age 24
2021 (4) UCLA

93-95	FB	++++
85-87	SL	++++
83-86	CU	+++
77-79	CB	+++

Year	Lev	Team	W	L	Sv	IP	K	ERA	WHIP	BF/G	OBA	H%	S%	xERA	Ctl	Dom	Cmd	hr/9	BPV
2022	A+	Great Lakes	5	3	0	86	127	3.87	1.16	16.3	201	30	72	3.08	4.1	13.3	3.3	1.3	147
2022	AA	Tulsa	1	1	0	30	42	4.19	1.00	19.1	142	17	64	2.26	4.8	12.6	2.6	1.5	115
2023	AA	Birmingham	3	0	0	22	31	4.13	1.24	22.1	245	38	65	3.05	2.9	12.8	4.4	0.4	170
2023	AA	Tulsa	5	3	0	73	85	4.06	1.41	18.2	242	32	74	3.99	4.5	10.5	2.3	1.0	83
2023	AAA	Charlotte	1	2	0	19	23	4.22	1.04	18.5	156	20	61	2.01	4.7	10.8	2.3	0.9	86

Hard-throwing RHP, acquired from LAD midseason, has makings of mid-tier MLB SP. Repeatable 3/4s delivery with solid extension. Body is at physical projection. Flat-angled FB is best offering with plus ride and controllable run. Tight SL has plus tendencies. 12-to-6 CB has plus movement profile but cannot throw in zone. CU is an average offering.

Nicolas, Kyle — RP — Pittsburgh

EXP MLB DEBUT: 2023 | H/W: 6-4 223 | FUT: Setup reliever | **7C**

Thrws R | Age 25
2020 (2) Ball State

91-95	FB	+++
80-83	CB	++
82-86	SL	+++
84-87	CU	+

Year	Lev	Team	W	L	Sv	IP	K	ERA	WHIP	BF/G	OBA	H%	S%	xERA	Ctl	Dom	Cmd	hr/9	BPV
2021	AA	Pensacola	3	2	0	39	50	2.53	1.23	19.8	173	25	82	2.42	5.8	11.5	2.0	0.7	70
2022	AA	Altoona	2	4	0	90	101	3.99	1.31	15.5	218	29	72	3.36	4.7	10.1	2.1	0.9	73
2023	AA	Altoona	3	5	0	53	63	4.40	1.48	19.1	272	36	75	4.93	3.9	10.7	2.7	1.4	105
2023	AAA	Indianapolis	1	2	2	45	64	6.20	1.58	8.6	249	35	63	5.06	5.8	12.8	2.2	1.6	92
2023	MLB	Pittsburgh	0	0	0	5	7	12.35	2.16	6.3	327	45	40	7.84	7.1	12.4	1.8	1.8	50

Versatile arm who operated as SP and RP in 2023. Mostly RP in AAA and appeared in 4 games with PIT. High-octane FB exhibits incredible movement and tough to barrel. Command has been far too erratic which limits effectiveness of heater. SL can be good but often can't use behind in count. Has trouble keeping ball in yard.

Nikhazy, Doug — SP — Cleveland

EXP MLB DEBUT: 2024 | H/W: 6-0 210 | FUT: #4 starter | **7D**

Thrws L | Age 24
2021 (2) Mississippi

88-93	FB	+++
74-76	CB	+++
83-85	SL	+++
78-82	CU	++

Year	Lev	Team	W	L	Sv	IP	K	ERA	WHIP	BF/G	OBA	H%	S%	xERA	Ctl	Dom	Cmd	hr/9	BPV
2022	A+	Lake County	4	4	0	93	118	3.19	1.37	18.5	184	26	79	2.97	6.6	11.4	1.7	0.8	46
2022	AA	Akron	0	2	0	9	10	11.87	2.75	16.9	353	45	54	9.07	10.9	9.9	0.9	1.0	-98
2023	AA	Akron	4	8	0	102	128	4.94	1.62	17.4	242	33	72	4.67	6.4	11.3	1.8	1.1	47

Short, strong LHP who struggled late in season after mid-year dominance. Led EL in walks and has tendency to aim pitches. Velocity a little short but has deep repertoire and deceptive high 3/4 slot. Gets good extension in delivery and can spin a solid CB with big bending action. Allows lot of flyballs and may opt for cutter/slider hybrid.

Nowlin, Jaylen — SP — Minnesota

EXP MLB DEBUT: 2024 | H/W: 6-1 180 | FUT: Middle reliever | **7D**

Thrws L | Age 23
2021 (19) Chipola JC

89-93	FB	+++
81-84	SL	+++
82-85	CU	+++

Year	Lev	Team	W	L	Sv	IP	K	ERA	WHIP	BF/G	OBA	H%	S%	xERA	Ctl	Dom	Cmd	hr/9	BPV
2021	Rk	FCL Twins	0	1	0	0	1	####	40.00	4.3	876	156	25	#####	###	90.0	0.5	0.0	-3222
2022	A	Fort Myers	4	3	0	56	89	3.68	1.35	12.3	229	39	72	3.02	4.6	14.3	3.1	0.3	149
2022	A+	Cedar Rapids	1	1	0	14	22	4.47	1.42	19.9	246	38	72	4.31	4.5	14.0	3.1	1.3	150
2023	A+	Cedar Rapids	3	6	0	67	79	4.82	1.37	18.8	267	34	69	4.69	3.1	10.6	3.4	1.5	125
2023	AA	Wichita	3	1	0	37	35	3.87	1.42	17.5	228	28	76	3.86	5.3	8.5	1.6	1.0	27

Underrated LHP who continues to thrive based upon pitchability. Filthy against LHH with solid-average SL and changes speeds with aplomb. More of a flyball guy and will need to pitch lower in zone. Lacks plus pitch but could be ideal lefty RP who can dominate with FB/SL combo. Was better in AA than High-A.

Nunez, Juan — SP — Baltimore

EXP MLB DEBUT: 2026 | H/W: 5-11 190 | FUT: Middle reliever | **6C**

Thrws R | Age 23
2019 FA (DR)

93-95	FB	+++
83-87	SL	+++
80-83	CB	++
88-90	CU	++

Year	Lev	Team	W	L	Sv	IP	K	ERA	WHIP	BF/G	OBA	H%	S%	xERA	Ctl	Dom	Cmd	hr/9	BPV
2022	Rk	FCL Orioles B	0	0	0	6	9	3.00	1.67	13.5	347	47	100	8.10	1.5	13.5	9.0	3.0	221
2022	Rk	FCL Twins	0	2	0	29	47	4.93	1.27	14.9	247	41	60	3.31	3.1	14.5	4.7	0.6	196
2022	A	Delmarva	0	0	0	14	7	1.27	1.41	15.0	149	17	90	2.04	8.2	4.4	0.5	0.0	-125
2023	A	Delmarva	0	4	1	55	72	3.93	1.27	17.3	221	33	69	2.90	4.3	11.8	2.8	0.5	115
2023	A+	Aberdeen	0	2	1	49	53	4.02	1.46	16.2	224	29	75	3.84	5.9	9.7	1.7	0.9	34

Low 3/4s RHP overachieved as an older prospect on the lower levels in 2023. Struggles staying within delivery, flying out often Flat-angled four-seam FB plays up due to exceptional riding profile from lower slot. Doesn't throw enough FB strikes to stay as SP. Vertical breaking SL is best secondary offering. Also throws CB and CU.

Nunez, Edwin — RP — St. Louis

EXP MLB DEBUT: 2025 | H/W: 6-3 185 | FUT: Setup reliever | **6C**

Thrws R | Age 22
2020 FA (DR)

96-98	FB	++++
76-79	SL	+
83-86	CU	+++

Year	Lev	Team	W	L	Sv	IP	K	ERA	WHIP	BF/G	OBA	H%	S%	xERA	Ctl	Dom	Cmd	hr/9	BPV
2021	A	Palm Beach	3	3	0	53	59	11.00	2.26	8.4	299	39	49	7.12	9.5	10.0	1.1	1.2	-58
2022	Rk	FCL Cardinals	0	1	2	26	23	4.12	1.34	4.9	213	27	68	2.87	5.2	7.9	1.5	0.3	21
2022	A	Palm Beach	1	1	0	6	7	13.06	3.06	7.3	314	40	56	9.64	16.0	10.2	0.6	1.5	-230
2023	A	Palm Beach	3	5	0	27	35	3.65	1.37	6.0	231	35	72	3.12	4.6	11.6	2.5	0.3	102
2023	A+	Peoria	3	1	5	36	30	3.24	1.36	6.9	245	29	80	3.94	4.7	7.5	1.9	1.0	45

Tall, strong frame with quick tempo and arm action, but max effort delivery results in below-average command. FB sits at 96-98 with good sink, topping at 100. Upper-80 CU has good late sink and fade and gets plenty of swing-and-miss. Lack of a viable 3rd offering and struggles with control resulted in him moving to a relief role where he thrived.

O'Halloran,Connor

SP | Toronto | EXP MLB DEBUT: 2026 | H/W: 6-2 190 | FUT: #4 starter | 7D

Thrws L	Age 21		Year	Lev	Team	W	L	Sv	IP	K	ERA	WHIP	BF/G	OBA	H%	S%	xERA	Ctl	Dom	Cmd	hr/9	BPV
2023 (5) Michigan																						
89-93	FB	+++																				
81-82	SL	+++																				
83-85	CU	+++	2023	NCAA	Michigan	8	6	0	103	110	4.11	1.13	23.9	237	31	64	3.03	2.3	9.6	4.2	0.8	130
			2023	A	Dunedin	3	1	0	10	9	6.30	1.60	7.4	221	27	60	4.15	7.2	8.1	1.1	0.9	-31

Deceptive LHP with solid pitch mix and advanced pitchability. Generally throws quality strikes with three pitches, including FB with below-average velocity. Spots FB well to both sides of plate. SL is best pitch and particularly strong against LHH. Gets late tumble on CU and induces weak contact. Fits more of a back-end profile.

Olson,Emmett

SP | Miami | EXP MLB DEBUT: 2026 | H/W: 6-4 230 | FUT: #4 starter | 7D

Thrws L	Age 21		Year	Lev	Team	W	L	Sv	IP	K	ERA	WHIP	BF/G	OBA	H%	S%	xERA	Ctl	Dom	Cmd	hr/9	BPV
2023 (4) Nebraska																						
90-93	FB	+++																				
82-84	SL	++++																				
74-76	CB	++	2023	NCAA	Nebraska	6	3	0	82	80	4.50	1.20	21.9	227	26	68	3.80	3.3	8.8	2.7	1.5	87
83-86	CU	+++	2023	Rk	FCL Marlins	0	0	0	1	2	7.50	1.67	5.4	228	42	50	3.49	7.5	15.0	2.0	0.0	86

Former RP converted to SP in 2023 and had solid college season. Repeatable high 3/4s delivery with below-average extension. Flat-angled 4-seam FB features significant vertical rise. Sweeping SL is best secondary with late drop in horizontal breaking progression. Developing feel for CU. CB likely non-factor in pro ball.

Ottenbreit,Micah

SP | Philadelphia | EXP MLB DEBUT: 2026 | H/W: 6-4 190 | FUT: #4 starter | 7E

Thrws R	Age 20		Year	Lev	Team	W	L	Sv	IP	K	ERA	WHIP	BF/G	OBA	H%	S%	xERA	Ctl	Dom	Cmd	hr/9	BPV
2021 (4) HS (MI)																						
91-94	FB	++																				
76-79	CB	+++	2021	Rk	FCL Phillies	1	0	0	6	4	4.50	1.50	5.2	262	32	67	3.61	4.5	6.0	1.3	0.0	5
81-84	CU	++	2022	A	Clearwater	0	1	0	5	4	8.65	2.12	12.8	290	32	60	7.18	8.7	6.9	0.8	1.7	-91
			2023	Rk	FCL Phillies	0	0	0	2	0	12.86	2.38	5.5	336	34	40	7.02	8.6	0.0	0.0	0.0	-213

Recovery from mid-2022 Tommy John surgery was taken longer than expected, but should be back on the mound in 2024. Still some projection left and has a solid foundation from which to work, including a sturdy, 3-pitch arsenal featuring a high-spin curve. Had made strides before the injury, but a wild card until he pitches again.

Ovalles,Layonel

SP | New York (N) | EXP MLB DEBUT: 2025 | H/W: 6-3 216 | FUT: #4 starter | 7D

Thrws R	Age 20		Year	Lev	Team	W	L	Sv	IP	K	ERA	WHIP	BF/G	OBA	H%	S%	xERA	Ctl	Dom	Cmd	hr/9	BPV
2019 FA (DR)			2021	Rk	DSL Mets	0	2	1	31	30	1.16	0.51	10.4	120	17	75		1.2	8.7	7.5	0.0	143
91-93	FB	+++	2022	Rk	FCL Mets	1	2	1	29	44	2.78	1.07	10.3	241	41	71	2.15	1.5	13.6	8.8	0.0	221
82-85	SL	++++	2022	A	St. Lucie	0	1	1	17	22	6.32	1.58	15.0	237	31	63	4.91	6.3	11.6	1.8	1.6	56
89-91	CT	+++	2023	A	St. Lucie	3	6	0	83	84	4.76	1.25	15.4	225	28	64	3.48	3.9	9.1	2.3	1.1	76
83-85	CU	++	2023	A+	Brooklyn	0	1	0	10	9	3.53	1.86	23.9	327	41	79	5.49	4.4	7.9	1.8	0.0	42

Big-bodied RHP enjoyed solid season split between lower level affiliates. Maxed-out frame. Jerky 3/4s delivery with below-average extension. 4-pitch mix. 4-seam FB has ordinary profile, lacking spin efficiency. SL is a plus pitch with significant sweeping action. CT is a short breaker, keeping LHH honest. CU is fringe pitch.

Owen,Hunter

SP | Kansas City | EXP MLB DEBUT: 2026 | H/W: 6-6 261 | FUT: #5 SP/swingman | 6A

Thrws L	Age 22		Year	Lev	Team	W	L	Sv	IP	K	ERA	WHIP	BF/G	OBA	H%	S%	xERA	Ctl	Dom	Cmd	hr/9	BPV
2023 (4) Vanderbilt																						
92-94	FB	+++																				
77-79	CB	+++																				
83-86	SL	++																				
83-86	CU	++																				

Big-bodied SP prospect enjoyed solid college season prior to 4th round selection in draft. Repeats cross-fire 3/4s delivery with solid extension. Strike-thrower. FB plays up due to ability to command up in zone. Both secondaries performed well in college. However, CB projection outpaces SL as pro pitch. Has feel for CU.

Pacheco,Freddy

RP | Detroit | EXP MLB DEBUT: 2025 | H/W: 5-11 203 | FUT: Middle reliever | 6C

Thrws R	Age 25		Year	Lev	Team	W	L	Sv	IP	K	ERA	WHIP	BF/G	OBA	H%	S%	xERA	Ctl	Dom	Cmd	hr/9	BPV
2017 FA (VZ)			2021	AA	Springfield	1	0	3	19	33	1.88	0.78	4.6	114	22	79	0.45	3.8	15.5	4.1	0.5	195
95-97	FB	++++	2021	AAA	Memphis	0	0	0	3	5	0.00	0.67	5.2	106	22	100		3.0	15.0	5.0	0.0	207
82-84	SL	+++	2022	AA	Springfield	1	5	8	28	41	3.84	1.28	4.8	202	29	75	3.42	5.1	13.1	2.6	1.3	116
86-88	CU	+	2022	AAA	Memphis	2	2	4	33	43	2.44	0.87	4.7	154	23	74	1.18	3.3	11.7	3.6	0.5	140
			2023	--	Did Not Play																	

Claimed off waivers, had Tommy John surgery in June, and will miss all of 2024. When healthy, attacks hitters with an aggressive two-pitch mix. Quick arm action and max effort delivery on a plus mid-90s heater (T 99). Backs up the heat with a swing-and-miss SL. Struggles with control and command will need to be resolved once he returns to action.

Painter,Andrew

SP | Philadelphia | EXP MLB DEBUT: 2025 | H/W: 6-7 215 | FUT: #1 starter | 9B

Thrws R	Age 20		Year	Lev	Team	W	L	Sv	IP	K	ERA	WHIP	BF/G	OBA	H%	S%	xERA	Ctl	Dom	Cmd	hr/9	BPV
2021 (1) HS (FL)			2021	Rk	FCL Phillies	0	0	0	6	12	0.00	0.67	5.2	191	45	100	0.50	0.0	18.0		0.0	342
96-99	FB	+++++	2022	A	Clearwater	1	1	0	38	69	1.41	0.86	15.6	136	31	82	0.43	3.8	16.3	4.3	0.0	209
81-84	SL	++++	2022	A+	Jersey Shore	3	0	0	36	49	0.99	0.88	16.8	197	30	93	1.64	1.7	12.2	7.0	0.5	190
87-89	CU	++++	2022	AA	Reading	2	1	0	28	37	2.56	0.96	21.2	240	34	79	2.80	0.6	11.9	18.5	1.0	214
77-79	CB	++	2023	--	Did Not Play																	

Was set to compete for 2023 rotation spot as a teenager, but elbow barked after one spring training start and led to July Tommy John surgery. Has unique mix of elite stuff, poise, command and picturesque mechanics. High-90s FB and mid-80s SL lead the way, but has a four-pitch mix for Ks and soft contact and doesn't walk guys. Will debut in 2025.

Pallette,Peyton

SP | Chicago (A) | EXP MLB DEBUT: 2025 | H/W: 6-1 180 | FUT: #4 starter | 7C

Thrws R	Age 22		Year	Lev	Team	W	L	Sv	IP	K	ERA	WHIP	BF/G	OBA	H%	S%	xERA	Ctl	Dom	Cmd	hr/9	BPV
2022 (2) Arkansas																						
92-94	FB	++++																				
78-80	CB	+++																				
85-87	CU	+++																				
			2023	A	Kannapolis	0	4	0	72	78	4.13	1.36	13.7	219	28	72	3.60	5.1	9.8	1.9	1.0	55

Undersized, former second round pick made pro debut after missing previous season recovering from Tommy John surgery. Athletic, 3/4s delivery with below average extension. Live arm. 4-seam FB clearly plus pitch with flat-angled approach and plus riding action out of slot. Throws a lot of strikes with secondaries but both average offerings.

Palmquist,Carson

SP | Colorado | EXP MLB DEBUT: 2025 | H/W: 6-3 185 | FUT: Setup reliever | 6C

Thrws L	Age 23		Year	Lev	Team	W	L	Sv	IP	K	ERA	WHIP	BF/G	OBA	H%	S%	xERA	Ctl	Dom	Cmd	hr/9	BPV
2022 (3) Miami																						
90-92	FB	+++	2022	NCAA	Miami	9	4	0	84	118	2.89	1.21	21.2	228	32	85	3.79	3.4	12.6	3.7	1.5	153
	SL	+++	2022	Rk	ACL Rockies	0	0	0	1	1	0.00	2.00	4.8	0	0	100	2.18	18.0	9.0	0.5	0.0	-306
	CU	++	2023	A+	Spokane	7	2	0	70	106	3.73	1.27	19.1	236	36	75	3.70	3.6	13.6	3.8	1.2	166
			2023	AA	Hartford	0	2	0	22	28	4.48	1.27	22.6	234	30	71	4.12	3.7	11.4	3.1	1.6	124

Lean LHP attacks from a sidearm slot with funky mechanics and crossfire action that creates deception and an uncomfortable AB for LHB. Low-90s FB has nice horizontal break from low release point and pairs well with Sweeper that has two-plane break and plenty of swing-and-miss. CU is a work in progress and will determine his long-term role.

Pan,Wen Hui

RP | Philadelphia | EXP MLB DEBUT: 2025 | H/W: 6-3 220 | FUT: Middle reliever | 8D

Thrws R	Age 21		Year	Lev	Team	W	L	Sv	IP	K	ERA	WHIP	BF/G	OBA	H%	S%	xERA	Ctl	Dom	Cmd	hr/9	BPV
2023 FA (TW)																						
94-98	FB	+++++																				
80-83	SL	++++																				
82-85	SP	+++	2023	A	Clearwater	4	1	7	57	81	2.83	0.87	7.8	161	27	67	1.04	3.0	12.7	4.3	0.3	167
			2023	A+	Jersey Shore	0	0	0	6	7	15.00	3.00	5.8	434	55	47	11.85	7.5	10.5	1.4	1.5	5

Unheralded international sign announced his arrival in A-ball. Elite mid- to upper-90s FB with extreme ride profile gets chases and misses. SL is also plus, and SP gives him three pitches. Starting for now, but still probably a reliever in the end, as he seeks consistency and command. But a chance to move quickly and could be back-end impact arm.

Paniagua,Inohan

SP | St. Louis | EXP MLB DEBUT: 2025 | H/W: 6-1 148 | FUT: #4 starter | 7D

Thrws R	Age 24		Year	Lev	Team	W	L	Sv	IP	K	ERA	WHIP	BF/G	OBA	H%	S%	xERA	Ctl	Dom	Cmd	hr/9	BPV
2017 FA (DR)			2021	A	Palm Beach	4	1	2	46	62	3.90	1.21	11.6	222	33	68	2.85	3.7	12.1	3.3	0.6	136
90-92	FB	++	2022	A	Palm Beach	6	4	0	99	107	2.18	0.96	22.0	205	28	78	1.82	2.1	9.7	4.7	0.4	137
74-76	CB	+++	2022	A+	Peoria	2	2	0	38	38	4.48	1.31	19.7	240	27	74	4.57	3.8	9.0	2.4	1.9	77
80-83	CU	+++	2023	Rk	FCL Cardinals	0	0	0	3	6	0.00	1.56	4.7	250	50	100	3.49	5.6	16.9	3.0	0.0	170
			2023	A+	Peoria	0	3	0	44	41	4.49	1.36	16.8	210	26	67	3.14	5.5	8.4	1.5	0.6	20

Lean, projectable hurler missed 3 months of action with a shoulder injury. Starts motion with a high leg kick with a quick arm from a low 3/4 slot. Repeats mechanics well. Low-90s FB has good late sink and could add velo as he matures. Mid-70s CB is best secondary with good late sink and shows feel for CU. Will need more velo to reach his potential.

Paplham,Cole — RP — San Diego

EXP MLB DEBUT: 2024 | H/W: 6-3 215 | FUT: Closer | 7D

Thrws R Age 24
2022 FA (New Orleans)

Velo	Pitch	Grade
94-99	FB	++++
83-87	SL	+++

Year	Lev	Team	W	L	Sv	IP	K	ERA	WHIP	BF/G	OBA	H%	S%	xERA	Ctl	Dom	Cmd	hr/9	BPV
2023	A	Lake Elsinore	0	0	8	21	25	4.29	1.38	4.0	223	33	66	2.75	5.1	10.7	2.1	0.0	72
2023	A+	Fort Wayne	1	0	3	8	11	1.13	0.63	3.4	151	21	100	1.07	1.1	12.4	11.0	1.1	210
2023	AA	San Antonio	0	0	0	1	0	9.00	2.00	4.8	415	41	50	7.58	0.0	0.0		0.0	18

Made pro debut and pitched on 3 levels. Got better as season progressed and served as closer in lower minors. Throws hard with drop and drive delivery, though lot of moving parts can be difficult to repeat. FB explodes out of hand and gets good arm side run. Can get hitters to chase SL but it often lacks enough break to miss bats.

Parker,Mitchell — SP — Washington

EXP MLB DEBUT: 2024 | H/W: 6-4 224 | FUT: #5 SP/swingman | 7C

Thrws L Age 24
2020 (5) San Jacinto JC

Velo	Pitch	Grade
91-93	FB	+++
81-83	SL	++++
80-82	CB	+++
83-85	CT	++

Year	Lev	Team	W	L	Sv	IP	K	ERA	WHIP	BF/G	OBA	H%	S%	xERA	Ctl	Dom	Cmd	hr/9	BPV
2021	A	Fredericksburg	3	7	0	57	85	4.10	1.19	19.1	226	34	70	3.47	3.3	13.4	4.0	1.3	170
2021	A+	Wilmington	1	5	0	44	59	5.92	1.66	17.9	310	44	64	5.42	3.5	12.0	3.5	0.8	141
2022	A+	Wilmington	6	4	0	100	117	2.88	1.43	17.7	212	31	79	3.00	6.0	10.5	1.7	0.3	45
2023	AA	Harrisburg	9	6	0	113	132	4.21	1.36	18.9	239	32	70	3.65	4.3	10.5	2.4	0.8	91
2023	AAA	Rochester	0	1	0	10	18	10.69	2.18	16.8	345	53	53	9.01	6.2	16.0	2.6	2.7	138

Tall lefty that gets good ride and extension on low-90s FB. Pairsthe heater with two good breaking pitches—a big-drop CB and newer SL. Cutter and split-change work their way into his arsenal as well. Most pitches get good whiff rates, though walks have plagued him some. Should see time in MLB in 2024. Sleeper swingman.

Perales,Luis — SP — Boston

EXP MLB DEBUT: 2026 | H/W: 6-1 160 | FUT: #3 starter | 8D

Thrws R Age 20
2019 FA (VZ)

Velo	Pitch	Grade
94-98	FB	++++
84-87	SL	+++
85-88	CU	+

Year	Lev	Team	W	L	Sv	IP	K	ERA	WHIP	BF/G	OBA	H%	S%	xERA	Ctl	Dom	Cmd	hr/9	BPV
2021	Rk	DSL Red Sox R	0	0	0	2		4.50	1.00	7.6	151	27	50	0.94	4.5	13.5	3.0	0.0	140
2022	Rk	FCL Red Sox	0	1	0	25	34	1.08	0.76	9.9	124	22	84	0.08	3.2	12.2	3.8	0.0	151
2022	A	Salem	0	1	0	10	16	3.53	2.06	12.4	258	41	85	5.71	9.7	14.1	1.5	0.9	10
2023	A	Salem	4	4	0	53	71	3.22	1.24	16.6	202	31	73	2.46	4.7	12.0	2.5	0.3	106
2023	A+	Greenville	0	3	0	36	44	4.99	1.69	20.4	277	35	77	6.12	5.5	11.0	2.0	2.0	67

Lean, quick-armed RHP with electric FB that can dominate on its own. While SL has plus potential with natural cutting action, he has trouble locating it. Secondary offerings need major refining but has pitch mix to be lethal. Not enough separation between FB and CU. Could eventually move to pen where FB/SL could play up.

Perez,Fernando — SP — Toronto

EXP MLB DEBUT: 2027 | H/W: 6-3 170 | FUT: #4 starter | 7D

Thrws R Age 20
2022 FA (NI)

Velo	Pitch	Grade
91-94	FB	+++
82-84	SL	++
85-86	CU	+++

Year	Lev	Team	W	L	Sv	IP	K	ERA	WHIP	BF/G	OBA	H%	S%	xERA	Ctl	Dom	Cmd	hr/9	BPV
2022	Rk	DSL Blue Jays	1	4	0	43	48	4.58	1.27	14.7	291	38	65	4.19	1.0	10.0	9.6	0.8	170
2023	Rk	FCL Blue Jays	2	2	0	49	57	2.74	0.96	16.9	201	29	70	1.59	2.2	10.4	4.8	0.2	146

Tall, slender RHP who led FCL in ERA and 2nd in Ks. Has room to add strength and muscle to add to durability and stamina. Lacks frontline velocity and has to improve secondary pitch consistency. CU shows flashes of being above average. Already spots ball well and hope is he keeps command while adding bulk to frame.

Perkins,Jack — SP — Oakland

EXP MLB DEBUT: 2025 | H/W: 6-1 220 | FUT: #4 starter | 7C

Thrws R Age 24
2022 (5) Indiana

Velo	Pitch	Grade
92-95	FB	+++
82-84	CB	+++
87-90	CT	+++

Year	Lev	Team	W	L	Sv	IP	K	ERA	WHIP	BF/G	OBA	H%	S%	xERA	Ctl	Dom	Cmd	hr/9	BPV
2022	NCAA	Indiana	3	4	0	83	91	5.10	1.49	22.4	248	33	65	3.97	5.1	9.9	1.9	0.7	58
2022	Rk	ACL Athletics	0	1	0	1	3	9.00	2.00	4.8	415	110	50	7.31	0.0	27.0		0.0	504
2022	A	Stockton	0	0	0	9	11	2.00	0.78	6.5	165	26	71	0.56	2.0	11.0	5.5	0.0	162
2023	A+	Lansing	3	3	0	53	49	2.54	0.98	20.2	185	23	76	1.78	3.0	8.3	2.7	0.5	85
2023	AA	Midland	1	0	0	54	44	5.67	1.83	20.9	315	39	67	5.53	4.8	7.3	1.5	0.3	20

Sinkerballer with solid power stuff and ability to mess with hitters timing. Doesn't allow many HR but also doesn't miss as many bats as repertoire would indicate. Nasty CT at times from short arm action is tough to pick up out of hand. Manipulates hard breaking ball well but is far too inconsistent. Pitched well in High-A before struggles in AA.

Perry,Nolan — SP — Toronto

EXP MLB DEBUT: 2027 | H/W: 6-2 195 | FUT: #3 starter | 8E

Thrws R Age 20
2022 (12) HS (NM)

Velo	Pitch	Grade
91-94	FB	+++
81-84	SL	++
81-82	CB	++
83-85	CU	++

Year	Lev	Team	W	L	Sv	IP	K	ERA	WHIP	BF/G	OBA	H%	S%	xERA	Ctl	Dom	Cmd	hr/9	BPV
2023	Rk	FCL Blue Jays	2	3	0	38	51	7.32	1.63	18.8	300	43	53	5.30	3.8	12.0	3.2	0.9	133

Projectable RHP who struggled in first pro experience but has intriguing upside. Clean arm action portends good future. Has present velocity and potential to add more. FB features late action from flat angle to plate. Mixes in both SL and CB with similar velo but different breaks. Must enhance CU and maintain arm speed.

Petty,Chase — SP — Cincinnati

EXP MLB DEBUT: 2025 | H/W: 6-1 190 | FUT: #3 starter | 8D

Thrws R Age 21
2021 (1) HS (NJ)

Velo	Pitch	Grade
87-89	SL	++++
92-94	FB	+++
87-89	CU	++++

Year	Lev	Team	W	L	Sv	IP	K	ERA	WHIP	BF/G	OBA	H%	S%	xERA	Ctl	Dom	Cmd	hr/9	BPV
2021	Rk	FCL Twins	0	0	0	5	6	5.40	1.40	10.6	299	43	57	3.84	1.8	10.8	6.0	0.0	164
2022	A	Daytona	0	4	0	67	63	3.08	1.21	15.0	231	29	76	3.06	3.2	8.4	2.6	0.7	83
2022	A+	Dayton	1	2	0	30	33	4.47	1.13	17.0	241	32	59	2.90	2.1	9.8	4.7	0.6	139
2023	A+	Dayton	0	2	0	60	61	1.95	1.20	15.1	255	35	82	2.73	2.1	9.2	4.4	0.0	126
2023	AA	Chattanooga	0	0	0	8	5	0.00	0.75	14.3	181	22	100	0.72	1.1	5.6	5.0	0.0	89

Former 1st round pick has molded into complete pitcher at relatively young age. Athletic, low 3/4s delivery. Relies on SL-heavy arsenal; it's a tight, two-plane breaker mostly. Can manipulate grip to get additional break. 2-seam FB has sinker characteristics with plus arm-side run. Has feel for near-plus CU. Commands everything well.

Pham,Alex — SP — Baltimore

EXP MLB DEBUT: 2025 | H/W: 5-11 165 | FUT: Setup reliever | 7D

Thrws R Age 24
2021 (19) San Francisco

Velo	Pitch	Grade
90-93	FB	+++
83-86	SL	+++
83-86	CU	++
76-79	CB	++

Year	Lev	Team	W	L	Sv	IP	K	ERA	WHIP	BF/G	OBA	H%	S%	xERA	Ctl	Dom	Cmd	hr/9	BPV
2022	Rk	FCL Orioles B	0	0	0	1	1	0.00	0.00	2.8	0	0			0.0	9.0		0.0	180
2022	A	Delmarva	0	0	2	11	15	1.62	1.35	7.7	204	33	87	2.43	5.7	12.2	2.1	0.0	84
2022	A+	Aberdeen	5	2	0	20	30	5.79	1.44	7.8	240	37	59	3.92	4.9	13.4	2.7	0.9	126
2023	A+	Aberdeen	3	3	0	51	76	2.47	1.06	16.5	168	26	82	2.09	4.4	13.4	3.0	0.9	140
2023	AA	Bowie	0	2	1	60	54	2.69	1.00	16.4	202	25	76	2.26	2.5	8.1	3.2	0.7	95

Over-the-top slot RHP pitched well between two levels in 2023. Short-statured with deceptive delivery, plays up overall stuff. FB/SL each have above-average upside. FB has exceptional ride profile and pounds zone with strikes. SL is a two-plane breaker with later horizontal drop in pitch progression. Utilizes CB to change eye levels. Also throws CU.

Phillips,Cole — SP — Seattle

EXP MLB DEBUT: 2025 | H/W: 6-3 200 | FUT: #3 starter | 8E

Thrws R Age 20
2022 (2) HS (TX)

Velo	Pitch	Grade
95-98	FB	++++
80-83	SL	+++
74-78	CB	++
85-87	CU	++

Year	Lev	Team	W	L	Sv	IP	K	ERA	WHIP	BF/G	OBA	H%	S%	xERA	Ctl	Dom	Cmd	hr/9	BPV

Acquired from ATL in December 2023. Missed season rehabbing from Tommy surgery. Lean, athletic frame with room to mature. Refined 3/4 delivery off-season prior to draft, picking up velocity. 4-seam FB has carry and arm-side run, exploding late up in the zone. Tight 2-plane SL has late vertical movement down, contributing to high whiff rate.

Phillips,Connor — SP — Cincinnati

EXP MLB DEBUT: 2023 | H/W: 6-2 209 | FUT: #3 starter | 8D

Thrws R Age 22
2020 (2) McLennan CC

Velo	Pitch	Grade
95-97	FB	++++
81-83	CB	++++
85-87	SL	+++
87-89		+

Year	Lev	Team	W	L	Sv	IP	K	ERA	WHIP	BF/G	OBA	H%	S%	xERA	Ctl	Dom	Cmd	hr/9	BPV
2022	A+	Dayton	4	3	0	64	90	2.95	1.11	21.0	178	27	76	2.18	4.5	12.7	2.8	0.7	124
2022	AA	Chattanooga	1	5	0	45	60	4.98	1.81	17.5	274	40	72	5.06	6.8	11.9	1.8	0.6	50
2023	AA	Chattanooga	2	2	0	64	111	3.36	1.32	19.0	243	41	80	4.00	3.8	15.6	4.1	1.3	196
2023	AAA	Louisville	2	3	1	40	43	4.71	1.57	16.0	226	31	68	3.49	6.7	9.7	1.4	0.2	10
2023	MLB	Cincinnati	1	1	0	20	26	7.13	1.53	17.6	240	30	58	5.44	5.8	11.6	2.0	2.2	70

High 3/4s RHP with premium stuff struggled in big league debut due to command and control. Athletic delivery with frame near physical projection. 4-seam FB has flat approach angle and achieves significant riding action late. FB command varies from start to start. SL has significant sweep with late downward action. 12-to-6 CB has average upside.

Pinto,Jean — SP — Baltimore

EXP MLB DEBUT: 2025 | H/W: 5-11 175 | FUT: Middle reliever | 6C

Thrws R Age 23
2019 FA (VZ)

Velo	Pitch	Grade
90-93	FB	++
82-85	SL	+++
80-83	CB	+++

Year	Lev	Team	W	L	Sv	IP	K	ERA	WHIP	BF/G	OBA	H%	S%	xERA	Ctl	Dom	Cmd	hr/9	BPV
2021	Rk	FCL Orioles Black	1	1	0	20	28	1.80	0.75	14.3	163	24	85	1.30	1.8	12.6	7.0	0.9	196
2021	A	Delmarva	1	1	0	46	56	2.53	0.91	19.1	182	27	71	1.26	2.5	10.9	4.3	0.2	146
2022	A+	Aberdeen	4	6	2	91	103	3.85	1.37	15.9	235	31	75	3.90	4.5	10.2	2.2	1.1	78
2023	A+	Aberdeen	1	1	0	52	73	2.76	1.11	15.8	214	33	78	2.60	3.1	12.6	4.1	0.7	161
2023	AA	Bowie	2	1	0	29	28	3.72	1.52	14.0	281	34	80	5.06	3.7	8.7	2.3	1.2	74

Shorter-stature RHP with 3/4s delivery struggled after mid-season Double-A promotion. Stocky, muscular frame at physical projection. Has two nice secondaries, both whiff inducers.Mostly ditched two-seam FB for four-seam variating. FB needs improvement in shape and command to hold down SP role. A breaking ball heavy arsenal plays as RP.

Porter,Brock

SP | Texas | EXP MLB DEBUT: 2026 | H/W: 6-4 208 | FUT: #2 starter | 9D

Thrws R Age 20 — 2022 (4) HS (MI)

Velo	Pitch	Grade
92-95	FB	++++
79-82	CU	++++
91-94	CT	++
80-83	SL	++

Year	Lev	Team	W	L	Sv	IP	K	ERA	WHIP	BF/G	OBA	H%	S%	xERA	Ctl	Dom	Cmd	hr/9	BPV
2023	A	Down East	0	3	0	69	95	2.47	1.17	13.1	167	28	78	1.68	5.5	12.4	2.3	0.1	93

Excellent 2023 debut with both the fastball and change plus, and slider now flashing same. Developed cutter and curve looks average, though command is still spotty. Got stronger as year waned; only 4 BB last 4 GS. Big #2 upside on premium frame, will take time - 4 IP max/GS - but may move quicker than most prep pitchers.

Povich,Cade

SP | Baltimore | EXP MLB DEBUT: 2024 | H/W: 6-3 185 | FUT: #3 starter | 7B

Thrws L Age 23 — 2021 (3) Nebraska

Velo	Pitch	Grade
91-94	FB	+++
88-90	CT	+++
76-78	CB	+++
84-86	CU	+++

Year	Lev	Team	W	L	Sv	IP	K	ERA	WHIP	BF/G	OBA	H%	S%	xERA	Ctl	Dom	Cmd	hr/9	BPV
2022	A+	Aberdeen	2	0	0	12	15	0.00	0.50	19.9	106	18	100		1.5	11.3	7.5	0.0	180
2022	A+	Cedar Rapids	6	8	0	78	107	4.49	1.24	19.8	244	35	66	3.62	3.0	12.3	4.1	1.0	159
2022	AA	Bowie	2	2	0	23	26	7.01	1.39	16.2	244	29	52	4.86	4.3	10.1	2.4	1.9	85
2023	AA	Bowie	6	7	0	81	118	4.88	1.37	18.9	244	36	68	4.22	4.1	13.1	3.2	1.3	143
2023	AAA	Norfolk Tides	2	3	0	45	53	5.39	1.35	18.8	201	26	62	3.54	5.8	10.6	1.8	1.2	52

Crafty LHP made it up to Triple-A in 2023. Has bevy of pitches at disposal, including FB, CT, CU, SL and CB. FB usage is 50% where the other pitches fill up near equal pieces of the remaining pie. SL is the best of the secondaries, but none of the others are far behind. Struggles throwing FB consistently in zone. Has better feel for CT and SL command.

Prielipp,Connor

SP | Minnesota | EXP MLB DEBUT: 2025 | H/W: 6-2 210 | FUT: #2 starter | 9E

Thrws L Age 23 — 2022 (2) Alabama

Velo	Pitch	Grade
93-97	FB	++++
86-89	SL	++++
81-84	CU	++

Year	Lev	Team	W	L	Sv	IP	K	ERA	WHIP	BF/G	OBA	H%	S%	xERA	Ctl	Dom	Cmd	hr/9	BPV
2023	Rk	FCL Twins	0	0	0	2	4	8.18	2.27	11.2	326	58	60	6.41	8.2	16.4	2.0	0.0	92
2023	A+	Cedar Rapids	0	0	0	4	3	6.75	1.75	18.3	307	38	57	4.89	4.5	6.8	1.5	0.0	18

Likely to miss most if not all of 2024 due to another elbow surgery. Only 6.2 IP as pro. Possesses very high upside when healthy. Flashes two plus pitches in FB and incredible SL. Both FB and SL miss bats and can be thrown for strikes. Repeats delivery consistently along with arm slot. Hasn't used CU much but throws with good arm speed.

Rajcic,Max

SP | St. Louis | EXP MLB DEBUT: 2025 | H/W: 6-0 210 | FUT: #4 starter | 7D

Thrws R Age 22 — 2022 (6) UCLA

Velo	Pitch	Grade
92-94	FB	++
76-78	CB	++++
80-82	CU	+++

Year	Lev	Team	W	L	Sv	IP	K	ERA	WHIP	BF/G	OBA	H%	S%	xERA	Ctl	Dom	Cmd	hr/9	BPV
2023	A	Palm Beach	6	3	0	62	68	1.89	0.81	18.7	190	26	80	1.47	1.3	9.9	7.6	0.6	160
2023	A+	Peoria	3	3	0	61	55	3.09	1.23	22.5	249	32	74	3.00	2.7	8.1	3.1	0.3	92

Had a solid pro debut between Low and High-A. Short, thick frame with high ¾ arm slot. Arm slot results in good sink on low-90s FB but with little ride or deception. Works mostly north/south with above-average 12-to-6 CB his best secondary. Shows some feel for CU that has good late fade and sink. Lack of FB velocity limits upside.

Ray,Dylan

SP | Arizona | EXP MLB DEBUT: 2025 | H/W: 6-3 230 | FUT: #4 starter | 7C

Thrws R Age 22 — 2022 (4) Alabama

Velo	Pitch	Grade
92-95	FB	++
86-88	SL	+++
83-85	CB	++++
78-81	CU	++

Year	Lev	Team	W	L	Sv	IP	K	ERA	WHIP	BF/G	OBA	H%	S%	xERA	Ctl	Dom	Cmd	hr/9	BPV
2022	NCAA	Alabama	1	4	8	31	49	4.63	1.22	7.0	208	29	71	4.03	4.3	14.2	3.3	2.0	156
2022	Rk	ACL DBacks R	0	0	0	2	3	0.00	0.50	3.3	0	0	100		4.5	13.5	3.0	0.0	140
2022	A	Visalia	0	3	0	11	14	8.04	1.70	8.4	336	38	64	8.96	2.4	11.3	4.7	4.0	155
2023	A+	Hillsboro	7	6	0	99	123	3.81	1.17	18.0	231	33	69	3.00	2.9	11.2	3.8	0.7	141
2023	AA	Amarillo	1	2	0	14	15	8.36	1.79	21.5	301	36	55	6.67	5.1	9.6	1.9	1.9	53

Imposing RHP impressed in first full pro season. Strike thrower with easy, repeatable delivery. Peppers zone with mid-to-low 90s FB. CU and SL miss bats and get plenty of bites outside of the zone, helping drive down BB%. Success rests on getting chases outside given high contact% on in-zone pitches.

Raya,Marco

SP | Minnesota | EXP MLB DEBUT: 2025 | H/W: 6-1 170 | FUT: #3 starter | 8C

Thrws R Age 21 — 2020 (4) HS (TX)

Velo	Pitch	Grade
92-96	FB	++++
78-80	CB	++
82-84	SL	+++
83-85	CU	++

Year	Lev	Team	W	L	Sv	IP	K	ERA	WHIP	BF/G	OBA	H%	S%	xERA	Ctl	Dom	Cmd	hr/9	BPV
2021	--	Did Not Play																	
2022	A	Fort Myers	3	2	0	65	76	3.05	1.08	13.3	204	27	77	2.80	3.2	10.5	3.3	1.1	121
2023	A+	Cedar Rapids	0	1	0	33	39	2.98	0.93	11.3	197	26	74	2.34	2.2	10.6	4.9	1.1	150
2023	AA	Wichita	0	3	0	29	26	5.28	1.24	10.7	212	26	56	2.88	4.3	8.1	1.9	0.6	46

Undersized RHP who is tough to barrel as evidenced by low oppBA. Mostly shorter outings but continued to show outstanding pitches with high spin rates. Owns 4 pitches that all project as average to plus, highlighted by electric FB with great arm speed. SL features big break and slower CB serves as change-of-pace. Upgrading CU.

Reed,Carlson

RP | Pittsburgh | EXP MLB DEBUT: 2025 | H/W: 6-4 200 | FUT: Setup reliever | 7D

Thrws R Age 21 — 2023 (4) West Virginia

Velo	Pitch	Grade
92-95	FB	+++
81-84	SL	+++
84-86	CU	+++

Year	Lev	Team	W	L	Sv	IP	K	ERA	WHIP	BF/G	OBA	H%	S%	xERA	Ctl	Dom	Cmd	hr/9	BPV
2023	NCAA	West Virginia	2	1	7	38	60	2.61	1.53	6.6	235	40	84	3.69	5.9	14.2	2.4	0.5	114
2023	Rk	FCL Pirates B	1	2	0	7	6	2.57	1.43	7.4	262	34	80	3.41	3.9	7.7	2.0	0.0	53

Tall, lean RP with natural pitch mix to be effective in short stints. Long arm action impacts ability to repeat and throw strikes. Has FB and SL that both miss bats. FB appears quicker than mid-90s mph as he gets great extension. Some projection remaining but has to repeat delivery. Able to change speeds with solid-average CU.

Reynolds,Sean

RP | San Diego | EXP MLB DEBUT: 2024 | H/W: 6-8 250 | FUT: Setup reliever | 6B

Thrws R Age 25 — 2016 (4) HS (CA)

Velo	Pitch	Grade
95-99	FB	++++
84-86	SL	+++
87-89	CU	+++

Year	Lev	Team	W	L	Sv	IP	K	ERA	WHIP	BF/G	OBA	H%	S%	xERA	Ctl	Dom	Cmd	hr/9	BPV
2022	A+	Beloit	0	1	6	27	39	3.31	1.14	4.1	181	28	72	2.25	4.6	12.9	2.8	0.7	125
2022	AA	Pensacola	2	0	4	24	27	6.01	1.33	4.3	244	32	62	3.92	3.7	10.0	2.7	1.1	98
2023	AA	Pensacola	1	1	9	30	37	2.38	1.23	5.1	198	29	81	2.33	4.8	11.0	2.3	0.3	88
2023	AAA	Jacksonville	2	0	3	18	17	3.50	1.17	5.1	216	28	70	2.62	3.5	8.5	2.4	0.5	77
2023	AAA	El Paso	0	1	0	16	19	13.50	3.31	5.8	366	47	58	11.37	15.2	10.7	0.7	1.7	-200

Career RP acquired from MIA in Aug 2023. Former position player who moved to mound in 2021. Owns outstanding FB that can blow by hitters up in zone. Hard CU also has moments of baffling hitters. Struggles to maintain command of pitches and inconsistent release point could be issue. Could be successful with FB/CU only.

Richardson,Lyon

SP | Cincinnati | EXP MLB DEBUT: 2023 | H/W: 6-2 207 | FUT: Setup reliever | 7D

Thrws R Age 24 — 2018 (2) HS (FL)

Velo	Pitch	Grade
96-98	FB	+++
86-88	CU	+++
76-80	CB	+++
83-85	SL	+++

Year	Lev	Team	W	L	Sv	IP	K	ERA	WHIP	BF/G	OBA	H%	S%	xERA	Ctl	Dom	Cmd	hr/9	BPV
2021	A+	Dayton	2	5	0	76	91	5.09	1.47	17.2	257	35	67	4.42	4.5	10.8	2.4	1.1	90
2023	A	Daytona	0	0	0	9	18	1.00	0.67	10.5	165	40	83	0.21	1.0	18.0	18.0	0.0	315
2023	AA	Chattanooga	0	2	0	46	58	2.15	1.24	12.4	212	32	84	2.63	4.3	11.3	2.6	0.4	106
2023	AAA	Louisville	0	1	0	14	24	9.57	1.84	11.0	217	41	42	3.79	9.6	15.3	1.6	0.0	35
2023	MLB	Cincinnati	0	2	0	16	12	8.89	1.98	19.4	271	25	62	8.06	8.3	6.7	0.8	3.3	-87

Athletic, low 3/4s RHP made return from several arm issues, making MLB debut. Power driven delivery with below-average extension. Struggles to repeat. Has SP quality arsenal but, control/command issues persist. Struggles command high-riding 4-seam FB. Does better with sinker. All secondaries are average-to-above offerings.

Ritchie,JR

SP | Atlanta | EXP MLB DEBUT: 2026 | H/W: 6-2 185 | FUT: #3 starter | 8D

Thrws R Age 20 — 2022 (1) HS (WA)

Velo	Pitch	Grade
92-95	FB	++++
82-84	SL	+++
83-85	CU	+++

Year	Lev	Team	W	L	Sv	IP	K	ERA	WHIP	BF/G	OBA	H%	S%	xERA	Ctl	Dom	Cmd	hr/9	BPV
2022	Rk	FCL Braves	0	0	0	4	4	0.00	0.73	7.3	147	21	100	0.28	2.2	8.8	4.0	0.0	117
2022	A	Augusta	0	0	0	10	10	2.70	1.10	13.1	199	25	80	2.62	3.6	9.0	2.5	0.9	83
2023	A	Augusta	0	1	0	13	25	5.50	1.07	12.7	229	48	43	1.98	2.1	17.2	8.3	0.0	272

Low 3/4s RHP looked poised to breakout in Low-A before Tommy John surgery sidelined him through the 2024 season. Athletic build with easy, repeatable delivery. Flat-angled FB has deceptive ride profile, playing up due to slot. SL is best secondary with short, 2-plane break. Has feel for CU with solid arm-side fade.

Robaina,Julio

SP | Houston | EXP MLB DEBUT: 2025 | H/W: 5-11 170 | FUT: #5 SP/swingman | 6C

Thrws L Age 22 — 2017 FA (CU)

Velo	Pitch	Grade
91-92	FB	++
77-79	CB	+
81-83	SL	++++
84-86	CU	++

Year	Lev	Team	W	L	Sv	IP	K	ERA	WHIP	BF/G	OBA	H%	S%	xERA	Ctl	Dom	Cmd	hr/9	BPV
2019	A	Quad Cities	0	1	1	5	6	0.00	1.92	12.3	120	19	100	2.99	13.8	10.4	0.8	0.0	-169
2021	A	Fayetteville	4	1	0	44	46	3.67	1.29	16.5	238	33	70	2.92	3.7	9.4	2.6	0.2	88
2021	A+	Asheville	3	2	0	32	42	3.93	1.21	21.6	261	37	69	3.61	2.0	11.8	6.0	0.8	177
2022	AA	Corpus Christi	2	6	0	80	84	6.85	1.92	16.5	291	37	65	6.21	6.8	9.4	1.4	1.2	3
2023	AA	Corpus Christi	10	6	0	116	114	3.18	1.32	18.5	243	32	76	3.31	3.7	8.8	2.4	0.5	77

Spent 2023 at Double-A. Gets on hitters with horizontal plane from 3/4 arm slot, good extension down mound. Excellent command of sweepy SL. Has good command of arsenal, but stiff FB leads to too much contact, limiting K% upside. Maintaining above-average GB% crucial to run prevention. Likely backend starter without more Ks.

Robberse,Sem | SP | St. Louis | EXP MLB DEBUT: 2024 | H/W: 6-1 185 | FUT: #4 starter | 7D

Thrws R Age 22	Year	Lev	Team	W	L	Sv	IP	K	ERA	WHIP	BF/G	OBA	H%	S%	xERA	Ctl	Dom	Cmd	hr/9	BPV
2019 FA (NT)	2021	A+	Vancouver	0	3	0	31	29	5.23	1.84	20.6	308	38	72	5.94	5.2	8.4	1.6	0.9	28
89-92 FB ++	2022	A+	Vancouver	4	4	0	86	78	3.13	1.16	20.2	238	29	75	3.10	2.5	8.1	3.3	0.7	97
83-86 SL +++	2022	AA	New Hampshire	0	3	0	24	19	3.72	1.20	19.4	218	23	76	3.66	3.7	7.1	1.9	1.5	45
88-90 CT +++	2023	AA	New Hampshire	3	5	0	88	86	4.08	1.18	19.6	222	26	71	3.59	3.4	8.8	2.6	1.4	85
84-86 CU ++	2023	AAA	Memphis	2	1	0	35	44	4.87	1.79	20.2	283	38	77	6.04	6.2	11.3	1.8	1.5	55

Signed out of the Netherlands, came over as part of Jordan Hicks deal. Tall, athletic frame and works primarily off low-90s FB that has arm-side run, but lacks velocity or carry. Mixes in a CT to work both sides of the plate. Best pitch is short mid-80s SL that induces weak contact. Improved CU gives him the potential for 3 above-average offerings.

Robertson,Nick | RP | St. Louis | EXP MLB DEBUT: 2023 | H/W: 6-6 265 | FUT: Setup reliever | 6A

Thrws R Age 25	Year	Lev	Team	W	L	Sv	IP	K	ERA	WHIP	BF/G	OBA	H%	S%	xERA	Ctl	Dom	Cmd	hr/9	BPV
2019 (7) James Madison	2022	AAA	Oklahoma City	0	0	2	11	15	2.41	1.16	5.0	240	38	77	2.41	2.4	12.1	5.0	0.0	170
94-97 FB +++	2023	AAA	Oklahoma City	2	0	7	28	42	2.56	1.00	4.0	193	31	77	2.00	2.9	13.5	4.7	0.6	182
85-87 SL ++	2023	AAA	Worcester	2	1	2	14	16	4.47	1.28	3.9	260	32	73	4.78	2.6	10.2	4.0	1.9	133
87-89 CU +++	2023	MLB	Boston	0	0	0	12	13	6.00	1.50	5.8	278	35	63	5.20	3.8	9.8	2.6	1.5	92
	2023	MLB	Los Angeles	0	1	0	10	13	6.24	2.08	5.5	374	51	70	7.66	3.6	11.6	3.3	0.9	130

On shuttle between AAA and majors with LA and BOS and then sent to STL in Dec 2023. Spent all career in pen and pitches aggressively. Lot of effort but is effective as he pitches inside and out. FB lacks movement and CU can be too firm. Uses imposing figure and quick delivery to fool hitters. Has good velocity and can register Ks.

Roby,Tekoah | SP | St. Louis | EXP MLB DEBUT: 2024 | H/W: 6-1 185 | FUT: #3 starter | 8D

Thrws R Age 22	Year	Lev	Team	W	L	Sv	IP	K	ERA	WHIP	BF/G	OBA	H%	S%	xERA	Ctl	Dom	Cmd	hr/9	BPV
2020 (3) HS (FL)																				
93-96 FB +++	2021	A	Down East	2	2	0	22	35	2.45	0.95	13.8	184	32	75	1.57	2.9	14.3	5.0	0.4	198
76-78 CB ++++	2022	A+	Hickory	3	11	0	104	126	4.66	1.25	19.3	244	31	68	4.23	3.0	10.9	3.6	1.6	132
83-85 SL +++	2023	AA	Frisco	2	3	0	46	50	5.08	1.32	19.1	274	35	63	4.21	2.3	9.8	4.2	1.0	130
79-82 CU +++	2023	AA	Springfield	0	0	0	12	19	3.00	0.75	10.7	151	25	63	1.01	2.3	14.3	6.3	0.8	214

Centerpiece of the J. Montgomery deal has four above-average offerings. Thick lower half and comes at hitters from a high 3/4 arm slot working mostly north/south. Uptick in FB velo; backs up FB with a high spin CB. CU and recently added SL round out the mix. Shoulder injury limited him to just 14 starts, but he was healthy in the AFL.

Rock,Joe | SP | Colorado | EXP MLB DEBUT: 2024 | H/W: 6-6 200 | FUT: #5 SP/swingman | 7D

Thrws L Age 23	Year	Lev	Team	W	L	Sv	IP	K	ERA	WHIP	BF/G	OBA	H%	S%	xERA	Ctl	Dom	Cmd	hr/9	BPV
2021 (2) Ohio	2021	Rk	ACL Rockies	1	0	0	8	11	1.13	0.75	7.1	181	30	83	0.66	1.1	12.4	11.0	0.0	210
91-94 FB +++	2022	A+	Spokane	7	8	0	107	109	4.45	1.23	21.7	223	28	65	3.19	3.8	9.2	2.4	0.8	81
82-84 SL +++	2022	AA	Hartford	0	0	0	8	11	10.13	1.75	18.3	285	38	42	6.62	5.6	12.4	2.2	2.3	89
83-85 CU ++	2023	AA	Hartford	1	10	0	90	108	4.50	1.40	20.0	270	36	72	4.65	3.2	10.8	3.4	1.3	126
	2023	AAA	Albuquerque	0	0	0	2	4	12.27	2.27	11.2	326	48	50	10.26	8.2	16.4	2.0	4.1	92

LHP uses a tall-and-fall low 3/4 delivery with a surprisingly short stride but good extension on release. Quick arm action leads to low-90s FB that gets on hitters quickly and tops at 97. Late-breaking SL is best secondary and a CU that still needs refinement and separation from FB. Showed improved command but was also more hittable in 2023.

Rocker,Kumar | SP | Texas | EXP MLB DEBUT: 2025 | H/W: 6-5 245 | FUT: #2 SP/closer | 8D

Thrws R Age 24	Year	Lev	Team	W	L	Sv	IP	K	ERA	WHIP	BF/G	OBA	H%	S%	xERA	Ctl	Dom	Cmd	hr/9	BPV
2022 (1) Vanderbilt																				
93-96 FB ++++																				
83-86 SL ++++																				
87-90 CU +++																				
80-84 CB ++++	2023	A+	Hickory	2	2	0	28	42	3.86	1.00	17.8	210	34	62	2.21	2.3	13.5	6.0	0.6	200

On stuff alone, he would rank near top of system. His fastball and curve are both plus, slider is a monster, and rounded out with average change and control. But he went under the Tommy John knife after six 2023 starts. Whether this hastens bullpen future is unknown, he just needs health and reps now.

Rodriguez Cruz,Elmer | SP | Boston | EXP MLB DEBUT: 2026 | H/W: 6-3 190 | FUT: #4 starter | 7D

Thrws R Age 20	Year	Lev	Team	W	L	Sv	IP	K	ERA	WHIP	BF/G	OBA	H%	S%	xERA	Ctl	Dom	Cmd	hr/9	BPV
2021 (4) HS (PR)																				
91-95 FB +++																				
78-82 CB +++	2022	Rk	FCL Red Sox	0	3	0	32	36	1.96	1.25	11.9	236	34	83	2.59	3.4	10.1	3.0	0.0	109
83-86 SL ++	2022	A	Salem	0	0	0	6	6	1.50	1.00	11.5	151	22	83	0.99	4.5	9.0	2.0	0.0	59
83-85 CU ++	2023	A	Salem	6	3	0	55	51	2.61	1.27	16.1	217	27	82	3.03	4.4	8.3	1.9	0.7	49

Thin, projectable SP who missed development time in Low-A due to injuries. Has clean, smooth mechanics with ideal extension to produce potential plus FB. Relies almost exclusively on heater as secondary stuff not dynamic. Likes to pitch inside and proven effective against LHH. Needs one of two breakers to evolve.

Rodriguez,Carlos | SP | Milwaukee | EXP MLB DEBUT: 2024 | H/W: 6-0 206 | FUT: #4 starter | 7B

Thrws R Age 22	Year	Lev	Team	W	L	Sv	IP	K	ERA	WHIP	BF/G	OBA	H%	S%	xERA	Ctl	Dom	Cmd	hr/9	BPV
2021 (6) Florida SW JC																				
91-94 FB +++																				
74-78 CB ++	2022	A	Carolina	3	4	1	71	84	3.54	1.13	14.8	209	28	71	2.77	3.4	10.6	3.1	0.9	117
81-85 SL ++	2023	AA	Biloxi	9	6	0	123	152	2.78	1.10	19.3	191	27	78	2.33	3.9	11.1	2.9	0.7	113
82-85 CU +++	2023	AAA	Nashville	0	0	0	4	6	6.43	2.14	20.8	297	46	67	5.66	8.6	12.9	1.5	0.0	18

Durable, strong SP who led SL in ERA and 2nd in Ks. Tough to barrel as he changes speeds well and can be effectively wild. Locates FB but has trouble spotting secondary offerings in zone. Works with both CB and SL that need work. SL lacks projection while CB has moments. Effective CU against LHH. Has been more of a flyball guy.

Rodriguez,Luis | SP | New York (N) | EXP MLB DEBUT: 2026 | H/W: 6-3 190 | FUT: #4 starter | 7D

Thrws L Age 21	Year	Lev	Team	W	L	Sv	IP	K	ERA	WHIP	BF/G	OBA	H%	S%	xERA	Ctl	Dom	Cmd	hr/9	BPV
2019 FA (DR)																				
94-96 FB ++++	2021	Rk	FCL Mets	0	1	0	5	11	1.76	0.98	4.8	122	37	80	0.55	5.3	19.4	3.7	0.0	224
83-85 SL +++	2021	A	St. Lucie	0	1	0	7	5	7.71	1.71	10.6	336	38	55	6.49	2.6	6.4	2.5	1.3	64
88-89 CU +++	2023	Rk	FCL Mets	0	1	0	5	4	7.06	1.76	5.8	327	37	63	6.91	3.5	7.1	2.0	1.8	50
	2023	A	St. Lucie	0	0	0	5	6	1.76	1.37	10.7	122	19	86	1.62	8.8	10.6	1.2	0.0	-30

Hard-throwing, projectable LHP with pitch arsenal to start. Repeatable, 3/4s delivery. Near physical projection. Primary 2-seam FB usage with solid sinking action. Works in 4-seam FB as well, but it's not as effective. SL has solid sweeping characteristics and could be above-average offering at projection. Sells CU well out of motion.

Rodriguez,Randy | RP | San Francisco | EXP MLB DEBUT: 2024 | H/W: 6-0 166 | FUT: Setup reliever | 7C

Thrws R Age 24	Year	Lev	Team	W	L	Sv	IP	K	ERA	WHIP	BF/G	OBA	H%	S%	xERA	Ctl	Dom	Cmd	hr/9	BPV
2017 FA (DR)																				
93-97 FB ++++	2022	AAA	Sacramento	0	1	0	6	7	10.50	2.33	6.2	151	23	50	4.33	16.5	10.5	0.6	0.0	-239
83-85 SL +++	2023	Rk	ACL Giants O	0	0	0	2	3	0.00	1.50	4.3	151	27	100	2.20	9.0	13.5	1.5	0.0	18
82-84 CB ++	2023	AA	Richmond	2	1	1	30	40	2.99	1.23	7.6	183	29	75	2.17	5.4	12.0	2.2	0.3	88
83-85 CU ++	2023	AAA	Sacramento	0	1	0	37	41	5.81	1.85	6.4	234	31	68	4.77	9.0	9.9	1.1	0.7	-45

Short RP who has spent most of last 2 seasons in bullpen. Few can match outstanding FB/SL combo but continues to suffer from well below average control and injury history. Very inconsistent production as result of inability to spot FB within zone. Quick arm produces plus spin and sweep to SL. Has hard CU at disposal, but not used often.

Rogers,Dalton | SP | Boston | EXP MLB DEBUT: 2025 | H/W: 5-11 172 | FUT: #4 starter | 7C

Thrws L Age 23	Year	Lev	Team	W	L	Sv	IP	K	ERA	WHIP	BF/G	OBA	H%	S%	xERA	Ctl	Dom	Cmd	hr/9	BPV
2022 (3) Southern Miss																				
91-95 FB +++	2022	NCAA	Southern Miss	1	1	6	37	57	1.95	1.05	6.2	133	24	82	1.12	5.6	13.9	2.5	0.2	117
81-83 SL +++	2022	Rk	FCL Red Sox	0	0	0	2	3	9.00	2.00	4.8	262	43	50	4.79	9.0	13.5	1.5	0.0	18
82-84 CU ++	2023	A	Salem	0	1	0	21	38	2.55	1.13	14.0	155	34	75	1.30	5.5	16.1	2.9	0.0	159
	2023	A+	Greenville	2	6	0	75	102	5.52	1.52	19.1	238	35	64	4.06	5.8	12.2	2.1	0.8	83

Short SP who had 2nd highest K/9 in org but was sluggish upon promotion to High-A. Lacks plus stuff in arsenal and relies on ability to hide ball in drop-and-drive delivery. FB features a lot of movement but isn't effective up in zone. Gets good mileage out of SL with depth. CU has moments and pairs well with high-spin FB.

Rojas,Kendry | SP | Toronto | EXP MLB DEBUT: 2026 | H/W: 6-2 190 | FUT: #3 starter | 8D

Thrws L Age 21	Year	Lev	Team	W	L	Sv	IP	K	ERA	WHIP	BF/G	OBA	H%	S%	xERA	Ctl	Dom	Cmd	hr/9	BPV
2020 FA (CU)																				
91-94 FB +++	2021	Rk	FCL Blue Jays	0	0	0	23	39	2.33	0.82	10.6	176	33	72	1.11	1.9	15.1	7.8	0.4	238
82-84 SL +++	2022	Rk	FCL Blue Jays	0	0	0	1	3	0.00	0.00	2.8	0	0			0.0	27.0		0.0	504
84-87 CU +++	2022	A	Dunedin	2	2	0	39	43	4.13	1.40	13.8	246	34	69	3.32	4.4	9.9	2.3	0.2	78
	2023	A	Dunedin	4	6	0	84	82	3.75	1.24	17.0	231	29	72	3.31	3.5	8.8	2.5	0.9	81

Repeated Low-A and showed improved control and more consistent secondary offerings. Leverages low ¾ slot and whip-like arm action to produce good velocity and cutting action to above average FB. Hard SL is used as chase pitch but has trouble commanding it. Can slow arm speed on CU but still solid pitch. Has K ability and upside.

Romero,Jose

RP | Chicago (N) | EXP MLB DEBUT: 2025 | H/W: 5-10 185 | FUT: Setup reliever | 6C

Thrws R Age 22	Year	Lev	Team	W	L	Sv	IP	K	ERA	WHIP	BF/G	OBA	H%	S%	xERA	Ctl	Dom	Cmd	hr/9	BPV
2020 FA (VZ)																				
92-94 FB +++	2021	Rk	DSL Cubs Blue	3	0	1	30	42	2.69	1.23	6.8	191	31	78	2.25	5.1	12.6	2.5	0.3	107
80-83 SL +++	2022	Rk	ACL Cubs	2	1	0	22	29	2.04	1.00	9.4	138	21	81	1.20	4.9	11.8	2.4	0.4	99
	2022	A	Myrtle Beach	0	1	0	2	2	54.00	5.00	7.8	470	52		20.61	22.5	9.0	0.4	4.5	-428
	2023	A	Myrtle Beach	3	1	3	48	68	2.80	1.20	6.9	205	32	78	2.59	4.3	12.7	3.0	0.6	131

Short, stocky RHP from Venezuela had a breakout campaign at Low-A and impressed in the AFL. Pounds the zone with a low-90s FB that has good late arm-side run and ride and low-80s SL that has tight late break and generates plenty of swing-and-miss. Now owns a 31% K rate and could develop into a viable setup reliever.

Roupp,Landen

SP | San Francisco | EXP MLB DEBUT: 2024 | H/W: 6-2 205 | FUT: #4 starter | 7B

Thrws R Age 25	Year	Lev	Team	W	L	Sv	IP	K	ERA	WHIP	BF/G	OBA	H%	S%	xERA	Ctl	Dom	Cmd	hr/9	BPV
2021 (12) UNC Wilmington	2021	A	San Jose	0	0	0	2	2	0.00	0.50	6.6	151	22	100		0.0	9.0		0.0	180
91-95 FB +++	2022	A	San Jose	5	2	0	48	69	2.61	1.04	13.3	195	32	75	1.88	3.2	12.9	4.1	0.4	164
79-82 CB ++++	2022	A+	Eugene	3	0	0	32	52	1.68	0.87	16.9	173	32	81	1.12	2.5	14.6	5.8	0.3	212
80-83 SL +++	2022	AA	Richmond	2	1	0	26	31	3.79	1.15	20.7	205	27	70	2.92	3.8	10.7	2.8	1.0	108
83-84 CU ++	2023	AA	Richmond	0	0	0	31	42	1.74	1.00	11.8	201	32	83	1.79	2.6	12.2	4.7	0.3	167

Followed up breakout 2022 with injury-riddled campaign in 2023, all in AA. Ended season in June but beforehand continued to showcase a deceptive delivery and incredible bat-missing CB with lots of spin and late action. Commands sinking FB well and gets high amount of GB. Minimizes walks but will need better CU to combat LHH.

Rutledge,Jackson

SP | Washington | EXP MLB DEBUT: 2023 | H/W: 6-8 251 | FUT: #4 starter | 7B

Thrws R Age 25	Year	Lev	Team	W	L	Sv	IP	K	ERA	WHIP	BF/G	OBA	H%	S%	xERA	Ctl	Dom	Cmd	hr/9	BPV
2019 (1) San Jacinto JC	2021	A+	Wilmington	0	3	0	10		13.24	2.55	13.7	371	48	42	7.99	7.9	8.8	1.1	0.0	-38
94-97 FB +++	2022	A	Fredericksburg	8	6	0	97	99	4.91	1.39	20.4	279	36	64	4.15	2.7	9.2	3.4	0.6	111
84-87 SL +++	2023	AA	Harrisburg	6	1	0	68	62	3.17	1.10	22.3	207	26	73	2.49	3.3	8.2	2.5	0.7	76
87-90 CU ++	2023	AAA	Rochester	2	3	0	50	44	4.48	1.51	19.8	245	29	74	4.58	5.4	7.9	1.5	1.3	15
78-81 CB ++	2023	MLB	Washington	1	1	0	20	12	6.75	1.50	21.6	299	31	58	5.83	2.7	5.4	2.0	1.8	42

Worked his way through early-career injuries to make his MLB debut in 2023. Coachable and has shown the ability to make changes. His four-pitch arsenal is a bit underwhelming given his physical size. SL is his best pitch even with a mid-90s fastball; would benefit overall from throwing more strikes. Still some reliever risk, but a SP for now.

Ryan,River

SP | Los Angeles (N) | EXP MLB DEBUT: 2024 | H/W: 6-2 195 | FUT: #3 starter | 8D

Thrws R Age 25	Year	Lev	Team	W	L	Sv	IP	K	ERA	WHIP	BF/G	OBA	H%	S%	xERA	Ctl	Dom	Cmd	hr/9	BPV
2021 (11) UNC-Pembroke	2021	NCAA	UNC-Pembroke	5	1	6	51	68	3.69	1.11	11.8	213	31	69	2.76	3.2	12.0	3.8	0.9	148
94-96 FB ++++	2022	A	Rancho Cuca	1	3	0	33	48	2.71	1.27	13.6	236	37	80	3.12	3.5	13.0	3.7	0.5	157
88-92 SL +++	2022	A+	Great Lakes	1	1	0	14	22	1.93	1.21	11.3	186	29	93	3.06	5.1	14.1	2.8	1.3	134
79-82 CB +++	2023	AA	Tulsa	1	6	0	97	98	3.34	1.26	16.5	222	28	75	3.14	4.1	9.1	2.2	0.7	71
86-88 CU +++	2023	AAA	Oklahoma City	0	1	0	7	12	10.29	2.00	16.9	378	56	50	9.08	2.6	15.4	6.0	2.6	226

Has an exciting 4-pitch mix and attacks hitters with a plus 4-seamer that sits at 94-96 with arm-side run and carry both at top and bottom of the zone. Best secondary is a low-90s CT that keeps hitters off the FB, and above-average SL, CB, and CU with good late fade. Athletic frame and easy, repeatable mechanics. Could surprise.

Salinas,Royber

SP | Oakland | EXP MLB DEBUT: 2024 | H/W: 6-3 205 | FUT: #4 starter | 7C

Thrws R Age 22	Year	Lev	Team	W	L	Sv	IP	K	ERA	WHIP	BF/G	OBA	H%	S%	xERA	Ctl	Dom	Cmd	hr/9	BPV
2018 FA (VZ)	2021	A	Augusta	2	0	0	14	18	0.64	1.00	17.8	132	22	93	0.77	5.1	11.6	2.3	0.0	87
92-95 FB ++++	2022	A	Augusta	0	1	0	23	52	1.55	0.95	17.5	133	40	86	0.93	4.7	20.2	4.3	0.4	255
80-83 CB ++	2022	A+	Rome	5	7	0	85	123	4.12	1.34	17.7	208	33	69	3.04	5.4	13.0	2.4	0.6	107
82-85 SL +++	2023	Rk	ACL Athletics	0	0	0	4	4	4.39	1.46	8.8	342	44	67	4.72	0.0	8.8		0.0	176
83-87 CU ++	2023	AA	Midland	1	5	1	67	89	5.50	1.34	15.5	238	33	60	3.96	4.2	11.9	2.9	1.2	121

Strong-framed SP who is progressing one level per year. Stuff better than results but has limited upside due to struggles with LHH and lack of durability. Max effort delivery may move to pen and has plus FB and SL to be potent. Fails to throw consistent strikes, mostly due to erratic arm slot. Still young enough to polish game.

Sanchez,Sixto

SP | Miami | EXP MLB DEBUT: 2020 | H/W: 6-0 234 | FUT: Setup reliever | 8E

Thrws R Age 25	Year	Lev	Team	W	L	Sv	IP	K	ERA	WHIP	BF/G	OBA	H%	S%	xERA	Ctl	Dom	Cmd	hr/9	BPV
2015 FA (DR)	2018	A+	Clearwater	4	3	0	46	45	2.53	1.08	22.5	230	31	76	2.29	2.1	8.8	4.1	0.2	118
96-100 FB ++++	2019	A+	Jupiter	0	2	0	11	6	4.91	1.45	23.5	311	34	67	4.99	1.6	4.9	3.0	0.8	62
88-90 CT +++	2019	AA	Jacksonville	8	4	0	103	97	2.53	1.03	22.0	230	30	76	2.39	1.7	8.5	5.1	0.4	126
84-97 SL +++	2020	MLB	Miami	3	2	0	39	33	3.46	1.21	22.4	247	30	73	3.29	2.5	7.6	3.0	0.7	87
87-92 CU +++	2023	AA	Pensacola	0	0	0	1	2	0.00	2.00	4.8	262	55	100	4.75	9.0	18.0	2.0	0.0	99

Oft injured RHP with electric FB finally appeared in a game, the 1st since 2020. Pitching an inning, the once mighty FB topped out at 88 MPH, a far cry from the 96-100 MPH FB during 2020 MLB debut. With all the missed development time, still only 25. Being kept alive as prospect solely based on past glory.

Sandlin,David

SP | Kansas City | EXP MLB DEBUT: 2026 | H/W: 6-4 215 | FUT: Setup reliever | 7C

Thrws R Age 23	Year	Lev	Team	W	L	Sv	IP	K	ERA	WHIP	BF/G	OBA	H%	S%	xERA	Ctl	Dom	Cmd	hr/9	BPV
2022 (11) Oklahoma																				
95-97 FB ++++	2022	NCAA	Oklahoma	9	4	0	95	102	5.59	1.38	21.0	272	34	62	4.74	2.9	9.7	3.3	1.4	113
83-87 SL +++	2022	Rk	ACL Royals Blue	0	0	0	2	3	0.00	0.50	6.6	151	27	100		0.0	13.5		0.0	261
87-90 CU ++	2023	A	Columbia	4	1	0	58	79	3.40	1.20	19.5	258	37	77	3.90	2.0	12.2	6.1	1.2	184
	2023	A+	Quad Cities	0	1	0	8	8	4.50	1.38	16.8	210	26	70	3.65	5.6	9.0	1.6	1.1	28

Tall, near-physical projection RHP split time between lower minor affiliates. Missed last 3 months due to oblique injury. Throws hard and features a tight breaking SL. Raw stuff is very good but plays down due to limited extension in delivery, which will ultimately leads to RP future.

Santa,Alimber

RP | Houston | EXP MLB DEBUT: 2027 | H/W: 5-10 163 | FUT: #3 starter | 8E

Thrws R Age 20	Year	Lev	Team	W	L	Sv	IP	K	ERA	WHIP	BF/G	OBA	H%	S%	xERA	Ctl	Dom	Cmd	hr/9	BPV
2020 FA (DR)	2021	Rk	DSL Astros	0	2	1	13	14	3.41	1.52	9.5	273	38	75	3.77	4.1	9.5	2.3	0.0	79
94-97 FB +++	2021	Rk	FCL Astros	0	0	0	7	8	3.80	0.99	9.0	200	20	80	3.87	2.5	10.1	4.0	2.5	132
79-81 CB ++	2022	Rk	FCL Astros O	0	0	0	2	4	9.00	1.50	4.3	347	65	33	4.81	0.0	18.0		0.0	342
84-87 SL +++	2022	A	Fayetteville	0	0	0	0	0			3.0	1000	100	67				0.0		
85-87 CU ++	2023	A	Fayetteville	3	9	0	87	119	5.99	1.84	15.6	259	39	66	4.84	7.6	12.3	1.6	0.5	33

Young RHP with big arm has good raw stuff, rough command. Pushes off mound well, throws with quick arm action. FB is potential plus pitch with good movement. Struggles to get bites on secondaries. Raw, but further offspeed pitch development could yield big results.

Santos,Dahian

SP | Toronto | EXP MLB DEBUT: 2026 | H/W: 5-11 160 | FUT: #4 starter | 7D

Thrws R Age 21	Year	Lev	Team	W	L	Sv	IP	K	ERA	WHIP	BF/G	OBA	H%	S%	xERA	Ctl	Dom	Cmd	hr/9	BPV
2019 FA (VZ)	2021	Rk	FCL Blue Jays	1	2	0	35	53	4.62	1.20	14.1	233	35	65	3.58	3.1	13.6	4.4	1.3	180
90-94 FB +++	2021	A	Dunedin	0	2	0	5	5	12.60	2.40	13.1	362	43	45	9.13	7.2	9.0	1.3	1.8	-14
82-84 SL +++	2022	A	Dunedin	4	5	0	73	120	3.45	1.12	15.2	186	31	73	2.54	4.3	14.8	3.4	1.0	168
83-84 CU ++	2022	A+	Vancouver	0	2	0	12	22	11.07	2.13	15.1	331	53	48	8.22	6.6	16.2	2.4	2.2	131
	2023	A+	Vancouver	3	3	0	48	56	3.56	1.19	16.1	181	24	73	2.65	5.1	10.5	2.1	0.9	70

Short-framed SP who ended season in early July due to injury. Has room to add strength yet has very good FB now. Very tough to barrel and consistently posts low oppBA because of arm action and quick delivery. Control has room to improve. Tends to slow arm speed on CU SL is best secondary pitch and features lot of spin.

Santos,Junior

SP | New York (N) | EXP MLB DEBUT: 2024 | H/W: 6-7 244 | FUT: Setup reliever | 7D

Thrws R Age 22	Year	Lev	Team	W	L	Sv	IP	K	ERA	WHIP	BF/G	OBA	H%	S%	xERA	Ctl	Dom	Cmd	hr/9	BPV
2018 FA (DR)	2018	Rk	DSL Mets	1	1	0	45	36	2.80	0.91	15.3	216	27	68	1.71	1.2	7.2	6.0	0.2	115
95-98 FB ++++	2019	Rk	Kingsport	0	5	0	40	36	5.15	1.77	13.2	289	35	72	5.48	5.6	8.1	1.4	0.9	12
84-86 SL +++	2021	A	St. Lucie	6	6	0	96	79	4.59	1.52	19.8	285	34	70	4.68	3.6	7.4	2.1	0.8	55
86-88 CU +	2022	A+	Brooklyn	8	13	0	116	105	4.49	1.46	19.1	278	35	67	4.01	3.4	8.1	2.4	0.3	72
	2023	AA	Binghamton	4	8	3	97	71	5.94	1.65	15.5	303	35	64	5.45	3.8	6.6	1.7	0.9	34

Hard-throwing sinkerballer began conversion to RP role in 2024. Low 3/4s delivery with solid extension. Improved command and fitness overall. Throws heavy 2-seam FB with plus arm-side run for strikes. Not a bat missing pitch. Secondary development continues to lag behind. Vertical breaking SL has best shot at developing. Has no feel for CU grip.

Sauer,Matt

SP | Kansas City | EXP MLB DEBUT: 2024 | H/W: 6-4 230 | FUT: Setup reliever | 7C

Thrws R Age 25	Year	Lev	Team	W	L	Sv	IP	K	ERA	WHIP	BF/G	OBA	H%	S%	xERA	Ctl	Dom	Cmd	hr/9	BPV
2017 (2) HS (CA)	2022	A+	Hudson Valley	5	3	0	88	100	3.78	1.25	19.9	232	31	72	3.30	3.6	10.2	2.9	0.8	105
92-94 FB +++	2022	AA	Somerset	0	2	0	20	34	8.02	1.44	21.5	279	43	46	5.68	3.1	15.1	4.9	2.2	206
83-85 SL ++++	2023	Rk	FCL Yankees	0	1	0	3	5	5.63	1.25	6.5	181	20	67	4.54	5.6	14.1	2.5	2.8	119
79-81 CB +++	2023	A+	Hudson Valley	0	0	0	2	5	0.00	1.50	8.6	0	0	100	0.79	13.5	22.5	1.7	0.0	59
	2023	AA	Somerset	6	4	0	68	83	3.44	1.15	19.3	203	26	78	3.28	3.8	11.0	2.9	1.5	112

Over-the-top RHP with SP pitch mix continues to struggle with health despite statistical gains. Athletic delivery with solid extension, will lose release point from time to time. 4-seam FB has tremendous ride profile but struggles with command in zone. Sweeping SL is best pitch. Has better command of SL than FB. An average CB rounds out pitches.

Schoenwetter,Cole — SP — Cincinnati

EXP MLB DEBUT: 2027 | H/W: 6-3 190 | FUT: #3 starter | 8E

Thrws R Age 19 — 2023 (4) HS (CA)

Velo	Pitch	Grade
92-95	FB	++++
76-79	CB	++++
81-83	CU	++

Tall, projectable RHP was an over-slot 4th round signing in 2023. Thin frame with room to grow. Uneven low 3/4s delivery. Struggles maintaining balance and flying open. FB sits mid 90s with solid ride/run profile. 11-to-5 CB has solid depth and late breaking action. Telegraphs CU. Area scouts were concerned with RP risk leading up to draft.

Schultz,Noah — SP — Chicago (A)

EXP MLB DEBUT: 2026 | H/W: 6-9 220 | FUT: #1 starter | 9D

Thrws L Age 20 — 2022 (1) HS (IL)

Velo	Pitch	Grade
93-95	FB	++++
79-81	SL	++++
85-87	CU	+++

Year	Lev	Team	W	L	Sv	IP	K	ERA	WHIP	BF/G	OBA	H%	S%	xERA	Ctl	Dom	Cmd	hr/9	BPV
2023	A	Kannapolis	1	2	0	27	38	1.33	0.85	9.9	183	27	95	1.86	2.0	12.7	6.3	1.0	192

Tall, projectable LHP was eased into pro ball after flexor sprain injury in spring training. Low 3/4s delivery creates deception through slot and lengthy frame. FB is potential double-plus due to slot and break profile. Sweeping SL is best secondary with near 50% whiff rate. Also throws occasional CU, which projects as solid 3rd offering.

Schweitzer,Tyler — SP — Chicago (A)

EXP MLB DEBUT: 2025 | H/W: 6-0 185 | FUT: #4 starter | 7D

Thrws L Age 23 — 2022 (5) Ball State

Velo	Pitch	Grade
90-92	FB	++++
77-79	CB	+++
82-84	SL	+++
83-85	CU	+++

Year	Lev	Team	W	L	Sv	IP	K	ERA	WHIP	BF/G	OBA	H%	S%	xERA	Ctl	Dom	Cmd	hr/9	BPV
2023	A	Kannapolis	7	2	0	67	76	3.88	1.24	21.0	247	33	69	3.32	2.8	10.2	3.6	0.7	125
2023	A+	Winston Salem	0	2	0	39	45	4.13	1.43	16.7	224	29	75	3.97	5.5	10.3	1.9	1.1	55

Undersized, 3/4s RHP with solid assortment of pitches performed well in first full pro season. Repeatable, crossfire delivery with solid strike throwing tendencies. High-riding 4-seam FB is best pitch with flat angled approach. Varies between average SL and average CB as main secondaries. SL is better offering. CU lacks fade.

Schwellenbach,Spencer — SP — Atlanta

EXP MLB DEBUT: 2024 | H/W: 6-1 200 | FUT: #4 starter | 7B

Thrws R Age 23 — 2021 (2) Nebraska

Velo	Pitch	Grade
95-96	FB	++++
83-85	SL	+++
79-81	CB	+++
83-85	CU	++

Year	Lev	Team	W	L	Sv	IP	K	ERA	WHIP	BF/G	OBA	H%	S%	xERA	Ctl	Dom	Cmd	hr/9	BPV
2021	--	Did Not Play																	
2023	A	Augusta	4	2	0	51	41	2.64	1.15	15.6	234	28	79	2.85	2.6	7.2	2.7	0.5	77
2023	A+	Rome	1	0	0	13	14	2.05	0.38	14.1	97	15	40		0.7	9.5	14.0	0.0	171

Athletic, command/control former 2-way player emerged from Tommy John surgery to have successful debut. Double-plus command plays up arsenal. Low 3/4s slot delivery with solid extension. 4-seam FB has flat-angled approach and solid ride, which plays up due to slot. SL and CB have similar action, but varied speed. CU is below-average; mixes in CT.

Scott,Christian — SP — New York (N)

EXP MLB DEBUT: 2024 | H/W: 6-4 215 | FUT: #3 starter | 8C

Thrws R Age 24 — 2021 (5) Florida

Velo	Pitch	Grade
93-95	FB	++++
83-85	SL	+++
84-86	SP	++++
78-79	CB	++

Year	Lev	Team	W	L	Sv	IP	K	ERA	WHIP	BF/G	OBA	H%	S%	xERA	Ctl	Dom	Cmd	hr/9	BPV
2022	A	St. Lucie	3	3	0	37	52	4.85	1.40	13.1	277	42	64	3.95	2.9	12.6	4.3	0.5	166
2022	A+	Brooklyn	0	0	0	21	25	3.84	1.47	15.1	261	38	71	3.47	4.3	10.7	2.5	0.0	95
2023	A	St. Lucie	0	1	0	2	3	9.00	2.00	9.6	415	60	50	7.45	0.0	13.5		0.0	261
2023	A+	Brooklyn	1	0	0	23	27	2.33	0.82	14.1	187	28	68	0.91	1.6	10.5	6.8	0.0	165
2023	AA	Binghamton	4	3	0	62	77	2.47	0.84	18.9	201	29	74	1.80	1.2	11.2	9.6	0.7	188

Tall, projectable RHP enjoyed breakout season after refining his pitch mix the past two off-seasons. Long frame; is near physical projection. Easy, repeatable delivery with plus extension. 4-seam FB has plus ride and run from lower arm slot. SP has natural arm-side fade and late drop. SL is a solid offering. Will mix in 2-seam FB and CB.

Segura,Enrique — SP — Philadelphia

EXP MLB DEBUT: 2027 | H/W: 6-3 175 | FUT: #4 starter | 7D

Thrws R Age 19 — 2022 FA (DR)

Velo	Pitch	Grade
90-93	FB	+++
78-80	CB	++
79-83	SL	+
82-85	CU	++

Year	Lev	Team	W	L	Sv	IP	K	ERA	WHIP	BF/G	OBA	H%	S%	xERA	Ctl	Dom	Cmd	hr/9	BPV
2022	Rk	DSL Phillies R	5	1	0	42	39	2.35	1.37	13.6	232	30	82	3.08	4.7	8.3	1.8	0.2	41
2023	Rk	FCL Phillies	1	3	0	36	33	6.96	1.69	14.8	239	29	58	4.68	7.2	8.2	1.1	1.0	-29

After an impressive debut in the DSL in 2022, encountered some rough patches in the Complex league in 2023. Control waned, but is still young and growing into his lanky frame. Gets good extension; FB gets some ride, but lack of strikes across four-pitch arsenal (CB/SL/CU) needs addressed. Likely heads to Single-A.

Selvidge,Brock — SP — New York (A)

EXP MLB DEBUT: 2025 | H/W: 6-3 205 | FUT: #3 starter | 8E

Thrws L Age 21 — 2021 (3) HS (AZ)

Velo	Pitch	Grade
84-86	SL	++++
91-94	FB	+++
85-87	CU	+++
87-89	CT	++

Year	Lev	Team	W	L	Sv	IP	K	ERA	WHIP	BF/G	OBA	H%	S%	xERA	Ctl	Dom	Cmd	hr/9	BPV
2021	Rk	FCL Yankees	0	0	0	3	4	2.81	0.94	4.0	181	28	67	1.14	2.8	11.3	4.0	0.0	145
2022	Rk	FCL Yankees	3	1	0	42	53	2.99	1.28	15.7	237	35	77	3.07	3.6	11.3	3.1	0.4	124
2023	A	Tampa	4	4	0	77	91	3.39	1.21	20.7	249	35	71	2.97	2.5	10.6	4.3	0.4	143
2023	A+	Hudson Valley	4	1	0	50	46	3.59	1.16	22.1	237	31	68	2.73	2.5	8.3	3.3	0.4	99

Projectable LHP had strong full season debut, relying heavily on SL/FB mix. Athletic, 3/4s delivery. Fights flying open. Commands two-plane SL well, varies profile of pitch to achieve deception. 4-seam FB has high spin rate but struggles with identity, living best up. Fading CU could become above-average pitch. CT is newer wrinkle.

Serna,Luis — SP — New York (A)

EXP MLB DEBUT: 2026 | H/W: 5-11 162 | FUT: #3 starter | 8E

Thrws R Age 19 — 2021 FA (MX)

Velo	Pitch	Grade
91-93	FB	+++
79-81	SL	+++
76-78	CU	++++
76-78	CB	+++

Year	Lev	Team	W	L	Sv	IP	K	ERA	WHIP	BF/G	OBA	H%	S%	xERA	Ctl	Dom	Cmd	hr/9	BPV
2021	Rk	DSL Yankees	1	5	0	40	46	2.25	1.05	12.9	181	27	76	1.43	3.8	10.4	2.7	0.0	101
2022	Rk	FCL Yankees	0	0	0	41	56	1.97	1.22	15.1	222	36	82	2.30	3.7	12.3	3.3	0.0	138
2023	Rk	FCL Yankees	0	1	0	19	23	4.24	1.31	9.9	240	33	70	3.67	3.8	10.8	2.9	0.9	111

Low 3/4s RHP struggled to maintain health after breakout 2022. Stayed with complex team, attempting to manage workload post shoulder injury. 4-pitch pitcher. Best pitch is late-fading CU with drop off the table sink. 4-Seam FB backed up, struggled to find whiffs. SL and CB project as average pitches. RP risk with health and delivery concerns.

Serwinowski,Adam — SP — Cincinnati

EXP MLB DEBUT: 2026 | H/W: 6-5 190 | FUT: #3 starter | 8E

Thrws L Age 19 — 2022 (15) HS (SC)

Velo	Pitch	Grade
94-96	FB	++++
79-82	CB	++++

Year	Lev	Team	W	L	Sv	IP	K	ERA	WHIP	BF/G	OBA	H%	S%	xERA	Ctl	Dom	Cmd	hr/9	BPV
2022	Rk	ACL Reds	0	0	0	1	1	0.00	2.00	4.8	262	35	100	4.84	9.0	9.0	1.0	0.0	-63
2023	Rk	ACL Reds	0	0	0	27	43	3.65	1.07	9.6	145	26	64	1.37	5.3	14.3	2.7	0.3	132

Hard-throwing, low 3/4s LHP was one of the best pitchers in Arizona Complex League. Struggles to repeat raw delivery, throw strikes. Long frame with room to grow. 3-pitch pitcher. Easy velocity with 4-seam FB. Improved FB action helps play up pitch. Slurvy CB is best pitch, which may refine into true sweeping SL at projection.

Seymour,Carson — SP — San Francisco

EXP MLB DEBUT: 2024 | H/W: 6-6 260 | FUT: #4 starter | 7C

Thrws R Age 25 — 2021 (6) Kansas State

Velo	Pitch	Grade
92-95	FB	++++
80-82	CB	++
85-88	SL	+++
84-86	CU	+++

Year	Lev	Team	W	L	Sv	IP	K	ERA	WHIP	BF/G	OBA	H%	S%	xERA	Ctl	Dom	Cmd	hr/9	BPV
2021	Rk	FCL Mets	0	0	0	4	4	2.20	2.20	5.1	206	28	89	4.62	13.2	8.8	0.7	0.0	-180
2022	A	St. Lucie	4	0	0	30	27	1.20	1.06	16.7	213	28	88	1.86	2.7	8.1	3.0	0.0	91
2022	A+	Brooklyn	1	5	0	51	65	3.70	1.12	18.3	238	32	73	3.59	2.1	11.4	5.4	1.4	167
2022	A+	Eugene	2	3	0	29	43	4.02	1.20	19.5	234	38	65	2.70	3.1	13.3	4.3	0.3	174
2023	AA	Richmond	5	3	0	112	114	4.01	1.24	16.3	233	30	68	3.14	3.4	9.1	2.7	0.6	89

Tall, large RHP with exceptional sinker that helped to post 4th lowest oppBA in EL. Induces weak contact with lively sinker and enhanced by downhill plane to plate. Keeps ball on ground and can complement FB with interesting SL with cutting action. Particularly stingy against LHH, but RHH are another story with sub-par command and control.

Seymour,Ian — SP — Tampa Bay

EXP MLB DEBUT: 2024 | H/W: 6-0 210 | FUT: Middle reliever | 7C

Thrws L Age 25 — 2020 (2) Virginia Tech

Velo	Pitch	Grade
88-90	FB	++++
81-83	CU	++++
81-84	SL	++
73-76	CB	++

Year	Lev	Team	W	L	Sv	IP	K	ERA	WHIP	BF/G	OBA	H%	S%	xERA	Ctl	Dom	Cmd	hr/9	BPV
2022	AA	Montgomery	0	2	0	16	23	8.33	2.10	15.9	325	47	59	7.04	6.7	12.8	1.9	1.1	68
2023	Rk	FCL Rays	0	0	0	6	11	1.45	1.29	6.4	186	38	88	2.03	5.8	16.0	2.8	0.0	149
2023	A	Charleston	1	0	0	22	22	1.64	0.77	13.2	162	22	81	0.92	2.0	9.0	4.4	0.4	125
2023	A+	Bowling Green	0	0	0	8	9	2.20	1.10	16.1	147	18	88	2.22	5.5	9.9	1.8	1.1	48
2023	AA	Montgomery	0	0	0	4	4	0.00	0.71	14.8	78	11	100		4.3	8.6	2.0	0.0	57

Crossfire LHP with deception made it back from Tommy John surgery to post solid numbers at three levels. Creates deception with over-the-top slot and late release. Thrives despite low velocity FB due to plus ride and deceptive delivery. CU is best secondary with over 50% whiff rate. CU thrives in zone. Struggles to spin both SL and CB consistently.

Shim,Jun Seok
SP | Pittsburgh | EXP MLB DEBUT: 2026 | H/W: 6-4 215 | FUT: #3 starter | 8D

Thrws R Age 19
2023 FA (KR)

Velo	Pitch	Grade
92-96	FB	++++
75-78	CB	+++
80-82	SL	++
82-84	CU	++

Year	Lev	Team	W	L	Sv	IP	K	ERA	WHIP	BF/G	OBA	H%	S%	xERA	Ctl	Dom	Cmd	hr/9	BPV
2023	Rk	FCL Pirates B	0	0	0	8	13	3.38	0.75	7.1	117	17	60	1.03	3.4	14.6	4.3	1.1	190

Exciting, tall RHP with intriguing upside. Started 4 games in US debut and impressed with quick, electric arm that produces plus FB. Lot of riding life on FB and tough to hit hard. CB ahead of SL at present and could develop into above average offering. More oomph to SL would be ideal. Will need to add muscle and weight to lean frame.

Showalter,Zack
SP | St. Louis | EXP MLB DEBUT: 2026 | H/W: 6-2 195 | FUT: #4 starter | 7D

Thrws R Age 20
2022 (11) HS (FL)

Velo	Pitch	Grade
93-96	FB	++++
76-78	SL	++
86-88	CU	+

Year	Lev	Team	W	L	Sv	IP	K	ERA	WHIP	BF/G	OBA	H%	S%	xERA	Ctl	Dom	Cmd	hr/9	BPV
2023	Rk	FCL Orioles B	0	0	0	10	16	0.90	1.10	13.1	199	36	91	1.72	3.6	14.4	4.0	0.0	180
2023	A	Palm Beach	0	0	0	1	1	0.00	1.00	3.8	0	0	100		9.0	9.0	1.0	0.0	-63
2023	A	Delmarva	0	2	0	20	25	3.13	1.44	14.3	251	36	79	3.68	4.5	11.2	2.5	0.4	99

Uses a short arm action and high arm slot to hide the ball. Release point is inconsistent and close to max effort delivery results in below-average control and command. Fringe control and command. Mid-90s FB does have carry and run with plus potential. Slurvy SL lacks depth while upper-80s CU shows potential; needs greater separation from FB.

Silva,Eric
SP | San Francisco | EXP MLB DEBUT: 2025 | H/W: 6-1 185 | FUT: #3 starter | 8E

Thrws R Age 21
2021 (4) HS (CA)

Velo	Pitch	Grade
92-95	FB	+++
79-80	CB	+++
82-84	SL	+++
83-85	CU	++

Year	Lev	Team	W	L	Sv	IP	K	ERA	WHIP	BF/G	OBA	H%	S%	xERA	Ctl	Dom	Cmd	hr/9	BPV
2021	Rk	ACL Giants O	0	1	0	1	2	36.00	7.00	4.9	587	83	43	25.31	27.0	18.0	0.7	0.0	-387
2022	A	San Jose	3	7	0	85	99	5.92	1.36	16.2	243	32	57	4.05	4.1	10.5	2.5	1.2	95
2023	Rk	ACL Giants B	0	0	0	5	13	5.29	1.37	10.7	327	84	57	4.10	0.0	22.9		0.0	431
2023	A+	Eugene	2	7	0	76	73	5.92	1.54	11.8	267	33	61	4.53	4.6	8.6	1.9	0.8	49

Quick-armed SP with very intriguing pitch mix but has found the going tough the last two seasons. Gets hit hard as he can nibble at the corners. Also falls behind in count and forced to use straight FB. Uses four pitches and all should get to at least average status. Has shown some feel for spin and is very athletic.

Sims,Landon
RP | Arizona | EXP MLB DEBUT: 2024 | H/W: 6-2 227 | FUT: Setup reliever | 7E

Thrws R Age 23
2022 (1) Mississippi State

Velo	Pitch	Grade
91-93	FB	+++
82-84	SL	+++
84-86	CU	++

Year	Lev	Team	W	L	Sv	IP	K	ERA	WHIP	BF/G	OBA	H%	S%	xERA	Ctl	Dom	Cmd	hr/9	BPV
2023	Rk	ACL DBacks R	0	0	0	7	6	0.00	1.13	4.0	200	26	100	1.86	3.8	7.6	2.0	0.0	52
2023	Rk	ACL Dbacks	0	1	0	2	3	14.21	1.58	8.4	272	46	0	3.86	4.7	14.2	3.0	0.0	146
2023	A	Visalia	0	3	0	15	19	7.11	1.58	9.6	272	35	57	5.56	4.7	11.3	2.4	1.8	93

Former college star made return from Tommy John surgery in short 24 IP pro debut. FB/SL heavy approach, mixes in occasional CU. Low-90s FB showing signs of regression, given mid-90s pre-TJ velo. SL has potential to be effective out pitch. May develop as starter yet if CU comes along, but likely headed for bullpen.

Skenes,Paul
SP | Pittsburgh | EXP MLB DEBUT: 2024 | H/W: 6-6 235 | FUT: #1 starter | 9B

Thrws R Age 21
2023 (1) LSU

Velo	Pitch	Grade
94-99	FB	+++++
85-88	SL	++++
88-90	CU	+++

Year	Lev	Team	W	L	Sv	IP	K	ERA	WHIP	BF/G	OBA	H%	S%	xERA	Ctl	Dom	Cmd	hr/9	BPV
2023	NCAA	LSU	13	2	0	122	209	1.69	0.75	23.0	173	32	81	1.02	1.5	15.4	10.5	0.5	255
2023	Rk	FCL Pirates B	0	0	0	1	1	0.00	0.00	2.8	0	0			0.0	9.0		0.0	180
2023	A	Bradenton	0	0	0	3	4	0.00	0.33	4.7	106	18	100		0.0	12.0		0.0	234
2023	AA	Altoona	0	0	0	2	5	16.36	2.73	6.1	392	77	33	8.73	8.2	20.5	2.5	0.0	165

Potential ace with both high ceiling and high floor. Reaches triple digits with ease and thrown with clean, easy mechanics. Has large, durable frame to hold velo deep into games. Ton of movement to elite FB and gets sharp, late break on plus SL. CU is solid-average and shows flashes of being even better. Led NCAA in K and K/9.

Slaten,Justin
RP | Boston | EXP MLB DEBUT: 2024 | H/W: 6-4 222 | FUT: Setup reliever | 7D

Thrws R Age 26
2019 (3) New Mexico

Velo	Pitch	Grade
95-98	FB	+++
83-90	SL	++++
89-92	CT	++
80-84	CB	++

Year	Lev	Team	W	L	Sv	IP	K	ERA	WHIP	BF/G	OBA	H%	S%	xERA	Ctl	Dom	Cmd	hr/9	BPV
2021	A+	Hickory	4	8	0	82	110	6.03	1.51	17.8	287	38	64	5.67	3.4	12.1	3.5	1.9	143
2022	Rk	ACL Rangers	0	0	0	1	2	0.00	0.00	2.8	0	0			0.0	18.0		0.0	342
2022	AA	Frisco	1	6	0	50	64	6.99	1.93	9.5	257	36	64	5.59	8.6	11.5	1.3	1.1	-8
2023	AA	Frisco	4	3	2	51	76	3.17	1.12	5.7	221	32	81	3.53	2.8	13.4	4.8	1.6	183
2023	AAA	Round Rock	1	0	0	8	10	1.11	0.86	6.0	116	13	100	1.32	4.4	11.1	2.5	1.1	98

Has 4 distinct pitches - FF, SL CT, CB - all in different velocity bands, with lowest whiff rate 29% on 97-mph plus FF with 18.5" of IVB. The SL is a plus-plus demon & new CT was at least average. He ate up AA, struggled some against LHB with loud contact when made but still showed impact stuff prime for leverage. Command better but still below average.

Small,Ethan
RP | Milwaukee | EXP MLB DEBUT: 2022 | H/W: 6-2 200 | FUT: #5 SP/swingman | 7C

Thrws L Age 27
2019 (1) Mississippi State

Velo	Pitch	Grade
90-94	FB	+++
78-82	SL	++
80-82	CU	+++

Year	Lev	Team	W	L	Sv	IP	K	ERA	WHIP	BF/G	OBA	H%	S%	xERA	Ctl	Dom	Cmd	hr/9	BPV
2021	AAA	Nashville	2	0	0	35	24	2.06	1.37	16.3	215	24	89	3.40	5.4	6.2	1.1	0.8	-17
2022	AAA	Nashville	7	6	0	103	114	4.46	1.36	15.9	220	30	67	3.33	5.1	10.0	2.0	0.7	60
2022	MLB	Milwaukee	0	0	0	6	7	7.38	2.62	16.6	317	41	73	8.61	11.8	10.3	0.9	1.5	-115
2023	AAA	Nashville	2	4	3	51	61	3.18	1.25	5.5	218	30	78	3.20	4.2	10.8	2.5	0.9	97
2023	MLB	Milwaukee	0	0	1	4	6	11.25	2.75	11.1	444	60	60	12.11	4.5	13.5	3.0	2.3	140

Durable LHP who was moved to pen and fared very well at AAA. Pitched mostly 1 IP at a time and proved effective with quality extension in delivery. Uses height well and quick arm delivers deceptive CU. SL hasn't developed as much as hoped. Always has posted low oppBA in minors. Tough for hitters to pick up ball out of hand.

Smith Shawver,AJ
SP | Atlanta | EXP MLB DEBUT: 2023 | H/W: 6-3 205 | FUT: #3 starter | 8C

Thrws R Age 21
2021 (7) HS (TX)

Velo	Pitch	Grade
94-96	FB	++++
84-87	SL	+++
77-79	CB	+++
85-87	CU	++

Year	Lev	Team	W	L	Sv	IP	K	ERA	WHIP	BF/G	OBA	H%	S%	xERA	Ctl	Dom	Cmd	hr/9	BPV
2022	A	Augusta	3	4	0	68	103	5.15	1.36	16.8	219	36	61	3.13	5.1	13.6	2.6	0.5	124
2023	A+	Rome	1	0	0	14	23	0.00	0.71	16.5	132	27	100	0.02	2.6	14.8	5.8	0.0	215
2023	AA	Mississippi	1	0	0	7	9	0.00	1.14	13.9	202	32	100	1.89	3.9	11.6	3.0	0.0	122
2023	AAA	Gwinnett	2	2	0	41	47	4.17	1.27	16.8	184	24	69	2.83	5.7	10.3	1.8	0.9	50
2023	MLB	Atlanta	1	0	0	25	20	4.30	1.12	16.5	194	16	76	4.13	3.9	7.2	1.8	2.5	41

High 3/4s SP accelerated to the big leagues after starting at High-A in 2024. Repeatable delivery with solid extension. Struggles sometimes with consistent slot for breakers. 4-seam FB clearly best pitch with flat-angled and significant ride profile. 11-5 CB is best whiff inducing secondary. Needs to throw all secondaries for higher strike rate.

Smith,Brady
SP | Los Angeles (N) | EXP MLB DEBUT: 2027 | H/W: 6-2 170 | FUT: #3 starter | 8D

Thrws R Age 19
2023 (3) HS (TN)

Velo	Pitch	Grade
90-93	FB	+++
80-83	SL	+++
75-77	CB	++++
82-84	CU	++

Year	Lev	Team	W	L	Sv	IP	K	ERA	WHIP	BF/G	OBA	H%	S%	xERA	Ctl	Dom	Cmd	hr/9	BPV

Physically mature two-sport prepster is raw on the mound, but has quick arm action and already owns low-90s FB with room for more once he gains experience. Shows advanced feel for spin and CB and SL project as above-average to plus. Long stride with ¾ arm slot and close to max-effort delivery that will need to be smoothed out

Smith,Dylan
SP | Detroit | EXP MLB DEBUT: 2025 | H/W: 6-2 180 | FUT: #4 starter | 7D

Thrws R Age 23
2021 (3) Alabama

Velo	Pitch	Grade
92-95	FB	+++
77-80	CB	++
83-85	SL	+++
	CU	++

Year	Lev	Team	W	L	Sv	IP	K	ERA	WHIP	BF/G	OBA	H%	S%	xERA	Ctl	Dom	Cmd	hr/9	BPV
2022	A	Lakeland	0	0	0	5	3	0.00	0.60	8.6	175	21	100	0.28	0.0	5.4		0.0	115
2022	A+	West Michigan	8	6	0	83	86	4.01	1.19	16.7	250	33	67	3.24	2.3	9.3	4.1	0.6	124
2023	Rk	FCL Tigers East	0	0	0	4	5	6.43	1.90	6.6	297	42	63	5.08	6.4	10.7	1.7	0.0	37
2023	A+	West Michigan	1	1	0	27	23	3.67	1.33	18.7	289	35	76	4.50	1.7	7.7	4.6	1.0	111
2023	AA	Erie	0	1	0	5	10	13.85	3.08	10.2	429	70	50	10.43	8.7	17.3	2.0	0.0	96

Breakout prospect from a year ago was limited to just 37.1 IP due to a right forearm strain. When healthy features a lively 92-95 heater that tops at 98 with nice carry and a bit of arm side run, but the shape of the pitch profiles better in relief, especially when paired with an above-average tight SL and fringy CB and CU.

Snelling,Robby
SP | San Diego | EXP MLB DEBUT: 2025 | H/W: 6-3 210 | FUT: #2 starter | 8B

Thrws L Age 20
2022 (1) HS (NV)

Velo	Pitch	Grade
93-97	FB	+++
81-83	CB	++++
84-85	CU	+++

Year	Lev	Team	W	L	Sv	IP	K	ERA	WHIP	BF/G	OBA	H%	S%	xERA	Ctl	Dom	Cmd	hr/9	BPV
2023	A	Lake Elsinore	5	1	0	51	59	1.58	1.02	17.9	213	30	86	2.04	2.3	10.4	4.5	0.4	143
2023	A+	Fort Wayne	4	2	0	34	40	2.37	1.23	19.8	243	35	80	2.87	2.9	10.5	3.6	0.3	129
2023	AA	San Antonio	2	0	0	17	19	1.58	1.29	17.6	199	27	90	2.73	5.3	10.0	1.9	0.5	56

Aggressive, athletic LHP who posted lowest ERA in org and only allowed more than 2 ERA once. Pitched great on three levels with outstanding pitch mix. Pitches above age class with clean delivery and feel for spotting pitches in strike zone. Tough to barrel up with plus CB and dynamic FB up in zone. Keeps ball on ground, but will need better CU.

Solometo,Anthony

SP | Pittsburgh | EXP MLB DEBUT: 2024 | H/W: 6-5 220 | FUT: #3 starter | 8C

Thrws L Age 21 — 2021 (2) HS (NJ)

Velo	Pitch	Grade
90-93	FB	+++
83-85	SL	+++
80-84	CU	+++

Year	Lev	Team	W	L	Sv	IP	K	ERA	WHIP	BF/G	OBA	H%	S%	xERA	Ctl	Dom	Cmd	hr/9	BPV
2021	--	Did Not Play																	
2022	A	Bradenton	5	1	0	47	51	2.67	1.06	14.1	189	27	72	1.55	3.6	9.7	2.7	0.0	95
2023	A+	Greensboro	2	3	0	58	68	2.32	1.17	19.3	208	30	80	2.32	3.9	10.5	2.7	0.3	103
2023	AA	Altoona	2	4	0	51	50	4.39	1.23	17.3	253	31	67	3.78	2.5	8.8	3.6	1.1	110

Tall LHP who may be put on fast track after splitting season between High-A and AA. Leverages unusual delivery for deception and makes FB look even quicker. Added cutting SL to arsenal and mixes with average CU to be effective against LHH and RHH. Allows very few HR and keeps ball on ground. K rate could climb higher.

Soto,Charlee

SP | Minnesota | EXP MLB DEBUT: 2028 | H/W: 6-3 210 | FUT: #3 starter | 8D

Thrws R Age 18 — 2023 (2) HS (FL)

Velo	Pitch	Grade
92-96	FB	++++
82-85	SL	+++
83-87	CU	++

Year	Lev	Team	W	L	Sv	IP	K	ERA	WHIP	BF/G	OBA	H%	S%	xERA	Ctl	Dom	Cmd	hr/9	BPV

Tall, projectable SP with tremendous upside due to size and arsenal. Very raw arm action and delivery from ¾ slot. Some effort with mechanics and impacts ability to change speeds. Leverages plus FB to advantage and has shown flashes of solid split CU. Everything out of hand is hard and a few more ticks to FB are in the offing.

Speas,Alex

RP | Texas | EXP MLB DEBUT: 2023 | H/W: 6-3 225 | FUT: Setup reliever | 8E

Thrws R Age 26 — 2016 (2) HS (GA)

Velo	Pitch	Grade
91-95	CT	++++
97-102	FB	++++
90-93	SL	+++

Year	Lev	Team	W	L	Sv	IP	K	ERA	WHIP	BF/G	OBA	H%	S%	xERA	Ctl	Dom	Cmd	hr/9	BPV
2021	Rk	ACL Rangers	1	1	0	3		11.61	2.26	5.2	186	53	43	4.43	14.5	20.3	1.4	0.0	-8
2021	AA	Frisco	1	2	0	12	23	11.25	2.58	5.4	228	42	55	7.19	15.8	17.3	1.1	1.5	-97
2023	AA	Frisco	3	0	2	28	47	0.64	0.93	4.6	141	29	92	0.64	4.2	15.1	3.6	0.0	177
2023	AAA	Round Rock	2	2	2	28	38	5.12	1.64	4.8	209	32	68	3.82	8.0	12.2	1.5	0.6	21
2023	MLB	Texas	0	2	0	2	4	13.50	3.50	4.2	262	55	57	8.53	22.5	18.0	0.8	0.0	-266

Unretiree hit like a bomb, but despite elite stuff red flags remain. CT/ FB /SL all arguably plus plus offerings, with SL newest wrinkle that ate batters alive. Big GB rate and swings and misses highlight huge leveraged upside, but control still below average. Disastrous MLB debut (5 BB in 2.0 IP) says to temper expectations for now.

Spiers,Carson

SP | Cincinnati | EXP MLB DEBUT: 2023 | H/W: 6-3 205 | FUT: #5 SP/swingman | 6B

Thrws R Age 26 — 2020 FA (Clemson)

Velo	Pitch	Grade
93-95	FB	+++
82-84	SL	+++
85-87	CU	+++
87-90	CT	+++

Year	Lev	Team	W	L	Sv	IP	K	ERA	WHIP	BF/G	OBA	H%	S%	xERA	Ctl	Dom	Cmd	hr/9	BPV
2022	AA	Chattanooga	2	5	0	104	90	5.01	1.47	20.3	280	31	74	5.71	3.4	7.8	2.3	2.1	67
2022	AAA	Louisville	2	1	0	17	15	7.41	1.88	16.0	352	41	62	7.45	3.2	7.9	2.5	1.6	75
2023	AA	Chattanooga	8	3	0	83	106	3.69	1.35	12.4	233	34	74	3.40	4.4	11.5	2.6	0.7	105
2023	AAA	Louisville	1	0	0	2	0	0.00	0.00	5.6	0	0			0.0	0.0		0.0	18
2023	MLB	Cincinnati	0	1	1	13	12	6.92	1.92	15.4	329	41	63	6.32	4.8	8.3	1.7	0.7	37

Unheralded RHP prospect filled variety of roles throughout season, earning MLB stint. Low 3/4s slot delivery. Will fly open, effecting overall control. Has average stuff across the board, plays up due to pitchability. Horizontal SL is best pitch with above-average potential. Also throws 4-seam FB, 2-seam FB, fading CU, tight CT and loopy CB.

Sproat,Brandon

SP | New York (N) | EXP MLB DEBUT: 2025 | H/W: 6-3 215 | FUT: #3 starter | 8D

Thrws R Age 23 — 2023 (2) Florida

Velo	Pitch	Grade
95-97	FB	++++
86-89	CU	++++
79-81	CB	+++
86-89	SL	++

Year	Lev	Team	W	L	Sv	IP	K	ERA	WHIP	BF/G	OBA	H%	S%	xERA	Ctl	Dom	Cmd	hr/9	BPV

Hard-throwing RHP starred for College World Series runner-up in 2023. Athletic, crossfire delivery with long arm circle. Struggles to stay on time with release, effecting control. 4-pitch arsenal. Mid-90s FB has plus profile due to ride/run. Sells plus CU with significant downward break well. CB has above-average 11-to-5 break.

Stephan,Josh

SP | Texas | EXP MLB DEBUT: 2024 | H/W: 6-3 185 | FUT: #4 starter | 7C

Thrws R Age 22 — 2020 FA (TX)

Velo	Pitch	Grade
82-85	SL	+++
90-93	FB	++
85-88	CU	+++
89-92	CT	++

Year	Lev	Team	W	L	Sv	IP	K	ERA	WHIP	BF/G	OBA	H%	S%	xERA	Ctl	Dom	Cmd	hr/9	BPV
2021	A	Down East	0	1	0	12	19	8.25	1.58	17.6	307	43	53	7.22	3.0	14.3	4.8	3.0	194
2022	A	Down East	4	4	1	91	102	3.36	1.11	19.9	230	30	74	3.09	2.4	10.1	4.3	1.0	135
2022	A+	Hickory	2	1	0	11	13	1.61	1.25	15.2	181	24	92	2.69	5.6	10.4	1.9	0.8	54
2023	A+	Hickory	6	3	0	62	73	2.17	0.81	18.8	178	23	83	1.87	1.7	10.6	6.1	1.2	161
2023	AA	Frisco	0	0	0	4	5	4.39	1.46	17.6	302	43	67	4.05	2.2	11.0	5.0	0.0	156

Though an NDFA, it was only because of short 2020 draft. He continues to well outpace tool grades due to above-average command of 4-pitch repertoire led by plus slider (42% whiff). 2S and 4S fastball are used equally, an above-average change is second best pitch but new cutter helped neutralize lefties. Shut down in July with back injury.

Stone,Gavin

SP | Los Angeles (N) | EXP MLB DEBUT: 2023 | H/W: 6-1 175 | FUT: #3 starter | 8D

Thrws R Age 25 — 2020 (5) Central Arkansas

Velo	Pitch	Grade
94-96	FB	+++
83-86	SL	++
84-86	CU	++++
89-91	CT	+

Year	Lev	Team	W	L	Sv	IP	K	ERA	WHIP	BF/G	OBA	H%	S%	xERA	Ctl	Dom	Cmd	hr/9	BPV
2022	A+	Great Lakes	1	1	0	25	28	1.44	1.00	15.9	212	30	88	2.01	2.2	10.1	4.7	0.4	141
2022	AA	Tulsa	6	4	0	73	107	1.60	1.22	21.1	223	37	86	2.43	3.7	13.2	3.6	0.1	155
2022	AAA	Oklahoma City	2	1	0	23	33	1.17	0.95	14.5	177	29	90	1.48	3.1	12.9	4.1	0.4	165
2023	AAA	Oklahoma City	7	4	0	100	120	4.76	1.32	19.7	233	31	66	3.73	4.1	10.8	2.6	1.1	100
2023	MLB	Los Angeles	1	1	1	31	22	9.00	1.90	18.3	345	37	55	8.09	3.8	6.4	1.7	2.3	31

Got hammered in MLB debut as he struggled with command and gave up 8 HR in 31 IP. Attacks hitters with a four-pitch mix. 4-seam FB sits in the mid-90s but with low spin and lack of command. Also throws a 2-seamer and power SL. Plus CU has swing-and-miss sink and fade, but other offerings need to improve. Look for better results in 2024.

Storm,Justin

RP | Miami | EXP MLB DEBUT: 2026 | H/W: 6-7 232 | FUT: Setup reliever | 7D

Thrws L Age 22 — 2023 (7) Southern Miss

Velo	Pitch	Grade
90-93	FB	++++
82-85	SL	+++
82-84	CU	++

Year	Lev	Team	W	L	Sv	IP	K	ERA	WHIP	BF/G	OBA	H%	S%	xERA	Ctl	Dom	Cmd	hr/9	BPV
2023	NCAA	Southern Miss	7	2	8	45	72	2.39	0.95	5.9	169	27	82	1.95	3.4	14.3	4.2	1.0	185
2023	Rk	FCL Marlins	0	0	0	4	4	6.59	1.95	4.9	147	21	63	3.35	13.2	8.8	0.7	0.0	-180

Tall, projectable LHP was selected in 7th round of 2023 draft. Over-the-top delivery with solid extension. Could use height even more in delivery. Best pitch is flat-angled FB with double-plus riding action. Sweeping SL has above-average potential, racking up whiffs in college, even against better competition. CU is below-average offering.

Stuart,Tyler

SP | New York (N) | EXP MLB DEBUT: 2025 | H/W: 6-9 250 | FUT: Setup reliever | 7D

Thrws R Age 24 — 2022 (6) Southern Miss

Velo	Pitch	Grade
81-84	SL	++++
92-95	FB	+++
85-87	CU	++
81-83	CB	+++

Year	Lev	Team	W	L	Sv	IP	K	ERA	WHIP	BF/G	OBA	H%	S%	xERA	Ctl	Dom	Cmd	hr/9	BPV
2022	NCAA	Southern Miss	4	0	1	40	38	3.38	1.18	7.3	232	31	70	2.57	2.9	8.6	2.9	0.2	93
2022	Rk	FCL Mets	0	0	0	1	1	0.00	0.00	2.8	0	0			0.0	9.0		0.0	180
2022	A	St. Lucie	0	0	0	2	6	16.36	3.18	6.6	392	95	43	9.83	12.3	24.5	2.0	0.0	128
2023	A+	Brooklyn	4	0	0	75	84	1.56	1.05	20.8	209	29	87	2.09	2.8	10.1	3.7	0.4	125
2023	AA	Binghamton	3	2	0	35	28	3.60	1.23	20.2	256	30	74	3.80	2.3	7.2	3.1	1.0	85

Tall, XXL frame RHP has tremendous feel for spin. Low 3/4s delivery. Stays balance despite longer limbs. Primary SL/FB pitcher. SL is plus pitch with sharp 2-plane break and above-average command. Misses lots of bats. 2-seam FB has solid sink and running profile but not a whiff inducer. 11-to-5 CB flashes above-average movement. CU lags behind.

Suarez,Santiago

SP | Tampa Bay | EXP MLB DEBUT: 2026 | H/W: 6-2 175 | FUT: #3 starter | 8E

Thrws R Age 19 — 2022 FA (VZ)

Velo	Pitch	Grade
92-94	FB	++++
77-80	CB	+++
85-87	CU	++

Year	Lev	Team	W	L	Sv	IP	K	ERA	WHIP	BF/G	OBA	H%	S%	xERA	Ctl	Dom	Cmd	hr/9	BPV
2022	Rk	DSL Miami	1	1	0	39	38	2.31	1.08	13.8	247	33	78	2.52	1.4	8.8	6.3	0.2	138
2023	Rk	FCL Rays	4	0	1	39	38	1.15	0.92	14.7	202	28	86	1.35	1.8	8.7	4.8	0.0	125
2023	A	Charleston	1	2	0	19	14	2.34	1.25	15.6	279	33	83	3.66	1.4	6.6	4.7	0.5	98

Pitchability RHP excelled in US debut. Low 3/4s repeatable crossfire delivery with solid extension. Three pitches highlighted by plus-plus FB command. Average movement plays up due to low release height and command. CB has solid 11-to-5 profile but doesn't get enough strikes. Struggles with feel of CU.

Sullivan,Sean

SP | Colorado | EXP MLB DEBUT: 2026 | H/W: 6-4 190 | FUT: #4 starter | 7E

Thrws L Age 21 — 2023 (2) Wake Forest

Velo	Pitch	Grade
89-92	FB	++++
77-79	SP	+
80-83	CU	++

Year	Lev	Team	W	L	Sv	IP	K	ERA	WHIP	BF/G	OBA	H%	S%	xERA	Ctl	Dom	Cmd	hr/9	BPV
2023	NCAA	Wake Forest	5	3	3	69	111	2.47	0.92	15.2	181	29	80	2.04	2.7	14.4	5.3	1.0	204
2023	Rk	ACL Rockies	0	0	0	2	4	0.00	0.50	3.3	0	0	100		4.5	18.0	4.0	0.0	221
2023	A	Fresno	1	0	0	2	6	0.00	0.00	5.6	0	0			0.0	27.0		0.0	504

Lefty attacks hitters from a low ¾, almost sidearm slot with crossfire action and is especially tough vs LHB. Pounds the strike zone with good command and works mostly east/west, running his bread and butter low-90s FB in on RHB, SL and CU are both average to a tick above. Repeats mechanics, but will need to improve his secondaries.

Susana,Jarlin — SP — Washington

EXP MLB DEBUT: 2026 | H/W: 6-6 235 | FUT: #2 SP/closer | 9D

Thrws R Age 20 — 2022 FA (DR)

Velo	Pitch	Grade
96-99	FB	++++
86-89	SL	+++
90-92	CT	+++
89-91	CU	+

Year	Lev	Team	W	L	Sv	IP	K	ERA	WHIP	BF/G	OBA	H%	S%	xERA	Ctl	Dom	Cmd	hr/9	BPV
2022	Rk	ACL Padres	0	0	0	29	44	2.47	0.89	13.5	155	27	72	1.00	3.4	13.6	4.0	0.3	171
2022	Rk	FCL Nationals	0	0	0	5	9	1.76	1.57	11.2	218	43	88	3.11	7.1	15.9	2.3	0.0	113
2022	A	Fredericksburg	0	0	0	10	13	2.67	1.39	14.2	240	34	85	3.81	4.5	11.6	2.6	0.9	106
2023	A	Fredericksburg	1	6	0	63	62	5.14	1.52	16.1	240	31	65	3.74	5.7	8.9	1.6	0.4	23

Hard thrower from the Soto trade struggled with walks and control in Low-A, but some promising pitch characteristics: Elite FB that can touch 100, lots of swing and miss on his SL, and a new low-90s cutter flashed some promise. Would benefit from strike consistency, but still just 20 years old. If he can harness stuff, there's considerable upside.

Swiney,Nick — RP — San Francisco

EXP MLB DEBUT: 2024 | H/W: 6-3 185 | FUT: Setup reliever | 6B

Thrws L Age 25 — 2020 (2) NC State

Velo	Pitch	Grade
87-90	FB	++
72-74	CB	+++
80-84	CU	+++

Year	Lev	Team	W	L	Sv	IP	K	ERA	WHIP	BF/G	OBA	H%	S%	xERA	Ctl	Dom	Cmd	hr/9	BPV
2021	Rk	ACL Giants B	0	0	0	8	16	1.13	1.63	7.1	237	52	92	3.47	6.8	18.0	2.7	0.0	160
2021	A	San Jose	0	0	0	24	42	0.75	1.16	13.7	191	38	93	1.76	4.5	15.7	3.5	0.0	179
2022	A+	Eugene	4	6	0	89	105	3.84	1.21	17.1	201	28	69	2.73	4.6	10.6	2.3	0.7	86
2023	AA	Richmond	3	0	0	15	18	1.18	1.05	9.8	174	24	93	1.90	4.1	10.7	2.6	0.6	98
2023	AAA	Sacramento	0	2	1	40	30	5.63	1.78	7.1	294	34	70	5.81	5.4	6.8	1.3	1.1	-6

Sinkerballer who was moved to relief in 2023. Despite move to pen, saw K rate plummet and control go awry. Likes to pitch backwards with nifty CU that can flash plus. FB is limited in effectiveness due to lack of velocity and movement. CB can be average offering when he throws for strikes. Tough on LHH and could be lefty specialist.

Sykora,Travis — SP — Washington

EXP MLB DEBUT: 2028 | H/W: 6-6 232 | FUT: #2 starter | 8E

Thrws R Age 19 — 2023 (3) HS (TX)

Velo	Pitch	Grade
95-97	FB	+++
83-85	SL	+++
84-86	SP	+++

Year	Lev	Team	W	L	Sv	IP	K	ERA	WHIP	BF/G	OBA	H%	S%	xERA	Ctl	Dom	Cmd	hr/9	BPV

Huge and physical right hander with monster upper-90s fastball that runs and has swing and miss characteristics. Slider is also above average and features a short, tight break. Also throws a split-change that drops out of sight. Solid mechanics, throws strikes, gets praise for makeup. Will start in the complex but intriguing package.

Tamarez,Misael — SP — Houston

EXP MLB DEBUT: 2024 | H/W: 6-1 206 | FUT: #3 starter | 8D

Thrws R Age 24 — 2019 FA (DR)

Velo	Pitch	Grade
95-97	FB	+++
87-90	CT	++++
89-91	CU	+++
81-83	CB	++

Year	Lev	Team	W	L	Sv	IP	K	ERA	WHIP	BF/G	OBA	H%	S%	xERA	Ctl	Dom	Cmd	hr/9	BPV
2021	A	Fayetteville	4	2	1	43	64	3.98	1.30	14.8	188	30	70	2.70	5.9	13.4	2.3	0.6	101
2021	A+	Asheville	2	1	0	33	39	3.52	1.20	19.1	243	32	75	3.58	2.7	10.6	3.9	1.1	135
2022	AA	Corpus Christi	3	6	1	103	122	4.63	1.27	17.6	207	26	69	3.76	4.8	10.6	2.2	1.6	80
2022	AAA	Sugar Land	1	1	0	18	20	2.50	1.17	17.9	106	12	84	1.90	7.5	10.0	1.3	1.0	-5
2023	AAA	Sugar Land	1	10	2	101	100	5.08	1.48	16.7	238	28	70	4.71	5.3	8.9	1.7	1.6	34

Righty starter spent 2023 season in AAA. FB/CT heavy approach, mixes in CU against LHB. FB sits mid-to-high-90s with good run. High-spin CT is best pitch, works as ersatz slider with excellent command and movement. Overall command is better than BB% suggests, but struggles locating high FB. Slight tweaks could unlock big upside.

Tarnok,Freddy — SP — Oakland

EXP MLB DEBUT: 2022 | H/W: 6-3 185 | FUT: #4 starter | 7B

Thrws R Age 25 — 2017 (3) HS (FL)

Velo	Pitch	Grade
92-96	FB	++++
78-81	CB	+++
85-87	SL	++
84-87	CU	+++

Year	Lev	Team	W	L	Sv	IP	K	ERA	WHIP	BF/G	OBA	H%	S%	xERA	Ctl	Dom	Cmd	hr/9	BPV
2022	AAA	Gwinnett	2	1	0	44	49	3.68	1.25	17.9	234	29	77	3.92	3.5	10.0	2.9	1.4	105
2022	MLB	Atlanta	0	0	0	0	1	0.00	5.00	1.6	639	177	100	22.66	0.0	45.0		0.0	828
2023	Rk	ACL Athletics	0	0	0	2	2	0.00	1.00	7.6	151	22	100	0.99	4.5	9.0	2.0	0.0	59
2023	AAA	Las Vegas	1	1	0	19	11	1.88	1.20	15.4	181	19	90	2.74	5.2	5.2	1.0	0.9	-28
2023	MLB	Oakland	1	1	0	14	14	5.07	1.55	12.4	216	21	78	5.49	7.0	8.9	1.3	2.5	-11

Missed most of season with shoulder strain and hip surgery. Health and control stand in way of bright future. Can dominate with high-octane FB and solid CU thrown with deceptive arm speed. Misses bats with variety of offerings, though FB velocity is too inconsistent. Has pitched in majors and could stick as RP if can't prove durability.

Taylor,Andrew — SP — Houston

EXP MLB DEBUT: 2026 | H/W: 6-5 190 | FUT: #5 SP/swingman | 7D

Thrws R Age 22 — 2022 (2) Central Michigan

Velo	Pitch	Grade
91-93	FB	+++
81-85	SL	+++
77-79	CB	++
83-85	CU	+

Year	Lev	Team	W	L	Sv	IP	K	ERA	WHIP	BF/G	OBA	H%	S%	xERA	Ctl	Dom	Cmd	hr/9	BPV
2023	A	Fayetteville	4	8	1	84	126	4.61	1.55	15.3	269	40	74	4.95	4.6	13.5	2.9	1.3	137

Tall RHP made major league debut at Low-A. Uses long legs to get extension down mound with clean low-effort delivery. Low-90s FB plays up with extension, misses bats in zone. Primary secondary is low-80s SL with makings of true out pitch when located well. SL plays off FB well against RHB, but lack of reliable CU makes lefties tough outs.

Taylor,Grant — SP — Chicago (A)

EXP MLB DEBUT: 2026 | H/W: 6-3 230 | FUT: Setup reliever | 7D

Thrws R Age 21 — 2023 (2) Louisiana State

Velo	Pitch	Grade
93-95	FB	++++
83-86	SL	+++
78-80	CB	+++

Year	Lev	Team	W	L	Sv	IP	K	ERA	WHIP	BF/G	OBA	H%	S%	xERA	Ctl	Dom	Cmd	hr/9	BPV

Over-the-top RHP was drafted in 2023 despite missing entire season due to Spring Tommy John surgery. Uses height well in delivery but longer arm path and inconsistent release bring heavy RP risk. Flat-angled FB has plus ride profile. Best secondary is 12-to-6 CB with above-average potential. Needs to tighten up mid-80s SL to complete arsenal.

Teodo,Emiliano — SP — Texas

EXP MLB DEBUT: 2025 | H/W: 6-1 165 | FUT: Closer | 8E

Thrws R Age 23 — 2020 FA (DR)

Velo	Pitch	Grade
95-100	FB	++++
83-89	SL	+++
	CB	

Year	Lev	Team	W	L	Sv	IP	K	ERA	WHIP	BF/G	OBA	H%	S%	xERA	Ctl	Dom	Cmd	hr/9	BPV
2021	Rk	ACL Rangers	4	2	0	29	48	3.40	1.44	6.5	226	41	74	2.91	5.6	14.8	2.7	0.0	135
2022	A	Down East	3	6	0	84	115	3.10	1.13	15.1	177	26	75	2.27	4.7	12.3	2.6	0.7	112
2023	A+	Hickory	5	3	0	61	84	4.56	1.41	14.4	235	33	72	4.33	4.9	12.4	2.5	1.5	109

Lithe and slightly undersized, he has tantalized with 100+ mph heat and huge bender but command issues and lack of a third pitch have led to noisy rotation performances. Though athletic, can lose command that leads to blow-ups. Still starting, but most evaluators see eventual transition to bullpen where he has closer upside.

Thompson,Matthew — SP — Chicago (A)

EXP MLB DEBUT: 2024 | H/W: 6-3 195 | FUT: #5 SP/swingman | 6C

Thrws R Age 23 — 2019 (2) HS (TX)

Velo	Pitch	Grade
92-94	FB	++
77-79	CB	+++
84-86	CU	+++
83-85	SL	++

Year	Lev	Team	W	L	Sv	IP	K	ERA	WHIP	BF/G	OBA	H%	S%	xERA	Ctl	Dom	Cmd	hr/9	BPV
2021	Rk	ACL White Sox	0	1	0	2	1	9.00	1.50	8.6	347	30	50	9.18	0.0	4.5		4.5	99
2021	A	Kannapolis	2	8	0	71	77	5.94	1.70	16.9	292	38	65	5.34	4.8	9.7	2.0	0.9	64
2022	A+	Winston-Salem	4	5	0	84	73	4.71	1.32	19.3	257	30	68	4.37	3.1	7.8	2.5	1.4	75
2022	AA	Birmingham	0	2	0	25	31	5.38	1.47	15.4	269	37	65	4.59	3.9	11.1	2.8	1.1	112
2023	AA	Birmingham	6	15	0	124	136	4.86	1.57	20.2	239	31	71	4.47	6.2	9.9	1.6	1.1	29

Athletic hurler continues to struggle with subpar FB shape and inability to control arsenal. Struggles with release point in over-the-top delivery. 4-seam FB doesn't perform well and has never taken step forward in development. Best pitches are 12-to-6 CB and late-fading CU but they play down due to strike throwing struggles. Also throws SL.

Thorpe,Drew — SP — San Diego

EXP MLB DEBUT: 2024 | H/W: 6-4 212 | FUT: #3 starter | 8C

Thrws R Age 23 — 2022 (2) Cal Poly

Velo	Pitch	Grade
91-95	FB	+++
83-85	SL	++++
81-84	CU	+++
88-89	CT	++

Year	Lev	Team	W	L	Sv	IP	K	ERA	WHIP	BF/G	OBA	H%	S%	xERA	Ctl	Dom	Cmd	hr/9	BPV
2023	A+	Hudson Valley	10	2	0	109	138	2.81	1.07	23.6	215	30	78	2.64	2.7	11.4	4.2	0.8	150
2023	AA	Somerset	4	0	0	30	44	1.50	0.66	21.0	150	23	88	0.94	1.5	13.2	8.8	0.9	214

Athletic RHP made pro debut, improving as season went on. Repeats over-the-top delivery with above-average extension. 4-seam FB has solid rate profile but needs shape development. CU is plus offering and best pitch with plus vertical and horizontal movement. Two-plane breaking SL best breaker. Also throws CT.

Tidwell,Blade — SP — New York (N)

EXP MLB DEBUT: 2024 | H/W: 6-4 207 | FUT: #3 starter | 8D

Thrws R Age 22 — 2022 (2) Tennessee

Velo	Pitch	Grade
93-96	FB	++++
81-83	SL	++++
79-81	CU	+++

Year	Lev	Team	W	L	Sv	IP	K	ERA	WHIP	BF/G	OBA	H%	S%	xERA	Ctl	Dom	Cmd	hr/9	BPV
2022	NCAA	Tennessee	3	2	0	39	51	3.00	1.08	11.7	220	30	81	3.24	2.5	11.8	4.6	1.4	161
2022	Rk	FCL Mets	0	0	0	1	2	0.00	1.00	3.8	0	0	100		9.0	18.0	2.0	0.0	99
2022	A	St. Lucie	0	1	0	8	9	2.22	1.23	8.2	149	22	80	1.55	6.7	10.0	1.5	0.0	18
2023	A+	Brooklyn	8	3	0	81	112	3.10	1.24	19.4	194	29	78	2.87	5.1	12.4	2.4	0.9	104
2023	AA	Binghamton	3	3	0	34	41	4.75	1.44	18.1	250	32	72	4.72	4.5	10.8	2.4	1.6	92

Athletic 3/4s RHP showcased his loud arsenal in 2023. Strong build, near physical projection. Deceptive delivery with solid extension plays up pitch mix. 4-seam FB has significant rise from lower slot; it's near plus-plus. SL has significant horizontal movement and natural sweep. Improved feel for CU, now average offering.

Tiedemann,Ricky | SP | Toronto | EXP MLB DEBUT: 2024 | H/W: 6-4 220 | FUT: #1 starter | 9C

Thrws L Age 21	Year	Lev	Team	W	L	Sv	IP	K	ERA	WHIP	BF/G	OBA	H%	S%	xERA	Ctl	Dom	Cmd	hr/9	BPV
2021 (3) Golden West JC	2022	AA	New Hampshire	0	1	0	11	14	2.45	0.82	10.0	139	23	67	0.38	3.3	11.5	3.5	0.0	136
94-97 FB ++++	2023	Rk	FCL Blue Jays	0	0	0	2	3	0.00	0.00	5.6	0	0			0.0	13.5		0.0	261
82-84 SL ++++	2023	A	Dunedin	0	0	0	6	15	0.00	0.33	9.5	56	34	100		1.5	22.5	15.0	0.0	383
83-86 CU ++++	2023	AA	New Hampshire	0	5	0	32	58	5.06	1.50	12.6	237	46	64	3.43	5.6	16.3	2.9	0.3	160
	2023	AAA	Buffalo	0	0	0	4	6	0.00	1.00	15.3	151	27	100	0.94	4.5	13.5	3.0	0.0	140

Dominating LHP with height, delivery, pitch mix and dominance to be ace. Pitcher of Year in AFL. Missed time with biceps injury but got to AA. Exceptional K rate and can miss bats with all 3 pitches. Throws from low slot that makes deceptive, hard FB even quicker. Sl and CU exhibit late action. CU gives him plus offering against RHH.

Tillero,Jesus | SP | Los Angeles (N) | EXP MLB DEBUT: 2028 | H/W: 6-0 190 | FUT: #3 starter | 8D

Thrws R Age 17	Year	Lev	Team	W	L	Sv	IP	K	ERA	WHIP	BF/G	OBA	H%	S%	xERA	Ctl	Dom	Cmd	hr/9	BPV
2023 FA (VZ)																				
92-95 FB ++++																				
83-86 SL +++																				
CU ++																				
	2023	Rk	DSL Dodgers Bautista	0	1	0	30	34	1.49	0.83	11.0	182	27	80	0.89	1.8	10.1	5.7	0.0	152

17-year-old from Venezuela signed for $500,000 in 2023. Shows advanced feel for pitching and FB already tops out at 97 mph. SL is best secondary and shows feel for spin and command. Future development hinges on refinement of fringe CU. Showed lots of potential in professional debut with 5.7 K/BB and plenty of arm talent.

Tredwell,Alonzo | SP | Houston | EXP MLB DEBUT: 2026 | H/W: 6-8 230 | FUT: #3 starter | 8E

Thrws R Age 21	Year	Lev	Team	W	L	Sv	IP	K	ERA	WHIP	BF/G	OBA	H%	S%	xERA	Ctl	Dom	Cmd	hr/9	BPV
2023 (2) UCLA																				
91-93 FB +++																				
82-84 SL +++																				
76-78 CB ++																				
85-87 CU ++																				

Oft-injured 2023 college draftee pitched well after move from bullpen to rotation before being shutdown for year with more injuries. Very tall, gets great extension to help low-to-mid-90s FB play up. Falls off mound with noticeable head whack, effort in delivery. Locates SL consistently, getting plenty of whiffs. Potential #3 package.

Ullola,Miguel | SP | Houston | EXP MLB DEBUT: 2026 | H/W: 6-1 205 | FUT: Setup reliever | 6B

Thrws R Age 21	Year	Lev	Team	W	L	Sv	IP	K	ERA	WHIP	BF/G	OBA	H%	S%	xERA	Ctl	Dom	Cmd	hr/9	BPV
2021 FA (DR)																				
94-95 FB +++	2021	Rk	FCL Astros	0	0	0	3	4	3.00	2.00	7.2	191	31	83	3.92	12.0	12.0	1.0	0.0	-90
86-87 SL ++	2021	Rk	DSL Astros	1	1	0	21	34	4.27	1.28	10.8	144	26	65	1.97	7.3	14.5	2.0	0.4	83
79-81 CB ++	2022	A	Fayetteville	2	2	2	72	120	3.25	1.31	13.5	161	30	75	2.16	6.9	15.0	2.2	0.4	102
88-90 CU ++	2023	A+	Asheville	3	9	0	90	116	5.89	1.66	16.2	255	35	66	4.99	6.3	11.6	1.8	1.2	57

Part-time starter oscillated between short and long outings all season. Predominately FB/SL pitcher. Good command of mid-90s FB but struggles with command of secondaries. Has raw stuff to succeed, but needs to shore up secondaries in order to project as starter. Repertoire, command make relief role more likely.

Urena,Walbert | SP | Los Angeles (A) | EXP MLB DEBUT: 2025 | H/W: 6-0 170 | FUT: Setup reliever | 7E

Thrws R Age 20	Year	Lev	Team	W	L	Sv	IP	K	ERA	WHIP	BF/G	OBA	H%	S%	xERA	Ctl	Dom	Cmd	hr/9	BPV
2021 FA (DR)																				
93-97 FB ++++																				
79-81 CB ++																				
82-84 SL ++	2022	Rk	ACL Angels	3	4	0	37	45	3.88	1.54	13.5	193	28	75	3.24	7.8	10.9	1.4	0.5	5
86-88 CU ++	2023	A	Inland Empire	4	7	0	98	97	5.68	1.57	19.6	253	33	62	4.07	5.5	8.9	1.6	0.5	30

Hard-throwing, athletic RHP struggled in first taste of full-season ball. 3/4s delivery with poor extension and RP jerkiness. Best pitch is 2-seam FB with solid sinking action and plus arm-side run. Low-A hitters chased it frequently out of zone. Struggles with feel for spin. Best secondary is horizontal SL. Lost feel for CU early, never returned.

Valdez,Luis | SP | Texas | EXP MLB DEBUT: 2026 | H/W: 6-2 158 | FUT: #4 starter | 7D

Thrws L Age 20	Year	Lev	Team	W	L	Sv	IP	K	ERA	WHIP	BF/G	OBA	H%	S%	xERA	Ctl	Dom	Cmd	hr/9	BPV
2019 FA (MX)	2022	Rk	ACL Dodgers	3	0	0	28	37	2.88	0.82	12.8	217	32	67	1.85	0.3	11.9	37.0	0.6	223
90-93 FB ++	2022	A	Rancho Cuca	0	1	0	5	8	7.20	1.60	11.1	299	50	50	4.30	3.6	14.4	4.0	0.0	180
83-86 SL ++	2023	Rk	ACL Rangers	0	1	0	11	11	4.09	1.18	8.8	244	31	67	3.30	2.5	9.0	3.7	0.8	114
82-85 CU +++	2023	A	Down East	0	0	0	2	2	13.50	2.50	10.6	415	52	40	8.75	4.5	9.0	2.0	0.0	59
	2023	A	Rancho Cuca	0	2	0	17	24	3.16	1.64	9.5	225	35	81	3.90	7.4	12.6	1.7	0.5	46

LHP with plus CU can carve up A-ball so noteworthy FB development will make-or-break profile, and helps explain otherwise meh 2023 surface stats. Frame has room for good weight on repeatable delivery and plus command projection says 91-mph FB velo will tick up. Mid-rotation projection upside, back-end now but definite major league floor.

Vargas,Jordy | SP | Colorado | EXP MLB DEBUT: 2026 | H/W: 6-3 153 | FUT: #4 starter | 7D

Thrws R Age 20	Year	Lev	Team	W	L	Sv	IP	K	ERA	WHIP	BF/G	OBA	H%	S%	xERA	Ctl	Dom	Cmd	hr/9	BPV
2021 FA (DR)																				
93-95 FB +++	2021	Rk	DSL Colorado	2	0	0	34	46	1.32	0.99	11.9	157	26	85	1.01	4.2	12.1	2.9	0.0	122
75-77 CB ++++	2022	Rk	ACL Rockies	2	1	0	26	40	2.40	0.65	13.0	150	28	59	0.05	1.4	13.7	10.0	0.0	228
83-85 CU ++	2022	A	Fresno	2	0	0	24	24	3.72	1.36	16.9	227	25	82	4.52	4.8	8.9	1.8	1.9	48
	2023	A	Fresno	6	3	0	64	69	4.22	1.23	20.0	234	31	65	3.05	3.4	9.7	2.9	0.6	102

Lean and projectable with a solid three-pitch mix, though had Tommy John surgery. Coils well pre-pitch with quick arm action, but doesn't use his lower half effectively. Prior to the injury FB sat 93-95 with arm-side run and 11-to-6 slurve and above-average CU give him the tools to remain a starter, but there is some reliever risk.

Vasil,Mike | SP | New York (N) | EXP MLB DEBUT: 2024 | H/W: 6-5 225 | FUT: #4 starter | 7C

Thrws R Age 24	Year	Lev	Team	W	L	Sv	IP	K	ERA	WHIP	BF/G	OBA	H%	S%	xERA	Ctl	Dom	Cmd	hr/9	BPV
2021 (8) Virginia	2022	Rk	FCL Mets	0	0	0	1	2	0.00	1.00	3.8	262	55	100	2.23	0.0	18.0		0.0	342
92-94 FB +++	2022	A	St. Lucie	3	1	0	37	39	2.19	1.00	15.7	199	28	78	1.75	2.7	9.5	3.5	0.2	117
85-87 SL +++	2022	A+	Brooklyn	1	1	0	33	44	5.17	1.18	16.5	205	30	56	2.77	4.1	12.0	2.9	0.8	123
83-85 CU +++	2023	AA	Binghamton	1	2	0	51	57	3.71	0.84	18.7	196	24	63	2.40	1.4	10.1	7.1	1.4	161
79-81 CB ++	2023	AAA	Syracuse	4	4	0	73	81	5.30	1.48	19.6	254	32	66	4.56	4.7	10.0	2.1	1.2	71

3/4s RHP wasn't able to follow up strong 2022 season. Workhorse frame near physical projection. Repeatable delivery but cuts off lower half, limiting extension. Throws a lot of strikes but struggles to put away hitters. Plus riding action on FB plays up pitch to plus. CU is best secondary but struggles throwing it for strikes.

Vasquez,Randy | SP | San Diego | EXP MLB DEBUT: 2023 | H/W: 6-0 165 | FUT: #4 starter | 6B

Thrws R Age 25	Year	Lev	Team	W	L	Sv	IP	K	ERA	WHIP	BF/G	OBA	H%	S%	xERA	Ctl	Dom	Cmd	hr/9	BPV
2018 FA (DR)	2021	A+	Hudson Valley	3	0	0	36	53	1.75	1.14	23.8	245	40	83	2.40	2.0	13.3	6.6	0.0	203
92-94 FB +++	2021	AA	Somerset	2	1	0	21	19	4.27	1.42	22.4	279	34	71	4.43	3.0	8.1	2.7	0.9	83
87-89 CT +++	2022	AA	Somerset	2	7	0	115	120	3.91	1.28	18.9	246	32	71	3.61	3.2	9.4	2.9	0.9	100
86-88 CU +++	2023	AAA	Scranton/WB	3	8	0	80	96	4.61	1.47	20.2	257	34	71	4.48	4.5	10.8	2.4	1.1	91
80-82 CB ++	2023	MLB	New York (A)	2	2	0	37	33	2.90	1.29	13.9	222	26	84	3.68	4.4	8.0	1.8	1.2	44

Low 3/4s RHP kept hitters off balance during MLB debut. Repeatable delivery with near average extension. Mixes and matches with 6 pitches, all sitting around average in performance and stuff. Heavy FB usage with 2-seam, 4-seam and cutter. Sweeping SL is best secondary offering. Throws late-fading CU with conviction. Fringe CB adjusts eye levels.

Vela,Noel | SP | San Diego | EXP MLB DEBUT: 2025 | H/W: 6-1 185 | FUT: #4 starter | 7D

Thrws L Age 24	Year	Lev	Team	W	L	Sv	IP	K	ERA	WHIP	BF/G	OBA	H%	S%	xERA	Ctl	Dom	Cmd	hr/9	BPV
2017 (28) HS (TX)	2021	A	Lake Elsinore	1	8	0	54	63	3.99	1.33	17.3	216	29	72	3.32	5.0	10.5	2.1	0.8	72
91-95 FB +++	2021	A+	Fort Wayne	0	3	0	33	44	3.81	1.42	17.5	249	37	73	3.69	4.4	12.0	2.8	0.5	116
78-80 CB +++	2022	A+	Fort Wayne	6	7	0	87	101	3.83	1.39	18.3	232	32	73	3.47	4.9	10.4	2.1	0.6	75
81-83 CU +++	2022	AA	San Antonio	1	3	0	22	24	6.49	2.03	12.0	285	38	66	5.61	8.1	9.7	1.2	0.4	-26
	2023	Rk	ACL Padres	0	0	0	0	0	0.00	20.00	4.6	780	78	100	74.18	90.0	0.0	0.0	0.0	-2412

Intriguing SP who missed most of season with bone spurs in elbow. Has makings of back-end starter with three quality offerings. Could be moved to pen if can't prove durability. Has added strength and velocity to FB and features lot of carry at top of zone. Likes to mix in effective, slower CB and solid-average CU. Walks have been an issue.

Vines,Darius | SP | Atlanta | EXP MLB DEBUT: 2023 | H/W: 6-1 190 | FUT: #4 starter | 7C

Thrws R Age 25	Year	Lev	Team	W	L	Sv	IP	K	ERA	WHIP	BF/G	OBA	H%	S%	xERA	Ctl	Dom	Cmd	hr/9	BPV
2019 (7) Cal State Bakersfield	2022	AAA	Gwinnett	1	0	0	33	29	3.25	1.30	19.5	236	30	74	2.99	3.8	7.9	2.1	0.3	57
88-91 FB +++	2023	Rk	FCL Braves	0	0	0	6	7	0.00	0.50	10.0	151	23	100		0.0	10.5		0.0	207
81-83 SL +++	2023	A+	Rome	0	0	0	9	14	4.00	1.00	17.2	191	26	71	3.26	3.0	14.0	4.7	2.0	189
80-82 CU ++++	2023	AAA	Gwinnett	3	2	0	34	28	2.38	1.23	23.0	232	26	89	3.76	3.4	7.4	2.2	1.3	58
84-87 CT +++	2023	MLB	Atlanta	1	0	0	20	14	4.03	1.09	15.7	209	22	68	3.17	3.1	6.3	2.0	1.3	46

At-projection SP prospect made MLB debut after season struggling with shoulder health. Repeats 3/4s delivery with long arm circle and average extension. Struggled throwing 4-seam FB for strikes entire season. Threw double-plus CU with late dropping profile more than 4-seam FB. Two-plane SL is above-average pitch. Added a CT with good results.

Vodnik,Victor — RP — Colorado — EXP MLB DEBUT: 2023 — H/W: 6-0 200 — FUT: Setup reliever — 6B

Thrws R Age 22	Year	Lev	Team	W	L	Sv	IP	K	ERA	WHIP	BF/G	OBA	H%	S%	xERA	Ctl	Dom	Cmd	hr/9	BPV
2018 (14) HS (CA)	2022	AAA	Gwinnett	2	0	2	27	33	2.98	1.54	4.9	253	35	83	4.17	5.3	10.9	2.1	0.7	72
95-97 FB ++++	2023	AA	Hartford	0	0	2	6	9	0.00	0.83	5.5	191	34	100	0.96	1.5	13.5	9.0	0.0	221
86-88 CU ++++	2023	AA	Mississippi	3	1	4	40	56	3.13	1.27	5.5	187	29	76	2.44	5.6	12.5	2.2	0.4	93
CB +	2023	AAA	Albuquerque	1	1	0	7	4	7.71	2.29	4.5	358	34	77	10.74	6.4	5.1	0.8	3.9	-63
	2023	MLB	Colorado	1	0	0	8	12	8.78	2.20	6.9	393	57	56	7.49	3.3	13.2	4.0	0.0	166

Reliever was acquired from the Braves in the Pierce Johnson trade. His brief MLB debut was a rocky one and he struggles with poor command, but his upper-90s FB tops at 100 with plenty of swing-and-miss. He backs up the heater with a plus upper-80s CU and a fringe CB. Mechanics are stiff and he struggles to maintain a consistent release point.

Waites,Cole — RP — San Francisco — EXP MLB DEBUT: 2022 — H/W: 6-3 180 — FUT: Setup reliever — 7C

Thrws R Age 25	Year	Lev	Team	W	L	Sv	IP	K	ERA	WHIP	BF/G	OBA	H%	S%	xERA	Ctl	Dom	Cmd	hr/9	BPV
2019 (18) West Alabama	2022	AA	Richmond	2	2	4	21	38	1.71	1.29	4.8	168	36	85	1.82	6.4	16.3	2.5	0.0	138
94-98 FB ++++	2022	AAA	Sacramento	1	0	1	8	11	0.00	0.75	4.1	117	21	100		3.4	12.4	3.7	0.0	150
82-85 SL ++++	2022	MLB	San Francisco	0	0	0	5	4	3.46	1.92	3.5	290	32	89	6.70	6.9	6.9	1.0	1.7	-44
	2023	AAA	Sacramento	3	4	1	30	32	6.26	1.75	4.3	234	30	64	4.68	8.0	9.5	1.2	0.9	-28
	2023	MLB	San Francisco	0	0	0	2	2	17.14	3.81	4.6	503	60	50	14.33	8.6	8.6	1.0	0.0	-59

Career RP who suffered thru horrendous season and underwent Tommy John surgery in September. Will likely miss all of 2024. Has two plus-to-elite offerings in incredible FB and nasty SL. K rate plummeted in 2023 as he fell behind in counts and was forced to aim FB to keep in zone. Rarely allows hard contact. One to keep eye on upon return.

Waldrep,Hurston — SP — Atlanta — EXP MLB DEBUT: 2024 — H/W: 6-2 210 — FUT: #2 SP/closer — 8C

Thrws R Age 22	Year	Lev	Team	W	L	Sv	IP	K	ERA	WHIP	BF/G	OBA	H%	S%	xERA	Ctl	Dom	Cmd	hr/9	BPV
2023 (1) Florida	2023	NCAA	Florida	10	3	0	101		4.18	1.40	22.5	229	36	73	3.86	5.1	13.9	2.7	1.1	131
95-97 FB ++++	2023	A	Augusta	0	0	0	3	8	3.00	1.33	12.5	262	87	75	3.01	3.0	24.0	8.0	0.0	369
86-88 SL ++++	2023	A+	Rome	0	0	0	12	17	0.75	0.75	14.3	106	19	89		3.8	12.8	3.4	0.0	146
86-89 SP ++++	2023	AA	Mississippi	0	1	0	10	11	2.70	1.50	14.4	221	29	86	3.88	6.3	9.9	1.6	0.9	26
91-93 CT ++	2023	AAA	Gwinnett	0	0	0	4	5	0.00	1.71	18.6	257	38	100	4.01	6.6	11.0	1.7	0.0	38

Hard-throwing 2023 College World Series star was Braves 1st round pick, making it to Triple-A. Up-tempo, over-the-top delivery with head whack. Struggles with control/command. Amped-up arsenal. Mid-90s FB plays up due to flat angle and secondaries. SP is double-plus offering with significant whiff potential. Gyro SL is nasty too.

Waldron,Matt — SP — San Diego — EXP MLB DEBUT: 2023 — H/W: 6-2 185 — FUT: #5 SP/swingman — 6B

Thrws R Age 27	Year	Lev	Team	W	L	Sv	IP	K	ERA	WHIP	BF/G	OBA	H%	S%	xERA	Ctl	Dom	Cmd	hr/9	BPV
2019 (18) Nebraska	2021	AA	San Antonio	0	4	0	31	31	6.66	1.64	19.8	285	37	57	4.80	4.6	9.0	1.9	0.6	54
91-93 FB ++	2022	AA	San Antonio	2	1	0	44	38	2.86	1.18	19.6	252	32	76	3.04	2.0	7.8	3.8	0.4	102
80-81 SL ++	2022	AAA	El Paso	3	9	0	69	58	8.47	1.75	19.7	321	37	51	6.57	3.8	7.6	2.0	1.6	52
77-80 KB +++	2023	AAA	El Paso	2	10	0	92	99	7.33	1.61	20.4	312	38	56	6.24	2.9	9.7	3.3	1.8	113
	2023	MLB	San Diego	1	3	0	41	31	4.38	1.24	20.9	252	26	74	4.66	2.6	6.8	2.6	2.0	69

Knuckleballer who was actually better in majors than in AAA. Hasn't pitched well in minors over last 2 years but remains option due to knuckler. Exhibits surprisingly good control of it and will mix in low 90s FB to keep hitters off guard. K rate jumped in 2023 but still struggles to keep ball in yard. Likely swingman profile and can eat innings.

Walston,Blake — SP — Arizona — EXP MLB DEBUT: 2025 — H/W: 6-5 175 — FUT: #5 SP/swingman — 6C

Thrws L Age 22	Year	Lev	Team	W	L	Sv	IP	K	ERA	WHIP	BF/G	OBA	H%	S%	xERA	Ctl	Dom	Cmd	hr/9	BPV
2019 (1) HS (NC)	2021	A	Visalia	2	2	0	43	60	3.34	1.18	21.6	219	33	74	2.97	3.5	12.5	3.5	0.8	148
90-92 FB +	2021	A+	Hillsboro	2	3	0	52	57	4.15	1.31	19.5	261	31	79	5.02	2.8	9.8	3.6	2.1	121
85-88 CT ++	2022	A+	Hillsboro	1	0	0	17	27	2.62	1.16	17.1	211	38	75	2.03	3.7	14.1	3.9	0.0	173
84-86 CU +	2022	AA	Amarillo	7	3	0	106	110	5.17	1.45	21.6	278	34	67	4.95	3.3	9.3	2.8	1.4	97
81-83 SL ++	2023	AAA	Reno	12	6	0	149	104	4.53	1.58	21.8	252	30	71	4.18	5.6	6.3	1.1	0.5	-21

Big-bodied, precocious lefty struggled in first taste of AAA. Stuff backed up with sharp decline in K%, no velo growth. Low-90s FB is liability. CB has good shape but batters have no issues sitting FB. Mechanics are clean but need work to unlock more velo, movement on pitches. Has shown ability to adapt, but needs to do so now more than ever.

Walter,Brandon — SP — Boston — EXP MLB DEBUT: 2023 — H/W: 6-2 201 — FUT: #4 starter — 7C

Thrws L Age 27	Year	Lev	Team	W	L	Sv	IP	K	ERA	WHIP	BF/G	OBA	H%	S%	xERA	Ctl	Dom	Cmd	hr/9	BPV
2019 (26) Delaware	2021	A+	Greenville	4	3	0	58	86	3.72	1.03	18.7	219	34	67	2.67	2.2	13.3	6.1	0.9	199
88-92 FB ++	2022	AA	Portland	2	2	0	50	68	2.88	0.78	20.0	203	29	70	2.00	0.5	12.2	22.7	1.1	224
78-82 SL +++	2022	AAA	Worcester	1	1	0	7	7	8.75	1.81	16.7	307	40	46	5.01	5.0	8.8	1.8	0.0	41
79-83 CU +++	2023	AAA	Worcester	3	5	0	94	88	4.60	1.43	19.0	272	33	69	4.43	3.4	8.4	2.5	1.0	79
	2023	MLB	Boston	0	0	1	23	16	6.26	1.70	11.5	330	37	64	6.24	2.7	6.3	2.3	1.2	57

Sinkerballer with versatility to start or relieve. Walk rate regressed along with K rate, though was previously all about command. Low ¾ slot results in GB. Best pitch may be tumbling CU thrown with deceptive arm speed. SL shows flashes of plus action. Has lost some velocity and FB now is below average offering.

Walters,Andrew — RP — Cleveland — EXP MLB DEBUT: 2025 — H/W: 6-4 222 — FUT: Closer — 7C

Thrws R Age 23	Year	Lev	Team	W	L	Sv	IP	K	ERA	WHIP	BF/G	OBA	H%	S%	xERA	Ctl	Dom	Cmd	hr/9	BPV
2023 (2) Miami																				
94-98 FB ++++																				
84-87 SL ++																				
87-89 CU +																				

College closer who could reach majors very quickly. Primarily FB guy with solid command. Pitches up in zone effectively with ride and carry on FB. Doesn't leverage height in delivery but still solid, particularly with sweeping SL. Has CU in holster but not overly impressive as it has little separation with FB. Will need to use SL more as pro.

Warren,Will — SP — New York (A) — EXP MLB DEBUT: 2024 — H/W: 6-2 175 — FUT: #4 starter — 7C

Thrws R Age 24	Year	Lev	Team	W	L	Sv	IP	K	ERA	WHIP	BF/G	OBA	H%	S%	xERA	Ctl	Dom	Cmd	hr/9	BPV
2021 (8) SE Louisiana																				
92-94 FB ++++	2022	A+	Hudson Valley	2	3	0	35	42	3.60	1.11	17.2	233	33	68	2.69	2.3	10.8	4.7	0.5	150
84-87 SL +++	2022	AA	Somerset	7	6	0	94	83	4.02	1.30	21.5	251	31	70	3.65	3.2	7.9	2.5	0.8	76
87-89 CU ++	2023	AA	Somerset	3	0	0	29	39	2.47	1.31	20.0	241	38	79	2.77	3.7	12.1	3.3	0.0	135
79-81 CB ++	2023	AAA	Scranton/WB	7	4	0	99	110	3.63	1.31	19.5	229	29	78	3.93	4.3	10.0	2.3	1.4	83

Athletic RHP with a slew of pitches saw effectiveness suffer after promotion to Triple-A. Low 3/4s delivery with solid extension. 2-seam FB is plus pitch with sink/run profile. Struggles with 4-seam FB shape and command. Features an above-average sweeping SL. Sells CU well but lacks downward fade with arm-side run. Mixes in CB and CT.

Watson,Danny — RP — New York (A) — EXP MLB DEBUT: 2024 — H/W: 6-7 235 — FUT: Middle reliever — 6C

Thrws R Age 23	Year	Lev	Team	W	L	Sv	IP	K	ERA	WHIP	BF/G	OBA	H%	S%	xERA	Ctl	Dom	Cmd	hr/9	BPV
2021 (15) VCU	2021	NCAA	VCU	2	4	1	44	55	4.08	1.34	9.7	234	35	67	2.97	4.3	11.2	2.6	0.2	104
89-92 FB +++	2021	A	Tampa	0	1	0	2	2	20.45	3.18	4.4	326	42	29	8.79	16.4	8.2	0.5	0.0	-277
80-84 SL ++++	2022	A	Tampa	5	5	1	58	66	4.03	1.39	6.4	215	30	71	3.13	5.6	10.2	1.8	0.5	51
84-86 CT +++	2023	A+	Hudson Valley	3	1	0	24	39	1.49	0.87	5.9	150	28	85	0.95	3.4	14.6	4.3	0.4	189
	2023	AA	Somerset	4	0	5	38	43	1.65	0.89	4.7	143	17	93	1.74	3.8	10.2	2.7	1.2	99

Sidearm RP saw stuff tick up during successful 2023 season. Low release height, combined with deceptive delivery, hides pitch until late in delivery progression. Frisbee SL is best pitch, especially when vertical drop is present. Throws flat-angled 4-seam FB and CT to compliment the SL. CT has helped profile stay honest versus LHH.

Watts Brown,Juaron — SP — Toronto — EXP MLB DEBUT: 2025 — H/W: 6-3 190 — FUT: #4 starter — 7D

Thrws R Age 22	Year	Lev	Team	W	L	Sv	IP	K	ERA	WHIP	BF/G	OBA	H%	S%	xERA	Ctl	Dom	Cmd	hr/9	BPV
2023 (3) Oklahoma State																				
90-93 FB +++																				
82-85 SL ++++																				
81-83 CB ++																				
83-85 CU ++																				

Lean, athletic SP with one of better SL in org. Features plus spin and horizontal action to befuddle hitters. Operates as true K pitch. FB command comes and goes and is key to ultimate upside. Could add more velocity with added bulk. Mixes in sub-par CB and CU that has above average potential. Exhibits smooth, quick delivery.

Wells,Levi — SP — Baltimore — EXP MLB DEBUT: 2025 — H/W: 6-2 216 — FUT: Setup reliever — 7D

Thrws R Age 22	Year	Lev	Team	W	L	Sv	IP	K	ERA	WHIP	BF/G	OBA	H%	S%	xERA	Ctl	Dom	Cmd	hr/9	BPV
2023 (4) Texas State																				
90-95 FB +++																				
78-82 CB +++																				
84-89 SL ++																				

Over-the-top slot college RHP did not make professional debut after heavy workload in spring. Does well repeating delivery with solid extension. Flat-angled FB lives in the upper half of zone, piling whiffs. CB is solid downer with above-average potential. There's talk of a CU, too, but rarely uses it.

Whisenhunt,Carson

SP | San Francisco | EXP MLB DEBUT: 2024 | H/W: 6-3 209 | FUT: #3 starter | 8C

Thrws L Age 23			Year	Lev	Team	W	L	Sv	IP	K	ERA	WHIP	BF/G	OBA	H%	S%	xERA	Ctl	Dom	Cmd	hr/9	BPV
2022 (2) East Carolina			2022	Rk	ACL Giants O	0	0	0	3	7	0.00	0.33	4.7	106	41	100		0.0	21.0		0.0	396
92-96	FB	+++	2022	A	San Jose	0	0	0	4	7	0.00	1.43	8.9	297	51	100	3.84	2.1	15.0	7.0	0.0	230
79-81	CB	+++	2023	A	San Jose	0	0	0	13	20	3.41	1.21	13.3	244	39	73	3.20	2.7	13.6	5.0	0.7	190
82-84	CU	++++	2023	A+	Eugene	1	0	0	25	36	1.43	0.68	14.6	113	19	81	0.10	2.9	12.9	4.5	0.4	173
			2023	AA	Richmond	0	1	0	19	27	3.28	1.41	13.5	228	36	77	3.30	5.2	12.7	2.5	0.5	107

Ended season in July due to left elbow sprain but was dynamic on three levels in 1st full pro season. Mostly pitched shorter outings, but flashed dominance with three pitches. Misses ton of bats with one of best CU in minors. Throws with same arm speed as FB that features late sinking action. Needs to polish FB command to stay ahead in counts.

White,Owen

SP | Texas | EXP MLB DEBUT: 2023 | H/W: 6-3 199 | FUT: #3 starter | 8D

Thrws R Age 24			Year	Lev	Team	W	L	Sv	IP	K	ERA	WHIP	BF/G	OBA	H%	S%	xERA	Ctl	Dom	Cmd	hr/9	BPV
2018 (2) HS (NC)			2022	A+	Hickory	6	2	0	58	81	4.02	1.20	21.3	237	35	70	3.48	2.9	12.5	4.3	1.1	164
91-95	FB	+++	2022	AA	Frisco	3	0	0	21	23	2.55	1.08	20.7	241	33	77	2.64	1.7	9.8	5.8	0.4	148
84-89	SL	+++	2023	AA	Frisco	2	3	0	56	48	3.53	1.12	18.4	202	24	71	2.63	3.7	7.7	2.1	0.8	57
87-90	CT	++	2023	AAA	Round Rock	2	2	0	52	32	5.01	1.61	17.8	261	27	74	5.51	5.5	5.5	1.0	1.7	-32
77-81	CB	++	2023	MLB	Texas	0	1	0	4	4	11.25	1.75	9.1	307	29	40	9.10	4.5	9.0	2.0	4.5	59

Stuff regressed nearly across board, losing 2 mph on fastball and consistency despite making MLB debut. SL may still be plus but otherwise it's now lots average and slightly above pitches. Highly athletic, repeats delivery well with little arm mileage and fluky injury history, so too soon to give up on. Still mid-rotation upside, but stock is down.

White,Thomas

SP | Miami | EXP MLB DEBUT: 2027 | H/W: 6-5 210 | FUT: #2 starter | 9E

Thrws L Age 19			Year	Lev	Team	W	L	Sv	IP	K	ERA	WHIP	BF/G	OBA	H%	S%	xERA	Ctl	Dom	Cmd	hr/9	BPV
2023 (1) HS (MA)																						
92-96	FB	++++																				
78-82	CB	++++																				
86-88	CU	+++	2023	Rk	FCL Marlins	0	0	0	0	2	0.00	10.00	2.6	0	0	100	21.53	90.0	90.0	1.0	0.0	-792
			2023	A	Jupiter	0	1	0	3	5	8.44	2.19	8.0	250	43	57	5.09	11.3	14.1	1.3	0.0	-33

Strong, tall projectable LHP signed for mid-1st round money despite being selected in the supplemental round. Athletic, low 3/4s delivery with plus extension. 4-seam FB has significant ride profile and will add MPH with strength gains with frame development. CB has devastating 1-to-5 break profile. Low spin rate CU has above-average upside.

Whitman,Joe

SP | San Francisco | EXP MLB DEBUT: 2025 | H/W: 6-5 200 | FUT: #4 starter | 7C

Thrws L Age 22			Year	Lev	Team	W	L	Sv	IP	K	ERA	WHIP	BF/G	OBA	H%	S%	xERA	Ctl	Dom	Cmd	hr/9	BPV
2023 (2) Kent State																						
91-94	FB	+++																				
81-83	SL	+++	2023	NCAA	Kent St.	9	2	0	81	100	2.56	1.14	21.4	216	32	77	2.26	3.2	11.1	3.4	0.2	131
82-84	CU	++	2023	Rk	ACL Giants B	0	0	0	4	4	0.00	0.50	4.4	81	12	100		2.3	9.0	4.0	0.0	119
			2023	A	San Jose	1	0	0	5	9	3.46	0.96	6.6	170	35	60	1.03	3.5	15.6	4.5	0.0	205

Tall LHP with impressive repertoire and ability to thrive with unique delivery. Throws with effort, but athletic enough to repeat and could withstand professional modifications. Possesses good control and command and features quick arm action. Gets good spin on FB and knocks out hitters with sharp SL. Development of CU will be key.

Wicks,Jordan

SP | Chicago (N) | EXP MLB DEBUT: 2023 | H/W: 6-3 220 | FUT: #4 starter | 7D

Thrws L Age 24			Year	Lev	Team	W	L	Sv	IP	K	ERA	WHIP	BF/G	OBA	H%	S%	xERA	Ctl	Dom	Cmd	hr/9	BPV
2021 (1) Kansas State			2022	A+	South Bend	4	3	0	66	86	3.67	1.25	16.9	261	38	72	3.56	2.3	11.7	5.1	0.7	166
91-94	FB	++	2022	AA	Tennessee	0	3	0	28	35	4.18	1.25	14.2	233	30	73	4.05	3.5	11.3	3.2	1.6	125
76-78	CB	+	2023	AA	Tennessee	4	0	0	58	69	3.41	1.17	17.8	230	30	78	3.62	2.9	10.7	3.6	1.4	131
81-84	SL	++	2023	AAA	Iowa	3	0	0	33	30	3.82	1.18	18.9	218	27	69	2.99	3.5	8.2	2.3	0.8	70
80-83	CU	+++++	2023	MLB	Chicago (N)	4	1	0	34	24	4.47	1.29	20.1	255	28	69	4.21	2.9	6.3	2.2	1.3	54

1st rounder made MLB debut where he held his own, but also failed to dominate. Big lefty has simple, repeatable mechanics and pounds the zone with a low-90s FB. Best offering is a double-plus CU that has excellent fade and sink and generates plenty of swing-and-miss (.171 BAA). SL and CB give him a 4-pitch mix, but the CU is his bread and butter.

Wiggins,Jaxon

SP | Chicago (N) | EXP MLB DEBUT: 2026 | H/W: 6-6 225 | FUT: #3 starter | 8E

Thrws R Age 22			Year	Lev	Team	W	L	Sv	IP	K	ERA	WHIP	BF/G	OBA	H%	S%	xERA	Ctl	Dom	Cmd	hr/9	BPV
2023 (2) Arkansas																						
94-97	FB	++++																				
85-87	SL	+++																				
77-79	CB	++																				
83-86	CU	+++																				

2nd round compensation pick had Tommy John surgery and has yet to make his professional debut. Athletic frame, fluid delivery, and attacks from a high ¾ arm slot. Prior to the injury featured a 4-pitch mix highlighted by a plus mid-90s FB. Power SL is best secondary and shows feel for CU and 12-to-6 CB. Struggles to find the strike zone.

Wilcox,Cole

SP | Tampa Bay | EXP MLB DEBUT: 2024 | H/W: 6-5 232 | FUT: Middle reliever | 6C

Thrws R Age 24			Year	Lev	Team	W	L	Sv	IP	K	ERA	WHIP	BF/G	OBA	H%	S%	xERA	Ctl	Dom	Cmd	hr/9	BPV
2020 (3) Georgia			2020	NCAA	Georgia	3	0	0	23	32	1.57	0.87	21.2	217	33	89	2.11	0.8	12.5	16.0	0.8	222
92-94	FB	+++	2021	A	Charleston	1	0	0	44	52	2.04	0.86	16.2	210	31	76	1.47	1.0	10.6	10.4	0.2	181
84-86	SL	++++	2022	Rk	FCL Rays	0	1	0	5	9	7.20	1.80	7.7	332	58	56	5.32	3.6	16.2	4.5	0.0	212
86-88	CU	++	2022	A	Charleston	0	1	0	11	15	2.45	0.91	10.3	205	30	78	2.10	1.6	12.3	7.5	0.8	195
			2023	AA	Montgomery	6	8	0	106	99	5.25	1.31	17.5	241	29	62	3.93	3.7	8.4	2.3	1.2	68

Strong-bodied RHP struggled in first full season back from Tommy John surgery. Healthy but stuff hasn't come back to pre-surgery form. Low 3/4s delivery with RP jerkiness. Struggles to maintain FB slot. Low strike% with 2-seam FB due to uncontrollable arm-side run. Two-plane SL still has plus markers. CU hasn't progressed.

Williams,Henry

SP | Kansas City | EXP MLB DEBUT: 2026 | H/W: 6-5 200 | FUT: Middle reliever | 7E

Thrws R Age 22			Year	Lev	Team	W	L	Sv	IP	K	ERA	WHIP	BF/G	OBA	H%	S%	xERA	Ctl	Dom	Cmd	hr/9	BPV
2022 (3) Duke																						
90-93	FB	+++																				
80-84	SL	+++																				
84-86	CU	++	2023	A	Columbia	2	1	0	24	23	3.38	1.29	19.7	210	25	79	3.45	4.9	8.6	1.8	1.1	42
			2023	A	Lake Elsinore	1	5	0	42	40	5.77	1.43	14.9	247	30	61	4.40	4.5	8.6	1.9	1.3	51

Tall college RHP made professional debut in 2023 after recovering from Tommy John surgery. Acquired from SD at trade deadline in 2023. Easy, 3/4s delivery with solid extension. Has a solid FB and SL combination while also developing a CU, throwing with convection. FB is lively and lives in the zone but struggles with inconsistent shape. Long term, likely RP.

Wilson,Paul

SP | Detroit | EXP MLB DEBUT: 2027 | H/W: 6-3 205 | FUT: #4 starter | 7D

Thrws L Age 19			Year	Lev	Team	W	L	Sv	IP	K	ERA	WHIP	BF/G	OBA	H%	S%	xERA	Ctl	Dom	Cmd	hr/9	BPV
2023 (3) HS (OR)																						
94-97	FB	+++																				
76-78	CB	++																				
78-81	CU	+																				
80-83	SL	++																				

Projectable, saw a velo uptick that gives him two above-average offerings. FB sits in the mid-90s with good life up, touching 98. Power 12-to-6 CB has swing-and-miss break, but needs better command. Comes at hitters from high 3/4 arm slot and works mostly north/south in the zone. Could develop as a mid-rotation arm if CU and command improve.

Winans,Allan

SP | Atlanta | EXP MLB DEBUT: 2023 | H/W: 6-2 165 | FUT: #5 SP/swingman | 6A

Thrws R Age 28			Year	Lev	Team	W	L	Sv	IP	K	ERA	WHIP	BF/G	OBA	H%	S%	xERA	Ctl	Dom	Cmd	hr/9	BPV
2018 (17) Campbell			2022	Rk	FCL Braves	0	0	0	5	5	0.00	0.80	9.1	124	18	100	0.22	3.6	9.0	2.5	0.0	83
88-90	FB	++	2022	AA	Mississippi	1	4	0	44	44	2.45	1.18	22.0	257	34	80	3.08	1.8	9.0	4.9	0.4	130
82-84	CU	++++	2022	AAA	Gwinnett	0	1	0	15	16	6.00	1.33	15.6	249	31	56	4.10	3.6	9.6	2.7	1.2	94
78-80	CB	+++	2023	AAA	Gwinnett	9	4	1	126	113	2.85	1.09	21.4	221	27	77	2.75	2.6	8.1	3.1	0.8	94
			2023	MLB	Atlanta	1	2	0	32	34	5.33	1.40	22.6	290	36	65	5.05	2.2	9.5	4.3	1.4	129

Journeyman, former MiLB phase Rule 5 pick made MLB debut, starting 6 games. Repeatable 3/4s delivery with above-average extension. Throws 3 pitches. Varies between fastballs, neither would be considered solid. Late-fading CU is plus offering with late tumble. CB is an above-average offering with solid sweeping action. No projection left.

Winn,Cole

RP | Texas | EXP MLB DEBUT: 2024 | H/W: 6-2 190 | FUT: #5 SP/swingman | 7E

Thrws R Age 24			Year	Lev	Team	W	L	Sv	IP	K	ERA	WHIP	BF/G	OBA	H%	S%	xERA	Ctl	Dom	Cmd	hr/9	BPV
2018 (1) HS (CA)			2019	A	Hickory	4	4	0	68	65	4.49	1.44	16.1	235	30	69	3.68	5.1	8.6	1.7	0.7	33
92-95	FB	++	2021	AA	Frisco	3	3	0	78	97	2.31	0.82	14.9	147	21	76	1.13	3.0	11.2	3.7	0.7	138
85-88	SL	+++	2021	AAA	Round Rock	1	0	0	8	10	3.38	1.25	16.3	181	24	78	2.98	5.6	11.3	2.0	1.1	69
78-81	CB	+	2022	AAA	Round Rock	9	8	0	121	123	6.53	1.75	19.8	268	34	62	5.19	6.5	9.1	1.4	1.0	8
84-87	CU	++	2023	AAA	Round Rock	9	8	0	101	97	7.22	1.91	16.5	286	34	64	6.38	7.0	8.6	1.2	1.5	-16

In isolation, all 4 offerings (FS, SL, CB, CU) have excellent whiff rates; SL leads the way. Good news ends there. Homers, walks in repeat of AAA season suggest mop-up/long reliever. Winter ball stats (0 HRA, 16 H, 24/10 K/BB in 24 IP) offer glimmer but otherwise former 1st-rounder is purely depth.

Winn,Keaton — SP — San Francisco

EXP MLB DEBUT: 2023 | H/W: 6-4 238 | FUT: #4 starter | 7B

Thrws R Age 26 — 2018 (5) Iowa Western CC

Velo	Pitch	Grade
94-96	FB	+ + + +
84-87	SL	+ + +
87-89	SP	+ + + +

Year	Lev	Team	W	L	Sv	IP	K	ERA	WHIP	BF/G	OBA	H%	S%	xERA	Ctl	Dom	Cmd	hr/9	BPV
2022	A	San Jose	1	1	0	40	55	4.93	1.34	12.9	251	37	63	3.63	3.6	12.3	3.4	0.7	143
2022	A+	Eugene	3	2	0	37	46	3.16	1.30	19.0	267	38	76	3.57	2.4	11.2	4.6	0.5	154
2022	AA	Richmond	2	3	0	30	24	4.19	1.36	21.0	292	34	73	4.80	1.8	7.2	4.0	1.2	99
2023	AAA	Sacramento	0	6	0	58	66	4.81	1.59	15.0	288	38	72	5.17	4.0	10.2	2.5	1.1	93
2023	MLB	San Francisco	1	3	1	42	35	4.70	1.05	18.1	233	26	58	3.26	1.7	7.5	4.4	1.3	107

Big-framed SP who reached majors and has the pitch mix and moxie to thrive at any level. Added spitter and can register Ks with it. Has demonstrated durability and stamina all while maintaining good velocity to FB with armside run. Throws strikes with breaking ball, but command took a step back.

Wolf,Jackson — SP — Pittsburgh

EXP MLB DEBUT: 2023 | H/W: 6-7 205 | FUT: #4 starter | 7B

Thrws L Age 24 — 2021 (4) West Virginia

Velo	Pitch	Grade
88-91	FB	+ + +
77-79	SL	+ + +
75-78	CB	+ + +
81-84	CU	+ +

Year	Lev	Team	W	L	Sv	IP	K	ERA	WHIP	BF/G	OBA	H%	S%	xERA	Ctl	Dom	Cmd	hr/9	BPV
2022	A+	Fort Wayne	7	8	0	119	134	4.01	1.13	20.5	213	27	69	3.16	3.3	10.1	3.0	1.2	111
2022	AA	San Antonio	0	2	0	10	8	8.82	1.76	23.4	294	35	47	5.56	5.3	7.1	1.3	0.9	2
2023	AA	Altoona	0	4	0	36	30	4.25	1.17	17.9	240	27	68	3.63	2.5	7.5	3.0	1.3	86
2023	AA	San Antonio	8	9	0	88	105	4.09	1.09	19.1	229	30	67	3.25	2.2	10.7	4.8	1.2	150
2023	MLB	San Diego	1	0	0	5	1	5.40	1.40	21.1	299	31	57	3.93	1.8	1.8	1.0	0.0	2

Very tall LHP who was acquired from SD at deadline. Uses angle to plate to keep hitters guessing. Tough to pick up average FB out of hand due to release. Gets lot of sink to FB but has been effective up in zone too. No other above average pitch in arsenal but sequences well and has been stingy against LHH. Lot of drop on CB while SL shows sweep.

Wolters,Blake — SP — Kansas City

EXP MLB DEBUT: 2028 | H/W: 6-4 210 | FUT: #2 SP/closer | 9E

Thrws R Age 19 — 2023 (2) HS (IL)

Velo	Pitch	Grade
95-98	FB	+ + + +
83-85	SL	+ + + +
78-80	CU	+ +

Year	Lev	Team	W	L	Sv	IP	K	ERA	WHIP	BF/G	OBA	H%	S%	xERA	Ctl	Dom	Cmd	hr/9	BPV

Tall, projectable RHP possess top end SP profile. Drafted in 2nd round despite limited events on the prep showcase circuit. FB sat low-90s as a junior in high school to upper-90s as a senior. Also has feel for spin. SL has plus attributes. 3/4s RHP with plus extension will need to shorten arm circle to achieve upside potential.

Woods Richardson,Sime — SP — Minnesota

EXP MLB DEBUT: 2022 | H/W: 6-3 210 | FUT: #4 starter | 7D

Thrws R Age 23 — 2018 (2) HS (TX)

Velo	Pitch	Grade
89-92	FB	+ + +
72-75	CB	+ + +
82-86	SL	+ + +
80-84	CU	+ + +

Year	Lev	Team	W	L	Sv	IP	K	ERA	WHIP	BF/G	OBA	H%	S%	xERA	Ctl	Dom	Cmd	hr/9	BPV
2022	AA	Wichita	3	3	0	70	77	3.08	1.17	17.5	221	30	74	2.67	3.3	9.9	3.0	0.5	106
2022	AAA	St. Paul	2	0	0	36	38	2.24	0.86	19.0	171	23	76	1.30	2.5	9.4	3.8	0.5	121
2022	MLB	Minnesota	0	1	0	5	3	3.60	1.00	19.1	175	15	75	2.98	3.6	5.4	1.5	1.8	18
2023	AAA	St. Paul	7	6	0	113	96	4.93	1.50	20.4	255	30	69	4.47	4.8	7.6	1.6	1.0	24
2023	MLB	Minnesota	0	0	0	4	5	10.71	2.38	21.8	371	47	56	9.56	6.4	10.7	1.7	2.1	37

Athletic RHP who was dreadful in first 3 months before turning it around midseason. Hasn't improved stuff and control regressed. Complicated delivery is tough to repeat. Best pitch remains good CU with depth and fade. Used to have plus CB but has fallen backward. When on, he looks usable. Still young and hope abounds.

Workman,Logan — SP — Tampa Bay

EXP MLB DEBUT: 2024 | H/W: 6-4 215 | FUT: Setup reliever | 7D

Thrws R Age 25 — 2021 (7) Lee University

Velo	Pitch	Grade
93-95	FB	+ + +
84-86	SL	+ + +
83-85	CU	+ + +
88-90	CT	+ +

Year	Lev	Team	W	L	Sv	IP	K	ERA	WHIP	BF/G	OBA	H%	S%	xERA	Ctl	Dom	Cmd	hr/9	BPV
2021	Rk	FCL Rays	1	0	0	10	14	0.89	1.09	6.6	174	29	91	1.43	4.5	12.5	2.8	0.0	122
2022	A	Charleston	1	0	0	23	34	0.78	0.78	13.9	187	33	89	0.79	1.2	13.2	11.3	0.0	225
2022	A+	Bowling Green	5	3	0	90	81	3.50	1.21	18.2	246	29	77	3.86	2.6	8.1	3.1	1.3	94
2023	Rk	FCL Rays	0	0	0	6	7	0.00	0.65	7.2	146	22	100	0.04	1.5	10.2	7.0	0.0	162
2023	AA	Montgomery	4	4	0	63	71	4.14	1.39	17.7	274	36	73	4.40	3.0	10.1	3.4	1.0	119

3/4 RHP missed first half with injury, posted solid stats in Double-A. Repeats deceptive delivery well. Primarily a 3-pitch pitcher, all average offerings, played up by deception. 4-seam FB has above-average ride/run profile. CU has become best secondary with late fade and occasional drop. Lost feel for SL at times incorporating CT into arsenal.

Wrobleski,Justin — SP — Los Angeles (N)

EXP MLB DEBUT: 2025 | H/W: 6-1 194 | FUT: #4 starter | 7D

Thrws L Age 23 — 2021 (11) Oklahoma State

Velo	Pitch	Grade
93-96	FB	+ + + +
80-83	CB	+ +
84-86	SL	+ + + +
83-85	CU	+ +

Year	Lev	Team	W	L	Sv	IP	K	ERA	WHIP	BF/G	OBA	H%	S%	xERA	Ctl	Dom	Cmd	hr/9	BPV
2022	Rk	ACL Dodgers	0	1	0	15	21	1.80	0.80	5.4	221	36	75	1.24	0.0	12.6		0.0	245
2022	A	Rancho Cuca	1	2	0	6	5	5.81	2.10	10.2	314	36	75	7.23	7.3	7.3	1.0	1.5	-47
2023	A+	Great Lakes	4	4	0	102	109	2.91	1.25	16.6	244	33	78	3.21	3.1	9.6	3.1	0.5	108

Had Tommy John surgery before the 2021 draft, causing him to fall. Coils well with quick arm action and good command. FB sits at 93-96 with arm side run and positive induced vertical break. Mid-80s SL is second plus offering with two-plane break while CB, CT, and CU show potential but need refinement. With health, could move up quickly.

Wyatt,Hiro — SP — Kansas City

EXP MLB DEBUT: 2028 | H/W: 6-1 190 | FUT: #5 SP/swingman | 7C

Thrws R Age 19 — 2023 (3) HS (CT)

Velo	Pitch	Grade
91-94	FB	+ + +
80-81	SL	+ + + +
88-89	CT	+ +
84-86	CU	+ +

Year	Lev	Team	W	L	Sv	IP	K	ERA	WHIP	BF/G	OBA	H%	S%	xERA	Ctl	Dom	Cmd	hr/9	BPV

Projectable, cold weather RHP has low-3/4s delivery with long arm circle. Creates deception with late release. FB sat low-90s at draft combine with a solid ride profile and potential for big velocity. SL is two-plane breaker with plus shape and tight spin. Also employs CT and CU as distant 3rd and 4th pitches.

Yan,Ricardo — SP — Arizona

EXP MLB DEBUT: 2026 | H/W: 6-4 180 | FUT: Closer | 7E

Thrws R Age 21 — 2021 FA (DR)

Velo	Pitch	Grade
90-91	FB	+ +
74-75	CB	+ + + +
83-89	CU	+ +
75-77	SL	+ + +

Year	Lev	Team	W	L	Sv	IP	K	ERA	WHIP	BF/G	OBA	H%	S%	xERA	Ctl	Dom	Cmd	hr/9	BPV
2021	Rk	DSL Dbacks 2	0	4	0	26	24	6.70	1.66	9.6	221	37	79	4.19	6.9	8.2	1.2	1.0	-19
2022	Rk	ACL Dbacks	1	1	0	24	31	3.75	1.21	10.7	201	30	68	2.39	4.5	11.6	2.6	0.4	106
2023	A	Visalia	1	9	0	81	105	4.33	1.14	17.8	202	30	61	2.40	3.8	11.7	3.1	0.6	126
2023	A+	Hillsboro	1	0	0	22	33	1.22	0.95	16.7	138	23	90	1.06	4.5	13.4	3.0	0.4	138

Tall RHP has premier bat-missing stuff, but struggles with command. Best pitch is mid-70s CB that misses bats and generates GBs. Opposing batters not easily fooled by FB, make plenty of contact in zone. Lack of deception, command allows batters to lay off secondaries. Could find success in relief given stuff with more CB heavy approach.

Ziegler,Calvin — SP — New York (N)

EXP MLB DEBUT: 2025 | H/W: 6-0 205 | FUT: #3 starter | 8E

Thrws R Age 21 — 2021 (2) HS (FL)

Velo	Pitch	Grade
91-94	FB	+ + +
80-83	CB	+ + +
82-85	SP	+ + + +

Year	Lev	Team	W	L	Sv	IP	K	ERA	WHIP	BF/G	OBA	H%	S%	xERA	Ctl	Dom	Cmd	hr/9	BPV
2021	--	Did Not Play																	
2022	A	St. Lucie	0	6	0	46	70	4.48	1.32	12.0	166	28	66	2.46	6.8	13.6	2.0	0.6	79
2023	A	St. Lucie	0	0	0	1	3	0.00	0.00	2.8	0	0			0.0	27.0		0.0	504

Athletic, high 3/4s RHP missed nearly the entire season due to injuries. Underwent surgery to remove bone spurs in elbow in March. During rehab, tore right quad, ending season. Flat-angled FB is best pitch with plus ride. SP has arm-side fade with late drop. A plus pitch. 12-to-6 CB is solid when throwing strikes. Struggles maintaining slot. High BB%.

Zobac,Steven — SP — Kansas City

EXP MLB DEBUT: 2026 | H/W: 6-3 185 | FUT: Setup reliever | 7D

Thrws R Age 23 — 2022 (4) California

Velo	Pitch	Grade
93-95	FB	+ + + +
84-87	SL	+ + +
83-86	CU	+ +

Year	Lev	Team	W	L	Sv	IP	K	ERA	WHIP	BF/G	OBA	H%	S%	xERA	Ctl	Dom	Cmd	hr/9	BPV
2023	A	Columbia	1	2	0	51	61	2.11	1.07	14.2	229	33	81	2.39	2.1	10.7	5.1	0.4	154
2023	A+	Quad Cities	1	4	0	39	37	5.31	1.44	20.7	286	36	62	4.41	2.8	8.5	3.1	0.7	97

High 3/4s slot RHP prospect struggled after mid-season promotion to High-A. RP profile with explosive FB and average SL, filling up the zone with strikes. FB is a plus offering with flat-angled approach and late riding action. Also flashed fringe CU to round out arsenal. Exclusively a SP in High-A, but fits better in RP role at Low-A.

Zulueta,Yosver — RP — Toronto

EXP MLB DEBUT: 2024 | H/W: 6-1 190 | FUT: Closer | 7C

Thrws R Age 26 — 2019 FA (CU)

Velo	Pitch	Grade
94-97	FB	+ + + +
80-82	CB	+ + +
83-85	SL	+ + +
86-87	CU	+ + +

Year	Lev	Team	W	L	Sv	IP	K	ERA	WHIP	BF/G	OBA	H%	S%	xERA	Ctl	Dom	Cmd	hr/9	BPV
2022	A	Dunedin	0	0	0	12	23	3.00	1.00	15.3	210	45	67	1.57	2.3	17.3	7.7	0.0	268
2022	A+	Vancouver	1	3	0	23	31	3.88	1.25	15.7	216	33	68	2.68	4.3	12.0	2.8	0.4	119
2022	AA	New Hampshire	1	1	0	15	25	4.17	1.59	7.4	190	34	74	3.40	8.3	14.9	1.8	0.6	61
2022	AAA	Buffalo	0	1	0	4	5	4.29	1.67	6.3	202	30	71	3.22	8.6	10.7	1.3	0.0	-21
2023	AAA	Buffalo	4	4	0	64	73	4.08	1.53	6.2	227	33	71	3.32	6.3	10.3	1.6	0.1	32

Aggressive, high-octane RHP who was moved to bullpen in mid May. Owns outstanding stuff and can dominate in short stints. Big problem has been inability to get ahead of hitters. Induces ton of GB with hard sinker and mixes in two breaking balls. Hitters often sit on FB. Throws above average CU and could evolve into special FB/CU RP.

MAJOR LEAGUE EQUIVALENTS

In his 1985 *Baseball Abstract*, Bill James introduced the concept of major league equivalencies. His assertion was that, with the proper adjustments, a minor leaguer's statistics could be converted to an equivalent major league level performance with a great deal of accuracy.

Because of wide variations in the level of play among different minor leagues, it is difficult to get a true reading on a player's potential. For instance, a .300 batting average achieved in the high-offense Triple-A West is not nearly as much of an accomplishment as a similar level in the Double-A Northeast. MLEs normalize these types of variances, for all statistical categories.

The actual MLEs are not projections. They represent how a player's previous performance might look at the major league level. However, the MLE stat line can be used in forecasting future performance in just the same way as a major league stat line would.

The model we use contains a few variations to James' version and updates all of the minor league and ballpark factors. In addition, we designed a module to convert pitching statistics, which is something James did not originally do.

Do MLEs really work?

Used correctly, MLEs are excellent indicators of potential. But just like we cannot take traditional major league statistics at face value, the same goes for MLEs. The underlying measures of base skill—batting eye ratios, pitching command ratios, etc.—are far more accurate in evaluating future talent than raw home runs, batting averages or ERAs.

The charts we present here also provide the unique perspective of looking at up to five years' worth of data. Ironically, the longer the history, the less likely the player is a legitimate prospect—he should have made it to the majors before compiling a long history in AA and/or AAA ball. Of course, the shorter trends

are more difficult to read despite them often belonging to players with higher ceilings. But even here we can find small indications of players improving their skills, or struggling, as they rise through more difficult levels of competition. Since players—especially those with any talent—are promoted rapidly through major league systems, a two or three-year scan is often all we get to spot any trends.

Here are some things to look for as you scan these charts:

Target players who...

- spent a full year in AA and then a full year in AAA
- had consistent playing time from one year to the next
- improved their base skills as they were promoted

Raise the warning flag for players who...

- were stuck at a level for multiple seasons, or regressed
- displayed marked changes in playing time from one year to the next
- showed large drops in BPIs from one year to the next

Players are listed on the charts if they spent at least part of 2018-2022 in AAA or AA and had at least 100 AB or 30 IP within those two levels. Each is listed with the organization with which they finished the season.

Only statistics accumulated in AAA and AA ball are included (players who split a season are indicated as a/a); Single-A stats are excluded.

Each player's actual AB and IP totals are used as the base for the conversion. However, it is more useful to compare performances using common levels, so rely on the ratios and sabermetric gauges. Complete explanations of these formulas appear in the Glossary.

BATTER	B	Yr	Age	Pos	Lvl	Tm	AB	R	H	D	T	HR	RBI	BB	K	SB	CS	BA	OB	Slg	OPS	bb%	ct%	Eye	PX	SX	RC/G	BPV
Abreu,Wilyer	L	22	23	CF	aa	BOS	457	72	98	28	0	12	49	77	167	21	3	213	327	356	683	14%	63%	0.46	119	103	3.29	10
		23	24	LF	aaa	BOS	299	45	69	9	1	15	43	38	83	5	1	232	319	426	745	11%	72%	0.46	111	80	4.13	26
Acuna,Luisangel	R	22	20	SS	aa	TEX	152	14	28	5	1	2	12	12	38	8	3	187	244	274	519	7%	75%	0.30	59	124	1.75	-1
		23	21	SS	aa	NYM	510	85	137	25	2	7	57	50	119	52	11	269	335	368	704	9%	77%	0.42	65	126	3.95	16
Adams,Jordyn	R	22	23	CF	aa	LAA	209	21	42	6	1	3	13	14	81	9	0	199	248	275	523	6%	61%	0.17	62	127	2.07	-52
		23	24	CF	aaa	LAA	415	46	90	20	4	10	42	33	157	27	6	216	273	360	633	7%	62%	0.21	105	132	2.73	-11
Alexander,Blaze	R	22	23	SS	a/a	ARI	344	32	81	15	2	10	33	21	116	6	7	236	280	380	660	6%	66%	0.18	105	78	2.83	-14
		23	24	SS	aaa	ARI	247	27	56	11	1	4	31	25	97	1	2	226	297	328	625	9%	61%	0.26	81	55	2.60	-56
Aliendo,Pablo	R	23	22	C	aa	CHC	321	37	63	20	1	11	46	31	125	4	0	198	268	368	636	9%	61%	0.25	130	73	2.62	-10
Amador,Adael	B	23	20	2B	aa	COL	35	2	5	0	0	1	1	3	8	2	1	136	202	212	414	8%	78%	0.38	36	66	1.23	-20
Amaya,Jacob	R	21	23	SS	aa	LA	417	42	74	12	1	9	33	34	117	3	0	177	239	272	511	8%	72%	0.29	59	68	1.81	-27
		22	24	SS	a/a	LA	476	51	97	15	2	12	43	47	132	4	2	203	274	316	590	9%	72%	0.35	75	69	2.40	-11
		23	25	SS	aaa	MIA	484	59	102	23	2	11	45	48	121	4	2	211	282	330	611	9%	75%	0.40	75	68	2.50	1
Anthony,Roman	L	23	19	CF	aa	BOS	35	8	12	4	0	1	7	6	6	2	0	333	436	520	957	15%	82%	1.05	121	81	7.45	84
Antico,Mike	L	22	24	CF	aa	STL	240	23	39	8	0	4	16	15	76	16	5	165	215	248	463	6%	68%	0.20	64	116	1.46	-27
		23	25	CF	aa	STL	476	58	99	19	3	12	48	35	146	35	9	209	264	334	597	7%	69%	0.24	81	126	2.48	-4
Auer,Mason	R	23	22	CF	aa	TAM	454	45	80	16	5	9	39	37	207	36	12	176	238	291	529	8%	54%	0.18	93	141	1.77	-48
Baldwin,Drake	L	23	22	C	a/a	ATL	65	5	19	1	0	2	6	5	16	0	0	294	344	382	726	7%	75%	0.31	48	8	4.58	-42
Ballesteros,Moises	L	23	20	1B	aa	CHC	21	2	5	0	0	0	1	1	3	0	0	216	244	216	460	4%	85%	0.24	0	40	1.71	-39
Banfield,Will	R	22	23	C	aa	MIA	116	11	27	4	1	2	12	4	28	0	0	236	260	343	603	3%	76%	0.13	70	58	2.52	-16
		23	24	C	aa	MIA	458	51	103	23	2	17	56	18	135	2	0	224	253	393	647	4%	70%	0.13	108	65	2.82	-3
Barber,Colin	L	23	23	LF	aa	HOU	270	31	57	14	1	9	30	33	85	4	2	211	298	365	663	11%	69%	0.39	103	63	2.93	0
Barger,Addison	L	22	23	SS	a/a	TOR	207	24	56	10	0	9	27	16	62	1	3	271	322	456	777	7%	70%	0.25	127	37	4.29	9
		23	24	RF	aaa	TOR	340	35	70	21	0	6	31	33	99	3	3	204	275	322	597	9%	71%	0.33	84	47	2.24	-15
Barrosa,Jorge	B	22	21	CF	aa	ARI	434	52	98	25	1	7	31	39	89	14	12	226	290	339	629	8%	80%	0.44	78	94	2.44	28
		23	22	CF	aaa	ARI	412	56	91	17	5	7	40	49	92	9	8	221	304	335	639	11%	78%	0.54	67	96	2.59	17
Beavers,Dylan	L	23	22	RF	aa	BAL	134	24	38	8	2	1	10	16	35	4	4	287	364	406	771	11%	74%	0.47	78	109	3.84	15
Beck,Jordan	R	23	22	LF	aa	COL	192	16	43	14	1	4	14	21	69	7	2	225	302	377	679	10%	64%	0.31	119	76	2.95	-4
Bericoto,Victor	R	23	22	RF	aa	SF	186	24	40	10	1	8	26	12	59	0	1	213	260	404	664	6%	68%	0.20	123	62	2.80	4
Bernabel,Warming	R	23	21	3B	aa	COL	302	22	64	14	1	5	21	11	66	1	0	212	239	315	555	3%	78%	0.16	64	47	2.07	-13
Berry,Jacob	B	23	22	1B	aa	MIA	113	17	25	5	1	4	17	7	28	4	0	225	269	385	654	6%	76%	0.25	93	114	3.06	24
Bigbie,Justice	R	23	24	LF	a/a	DET	294	41	85	14	0	8	37	20	56	4	1	291	336	422	758	6%	81%	0.36	76	56	4.53	17
Black,Tyler	L	23	23	3B	a/a	MIL	450	77	110	22	8	14	54	66	118	41	14	244	341	426	767	13%	74%	0.56	107	147	3.98	52
Bliss,Ryan	R	23	24	2B	a/a	SEA	540	75	129	27	4	16	59	37	146	38	18	240	288	391	679	6%	73%	0.25	94	122	3.02	18
Bonaci,Brainer	B	23	21	SS	aa	BOS	61	8	16	3	0	2	6	7	18	1	1	259	334	387	721	10%	71%	0.38	85	45	3.71	-14
Bowman,Cooper	R	23	23	2B	aa	OAK	271	34	59	15	2	5	26	26	75	24	3	216	284	340	624	9%	72%	0.34	83	134	2.77	15
Bradley,Tucker	L	22	24	LF	aa	KC	396	44	95	20	2	6	32	32	92	12	7	240	297	351	647	7%	77%	0.35	77	97	2.81	15
		23	25	LF	a/a	KC	303	34	70	20	3	4	38	29	82	8	5	233	299	361	661	9%	73%	0.35	88	94	2.69	9
Brito,Juan	B	23	22	2B	a/a	CLE	329	37	78	19	1	8	47	45	74	3	8	238	330	371	701	12%	78%	0.61	83	42	3.16	15
Brown,Vaun	R	23	25	CF	aa	SF	190	21	36	9	2	5	27	10	90	12	0	189	231	342	573	5%	52%	0.11	130	147	2.24	-30
Buelvas,Brayan	R	23	21	CF	aa	OAK	75	9	12	3	1	1	13	4	22	0	0	157	196	236	432	5%	71%	0.16	54	87	1.07	-37
Busch,Michael	L	21	24	2B	aa	LA	409	57	89	22	1	14	46	45	151	1	3	217	295	379	673	10%	63%	0.30	117	49	2.99	-17
		22	25	2B	a/a	LA	552	70	116	29	0	21	64	42	202	2	1	211	266	379	645	7%	63%	0.21	131	57	2.80	-8
		23	26	3B	aaa	LA	390	55	101	21	3	19	58	41	110	3	0	260	331	473	804	10%	72%	0.38	130	71	4.67	34
Bush,Homer	R	23	22	CF	aa	SD	28	2	11	1	0	0	3	1	2	1	1	383	402	413	815	3%	92%	0.36	21	36	5.63	2
Cabbage,Trey	L	21	24	RF	aa	MIN	244	29	54	9	1	13	35	23	126	1	0	222	289	420	709	9%	48%	0.18	171	61	3.60	-32
		22	25	1B	aa	LAA	113	13	29	5	1	7	20	13	57	6	2	258	332	484	816	10%	49%	0.22	208	99	4.83	15
		23	26	1B	aaa	LAA	418	50	100	19	2	20	53	27	177	19	4	239	285	439	725	6%	58%	0.15	149	107	3.75	-4
Caissie,Owen	L	23	21	RF	aa	CHC	439	59	112	27	2	15	64	58	180	5	10	255	342	430	773	12%	59%	0.32	138	59	3.93	-10
Callihan,Tyler	L	23	23	2B	aa	CIN	87	8	24	9	0	1	8	10	23	3	1	272	345	404	749	10%	74%	0.42	103	52	3.69	14
Caminero,Junior	R	23	20	3B	aa	TAM	314	44	87	8	2	16	49	25	67	2	4	278	332	476	809	7%	79%	0.38	102	60	4.87	32
Canario,Alexander	R	22	22	CF	a/a	CHC	375	44	74	16	2	19	49	32	126	13	3	198	261	405	666	8%	66%	0.25	144	109	2.96	31
		23	23	RF	aaa	CHC	145	15	32	10	0	5	23	10	52	1	0	223	273	391	664	6%	64%	0.19	125	45	2.95	-14
Cartaya,Diego	R	23	22	C	aa	LA	354	40	60	9	0	16	44	28	130	0	0	171	232	332	564	7%	63%	0.22	105	28	2.19	-38
Carter,Evan	L	22	20	RF	aa	TEX	21	6	8	2	0	1	5	4	7	1	1	376	467	558	1	15%	68%	0.53	144	92	8.08	45
		23	21	CF	a/a	TEX	411	54	104	14	4	9	46	57	120	18	12	252	343	377	720	12%	71%	0.47	77	103	3.58	2
Castanon,Marcos	R	23	24	2B	aa	SD	211	19	49	15	1	3	21	14	58	0	0	230	279	354	633	6%	72%	0.24	89	35	2.57	-14
Castillo,Neyfy	R	23	22	RF	aa	ARI	348	41	68	14	2	10	42	23	141	13	7	196	247	331	578	6%	60%	0.17	102	106	2.12	-34
Cheng,Tsung Che	L	23	22	SS	aa	PIT	247	29	57	10	1	3	21	15	54	11	3	231	274	319	593	6%	78%	0.27	55	100	2.53	-1
Chourio,Jackson	R	22	18	CF	aa	MIL	23	0	2	1	0	0	3	2	11	1	1	75	133	112	245	6%	51%	0.14	50	69	0.27	-119
		23	19	CF	a/a	MIL	531	70	137	25	2	19	72	35	115	35	9	258	304	419	723	6%	78%	0.30	92	108	3.86	34
Clarke,Denzel	R	23	23	CF	aa	OAK	234	37	50	10	3	7	30	26	94	8	1	213	293	372	665	10%	60%	0.28	114	128	3.01	-8
Clarke,Wes	R	22	23	1B	aa	MIL	59	6	12	2	0	4	6	5	25	0	0	208	269	414	683	8%	58%	0.20	156	14	3.36	-22
		23	24	1B	aa	MIL	398	48	80	21	0	20	57	65	176	4	1	201	314	404	718	14%	56%	0.37	160	45	3.55	-5
Clase,Jonatan	B	23	21	CF	aa	SEA	414	60	77	16	4	10	39	45	156	47	12	186	266	314	580	10%	62%	0.29	91	153	2.32	-10
Cook,Billy	R	23	24	RF	aa	BAL	447	49	94	13	1	17	63	33	140	23	3	211	265	357	622	7%	69%	0.23	90	103	2.89	-7
Corona,Kenedy	R	23	23	CF	aa	HOU	434	47	92	18	3	16	45	35	147	24	10	212	272	379	650	8%	66%	0.24	109	109	2.77	1
Cowser,Colton	L	22	22	CF	a/a	BAL	281	48	71	14	0	12	29	32	104	1	2	251	328	425	753	10%	63%	0.31	135	54	4.08	-2
		23	23	CF	aaa	BAL	323	51	80	14	1	11	44	46	120	6	3	248	342	397	739	12%	63%	0.38	106	71	4.00	-16
Crews,Dylan	R	23	21	CF	aa	WAS	72	6	14	5	0	0	4	7	21	3	3	194	267	264	531	9%	71%	0.35	62	64	1.46	-26
Crow Armstrong,Pete	L	23	21	CF	a/a	CHC	438	71	108	22	6	13	59	33	142	27	11	246	299	413	712	7%	68%	0.23	110	143	3.33	17
Davidson,Logan	B	21	24	SS	aa	OAK	448	37	78	19	1	5	34	44	177	3	3	174	248	253	501	9%	61%	0.25	67	53	1.55	-68
		22	25	SS	aa	OAK	424	45	81	17	1	8	35	33	160	3	1	192	250	291	541	7%	62%	0.21	82	64	1.96	-49
		23	26	1B	a/a	OAK	390	30	81	18	1	5	35	26	128	4	4	208	258	301	559	6%	67%	0.21	69	54	2.00	-45
Davis,Brennen	R	21	22	CF	a/a	CHC	323	44	71	21	0	12	35	35	122	4	4	221	298	398	696	10%	62%	0.29	132	59	3.14	-6
		22	23	CF	aaa	CHC	141	11	21	5	0	3	9	15	59	0	1	151	233	240	473	10%	58%	0.25	78	29	1.39	-75
		23	24	RF	aaa	CHC	219	17	32	6	0	2	17	14	66	6	3	147	198	207	405	6%	70%	0.21	43	71	1.04	-51

BATTER	B	Yr	Age	Pos	Lvl	Tm	AB	R	H	D	T	HR	RBI	BB	K	SB	CS	BA	OB	Slg	OPS	bb%	ct%	Eye	PX	SX	RC/G	BPV
De La Cruz,Carlos	R	22	23	LF	aa	PHI	151	15	35	10	1	5	16	6	51	1	0	232	259	409	668	4%	66%	0.11	135	62	2.90	0
		23	24	1B	aa	PHI	509	63	115	22	1	20	52	42	181	2	0	226	285	390	676	8%	64%	0.23	113	57	3.26	-17
De Los Santos,Deyvis	R	22	19	3B	aa	ARI	39	3	8	2	0	1	4	3	9	0	0	193	252	283	535	7%	76%	0.33	65	23	1.90	-22
		23	20	3B	aa	ARI	452	51	98	15	1	12	42	17	134	3	1	216	245	333	577	4%	70%	0.13	74	70	2.34	-29
Del Castillo,Adrian	L	23	24	C	a/a	ARI	357	33	73	16	1	7	42	37	131	1	2	206	280	319	599	9%	63%	0.28	85	44	2.35	-45
DeLauter,Chase	L	23	22	LF	aa	CLE	22	3	7	1	0	0	4	5	3	0	0	336	453	378	831	18%	85%	1.42	31	16	5.85	7
DeLoach,Zach	L	21	23	RF	aa	SEA	185	22	36	8	1	4	17	22	69	1	2	193	280	316	596	11%	63%	0.33	90	74	2.16	-31
		22	24	RF	aa	SEA	418	52	83	11	1	9	48	46	145	3	1	199	279	298	577	10%	65%	0.32	73	74	2.34	-36
		23	25	RF	aaa	SEA	528	56	113	23	1	14	55	48	218	5	4	214	280	342	622	8%	59%	0.22	100	57	2.65	-49
Dingler,Dillon	R	21	23	C	aa	DET	188	18	34	3	3	3	15	7	65	1	0	181	209	274	483	3%	66%	0.10	56	105	1.51	-52
		22	24	C	aa	DET	387	38	75	18	3	9	39	31	159	1	0	194	253	326	579	7%	59%	0.19	112	77	2.11	-35
		23	25	C	a/a	DET	281	34	53	15	1	7	35	25	110	2	1	189	255	327	582	8%	61%	0.23	107	69	2.13	-32
Dominguez,Jasson	B	23	20	CF	a/a	NYY	456	70	109	21	3	12	60	66	148	32	9	238	334	374	708	13%	68%	0.44	91	116	3.68	5
Dunn,Blake	R	23	25	CF	aa	CIN	295	52	84	11	2	13	36	29	100	21	6	284	349	408	816	9%	66%	0.29	117	134	5.36	18
Fabian,Jud	R	23	23	CF	aa	BAL	238	28	35	5	1	10	24	35	117	9	2	148	256	306	562	13%	51%	0.30	126	94	2.22	-41
Feduccia,Hunter	L	21	24	C	aa	LA	284	30	58	7	1	7	31	25	72	0	0	205	270	310	580	8%	75%	0.35	61	37	2.43	-24
		22	25	C	a/a	LA	294	27	53	15	0	10	30	23	99	0	0	181	241	337	577	7%	66%	0.23	117	33	2.12	-15
		23	26	C	aaa	LA	319	39	71	14	1	8	37	37	98	0	0	221	302	347	649	10%	69%	0.37	84	45	2.90	-20
Fernandez,Yanquiel	L	23	20	RF	aa	COL	218	15	43	10	0	7	19	11	74	0	0	199	237	342	579	5%	66%	0.15	99	10	2.24	-42
Foscue,Justin	R	21	22	2B	aa	TEX	93	12	21	7	0	2	11	7	31	0	1	226	279	351	630	7%	66%	0.22	98	49	2.45	-26
		22	23	2B	aa	TEX	400	39	92	25	1	9	53	30	75	2	5	231	284	368	652	7%	81%	0.39	90	43	2.72	25
		23	24	2B	aaa	TEX	462	61	101	26	3	13	55	57	81	9	8	218	304	369	673	11%	82%	0.71	86	78	2.87	46
Gauthier,Austin	R	23	24	SS	aa	LA	321	54	82	17	3	5	26	47	63	11	7	255	351	372	722	13%	80%	0.75	70	102	3.54	35
Gentry,Tyler	R	22	23	RF	aa	KC	274	36	73	15	0	9	40	24	71	5	5	268	326	421	747	8%	74%	0.33	106	61	3.97	17
		23	24	RF	aaa	KC	475	46	100	25	2	10	48	53	135	9	5	210	289	331	620	10%	71%	0.39	82	70	2.53	-5
Gomez,Moises	R	21	23	RF	aa	TAM	269	25	38	11	0	6	17	20	133	4	3	142	201	247	448	7%	51%	0.15	97	69	1.19	-83
		22	24	RF	a/a	STL	442	52	96	19	1	21	55	30	201	6	4	218	267	406	673	6%	55%	0.15	161	79	3.07	-14
		23	25	RF	aaa	STL	514	50	92	16	2	19	51	24	208	3	1	179	215	325	541	4%	60%	0.12	105	71	1.92	-46
Gonzalez,Jacob	R	23	25	1B	aa	PIT	308	24	63	8	1	6	35	13	65	0	1	205	237	296	533	4%	79%	0.20	51	32	1.98	-24
Goodman,Hunter	R	22	23	DH	aa	COL	44	3	8	0	0	1	2	2	12	1	0	192	223	283	506	4%	72%	0.14	51	40	2.04	-51
		23	24	LF	a/a	COL	410	43	92	26	0	25	69	27	119	0	1	224	272	473	745	6%	71%	0.23	154	15	3.60	26
Gorski,Matt	R	22	25	CF	a/a	PIT	143	17	32	7	1	3	18	10	56	7	2	222	272	363	635	7%	61%	0.18	115	137	2.65	-8
		23	26	CF	a/a	PIT	415	47	78	16	2	14	44	24	130	17	5	189	234	338	572	6%	69%	0.19	95	105	2.17	-5
Hackenberg,Adam	R	22	23	C	aa	CHW	42	2	6	1	0	1	1	2	16	0	0	132	173	205	378	5%	62%	0.13	56	13	0.95	-90
		23	24	C	a/a	CHW	340	34	75	13	0	6	26	30	101	2	0	221	283	314	598	8%	70%	0.29	64	44	2.59	-36
Halpin,Petey	L	23	21	CF	aa	CLE	452	48	101	21	3	8	33	44	135	10	2	223	292	335	627	9%	70%	0.33	76	91	2.71	-12
Hamilton,David	L	21	24	SS	aa	MIL	133	12	28	4	3	2	9	12	38	8	3	213	277	343	620	8%	72%	0.31	76	132	2.41	5
		22	25	2B	aa	BOS	463	53	96	15	6	7	27	36	136	45	9	207	264	313	577	7%	71%	0.26	72	167	2.38	7
		23	26	SS	aaa	BOS	393	47	80	13	5	11	34	43	127	36	17	203	282	346	628	10%	68%	0.34	90	131	2.52	4
Hardman,Tyler	R	23	24	3B	aa	NYY	283	43	57	8	2	20	43	31	130	7	3	203	281	458	739	10%	54%	0.24	188	100	3.67	19
Harris,Brett	R	22	24	3B	aa	OAK	315	33	71	12	1	6	29	20	73	7	5	224	270	327	597	6%	77%	0.27	68	88	2.41	2
		23	25	3B	a/a	OAK	387	38	82	19	2	5	38	31	80	6	1	212	271	307	578	7%	79%	0.39	60	81	2.23	6
Harris,Dustin	L	22	23	LF	aa	TEX	331	38	68	13	1	11	43	27	84	12	7	205	266	347	613	8%	75%	0.33	91	100	2.48	19
		23	24	LF	a/a	TEX	471	59	101	21	5	10	40	58	147	27	6	214	300	345	645	11%	69%	0.39	86	123	2.87	5
Haskin,Hudson	R	22	23	CF	aa	BAL	387	38	85	19	2	12	37	28	112	3	3	220	273	368	641	7%	71%	0.25	103	68	2.69	3
		23	24	CF	a/a	BAL	103	12	24	5	1	2	11	4	45	4	1	233	265	348	613	4%	56%	0.10	97	110	2.62	-55
Hassell III,Robert	L	22	21	CF	aa	WAS	108	7	22	5	0	1	10	10	37	1	0	201	270	267	537	9%	66%	0.27	60	35	1.96	-60
		23	22	CF	aa	WAS	414	48	86	15	1	7	33	46	167	12	5	207	287	301	588	10%	60%	0.28	74	78	2.41	-57
Helman,Michael	R	22	26	CF	a/a	MIN	512	61	99	18	2	11	36	38	136	24	6	194	249	304	553	7%	73%	0.28	74	126	2.13	6
		23	27	SS	a/a	MIN	130	15	28	6	1	4	23	5	27	3	1	218	249	377	626	4%	79%	0.20	90	86	2.58	25
Hernaiz,Darell	R	22	21	SS	aa	BAL	53	4	5	1	0	1	5	3	17	1	1	95	147	154	301	6%	68%	0.20	41	81	0.51	-55
		23	22	SS	a/a	OAK	498	57	131	28	3	5	46	34	83	8	6	263	310	361	671	6%	83%	0.40	61	77	3.09	20
Hernandez,Heriberto	R	23	24	RF	aa	TAM	389	47	80	15	2	10	44	56	158	5	2	207	306	333	639	13%	59%	0.35	96	76	2.79	-36
Hickey,Nathan	L	23	24	C	aa	BOS	291	37	66	16	0	12	42	29	101	2	0	227	297	404	701	9%	65%	0.29	123	49	3.46	-5
Hicks,Liam	L	23	24	C	aa	TEX	253	21	56	12	1	2	28	35	60	3	0	223	317	303	619	12%	76%	0.58	55	50	2.65	-10
Hinds,Rece	R	22	22	RF	aa	CIN	29	2	8	2	0	2	3	0	14	0	1	271	271	532	803	0%	53%	0.00	231	83	3.37	22
		23	23	RF	aa	CIN	412	45	99	25	4	20	70	25	171	14	7	240	283	466	749	6%	58%	0.15	170	106	3.57	15
Hiraldo,Miguel	R	23	23	2B	aa	TOR	320	32	78	19	0	10	42	19	123	12	6	244	288	397	684	6%	61%	0.16	118	69	3.21	-26
Holliday,Jackson	L	23	20	SS	a/a	BAL	217	36	61	11	2	4	19	29	54	3	2	281	367	399	766	12%	75%	0.55	75	84	4.24	11
Horwitz,Spencer	L	22	25	1B	a/a	TOR	403	52	89	27	1	9	34	47	111	5	2	222	303	358	661	10%	72%	0.42	102	75	2.85	17
		23	26	1B	aaa	TOR	392	39	105	24	1	7	47	48	88	6	2	268	349	386	734	11%	78%	0.55	77	51	3.90	11
House,Brady	R	23	20	3B	aa	WAS	139	18	43	8	2	3	11	6	45	1	1	311	342	459	801	4%	68%	0.14	103	82	4.63	-12
Hunt,Blake	R	21	23	C	aa	TAM	56	4	6	2	0	0	0	4	29	0	0	103	169	132	300	7%	49%	0.16	38	35	0.49	-146
		22	24	C	aa	TAM	273	21	53	12	1	3	26	14	85	1	0	193	234	277	511	5%	69%	0.17	68	57	1.70	-41
		23	25	C	a/a	TAM	246	28	50	17	0	9	28	15	74	1	2	205	251	377	628	6%	70%	0.21	117	46	2.41	1
Jackson,Jeremiah	R	22	22	2B	aa	LAA	307	28	53	13	0	10	28	25	86	4	4	174	236	309	546	7%	72%	0.29	93	58	1.86	-3
		23	23	3B	aa	NYM	440	54	98	16	1	18	71	45	166	24	10	222	294	382	676	9%	62%	0.27	112	89	3.22	-15
Jimenez,Leo	R	23	22	SS	a/a	TOR	352	46	83	16	1	6	35	29	75	6	2	237	295	343	638	8%	79%	0.39	65	81	2.87	9
Jones,Greg	L	21	23	SS	aa	TAM	54	6	9	1	1	1	1	3	24	5	0	158	202	244	446	5%	55%	0.12	62	175	1.53	-64
		22	24	SS	aa	TAM	319	36	60	16	2	5	27	18	156	25	6	188	232	295	527	5%	51%	0.12	111	161	1.83	-45
		23	25	CF	a/a	TAM	250	30	49	9	2	7	24	17	132	17	5	195	245	333	578	6%	47%	0.13	127	137	2.23	-54
Jones,Spencer	L	23	22	CF	aa	NYY	69	7	16	1	0	2	8	6	25	6	3	230	289	350	639	8%	64%	0.23	76	79	2.97	-44
Jordan,Blaze	R	23	21	1B	aa	BOS	189	15	44	9	0	5	24	9	29	0	0	235	270	364	634	5%	84%	0.31	72	14	2.83	11
Jung,Jace	L	23	23	2B	aa	DET	183	22	44	8	0	9	30	18	61	0	0	242	310	441	752	9%	66%	0.30	129	17	4.15	-6
Keirsey,DaShawn	L	22	25	CF	aa	MIN	425	38	89	21	2	4	30	20	129	26	8	210	246	298	545	5%	70%	0.16	71	127	1.96	-15
		23	26	CF	a/a	MIN	490	52	113	15	4	10	40	35	155	26	6	230	281	337	618	7%	68%	0.22	68	114	2.80	-23
Keith,Colt	L	23	22	3B	a/a	DET	507	66	135	34	3	18	75	46	131	2	2	265	327	450	776	8%	74%	0.35	116	61	4.15	27
Kjerstad,Heston	L	23	24	RF	a/a	BAL	479	64	120	23	5	14	40	31	114	4	5	251	297	406	703	6%	76%	0.27	91	82	3.31	17

BATTER	B	Yr	Age	Pos	Lvl	Tm	AB	R	H	D	T	HR	RBI	BB	K	SB	CS	BA	OB	Slg	OPS	bb%	ct%	Eye	PX	SX	RC/G	BPV
Langford,Wyatt	R	23	22	LF	a/a	TEX	61	8	21	5	0	3	8	13	15	3	2	346	458	589	1	17%	76%	0.85	150	43	8.28	72
Lawlar,Jordan	R	22	20	SS	aa	ARI	85	11	15	0	0	2	7	6	30	1	1	171	226	252	478	7%	65%	0.20	51	81	1.69	-61
		23	21	SS	a/a	ARI	417	62	96	20	3	11	44	36	112	23	6	229	291	370	661	8%	73%	0.33	88	123	3.08	18
Lee,Brooks	B	23	22	SS	a/a	MIN	501	59	117	34	2	11	60	42	104	5	4	234	294	376	670	8%	79%	0.40	89	65	2.88	25
León,Pedro	R	21	23	SS	a/a	HOU	246	29	45	7	1	7	25	28	103	12	11	183	267	302	569	10%	58%	0.27	88	97	1.98	-45
		22	24	CF	aaa	HOU	413	44	73	21	2	11	39	44	173	24	21	176	256	314	569	10%	58%	0.26	120	118	1.75	-15
		23	25	CF	aaa	HOU	483	47	93	18	2	14	45	40	196	13	8	192	254	327	580	8%	59%	0.20	100	83	2.17	-40
Leonard,Eddys	R	23	23	SS	a/a	DET	499	49	113	26	1	12	55	34	134	4	5	226	276	356	632	6%	73%	0.26	85	49	2.65	-9
Locklear,Tyler	R	23	23	1B	aa	SEA	77	8	16	5	1	1	6	8	17	1	0	213	284	320	603	9%	79%	0.46	72	77	2.32	15
Loftin,Nick	R	22	24	CF	a/a	KC	516	62	105	22	1	9	39	31	107	17	7	204	249	301	550	6%	79%	0.29	65	106	2.04	15
		23	25	3B	aaa	KC	315	27	69	11	0	8	37	22	51	4	5	218	269	335	604	7%	84%	0.43	64	41	2.49	13
Loperfido,Joey	L	23	24	CF	a/a	HOU	433	51	100	21	1	18	50	43	151	17	5	232	301	405	707	9%	65%	0.29	118	84	3.59	0
Lopez,Otto	R	21	23	2B	a/a	TOR	451	72	128	31	3	4	52	33	98	18	4	283	331	393	725	7%	78%	0.33	74	125	3.76	25
		22	24	2B	aaa	TOR	340	40	86	17	4	2	26	29	69	11	6	254	313	350	663	8%	80%	0.42	65	120	2.91	24
		23	25	SS	aaa	TOR	318	31	65	7	3	1	23	14	65	8	5	205	240	261	501	4%	80%	0.22	32	102	1.66	-15
Luciano,Marco	R	23	22	SS	a/a	SF	269	32	52	13	0	10	30	36	111	5	0	192	286	350	636	12%	59%	0.32	122	61	2.81	-23
Malloy,Justyn Henry	R	22	22	LF	a/a	ATL	215	32	52	11	0	6	29	40	72	2	0	243	362	375	737	16%	67%	0.56	102	50	3.99	-3
		23	23	3B	aaa	DET	487	62	112	21	1	14	58	79	168	3	1	229	337	364	701	14%	66%	0.47	94	53	3.53	-17
Manzardo,Kyle	L	22	22	1B	aa	TAM	99	13	27	9	0	3	19	10	23	1	1	269	338	456	794	9%	77%	0.45	131	46	4.19	48
		23	23	1B	aaa	CLE	343	34	67	22	1	12	37	40	90	1	1	196	280	366	645	10%	74%	0.44	108	31	2.62	14
Marsee,Jakob	L	23	22	CF	aa	SD	56	10	14	0	0	3	4	9	17	4	0	254	357	393	750	14%	70%	0.53	74	80	5.29	-9
Marte,Noelvi	R	23	22	3B	a/a	CIN	339	46	83	17	2	9	31	29	78	12	4	244	304	390	694	8%	77%	0.38	87	103	3.34	27
Martin,Austin	R	21	22	CF	aa	MIN	330	50	79	17	2	4	26	46	91	10	4	240	333	333	666	12%	72%	0.51	66	100	3.07	-1
		22	23	SS	aa	MIN	336	38	65	11	2	1	21	31	61	22	6	194	262	249	511	8%	82%	0.50	38	132	1.84	16
		23	24	2B	aaa	MIN	205	22	44	9	0	4	19	26	51	11	5	214	301	317	618	11%	75%	0.50	67	73	2.67	0
Martinez,Angel	B	22	20	2B	aa	CLE	82	8	18	6	1	2	13	9	20	2	1	219	296	388	685	10%	76%	0.46	114	80	2.88	42
		23	21	2B	a/a	CLE	525	56	116	20	3	11	62	39	130	9	3	220	275	333	608	7%	75%	0.30	68	88	2.56	-2
Martinez,Orelvis	R	22	21	SS	aa	TOR	433	38	73	13	0	22	50	25	151	3	3	169	215	348	563	5%	65%	0.17	124	44	2.04	-14
		23	22	SS	a/a	TOR	448	52	96	22	1	22	69	47	138	1	0	214	289	415	704	10%	69%	0.34	127	49	3.39	14
Martinez,Orlando	L	21	23	LF	aa	LAA	400	44	87	20	1	12	41	24	136	4	3	219	263	365	627	6%	66%	0.18	101	71	2.58	-21
		22	24	RF	a/a	LAA	385	30	80	14	3	6	39	22	109	5	8	207	251	303	554	5%	72%	0.20	68	76	1.87	-24
		23	25	RF	a/a	LAA	439	34	92	22	3	9	45	24	113	5	5	209	251	331	582	5%	74%	0.22	77	67	2.11	-9
Martorella,Nathan	L	23	22	1B	aa	SD	89	10	18	3	0	3	12	7	16	0	0	204	265	327	592	8%	82%	0.46	67	28	2.47	8
Mauricio,Ronny	R	21	20	SS	aa	NYM	31	2	9	1	0	1	1	2	13	2	0	277	310	375	686	5%	59%	0.12	74	50	4.11	-79
		22	21	SS	aa	NYM	509	49	109	21	1	18	62	17	146	14	12	214	240	368	608	3%	71%	0.12	104	86	2.30	3
		23	22	2B	aaa	NYM	490	53	115	24	2	14	49	26	115	17	8	235	274	380	654	5%	77%	0.23	86	88	2.89	14
Mayer,Marcelo	L	23	21	SS	aa	BOS	169	16	30	7	1	5	16	11	51	3	3	178	229	327	556	6%	70%	0.22	95	89	1.77	-3
Mayo,Coby	R	22	21	3B	aa	BAL	128	14	28	3	0	4	14	8	54	0	0	215	261	334	596	6%	58%	0.15	96	32	2.62	-67
		23	22	3B	a/a	BAL	504	64	124	37	2	20	76	72	162	4	1	247	341	447	788	13%	68%	0.45	138	63	4.23	28
McGeary,Haydn	R	23	24	1B	aa	CHC	361	41	77	12	1	11	54	49	120	3	3	213	306	340	646	12%	67%	0.40	84	47	2.91	-26
Mead,Curtis	R	22	22	3B	a/a	TAM	282	31	70	23	0	9	36	26	73	5	2	249	313	423	736	9%	74%	0.36	128	61	3.59	36
		23	23	3B	aaa	TAM	235	29	57	18	1	7	31	24	57	3	2	243	315	414	729	9%	76%	0.43	110	66	3.39	32
Meadows,Parker	L	22	23	CF	aa	DET	425	45	99	18	7	10	35	36	99	12	2	234	294	380	674	8%	77%	0.37	90	127	3.07	35
		23	24	CF	aaa	DET	449	53	94	23	6	11	44	40	137	13	2	210	274	365	639	8%	69%	0.29	100	121	2.61	12
Meckler,Wade	L	23	23	LF	a/a	SF	231	36	70	10	3	3	25	33	56	8	3	301	389	402	791	13%	76%	0.59	63	104	4.77	12
Meidroth,Chase	R	23	22	3B	aa	BOS	325	46	77	15	1	6	33	44	83	7	1	236	328	344	671	12%	75%	0.54	69	88	3.25	6
Melton,Jacob	L	23	23	CF	aa	HOU	52	7	11	1	0	4	10	3	19	4	0	218	260	464	724	5%	64%	0.16	149	86	4.12	15
Merrill,Jackson	L	23	20	SS	aa	SD	187	22	45	11	1	4	27	15	28	4	1	242	299	387	686	8%	85%	0.55	80	87	3.21	48
Mervis,Matt	L	22	24	1B	a/a	CHC	412	48	97	24	2	18	57	28	97	1	0	234	284	434	718	6%	77%	0.29	127	59	3.49	40
		23	25	1B	aaa	CHC	362	49	79	18	1	13	50	43	120	1	1	219	302	380	682	11%	67%	0.36	108	50	3.19	-7
Millas,Drew	B	22	24	C	aa	WAS	152	9	28	4	0	2	12	11	59	1	1	181	236	250	487	7%	61%	0.19	57	31	1.63	-85
		23	25	C	a/a	WAS	278	30	68	13	2	6	32	32	59	5	2	244	321	367	689	10%	79%	0.54	74	72	3.27	19
Misner,Kameron	L	21	23	CF	aa	MIA	55	10	15	6	0	1	3	6	19	2	2	269	342	421	762	10%	65%	0.31	130	85	3.32	10
		22	24	CF	aa	TAM	410	54	[illegible]	20	1	10	42	59	189	22	9	197	296	320	616	12%	55%	0.31	117	105	2.53	-30
		23	25	CF	aaa	TAM	421	56	75	20	3	14	38	60	225	14	7	178	280	343	623	12%	47%	0.27	137	112	2.41	27
Montgomery,Colson	L	22	20	SS	aa	CHW	48	3	6	1	0	2	5	1	16	0	0	124	149	241	390	3%	67%	0.09	78	31	0.97	-53
		23	21	SS	aa	CHW	131	19	27	7	1	3	15	19	39	0	1	210	308	355	663	12%	71%	0.48	95	71	2.74	6
Muncy,Max	R	19	25	LF	aaa	COL	390	44	113	29	4	8	39	27	93	1	0	289	336	442	778	7%	76%	0.29	117	106	5.33	42.7
		22	24	1B	aa	BAL	234	15	41	12	0	6	25	18	95	0	0	176	234	304	539	7%	59%	0.19	112	11	1.84	-54
		23	25	LF	aa	SF	294	40	71	13	0	4	25	19	53	13	5	243	290	328	618	6%	82%	0.37	52	88	2.80	11
Murray,BJ	B	23	23	3B	aa	CHC	452	53	102	29	3	11	55	61	145	10	3	225	317	376	693	12%	68%	0.42	106	90	3.13	9
Muzziotti,Simon	L	21	23	CF	a/a	PHI	41	2	9	2	0	0	6	4	7	1	0	217	290	256	546	9%	83%	0.61	30	43	2.23	-10
		22	24	CF	a/a	PHI	159	17	34	4	3	4	13	14	39	5	3	217	280	344	625	8%	75%	0.36	75	124	2.49	17
		23	25	LF	aaa	PHI	473	45	112	18	3	5	41	30	96	17	14	238	283	319	602	6%	80%	0.31	50	84	2.37	-2
Myers,Dane	R	21	25	3B	aa	DET	97	6	23	4	1	2	10	3	30	0	1	238	260	370	630	3%	69%	0.10	85	55	2.52	-30
		22	26	LF	a/a	DET	450	42	93	17	2	15	50	16	156	14	6	207	234	354	587	3%	65%	0.10	106	105	2.26	-14
		23	27	CF	a/a	MIA	374	52	96	12	2	10	42	34	96	14	4	257	318	385	703	8%	74%	0.35	74	102	3.77	6
Noel,Jhonkensy	R	22	21	RF	a/a	CLE	257	30	51	15	1	9	28	20	78	1	0	198	257	367	624	7%	69%	0.26	121	75	2.48	14
		23	22	LF	aaa	CLE	519	56	94	19	0	19	59	37	160	1	3	182	235	327	563	7%	69%	0.23	92	34	2.07	-24
Norby,Connor	R	22	22	2B	a/a	BAL	291	43	76	13	1	16	35	24	70	7	3	262	319	484	803	8%	76%	0.35	135	93	4.64	57
		23	23	2B	aaa	BAL	565	74	135	32	2	13	65	41	154	7	5	239	291	372	663	7%	73%	0.27	88	76	2.98	0
Nunez,Malcom	R	21	20	3B	aa	STL	202	19	43	4	0	4	13	13	47	1	1	212	261	288	549	6%	77%	0.29	44	43	2.23	-31
		22	21	1B	a/a	PIT	416	49	91	15	0	14	60	49	112	3	2	219	302	359	661	11%	73%	0.44	92	50	3.16	4
		23	22	1B	aaa	PIT	241	22	49	7	0	5	25	14	67	0	2	205	249	296	545	6%	72%	0.21	57	28	2.04	-44
Nunez,Nasim	B	22	22	SS	aa	MIA	142	17	32	5	0	0	11	18	40	16	6	227	315	264	579	11%	72%	0.46	36	108	2.55	-27
		23	23	SS	aa	MIA	490	63	97	10	2	4	32	64	116	39	8	198	291	249	540	12%	76%	0.55	32	114	2.28	-10
Nunez,Rainer	R	23	23	1B	aa	TOR	304	20	60	8	0	8	32	16	97	0	0	198	237	305	542	5%	68%	0.16	69	11	2.09	-58

BATTER	B	Yr	Age	Pos	Lvl	Tm	AB	R	H	D	T	HR	RBI	BB	K	SB	CS	BA	OB	Slg	OPS	bb%	ct%	Eye	PX	SX	RC/G	BPV
Ornelas,Jonathan	R	22	22	SS	aa	TEX	525	56	130	17	1	9	43	30	135	9	7	247	288	334	622	5%	74%	0.22	60	76	2.83	-20
		23	23	SS	aaa	TEX	434	52	91	15	1	6	35	51	137	10	1	210	293	292	584	10%	68%	0.37	58	88	2.45	-30
Ornelas,Tirso	L	22	22	LF	a/a	SD	455	40	101	23	1	4	33	28	103	4	2	223	268	305	574	6%	77%	0.28	62	67	2.20	-7
		23	23	RF	a/a	SD	478	50	107	23	1	11	52	46	126	6	7	225	293	345	638	9%	74%	0.36	78	53	2.70	-8
Ortiz,Joey	R	22	24	SS	a/a	BAL	539	58	124	28	4	14	54	31	112	5	2	230	273	373	646	5%	79%	0.28	91	88	2.78	29
		23	25	SS	aaa	BAL	349	45	89	23	2	6	40	22	81	8	5	256	300	382	682	6%	77%	0.27	83	91	3.05	15
Packard,Spencer	L	23	26	LF	aa	SEA	466	46	106	21	1	10	57	44	109	1	1	227	294	340	634	9%	77%	0.41	70	36	2.79	-7
Pages,Andy	R	22	22	RF	aa	LA	487	46	96	24	1	20	54	40	156	4	3	198	259	375	634	8%	68%	0.26	125	62	2.58	7
		23	23	CF	a/a	LA	112	17	27	10	1	2	18	18	39	5	3	239	347	409	756	14%	65%	0.47	134	93	3.40	25
Pages,Pedro	R	22	24	C	a/a	STL	291	22	48	11	0	5	25	21	115	1	0	165	222	257	479	7%	60%	0.18	79	35	1.49	-69
		23	25	C	aa	STL	424	42	89	19	1	10	49	39	112	2	0	210	276	333	609	8%	74%	0.35	77	56	2.54	-8
Palmegiani,Damiano	R	23	23	3B	a/a	TOR	467	51	103	29	1	18	67	51	171	5	0	220	296	397	693	10%	63%	0.30	130	59	3.27	-3
Parada,Kevin	R	23	22	C	aa	NYM	54	4	9	2	0	2	10	4	26	0	0	163	218	330	548	7%	52%	0.15	136	4	1.98	-66
Paris,Kyren	R	22	21	2B	aa	LAA	39	7	12	2	0	2	5	7	16	3	0	305	409	513	921	15%	59%	0.43	164	83	7.75	23
		23	22	SS	aa	LAA	415	58	93	20	1	11	33	64	169	32	5	225	328	359	687	13%	59%	0.38	106	103	3.57	-18
Pauley,Graham	L	23	23	3B	aa	SD	81	12	22	8	0	3	10	6	14	2	0	272	320	467	787	7%	83%	0.40	120	65	4.25	61
Pereira,Everson	R	22	21	CF	aa	NYY	113	16	28	3	2	4	10	7	42	2	2	244	288	410	698	6%	63%	0.17	117	119	3.15	-6
		23	22	LF	a/a	NYY	303	41	80	15	2	14	49	25	113	8	2	264	319	465	784	8%	63%	0.22	140	91	4.48	7
Perez, Jr.,Robert	R	19	19	DH	aaa	SEA	64	7	14	3	1	2	6	3	26	0	0	225	262	402	664	5%	59%	0.12	151	128	3.46	5.68
		23	23	RF	aa	SEA	450	41	89	18	2	12	46	26	182	1	2	199	242	326	569	5%	60%	0.14	97	58	2.09	-54
Perez,Wenceel	B	22	23	2B	aa	DET	150	19	40	8	6	3	19	10	25	3	4	269	317	465	781	6%	83%	0.41	109	121	3.35	72
		23	24	2B	a/a	DET	428	60	97	19	6	6	33	45	90	18	8	226	300	336	637	10%	79%	0.50	65	121	2.63	25
Perlaza,Yonathan	B	22	24	RF	aa	CHC	470	49	92	27	2	14	45	43	150	9	7	196	264	351	615	8%	68%	0.29	116	89	2.29	10
		23	25	LF	aaa	CHC	461	64	102	31	2	13	54	49	142	8	6	222	296	387	683	10%	69%	0.34	114	83	2.93	14
Pineda,Israel	R	22	22	C	a/a	WAS	114	13	25	4	0	6	19	10	27	1	0	216	280	409	688	8%	76%	0.37	114	40	3.46	27
		23	23	C	aa	WAS	98	5	13	3	0	1	8	6	38	0	0	137	187	195	382	6%	61%	0.16	48	17	0.91	-97
Placencia,Adrian	B	23	20	2B	aa	LAA	53	4	8	0	0	1	3	3	26	0	0	152	196	199	395	5%	52%	0.11	34	23	1.17	-147
Prieto,Cesar	L	22	23	3B	aa	BAL	368	29	78	18	0	3	24	10	64	1	6	211	231	285	516	3%	83%	0.15	53	41	1.63	-8
		23	24	2B	a/a	STL	498	50	131	21	2	7	47	20	60	6	8	263	291	352	643	4%	88%	0.33	50	61	2.88	20
Quero,Edgar	B	23	20	C	aa	CHW	368	38	82	15	0	5	42	55	80	1	2	223	324	304	628	13%	78%	0.68	52	25	2.76	-10
Quero,Jeferson	R	23	21	C	aa	MIL	335	35	76	11	0	13	37	29	78	4	0	227	289	376	664	8%	77%	0.37	84	50	3.32	7
Rafaela,Ceddanne	R	22	22	CF	aa	BOS	284	31	70	15	4	8	35	11	67	10	5	246	274	412	686	4%	76%	0.16	106	131	2.94	39
		23	23	CF	a/a	BOS	444	58	120	28	4	15	57	18	113	26	15	269	298	453	751	4%	75%	0.16	112	120	3.60	34
Ramirez,Agustin	R	23	22	C	aa	NYY	128	14	24	6	0	2	9	8	31	2	0	186	234	274	507	6%	76%	0.26	61	70	1.71	-12
Ramos,Bryan	R	22	20	3B	aa	CHW	80	6	15	2	0	2	8	4	16	0	1	191	226	313	539	4%	80%	0.22	73	29	1.87	-4
		23	21	3B	aa	CHW	291	33	69	8	1	12	34	28	81	3	3	236	304	389	693	9%	72%	0.35	89	48	3.49	-5
Ramos,Heliot	R	21	22	CF	a/a	SF	449	50	98	22	3	9	43	32	152	11	3	218	270	341	611	7%	66%	0.21	88	106	2.50	-18
		22	23	CF	aaa	SF	427	37	77	15	1	6	27	26	128	4	7	179	226	260	487	6%	70%	0.20	61	62	1.46	-40
		23	24	RF	aaa	SF	227	30	56	12	2	7	31	19	78	6	5	246	303	414	717	8%	66%	0.24	115	102	3.31	3
Ramos,Jose	R	23	22	CF	aa	LA	416	43	90	12	0	16	53	41	156	5	2	217	288	362	650	9%	62%	0.26	98	48	3.12	-38
Rhodes,John	R	22	22	RF	aa	BAL	90	8	14	2	1	0	6	8	24	0	0	157	225	212	437	8%	74%	0.33	39	77	1.07	-32
		23	23	LF	aa	BAL	408	47	79	18	2	12	54	42	134	6	1	194	270	336	606	9%	67%	0.31	96	83	2.45	-9
Ritter,Ryan	R	23	23	SS	aa	COL	25	3	4	1	0	0	1	2	11	1	0	144	210	182	392	8%	56%	0.19	43	91	1.10	-96
Rocchio,Brayan	B	21	20	SS	aa	CLE	184	28	51	13	3	5	25	11	44	6	4	275	315	457	773	6%	76%	0.25	110	128	3.75	43
		22	21	SS	a/a	CLE	510	55	110	23	1	12	43	36	115	9	10	215	266	335	601	7%	77%	0.31	80	72	2.33	11
		23	22	SS	aaa	CLE	468	57	109	27	3	5	46	45	74	18	8	233	301	338	640	9%	84%	0.61	64	101	2.66	38
Roden,Alan	L	23	24	RF	aa	TOR	174	27	47	5	1	5	21	19	37	7	2	271	343	392	736	10%	79%	0.52	67	87	4.29	18
Rodriguez,Alberto	L	23	23	RF	aa	SEA	179	13	43	7	0	2	20	14	61	4	2	241	296	316	611	7%	66%	0.23	57	43	2.72	-60
Rodriguez,Johnathan	R	22	23	RF	aa	CLE	107	7	19	6	1	4	11	4	49	0	1	175	201	359	560	3%	54%	0.07	164	82	1.62	-18
		23	24	RF	a/a	CLE	497	55	119	22	2	22	66	47	188	2	2	240	306	425	730	9%	62%	0.25	128	55	3.76	-13
Rodriguez,Jose	R	22	21	SS	aa	CHW	440	52	102	17	3	9	47	28	74	28	11	232	278	347	624	6%	83%	0.37	68	132	2.68	40
		23	22	2B	aa	CHW	469	52	105	16	0	17	44	15	117	22	10	225	248	368	616	3%	75%	0.12	83	87	2.62	1
Romo,Drew	B	23	22	C	a/a	COL	344	31	80	18	2	10	33	18	70	4	8	232	271	384	655	5%	80%	0.26	87	61	2.63	18
Rosario,Eguy	R	21	22	SS	aa	SD	420	50	102	27	2	9	47	40	121	23	16	243	308	380	688	9%	71%	0.33	94	104	2.95	11
		22	23	2B	aaa	SD	490	54	103	26	2	12	45	34	133	12	9	211	262	342	604	7%	73%	0.26	93	92	2.28	9
		23	24	3B	aaa	SD	166	14	32	6	0	3	16	12	48	2	5	192	244	289	534	6%	71%	0.24	64	61	1.69	-31
Rudick,Matt	L	23	25	LF	aa	NYM	214	38	49	9	0	7	26	41	51	10	1	229	354	368	722	16%	76%	0.81	83	84	4.04	31
Saggese,Thomas	R	22	20	2B	aa	TEX	21	3	7	3	1	1	6	1	3	1	0	331	353	672	1	3%	84%	0.21	198	133	6.01	143
		23	21	2B	a/a	STL	555	73	145	30	4	18	80	36	157	9	2	261	306	425	731	6%	72%	0.23	104	95	3.79	13
Salas,Ethan	L	23	17	C	aa	SD	28	2	5	1	0	0	3	4	8	0	1	166	260	198	458	11%	71%	0.44	28	35	1.12	-59
Schanuel,Nolan	L	23	21	1B	aa	LAA	60	11	18	3	1	1	9	12	10	1	0	301	416	415	831	16%	83%	1.17	64	83	5.29	44
Schobel,Tanner	R	23	22	2B	aa	MIN	177	14	34	5	1	1	13	19	45	2	1	191	269	251	520	10%	74%	0.41	40	55	1.82	-33
Schunk,Aaron	R	22	25	3B	aa	COL	450	37	95	27	1	9	46	20	125	4	2	211	245	335	580	4%	72%	0.16	93	62	2.13	-8
		23	26	3B	aaa	COL	458	39	105	20	4	9	42	23	134	7	8	230	268	350	617	5%	71%	0.17	78	72	2.41	-22
Scott,Victor	L	23	22	CF	aa	STL	282	37	77	10	1	5	25	13	50	32	9	275	306	370	675	4%	82%	0.25	53	126	3.60	20
Serretti,Danny	B	23	23	3B	aa	DET	156	11	27	6	0	1	11	19	39	1	1	176	267	228	495	11%	75%	0.50	40	31	1.53	-34
Severino,Yunior	B	22	23	3B	aa	MIN	143	12	31	7	0	5	16	9	55	0	1	220	267	371	638	6%	62%	0.17	122	25	2.71	-35
		23	24	3B	a/a	MIN	467	55	103	14	2	24	57	37	207	2	5	221	278	410	688	7%	56%	0.18	140	51	3.26	-33
Shenton,Austin	L	21	23	3B	aa	TAM	91	8	23	7	0	2	13	5	30	0	0	251	287	400	687	5%	68%	0.16	110	20	3.19	-24
		22	24	3B	aa	TAM	195	19	36	7	1	5	19	19	85	0	0	185	258	305	563	9%	56%	0.22	105	46	2.10	-57
		23	25	3B	a/a	TAM	473	71	117	38	0	21	69	66	188	0	0	246	338	458	797	12%	60%	0.35	166	26	4.34	8
Shewmake,Braden	L	21	24	SS	aa	ATL	324	34	67	13	2	10	34	14	83	3	2	206	239	352	592	4%	74%	0.17	86	86	2.25	3
		22	25	SS	aaa	ATL	278	28	62	12	1	5	19	18	66	7	0	222	269	337	606	6%	76%	0.27	77	104	2.60	11
		23	26	2B	aaa	ATL	474	56	88	22	2	11	49	27	130	19	1	186	231	309	540	5%	73%	0.21	80	119	1.98	3
Siani,Michael	L	22	23	CF	a/a	CIN	492	58	107	17	4	11	39	47	109	37	13	217	285	335	620	9%	78%	0.43	73	131	2.69	28
		23	24	CF	aaa	STL	409	46	74	14	2	6	32	49	132	15	5	180	268	264	532	11%	68%	0.37	59	99	1.91	-29

BATTER	B	Yr	Age	Pos	Lvl	Tm	AB	R	H	D	T	HR	RBI	BB	K	SB	CS	BA	OB	Slg	OPS	bb%	ct%	Eye	PX	SX	RC/G	BPV
Smith Njigba, Canaan	L	21	22	LF	a/a	PIT	240	27	54	10	0	4	31	36	80	10	1	225	326	321	647	13%	67%	0.45	70	76	3.16	-26
		22	23	LF	aaa	PIT	184	21	43	14	2	1	13	23	58	5	3	233	317	339	656	11%	69%	0.39	92	111	2.52	5
		23	24	LF	aaa	PIT	389	41	91	23	1	11	53	38	129	15	6	234	303	378	681	9%	67%	0.30	104	78	3.17	-6
Soto, Livan	L	21	21	SS	aa	LAA	40	2	8	1	0	0	3	2	12	0	0	195	241	218	458	6%	70%	0.20	20	19	1.49	-87
		22	22	SS	aa	LAA	456	45	105	14	1	4	37	47	116	12	9	230	302	290	593	9%	75%	0.41	44	69	2.49	-25
		23	23	SS	a/a	LAA	405	44	80	15	2	7	31	42	134	1	1	198	273	292	565	9%	67%	0.31	66	49	2.13	-44
Susac, Daniel	R	23	22	C	aa	OAK	50	1	12	1	0	1	6	1	15	1	0	234	256	289	545	3%	70%	0.10	36	19	2.38	-79
Sweeney, Trey	L	22	22	SS	aa	NYY	43	4	8	1	0	2	4	5	11	1	1	197	285	323	608	11%	74%	0.47	76	60	2.61	-3
		23	23	SS	aa	NYY	397	53	87	18	2	10	39	51	104	16	8	219	309	353	661	11%	74%	0.49	83	93	2.97	14
Tatum, Terrell	L	23	24	CF	aa	CHW	222	24	41	7	1	2	15	30	90	10	0	186	282	250	531	12%	59%	0.33	54	106	2.05	-62
Taylor, Samad	R	21	23	2B	aa	TOR	319	51	81	15	1	12	38	30	124	22	9	254	318	423	741	9%	61%	0.24	122	112	3.94	-5
		22	24	2B	aaa	TOR	244	31	54	9	1	7	34	20	70	17	6	220	279	358	637	8%	71%	0.28	91	133	2.86	15
		23	25	2B	aaa	KC	335	43	83	20	3	5	36	43	93	28	12	249	334	371	705	11%	72%	0.46	84	116	3.33	15
Teel, Kyle	L	23	21	DH	aa	BOS	31	2	9	2	0	1	9	6	12	2	0	301	417	443	859	17%	62%	0.53	111	35	6.23	-16
Tena, Jose	L	22	21	SS	a/a	CLE	535	54	120	23	4	10	45	19	160	5	6	224	251	335	586	3%	70%	0.12	81	87	2.21	-20
		23	22	SS	a/a	CLE	368	41	88	22	1	6	37	37	134	12	9	239	309	356	665	9%	64%	0.28	92	78	2.88	-28
Thompson, Sterlin	L	23	22	2B	COL		126	10	28	3	0	6	12	11	31	2	1	223	284	390	674	8%	75%	0.34	91	34	3.37	1
Tolbert, Tyler	R	23	25	SS	aa	KC	518	68	122	22	8	7	36	28	137	36	9	236	275	347	622	5%	74%	0.20	69	148	2.62	6
Tolentino, Milan	L	23	22	SS	aa	CLE	116	13	22	4	0	0	5	14	39	2	0	188	274	219	493	11%	67%	0.36	30	57	1.68	-69
Valdes, Javier	R	22	24	C	aa	ATL	78	10	15	3	1	2	8	13	24	1	0	197	309	307	616	14%	69%	0.53	77	84	2.56	-6
		23	25	C	aa	ATL	239	27	49	12	1	6	22	38	76	1	2	203	313	340	653	14%	68%	0.51	94	43	2.76	-9
Valenzuela, Brandon	B	23	23	C	aa	SD	94	8	14	3	0	1	5	10	33	2	0	150	234	210	444	10%	65%	0.31	48	53	1.31	-65
Valera, George	L	21	21	RF	aa	CLE	86	5	21	3	0	2	18	9	33	1	0	244	316	363	679	9%	62%	0.27	85	20	3.58	-59
		22	22	RF	a/a	CLE	484	59	100	21	2	16	54	48	165	1	2	207	279	359	637	9%	66%	0.29	111	63	2.66	-8
		23	23	CF	aaa	CLE	256	27	44	8	1	7	24	36	96	1	2	170	274	286	560	12%	63%	0.38	82	40	2.04	-45
Vaz, Javier	L	23	23	LF	aa	KC	112	13	30	4	2	1	9	11	19	3	1	270	336	372	707	9%	83%	0.59	54	91	3.62	24
Vazquez, Luis	R	21	22	SS	aa	CHC	29	2	6	1	0	0	1	1	9	0	0	213	233	244	478	3%	70%	0.09	28	17	1.61	-85
		22	23	SS	a/a	CHC	409	32	73	14	2	6	27	17	113	6	8	178	211	261	472	4%	72%	0.15	60	78	1.32	-30
		23	24	SS	a/a	CHC	454	49	100	19	0	13	55	37	140	7	12	221	279	346	626	8%	69%	0.26	84	48	2.53	-25
Veen, Zac	L	22	21	RF	aa	COL	124	8	19	4	0	1	4	8	42	3	5	153	207	199	406	6%	66%	0.20	40	64	0.88	-69
		23	22	RF	aa	COL	172	11	34	7	2	2	17	16	42	16	2	196	265	286	551	9%	76%	0.39	56	117	2.20	2
Vera, Arol	B	23	21	SS	aa	LAA	56	6	14	1	0	2	6	1	11	1	0	255	265	359	624	1%	80%	0.07	54	58	3.24	-14
Veras, Wilfred	R	22	20	DH	aa	CHW	45	4	10	2	0	2	4	2	15	0	0	230	266	449	715	5%	66%	0.14	158	3	3.48	3
		23	21	RF	aa	CHW	152	17	41	12	1	5	22	6	48	4	0	269	297	455	751	4%	69%	0.13	131	85	3.97	14
Vivas, Jorbit	L	23	22	2B	a/a	LA	506	73	120	22	2	10	47	50	80	19	5	237	305	351	657	9%	84%	0.62	64	100	3.11	38
Vukovich, A.J.	R	22	21	LF	aa	ARI	44	4	11	0	0	1	6	1	15	1	0	240	250	319	569	1%	67%	0.04	48	46	2.74	-75
		23	22	CF	aa	ARI	456	57	99	17	3	14	65	31	159	13	10	217	267	359	626	6%	65%	0.19	95	101	2.53	-19
Wagner, Max	R	23	22	3B	aa	BAL	111	13	25	6	1	2	14	6	37	1	1	221	259	345	604	5%	67%	0.16	88	76	2.29	-27
Wagner, Will	L	22	24	2B	aa	HOU	251	25	49	9	1	4	18	22	68	3	1	196	262	290	551	8%	73%	0.33	66	83	2.02	-13
		23	25	2B	a/a	HOU	233	27	65	16	2	5	24	19	61	3	2	278	332	423	756	8%	74%	0.31	96	70	3.95	10
Wallace, Cayden	R	23	22	3B	aa	KC	127	14	27	5	1	2	15	9	23	2	0	212	263	312	576	7%	82%	0.38	57	86	2.31	13
Wells, Austin	L	22	23	C	aa	NYY	211	25	46	6	1	9	32	22	68	5	0	217	290	382	672	9%	68%	0.32	110	88	3.40	7
		23	24	C	a/a	NYY	354	32	72	21	0	12	51	33	112	5	1	202	270	361	632	9%	68%	0.30	109	52	2.64	-4
Wendzel, Davis	R	21	24	SS	aa	TEX	187	21	38	9	0	5	19	18	58	1	2	201	270	334	604	9%	69%	0.30	89	43	2.36	-20
		22	25	SS	aaa	TEX	314	25	48	7	0	9	29	22	110	1	1	152	207	264	471	6%	65%	0.20	79	40	1.49	-50
		23	26	SS	aaa	TEX	453	52	84	15	0	20	46	49	154	2	4	184	265	353	617	10%	66%	0.32	108	38	2.57	-17
Whitcomb, Shay	R	22	24	2B	aa	HOU	461	42	78	17	1	12	38	23	196	13	2	170	209	291	500	5%	57%	0.12	103	111	1.64	-43
		23	25	SS	aa	HOU	538	53	104	16	0	25	68	28	217	14	8	194	233	362	595	5%	60%	0.13	117	65	2.36	-36
Wilken, Brock	R	23	21	3B	aa	MIL	23	2	4	2	0	2	6	2	10	0	0	193	243	480	723	6%	56%	0.15	229	7	3.09	23
Williams, Carson	R	23	20	SS	a/a	TAM	34	5	9	3	0	0	3	5	12	2	1	258	346	339	685	12%	64%	0.37	81	80	3.09	-30
Williams, Jett	R	23	20	SS	aa	NYM	22	5	5	1	0	0	2	2	11	1	0	211	275	252	527	8%	50%	0.18	52	101	2.08	-109
Wilson, Ethan	L	22	23	LF	aa	PHI	70	5	12	2	0	1	2	3	24	1	2	176	215	230	445	5%	66%	0.15	43	53	1.17	-73
		23	24	LF	aa	PHI	419	41	92	21	2	14	48	23	124	9	8	219	260	382	642	5%	70%	0.19	105	81	2.56	2
		21	23	RF	aa	LAA	296	39	62	7	0	16	41	28	117	19	8	209	277	391	668	9%	61%	0.24	121	95	3.17	-13
Wilson, Peyton	B	23	24	2B	aa	KC	489	51	122	31	4	4	47	39	107	14	8	250	306	354	660	7%	78%	0.37	70	93	2.81	13
Winn, Masyn	R	22	20	SS	aa	STL	345	40	68	19	1	6	28	28	92	17	6	197	257	305	562	7%	73%	0.30	81	109	2.06	8
		23	21	SS	aaa	STL	445	70	108	13	5	12	43	30	90	12	2	243	291	374	665	6%	80%	0.33	70	123	3.25	26
Wood, James	L	23	21	RF	aa	WAS	323	43	76	20	3	17	49	35	134	9	2	235	310	470	780	10%	58%	0.26	177	100	4.09	27
Yorke, Nick	R	23	21	2B	aa	BOS	444	58	113	23	7	11	48	39	127	14	5	255	315	414	728	8%	71%	0.30	100	120	3.53	19
Young, Jacob	R	23	24	LF	a/a	WAS	221	25	57	10	2	3	23	13	46	13	3	259	300	369	669	6%	79%	0.29	65	112	3.23	16
Zamora, Freddy	R	22	24	SS	aa	MIL	91	7	15	3	0	1	3	3	26	3	0	164	194	220	414	4%	71%	0.13	46	80	1.20	-46
		23	25	SS	aa	MIL	377	45	77	14	1	5	36	38	110	12	4	205	278	289	567	9%	71%	0.35	58	88	2.27	-23
Zavala, Aaron	L	22	22	RF	aa	TEX	112	19	25	7	0	3	14	14	32	3	1	226	313	371	684	11%	71%	0.44	106	80	3.21	18
		23	23	LF	aa	TEX	341	33	55	14	0	4	28	51	177	5	3	162	271	235	507	13%	48%	0.29	79	50	1.60	-101

PITCHER	Th	Yr	Age	LvL	Org	W	L	G	Sv	IP	H	ER	HR	BB	K	ERA	WHIP	BF/G	OBA	K%	BB%	K-BB	hr/9	H%	S%	BPV
Abel,Mick	R	22	21	aa	PHI	1	3	5	0	23	20	9	5	11	24	3.48	1.32	19.1	231	24%	11%	13%	1.9	26%	84%	53
		23	22	a/a	PHI	5	6	23	0	116	85	57	16	62	114	4.42	1.26	20.7	206	24%	13%	11%	1.2	24%	69%	68
Acker,Dane	R	23	24	aa	TEX	1	1	12	0	46	36	15	4	26	42	2.93	1.34	16.0	218	22%	13%	9%	0.8	27%	81%	71
Aguiar,Julian	R	23	22	aa	CIN	4	4	11	0	56	63	30	8	13	54	4.75	1.35	21.3	285	23%	5%	17%	1.2	35%	68%	101
Albright,Luke	R	23	24	aa	ARI	8	5	25	0	112	123	66	8	63	112	5.27	1.66	20.1	280	22%	13%	10%	0.7	36%	68%	70
Armbruester,Justin	R	22	24	aa	BAL	4	1	14	2	64	53	27	14	15	51	3.77	1.06	17.7	226	20%	6%	14%	2.0	23%	76%	65
		23	25	a/a	BAL	6	6	26	0	122	122	54	13	51	87	4.02	1.42	19.9	262	17%	10%	7%	1.0	30%	74%	48
Arrighetti,Spencer	R	22	22	aa	HOU	1	1	5	0	21	13	7	3	8	25	3.13	0.99	16.0	179	31%	10%	21%	1.1	23%	74%	117
		23	23	a/a	HOU	9	7	28	0	126	102	62	11	54	124	4.40	1.24	18.3	223	24%	11%	14%	0.8	28%	65%	88
Ashcraft,Braxton	R	23	24	aa	PIT	0	1	8	0	20	17	4	0	5	18	1.75	1.11	9.8	231	23%	7%	16%	0.0	31%	83%	128
Askew,Keyshawn	L	23	23	aa	TAM	1	0	11	3	23	16	13	1	13	23	4.91	1.26	8.6	198	24%	14%	10%	0.4	26%	59%	93
Barnett,Mason	R	23	23	aa	KC	2	1	7	0	34	30	15	2	11	34	3.85	1.21	19.7	238	25%	8%	16%	0.5	31%	68%	108
Bastardo,Angel	R	23	21	aa	BOS	0	1	3	0	16	13	11	3	9	9	5.93	1.37	22.4	229	13%	13%	0%	1.9	22%	61%	2
Beers,Blake	R	23	25	aa	OAK	3	10	18	0	82	106	72	13	33	58	7.86	1.70	20.6	314	16%	9%	7%	1.4	35%	54%	25
Beeter,Clayton	R	21	23	aa	LA	0	2	5	0	15	10	7	2	6	20	4.10	1.09	11.7	197	33%	10%	23%	1.1	27%	66%	122
		22	24	aa	NYY	0	3	25	0	77	70	41	11	45	110	4.78	1.48	13.2	242	32%	13%	19%	1.3	35%	71%	98
		23	25	a/a	NYY	9	7	27	0	133	121	61	19	75	139	4.12	1.47	21.2	243	24%	13%	11%	1.3	30%	76%	63
Bellozo,Valente	R	23	23	aa	HOU	0	1	4	1	17	10	3	2	6	11	1.70	0.90	16.0	168	16%	9%	8%	1.1	17%	92%	60
Bergert,Ryan	R	23	23	aa	SD	1	2	9	0	44	35	15	1	17	44	3.10	1.18	19.5	220	25%	10%	16%	0.2	30%	72%	115
Berroa,Prelander	R	22	22	aa	SEA	2	1	9	0	35	20	15	2	21	48	3.93	1.17	15.5	166	32%	14%	18%	0.6	25%	67%	123
		23	23	aa	SEA	5	1	43	6	66	48	22	2	34	89	2.93	1.23	6.2	204	33%	13%	21%	0.3	32%	75%	135
Birdsong,Hayden	R	23	22	aa	SF	0	3	8	0	23	24	17	2	13	29	6.48	1.60	12.7	268	28%	13%	15%	0.7	38%	58%	93
Black,Mason	R	23	24	a/a	SF	4	9	29	0	125	109	57	14	52	130	4.07	1.29	17.7	237	25%	10%	15%	1.0	30%	71%	86
Bolton,Cody	R	19	21	aa	PIT	2	3	9	0	40	46	37	7	17	28	8.29	1.57	19.5	358	16%	10%	6%	1.6	31%	34%	25
		22	24	aaa	PIT	4	2	30	0	77	60	26	3	38	67	3.01	1.28	10.5	217	21%	12%	9%	0.4	27%	76%	83
		23	25	aaa	PIT	3	4	34	1	48	45	23	2	18	36	4.25	1.31	5.9	247	18%	9%	9%	0.4	30%	66%	76
Boyle,Joe	R	22	23	aa	CIN	0	2	6	0	26	23	15	3	24	27	5.15	1.81	20.1	237	23%	20%	2%	1.2	29%	74%	52
		23	24	a/a	OAK	8	8	25	0	118	84	45	5	84	135	3.44	1.42	20.0	201	27%	17%	10%	0.4	28%	75%	99
Brnovich,Kyle	R	21	24	aa	BAL	2	1	15	0	62	60	29	11	14	60	4.16	1.20	16.7	255	24%	6%	18%	1.6	30%	72%	94
Brown,Ben	R	22	23	aa	CHC	3	0	7	0	31	32	12	2	11	38	3.56	1.40	18.7	270	27%	8%	19%	0.7	38%	76%	117
		23	24	a/a	CHC	8	8	26	0	94	78	44	8	53	108	4.24	1.39	15.3	226	27%	13%	14%	0.8	31%	71%	90
Burke,Sean	R	22	23	a/a	CHW	2	9	21	0	80	85	44	12	33	91	4.99	1.47	16.4	273	26%	9%	16%	1.3	35%	69%	79
		23	24	aaa	CHW	1	4	9	0	38	40	34	10	27	28	7.96	1.75	19.4	270	16%	16%	0%	2.4	27%	59%	-11
Burns,Tanner	R	22	24	aa	CLE	3	7	21	0	90	83	38	14	43	78	3.77	1.39	18.1	245	20%	11%	9%	1.4	28%	79%	49
		23	25	aa	CLE	5	3	29	1	88	82	37	13	47	70	3.79	1.46	13.0	249	18%	12%	6%	1.3	28%	79%	40
Burrows, Michael	R	22	23	a/a	PIT	5	6	24	0	95	86	41	6	29	92	3.87	1.21	16.0	243	23%	7%	16%	0.6	31%	68%	107
Bush,Ky	L	22	23	aa	LAA	7	4	21	0	103	94	39	13	27	86	3.44	1.17	19.6	245	20%	6%	14%	1.1	29%	75%	86
		23	24	aa	CHW	4	7	15	0	69	79	53	19	37	56	6.92	1.67	20.7	289	18%	12%	6%	2.4	30%	64%	1
Caceres,Kelvin	R	23	23	a/a	LAA	6	1	41	3	45	37	23	3	25	55	4.48	1.37	4.6	226	29%	13%	16%	0.6	32%	67%	104
Cameron,Noah	L	23	24	aa	KC	3	10	17	0	73	99	56	13	25	57	6.94	1.70	19.4	324	17%	8%	10%	1.6	36%	61%	30
Cannon,Jonathan	R	23	23	aa	CHW	1	4	11	0	49	67	34	9	15	32	6.17	1.66	20.0	325	15%	7%	8%	1.7	35%	66%	21
Canterino,Matt	R	22	25	aa	MIN	0	1	11	0	35	18	7	1	21	41	1.71	1.09	12.5	152	28%	14%	14%	0.2	23%	84%	122
Cantillo,Joey	L	22	23	aa	CLE	4	3	14	0	62	41	14	2	26	75	1.99	1.08	17.3	189	31%	11%	20%	0.3	28%	82%	134
		23	24	a/a	CLE	7	4	26	0	120	115	60	18	72	121	4.48	1.56	20.2	253	23%	14%	9%	1.4	31%	75%	53
Cavalli,Cade	R	21	23	a/a	WAS	4	8	17	0	84	83	45	5	48	87	4.86	1.55	21.7	258	24%	13%	11%	0.5	34%	68%	82
		22	24	aaa	WAS	6	4	20	0	97	80	41	3	36	85	3.77	1.19	19.5	227	21%	9%	12%	0.3	29%	67%	99
Cecconi,Slade	R	22	23	aa	ARI	7	6	26	0	131	136	55	16	27	106	3.77	1.24	20.5	269	19%	5%	14%	1.1	31%	74%	95
		23	24	aaa	ARI	5	9	23	0	117	123	69	16	31	97	5.30	1.31	21.1	271	20%	6%	14%	1.2	31%	62%	73
Champlain,Chandler	R	23	24	aa	KC	5	5	14	0	73	73	36	11	24	49	4.40	1.33	21.6	261	16%	8%	8%	1.3	28%	71%	43
Church,Marc	R	22	21	aa	TEX	1	3	14	1	15	18	11	3	6	18	6.45	1.58	4.7	294	26%	9%	17%	1.9	37%	63%	68
		23	22	a/a	TEX	9	4	43	2	62	56	25	7	36	68	3.63	1.48	6.2	243	26%	13%	12%	1.0	32%	79%	76
Coffey,Isaac	R	23	23	aa	BOS	7	4	12	0	58	53	30	13	23	60	4.67	1.30	20.0	244	25%	9%	16%	2.0	28%	72%	58
Cooke,Connor	R	23	24	a/a	TOR	3	2	29	3	37	38	18	4	15	51	4.37	1.42	5.5	267	32%	9%	23%	1.0	38%	71%	117
Crow,Coleman	R	22	22	aa	LAA	9	3	24	0	128	132	63	18	31	112	4.46	1.28	21.9	268	20%	6%	14%	1.3	31%	69%	85
		23	22	aa	LAA	2	0	4	0	24	10	5	3	6	27	2.02	0.64	20.7	125	33%	7%	26%	1.2	14%	82%	157
Cusick,Ryan	R	22	23	aa	OAK	1	6	12	0	41	52	28	3	26	36	6.17	1.89	16.1	311	18%	13%	5%	0.6	38%	66%	52
		23	24	a/a	OAK	5	8	23	0	99	87	50	12	58	69	4.50	1.46	18.5	236	16%	14%	3%	1.1	26%	72%	37
Dallas,Chad	R	23	23	aa	TOR	7	3	18	0	98	95	50	16	35	91	4.56	1.32	22.6	255	22%	9%	14%	1.5	30%	70%	64
Daniel,Davis	R	21	24	a/a	LAA	1	5	14	0	68	80	38	10	13	76	5.01	1.37	20.4	295	27%	5%	22%	1.3	38%	66%	140
Danner,Hagen	R	23	25	a/a	TOR	1	2	31	1	38	32	16	8	8	41	3.86	1.07	4.8	232	28%	6%	22%	2.0	27%	76%	111
De Avila,Luis	L	23	22	a/a	ATL	6	10	26	0	129	114	52	8	62	116	3.64	1.36	20.8	238	21%	11%	10%	0.6	30%	74%	78
Del Rosario,Joelvis	R	23	22	aa	OAK	2	1	5	0	25	35	18	5	6	13	6.54	1.59	22.3	328	12%	5%	7%	1.6	34%	61%	20
Denoyer,Noah	R	22	24	aa	BAL	1	2	14	2	53	32	15	9	10	56	2.62	0.80	13.8	177	29%	5%	23%	1.5	20%	80%	147
		23	25	aaa	BAL	3	0	25	1	52	55	34	8	37	50	5.90	1.77	9.6	273	21%	16%	5%	1.3	33%	69%	40
Dodd,Dylan	L	22	24	a/a	ATL	3	4	10	0	55	60	23	4	14	52	3.75	1.34	23.0	276	24%	7%	17%	0.7	35%	73%	104
		23	25	aaa	ATL	4	6	16	0	76	97	55	14	30	57	6.47	1.67	21.4	312	17%	9%	8%	1.6	35%	64%	25
Dollard,Taylor	R	22	23	aa	SEA	16	2	27	0	144	106	33	7	27	115	2.06	0.93	20.0	208	20%	5%	15%	0.5	25%	80%	133
Drohan,Shane	L	22	23	aa	BOS	1	1	5	0	24	23	10	5	10	17	3.57	1.37	20.1	251	17%	10%	7%	1.7	26%	83%	28
		23	24	a/a	BOS	10	7	27	0	123	139	79	22	70	105	5.81	1.69	20.6	286	19%	13%	6%	1.6	33%	69%	27
Enlow,Blayne	R	22	23	aa	MIN	1	3	24	3	58	60	26	3	27	54	3.98	1.50	10.5	269	21%	10%	11%	0.5	34%	73%	79
		23	24	a/a	MIN	5	6	26	0	100	107	59	14	31	93	5.29	1.38	16.2	275	22%	7%	15%	1.3	33%	64%	75
Espino,Daniel	R	22	21	aa	CLE	1	0	4	0	19	9	5	4	4	31	2.41	0.68	16.7	149	46%	5%	40%	1.8	20%	86%	240
Estes,Joey	R	23	22	a/a	OAK	9	6	27	0	139	112	49	16	37	110	3.19	1.07	20.1	222	20%	7%	13%	1.1	25%	75%	83
Festa,David	R	23	23	a/a	MIN	4	4	24	0	93	89	42	8	40	104	4.06	1.39	16.3	253	26%	10%	16%	0.8	34%	72%	96
Fitts,Richard	R	23	24	aa	NYY	11	5	27	0	154	152	70	24	44	141	4.11	1.27	23.3	259	22%	7%	15%	1.4	30%	73%	78
Flores,Wilmer	R	22	21	aa	DET	6	4	19	0	85	68	27	7	19	80	2.89	1.02	17.2	222	23%	5%	18%	0.7	28%	74%	131
		23	22	aa	DET	5	3	18	0	82	78	38	4	31	69	4.21	1.34	19.0	253	20%	9%	11%	0.5	31%	68%	81
Fluharty,Mason	L	23	22	aa	TOR	2	5	36	4	43	54	22	6	17	47	4.62	1.63	5.3	306	24%	9%	16%	1.3	39%	75%	71
Franklin,Kohl	R	23	24	aa	CHC	4	10	21	0	87	99	61	17	37	71	6.33	1.55	18.2	287	19%	10%	9%	1.8	32%	63%	30

PITCHER	Th	Yr	Age	LvL	Org	W	L	G	Sv	IP	H	ER	HR	BB	K	ERA	WHIP	BF/G	OBA	K%	BB%	K-BB	hr/9	H%	S%	BPV
Frasso,Nick	R	23	25	a/a	LA	4	6	25	0	95	100	45	5	30	89	4.22	1.37	16.0	271	22%	8%	15%	0.4	35%	68%	100
Fulton,Dax	L	22	21	aa	MIA	1	1	4	0	21	10	6	2	6	26	2.73	0.76	18.8	139	33%	8%	25%	0.8	19%	68%	158
		23	22	aa	MIA	2	4	7	0	33	35	21	4	18	33	5.75	1.61	20.9	273	23%	12%	10%	1.1	34%	65%	59
Gasser,Robert	L	22	23	a/a	MIL	3	3	9	0	48	42	18	3	23	50	3.33	1.34	22.3	235	25%	11%	14%	0.5	31%	76%	95
		23	24	aaa	MIL	9	1	26	0	136	135	61	13	49	145	4.06	1.35	21.9	261	25%	9%	17%	0.8	34%	72%	97
Gil,Luis	R	21	23	a/a	NYY	5	1	20	1	82	67	41	10	46	101	4.49	1.37	17.3	224	29%	13%	16%	1.1	30%	70%	90
		22	24	aaa	NYY	0	3	6	0	23	23	20	6	14	26	7.67	1.60	17.1	258	26%	14%	12%	2.3	30%	56%	35
Ginn,J.T.	R	22	23	aa	OAK	1	4	10	0	36	37	21	2	12	35	5.26	1.37	15.1	268	21%	7%	14%	0.5	34%	60%	98
		23	24	aa	OAK	1	2	6	0	23	29	20	2	12	9	7.82	1.78	17.7	306	8%	12%	-3%	0.6	32%	53%	11
Gipson Long,Sawyer	R	22	25	aa	DET	5	6	15	0	74	91	50	10	14	55	6.12	1.42	21.0	304	17%	5%	13%	1.3	34%	58%	77
		23	26	a/a	DET	8	8	22	0	101	97	54	18	30	97	4.83	1.25	18.7	253	24%	7%	16%	1.6	29%	67%	76
Gomez,Yoendrys	R	22	23	aa	NYY	1	0	4	0	17	15	7	1	6	17	3.79	1.20	17.2	236	24%	8%	16%	0.5	31%	68%	106
		23	24	aa	NYY	0	3	19	0	66	54	31	7	38	67	4.23	1.39	14.7	226	24%	13%	11%	0.9	29%	71%	76
Gonzalez,Wikelman	R	23	21	aa	BOS	3	1	10	0	49	30	15	2	27	54	2.79	1.16	19.5	179	28%	14%	14%	0.4	25%	76%	109
Gordon,Colton	L	23	25	a/a	HOU	7	7	29	1	129	125	62	18	56	127	4.33	1.40	18.8	256	23%	10%	13%	1.2	31%	73%	68
Graceffo,Gordon	R	22	22	aa	STL	7	4	18	0	95	67	29	9	18	69	2.78	0.89	19.6	199	18%	5%	13%	0.9	22%	74%	108
		23	23	aaa	STL	4	3	21	0	86	89	45	7	39	67	4.68	1.49	17.6	268	18%	11%	8%	0.8	32%	69%	56
Granillo,Andre	R	23	23	a/a	STL	3	4	53	14	69	54	35	7	33	74	4.52	1.26	5.3	216	26%	12%	14%	0.9	28%	65%	90
Groome,Jay	L	21	23	aa	BOS	2	0	3	0	17	13	5	0	4	22	2.38	1.01	22.0	217	33%	6%	27%	0.0	34%	74%	200
Guerrero,Luis	R	23	23	a/a	BOS	3	3	49	19	57	33	16	3	35	56	2.47	1.19	4.7	171	24%	15%	9%	0.5	22%	81%	92
Hall,DL	L	21	23	aa	BAL	2	0	7	0	33	17	12	4	15	46	3.23	0.98	18.0	157	36%	12%	24%	1.2	21%	73%	126
		22	24	a/a	BAL	3	8	23	0	83	69	42	11	46	106	4.54	1.38	15.2	227	29%	13%	17%	1.2	31%	70%	93
		23	25	aaa	BAL	1	2	17	1	49	42	25	6	29	56	4.51	1.46	12.3	233	27%	14%	13%	1.1	30%	72%	76
Hamel,Dominic	R	23	24	aa	NYM	8	6	26	0	124	128	67	12	54	138	4.83	1.47	20.5	268	26%	10%	16%	0.9	35%	68%	88
Hancock,Emerson	R	21	22	aa	SEA	1	1	3	0	15	11	6	0	4	12	3.25	0.97	19.2	202	21%	7%	14%	0.0	26%	63%	122
		22	23	aa	SEA	7	4	21	0	99	80	38	13	33	81	3.41	1.14	18.7	223	20%	8%	12%	1.2	25%	76%	70
		23	24	aa	SEA	11	5	20	0	98	90	49	8	34	92	4.51	1.26	20.0	246	23%	8%	15%	0.8	31%	65%	91
Harrison,Kyle	L	22	21	aa	SF	4	2	18	0	84	63	30	9	37	112	3.17	1.19	18.7	209	32%	11%	21%	1.0	30%	78%	118
		23	22	aaa	SF	1	3	20	0	67	53	33	8	44	92	4.42	1.44	14.3	219	32%	15%	17%	1.0	32%	72%	98
Henry,Cole	R	22	23	a/a	WAS	1	0	9	0	33	15	6	2	10	28	1.72	0.76	13.2	139	24%	9%	15%	0.5	17%	81%	116
		23	24	aa	WAS	0	2	10	0	19	28	28	6	14	18	13.22	2.20	9.6	343	18%	15%	4%	3.0	38%	39%	-27
Hernandez,Daysbel	R	21	25	a/a	ATL	3	2	36	3	45	38	24	5	25	47	4.78	1.39	5.3	231	24%	13%	11%	0.9	29%	67%	76
		23	27	a/a	ATL	1	0	17	2	20	7	1	0	9	24	0.57	0.80	4.3	115	34%	12%	22%	0.0	19%	92%	157
Herz,DJ	L	22	21	aa	CHC	1	4	9	0	33	23	25	4	27	37	6.68	1.51	16.0	196	23%	17%	6%	1.0	25%	55%	73
		23	22	aa	WAS	3	3	22	0	95	79	46	6	59	117	4.37	1.45	18.4	227	29%	14%	14%	0.6	32%	70%	101
Hodge,Porter	R	23	22	aa	CHC	6	7	35	0	82	68	48	3	45	89	5.20	1.37	9.8	226	26%	13%	13%	0.3	31%	59%	101
Horton,Cade	R	23	22	aa	CHC	1	1	6	0	27	19	4	0	10	27	1.38	1.08	17.6	200	25%	10%	16%	0.0	28%	86%	124
Hughes, Garbriel	R	23	22	aa	COL	2	2	6	0	29	40	30	10	11	23	9.27	1.77	22.2	330	17%	8%	9%	3.0	34%	52%	-16
Hurt,Kyle	R	22	24	aa	LA	1	5	12	0	31	36	31	3	32	38	8.87	2.21	13.0	293	22%	19%	3%	0.9	40%	58%	61
		23	25	a/a	LA	4	4	26	0	92	79	46	11	43	127	4.48	1.33	14.7	234	33%	11%	22%	1.1	34%	69%	111
Hurter,Brant	L	22	24	aa	DET	0	2	4	0	15	23	12	1	4	14	7.29	1.73	17.3	345	21%	6%	15%	0.5	43%	55%	96
		23	25	aa	DET	6	7	26	0	118	125	50	7	34	105	3.83	1.35	18.9	273	21%	7%	14%	0.5	34%	71%	97
Ingram,Kolton	L	21	25	aa	LAA	0	0	12	4	15	10	2	0	6	14	1.38	1.09	4.9	196	24%	10%	13%	0.0	27%	86%	114
		22	26	aa	LAA	6	2	50	10	62	42	18	6	17	59	2.60	0.94	4.7	194	25%	7%	18%	0.8	24%	77%	116
		23	27	a/a	LAA	3	4	45	4	63	47	22	3	34	61	3.17	1.29	5.8	210	23%	13%	10%	0.5	27%	76%	88
Iriarte,Jairo	R	23	22	aa	SD	0	1	13	0	30	22	15	2	16	45	4.44	1.26	9.5	209	37%	13%	24%	0.6	34%	64%	138
Jacob,Alek	R	22	24	a/a	SD	2	1	39	4	50	45	15	4	14	52	2.65	1.15	5.1	239	25%	7%	19%	0.7	31%	80%	123
		23	25	aa	SD	1	0	18	5	28	22	5	1	8	27	1.44	1.05	6.0	214	25%	7%	17%	0.3	28%	88%	125
Jarvis,Bryce	R	21	24	aa	ARI	1	2	8	0	35	35	23	7	16	33	5.95	1.46	18.7	261	22%	11%	11%	1.9	30%	64%	41
		22	25	aa	ARI	3	6	25	0	108	144	89	21	53	88	7.41	1.82	20.1	321	18%	10%	7%	1.7	36%	61%	18
		23	26	a/a	ARI	9	6	27	0	107	106	57	7	49	89	4.82	1.45	16.9	260	19%	11%	9%	0.6	32%	66%	67
Jarvis,Justin	R	22	22	aa	MIL	2	1	4	0	20	15	6	1	14	14	2.64	1.47	21.5	215	17%	17%	0%	0.4	26%	83%	60
		23	23	a/a	NYM	6	11	26	0	120	139	73	17	60	121	5.49	1.65	20.7	290	23%	11%	11%	1.3	36%	69%	56
Jones,Jared	R	23	22	a/a	PIT	5	9	26	0	127	118	62	12	50	120	4.40	1.32	20.2	248	23%	9%	13%	0.9	31%	68%	80
Joyce,Ben	R	23	23	aa	LAA	0	1	14	4	17	8	9	1	12	21	4.59	1.17	4.9	137	30%	18%	12%	0.6	19%	60%	110
Joyce,Jimmy	R	23	24	aa	SEA	0	3	7	0	32	31	14	1	9	25	3.80	1.25	18.7	257	19%	7%	12%	0.3	32%	68%	97
Juenger,Hayden	R	22	22	a/a	TOR	3	7	38	2	90	66	37	18	32	86	3.71	1.08	9.3	205	24%	9%	15%	1.8	22%	76%	67
		23	23	aaa	TOR	5	2	54	2	76	89	52	10	34	78	6.09	1.61	6.2	293	23%	10%	13%	1.2	37%	63%	63
Kelley,Jared	R	23	22	aa	CHW	0	3	16	0	23	36	32	3	28	24	12.49	2.81	8.1	360	18%	22%	-4%	1.3	45%	53%	17
Kelly,Antoine	L	22	23	aa	TEX	0	0	7	0	20	12	14	0	16	20	6.17	1.39	12.2	175	23%	19%	5%	0.0	25%	51%	100
		23	24	a/a	TEX	3	1	49	11	60	49	14	4	22	65	2.01	1.18	4.9	222	27%	9%	18%	0.6	30%	86%	112
Kent,Zak	R	21	23	aa	TEX	0	4	6	0	30	40	21	10	9	33	6.29	1.62	22.4	318	25%	7%	18%	3.0	36%	72%	35
		22	24	a/a	TEX	3	4	24	0	111	101	44	10	38	90	3.55	1.26	18.9	244	20%	8%	11%	0.8	29%	74%	74
		23	25	aaa	TEX	0	1	10	0	34	28	16	4	10	28	4.11	1.12	13.4	228	21%	7%	13%	1.1	26%	66%	80
Kerkering,Orion	R	23	22	a/a	PHI	1	1	22	7	23	23	6	2	5	29	2.15	1.20	4.2	261	32%	5%	27%	0.8	37%	87%	176
Kilian,Caleb	R	21	24	aa	CHC	4	4	15	0	80	75	27	5	12	66	3.06	1.08	20.9	248	21%	4%	17%	0.6	30%	73%	145
Kloffenstein,Adam	R	22	22	aa	TOR	2	5	19	0	86	98	53	11	37	75	5.59	1.57	19.9	287	19%	9%	10%	1.2	34%	66%	53
		23	23	a/a	STL	7	6	26	0	128	111	43	12	48	116	3.05	1.25	20.0	236	22%	9%	13%	0.8	29%	79%	83
Knack,Landon	R	21	24	aa	LA	2	1	6	0	24	20	11	6	3	23	4.07	0.94	15.2	227	25%	3%	22%	2.1	24%	69%	178
		22	25	aa	LA	2	10	17	0	66	68	35	8	24	66	4.77	1.38	16.4	266	23%	9%	15%	1.1	33%	68%	80
		23	26	a/a	LA	5	1	22	0	101	101	33	10	30	81	2.92	1.29	18.9	261	19%	7%	12%	0.9	31%	81%	75
Kochanowicz,Jack	R	23	23	aa	LAA	4	5	16	0	71	89	56	17	21	47	7.08	1.55	19.4	307	15%	7%	9%	2.1	32%	58%	14
Kouba,Rhett	R	23	24	aa	HOU	8	7	28	0	128	125	51	14	35	117	3.55	1.25	18.6	257	23%	7%	16%	1.0	31%	75%	94
Leasure,Jordan	R	22	24	aa	LA	2	2	44	5	50	39	19	8	17	53	3.43	1.12	4.5	218	26%	8%	18%	1.4	26%	77%	93
		23	25	a/a	CHW	2	4	44	11	49	42	24	11	25	63	4.32	1.36	4.7	233	31%	12%	19%	1.9	29%	77%	72
Leiter,Jack	R	22	22	aa	TEX	3	10	23	0	94	87	52	9	49	93	4.93	1.44	17.5	247	22%	12%	10%	0.8	31%	66%	74
		23	23	a/a	TEX	2	6	20	0	87	79	50	16	47	96	5.15	1.45	18.6	244	26%	13%	13%	1.7	30%	69%	59
Lin,Yu-Min	L	23	20	aa	ARI	5	2	11	0	61	48	26	5	22	56	3.85	1.14	22.0	217	23%	9%	14%	0.7	27%	67%	94
Little,Luke	L	23	23	a/a	CHC	5	2	31	1	49	29	14	1	32	71	2.52	1.24	6.5	173	35%	16%	20%	0.1	29%	78%	140

PITCHER	Th	Yr	Age	LvL	Org	W	L	G	Sv	IP	H	ER	HR	BB	K	ERA	WHIP	BF/G	OBA	K%	BB%	K-BB	hr/9	H%	S%	BPV
Lopez,Jacob	L	23	25	a/a	TAM	4	5	26	0	108	79	34	9	54	110	2.81	1.23	16.8	206	25%	12%	13%	0.7	27%	80%	90
Madden,Ty	R	22	22	aa	DET	2	2	7	0	37	29	11	5	11	41	2.62	1.07	20.7	216	29%	8%	21%	1.2	27%	83%	115
		23	23	aa	DET	3	4	26	0	118	112	50	14	50	120	3.85	1.38	19.0	252	24%	10%	14%	1.1	31%	76%	77
Maldonado,Anthony	R	22	24	a/a	MIA	4	3	42	4	65	51	23	8	19	72	3.12	1.07	6.1	215	29%	8%	21%	1.1	27%	76%	117
		23	25	aaa	MIA	7	3	34	9	46	26	10	5	21	56	1.99	1.02	5.2	168	32%	12%	20%	1.0	22%	88%	114
Martinez,Justin	R	23	22	aaa	ARI	2	1	47	9	50	31	19	2	40	57	3.46	1.42	4.5	182	27%	19%	8%	0.3	26%	75%	100
Mata,Bryan	R	19	20	aa	BOS	4	6	11	0	55	65	41	7	24	51	6.73	1.62	22.3	364	21%	10%	11%	1.2	35%	50%	60
Mattison,Tyler	R	23	24	aa	DET	2	0	22	4	34	23	7	0	18	37	1.81	1.20	6.2	191	27%	13%	14%	0.0	28%	83%	118
Mazur,Adam	R	23	22	aa	SD	2	3	12	0	38	50	18	3	6	38	4.27	1.49	13.7	319	23%	4%	19%	0.7	41%	72%	149
McDermott,Chayce	R	22	24	aa	BAL	1	1	6	0	28	18	19	8	19	29	5.92	1.31	19.4	187	25%	16%	9%	2.4	17%	63%	33
		23	25	a/a	BAL	8	8	26	1	121	79	47	8	69	121	3.45	1.21	18.8	187	25%	14%	11%	0.6	24%	73%	90
McGarry,Griff	R	22	23	a/a	PHI	1	5	15	0	42	21	16	3	27	41	3.41	1.13	11.1	150	24%	16%	8%	0.6	19%	71%	90
		23	24	a/a	PHI	1	3	16	0	61	44	45	4	50	65	6.56	1.53	16.7	204	25%	19%	6%	0.7	27%	55%	80
McGreevy,Michael	R	22	22	aa	STL	6	4	20	0	99	96	37	8	19	63	3.32	1.16	19.7	256	15%	5%	11%	0.8	29%	74%	84
		23	23	a/a	STL	13	6	27	0	155	182	68	14	33	102	3.91	1.39	24.2	294	16%	5%	11%	0.8	33%	74%	72
Mederos,Victor	R	23	22	aa	LAA	4	9	20	0	92	100	62	23	40	87	6.10	1.53	20.0	279	22%	10%	12%	2.2	31%	66%	29
Mejia,Juan	L	23	24	a/a	TEX	0	1	9	0	17	23	14	3	10	10	7.16	1.91	8.9	321	12%	12%	0%	1.6	34%	64%	-5
Melendez,Jaime	R	22	21	aa	HOU	2	8	23	0	75	58	37	6	44	95	4.44	1.36	13.7	215	29%	14%	16%	0.7	31%	68%	104
Mena,Cristian	R	23	21	a/a	CHW	8	7	27	0	135	132	75	20	62	133	5.01	1.43	21.3	257	23%	11%	12%	1.3	31%	68%	63
Meyer,Max	R	21	22	a/a	MIA	6	4	22	0	111	102	33	8	42	113	2.70	1.30	20.8	246	25%	9%	16%	0.7	32%	82%	98
		22	23	aaa	MIA	3	4	12	0	58	41	25	4	17	56	3.81	1.02	18.5	202	24%	8%	17%	0.7	26%	63%	113
Miller,Erik	L	22	24	a/a	PHI	1	1	32	0	49	42	19	4	29	51	3.55	1.45	6.5	232	24%	14%	10%	0.7	30%	77%	80
		23	25	a/a	SF	3	1	54	15	63	34	19	2	46	72	2.75	1.27	4.8	161	28%	18%	10%	0.3	23%	78%	110
Miller,Mason	R	23	25	a/a	OAK	1	0	5	0	17	5	2	1	3	24	0.96	0.46	11.3	096	43%	5%	38%	0.8	13%	94%	274
Misiorowski,Jacob	R	23	21	aa	MIL	2	1	5	0	21	18	13	2	15	33	5.61	1.55	18.3	229	36%	16%	20%	0.8	37%	64%	115
Montero,Keider	R	23	23	a/a	DET	15	4	23	0	112	124	65	13	44	113	5.20	1.50	21.1	282	23%	9%	14%	1.0	35%	67%	77
Monteverde,Patrick	L	22	25	aa	MIA	1	0	6	0	32	42	19	5	6	26	5.42	1.50	23.2	318	20%	5%	15%	1.3	37%	66%	88
		23	26	a/a	MIA	11	6	23	0	124	125	67	19	53	94	4.87	1.43	23.0	263	18%	10%	8%	1.3	29%	69%	40
Montgomery,Mason	L	22	22	aa	TAM	3	1	11	0	55	39	13	4	14	48	2.20	0.97	19.0	202	22%	6%	16%	0.6	25%	80%	115
		23	23	a/a	TAM	7	4	29	0	127	111	56	19	55	126	3.92	1.30	18.1	236	24%	11%	13%	1.3	28%	75%	68
Murphy,Ryan	R	23	24	aa	SF	2	9	29	0	108	120	64	15	54	90	5.33	1.61	16.5	282	19%	11%	8%	1.2	33%	69%	42
Nastrini,Nick	R	22	22	aa	LA	1	1	6	0	31	14	13	5	13	37	3.71	0.88	19.2	137	31%	11%	20%	1.4	15%	64%	108
		23	23	a/a	CHW	9	5	25	0	116	105	56	12	54	115	4.34	1.36	19.4	242	24%	11%	13%	1.0	30%	70%	77
Nicolas,Kyle	R	21	22	aa	MIA	3	2	8	0	40	26	13	3	25	44	2.97	1.28	20.6	188	26%	15%	11%	0.7	25%	79%	92
		22	23	aa	PIT	2	4	24	0	92	74	39	7	44	84	3.80	1.28	15.7	220	21%	11%	10%	0.7	27%	71%	78
		23	24	a/a	PIT	4	7	35	2	100	114	68	17	54	100	6.14	1.67	12.9	287	22%	12%	10%	1.6	35%	66%	44
Nikhazy,Doug	L	23	24	aa	CLE	4	8	26	0	102	109	70	15	81	106	6.19	1.87	18.4	275	22%	17%	5%	1.3	34%	68%	44
Nowlin,Jaylen	L	23	22	aa	MIN	3	1	9	0	39	32	15	3	21	31	3.55	1.33	18.1	223	19%	13%	6%	0.8	26%	75%	61
Nuñez,Juan	R	23	27	aa	TOR	2	3	32	1	40	26	21	2	43	46	4.69	1.70	5.7	184	25%	24%	2%	0.5	26%	72%	86
Pacheco,Freddy	R	21	23	a/a	STL	1	0	17	3	24	8	4	1	8	32	1.35	0.65	4.9	105	38%	9%	28%	0.3	16%	81%	182
Palmquist,Carson	L	23	23	aa	COL	0	2	4	0	23	23	15	6	9	22	5.68	1.39	24.3	260	22%	9%	13%	2.2	28%	66%	36
Parker,Mitchell	L	23	24	a/a	WAS	9	7	28	0	126	132	77	15	61	127	5.47	1.54	19.7	271	23%	11%	12%	1.0	34%	65%	67
Perkins,Jack	R	21	24	a/a	PHI	3	5	18	0	85	105	47	14	26	63	4.94	1.54	20.6	304	17%	7%	10%	1.5	34%	72%	39
		22	25	a/a	PHI	3	5	28	0	63	84	55	11	32	47	7.86	1.84	10.5	321	16%	11%	5%	1.6	36%	58%	15
Pham,Alex	R	23	24	aa	BAL	0	2	14	1	62	50	21	5	17	44	3.09	1.08	17.3	221	18%	7%	11%	0.7	25%	73%	81
Phillips,Connor	R	22	21	aa	CIN	1	5	12	0	47	50	26	3	32	54	4.91	1.75	18.0	274	25%	15%	10%	0.6	37%	72%	78
		23	22	a/a	CIN	4	5	25	1	107	97	47	12	54	136	3.94	1.40	18.1	242	30%	12%	18%	1.0	34%	75%	98
Pinto,Jean	R	23	22	aa	BAL	2	1	9	0	29	35	14	4	12	24	4.25	1.63	14.3	303	18%	9%	9%	1.2	35%	77%	46
Povich,Cade	L	22	22	aa	BAL	2	2	6	0	24	22	18	5	10	22	6.66	1.31	16.6	242	21%	10%	12%	2.0	26%	52%	44
		23	23	a/a	BAL	8	10	28	0	128	116	77	16	64	142	5.43	1.40	19.3	243	26%	12%	14%	1.1	31%	63%	79
Raya,Marco	R	23	21	aa	MIN	0	3	11	0	29	22	16	2	13	23	5.06	1.22	10.6	214	20%	11%	9%	0.5	26%	57%	77
Reynolds,Sean	R	22	24	aa	MIA	2	0	24	4	26	25	16	3	10	23	5.37	1.31	4.5	250	21%	9%	12%	1.0	30%	59%	72
		23	25	a/a	SD	3	2	55	12	66	63	36	4	44	61	4.94	1.62	5.3	253	21%	15%	6%	0.6	32%	69%	65
Richardson,Lyon	R	23	23	a/a	CIN	0	3	21	0	61	50	28	2	36	71	4.08	1.40	12.3	224	27%	14%	14%	0.3	32%	70%	104
Robaina,Julio	L	22	21	aa	HOU	2	6	23	0	82	91	55	9	53	75	6.04	1.76	16.4	283	19%	14%	6%	1.0	34%	66%	47
		23	22	aa	HOU	10	6	26	0	116	112	44	6	45	102	3.38	1.36	18.6	256	21%	9%	12%	0.5	32%	75%	85
Robberse,Sem	R	22	21	aa	TOR	0	3	5	0	26	19	9	4	8	16	3.13	1.03	20.2	202	16%	8%	8%	1.2	21%	76%	53
		23	22	a/a	STL	5	6	26	0	126	111	56	16	49	110	3.97	1.27	19.9	238	21%	9%	12%	1.2	28%	73%	67
Robertson,Nick	R	21	23	aa	LA	2	4	39	4	60	57	22	5	14	54	3.36	1.19	6.2	251	22%	6%	16%	0.7	31%	73%	110
		22	24	a/a	LA	1	3	53	9	69	62	29	6	25	73	3.76	1.25	5.3	239	25%	8%	16%	0.8	31%	72%	100
		23	25	aaa	BOS	4	1	42	9	44	37	17	5	12	46	3.36	1.12	4.1	229	26%	7%	19%	1.1	29%	75%	111
Roby,Tekoah	R	23	22	aa	STL	2	3	14	0	59	56	29	5	13	58	4.38	1.17	16.8	251	25%	5%	19%	0.8	32%	63%	130
Rock,Joe	L	23	23	a/a	COL	1	10	20	0	94	110	56	18	33	86	5.35	1.51	20.4	293	21%	8%	13%	1.7	34%	69%	51
Rodriguez,Carlos	R	23	22	a/a	MIL	9	6	26	0	131	92	42	10	54	143	2.88	1.10	19.8	198	28%	10%	17%	0.7	26%	76%	110
Rodriguez,Randy	R	22	23	a/a	SF	0	2	11	0	16	10	13	2	18	22	7.57	1.75	6.7	186	27%	22%	5%	0.9	27%	55%	92
		23	24	a/a	SF	2	2	43	1	70	57	38	3	55	68	4.83	1.59	7.2	223	22%	18%	4%	0.4	29%	68%	75
Roupp,Landen	R	22	24	aa	SF	2	1	5	0	27	21	12	3	11	26	3.92	1.18	21.7	214	24%	10%	14%	0.9	26%	69%	86
		23	25	aa	SF	0	0	10	0	31	26	8	1	10	34	2.19	1.16	12.4	232	28%	8%	20%	0.3	32%	81%	135
Rutledge,Jackson	R	23	24	a/a	WAS	8	4	23	0	121	111	58	14	55	90	4.29	1.37	22.1	244	18%	11%	7%	1.0	28%	71%	50
Ryan,River	R	23	25	a/a	LA	1	7	26	0	105	103	50	11	45	92	4.32	1.41	17.1	258	21%	10%	11%	1.0	31%	72%	64
Salinas,Royber	R	23	22	aa	OAK	1	5	18	1	68	60	40	7	29	75	5.23	1.30	15.6	239	27%	10%	16%	0.9	31%	60%	94
Sanchez,Sixto	R	19	21	aa	MIA	8	4	18	0	103	111	45	6	22	85	3.90	1.29	23.5	314	20%	5%	15%	0.5	34%	65%	102
Santos,Junior	R	23	22	aa	NYM	4	8	28	3	97	136	77	10	43	64	7.16	1.85	16.2	332	14%	10%	5%	0.9	37%	60%	27
Sauer,Matt	R	22	23	aa	NYY	0	2	4	0	22	23	19	5	7	30	7.50	1.35	23.2	272	32%	7%	25%	2.0	36%	46%	107
		23	24	aa	NYY	6	4	14	0	69	57	31	12	29	72	4.04	1.25	20.1	226	25%	10%	15%	1.6	27%	74%	70
Scott,Christian	R	23	24	aa	NYM	4	3	12	0	62	52	21	5	9	66	3.10	0.99	19.7	230	28%	4%	24%	0.7	30%	71%	202
Seymour,Carson	R	23	25	aa	SF	5	3	28	0	114	115	63	8	46	93	4.96	1.41	17.3	264	19%	10%	10%	0.6	32%	64%	70
Seymour,Ian	L	22	24	aa	TAM	0	2	5	0	18	23	14	2	11	20	6.92	1.84	17.0	305	25%	14%	11%	0.8	40%	61%	69

PITCHER	Th	Yr	Age	LvL	Org	W	L	G	Sv	IP	H	ER	HR	BB	K	ERA	WHIP	BF/G	OBA	K%	BB%	K-BB	hr/9	H%	S%	BPV
Slaten, Justin	R	22	25	aa	TEX	1	6	25	0	52	52	38	5	45	51	6.47	1.84	9.7	259	21%	18%	3%	0.9	33%	64%	54
		23	26	a/a	TEX	5	3	40	2	61	50	21	11	20	68	3.03	1.14	6.1	223	28%	8%	20%	1.6	27%	83%	94
Small, Ethan	L	21	24	a/a	MIL	4	2	17	0	77	59	19	4	41	78	2.19	1.30	18.7	214	25%	13%	12%	0.5	28%	85%	92
		22	25	aaa	MIL	7	6	27	0	103	89	52	8	57	96	4.58	1.42	16.2	235	22%	13%	9%	0.7	30%	68%	74
		23	26	aaa	MIL	2	4	38	3	51	46	20	6	25	51	3.57	1.38	5.6	242	24%	11%	12%	1.0	30%	77%	75
Smith-Shawver, AJ	R	23	21	a/a	ATL	3	2	12	0	48	34	21	4	28	51	4.01	1.29	16.4	201	26%	14%	12%	0.7	26%	70%	89
Solometo, Anthony	L	23	21	aa	PIT	2	4	12	0	53	56	31	7	14	41	5.21	1.33	18.4	273	19%	7%	12%	1.1	31%	62%	69
Speas, Alex	R	23	25	a/a	TEX	5	2	49	4	58	38	19	2	38	69	2.96	1.29	4.9	186	29%	16%	13%	0.3	27%	77%	110
Spiers, Carson	R	22	25	a/a	CIN	4	6	27	0	123	162	84	33	47	88	6.15	1.70	20.6	318	16%	9%	8%	2.4	33%	71%	-4
		23	26	a/a	CIN	9	3	29	0	85	82	39	8	42	86	4.09	1.46	12.5	255	24%	12%	12%	0.8	33%	73%	77
Stone, Gavin	R	22	24	a/a	LA	8	5	20	0	98	72	14	2	32	117	1.29	1.06	19.1	207	30%	8%	22%	0.2	31%	88%	151
		23	25	aaa	LA	7	4	21	0	102	96	57	13	44	100	5.02	1.36	20.4	249	23%	10%	13%	1.1	31%	65%	72
Stuart, Tyler	R	23	24	aa	NYM	3	2	7	0	35	40	18	4	10	24	4.52	1.44	21.3	290	16%	7%	10%	1.1	33%	71%	53
Sullivan, Sean	R	23	23	aa	PIT	8	4	24	0	115	125	62	15	40	78	4.87	1.44	20.4	278	16%	8%	8%	1.2	31%	69%	42
Swiney, Nick	L	23	24	a/a	SF	3	2	32	1	57	63	30	5	31	40	4.72	1.63	8.0	279	16%	12%	4%	0.8	32%	72%	40
Tamarez, Misael	R	22	22	a/a	HOU	4	7	28	1	122	81	53	17	61	126	3.88	1.17	17.4	191	25%	12%	13%	1.2	23%	72%	79
		23	23	aaa	HOU	1	10	26	2	101	91	54	17	54	88	4.81	1.43	16.5	242	21%	12%	8%	1.5	27%	71%	44
Tarnok, Freddy	R	21	23	aa	ATL	3	2	9	0	45	42	17	2	16	51	3.46	1.29	20.6	250	28%	9%	19%	0.5	35%	73%	120
Thompson, Matthew	R	22	22	aa	CHW	0	2	7	0	26	26	14	3	10	27	4.88	1.39	15.7	263	24%	9%	15%	1.0	33%	67%	83
		23	23	aaa	CHW	6	15	27	0	125	120	73	17	85	113	5.23	1.64	20.7	254	20%	15%	5%	1.2	30%	70%	44
Tiedemann, Ricky	L	23	21	a/a	TOR	0	5	12	0	36	31	18	1	19	56	4.56	1.40	12.7	235	37%	13%	24%	0.2	40%	65%	145
Vasil, Mike	R	23	23	a/a	NYM	5	6	26	0	124	113	67	16	46	121	4.87	1.28	19.5	244	24%	9%	15%	1.1	30%	64%	81
Vasquez, Randy	R	21	23	aa	NYY	2	1	4	0	22	26	12	2	7	16	4.81	1.51	23.9	296	17%	7%	10%	0.9	34%	69%	57
		22	24	a/a	NYY	2	7	25	0	116	115	52	11	40	102	4.07	1.33	19.3	260	21%	8%	13%	0.8	32%	71%	80
		23	25	aaa	NYY	3	8	17	0	81	87	45	10	39	81	4.95	1.56	20.9	276	23%	11%	12%	1.1	34%	70%	64
Vela, Noel	L	22	24	aa	SD	1	3	9	0	24	26	16	1	19	20	5.85	1.87	12.6	278	19%	18%	1%	0.3	35%	67%	58
Vines, Darius	R	22	24	a/a	ATL	8	4	27	0	142	151	72	19	45	131	4.53	1.38	22.1	273	22%	8%	14%	1.2	33%	70%	74
		23	25	aaa	ATL	3	2	6	0	35	33	10	5	13	24	2.58	1.30	24.1	249	16%	9%	8%	1.3	27%	87%	43
Vodnik, Victor	R	21	22	aa	ATL	1	4	11	0	35	38	26	6	23	35	6.67	1.72	14.5	277	22%	14%	8%	1.5	33%	63%	42
		22	23	a/a	ATL	2	0	31	3	36	34	11	2	19	40	2.66	1.48	5.0	251	27%	13%	14%	0.5	34%	83%	92
		23	24	a/a	COL	4	2	42	6	55	47	24	6	30	52	3.88	1.41	5.6	233	22%	13%	9%	1.0	28%	76%	64
Waites, Cole	R	22	24	a/a	SF	3	2	25	5	29	16	4	0	17	41	1.22	1.14	4.6	162	34%	14%	20%	0.0	28%	88%	149
		23	25	aaa	SF	3	4	32	1	32	28	22	2	26	26	6.06	1.69	4.5	238	18%	18%	0%	0.7	29%	63%	52
Waldrep, Hurston	R	23	21	a/a	ATL	4	0	15	0	15	13	3	1	10	15	2.01	1.51	16.3	236	22%	15%	8%	0.6	30%	89%	75
Waldron, Matt	R	21	25	aa	SD	0	4	7	0	32	39	25	2	17	25	7.10	1.74	20.9	303	17%	11%	6%	0.5	36%	57%	53
		22	26	a/a	SD	5	10	25	0	115	138	72	11	37	79	5.62	1.52	20.0	299	15%	7%	8%	0.9	34%	63%	51
		23	27	aaa	SD	2	10	20	0	93	118	62	14	26	79	6.02	1.54	20.3	310	20%	6%	13%	1.4	36%	63%	63
Walston, Blake	L	22	21	aa	ARI	7	3	21	0	107	109	52	12	32	95	4.33	1.32	21.1	266	21%	7%	14%	1.0	32%	69%	84
		23	22	aaa	ARI	12	6	30	0	150	135	63	6	77	89	3.77	1.41	21.2	242	14%	12%	2%	0.3	28%	72%	52
Walter, Brandon	L	22	26	a/a	BOS	3	3	11	0	59	51	26	6	7	58	3.90	0.99	20.5	236	25%	3%	22%	0.9	30%	62%	211
		23	27	aaa	BOS	3	5	21	0	94	116	55	11	35	67	5.29	1.61	19.8	305	16%	8%	8%	1.1	35%	68%	41
Warren, Will	R	22	23	aa	NYY	7	6	18	0	94	95	43	8	31	72	4.13	1.34	21.7	263	18%	8%	10%	0.7	31%	70%	70
		23	24	a/a	NYY	7	7	27	0	131	123	54	16	58	128	3.71	1.38	20.4	249	23%	11%	13%	1.1	31%	77%	73
Whisenhunt, Carson	L	23	23	aa	SF	0	1	6	0	21	18	8	1	11	23	3.58	1.40	14.9	236	26%	13%	13%	0.4	32%	74%	97
White, Owen	R	22	23	aa	TEX	3	0	4	0	23	19	6	1	4	19	2.15	1.02	22.3	226	23%	5%	17%	0.3	28%	79%	136
		23	24	a/a	TEX	4	5	25	0	110	99	53	15	54	66	4.33	1.39	18.6	242	14%	12%	3%	1.3	26%	73%	27
Wicks, Jordan	L	22	23	aa	CHC	0	3	8	0	28	24	11	4	9	30	3.66	1.18	14.0	230	25%	8%	17%	1.3	29%	74%	96
		23	24	a/a	CHC	4	2	20	0	92	80	36	10	30	82	3.55	1.19	18.5	235	22%	8%	14%	1.0	28%	74%	84
Wilcox, Cole	R	23	24	aa	TAM	6	8	25	0	108	104	67	14	42	85	5.55	1.36	18.1	255	19%	9%	9%	1.2	29%	60%	53
Winans, Allan	R	21	26	aa	NYM	1	1	14	3	28	13	5	3	8	24	1.61	0.73	7.1	141	24%	8%	17%	0.8	16%	87%	115
		22	27	a/a	ATL	1	5	12	0	60	71	28	5	17	47	4.26	1.46	21.4	295	18%	6%	12%	0.7	35%	71%	77
		23	28	aaa	ATL	9	4	23	1	127	122	48	12	38	90	3.39	1.26	22.6	254	17%	7%	10%	0.8	29%	76%	68
Winn, Cole	R	21	22	a/a	TEX	3	2	11	0	86	48	26	7	30	92	2.74	0.90	15.3	164	29%	9%	19%	0.8	21%	73%	122
		22	23	aaa	TEX	9	8	28	0	123	122	76	10	75	103	5.57	1.60	19.5	260	18%	13%	5%	0.7	31%	65%	55
		23	24	aaa	TEX	9	8	29	0	101	122	82	17	76	80	7.32	1.96	16.6	299	17%	16%	1%	1.5	34%	64%	15
Winn, Keaton	R	22	24	aa	SF	2	3	6	0	31	38	15	4	6	20	4.35	1.43	22.0	305	16%	5%	11%	1.1	34%	72%	68
		23	25	aaa	SF	0	6	17	0	58	72	32	6	25	54	4.97	1.67	15.3	305	21%	10%	11%	0.9	38%	71%	63
Wolf, Jackson	L	23	24	aa	PIT	8	6	26	0	125	128	74	20	34	106	5.32	1.30	19.8	266	21%	7%	14%	1.4	30%	62%	70
Woods Richardson, Simeon	R	21	21	aa	MIN	3	5	15	0	54	51	37	5	33	67	6.19	1.55	15.8	251	28%	14%	14%	0.8	35%	59%	91
		22	22	a/a	MIN	5	3	23	0	110	75	29	5	32	99	2.40	0.97	18.2	195	23%	7%	16%	0.4	25%	76%	119
		23	23	aaa	MIN	7	6	24	0	115	112	60	11	58	84	4.67	1.48	20.6	257	17%	12%	5%	0.9	30%	69%	47
Workman, Logan	R	23	25	aa	TAM	4	4	15	0	64	75	32	7	21	59	4.48	1.50	18.4	294	21%	7%	14%	1.0	36%	72%	76
Zulueta, Yosver	R	22	24	a/a	TOR	1	2	12	0	22	14	9	1	16	25	3.80	1.36	7.8	183	26%	17%	9%	0.4	25%	71%	97
		23	25	aaa	TOR	4	4	45	0	64	57	29	1	41	59	4.13	1.53	6.2	240	21%	15%	7%	0.1	32%	71%	83
Zwack, Nick	L	23	25	aa	SF	5	7	24	0	81	112	74	14	34	75	8.25	1.80	15.6	328	20%	9%	11%	1.5	39%	54%	39

ORGANIZATION RATINGS/RANKINGS

Each organization is graded on a standard A-F scale in four separate categories, and then after weighing the categories and adding some subjectivity, a final grade and ranking are determined. The four categories are the following:

Hitting: The quality and quantity of hitting prospects, the balance between athleticism, power, speed, and defense, and the quality of player development.

Pitching: The quality and quantity of pitching prospects and the quality of player development.

Top-End Talent: The quality of the top players within the organization. Successful teams are ones that have the most star-quality players. These are the players who are a teams' above average regulars, front-end starters, and closers.

Depth: The depth of both hitting and pitching prospects within the organization.

Overall Grade: The four categories are weighted, with top-end talent being the most important and depth being the least.

TEAM	Hitting	Pitching	Top-End Talent	Depth	Overall
Baltimore Orioles	A	C+	A	B+	A-
Chicago Cubs	A-	B	A	B	A-
Milwaukee Brewers	A	C+	A-	B+	A-
Los Angeles Dodgers	B	B+	B	A	A-
Tampa Bay Rays	A	C	A	B-	B+
Texas Rangers	B+	B	A-	B+	B+
New York Yankees	A-	B-	A-	B+	B+
Cincinnati Reds	B+	B	B	B+	B+
Pittsburgh Pirates	C	A-	A	B	B
San Diego Padres	B	B	A-	B	B
Minnesota Twins	B+	C	B+	B	B
San Francisco Giants	B+	C+	B+	B	B
Boston Red Sox	B+	D	B	B	B
Detroit Tigers	A-	B	B	B-	B
New York Mets	B+	B-	B	C+	B
Oakland Athletics	B	C	B-	B	B
Washington Nationals	B	D	A-	C	B-
Cleveland Guardians	B+	D+	B	B-	B-
Seattle Mariners	B+	D	B	B-	B-
Chicago White Sox	B-	B	B-	C	B-
Colorado Rockies	A-	D-	B+	C	C+
Arizona Diamondbacks	B	D-	B	D-	C+
Miami Marlins	C	B+	B-	D	C+
Philadelphia Phillies	C	B-	B	D	C
Toronto Blue Jays	C-	C+	C	C-	C
Atlanta Braves	D	B+	C	C-	C-
Kansas City Royals	D	C-	C	D+	C-
St. Louis Cardinals	C	C+	C	C-	C-
Houston Astros	C-	D-	D	D	D
Los Angeles Angels	C-	D	D+	F	D

This section of the book may be the smallest as far as word count is concerned, but may be the most important, as this is where players' skills and potential are tied together and ranked against their peers. The rankings that follow are divided into long-term potential in the major leagues and shorter-term fantasy value.

ORGANIZATIONAL: Lists the top 15 minor league prospects within each organization in terms of long-range potential in the major leagues.

POSITIONAL: Lists the top 15 prospects, by position, in terms of long-range potential in the major leagues.

TOP POWER: Lists the top 25 prospects that have the potential to hit for power in the major leagues, combining raw power, plate discipline, and at the ability to make their power game-usable.

TOP BA: Lists the top 25 prospects that have the potential to hit for high batting average in the major leagues, combining contact ability, plate discipline, hitting mechanics and strength.

TOP SPEED: Lists the top 25 prospects that have the potential to steal bases in the major leagues, combining raw speed and base-running instincts.

TOP FASTBALL: Lists the top 25 pitchers that have the best fastball, combining velocity and pitch movement.

TOP BREAKING BALL: Lists the top 25 pitchers that have the best breaking ball, combining pitch movement, strikeout potential, and consistency.

2024 TOP FANTASY PROSPECTS: Lists the top 40 minor league prospects likely to have the most value to their respective fantasy teams in 2024, then 35 more players to consider who could get the call and have the skills to produce. Remember that this section addresses 2024 value, not long-term value.

TOP 100 ARCHIVE: Takes a look back at the top 100 lists from the past eight years.

The rankings in this book are the creation of the minor league department at BaseballHQ.com. While several baseball personnel contributed player information to the book, no opinions were solicited or received in comparing players.

TOP PROSPECTS BY ORGANIZATION

AL EAST

BALTIMORE ORIOLES
1. Jackson Holliday, SS
2. Coby Mayo, IF
3. Samuel Basallo, C
4. Colton Cowser, OF
5. Heston Kjerstad, OF
6. DL Hall, LHP
7. Connor Norby, IF
8. Enrique Bradfield Jr., OF
9. Dylan Beavers, OF
10. Joey Ortiz, SS
11. Cade Povich, LHP
12. Mac Horvath, IF
13. Justin Armbruester, RHP
14. Jackson Baumeister, RHP
15. Seth Johnson, RHP

BOSTON RED SOX
1. Marcelo Mayer, SS
2. Ceddanne Rafaela, OF
3. Roman Anthony, OF
4. Kyle Teel, C
5. Wikelman Gonzalez, RHP
6. Miguel Bleis, OF
7. Nick Yorke, 2B
8. Eddinson Paulino, IF
9. Luis Perales, RHP
10. Nazzan Zanetello, SS
11. Wilyer Abreu, OF
12. Blaze Jordan, IF
13. Nathan Hickey, C
14. Bryan Mata, RHP
15. Brandon Walter, LHP

NEW YORK YANKEES
1. Jasson Dominguez, OF
2. Spencer Jones, OF
3. Roderick Arias, SS
4. Everson Pereira, OF
5. Chase Hampton, RHP
6. George Lombard Jr., SS
7. Austin Wells, C
8. Henry Lalane, LHP
9. Ben Rice, C
10. Brando Mayea, OF
11. Will Warren, RHP
12. Clayton Beeter, RHP
13. Kyle Carr, LHP
14. John Cruz, OF
15. Carlos Lagrange, RHP

TAMPA BAY RAYS
1. Junior Caminero, IF
2. Curtis Mead, IF
3. Xavier Isaac, 1B
4. Carson Williams, SS
5. Brayden Taylor, 3B
6. Austin Shenton, IF
7. Dominic Keegan, C
8. Colton Ledbetter, OF
9. Yoniel Curet, RHP
10. Santiago Suarez, RHP
11. Trevor Martin, RHP
12. Marcus Johnson, RHP
13. Adrian Santana, SS
14. Mason Montgomery, LHP
15. Ian Seymour, LHP

TORONTO BLUE JAYS
1. Ricky Tiedemann, LHP
2. Arjun Nimmala, SS
3. Brandon Barriera, LHP
4. Orelvis Martinez, IF
5. Addison Barger, IF
6. Alan Roden, OF
7. Kendry Rojas, LHP
8. Leo Jimenez, IF
9. Adam Macko, LHP
10. Connor Cooke, RHP
11. Yosver Zulueta, RHP
12. Spencer Horwitz, 1B
13. Cade Doughty, IF
14. Chad Dallas, RHP
15. Juaron Watts Brown, RHP

AL CENTRAL

CHICAGO WHITE SOX
1. Colson Montgomery, SS
2. Noah Schultz, LHP
3. Bryan Ramos, 3B
4. Nick Nastrini, RHP
5. Edgar Quero, C
6. Jose G. Rodriguez, IF
7. Jacob Gonzalez, SS
8. Cristian Mena, RHP
9. Javier Mogollon, IF
10. Peyton Pallette, RHP
11. Jordan Leasure, RHP
12. Jacob Burke, OF
13. Juan Carela, RHP
14. Jonathan Cannon, RHP
15. Terrell Tatum, OF

CLEVELAND GUARDIANS
1. Chase DeLauter, OF
2. Brayan Rocchio, SS
3. Daniel Espino, RHP
4. Kyle Manzardo, 1B
5. Alex Clemmey, LHP
6. George Valera, OF
7. Jaison Chourio, OF
8. Angel Martinez, IF
9. Juan Brito, IF
10. Joey Cantillo, LHP
11. Ralphy Velazquez, C
12. Deyvison De Los Santos, IF
13. Johnathan Rodriguez, OF
14. Kahlil Watson, SS
15. Justin Campbell, RHP

DETROIT TIGERS
1. Colt Keith, 3B
2. Jackson Jobe, RHP
3. Max Clark, OF
4. Jace Jung, 2B
5. Parker Meadows, OF
6. Justyn Henry Malloy, OF
7. Kevin McGonigle, IF
8. Ty Madden, RHP
9. Wilmer Flores, RHP
10. Hao Yu Lee, 2B
11. Max Anderson, 2B
12. Paul Wilson, LHP
13. Justice Bigbie, OF
14. Dillon Dingler, C
15. Sawyer Gipson Long, RHP

KANSAS CITY ROYALS
1. Blake Mitchell, C
2. Cayden Wallace, 3B
3. Mason Barnett, RHP
4. Blake Wolters, RHP
5. Nick Loftin, IF
6. Chandler Champlain, RHP
7. Gavin Cross, OF
8. Frank Mozzicato, LHP
9. Tyler Gentry, OF
10. Noah Cameron, LHP
11. David Sandlin, RHP
12. Hiro Wyatt, RHP
13. Javier Vaz, IF
14. Carson Roccaforte, OF
15. Ramon Ramirez, C

MINNESOTA TWINS
1. Walker Jenkins, OF
2. Brooks Lee, SS
3. Emmanuel Rodriguez, OF
4. Marco Raya, RHP
5. Connor Prielipp, LHP
6. Kala i Rosario, OF
7. David Festa, RHP
8. Charlee Soto, RHP
9. Danny De Andrade, SS
10. Tanner Schobel, IF
11. Yasser Mercedes, OF
12. C.J. Culpepper, RHP
13. Brandon Winokur, UT
14. Luke Keaschall, 2B
15. Matt Canterino, RHP

AL WEST

HOUSTON ASTROS
1. Brice Matthews, SS
2. Nehomar Ochoa Jr., OF
3. Misael Tamarez, RHP
4. Alonzo Tredwell, RHP
5. Jacob Melton, OF
6. Spencer Arrighetti, RHP
7. Colton Gordon, LHP
8. Chase Jaworsky, SS
9. Colin Barber, OF
10. Zach Dezenzo, IF
11. Alimber Santa, RHP
12. Andrew Taylor, RHP
13. Joey Loperfido, UT
14. Kenedy Corona, OF
15. Will Wagner, IF

LOS ANGELES ANGELS
1. Caden Dana, RHP
2. Nolan Schanuel, 1B
3. Nelson Rada, OF
4. Alberto Rios, OF
5. Kyren Paris, IF
6. Joe Redfield, OF
7. Jack Kochanowicz, RHP
8. Ben Joyce, RHP
9. Davis Daniel, RHP
10. Denzer Guzman, SS
11. Jorge Ruiz, OF
12. Trey Cabbage, IF
13. Jordyn Adams, OF
14. Kelvin Caceres, RHP
15. Jadiel Sanchez, OF

OAKLAND ATHLETICS
1. Daniel Susac, C
2. Mason Miller, RHP
3. Denzel Clarke, OF
4. Jacob Wilson, SS
5. Max Muncy, SS
6. Joey Estes, RHP
7. Luis Morales, RHP
8. Colby Thomas, OF
9. Myles Naylor, IF
10. Freddy Tarnok, RHP
11. Cole Miller, RHP
12. Darell Hernaiz, SS
13. Brett Harris, 3B
14. Henry Bolte, OF
15. Steven Echavarria, RHP

SEATTLE MARINERS
1. Cole Young, SS
2. Harry Ford, C
3. Colt Emerson, SS
4. Emerson Hancock, RHP
5. Ryan Bliss, IF
6. Michael Arroyo, SS
7. Gabriel Gonzalez, OF
8. Felnin Celesten, SS
9. Tai Peete, IF
10. Jonny Farmelo, OF
11. Jonatan Clase, OF
12. Lazaro Montes, OF
13. Tyler Locklear, 1B
14. Aidan Smith, OF
15. Michael Morales, RHP

TEXAS RANGERS
1. Wyatt Langford, OF
2. Evan Carter, OF
3. Sebastian Walcott, SS
4. Brock Porter, RHP
5. Jack Leiter, RHP
6. Owen White, RHP
7. Kumar Rocker, RHP
8. Anthony Gutierrez, OF
9. Aidan Curry, RHP
10. Emiliano Teodo, RHP
11. Dustin Harris, IF
12. Justin Foscue, IF
13. Echedry Vargas, IF
14. Jose Corniell, RHP
15. Abimelec Ortiz, 1B

Top Prospects by Organization

NL EAST

ATLANTA BRAVES
1   AJ Smith Shawver, RHP
2   Hurston Waldrep, RHP
3   JR Ritchie, RHP
4   Owen Murphy, RHP
5   Spencer Schwellenbach, RHP
6   Drake Baldwin, C
7   Darius Vines, RHP
8   Ignacio Alvarez, SS
9   David McCabe, 3B
10 Jhancarlos Lara, RHP
11 Drue Hackenberg, RHP
12 Luis Guanipa, OF
13 Cade Kuehler, RHP
14 Keshawn Ogans, IF
15 Isaiah Drake, OF

MIAMI MARLINS
1   Noble Meyer, RHP
2   Max Meyer, RHP
3   Thomas White, LHP
4   Victor Mesa Jr, OF
5   Yidde Cappe, IF
6   Karson Milbrandt, RHP
7   Dax Fulton, LHP
8   Jacob Berry, IF
9   Kemp Alderman, OF
10 Emmett Olson, LHP
11 Dane Myers, OF
12 Brock Vradenburg, 1B
13 Jacob Miller, RHP
14 Jacob Amaya, IF
15 Will Banfield, C

NEW YORK METS
1   Jett Williams, OF
2   Drew Gilbert, OF
3   Luisangel Acuna, IF
4   Ronny Mauricio, IF
5   Ryan Clifford, OF
6   Christian Scott, RHP
7   Colin Houck, SS
8   Blade Tidwell, RHP
9   Mike Vasil, RHP
10 Brandon Sproat, RHP
11 Kevin Parada, C
12 Marco Vargas, IF
13 Kade Morris, RHP
14 Alex Ramirez, OF
15 Layonel Ovalles, RHP

PHILADELPHIA PHILLIES
1   Andrew Painter, RHP
2   Justin Crawford, OF
3   Aidan Miller, SS
4   Mick Abel, RHP
5   Orion Kerkering, RHP
6   Gabriel Rincones Jr, OF
7   Devin Saltiban, SS
8   Griff McGarry, RHP
9   Eduardo Tait, C
10 Starlyn Caba, SS
11 Carlos De La Cruz, 1B
12 Bryan Rincon, SS
13 Alex McFarlane, RHP
14 Jean Cabrera, RHP
15 William Bergolla, IF

WASHINGTON NATIONALS
1   Dylan Crews, OF
2   James Wood, OF
3   Brady House, 3B
4   Cade Cavalli, RHP
5   Elijah Green, OF
6   Yohandy Morales, 3B
7   Jackson Rutledge, RHP
8   Cristhian Vaquero, OF
9   Jarlin Susana, RHP
10 Robert Hasselll III, OF
11 Daylen Lile, OF
12 Jacob Young, OF
13 DJ Herz, LHP
14 Nasim Nunez, IF
15 Trey Lipscomb, IF

NL CENTRAL

CHICAGO CUBS
1   Pete Crow Armstrong, OF
2   Michael Busch, IF
3   Cade Horton, RHP
4   Matt Shaw, IF
5   Owen Caissie, OF
6   Kevin Alcantara, OF
7   Ben Brown, RHP
8   James Triantos, IF
9   Moises Ballesteros, C
10 Jordan Wicks, LHP
11 Alexander Canario, OF
12 Matt Mervis, 1B
13 Jefferson Rojas, SS
14 Cristian Hernandez, SS
15 Josh Rivera, IF

CINCINNATI REDS
1   Noelvi Marte, 3B
2   Rhett Lowder, RHP
3   Edwin Arroyo, SS
4   Blake Dunn, OF
5   Carlos Jorge, IF
6   Sal Stewart, IF
7   Connor Phillips, RHP
8   Chase Petty, RHP
9   Alfredo Duno, C
10 Cam Collier, 3B
11 Hector Rodriguez, OF
12 Ricardo Cabrera, IF
13 Julian Aguiar, RHP
14 Leonardo Balcazar, IF
15 Sammy Stafura, SS

MILWAUKEE BREWERS
1   Jackson Chourio, OF
2   Jacob Misiorowski, RHP
3   Tyler Black, 3B
4   Jeferson Quero, C
5   Brock Wilken, 3B
6   Robert Gasser, LHP
7   Luis Lara, OF
8   Eric Brown, Jr., SS
9   Eric Bitonti, IF
10 Carlos Rodriguez, RHP
11 Dylan O Rae, IF
12 Josh Knoth, RHP
13 Cooper Pratt, SS
14 Bradley Blalock, RHP
15 Logan Henderson, RHP

PITTSBURGH PIRATES
1   Paul Skenes, RHP
2   Termarr Johnson, 2B
3   Jared Jones, RHP
4   Thomas Harrington, RHP
5   Bubba Chandler, RHP
6   Braxton Ashcraft, RHP
7   Anthony Solometo, LHP
8   Jun Seok Shim, RHP
9   Mitch Jebb, IF
10 Tsung Che Cheng, IF
11 Lonnie White, OF
12 Jackson Wolf, LHP
13 Hunter Barco, LHP
14 Michael Burrows, RHP
15 Jack Brannigan, IF

ST LOUIS CARDINALS
1   Masyn Winn, SS
2   Tink Hence, RHP
3   Victor Scott, OF
4   Tekoah Roby, RHP
5   Chase Davis, OF
6   Cooper Hjerpe, LHP
7   Thomas Saggese, IF
8   Gordon Graceffo, RHP
9   Leonardo Bernal, C
10 Sem Robberse, RHP
11 Michael McGreevy, RHP
12 Cesar Prieto, IF
13 Zack Showalter, RHP
14 Jimmy Crooks, C
15 Won Bin Cho, OF

NL WEST

ARIZONA DIAMONDBACKS
1   Jordan Lawlar, SS
2   Druw Jones, OF
3   Jansel Luis, IF
4   Cristofer Torin, IF
5   Tommy Troy, SS
6   Yu Min Lin, LHP
7   Jorge Barrosa, OF
8   Gino Groover, 3B
9   Joe Elbis, RHP
10 Grayson Hitt, LHP
11 Dylan Ray, RHP
12 A.J. Vukovich, UT
13 Kristian Robinson, OF
14 Caden Grice, LHP
15 Manuel Pena, IF

COLORADO ROCKIES
1   Adael Amador, SS
2   Yanquiel Fernandez, OF
3   Jordan Beck, OF
4   Zac Veen, OF
5   Chase Dollander, RHP
6   Cole Carrigg, UT
7   Sterlin Thompson, OF
8   Drew Romo, C
9   Benny Montgomery, OF
10 Dyan Jorge, SS
11 Hunter Goodman, 1B
12 Gabriel Hughes, RHP
13 Jordy Vargas, RHP
14 Warming Bernabel, 3B
15 Joe Rock, LHP

LOS ANGELES DODGERS
1   Dalton Rushing, C
2   Andy Pages, OF
3   Gavin Stone, RHP
4   Diego Cartaya, C
5   Nick Frasso, RHP
6   River Ryan, RHP
7   Kyle Hurt, RHP
8   Josue De Paula, OF
9   Jackson Ferris, LHP
10 Landon Knack, RHP
11 Kendall George, OF
13 Joendry Vargas, SS
13 Thayron Liranzo, C
14 Jake Gelof, 3B
15 Trey Sweeney, SS

SAN DIEGO PADRES
1   Jackson Merrill, SS
2   Robby Snelling, LHP
3   Dylan Lesko, RHP
4   Ethan Salas, C
5   Drew Thorpe, RHP
6   Dillon Head, OF
7   Samuel Zavala, OF
8   Adam Mazur, RHP
9   Jakob Marsee, OF
10 Jairo Iriarte, RHP
11 Ryan Bergert, RHP
12 Nathan Martorella, OF
13 Homer Bush, OF
14 Graham Pauley, 3B
15 Eguy Rosario, IF

SAN FRANCISCO GIANTS
1   Kyle Harrison, LHP
2   Marco Luciano, SS
3   Bryce Eldridge, OF/RHP
4   Carson Whisenhunt, LHP
5   Reggie Crawford, LHP
6   Rayner Arias, OF
7   Walker Martin, SS
8   Hayden Birdsong, RHP
9   Mason Black, RHP
10 Landen Roupp, RHP
11 Wade Meckler, OF
12 Keaton Winn, RHP
13 Joe Whitman, LHP
14 Gerelmi Maldonado, RHP
15 Aeverson Arteaga, SS

TOP PROSPECTS BY POSITION

CATCHER
1. Ethan Salas, SD
2. Samuel Basallo, BAL
3. Harry Ford, SEA
4. Jeferson Quero, MIL
5. Kyle Teel, BOS
6. Dalton Rushing, LA
7. Moises Ballesteros, CHC
8. Daniel Susac, OAK
9. Austin Wells, NYY
10. Blake Mitchell, KC
11. Cole Carrigg, COL
12. Drew Romo, COL
13. Edgar Quero, CHW
14. Kevin Parada, NYM
15. Diego Cartaya, LA

FIRST BASEMEN
1. Kyle Manzardo, CLE
2. Xavier Isaac, TAM
3. Nolan Schanuel, LAA
4. Blaze Jordan, BOS
5. Tyler Locklear, SEA
6. Jhonkensy Noel, CLE
7. Abimelec Ortiz, TEX
8. Matt Mervis, CHC
9. Dustin Harris, TEX
10. Nathan Martorella, SD
11. Spencer Horwitz, TOR
12. Hunter Goodman, COL
13. Malcom Nunez, PIT
14. T.J. White, WAS
15. Tony Blanco, PIT

SECOND BASEMEN
1. Termarr Johnson, PIT
2. Michael Busch, CHC
3. Jace Jung, DET
4. Connor Norby, BAL
5. Thomas Saggese, STL
6. Kevin McGonigle, DET
7. Justin Foscue, TEX
8. Juan Brito, CLE
9. Nick Yorke, BOS
10. Jansel Luis, ARI
11. Ryan Bliss, SEA
12. Carlos Jorge, CIN
13. Leo Jimenez, TOR
14. Tanner Schobel, MIN
15. Max Anderson, DET

SHORTSTOP
1. Jackson Holliday, BAL
2. Jordan Lawlar, ARI
3. Jackson Merrill, SD
4. Adael Amador, COL
5. Colson Montgomery, CHW
6. Marcelo Mayer, BOS
7. Jett Williams, NYM
8. Matt Shaw, CHC
9. Masyn Winn, STL
10. Cole Young, SEA
11. Brooks Lee, MIN
12. Carson Williams, TAM
13. Luisangel Acuna, NYM
14. Ronny Mauricio, NYM
15. Marco Luciano, SF

THIRD BASEMEN
1. Junior Caminero, TAM
2. Noelvi Marte, CIN
3. Coby Mayo, BAL
4. Colt Keith, DET
5. Curtis Mead, TAM
6. Brady House, WAS
7. Tyler Black, MIL
8. Bryan Ramos, CHW
9. Aidan Miller, PHI
10. Sterlin Thompson, COL
11. Cam Collier, CIN
12. Sal Stewart, CIN
13. Brock Wilken, MIL
14. Deyvison De Los Santos, CLE
15. Brayden Taylor, TAM

OUTFIELDERS
1. Jackson Chourio, MIL
2. Wyatt Langford, TEX
3. Dylan Crews, WAS
4. Evan Carter, TEX
5. Walker Jenkins, MIN
6. James Wood, WAS
7. Pete Crow-Armstrong, CHC
8. Jasson Dominguez, NYY
9. Colton Cowser, BAL
10. Roman Anthony, BOS
11. Chase DeLauter, CLE
12. Max Clark, DET
13. Ceddanne Rafaela, BOS
14. Heston Kjerstad, BAL
15. Drew Gilbert, NYM
16. Emmanuel Rodriguez, MIN
17. Owen Caissie, CHC
18. Druw Jones, ARI
19. Spencer Jones, NYY
20. Yanquiel Fernandez, COL
21. Bryce Eldridge, SF
22. Justin Crawford, PHI
23. Josue De Paula, LA
24. Everson Pereira, NYY
25. Victor Scott, STL
26. Lazaro Montes, SEA
27. Gabriel Gonzalez, SEA
28. Jonatan Clase, SEA
29. Kevin Alcantara, CHC
30. Samuel Zavala, SD
31. Dylan Beavers, BAL
32. Ryan Clifford, NYM
33. Parker Meadows, DET
34. Dillon Head, SD
35. Jordan Beck, COL
36. Denzel Clarke, OAK
37. Andy Pages, LA
38. Jacob Melton, HOU
39. Luis Lara, MIL
40. Zac Veen, COL
41. Justyn-Henry Malloy, DET
42. Luis Baez, HOU
43. Nelson Rada, LAA
44. Jakob Marsee, SD
45. Enrique Bradfield, BAL

RIGHT-HANDED PITCHERS
1. Paul Skenes, PIT
2. Andrew Painter, PHI
3. Cade Horton, CHC
4. Jackson Jobe, DET
5. Jacob Misiorowski, MIL
6. AJ Smith-Shawver, ATL
7. Dylan Lesko, SD
8. Mason Miller, OAK
9. Jared Jones, PIT
10. Noble Meyer, MIA
11. Rhett Lowder, CIN
12. Hurston Waldrep, ATL
13. Tink Hence, STL
14. Max Meyer, MIA
15. Mick Abel, PHI
16. Drew Thorpe, SD
17. Gavin Stone, LA
18. Chase Hampton, NYY
19. Bubba Chandler, PIT
20. Connor Phillips, CIN
21. Tekoah Roby, STL
22. Brock Porter, TEX
23. Daniel Espino, CLE
24. Cade Cavalli, WAS
25. Chase Dollander, COL
26. Jose Corniell, TEX
27. Jairo Iriarte, SD
28. Caden Dana, LAA
29. Carlos F. Rodriguez, MIL
30. Will Warren, NYY
31. Chase Petty, CIN
32. Orion Kerkering, PHI
33. Luis Morales, OAK
34. Luis Perales, BOS
35. Coleman Crow, MIL
36. Wikelman Gonzalez, BOS
37. Kyle Hurt, LA
38. Angel Bastardo, BOS
39. Owen White, TEX
40. Owen Murphy, ATL
41. JR Ritchie, ATL
42. Ben Brown, CHC
43. Nick Nastrini, CHW
44. Cristian Mena, CHW
45. Emerson Hancock, SEA
46. Mike Vasil, NYM
47. Nick Frasso, LA
48. Thomas Harrington, PIT
49. Jarlin Susana, WAS
50. Wilmer Flores, DET

LEFT-HANDED PITCHERS
1. Ricky Tiedemann, TOR
2. Kyle Harrison, SF
3. Robby Snelling, SD
4. Noah Schultz, CHW
5. Carson Whisenhunt, SF
6. DL Hall, BAL
7. Anthony Solometo, PIT
8. Jordan Wicks, CHC
9. Cooper Hjerpe, STL
10. Thomas White, MIA
11. Robert Gasser, MIL
12. Henry Lalane, NYY
13. Reggie Crawford, SF
14. Brandon Barriera, TOR
15. Frank Mozzicato, KC
16. Jake Eder, CHW
17. Jackson Ferris, LA
18. Cade Povich, BAL
19. Connor Prielipp, MIN
20. Mason Montgomery, TAM

TOP PROSPECTS BY SKILLS

2024 TOP FANTASY IMPACT

TOP POWER

Owen Caissie, CHC
Colt Keith, DET
Jackson Chourio, MIL
Denzel Clarke, OAK
Chase DeLauter, CLE
Walker Jenkins, MIN
Blaze Jordan, BOS
Orelvis Martinez, TOR
Xavier Isaac, TAM
Jhonkensy Noel, CLE
Emmanuel Rodriguez, MIN
Dylan Crews, WAS
Brock Wilken, MIL
Wyatt Langford, TEX
James Wood, WAS
Noelvi Marte, CIN
Curtis Mead, TAM
Andy Pages, LA
Spencer Jones, NYY
Jasson Dominguez, NYY
Junior Caminero, TAM
Coby Mayo, BAL
Abimelec Ortiz, TEX
Samuel Basallo, BAL
Colson Montgomery, CHW

TOP BA

Dylan Crews, WAS
Wyatt Langford, TEX
Jackson Holliday, BAL
Tyler Black, MIL
Junior Caminero, TAM
Walker Jenkins, MIN
Max Clark, DET
Jackson Merrill, SD
Jacob Wilson, OAK
Cole Young, SEA
Jett Williams, NYY
Curtis Mead, TAM
Jace Jung, DET
Brooks Lee, MIN
Colt Emerson, SEA
Pete Crow-Armstrong, CHC
Nolan Schanuel, LAA
Sterlin Thompson, COL
Matt Shaw, CHC
Carlos Jorge, CIN
Daniel Susac, OAK
Colt Keith, DET
Kyle Manzardo, CLE
Wade Meckler, SF
Dylan O'Rae, MIL

TOP SPEED

Victor Scott, STL
Jonatan Clase, SEA
Dillon Head, SD
Dasan Brown, TOR
Jordyn Adams, LAA
Chandler Simpson, TAM
Enrique Bradfield, BAL
Cole Carrigg, COL
Emaarion Boyd, PHI
Dylan O'Rae, MIL
Tyler Tolbert, KC
Max Clark, DET
Henry Bolte, OAK
Isaiah Drake, ATL
Kendall George, LA
Jett Williams, NYM
Jackson Chourio, MIL
Ceddanne Rafaela, BOS
Kahlil Watson, CLE
Luis Lara, MIL
Denzel Clarke, OAK
Justin Crawford, PHI
David Hamilton, BOS
Pete Crow-Armstrong, CHC
Luisangel Acuna, NYM

TOP FASTBALL

Paul Skenes, PIT
Andrew Painter, RHP
Tink Hence, STL
Jackson Jobe, DET
Chase Dollander, COL
Cade Cavalli, WAS
Ben Brown, CHC
Joe Boyle, OAK
Daniel Espino, CLE
Mason Miller, OAK
Nick Frasso, LA
Ben Joyce, LAA
Ricky Tiedemann, TOR
Cade Horton, CHC
Jarlin Susana, WAS
Hurston Waldrep, ATL
Bubba Chandler, PIT
Kyle Harrison, SF
Jared Jones, PIT
Jacob Misiorowski, MIL
Orion Kerkering, PHI
Connor Phillips, CIN
AJ Smith-Shawver, ATL
David Festa, MIN
Noah Schultz, CHW

TOP BREAKING BALL

Cade Horton, CHC
Orion Kerkering, PHI
Kyle Harrison, SF
Paul Skenes, PIT
Rhett Lowder, CIN
Jackson Jobe, DET
Ricky Tiedemann, TOR
Jacob Misiorowski, MIL
Noah Schultz, CHW
Andrew Painter, PHI
Caden Dana, LAA
Noble Meyer, MIA
Chase Dollander, COL

DL Hall, BAL
Max Meyer, MIA
Robby Snelling, SD
Reggie Crawford, SF
Daniel Espino, CLE
Ben Brown, CHC
Mason Miller, OAK
Robert Gasser, MIL
Jake Eder, CHW
Cade Cavalli, WAS
Tekoah Roby, STL
Hurston Waldrep, ATL

THE TOP 40 • RANKED

1. Jackson Holliday (SS, BAL)
2. Junior Caminero (3B, TAM)
3. Evan Carter (OF, TEX)
4. Noelvi Marte (3B, CIN)
5. Colt Keith (3B, DET)
6. Wyatt Langford (OF, TEX)
7. Jackson Chourio (OF, MIL)
8. Jordan Lawlar (SS, ARI)
9. Dylan Crews (OF, WAS)
10. Pete Crow-Armstrong (OF, CHC)

11. Ronny Mauricio (IF, NYM)
12. Colton Cowser (OF, BAL)
13. Paul Skenes (RHP, PIT)
14. Kyle Harrison (LHP, SF)
15. Masyn Winn (SS, STL)
16. Kyle Manzardo (1B, CLE)
17. Marco Luciano (SS, SF)
18. Mason Miller (RHP, OAK)
19. Jasson Dominguez (OF, NYY)
20. Heston Kjerstad (OF, BAL)

21. Ceddanne Rafaela (SS/OF, BOS)
22. Nolan Schanuel (1B, LAA)
23. Curtis Mead (3B, TAM)
24. Nick Loftin (2B, KC)
25. Jordan Wicks (LHP, CHC)
26. James Wood (OF, WAS)
27. Coby Mayo (3B, BAL)
28. Brayan Rocchio (SS, CLE)
29. Gavin Stone (RHP, LAD)
30. Jace Jung (2B, DET)

31. Marcelo Mayer (SS, BOS)
32. Xavier Edwards (2B, MIA)
33. Mick Abel (RHP, PHI)
34. Justyn-Henry Malloy (OF, DET)
35. Parker Meadows (OF, DET)
36. Michael Busch (IF, CHC)
37. Adael Amador (SS, COL)
38. Austin Wells (C, NYY)
39. Matt Mervis (1B, CHC)
40. Cade Horton (RHP, CHC)

THE NEXT 35 • ALPHA ORDER

Luisangel Acuña (SS, NYM)
Jacob Amaya (SS, MIA)
Edwin Arroyo (SS, CIN)
Tyler Black (2B, MIL)
Ben Brown (RHP, CHC)
Owen Caissie (OF, CHC)
Jake Eder (LHP, CHW)
Yanquiel Fernandez (OF, COL)
Nick Frasso (RHP, LAD)
Robert Gasser (LHP, SD)
Drew Gilbert (OF, NYM)
Emerson Hancock (RHP, SEA)
Tink Hence (RHP, STL)
Brady House (3B, WAS)
Kyle Hurt (RHP, LAD)
Jared Jones (RHP, PIT)
Spencer Jones (OF, NYY)
Brooks Lee (SS, MIN)
Orelvis Martinez (SS, TOR)
Jackson Merrill (SS, SD)
Jacob Misiorowski (RHP, MIL)
Colson Montgomery (SS, CHW)
Connor Norby (2B, BAL)
Connor Phillips (RHP, CIN)
Edgar Quero (C, CHW)
Jeferson Quero (C, MIL)
Jackson Rutledge (RHP, WAS)
Thomas Saggese (IF, STL)
AJ Smith-Shawver (RHP, ATL)
Robby Snelling (LHP, SD)
Drew Thorpe (RHP, NYY)
Ricky Tiedemann (LHP, TOR)
Hurston Waldrep (RHP, ATL)
Owen White (RHP, TEX)
Carson Williams (SS, TAM)

TOP 100 PROSPECTS ARCHIVE

2023

1. Corbin Carroll (OF, ARI)
2. Gunnar Henderson (SS, BAL)
3. Jordan Lawlar (SS, ARI)
4. Jackson Chourio (OF, MIL)
5. Jordan Walker (OF, STL)
6. Anthony Volpe (SS, NYY)
7. Grayson Rodriguez (RHP, BAL)
8. Elly De La Cruz (SS, CIN)
9. Eury Perez (RHP, MIA)
10. Andrew Painter (RHP, PHI)

11. James Wood (OF, WAS)
12. Ezequiel Tovar (SS, COL)
13. Francisco Alvarez (C, NYM)
14. Jackson Holliday (SS, BAL)
15. Druw Jones (OF, ARI)
16. Marcelo Mayer (SS, BOS)
17. Ricky Tiedemann (LHP, TOR)
18. Miguel Vargas (3B, LA)
19. Josh Jung (3B, TEX)
20. Daniel Espino (RHP, CLE)

21. Triston Casas (1B, BOS)
22. Kyle Harrison (LHP, SF)
23. Royce Lewis (SS, MIN)
24. Evan Carter (OF, TEX)
25. Robert Hassell III (OF, WAS)
26. Noelvi Marte (SS, CIN)
27. Gavin Williams (RHP, CLE)
28. Colton Cowser (OF, BAL)
29. Marco Luciano (SS, SF)
30. Jasson Dominguez (OF, NYY)

31. Brett Baty (3B, NYM)
32. Curtis Mead (3B, TAM)
33. Termarr Johnson (2B, PIT)
34. Kyle Manzardo (1B, TAM)
35. Pete Crow-Armstrong (OF, CHC)
36. Tyler Soderstrom (C, OAK)
37. Bobby Miller (RHP, LA)
38. Hunter Brown (RHP, HOU)
39. Diego Cartaya (C, LA)
40. Taj Bradley (RHP, TAM)

41. Elijah Green (OF, WAS)
42. Colson Montgomery (SS, CHW)
43. Masyn Winn (SS, STL)
44. Bo Naylor (C, CLE)
45. Brooks Lee (SS, MIN)
46. Jackson Merrill (SS, SD)
47. Zac Veen (OF, COL)
48. Adael Amador (SS, COL)
49. Kevin Parada (C, NYM)
50. Gavin Stone (RHP, LA)

51. Brandon Pfaadt (RHP, ARI)
52. Sal Frelick (OF, MIL)
53. Oswald Peraza (SS, NYY)
54. Endy Rodriguez (C, PIT)
55. Edwn Arroyo (SS, CIN)
56. Max Meyer (RHP, MIA)
57. Henry Davis (C, PIT)
58. Harry Ford (C, SEA)
59. Brennen Davis (OF, CHC)
60. Cam Collier (3B, CIN)

61. Emmanuel Rodriguez (OF, MIN)
62. Mick Abel (RHP, PHI)
63. Logan O'Hoppe (C, LAA)
64. Brayan Rocchio (SS, CLE)
65. Tink Hence (RHP, STL)
66. Cade Cavalli (RHP, WAS)
67. Connor Norby (2B, BAL)
68. Zach Neto (SS, LAA)
69. George Valera (OF, CLE)
70. Coby Mayo (3B, BAL)

71. DL Hall (LHP, BAL)
72. Jackson Jobe (RHP, DET)
73. Brady House (SS, WAS)
74. Will Brennan (OF, CLE)
75. Esteury Ruiz (OF, OAK)
76. Jace Jung (2B, DET)
77. Matt Mervis (1B, CHC)
78. Tanner Bibee (RHP, CLE)
79. Gavin Cross (OF, KC)
80. Kevin Alcantara (OF, CHC)

81. Garrett Mitchell (OF, MIL)
82. Jordan Westburg (SS, BAL)
83. Yainer Diaz (C, HOU)
84. Quinn Priester (RHP, PIT)
85. Andy Pages (OF, LA)
86. Spencer Jones (OF, NYY)
87. Michael Busch (2B, LA)
88. Oscar Colas (OF, CHW)
89. Chase DeLauter (OF, CLE)
90. Jack Leiter (RHP, TEX)

91. Emerson Hancock (RHP, SEA)
92. Dustin Harris (OF, TEX)
93. Colt Keith (3B, DET)
94. Junior Caminero (3B, TAM)
95. Jacob Berry (3B, MIA)
96. Ceddanne Rafaela (OF, BOS)
97. Ryan Pepiot (RHP, LA)
98. Owen White (RHP, TEX)
99. Jose Acuña (SS, TEX)
100. Wilmer Flores (RHP, DET)

2022

1. Bobby Witt, Jr. (SS, KC)
2. Julio Rodriguez (OF, SEA)
3. Adley Rutschman (C, BAL)
4. Spencer Torkelson (1B, DET)
5. Riley Greene (OF, DET)
6. CJ Abrams (SS, SD)
7. Grayson Rodriguez (RHP, BAL)
8. Shane Baz (RHP, TAM)
9. Noelvi Marte (SS, SEA)
10. Marco Luciano (SS, SF)

11. Corbin Carroll (OF, ARI)
12. Oneil Cruz (SS, PIT)
13. Anthony Volpe (SS, NYY)
14. Francisco Alvarez (C, NYM)
15. George Kirby (RHP, SEA)
16. Brennen Davis (OF, CHC)
17. Jack Leiter (RHP, TEX)
18. Gabriel Moreno (C, TOR)
19. Jordan Walker (3B, STL)
20. Zac Veen (OF, COL)

21. Triston Casas (1B, BOS)
22. Josh Jung (3B, TEX)
23. Marcelo Mayer (SS, BOS)
24. Nolan Gorman (2B, STL)
25. Vidal Brujan (2B, TAM)
26. Hunter Greene (RHP, CIN)
27. Cade Cavalli (RHP, WAS)
28. Henry Davis (C, PIT)
29. Jasson Dominguez (OF, NYY)
30. Austin Martin (SS, MIN)

31. Robert Hassell (OF, SD)
32. Alek Thomas (OF, ARI)
33. Tyler Soderstrom (C, OAK)
34. Max Meyer (RHP, MIA)
35. Brett Baty (3B, NYM)
36. Josh Lowe (OF, TAM)
37. Reid Detmers (LHP, LAA)
38. Orelvis Martinez (SS, TOR)
39. Sixto Sanchez (RHP, MIA)
40. Khalil Watson (SS, MIA)

41. Royce Lewis (SS, MIN)
42. Jordan Lawlar (SS, ARI)
43. Nick Gonzales (2B, PIT)
44. MJ Melendez (C, KC)
45. Nick Lodolo (LHP, CIN)
46. Luis Matos (OF, SF)
47. Nick Pratto (1B, KC)
48. Brady House (SS, WAS)
49. Brayan Rocchio (SS, CLE)
50. Jackson Jobe (RHP, DET)

51. Michael Harris (OF, ATL)
52. Emerson Hancock (RHP, SEA)
53. Edward Cabrera (RHP, MIA)
54. George Valera (OF, CLE)
55. Jordan Groshans (3B, TOR)
56. Cole Winn (RHP, TEX)
57. Diego Cartaya (C, LA)
58. Joey Bart (C, SF)
59. Nick Yorke (2B, BOS)
60. Eury Perez (RHP, MIA)

61. DL Hall (LHP, BAL)
62. Garrett Mitchell (OF, MIL)
63. Daniel Espino (RHP, CLE)
64. Quinn Priester (RHP, PIT)
65. Asa Lacy (LHP, KC)
66. Jarren Duran (OF, BOS)
67. Bobby Miller (RHP, LA)
68. Luis Campusano (C, SD)
69. Mick Abel (RHP, PHI)
70. Ronny Mauricio (SS, NYM)

71. Colton Cowser (OF, BAL)
72. Matthew Liberatore (LHP, STL)
73. Roansy Contreras (RHP, PIT)
74. Oswald Peraza (SS, NYY)
75. MacKenzie Gore (LHP, SD)
76. Tyler Freeman (SS, CLE)
77. Cristian Hernandez (SS, CHC)
78. Coby Mayo (3B, BAL)
79. Greg Jones (SS, TAM)
80. Cristian Pache (OF, ATL)

81. Miguel Vargas (3B, LA)
82. Gunnar Henderson (SS, BAL)
83. Kyle Harrison (LHP, SF)
84. Shea Langeliers (C, ATL)
85. Taj Bradley (RHP, TAM)
86. Bryson Stott (SS, PHI)
87. Elly De La Cruz (3B, CIN)
88. Matt McLain (SS, CIN)
89. Benny Montgomery (OF, COL)
90. Drew Waters (OF, ATL)

91. Heliot Ramos (OF, SF)
92. Drey Jameson (RHP, ARI)
93. Kevin Alcantara (OF, CHC)
94. Mark Vientos (3B, NYM)
95. Curtis Mead (3B, TAM)
96. Jordan Balazovic (RHP, MIN)
97. Spencer Strider (RHP, ATL)
98. Jeremy Pena (SS, HOU)
99. Matt Brash (RHP, SEA)
100. Gavin Williams (RHP, CLE)

TOP 100 PROSPECTS ARCHIVE

2021

1. Wander Franco (SS, TAM)
2. Adley Rutschman (C, BAL)
3. Spencer Torkelson (3B, DET)
4. Jarred Kelenic (OF, SEA)
5. Julio Rodriguez (OF, SEA)
6. Marco Luciano (SS, SF)
7. MacKenzie Gore (LHP, SD)
8. Royce Lewis (SS, MIN)
9. Bobby Witt, Jr. (SS, KC)
10. CJ Abrams (SS, SD)

11. Andrew Vaughn (1B, CHW)
12. Sixto Sanchez (RHP, MIA)
13. Dylan Carlson (OF, STL)
14. Casey Mize (RHP, DET)
15. Austin Martin (SS, TOR)
16. Ke'Bryan Hayes (3B, PIT)
17. Alex Kirilloff (OF, MIN)
18. Forrest Whitley (RHP, HOU)
19. Nate Pearson (RHP, TOR)
20. Ian Anderson (RHP, ATL)

21. Michael Kopech (RHP, CHW)
22. Joey Bart (C, SF)
23. Matthew Manning (RHP, DET)
24. Spencer Howard (RHP, PHI)
25. Cristian Pache (OF, ATL)
26. Asa Lacy (LHP, KC)
27. Kristian Robinson (OF, ARI)
28. Jasson Dominguez (OF, NYY)
29. Max Meyer (RHP, MIA)
30. Vidal Brujan (2B, TAM)

31. JJ Bleday (OF, MIA)
32. Grayson Rodriguez (RHP, BAL)
33. Riley Greene (OF, DET)
34. Corbin Carroll (OF, ARI)
35. Randy Arozarena (OF, TAM)
36. Nick Madrigal (2B, CHW)
37. Nick Gonzales (SS, PIT)
38. Oneil Cruz (SS, PIT)
39. Jeter Downs (2B/SS, BOS)
40. Drew Waters (OF, ATL)

41. Tarik Skubal (LHP, DET)
42. Nolan Jones (3B, CLE)
43. Luis Patino (RHP, TAM)
44. Nolan Gorman (3B, STL)
45. Daniel Lynch (LHP, KC)
46. Jazz Chisholm (SS, MIA)
47. Zac Veen (OF, COL)
48. Jordan Groshans (SS, TOR)
49. Josiah Gray (RHP, LA)
50. Emerson Hancock (RHP, SEA)

51. Brennen Davis (OF, CHC)
52. A.J. Puk (LHP, OAK)
53. Trevor Larnach (OF, MIN)
54. Heliot Ramos (OF, SF)
55. Triston Casas (1B, BOS)
56. Brandon Marsh (OF, LAA)
57. Ronny Mauricio (SS, NYM)
58. Noelvi Marte (SS, SEA)
59. Logan Gilbert (RHP, SEA)
60. Alek Thomas (OF, ARI)

61. Brendan McKay (LHP, TAM)
62. Deivi Garcia (RHP, NYY)
63. Hunter Bishop (OF, SF)
64. Luis Campusano (C, SD)
65. Josh Jung (3B, TEX)
66. Triston McKenzie (RHP, CLE)
67. Heston Kjerstad (OF, BAL)
68. Matthew Liberatore (LHP, STL)
69. DL Hall (LHP, BAL)
70. Francisco Alvarez (C, NYM)

71. Leody Taveras (OF, TEX)
72. George Valera (OF, CLE)
73. Hunter Greene (RHP, CIN)
74. Brailyn Marquez (LHP, CHC)
75. Garrett Mitchell (OF, MIL)
76. Nick Lodolo (LHP, CIN)
77. Clarke Schmidt (RHP, NYY)
78. Xavier Edwards (2B/SS, TAM)
79. Geraldo Perdomo (SS, ARI)
80. Jordyn Adams (OF, LAA)

81. Tyler Freeman (SS, CLE)
82. Ryan Mountcastle (1B, BAL)
83. Edward Cabrera (RHP, MIA)
84. Robert Hassell (OF, SD)
85. Jordan Balazovic (RHP, MIN)
86. Austin Hendrick (OF, CIN)
87. Reid Detmers (LHP, LAA)
88. Taylor Trammell (OF, SEA)
89. Bo Naylor (C, CLE)
90. Shane Baz (RHP, TAM)

91. Bobby Dalbec (1B/3B, BOS)
92. Erick Pena (OF, KC)
93. Greg Jones (SS, TAM)
94. Matthew Allan (RHP, NYM)
95. Jesus Sanchez (OF, MIA)
96. Garrett Crochet (LHP, CHW)
97. Mick Abel (RHP, PHI)
98. Josh Lowe (OF, TAM)
99. Simeon Woods-Richardson (RHP, TOR)
100. Keibert Ruiz (C, LA)

2020

1. Wander Franco (SS, TAM)
2. Jo Adell (OF, LAA)
3. Luis Robert (OF, CHW)
4. Gavin Lux (SS, LA)
5. MacKenzie Gore (LHP, SD)
6. Royce Lewis (SS, MIN)
7. Jarred Kelenic (OF, SEA)
8. Adley Rutschman (C, BAL)
9. Forrest Whitley (RHP, HOU)
10. Julio Rodriguez (OF, SEA)

11. Jesus Luzardo (LHP, OAK)
12. Andrew Vaughn (1B, CHW)
13. Casey Mize (RHP, DET)
14. Carter Kieboom (SS, WAS)
15. Dylan Carlson (OF, STL)
16. Nate Pearson (RHP, TOR)
17. Dustin May (RHP, LA)
18. Alex Kirilloff (OF, MIN)
19. Bobby Witt, Jr. (SS, KC)
20. Marco Luciano (SS, SF)

21. Joey Bart (C, SF)
22. Michael Kopech (RHP, CHW)
23. Cristian Pache (OF, ATL)
24. Matt Manning (RHP, DET)
25. C.J. Abrams (SS, SD)
26. Sixto Sanchez (RHP, MIA)
27. Drew Waters (OF, ATL)
28. Alec Bohm (3B, PHI)
29. Brendan McKay (LHP/DH, TAM)
30. Kristian Robinson (OF, ARI)

31. Vidal Brujan (2B, TAM)
32. A.J. Puk (LHP, OAK)
33. Brendan Rodgers (SS, COL)
34. Luis Patino (RHP, SD)
35. Spencer Howard (RHP, PHI)
36. J.J. Bleday (OF, MIA)
37. Nolan Gorman (3B, STL)
38. Heliot Ramos (OF, SF)
39. Jazz Chisholm (SS, MIA)
40. Mitch Keller (RHP, PIT)

41. Nolan Jones (3B, CLE)
42. Taylor Trammell (OF, SD)
43. Jasson Dominguez (OF, NYY)
44. Grayson Rodriguez (RHP, BAL)
45. Brusdar Graterol (RHP, MIN)
46. Ian Anderson (RHP, ATL)
47. Oneil Cruz (SS, PIT)
48. Jesus Sanchez (OF, MIA)
49. Hunter Bishop (OF, SF)
50. Trevor Larnach (OF, MIN)

51. Nick Madrigal (2B, CHW)
52. Riley Greene (OF, DET)
53. Ryan Mountcastle (1B, BAL)
54. Ke'Bryan Hayes (3B, PIT)
55. Jordan Groshans (SS, TOR)
56. Ronny Mauricio (SS, NYM)
57. Daniel Lynch (LHP, KC)
58. Xavier Edwards (SS, TAM)
59. Matthew Liberatore (LHP, TAM)
60. D.L. Hall (LHP, BAL)

61. Alek Thomas (OF, ARI)
62. Brennen Davis (OF, CHC)
63. Hunter Greene (RHP, CIN)
64. Deivi Garcia (RHP, NYY)
65. Logan Gilbert (RHP, SEA)
66. Nico Hoerner (SS, CHC)
67. Kyle Wright (RHP, ATL)
68. George Valera (OF, CLE)
69. Sean Murphy (C, OAK)
70. Corbin Carroll (OF, ARI)

71. Keibert Ruiz (C, LA)
72. Josiah Gray (RHP, LA)
73. Josh Jung (3B, TEX)
74. Evan White (1B, SEA)
75. Tyler Freeman (SS, CLE)
76. Luis Garcia (SS, WAS)
77. Shane Baz (RHP, TAM)
78. Daulton Varsho (C, ARI)
79. Triston Casas (1B, BOS)
80. Nick Lodolo (LHP, CIN)

81. Hans Crouse (RHP, TEX)
82. Tarik Skubal (LHP, DET)
83. Brandon Marsh (OF, LAA)
84. Jeter Downs (SS, LA)
85. Greg Jones (SS, TAM)
86. Luis Campusano (C, SD)
87. Clarke Schmidt (RHP, NYY)
88. Noelvi Marte (SS, SEA)
89. Jordan Balazovic (RHP, MIN)
90. Ethan Hankins (RHP, CLE)

91. Sherten Apostel (3B, TEX)
92. Robert Puason (SS, OAK)
93. Brent Honeywell (RHP, TAM)
94. Brady Singer (RHP, KC)
95. Leody Taveras (OF, TEX)
96. Francisco Alvarez (C, NYM)
97. Geraldo Perdomo (SS, ARI)
98. Adrian Morejon (LHP, SD)
99. Monte Harrison (OF, MIA)
100. Brailyn Marquez (LHP, CHC)

TOP 100 PROSPECTS ARCHIVE

2019

1. Vladimir Guerrero Jr., (3B, TOR)
2. Eloy Jimenez, (OF, CHW)
3. Fernando Tatis Jr., (SS, SD)
4. Victor Robles, (OF, WAS)
5. Royce Lewis, (SS, MIN)
6. Kyle Tucker, (OF, HOU)
7. Forrest Whitley, (RHP, HOU)
8. Bo Bichette, (SS, TOR)
9. Nick Senzel, (2B, CIN)
10. Alex Kirilloff, (OF, MIN)

11. Jo Adell, (OF, LAA)
12. Wander Franco, (SS, TAM)
13. Jesus Luzardo, (LHP, OAK)
14. Brendan Rodgers, (SS, COL)
15. Michael Kopech, (RHP, CHW)
16. MacKenzie Gore, (LHP, SD)
17. Taylor Trammell, (OF, CIN)
18. Keston Hiura, (2B, MIL)
19. Sixto Sanchez, (RHP, PHI)
20. Casey Mize, (RHP, DET)

21. Dylan Cease, (RHP, CHW)
22. Mike Soroka, (RHP, ATL)
23. Joey Bart, (C, SF)
24. Carter Kieboom, (SS, WAS)
25. Alex Reyes, (RHP, STL)
26. Luis Urias, (2B, SD)
27. Ian Anderson, (RHP, ATL)
28. Brent Honeywell, (RHP, TAM)
29. Mitch Keller, (RHP, PIT)
30. Keibert Ruiz, (C, LA)

31. Peter Alonso, (1B, NYM)
32. Chris Paddack, (RHP, SD)
33. Hunter Greene, (RHP, CIN)
34. A.J. Puk, (LHP, OAK)
35. Austin Riley, (3B, ATL)
36. Kyle Wright, (RHP, ATL)
37. Alex Verdugo, (OF, LA)
38. Luis Robert, (OF, CHW)
39. Jesus Sanchez, (OF, TAM)
40. Nick Madrigal, (SS, CHW)

41. Triston McKenzie, (RHP, CLE)
42. Yordan Alvarez, (OF, HOU)
43. Brendan McKay, (1B/LHP, TAM)
44. Jonathan India, (3B, CIN)
45. Touki Toussaint, (RHP, ATL)
46. Matt Manning, (RHP, DET)
47. Francisco Mejia, (C, SD)
48. Ke'Bryan Hayes, (3B, PIT)
49. Nolan Gorman, (3B, STL)
50. Adrian Morejon, (LHP, SD)

51. Danny Jansen, (C, TOR)
52. Alec Bohm, (3B, PHI)
53. Justus Sheffield, (LHP, SEA)
54. Yusinel Diaz, (OF, BAL)
55. Jarred Kelenic, (OF, SEA)
56. Andres Gimenez, (SS, NYM)
57. Estevan Florial, (OF, NYY)
58. Luis Garcia, (SS/3B, WAS)
59. Jon Duplantier, (RHP, ARI)
60. Luis Patino, (RHP, SD)

61. Leody Taveras, (OF, TEX)
62. Nolan Jones, (3B, CLE)
63. Gavin Lux, (2B, LA)
64. Adonis Medina, (RHP, PHI)
65. Michel Baez, (RHP, SD)
66. Brusdar Graterol, (RHP, MIN)
67. Julio Pablo Martinez, (OF, TEX)
68. Matthew Liberatore, (LHP, TAM)
69. Cristian Pache, (OF, ATL)
70. Dustin May, (RHP, LA)

71. Josh James, (RHP, HOU)
72. Jonathan Loaisiga, (RHP, NYY)
73. Sean Murphy, (C, OAK)
74. Brady Singer, (RHP, KC)
75. Dane Dunning, (RHP, CHW)
76. Khalil Lee, (OF, KC)
77. Ryan Mountcastle, (3B, BAL)
78. Heliot Ramos, (OF, SF)
79. Nate Pearson, (RHP, TOR)
80. Drew Waters, (OF, ATL)

81. Jazz Chisholm, (SS, ARI)
82. Hans Crouse, (RHP, TEX)
83. DL Hall, (LHP, BAL)
84. MJ Melendez, (C, KC)
85. Oneil Cruz, (SS, PIT)
86. Kristian Robinson, (OF, ARI)
87. Ronaldo Hernandez, (C, TAM)
88. Vidal Brujan, (2B, TAM)
89. Colton Welker, (3B, COL)
90. Franklin Perez, (RHP, DET)

91. Travis Swaggerty, (OF, PIT)
92. Daz Cameron, (OF, DET)
93. Griffin Canning, (RHP, LAA)
94. Bryse Wilson, (RHP, ATL)
95. Brandon Marsh, (OF, LAA)
96. Bubba Thompson, (OF, TEX)
97. Logan Allen, (LHP, SD)
98. Justin Dunn , (RHP, SEA)
99. Miguel Amaya, (C, CHC)
100. Dakota Hudson, (RHP, STL)

2018

1. Ronald Acuna (OF, ATL)
2. Victor Robles (OF, WAS)
3. Vladimir Guerrero Jr. (3B, TOR)
4. Eloy Jimenez (OF, CHW)
5. Gleyber Torres (SS, NYY)
6. Brendan Rodgers (SS, COL)
7. Nick Senzel (3B, CIN)
8. Alex Reyes (RHP, STL)
9. Walker Buehler (RHP, LA)
10. Michael Kopech (RHP, CHW)

11. Fernando Tatis Jr. (SS, SD)
12. Kyle Tucker (OF, HOU)
13. Bo Bichette (SS, TOR)
14. Lewis Brinson (OF, MIL)
15. Brent Honeywell (RHP, TAM)
16. MacKenzie Gore (LHP, SD)
17. Forrest Whitley (RHP, HOU)
18. Willy Adames (SS, TAM)
19. Leody Taveras (OF, TEX)
20. Royce Lewis (SS, MIN)

21. Mitch Keller (RHP, PIT)
22. Francisco Mejia (C, CLE)
23. Kyle Wright (RHP, ATL)
24. A.J. Puk (LHP, OAK)
25. Sixto Sanchez (RHP, PHI)
26. Hunter Greene (RHP, CIN)
27. Franklin Barreto (SS, OAK)
28. Juan Soto (OF, WAS)
29. Triston McKenzie (RHP, CLE)
30. Luiz Gohara (LHP, ATL)

31. Alex Verdugo (OF, LA)
32. Franklin Perez (RHP, DET)
33. Luis Robert (OF, CHW)
34. Keston Huira (2B, MIL)
35. Ryan McMahon (1B, COL)
36. Scott Kingery (2B, PHI)
37. Mike Soroka (RHP, ATL)
38. Willie Calhoun (OF/2B, TEX)
39. Kolby Allard (LHP, ATL)
40. Austin Hays (OF, BAL)

41. Jack Flaherty (RHP, STL)
42. J.P. Crawford (SS, PHI)
43. Anthony Alford (OF, TOR)
44. Austin Meadows (OF, PIT)
45. Brendan McKay (1B/LHP, TAM)
46. Luis Urias (2B/SS, SD)
47. Kyle Lewis (OF, SEA)
48. Taylor Trammell (OF, CIN)
49. Yadier Alvarez (RHP, LA)
50. Estevan Florial (OF, NYY)

51. Jay Groome (LHP, BOS)
52. Cal Quantrill (RHP, SD)
53. Nick Gordon (SS, MIN)
54. Jesus Sanchez (OF, TAM)
55. Chance Adams (RHP, NYY)
56. Jorge Mateo (SS, OAK)
57. Ian Anderson (RHP, ATL)
58. Michel Baez (RHP, SD)
59. Alec Hansen (RHP, CHW)
60. Monte Harrison (OF, MIL)

61. Keibert Ruiz (C, LA)
62. Carson Kelly (C, STL)
63. Kevin Maitan (3B, LAA)
64. Riley Pint (RHP, COL)
65. Anderson Espinoza (RHP, SD)
66. Matt Manning (RHP, DET)
67. Austin Beck (OF, OAK)
68. Dylan Cease (RHP, CHW)
69. Jorge Alfaro (C, PHI)
70. Justus Sheffield (LHP, NYY)

71. Blake Rutherford (OF, CHW)
72. Chance Sisco (C, BAL)
73. Ryan Mountcastle (3B, BAL)
74. Corbin Burnes (RHP, MIL)
75. Jake Bauers (OF/1B, TAM)
76. Pavin Smith (1B, ARI)
77. Adonis Medina (RHP, PHI)
78. Jon Duplantier (RHP, ARI)
79. Heliot Ramos (OF, SF)
80. Adrian Morejon (LHP, SD)

81. Dustin Fowler (OF, OAK)
82. Mickey Moniak (OF, PHI)
83. Shane Baz (RHP, PIT)
84. Yusniel Diaz (OF, LA)
85. Jesse Winker (OF, CIN)
86. Stephen Gonsalves (LHP, MIN)
87. Isan Diaz (2B, MIL)
88. Joey Wentz (LHP, ATL)
89. Tyler O'Neill (OF, STL)
90. Alex Faedo (RHP, DET)

91. Jo Adell (OF, LAA)
92. Austin Riley (3B, ATL)
93. Corey Ray (OF, MIL)
94. Brandon Woodruff (RHP, MIL)
95. Mitchell White (RHP, LA)
96. Yordan Alvarez (1B, HOU)
97. Michael Chavis (3B, BOS)
98. Jose De Leon (RHP, TAM)
99. Christian Arroyo (3B, TAM)
100. Chris Shaw (1B, SF)

TOP 100 PROSPECTS ARCHIVE

2017

1. Yoan Moncada (2B, CHW)
2. Andrew Benintendi (OF, BOS)
3. Dansby Swanson (SS, ATL)
4. Alex Reyes (RHP, STL)
5. Lucas Giolito (RHP, CHW)
6. Victor Robles (OF, WAS)
7. J.P. Crawford (SS, PHI)
8. Tyler Glasnow (RHP, PIT)
9. Brendan Rodgers (SS, COL)
10. Austin Meadows (OF, PIT)

11. Gleyber Torres (SS, NYY)
12. Amed Rosario (SS, NYM)
13. Rafael Devers (3B, BOS)
14. Lewis Brinson (OF, MIL)
15. Anderson Espinoza (RHP, SD)
16. Willy Adames (SS, TAM)
17. Eloy Jimenez (OF, CHC)
18. Manuel Margot (OF, SD)
19. Ozzie Albies (2B, ATL)
20. Clint Frazier (OF, NYY)

21. Bradley Zimmer (OF, CLE)
22. Franklin Barreto (SS, OAK)
23. Brent Honeywell (RHP, TAM)
24. Cody Bellinger (1B, LAD)
25. Francis Martes (RHP, HOU)
26. Reynaldo Lopez (RHP, CHW)
27. Jose De Leon (RHP, LAD)
28. Mickey Moniak (OF, PHI)
29. Ian Happ (2B, CHC)
30. Kyle Tucker (OF, HOU)

31. Nick Senzel (3B, CIN)
32. Michael Kopech (RHP, CHW)
33. Aaron Judge (OF, NYY)
34. Josh Bell (1B, PIT)
35. Kyle Lewis (OF, SEA)
36. Hunter Renfroe (OF, SD)
37. Jorge Mateo (SS, NYY)
38. Amir Garrett (LHP, CIN)
39. Corey Ray (OF, MIL)
40. Jeff Hoffman (RHP, COL)

41. Tyler O'Neill (OF, SEA)
42. Josh Hader (LHP, MIL)
43. Kolby Allard (LHP, ATL)
44. Jason Groome (LHP, BOS)
45. Jorge Alfaro (C, PHI)
46. Nick Williams (OF, PHI)
47. Nick Gordon (SS, MIN)
48. Sean Newcomb (LHP, ATL)
49. Alex Verdugo (OF, LAD)
50. Blake Rutherford (OF, NYY)

51. Carson Fulmer (RHP, CHW)
52. Vladimir Guerrero, Jr. (3B, TOR)
53. David Paulino (RHP, HOU)
54. Mitch Keller (RHP, PIT)
55. Riley Pint (RHP, COL)
56. Francisco Mejia (C, CLE)
57. Brady Aiken (LHP, CLE)
58. Yulieski Gurriel (3B, HOU)
59. Braxton Garrett (LHP, MIA)
60. Tyler Jay (LHP, MIN)

61. A.J. Puk (LHP, OAK)
62. Kevin Newman (SS, PIT)
63. Robert Stephenson (RHP, CIN)
64. Sean Reid-Foley (RHP, TOR)
65. Matt Manning (RHP, DET)
66. Anthony Alford (OF, TOR)
67. Jesse Winker (OF, CIN)
68. Dominic Smith (1B, NYM)
69. Raimel Tapia (OF, COL)
70. Zack Collins (C, CHW)

71. James Kaprielian (RHP, NYY)
72. Erick Fedde (RHP, WAS)
73. Luis Ortiz (RHP, MIL)
74. Phil Bickford (RHP, MIL)
75. Jake Bauers (OF, TAM)
76. Justus Sheffield (LHP, NYY)
77. Matt Chapman (3B, OAK)
78. Luke Weaver (RHP, STL)
79. Grant Holmes (RHP, OAK)
80. Bobby Bradley (1B, CLE)

81. Ronald Acuna (OF, ATL)
82. Derek Fisher (OF, HOU)
83. Brett Phillips (OF, MIL)
84. Yadier Alvarez (RHP, LAD)
85. Leody Taveras (OF, TEX)
86. Yohander Mendez (LHP, TEX)
87. Kevin Maitan (SS, ATL)
88. Triston McKenzie (LHP, CLE)
89. Willie Calhoun (2B, LAD)
90. Ryan McMahon (3B, COL)

91. Isan Diaz (2B, MIL)
92. Ian Anderson (RHP, ATL)
93. Trent Clark (OF, MIL)
94. Alex Kirilloff (OF, MIN)
95. Harrison Bader (OF, STL)
96. Tyler Beede (RHP, SF)
97. Richard Urena (SS, TOR)
98. Mike Soroka (RHP, ATL)
99. Dylan Cease (RHP, CHC)
100. Stephen Gonsalves (LHP, MIN)

2016

1. Byron Buxton (OF, MIN)
2. Corey Seager (SS, LAD)
3. Lucas Giolito (RHP, WAS)
4. J.P. Crawford (SS, PHI)
5. Alex Reyes (RHP, STL)
6. Julio Urias (LHP, LAD)
7. Yoan Moncada (2B, BOS)
8. Tyler Glasnow (RHP, PIT)
9. Joey Gallo (3B, TEX)
10. Steven Matz (LHP, NYM)

11. Rafael Devers (3B, BOS)
12. Jose Berrios (RHP, MIN)
13. Orlando Arcia (SS, MIL)
14. Blake Snell (LHP, TAM)
15. Trea Turner (SS, WAS)
16. Bradley Zimmer (OF, CLE)
17. Jose De Leon (RHP, LAD)
18. Brendan Rodgers (SS, COL)
19. Dansby Swanson (SS, ATL)
20. Robert Stephenson (RHP, CIN)

21. Nomar Mazara (OF, TEX)
22. Victor Robles (OF, WAS)
23. Aaron Judge (OF, NYY)
24. Manuel Margot (OF, SD)
25. Clint Frazier (OF, CLE)
26. Lewis Brinson (OF, TEX)
27. Alex Bregman (SS, HOU)
28. Jon Gray (RHP, COL)
29. Ryan McMahon (3B, COL)
30. Austin Meadows (OF, PIT)

31. Nick Williams (OF, PHI)
32. Franklin Barreto (SS, OAK)
33. David Dahl (OF, COL)
34. Brett Phillips (OF, MIL)
35. Gleyber Torres (SS, CHC)
36. Sean Newcomb (LHP, ATL)
37. Carson Fulmer (RHP, CHW)
38. Ozhaino Albies (SS, ATL)
39. Dillon Tate (RHP, TEX)
40. Andrew Benintendi (OF, BOS)

41. Jameson Taillon (RHP, PIT)
42. Raul Mondesi (SS, KC)
43. Archie Bradley (RHP, ARI)
44. Tim Anderson (SS, CHW)
45. Kolby Allard (LHP, ATL)
46. Jake Thompson (RHP, PHI)
47. Dylan Bundy (RHP, BAL)
48. Willy Adames (SS, TAM)
49. Anderson Espinoza (RHP, BOS)
50. Aaron Blair (RHP, ATL)

51. A.J. Reed (1B, HOU)
52. Jeff Hoffman (RHP, COL)
53. Jesse Winker (OF, CIN)
54. Brent Honeywell (RHP, TAM)
55. Josh Bell (1B, PIT)
56. Anthony Alford (OF, TOR)
57. Tyler Kolek (RHP, MIA)
58. Max Kepler (OF, MIN)
59. Hunter Renfroe (OF, SD)
60. Mark Appel (RHP, PHI)

61. Kyle Zimmer (RHP, KC)
62. Jose Peraza (2B, CIN)
63. Kyle Tucker (OF, HOU)
64. Cody Reed (LHP, CIN)
65. Billy McKinney (OF, CHC)
66. Nick Gordon (SS, MIN)
67. Braden Shipley (RHP, ARI)
68. Jorge Lopez (RHP, MIL)
69. Touki Toussaint (RHP, ATL)
70. Hector Olivera (3B, ATL)

71. Derek Fisher (OF, HOU)
72. Jorge Alfaro (C, PHI)
73. Raimel Tapia (OF, COL)
74. Grant Holmes (RHP, LAD)
75. Dominic Smith (1B, NYM)
76. Daz Cameron (OF, HOU)
77. Alex Jackson (OF, SEA)
78. Sean Manaea (LHP, OAK)
79. Amed Rosario (SS, NYM)
80. Reynaldo Lopez (RHP, WAS)

81. Javier Guerra (SS, SD)
82. Hunter Harvey (RHP, BAL)
83. Luis Ortiz (RHP, TEX)
84. Brady Aiken (LHP, CLE)
85. Matt Olson (1B, OAK)
86. Jorge Mateo (SS, NYY)
87. Daniel Robertson (SS, TAM)
88. Taylor Guerrieri (RHP, TAM)
89. Amir Garrett (LHP, CIN)
90. Willson Contreras (C, CHC)

91. Renato Nunez (3B, OAK)
92. Tyler Jay (LHP, MIN)
93. Tyler Stephenson (C, CIN)
94. Christian Arroyo (SS, SF)
95. Josh Naylor (1B, MIA)
96. Brian Johnson (LHP, BOS)
97. Tyler Beede (RHP, SF)
98. Garrett Whitley (OF, TAM)
99. Cody Bellinger (1B, LAD)
100. Michael Fulmer (RHP, DET)

GLOSSARY

AVG: Batting Average (see also BA)

BA: Batting Average (see also AVG)

Base Performance Indicator (BPI): A statistical formula that measures an isolated aspect of a player's situation-independent raw skill or a gauge that helps capture the effects of random chance has on a skill. Although there are many such formulas, there are only a few that we are referring to when the term is used in this book. For pitchers, our BPI's are control (bb%), dominance (k/9), command (k/bb), opposition on base average (OOB), ground/line/fly ratios (G/L/F), and expected ERA (xERA). Random chance is measured witih the hit rate (H%) and strand rate (S%).

*Base Performance Value (BPV): A single value that describes a pitcher's overall raw skill level. This is more useful than any traditional statistical gauge to track performance trends and project future statistical output. The BPV formula combines and weights several BPIs:

(Dominance Rate x 6) + (Command ratio x 21) – Opposition HR Rate x 30) – ((Opp. Batting Average - .275) x 200)

The formula combines the individual raw skills of power, command, the ability to keep batters from reaching base, and the ability to prevent long hits, all characteristics that are unaffected by most external team factors. In tandem with a pitcher's strand rate, it provides a complete picture of the elements that contribute to a pitcher's ERA, and therefore serves as an accurate tool to project likely changes in ERA. **BENCHMARKS:** We generally consider a BPV of 50 to be the minimum level required for long-term success. The elite of bullpen aces will have BPV's in the excess of 100 and it is rare for these stoppers to enjoy long-term success with consistent levels under 75.

Batters Faced per Game *(Craig Wright)*

((IP x 2.82) + H + BB) / G

A measure of pitcher usage and one of the leading indicators for potential pitcher burnout.

Batting Average (BA, or AVG)

(H/AB)

Ratio of hits to at-bats, though it is a poor evaluative measure of hitting performance. It neglects the offensive value of the base on balls and assumes that all hits are created equal.

Batting Eye (Eye)

(Walks / Strikeouts)

A measure of a player's strike zone judgment, the raw ability to distinguish between balls and strikes. **BENCHMARKS:** The best hitters have eye ratios over 1.00 (indicating more walks than strikeouts) and are the most likely to be among a league's .300 hitters. At the other end of the scale are ratios

less than 0.50, which represent batters who likely also have lower BAs.

bb%: Walk rate (hitters)

bb/9: Opposition Walks per 9 IP

BF/Gm: Batters Faced Per Game

BPI: Base Performance Indicator

*BPV: Base Performance Value

Cmd: Command ratio

Command Ratio (Cmd)

(Strikeouts / Walks)

This is a measure of a pitcher's raw ability to get the ball over the plate. There is no more fundamental a skill than this, and so it is accurately used as a leading indicator to project future rises and falls in other gauges, such as ERA. Command is one of the best gauges to use to evaluate minor league performance. It is a prime component of a pitcher's base performance value. **BENCHMARKS:** Baseball's upper echelon of command pitchers will have ratios in excess of 3.0. Pitchers with ratios under 1.0 — indicating that they walk more batters than they strike out — have virtually no potential for long term success. If you make no other changes in your approach to drafting a pitching staff, limiting your focus to only pitchers with a command ratio of 2.0 or better will substantially improve your odds of success.

Contact Rate (ct%)

((AB - K) / AB)

Measures a batter's ability to get wood on the ball and hit it into the field of play. **BENCHMARK:** Those batters with the best contact skill will have levels of 90% or better. The hackers of society will have levels of 75% or less.

Control Rate (bb/9), or Opposition Walks per Game

BB Allowed x 9 / IP

Measures how many walks a pitcher allows per game equivalent. **BENCHMARK:** The best pitchers will have bb/9 levels of 3.0 or less.

ct%: Contact rate

Ctl: Control Rate

Dom: Dominance Rate

Dominance Rate (k/9), or Opposition Strikeouts per Game

(K Allowed x 9 / IP)

Measures how many strikeouts a pitcher allows per game equivalent. **BENCHMARK:** The best pitchers will have k/9 levels of 6.0 or higher.

*Expected Earned Run Average (*Gill and Reeve*)

(.575 x H [per 9 IP]) + (.94 x HR [per 9 IP]) + (.28 x BB [per 9 IP]) - (.01 x K [per 9 IP]) - Normalizing Factor

"xERA represents the expected ERA of the pitcher based on a normal distribution of his statistics. It is not influenced by situation-dependent factors." xERA erases the inequity between starters' and relievers' ERA's, eliminating the effect that a pitcher's success or failure has on another pitcher's ERA.

Similar to other gauges, the accuracy of this formula changes with the level of competition from one season to the next. The normalizing factor allows us to better approximate a pitcher's actual ERA. This value is usually somewhere around 2.77 and varies by league and year. **BENCHMARKS:** In general, xERA's should approximate a pitcher's ERA fairly closely. However, those pitchers who have large variances between the two gauges are candidates for further analysis.

Extra-Base Hit Rate (X/H)

(2B + 3B + HR) / Hits

X/H is a measure of power and can be used along with a player's slugging percentage and isolated power to gauge a player's ability to drive the ball. **BENCHMARKS:** Players with above average power will post X/H of greater than 38% and players with moderate power will post X/H of 30% or greater. Weak hitters with below average power will have a X/H level of less than 20%.

Eye: Batting Eye

h%: Hit rate (batters)

H%: Hits Allowed per Balls in Play (pitchers)

Hit Rate (h% or H%)

(H—HR) / (AB – HR - K)

The percent of balls hit into the field of play that fall for hits.

hr/9: Opposition Home Runs per 9 IP

ISO: Isolated Power

Isolated Power (ISO)

(Slugging Percentage - Batting Average)

Isolated Power is a measurement of power skill. Subtracting a player's BA from his SLG, we are essentially pulling out all the singles and single bases from the formula. What remains are the extra-base hits. ISO is not an absolute measurement as it assumes that two doubles is worth one home run, which certainly is not the case, but is another statistic that is a good measurement of raw power. **BENCHMARKS:** The game's top sluggers will tend to have ISO levels over .200. Weak hitters will be under .100.

k/9: Dominance rate (opposition strikeouts per 9 IP)

Major League Equivalency (*Bill James*)

A formula that converts a player's minor or foreign league statistics into a comparable performance in the major leagues. These are not projections, but conversions of current performance.

Contains adjustments for the level of play in individual leagues and teams. Works best with Triple-A stats, not quite as well with Double-A stats, and hardly at all with the lower levels. Foreign conversions are still a work in process. James' original formula only addressed batting. Our research has devised conversion formulas for pitchers, however, their best use comes when looking at BPI's, not traditional stats.

MLE: Major League Equivalency

OBP: On Base Percentage (batters)

OBA: Opposition Batting Average (pitchers)

On Base Percentage (OBP)

(H + BB) / (AB + BB)

Addressing one of the two deficiencies in BA, OBP gives value to those events that get batters on base, but are not hits. By adding walks (and often, hit batsmen) into the basic batting average formula, we have a better gauge of a batter's ability to reach base safely. An OBP of .350 can be read as "this batter gets on base 35% of the time."

Why this is a more important gauge than batting average? When a run is scored, there is no distinction made as to how that runner reached base. So, two thirds of the time—about how often a batter comes to the plate with the bases empty—a walk really is as good as a hit. **BENCHMARKS:** We all know what a .300 hitter is, but what represents "good" for OBP? That comparable level would likely be .400, with .275 representing the level of futility.

On Base Plus Slugging Percentage (OPS): A simple sum of the two gauges, it is considered as one of the better evaluators of overall performance. OPS combines the two basic elements of offensive production — the ability to get on base (OBP) and the ability to advance baserunners (SLG). **BENCHMARKS:** The game's top batters will have OPS levels over .900. The worst batters will have levels under .600.

Opposition Batting Average (OBA)

(Hits Allowed / ((IP x 2.82) + Hits Allowed))

A close approximation of the batting average achieved by opposing batters against a particular pitcher. **BENCHMARKS:** The converse of the benchmark for batters, the best pitchers will have levels under .250; the worst pitchers levels over .300.

Opposition Home Runs per Game (hr/9)

(HR Allowed x 9 / IP)

Measures how many home runs a pitcher allows per game equivalent. **BENCHMARK:** The best pitchers will have hr/9 levels of under 1.0.

Opposition On Base Average (OOB)

(Hits Allowed + BB) / ((IP x 2.82) + H + BB)

A close approximation of the on base average achieved by opposing batters against a particular pitcher. **BENCHMARK:** The best pitchers will have levels under .300; the worst pitchers levels over .375.

Opposition Strikeouts per Game: See Dominance Rate.

Opposition Walks per Game: See Control Rate.

OPS: On Base Plus Slugging Percentage

RC: Runs Created

RC/G: Runs Created Per Game

Runs Created *(Bill James)*

(H + BB - CS) x (Total bases + (.55 x SB)) / (AB + BB)

A formula that converts all offensive events into a total of runs scored. As calculated for individual teams, the result approximates a club's actual run total with great accuracy.

Runs Created Per Game *(Bill James)*

Runs Created / ((AB - H + CS) / 25.5)

RC expressed on a per-game basis might be considered the hypothetical ERA compiled against a particular batter. **BENCHMARKS:** Few players surpass the level of a 10.00 RC/G in any given season, but any level over 7.50 can still be considered very good. At the bottom are levels below 3.00.

S%: Strand Rate

Save: There are six events that need to occur in order for a pitcher to post a single save...

1. The starting pitcher and middle relievers must pitch well.
2. The offense must score enough runs.
3. It must be a reasonably close game.
4. The manager must choose to put the pitcher in for a save opportunity.
5. The pitcher must pitch well and hold the lead.
6. The manager must let him finish the game.

Of these six events, only one is within the control of the relief pitcher. As such, projecting saves for a reliever has little to do with skill and a lot to do with opportunity. However, pitchers with excellent skills sets may create opportunity for themselves.

Situation Independent: Describing a statistical gauge that measures performance apart from the context of team, ballpark, or other outside variables. Strikeouts and Walks, inasmuch as they are unaffected by the performance of a batter's surrounding team, are considered situation independent stats.

Conversely, RBIs are situation dependent because individual performance varies greatly by the performance of other batters on the team (you can't drive in runs if there is nobody on base). Similarly, pitching wins are as much a measure of the success of a pitcher as they are a measure of the success of the offense and defense performing behind that pitcher, and are therefore a poor measure of pitching performance alone.

Situation independent gauges are important for us to be able to separate a player's contribution to his team and isolate his performance so that we may judge it on its own merits.

Slg: Slugging Percentage

Slugging Percentage (Slg)

(Singles + (2 x Doubles) + (3 x Triples) + (4 x HR)) / AB

A measure of the total number of bases accumulated per at bat. It is a misnomer; it is not a true measure of a batter's slugging ability because it includes singles. SLG also assumes that each type of hit has proportionately increasing value (i.e. a double is twice as valuable as a single, etc.) which is not true. **BENCHMARKS:** The top batters will have levels over .500. The bottom batters will have levels under .300.

Strand Rate (S%)

(H + BB - ER) / (H + BB - HR)

Measures the percentage of allowed runners a pitcher strands, which incorporates both individual pitcher skill and bullpen effectiveness. **BENCHMARKS:** The most adept at stranding runners will have S% levels over 75%. Once a pitcher's S% starts dropping down below 65%, he's going to have problems with his ERA. Those pitchers with strand rates over 80% will have artificially low ERAs, which will be prone to relapse.

Strikeouts per Game: See Opposition Strikeouts per game.

Walks + Hits per Innings Pitched (WHIP): The number of baserunners a pitcher allows per inning. **BENCHMARKS:** Usually, a WHIP of under 1.20 is considered top level and over 1.50 is indicative of poor performance. Levels under 1.00 — allowing fewer runners than IP — represent extraordinary performance and are rarely maintained over time.

Walk rate (bb%)

(BB / (AB + BB))

A measure of a batter's eye and plate patience. BENCHMARKS: The best batters will have levels of over 10%. Those with the least plate patience will have levels of 5% or less.

Walks per Game: See Opposition Walks per Game.

WHIP: Walks + Hits per Innings Pitched

Wins: There are five events that need to occur in order for a pitcher to post a single win...

1. He must pitch well, allowing few runs.
2. The offense must score enough runs.
3. The defense must successfully field all batted balls.
4. The bullpen must hold the lead.
5. The manager must leave the pitcher in for 5 innings, and not remove him if the team is still behind.

X/H: Extra-base Hit Rate

*xERA: Expected ERA

* Asterisked formulas have updated versions in the Baseball Forecaster. *However, those updates include statistics like Ground Ball Rate, Fly Ball Rate or Line Drive Rate, for which we do not have reliable data for minor leaguers. So we use the previous version of those formulas, as listed here, for the players in this book.*

Returning to Tampa!

March 1-3, 2024

St. Petersburg Clearwater Marriott, St. Petersburg, FL

Featuring:

Interactive sessions on topics like player analysis,

injury warning signs, and 2024 breakout picks

Current ADP discussions, plus strategies for auctions and drafts

Spring training games just a few miles away

Drafts! Live, in-person, plus the LABR experts leagues

... all with a group of the friendliest, most passionate baseball fans around!

Make your Spring Training Plans NOW and include First Pitch Florida weekend!

More details: www.baseballhq.com/first-pitch-florida

Get Forecaster Insights In a New Package!

The **Baseball Forecaster** provides the core concepts in player evaluation and gaming strategy. You can maintain that edge all season long.

For over 25 years, **BaseballHQ.com** builds on the insights found in the Forecaster and covers all aspects of what's happening on the field—all with the most powerful fantasy slant on the Internet, from spring training to the season's last pitch. And in 2024, a new mobile-friendly website design will make it even easier to get ahead of the competition! Though it will have a modern look and feel, our signature features will be as sharp as ever:

- Nationally-renowned baseball analysts.
- MLB news analysis; including anticipating the **next** move.
- Dedicated columns on starting pitching, relievers, batters, and our popular Fact or Fluke? player profiles.
- Minor-league coverage beyond just scouting and lists.
- FAB targets, starting pitcher reports, strategy articles, daily game resources, call-up profiles and more!

Plus, **BaseballHQ.com** gets personal, with customizable tools and valuable resources:

- New and improved Team Stat Tracker and Power Search tools
- Custom Draft Guide for YOUR league's parameters
- Sortable and downloadable stats and projection files

Visit **www.baseballhq.com/subscribe**

to lock down your path to a 2024 championship!

Full Season subscription $99
(prorated at the time of order; auto-renews each October)

Draft Prep subscription $45
(complete access from mid-January through April 30, 2024)

Please read our Terms of service at www.baseballhq.com/terms.html

Baseball Forecaster & BaseballHQ.com:
Your (updated!) season-long championship lineup.